Teaching, Learning, and the Net Generation:

Concepts and Tools for Reaching Digital Learners

Sharmila Pixy Ferris
William Paterson University, USA

Information Science
REFERENCE

Managing Director:	Lindsay Johnston
Senior Editorial Director:	Heather Probst
Book Production Manager:	Sean Woznicki
Development Manager:	Joel Gamon
Development Editor:	Hannah Abelbeck
Acquisitions Editor:	Erika Gallagher
Typesetter:	Christopher Shearer
Print Coordinator:	Jamie Snavely
Cover Design:	Nick Newcomer, Greg Snader

Published in the United States of America by
Information Science Reference (an imprint of IGI Global)
701 E. Chocolate Avenue
Hershey PA 17033
Tel: 717-533-8845
Fax: 717-533-8661
E-mail: cust@igi-global.com
Web site: http://www.igi-global.com

Library of Congress Cataloging-in-Publication Data

Teaching, learning, and the net generation: concepts and tools for reaching digital learners / Sharmila Pixy Ferris.
p. cm.
Includes bibliographical references and index.
Summary: "This book provides pedagogical resources for understanding digital learners, and effectively teaching and learning with today's generation of digital natives, offering a much-needed resource that moves beyond traditional disciplinary and geographical boundaries, bridges theories and practice, and addresses emerging issues in technology and pedagogy"--Provided by publisher.
ISBN 978-1-61350-347-8 (hardcover) -- ISBN 978-1-61350-348-5 (ebook) -- ISBN 978-1-61350-349-2 (print & perpetual access) 1. Educational technology. 2. Generation Y--Education. I. Ferris, Sharmila Pixy.
LB1028.3.T3857 2012
371.33--dc23

2011032912

British Cataloguing in Publication Data
A Cataloguing in Publication record for this book is available from the British Library.

Table of Contents

Foreword xvii

Preface xix

Acknowledgment xxv

Section 1
Theories and Concepts

Chapter 1
Developing Faculty to Integrate Innovative Learning into Their Practice with the SOLE Model 1
Simon Paul Atkinson, BPP University College, UK

Chapter 2
The Gloss and the Reality of Teaching Digital Natives: Taking the Long View 19
Star A. Muir, George Mason University, USA

Chapter 3
Personalized Integrated Educational Systems: Technology for the Information-Age Paradigm of Education in Higher Education 41
Charles M. Reigeluth, Indiana University, USA
William R. Watson, Purdue University, USA
Sunnie Lee Watson, Ball State University, USA

Chapter 4
Frustration Vaccination? Inoculation Theory and Digital Learning 61
Josh Compton, Dartmouth College, USA

Chapter 5
Face to Face Communication outside the Digital Realm to Foster Student Growth and Development 74
Charles F. Aust, Kennesaw State University, USA

Section 2
Theory and Practice

Section 3
Social Media for Digital Learners

Detailed Table of Contents

Foreword xvii

Preface xix

Acknowledgment xxv

Section 1
Theories and Concepts

Chapter 1
Developing Faculty to Integrate Innovative Learning into Their Practice with the SOLE Model 1
Simon Paul Atkinson, BPP University College, UK

A subtle blend of institutional approaches, customised to each institution, is necessary if the challenge of adopting the very best of educational technologies to meet the demands of new emerging generations of learners is to be met. The Student-Owned Learning-Engagement (SOLE) model is suggested as providing one possible institutional solution. The Net generation, both in its mythological state and its rudimentary reality, presents a challenge to contemporary universities, to teach in increasingly diverse ways, to increasingly diverse populations. Senior university leaders and faculty must acknowledge that the very nature of knowledge creation, stewardship, and propagation has changed. Staff, trained in one epistemological universe, must be supported in adapting their skills to a new one.

Chapter 2
The Gloss and the Reality of Teaching Digital Natives: Taking the Long View 19
Star A. Muir, George Mason University, USA

Characterizations of youth growing up with the Internet as Digital Natives have begun a revolution in teaching, but have also been problematized in the literature, opening up significant questions about stereotypical assumptions made by teachers about students in the classroom. Research indicates that a continuing gap exists between "power users" and "digital strangers," which has broad implications for educational priorities and classroom practice. Evidence is also mounting that heavy internet and concurrent media usage impacts both students' ability to focus and their evolving habits of mind as the brain responds to new sources of positive reinforcement. This chapter explores some of these tensions in characterizing and responding to Digital Natives, and seeks to identify a responsive pedagogy of classroom practices that tap into student passions, offer students some techniques to learn focus, attention, and other important skills for both digital and "analog" environments, and address persistent skill gaps between students.

Chapter 3
Personalized Integrated Educational Systems: Technology for the Information-Age Paradigm of Education in Higher Education 41
Charles M. Reigeluth, Indiana University, USA
William R. Watson, Purdue University, USA
Sunnie Lee Watson, Ball State University, USA

This chapter presents a detailed description of the powerful and necessary role technology can play in higher education in the current information-age. This article calls for a Personalized Integrated Educational System (PIES), a comprehensive and integrated application of technology to the learning process, which will provide four primary roles for student learning: record keeping, planning, instruction, and assessment. Each of these four major roles is described in terms of the functions it provides to support student learning. Finally, secondary roles such as communication and general data administration are described in order to illustrate the systemic nature of PIES technology necessary to fully support the learner-centered approach that is essential in the information-age paradigm of higher education.

Chapter 4
Frustration Vaccination? Inoculation Theory and Digital Learning 61
Josh Compton, Dartmouth College, USA

Inoculation theory is a classic theory of social influence, describing how exposure to weakened versions of challenges motivates a process of resistance to protect against future, stronger challenges. Inoculation theory can offer useful guidance to teachers as they talk with Net Generational students about digital learning projects. Discussions guided by inoculation theory raise and refute potential challenges students may have in the process of completing their digital learning projects, helping to protect students against discouraging frustration, but also, encouraging a more thoughtful, nuanced consideration of the use of technology in meeting learning objectives. Inoculation theory-guided discussions will not only impact what students are thinking about, but even how they are thinking—bolstering digital learning project objectives.

Chapter 5
Face to Face Communication outside the Digital Realm to Foster Student Growth and Development.. 74
Charles F. Aust, Kennesaw State University, USA

Benefits of college go beyond acquisition of skills and knowledge to include understanding, effective decision-making, personal growth, and maturation. While online courses and online social interactions grow, the benefits of and preference for face-to-face interaction remain important. Digital learners are human beings, so non-digital ways of fostering their development remain relevant. Face-to-face interactions of significance occur in the classroom, and the real physical presence of each other cannot always be replaced by digital tools and delivery, nor should it be. While not downplaying online and digital technologies' role in advancing academic progress online, in-person face-to-face learning experiences contribute in important ways to students' growth and adaptation. Each time instructors and students communicate, they co-construct their evolving social reality. Face-to-face interactions provide unique capabilities and benefits in that transformational process, as this chapter explores.

Section 2
Theory and Practice

Chapter 6
Millennials are Digital Natives? An Investigation into Digital Propensity and Age 90
Boaventura DaCosta, Solers Research Group, USA
Carolyn Kinsell, Solers Research Group, USA
Angelique Nasah, Solers Research Group, USA

The abundance of opinions about Millennials has made it very difficult to separate reality from conjecture, especially with regard to the suppositions made about their propensity towards technology. Labeled as digital natives, Millennials are thought to possess learning traits never before seen as a result of growing up in the digital information age. In this chapter, the authors present the findings of a study in which postsecondary students (N = 580) were surveyed to quantitatively investigate the differences between digital natives and digital immigrants. Findings revealed that of the ten traits investigated, only two showed significant difference, and of these two traits, only one favored the digital native notion, shedding doubt on the strong digital propensity claims made about today's Millennials. Although differences were found, it cannot be said with any certainty that there is an unambiguous delineation that merits the digital native and digital immigrant labels. The findings raise a variety of implications for institutions training pre-service teachers; educators interested in using digital media, devices, and social networks in their classroom; curriculum developers designing instructional material; educational leaders developing information and communication technology policy for school; and researchers investigating digital propensity with today's youth.

Chapter 7
Net Geners' Multi-Modal and Multi-Tasking Performance in Complex Problem Solving 107
Robert Z. Zheng, University of Utah, USA

This chapter examines the influence of multi-modal presentation and multi-tasking on Net Generation students' performance in complex problem solving. The goals of the chapter are to examine (a) the differences between multi-modal presentation/multi-tasking and non multi-modal presentation/multi-tasking, (b) the influence of visual cognitive style on both types of performances, and (c) the relationship among the variables under study. The findings of the study showed that participants performed best with multi-modal presentation as evidenced in their reduced cognitive load, and their improved self-efficacy and performance in multiple rule-based problem solving. The findings also revealed that multi-tasking could block learners' learning pathway due to an increase in cognitive load. Discussion on the significance of the findings and their implication for educational community is made with suggestions for future research.

As members of the Net Generation embrace digital communication and interactive technology, educators have increasingly integrated them into the classroom in an effort to attract and motivate digital learners, but often without considering how these approaches affect the learning process. This chapter examines the nature and impact of interactivity as a discrete element within an instructional setting. It explores whether the recognition of interactivity by students measurably contributes to actual cognitive learning and, more importantly, how. If the positive impact of interactivity within the teaching process is to be replicated and exploited, instructors must understand which elements contribute to online student learning, in what ways, and to what degree. Outcome Interactivity Theory is used as a framework to test the impact of interactive functionality in instructional content on knowledge acquisition and satisfaction learning outcomes for students. Results are described, and limitations and practical implications are discussed.

The role of communication technologies in the learning process is both a dynamic and complex issue. Yet, we know surprisingly little about how the use of specific communication technologies may influence classroom performance, key learning outcomes, and other measures of course satisfaction. The research reported here attempts to add to our knowledge about the role of communication in the technology-enhanced classroom (TEC) education and in technology-enhanced online (TEO) education through a direct comparison of two courses. The findings indicate additional support for "The No Significant Difference Phenomenon." Furthermore, the authors found that prior experiences lead students to gravitate towards their preferred learning environments, and that basic website elements are required in any learning environment to enhance student outcomes. Finally, it is found that when used appropriately, the benefits of communication technology use in education outweigh many of the drawbacks.

Section 3
Social Media for Digital Learners

Harnessing the potential of technology for increased student engagement may be a key strategy of teaching and learning successfully with Net Generation students. Interactive technology, such as wikis,

Social media, offer a means of engaging digital learners in critical thinking and collaborative learning. Interdisciplinary faculty at Otterbein University, a four year comprehensive university in the United States, explored the impact of integrating blogs and wikis into their courses by designing assignments based on Fink's Paradigm of Significant Learning (2003). This chapter presents the collective findings, reflections, and lessons learned from their professional learning community (PLC). First, even though students did improve in organizing and presenting data, their critical thinking skills did not. Second, collaborative learning was enhanced, and Fink's Paradigm of Significant Learning did help faculty integrate blogs and wikis into their courses. Third, student attitudes about using the technology were mostly positive; agreeing that interaction and quality of communication with the professor and other students increased. The authors conclude that even inexperienced faculty should adopt social media tools, as long as there is a clear connection between the courses' learning objectives and the particular technology being used.

The discourse surrounding digital natives and their learning needs often presupposes a level of social media knowledge or savviness that is equal, if not superior, to that of any other generation, including that of their teachers. Although it is undeniable that this new breed of students feels comfortable using social media as an integral part of their wired lives, the assumption that digital immersion results in digital literacy may end up preventing a whole generation of students from learning how to take full advantage of the digital tools they grew up with. As long as this assumption goes unchallenged, the net generation may very well continue navigating this digitally mediated world without ever truly understanding the strategic uses of social media technologies. If we are to prepare 21st century students for today's highly competitive global marketplace and rapidly changing world, we need to teach them how to direct their own learning. Fortunately, today's social media technologies make it easier than ever for students to develop independent learning skills. In this chapter we discuss how students can use various social media platforms to identify and connect to communities of experts capable of supporting their learning needs and how to incorporate these personal learning networks into everyday pedagogical practice.

Computer-mediated classrooms are proliferating and instructors are finding creative ways to reach the digital learners of today. But with all these technology tools, making decisions that are guided by solid pedagogical practices are vital. This study relies on instructional communication, multicommunication practices, and interactivity research and how they play key roles when creating a participatory classroom environment. The tool used to address the problems outlined in this case study is webconferencing—a synchronous Web-based platform that allows the instructor to share slides, create real-time surveys (polls), and provide text chat opportunities for students who are co-located or dispersed. By leveraging the webconferencing tools and the desires of the Net Generation, the classroom in this study became more inclusive, communicative, and interactive.

Chapter 16
New Media and Digital Learners: An Examination of Teaching and Learning................................. 289
William J. Gibbs, Duquesne University, USA

The proliferation of digital technologies coupled with technically sophisticated students with high educational expectations requires media educators to rethink conventional teaching and learning practices. Students enter the college experience with a wealth of background knowledge and experience that instructors must take into account when designing new/digital media courses. In this chapter, the author examines current principles of instruction, learning, instructional design, and learning theory and their relevance to the education of digital learners. In addition, the development of a digital media course premised on these teaching and learning precepts is outlined. Finally, the author reviews some of the challenges faced when instituting innovative instructional practices.

Section 4
Pedagogy and Technology for the Net Generational Classroom

Chapter 17
Action Learning: Inspire Lasting Learning through Truly Applied Projects..................................... 311
Scott P. Roberts, University of Maryland, USA
Steven G. Buzinksi, University of Maryland, USA

Students, and in particular those that have come to be known as members of the Net Generation, learn best when they are presented with the opportunity to engage relevant material using media which they perceive to be familiar and effective. Going beyond academic exercises, Action Learning assignments cater to the generational expectation that their actions have immediate and meaningful social implications. Through five component steps, Action Learning projects guide students through identifying, implementing, and evaluating an informed attempt to make a measurable impact on the world beyond their academic buildings. In doing so we create purposeful scholarship, move beyond basic demonstrations of learning, and enhance information encoding for future utilization.

Chapter 18
The Net Generation Illusion: Challenging Conformance to Social Expectations 324
Rachel Ellaway, Northern Ontario School of Medicine, Canada
Janet Tworek, University of Calgary, Canada

The thesis of this chapter is that the Net Generation concept has become a powerful meme that influences professional education in ways that can be both distracting and disruptive. The authors explore the interactions between the Net Generation meme and medical education and identify points of consonance and dissonance between them. In doing so a critical response to the idea of a Net Generation is presented, as well as its specific manifestations and impacts on the development of healthcare professionals. A digital professionalism framework is presented as a way to restore balance within medical education, as well as situating it within an increasingly digital social milieu.

Chapter 19
Utilizing Audio and Video Captures to Train and Engage the Net Generation in Effective Presentation Skills 340
Jessica Fargnoli, Bergen Community College, USA

This chapter examines the rationale and benefits for the use of audio and video capture as a pedagogical tool for engaging and instructing the Net Generation. It examines means of incorporating audio and video technology to guide students in developing effective presentation skills, and provides examples of how to utilize audio and video capture technology in other disciplines. Specifically, this chapter provides (1) a pedagogical resource and strategy to engage the Net Generation (2) provides an effective and applied approach for instruction through audio and video captures in the classroom, and (3) discusses increased level of student engagement through incorporating of technology in the classroom. As a case example, self-report and survey results from a college-level Speech Communication course and remedial Basic Communication courses in which Echo 360 audio and video capture technology will be explored in respect to engaging the Net Generation.

Chapter 20
Service-Learning as a Pedagogical Approach for Net Generation Learners: A Case Study.............. 358
Sally Blomstrom, Embry-Riddle Aeronautical University, USA

This chapter focuses on service-learning as a pedagogical approach for Net Generation learners, and presents a case study from a private technological institution in the United States as an example. The chapter covers details of the assignment as a case study, specific considerations in the assignment's design for Net Generation learners, ways in which the assignment followed principles of service-learning assignments, and how service-learning principles correspond with Net Generation learner characteristics. The case study focuses on an assignment for a speech class in which university students developed and delivered presentations on science topics to two audiences: children in an afterschool program and an online audience of teachers and adults. Issues and problems that arose are discussed followed by suggestions and recommendations for this service-learning project.

Chapter 21
Teaching with PowerPoint in the Net Generation.. 374
Chris Gurrie, University of Tampa, USA
Brandy Fair, Grayson County College, USA

This chapter focuses on students' perceptions of their professors' use, abuse, and success with PowerPoint presentation software. Both recent literature about the Net Generation and this study show that the novelty of PowerPoint is wearing off. The researchers found that student perceptions ranged from highly critical of professors' uses of PowerPoint, to delightfully engaged by the use of PowerPoint as a teaching tool. This research could benefit anyone looking to retool or calibrate current PowerPoint practices. The Net Generation of students has grown up with PowerPoint; its continued use is nothing new or novel when discussing student engagement and the transfer of knowledge. However, a return to best practices of teaching and engagement while implementing PowerPoint may help today's learners better retain course materials.

Chapter 22
Integrating Personal Experiences and Course Materials to Promote Net Generation Student Learning in an Online Health Communication Course 393
Rukhsana Ahmed, University of Ottawa, Canada

This study examines how technology-enhanced experiential learning methods, specifically the integration of personal experiences and course materials in an online course, can enhance Net Generation student learning. Drawing from undergraduate and graduate students' perspectives on their learning experiences gathered through an evaluation survey in an online health communication course, the study demonstrates how learning can be incorporated into everyday practice to meet the unique needs of digital learners. The study concludes with a discussion of implications of the findings for designing innovative methods of teaching and learning with the Net Generation in higher education institutions.

Afterword 409

Compilation of References 411

About the Contributors 448

Index 458

Foreword

THE NET GENERATION AND THE FUTURE OF LEARNING

Is it possible that colleges can turn their current and future students into independent, critically thinking, self motivated, pro-active learners or will they remain academically adrift with limited learning on college campuses as the title of a recent book suggests?[1] Are there successful academic learning concepts and practices that that can be employed successfully with this new student generation to prepare them for their future independent learning?

This book is a must read for educators who are interested in the future of learning at all levels, but especially in higher education. The measurable behavioral differences between the Net Generation (aka Millennials), and previous generations, have stimulated these educators and researchers to develop theories, as well as identify and test different technologies and pedagogies that may work more effectively and be better motivators. As a bonus, some of the new learning technologies and pedagogies may also prove more effective with preceding generations. As you read through these papers, and I encourage you to do so, please note that the evidence of what works may change the focus of where college and university students spend their in-class and out-of-class time.

I have conducted more than sixty Net Generation focus groups of college students in most states and even three foreign countries, most of them in front of live audiences consisting of college faculty and administrators. Using published research about Net Gen behaviors, I ask questions of a random group of 8 to 14 local college students questions in front of their faculty and administrators to prove or disprove the study results. The results, by and large, are confirmed; the Net Generation students do behave differently. Net Gen communication, gaming, and learning behaviors are different in many statistically significant ways. They expect much more personal interactivity, gaming, personal attention from expert faculty, collaboration with their fellow students, social networking, and balanced integrated learning technologies. Since college students do not behave the same as previous generations or learn in exactly the same fashion, is it possible to motivate these students to become independent self-learners?

The chapters in this book offer many questions and answers about what actually works and also what might work to improve Net Generation learning. For example, here are a few questions that have been raised and answered or investigated. Does heavy Internet and concurrent media usage impact Net Gen student ability to focus? Has the very nature of knowledge creation, stewardship, and propagation changed? Do Net Gen college students show a higher preference for play oriented educational material than older groups? Do students still want and need face to face education? Does interactive online instruction produce different results from traditional static instructional models? Does introducing interactive functionality in instructional technology and lesson content encourage students to pay closer attention, work harder and study longer? Do students generally have positive views about learning technologies when they are used appropriately? Do only a small percentage of Net Gen students prefer group work? These are only a small portion of the questions raised.

Many faculty teaching at colleges and universities throughout the United States, and some internationally, have noticed the change in their current college students from those a generation ago. Faculty have typically had one of three reactions. First, some faculty are in denial; in spite of compelling evidence, they do not believe this student generation is substantially different in any way that matters. Second, other faculty members recognize that this generation is different in significant ways, but they have been teaching for, say, XX years "effectively," and have no intention of changing. Third, the remainder of faculty recognize that this student generation is different in important ways and are looking for successful teaching and learning practices to deal with these differences effectively. This book is for that last group.

The future of learning is not limited to just what happens in the classroom, but rather, how current students develop their curiosity, critical thinking, and independent, proactive learning. The reason we should listen to such studies and ideas presented in the collection of papers in this book, is that the faculty and teachers on our campuses and schools will surely help shape how these students might become successful in their ever changing future learning environments.

Richard Sweeney
New Jersey Institute of Technology 7/25/2011

***Richard Sweeney** is the University Librarian at the New Jersey Institute of Technology and also leads the Department of Instructional Technology and Media Services. His career experience is extensive, spanning Vice Provost (for Libraries and Information Services at Polytechnic University in Brooklyn), Executive Director in libraries in Ohio, and positions in libraries in Flint, MI and Atlantic City. Rich has served on the Board of Trustees of Thomas Edison State College (NJ), has taught at the high school, college, and graduate levels, and as an Executive Committee member of VALE (Virtual Academic Library Committee of New Jersey) for over eleven years. Rich is a frequent speaker and consultant. As a speaker, he has conducted over 60 Millennial generation panels in front of live audiences in higher education and industry in over twenty states. His Millennial research has been featured in the Chronicle of Higher Education, the NJ Star Leger, and others. He has published a number of articles in journals.*

ENDNOTE

1 Richard Arum and Josipa Roska. Academically Adrift: limited learning on college campuses. The University of Chicago Press, Chicago and London, 2011.

Preface

As an undergraduate I was fortunate to have teachers who challenged and inspired me. When I entered the classroom, I wanted to *be* those teachers. What I didn't realize was the complexities involved! In speaking to like-minded colleagues, I realized that many of my colleagues were also wrestling with similar issues. Over the years I have continued a pursuit of better teaching, through both research and practice. This book represents a natural progression of my interests. Notwithstanding its title, the book is not a generational indictment, nor does it promote specific modes or techniques of teaching and learning; its goal is simply to promote better teaching through awareness and understanding.

Today no understanding of teaching and learning can occur in the absence of an understanding of technology. I am not advocating technology as the answer to all educational ills, nor am I dichotomizing technology as necessarily good or bad. As an early proponent of technorealism, I feel that educational discussions of technology generally fail to address its complexity. This book, then, represents an attempt to think "critically about the role that tools and interfaces play in human evolution and everyday life" (www.technorealism.org). It tries to reach a middle ground between blindly following educational practices that have remain unchanged for centuries, and the more recent trend of throwing new technologies at students in hopes that they will embrace and learn from them.

Clearly our technological choices alone have not necessarily led to better learning environments. This book is one attempt to address this issue. The specific focus of this book is pedagogy addressing the Net Generation, or Millennials. Because of this, it is of primary importance to note that making generalizations about generations is dangerous. But, as Taylor (2005) notes, some generalizations can help in understanding generational cohorts. As such, sociologists have labeled the various generations of the twentieth century: the Silent Generation, born 1901-1924, age today 86 and older; Baby Boomers born 1946-1964, age today 45-66; Generation X, born 1965-1978, age today 33-47 and the Net Generation, born 1979-1994, age today 17-32 (Sweeney, 2008).

Although generational labels are used in this book, they are used in ways that are both realistic and critical - critical in that we acknowledge that existing conceptualizations of Net Gen learning exist, but can and should be challenged; realistic in that we acknowledge that the learning needs of digital learners may not be unique to this generation, and that there is as much variation within generations as between them.

Conceptualizations of the Net Generation as a unique generation exist, and exist in plenty. The generation has many labels: Millennials, Generation Y, Generation Next, Generation Me, M Generation, and Echo Boomers. (The Net Generation was selected as the label of choice in this book because of its associations with the Internet and the digital revolution.) There is a wide body of research focusing on this generation's behaviors and characteristics, as the authors in this book will describe in some detail. Since you will read a great deal more about Net Generational behaviors and learning characteristics in the chapters to come, I will not discuss the issue in any depth here. I will, however, note that many researchers have found that the Net Generation learns differently from previous generations; a finding that has been confirmed by organizations like Educause and the Pew Internet Project.

So this book is predicated on the premise that educators today are dealing with a large number of students who were born digital and live wired, and that these students learn in ways that are sometimes distinctively different from their predecessors. In spite of this, research shows that traditional teaching methods continue to dominate the classroom. This edited book will provide pedagogical resources for better understanding teaching and learning with digital learners.

Given the premise stated above, this book does not blindly advocate adapting teaching to the perceived needs of a generation of learners. Rather, it takes a realistic and critical approach. It does so in three ways. Firstly, this book recognizes that the learning needs of digital learners may not be unique. Well before this Net Generation, educators have complaints that sound only too familiar -- from the professor in 1855 who lamented his students having "an undisciplined mind, and an uncultivated heart, yet with exalted ideas of personal dignity, and a scowling contempt for lawful authority" (quoted in Hoover, 2009) to Marshall McLuhan's (1957) statement about education and entertainment being synonymous. So it may be unrealistic to assume that this generation is any more unique than any previous generation. The Net Generation may have more in common with other generations than is popularly accepted, and the gap between Digital Natives and Digital Immigrants may be exaggerated.

Secondly, this book takes a realistic focus in acknowledging that existing conceptualizations of Net Gen learning can and should be challenged. Hoover's (2009) perspective that notions of the Net Generation may be over-hyped, is supported by several authors in this book. DaCosta, Kinsell, and Nasah note that the data to support many of the assumptions put forth about the Net Generation is contradictory, and that empirical data is often lacking. Their research is supported by several other authors in this book, including Atkinson, Ellaway, and Tworek, and Muir.

Thirdly, this book acknowledges that no generational overview can ever effectively reflect the range and diversity of the individuals within that generation. That there is as much variation within generations as between them is clearly recognized and emphasized in this book, as discussed by Muir. As well, DaCosta, Kinsell, and Nasah, provide clear evidence to show there is as much variation within the Net Generation as between generations. Not all members of the Net Generation share their commonly accepted characteristics of being wired, connected, and digitally literate!

Taking all the above factors into consideration, generation labels remain a convenient way to consider the pedagogical needs of students, but these needs remain important no matter what the generation. Higher education still needs to focus more fully on pedagogical practices, and to allocate more resources to the understanding and improvement of teaching. This book provides one such resource. It is important to remember that as a resource it does not blindly advocate tailoring our teaching to the needs of any students, whether a new generation or not. Nor does it advocate ignoring students' learning needs. The authors in the book do acknowledge the realities of a wired world and promote the ever-important need for improved pedagogy. This over-arching focus on pedagogy is the pervasive theme of the book, as can be seen in the chapter previews that follow.

The book begins with a Foreword, written by Richard Sweeney. Affectionately nicknamed "the Millennial Man," Sweeney has conducted focus groups in front of live audiences at 60 colleges and universities across the U.S. His knowledge of this generation places him in a unique position to explain the contribution of this book to the field.

The book is then divided into four sections: theories and concepts, theory and practice, social media for digital learners, and pedagogies for today's classroom.

Section 1 addresses the dearth of pedagogical theory by examining theories and concepts through the lens of educators, administrators, and students. Taking the position that theories are at the heart of practice, this section provides theories, concepts, and models to help us in teaching, planning, research, and practice.

In Chapter 1, Simon Atkinson proposes a model to help educators effectively meet the challenges of new generations of learners. He proposes a Student-Owned Learning-Engagement (SOLE) model as a customized and customizable model to help educators, trained in one epistemological universe, to adapt their skills to a new one.

In Chapter 2, Star Muir considers the tensions arising from the broad characterization of a generation of students as Digital Natives. In discussing contradictory research findings, he provides a larger picture of the Net Generation. Star's broad focus is the articulation of a responsive pedagogy of classroom practices that could be equally effective for what he terms "digital and analog" environments, addressing persistent skill gaps between students.

In Chapter 3, Charles Reigeluth, William Watson, and Sunnie Lee Watson examine the role of technology in higher education. They propose a model for a comprehensive and integrated application of technology to the learning process. This model addresses four primary roles for student learning: record keeping, planning, instruction, and assessment, and such secondary roles as communication and general data administration.

In Chapter 4, Josh Compton offers Inoculation theory as a device which can guide educators as they work with Net Generational students on digital learning projects. Inoculation theory is a classic theory of social influence, describing how exposure to weakened versions of challenges motivates a process of resistance to protect against future, stronger challenges. He demonstrates how discussions guided by Inoculation theory have the potential to impact both the content and the processes of students' thinking.

Finally, in Chapter 5, Charles Aust discusses the benefits of face-to-face interactions in fostering student development. Without belittling technology's role in advancing academic progress, Aust reminds us that digital learners are also human beings who can benefit from the transformational processes brought about in the physical presence of others. He considers the many ways face-to-face learning experiences contribute to students' growth and adaptation.

Section 2 develops the previous section by addressing theory and practice. While theory helps us understand and improve our teaching, without a link to classroom practice theories do not achieve their potential. The chapters in this section present research that has a strong theoretical focus, demonstrating the effectiveness of examining theory through empirical research.

In Chapter 6, Boaventura DaCosta, Carolyn Kinsell, and Angelique Nasah question the concept of digital propensity applied to the Net Generation. They present the findings of an empirical study in which 580 postsecondary students were surveyed to investigate the differences between digital natives and digital immigrants. Their findings revealed that of the ten traits investigated, only two showed significant difference, and of these two traits, only one favored the digital native notion, shedding doubt on the strong digital propensity claims made about the Net Generation.

In Chapter 7, Robert Zheng investigates the influence of multi-modal presentation and multi-tasking on Net Generation students' performance in complex problem solving. His findings show that participants performed best with multi-modal presentation as evidenced in their reduced cognitive load, improved self-efficacy and performance in multiple rule-based problem solving. The findings also revealed that multi-tasking could block learners' learning pathway due to an increase in cognitive load.

In Chapter 8, James Gleason and Laura Beth Daws study the nature and impact of interactivity as a discrete element within an instructional setting. They empirically explore whether the recognition of interactivity by students measurably contributes to actual cognitive learning and in what ways. Their results did not support the positive impact of interactivity on measurable student knowledge acquisition, but the recognition of interactivity did influence student satisfaction positively.

In Chapter 9, Scott D'Urso and Craig Scott examine the use of specific communication technologies as influencing classroom performance, key learning outcomes, and other measures of course satisfaction. Comparing communication in the technology-enhanced classroom education and in technology-enhanced online education, the authors found no significant difference between the two courses. Results also indicated that prior experiences lead students to gravitate towards their preferred learning environments, and that when used appropriately, the benefits of communication technology use in education outweigh many of the drawbacks.

Section 3 addresses uses of social media for digital learners. Social media use is the single most defining characteristic of the Net Generation. But while widely embraced by many, across the generations, social media are only cautiously utilized by educators. This section offers ways in which social media can be utilized effectively to expand our pedagogical toolbox.

In Chapter 10, Maureen Ebben, Russell Kivatisky, and Daniel Panici use a case study and survey data to explore three issues: students' perceptions of technology in teaching and learning, students' perceptions of wiki technology in teaching and learning, and students' attitudes about group work and collaboration. Their results suggest three contradictions in student behaviors and perceptions regarding group work and collaboration. They also offer five critical insights as to best practices for teaching and learning with wikis.

In Chapter 11, Susanne Croasdaile and her students Rachel Angel, Erin Carr, Lucy Hudson, & Carin Ursey analyze blogs created by Net Generation students enrolled in a Master's level research methods course designed according to the principles of Universal Design for Learning. The authors' blog postings demonstrate the possibilities inherent in the use of blogs in the classroom. They discuss the importance of formative assessment, particularly through the use of student self-assessment and instructor feedback to close the gap between current performance and learning goals, and provide best practices for blog use.

In Chapter 12, Hilary Wilder, Geraldine Mongillo, and Carrie Eunyoung Hong describe a pilot study using Twitter to afford anytime/anywhere writing by first-year students. Students tweeted weekly ideas, thoughts, and reflections on their first-year experience throughout the semester, with the goal of compiling all tweets into a formally written text (a "Freshman Survival Guide") to see if they could use a "new literacy" skill to promote traditional writing. Results indicated that Twitter use was not as high as expected, and that students were not overwhelmingly positive about using new technologies in the classroom, but many seemed open to that possibility.

In Chapter 13, Marsha Huber, Jean Kelly, and Shirine Mafi discuss their experiences integrating blogs and wikis into their courses, using assignments based on Fink's Paradigm of Significant Learning. Their results varied: even though students did improve in organizing and presenting data, their critical thinking skills did not; collaborative learning was enhanced, and Fink's Paradigm of Significant Learning was successful; student attitudes about using the technology were mostly positive. The authors concluded that even inexperienced faculty can adopt social media tools as long as there is a clear connection between the courses' learning objectives and the particular technology being used.

In Chapter 14, Shannan Butler and Corinne Weisgerber explore ways that Personal Learning Networks can be incorporated into everyday pedagogical practice. They consider ways students can use social media platforms (such as Twitter, blogs and social bookmarking, and others) to identify and connect with communities of experts. The authors suggest designing an independent learning project, and provide a model.

In Chapter 15, Keri Stephens, Melissa Murphy, and Kerk Kee provide a case study of a Communications course highlighting the role of instructional communication, multicommunication practices, and interactivity research in creating a participatory classroom environment. The authors utilize web conferencing to engage disconnected students. They conclude that web conferencing media is effective in improving participation, and in creating a more inclusive, communicative, and interactive community of learners.

In Chapter 16, William Gibbs examines current principles of instruction, learning, instructional design, and learning theory and their relevance to the education of digital learners. The discussion is developed and illustrated through the description of a digital media course premised on these teaching and learning precepts. He concludes with a review of some of the challenges faced when instituting innovative instructional practices.

Section 4 considers a broader range of pedagogies for today's classroom. The unique characteristics of the 21st century classroom are only in part due to the changes in students. A complex array of factors act on the classroom today, including increasing legislation directed at higher education, intensifying demands for accountability from both the general public and legislators, cost-cutting measures imposed by cash-strapped institutions, along with unprepared students, demands for graduates with better skills and knowledge than their predecessors, a rapidly changing workplace, and a rising faculty work load. In these circumstances, pedagogy often takes a back seat, but it is at just such times that pedagogy should assume greater importance. The chapters in this section offer a range of pedagogical resources

In Chapter 17, Scott Roberts and Steven Buzinksi discuss how Action Learning assignments can help Net Generation students learn by engaging relevant material using familiar media. The authors offer five component steps in Action Learning projects, which guide students through identifying, implementing, and evaluating an informed attempt to make a measurable impact on the world. In doing so they create purposeful scholarship, move beyond basic demonstrations of learning, and enhance information for future utilization.

In Chapter 18, Rachel Ellaway and Janet Tworek examine the influences of the Net Generation meme on professional education. They explore the interactions between the Net Generation meme and medical education and identify points of consonance and dissonance. In doing so they present a critical response to the idea of a Net Generation, as well as its specific manifestations and impacts on the development of healthcare professionals. They conclude by presenting a digital professionalism framework as a way to restore balance within medical education as well as situating it within an increasingly digital social milieu.

In Chapter 19, Jessica Fargnoli considers the rationale and benefits for the use of audio and video capture as a pedagogical tool for engaging and instructing the Net Generation. She examines means of incorporating audio and video technology to guide students in developing effective presentation skills, and provides examples of how to utilize audio and video capture technology in any discipline. She utilizes a case example, and data from self-report and surveys, to explore the utility of Echo 360 audio and video capture technology in engaging the Net Generation.

In Chapter 20, Sally Blomstrom focuses on service learning as a pedagogical approach for Net Generation learners, and presents a case study as an example. She discusses the case study assignment in a speech class. She specifically considers the assignment's design for Net Generation learners, ways in which the assignment followed principles of service-learning assignments, and how service-learning principles provide a complement to Net Generation learner characteristics.

In Chapter 21, Chris Gurrie and Brandy Fair consider students' perceptions of their professors' use, abuse, and success with PowerPoint presentation software. They found student perceptions ranged from highly critical to delightfully engaged. Their research and analyses highlight best practices of teaching and engagement while implementing PowerPoint as a way to help today's learners better retain course materials.

In Chapter 22, Rukhsana Ahmed examines how technology-enhanced experiential learning methods, specifically the integration of personal experiences and course materials in an online course, can enhance Net Generation student learning. Drawing from undergraduate and graduate students' perspectives on their learning experiences gathered through an evaluation survey in an online health communication course, her study demonstrates how learning can be incorporated into everyday practice to meet the unique needs of digital learners.

The Afterword is written by Ronald Jacobson, editor of the classic *Communication and Cyberspace: Social Interaction in an Electronic Environment*. His experience as an administrator, whose responsibilities include facilitating University initiatives in online learning and new program development, provide a unique perspective with which to close this book.

It is my hope that the wide range of issues and topics considered in this book will prove a solid resource for educators. Since technological change will continue to impact education, educators will need to continually think about pedagogies to more effectively prepare the young people who are our future. In doing so, this book accentuates the fine line educators must walk: we can not abdicate our role as authorities directing the learning experiences of our students, but we need to continually look at ways to maximize the skills they develop outside of class, without accommodating the poor learning habits sometimes promoted by technology.

As such, this book is a broad and inclusive pedagogical resource, offering sound learning theories, examples of practice, and a range of pedagogical ideas and resources. It should thus be of interest to anyone who seeks a deeper understanding of teaching and learning—academics and teachers, practitioners, and Net Geners.

REFERENCES

Hoover, E. (2009, October 11). The Millennial muddle: How stereotyping students has become a thriving industry and a bundle of contradictions. *Chronicle of Higher Education*. Retrieved from http://chronicle.com/article/The-Millennial-Muddle-How/48772/.

McLuhan, M. (1957). Classroom without walls: Explorations, 7. In Carpenter, E., & McLuhan, M. (Eds.), *Explorations in communication*. Boston, MA: Beacon.

Sweeney, R. P. (2008, September). *The Millennial generation goes to college: A focus group*. Presentation at William Paterson University, Wayne, NJ.

Taylor, M. (2005). *Working with generations*. Retrieved from http://www.taylorprograms.com/.

Acknowledgment

This book is dedicated to my mother, Joyce Ferris, who was a constant presence as this book developed. Although she could not see the book's completion, she is still with me.

Thanks also to my ever-supportive family. Jakers and Shayleigh are the best examples of the Net Generation anyone could want! Brian gave me lots of time and space to work and kept me in touch with the real world.

An edited book entails complex processes: of researching themes, seeking submissions, working with authors, setting up and coordinating peer reviews – all of which take place unacknowledged. So thanks to all who participated in these processes – colleagues and friends who helped post the Call, conference attendees who spread the word, all those who submitted proposals, even those not accepted.

This book could not have been completed without the reviewers who gave so generously of their time and effort. Special thanks go to super-reviewers Kelli Jean Smith, Kathleen Woods and Maureen Minielli – professional, prompt, and above all, friends whose value goes far beyond this simple acknowledgement can recognize.

Thanks also to the following who shared their expertise by blind-reviewing chapters: Rukhsana Ahmed, Simon Atkinson, Shannan Butler, Ryan Curtis, Ben DaCosta, Scott D'Urso, Susanne Croasdaile, Maureen Ebben, Bill Gibbs, Carrie Hong, Martin Guardado, Jim Gleason, Gerry Mongillo, Yuping Mao, Kevin Meyer, Keri Stephens, Charles Ruddick, and Hilary Wilder.

Finally, thanks go to my editor, Hannah Abelbeck from IGI Global, whose prompt responses and excellent guidance smoothed the path of this book.

Sharmila Pixy Ferris
William Paterson University, USA

Section 1
Theories and Concepts

He who loves practice without theory is like the sailor who boards ship without a rudder and compass and never knows where he may cast (Leonardo da Vinci).

Although pedagogy remains of interest to many educators, there is a dearth of pedagogical theory today. The main concerns of educators often seem to be practicalities, rather than research that develops theories. This is problematic, as theories are at the heart of practice. In education especially, theories are essential to planning and research, as well as practice.

The chapters in this section address this issue, examining theories and concepts through the lens of educators, administrators, and students. Atkinson proposes a model to help educators effectively meet the challenges of new generations of learners; his model focuses on students' learning needs, while acknowledging the perspectives of their teachers. Reiguleth, Watson, and Watson offer a model utilizing technology for student-centered learning, which builds on the strengths of technology to facilitate administration and education. Muir articulates a responsive pedagogy of classroom practices that are equally relevant to learners of all generations. Aust considers the benefits of face-to-face interpersonal communication as an essential factor in fostering student development.

The chapters in this section also address an equally important issue in the consideration of theory: that of implementation. Sometimes theories cannot be translated into practice; other times there's a lack of congruence between theory and actual classroom practice. The authors in this section make clear the correspondence between theory and practice. Atkinson's model is clearly articulated and can be adopted with ease by institutions of higher education, as can Reiguleth, Watson, and Watson's PIES model. Compton clearly demonstrates how Inoculation theory can positively impact both the content and the processes of students' thinking, and Aust presents ways to build on the power of physical presence.

Taken together, these chapters present sound learning theories to help us understand teaching and learning more effectively.

Chapter 1
Developing Faculty to Integrate Innovative Learning into Their Practice with the SOLE Model

Simon Paul Atkinson
BPP University College, UK

ABSTRACT

A subtle blend of institutional approaches, customised to each institution, is necessary if the challenge of adopting the very best of educational technologies to meet the demands of new emerging generations of learners is to be met. The Student-Owned Learning-Engagement (SOLE) model is suggested as providing one possible institutional solution. The Net generation, both in its mythological state and its rudimentary reality, presents a challenge to contemporary universities, to teach in increasingly diverse ways, to increasingly diverse populations. Senior university leaders and faculty must acknowledge that the very nature of knowledge creation, stewardship, and propagation has changed. Faculty, trained in one epistemological universe, must be supported in adapting their skills to a new one.

INTRODUCTION

This chapter identifies the myths that inform, and mis-inform, current policy, the actual challenges that result, and suggests a model that supports a professional, disciplined and sustainable response on the part of educators. The SOLE model is proposed as one means to meet this challenge. It builds on the educational theories that have dominated the last 70 years of higher education in the Anglo-Saxon world and much of Western Europe. Cognizant of behaviourist, cognitivist, and constructivist theories of learning, the SOLE model provides an opportunity to evaluate the conditions, identify strategies, and monitor performance of teaching and learning with each subsequent cohort, or generation of students. It supports a model of learning design that accommodates innovative

DOI: 10.4018/978-1-61350-347-8.ch001

methods, using emerging technologies, as readily as it supports 'traditional' models of classroom practice. It exposes existing pedagogic practice and suggests, but does not restrict, the initiative of the learning designer. It seeks to identify and support the learner's characteristics, self-understanding, and metacognitive development, and allow these to determine the learning process. It is intended to be suitable for this 'generation' and all those that come after.

BACKGROUND

There is a clear need for higher education to be responsive to its current learners' needs and for faculty to be supported in this process. Contemporary developments require the support of new models of academic practice and new approaches to learning. We must first clarify what, if anything, is genuinely new about our current cohorts of learners and then look for approaches to learning design that are capable of accommodating current and future changes.

It is unwise to suggest that an entire generation is digitally wired, connected and digitally literate, indeed the evidence suggests the contrary (Jones, Ramanau, Cross, & Healing, 2010). While it produces useful headlines and clear policy options, it does not necessarily produce effective education. Each course design, each member of faculty, needs the skills to profile, identify, and empathise with each subsequent cohort. Each course of study must be responsive, appropriate, and supportive of cohorts emerging and evolving modes of learning behaviour.

I would contest the notion that this generation is any more unique than any previous generation, or indeed the notion of a generation at all, but I support the need for pedagogical practices, resources, and faculty development that seeks to understand and optimize learning for contemporary learners, digital or otherwise. Institutions everywhere are challenged by the need to provide increasingly personalised learning experiences for increasingly diverse cohorts of students. This pressure, from national government policymakers worldwide and university managers, and indirectly from students themselves, is one that individual academics can either choose to resist, to embrace, or feel afflicted by. The individual response and the institutional response are often in disharmony. The question of whether it is *appropriate* to 'develop' existing and new academics to integrate e-learning into their practice is worth exploring. There is a danger that 'developing' suggests that this is something that requires additional effort, that it is not in the normal manner of things. Likewise, to suggest that this applies to existing and new academics rather than simply to refer to all academics, also implies that our current situation is something extraordinary. We might also take issue with the notion of 'to integrate,' which again implies that there is something 'other' that needs to be incorporated into established or recognised practice.

Our physical classrooms, our teaching spaces, laboratories, seminar rooms and lecture theatres have not undergone significant change. The assumptions on the part of both teachers and students of the nature of learning that takes place in these well-established, and well understood spaces, have been difficult to challenge. Indeed, it is remarkable how enduring these images of educational spaces are. The promise of technology-enhanced mega-universities designed to meet the needs of a growing global population of aspiring graduates (Daniel, 1996) appears to be stubbornly resisted by universities. For example, despite being freed of all the constraints of physical reality universities still persist in building large virtual 3-D representations of traditional lecture theatres in Second Life (www.secondlife.com). In this context, the question of academic development is a highly pertinent one. The e-learning agenda has demonstrated, perhaps more clearly than any other change in the educational space, how ill prepared many faculty are to teach in the contemporary environment in which they find themselves. Technology has become a diagnostic test of pedagogical understanding. The absence of effective reward and recognition systems for teaching in our universities is evidence of the persistent dominance of 19th and 20th century models of knowledge, of pre-digital epistemology. Higher education is one of the last, if not the only, remaining self-declared 'professions' in which it is possible to practice without being qualified.

THE CHALLENGE

E-learning should not be *integrated* into practice, it must *change* practice, in some cases radically and beyond all recognition. Academics should not be required to integrate e-learning, they should be supported to re-evaluate, to re-model, and redesign their teaching every year to account for new physical spaces, new student contexts, as well as new digital opportunities. Academics are higher education's greatest asset, they are an expensive resource, and one which must be adequate to the task. The professionalisation of faculty as teachers, researchers and administrators, is, in many respects, a question of identity. Just as the nature of knowledge and meaning making has evolved radically in the last 50 years, so too has the role of the academic (Henkel, 2005). But this evolving role has been, in many cases, resisted. In the same way that digital developments have influenced education as a whole, one might reasonably suggest that there is a large contingent of our population who are digitally literate, and net savvy. But this phenomena is not evenly distributed throughout societies in the developed world, or within any single nation state. There is a digital divide that is not simply generational but also educational, socio-economic and cultural. Whilst there are discernable age related variations in behaviours with respect to technology adoption and use, there is no definable generation (Jones et al., 2010). Yet the myth of the net generation persists. It has led to naive and impractical policies, unrealistic political ambitions for education and, as a result, has achieved relatively little.

What there has been is a significant cultural change. There has been a change in the way that individuals communicate, in the way that they store information, share resources, exchange views. Individuals from all generations are making new information, in new forms, they are creating knowledge and new interpretations of that knowledge, they are creating new meanings, sharing insight, learning to be critical, learning to compare and evaluate (Jenkins, 2009). Whether tagging others' content online, or engaging in some mash-up, individuals are manipulating information and the knowledge that it represents, to create new knowledge and share new representations. Indeed, in many cases, individuals are changing the world around themselves, developing user-generated contexts in which they can be the individuals they aspire to be.

Our universities, as well as our schools, have a mandate from the societies that validate them. There is a time delay in how this mandate is negotiated and a lack of public engagement with an agenda that is so influential. Nonetheless, there is an institutional need, and a social expectation, to prepare teaching staff in such a way as to enable students to benefit from the social realities in which they will function. There is a debate about institutional roles, about the level of control that an institution can, should or must influence over technology or whether to release the freedom of open source, open repositories, and the collective creativity of Web 2.0 applications (Atkinson, 2009). These are important questions which institutions, and associations or federations of institutions, must consider if they are serious about enabling their staff to fulfil their remit. Clarity about that remit is essential.

In practice, all of the approaches to technology adoption in our institutions are contextually dependent. The change that has occurred in the development and formation of information and knowledge exchange has changed the very identity of academics and of institutions. That this change appears to have gone largely unnoticed by many academics is as remarkable as it is problematic.

There is a significant task ahead in terms of this identity work. It is not simply about developing individuals' abilities to teach by making them aware of the new, or relatively new, learning theory. Nor is it merely about familiarising staff with new technologies that might enable them to do something more effective and progressive in their classrooms. Rather it is about re-describing what it means to be an academic, what it means to be a teacher in a contemporary university in a developing world (Davidson, 2009). The contemporary academic needs to understand enough learning theory to be able to make sound professional judgments about appropriate technology, they need to have a sufficiently profound understanding of the nature of the learner, of the context in which the learning is taking place, of the context of the discipline and its development, to be able to make judgments about technology. This is not a widely distributed ability; it is not a de facto requirement for successful completion of a doctorate or appointment to a tenured or secure academic position. It is a requirement though for an effective contemporary academic teaching in a modern university.

In an environment in which learning takes place through increasingly social networks, and in which content is often freely available, the notion of the academic as the guardian of canonical knowledge has surely evaporated. Staff themselves must adopt and adapt the communication practices of the society into which students will go to be effective in their practices (Luehmann & Tinelli, 2008). The barriers to open educational resources (OER) are rarely purely technical (De Liddo, 2010). Rather, there is a perception on the part of academics that only knowledge which they have created or contextualised, and transmitted, is suitable for their students. They do their students a disservice. Certainly to reuse learning resources will require their re-contextualisation, but since one of the most effective means of learning is to deconstruct and reconstruction knowledge, even that process of re-contextualisation may engage the student and form part of the learning process.

ISSUE: FRAMEWORKS FOR DEVELOPMENT

The question is not so much about the method, or appropriateness, of integration of alternative practices into existing practice. It is, instead, about the design of learning and the ability of staff, faculty and designers, to design, articulate and share appropriate models of learning. Whilst it is unrealistic to expect all academics to be specialists in learning theory, it is not unrealistic to expect that they be sufficiently versed in learning theory as to enable them to design appropriate learning opportunities. The danger of 'leading' change by adopting a technology focused redesign of learning is that teacher focused practices are simply remodelled through technology without the necessary shift towards a learner centred epistemology. It is not that we require faculty to develop learning with new technology in mind, but rather that we anticipate all staff should develop learning for an appropriate context. Boud and Prosser (2002) have suggested a learner-focused perspective that situates learning design in the context of quality lifelong learning outcomes. Learning and teaching are seen as 'relational phenomena,' stressing that learning is always situated in a unique context. It is important, therefore, that learning design encourages deep learning with specific subject matter but also that learners are aware of the design, structure and intent of the learning process. David Boud (1993) identifies five elements of effective adult learning that neatly encapsulates these learning centred perspectives. These are:

- Learning built on a foundation of experience;
- The active construction of learner's own experience;
- Learning as an holistic process;

- Learning as being socially and culturally constructed;
- Learning as being influenced by the 'socio-emotional context' in which it occurs (Boud, 1993).

Research from both higher education and professional contexts suggests that the learner experience, and the resultant outcomes, is greatly influenced by learners' perspectives of that experience. This suggests that transparency in learning design is a crucial element. Boud and Prosser (2002) suggest a framework is learner-centred and communicates learning as being 'holistic, relational, and problematic.' The resulting framework is structured around four areas which are:

- **Engagement of learners:** taking into account prior knowledge and expectations;
- **Acknowledgement of the learning context:** but the context of the learner and the context of learning;
- **Learner challenge:** taking learners beyond the immediate experience of provided materials;
- **The provision and practice:** with a stress on demonstration feedback reflection and the development of confidence (Boud & Prosser, 2002).

The framework is designed to produce high quality learning activities but also provides some indication of how individual courses, or programmes of study, might be approached. The framework outlined by Boyd and Prosser aligned closely with that detailed by Hung and Chen (2001) on e-learning design in the context of situated learning which resulted in six key principles. These are:

- Learning is embedded in rich cultural and social contexts;
- Learning is reflective and metacognitive;
- Learning is an identity formation or act of membership;
- Learning is a social act/construction mediating between social beings through language, science, the genres and tools;
- Learning is socially distributed between persons and tools;
- Learning is demand driven/dependent on engagement in practice (Hung & Chen, 2001).

These frameworks suggest that learning content and process should be transparent to the learner, and that learning is distributed between the individual and the tools at their disposal. The frameworks also stress the need for learner engagement regardless of whether or not the context includes technology. Indeed the level of technology adoption is largely irrelevant to the underlying principles of these frameworks. The primary importance is assigned to learning context and learner expectations, to the socially and culturally embedded nature of learning. To design learning with the stress on the subject content, devoid of the learner experience is ineffective and out of place. There is a tension between the design of learning that is overly contextualised, non-reusable, and subject specific, and designs which follow basic principles but which may prove less than practical to implement. What is required is a model of learning that places the learner at the centre, that stresses the need for learning challenge and engagement, reflection and metacognition, but which is valid regardless of the technology used to enable the model.

SOLUTION: A STUDENT-OWNED LEARNING-ENGAGEMENT (SOLE) MODEL

From Concept to Model

One model that attempts to fulfil the need for learner-centredness is the Student-Owned Learning-Engagement (SOLE) model (Atkinson, 2011). This model (see Figure 1) sees the learner

Figure 1. SOLE model June 2010

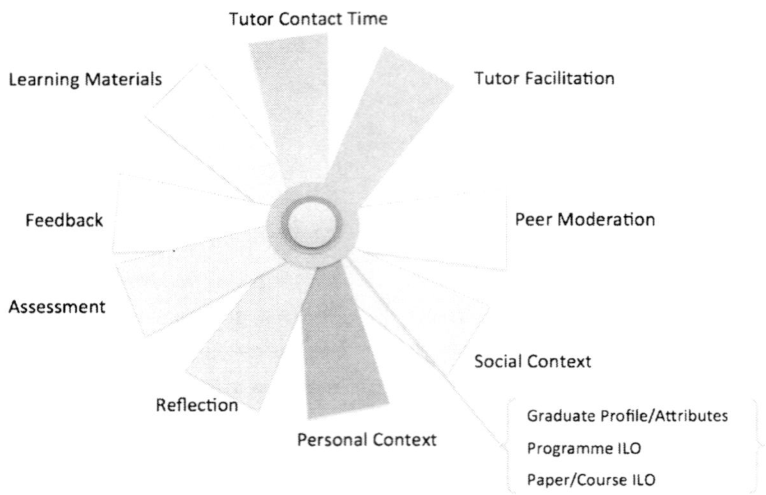

as 'owning' the learning design itself and attempts to embed and embody both theory and practice in a practical visual representation. It is a model that implicitly requires academics to design learning that takes account of both Boud and Prosser (2002), and Hung and Chen's (2001) recommendations.

Developed on the basis of an increasing demand from academics for support in designing within a blended institutional delivery environment, with the same learning outcomes expected of both face-to-face and online delivery, the SOLE model attempts to capture in its nine elements of student activity, or engagement, the pre-requisites for effective learning design. These elements, described in Table 1, are designed to reflect a comprehensive consideration of the students' learning experience that, if properly populated, would afford an effective balance of activity, of

Table 1. The nine learning-engagement elements of the SOLE model

Element	Definition
Feedback	Supportive guidance on quality and level of evidence being demonstrated in achievement of the learning outcomes.
Assessment	Both formative and summative assessment.
Reflection	Identified as a reflection-on-action to reflection-in action process through the course life-cycle.
Personal Context	The individual life context, which the learner occupies, is a source of real-world activity we can build on in our learning design.
Social Context	The non-course context in which the learner lives is a source of real-world activity we can build on in our course design.
Peer Moderation	The direct engagement with fellow students on the same learning cycle, which can be reasonably directed.
Tutor Facilitation	Time and activity allocated to asynchronous engagement involving the teacher.
Tutor Contact Time	Time and activity allocated for real-time synchronous engagement.
Learning Materials	The materials provided, usually in advance, to support domain knowledge acquisition.

learning ownership and opportunities, for higher-order thinking and deep learning.

It is worth noting that the names of the elements are intended to be customizable to different institutional contexts. It is possible, for instance, that 'tutor' could be substituted for 'lecturer,' and that 'learning materials' be redefined as 'resources.' It is also possible that in particular institutional contexts, an additional element might be added, although to date the author has not encountered any element of active learning engagement, defined from the perspective of what a student does, that is not reflected in the existing nine elements of the model.

The model was initially designed to serve as a faculty development tool, to be worked through at course team meetings or in professional development contexts. It is a tool for professional debate, allowing individual academics to reflect on their personal practice, to reflect the specific needs of their disciplines, and to draw on the recommendations of colleagues, former students, and current students. The model requires that the conversations that inform and populate it are necessarily current.

From Model to Toolkit

Educational theory should, perhaps, be of interest to all learning and teaching practitioners but a visual representation may still not be sufficient to make theory 'live' for many teachers. Whilst the opportunity exists for professional development around a presentation and discussion of the model itself, and these have been successfully undertaken in workshops, such a model needs to be as accessible as possible. Conole suggests, 'the development of toolkits provides a way for non-specialists to engage with such theories in a manner which supports careful design and prompts productive reflection and engagement' (Conole, Dyke, Oliver, & Seale, 2004, p. 18).

The need, therefore, is to support professional development and reflection with a means to 'actualise' the model in a practical and meaningful way. The SOLE model's stated aims (Atkinson, 2011) are to seek to;

- embody pedagogical guidance and learning theory within an accessible and transparent model shared by students and teachers;
- embody best practices regarding constructive alignment (Biggs & Tang, 2007) inside a learning design model easily accessible to, and shared by, staff and students;
- produce a practical model that 'captured' the lessons to be learnt from Laurillard's representations of conversational learning processes (Laurillard, 1993), whilst taking an inclusive approach to alternative conceptualisations of learning;
- enable the development of a practical toolkit that would make patterns of learning design shareable and transparent to students and colleagues (Conole & Fill, 2005).

Whilst the model incorporates pre-existing theory in its design, it does not enforce a specific pedagogical theory. Although neither advocating social-constructivism nor constructivism, the model does advocate the interconnectedness of the learner experience with the learner as central. This is not an advocacy of solipsism but rather of building on all the connections, present and past, that each individual values.

To enable faculty to design learning that is transparent to students, one of the underlying principles of the SOLE model is that a representation, or visualisation, of the learning can be made available to students. This serves to engage the learners, acknowledge their context, and make transparent the learning process. This visualisation takes the simple form of a printout from Microsoft Excel or as a PDF for upload into a virtual environment or email distribution. This visualisation acts as a form of advanced organiser, but is highly significant. By making available the learning design with all of the various elements of the SOLE model populated, the course designer is making it clear that the student takes possession of the *intended* learning process. The students have before them what is expected of them in all of the areas of learning previously distributed, often unevenly, between staff and student. The stress is on students owning the process. A toolkit using Microsoft Excel, the template made freely available via the web (www.solemodel.org), allows academics with no additional professional development beyond basic Excel use, to create an integrated and holistic view of the learning process that accounts the theory but is not constrained by it.

The model is accompanied by an Excel toolkit (see Figure 2) because:

Toolkits are designed to facilitate the identification of implications or recommend suitable approaches based on the information and assumptions elicited from the user. They provide a structured guiding framework, whilst also enabling flexibility and local contextualisation. Therefore rather than the toolkit deciding on the best approach on behalf of the user, the practitioner uses these interferences to make informed, professional decisions about whether certain changes would be appropriate. (Conole et al., 2004, p. 22)

The toolkit provides much the same opportunities for professional development as the model but supports the individual teacher, and ultimately the student, 'to work "within" a learning design, diagnosing expected activity, adjusting the balance of engagement through the development process, describing (as an advanced organiser) what the learning might look like and providing opportunities for on-going evaluation.' (Atkinson, 2011).

Embedded Pedagogical Guidance

The choice of Microsoft Excel as the software environment to support a toolkit was made to ensure that the skills acquisition required of faculty would be minimal, that use would build on existing practice, and add meaningfully to an individual's skill set regardless of whether they persisted with the toolkit. One feature of the Microsoft Excel environment that is particularly attractive for the toolkit is the ability to add comments to any cell within any spreadsheet (see Figure 3), and to add sheets containing bespoke guidance which can subsequently be deleted without impacting on the toolkit as a whole.

The ability to add comments to cells within a spreadsheet has led to the creation of a dedicated support environment, an annotated version of the model and its definitions with embedded advice at two levels. A series of meta-questions relating to how individual faculty might approach the elements of the model is provided, and a series of more detailed questions, references and guidance provided in such a way that they could be easily customised to a specific institutional context. This allows the toolkit to be used by staff development units, or course team leaders, to share established good practice and guide the implementation of new and existing courses. Each of these definitions is supported online (www.solemodel.org) with a short annotated video describing a function of the element and examples of its implications for learning design. These generic videos can be replaced with institutionally specific ones if more institutional guidance is required.

The toolkit can be downloaded freely and is customizable. Guidance sheets can be deleted without impacting on the weekly, or unit views, and the overview that they generate. It would be practical, therefore, for a course leader or staff developer to add a sheet by way of exemplar, or to embed specific guidance on some aspects of course design practice such as institutional guidelines on plagiarism or word length.

Embodied Best Practice

The toolkit provides a visualisation of where learners are spending their time. An automatically generated pie chart, reminiscent of the model, al-

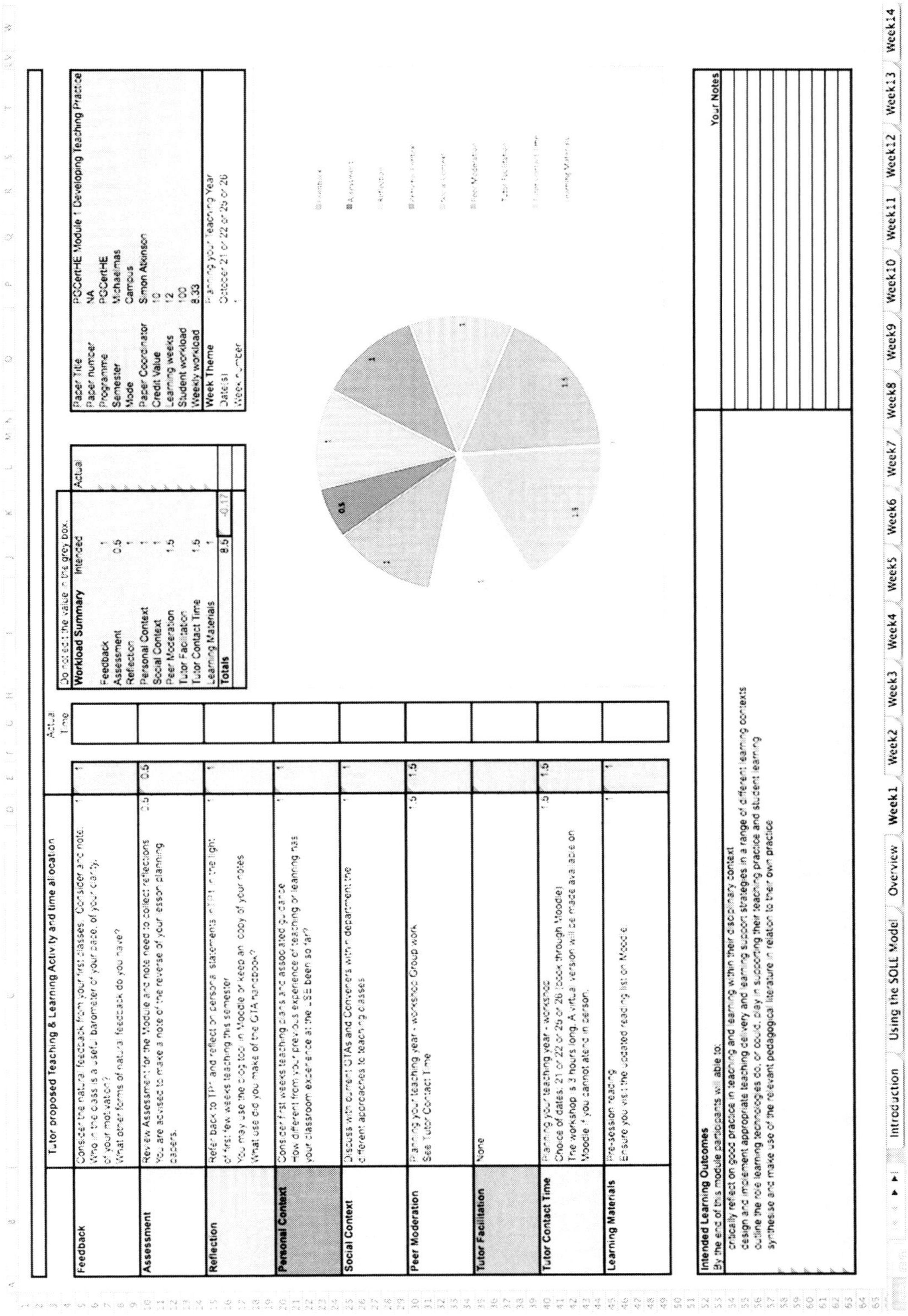

Figure 2. Using the SOLE model

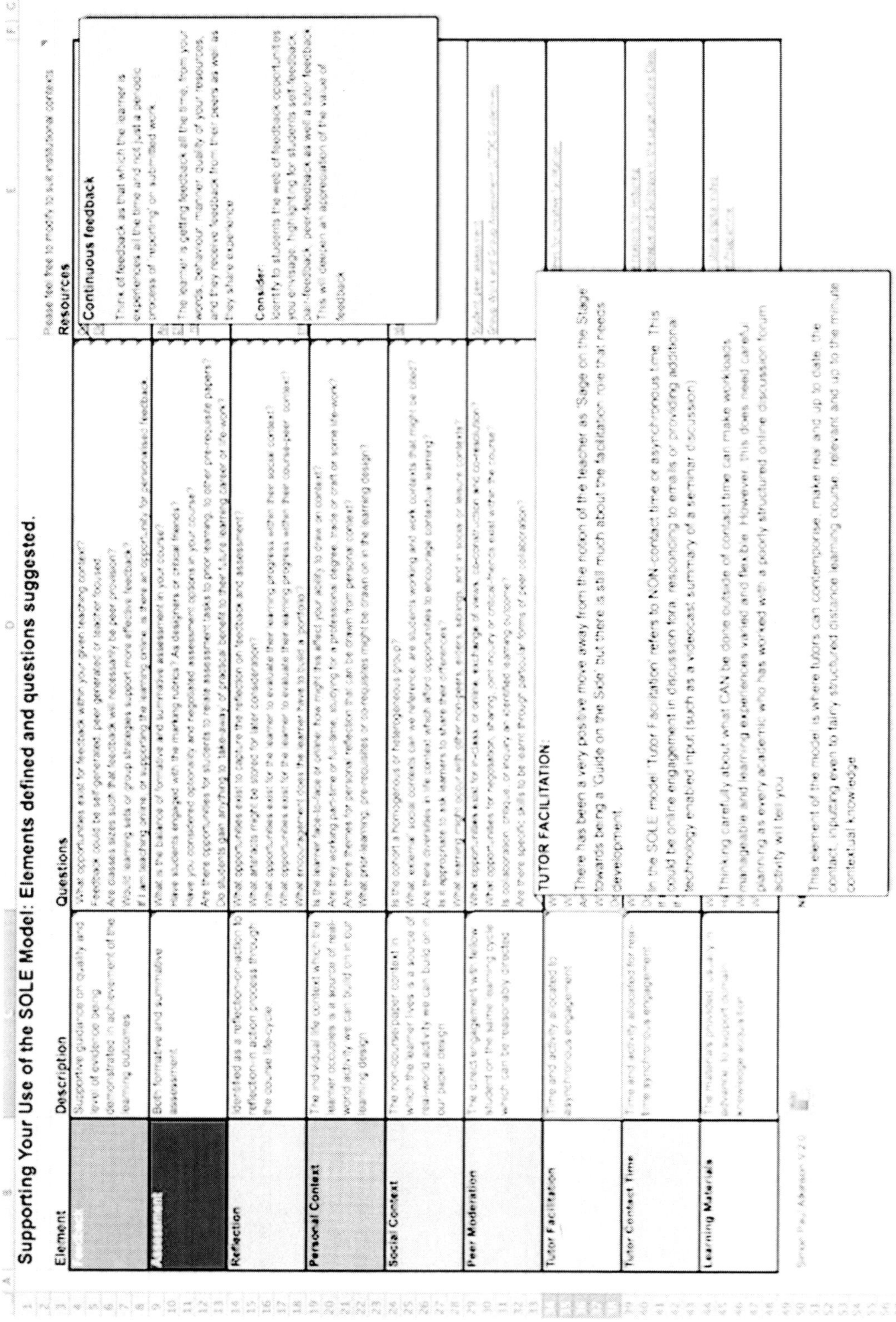

Figure 3. Embedded guidance as cell comments in Microsoft Excel

lows for a quick and easy visual reference. Both students and faculty can identify at a glance where the majority of time is being suggested for students to engage in aspects of their learning. The result is that the learning design can identify how the balance of activity, between faculty and student, varies over the course of a number of weeks. So, one might expect to see, for example, that in the early stages of a semester long course a greater degree of tutor contact time and tutor facilitation but perhaps less assessment. (Note that the term tutor is used here in the same sense as teaching assistants or lecturers.) Later in the period of study, one might expect to see significantly less direct tutor contact and a greater degree of independent learning, signified by more engagement activities being described in the reflection and feedback elements. Whilst the model and toolkit do not enforce this pattern, it makes it evident. The real benefit of this visualisation is that students themselves can see the degree to which their learning is dependent upon others and dependent upon them assuming ownership of its varied dimensions.

A degree of balance week by week, or unit by unit, might suggest good practice but the reality of each individual course design is down to the judgement of the individual learning designer. Whilst the model does not, in itself, represent best practice, it operates on the assumption that best practice is contextually specific, and that best practice will be established through first use of the model and toolkit. The use of a toolkit makes explicit the decisions that the learning designer takes, it provides both for them and for their students evidence of their intent.

Descriptive, Developmental, Evaluative, and Diagnostic

The toolkit is intended to fulfil four functions. The individual spreadsheets in the toolkit function as an advanced organiser, a personal planner, for students. The student might be provided with this as a PDF printout, as a guide for how to engage with the resources, of where to be for contact time, or provide questions for reflection. It does not replace course materials or other guidance that might be more expansive in the context of the virtual learning environment, but it does provide a quick identifiable structure to the complexity of learning. Beyond its descriptive function, the ability to plan and develop a period of study whilst maintaining an overview of the balance of learner activity, signifies the toolkit's developmental function. Conceived of as an instrument for collaborative design, for course teams to debate, discuss and share, the toolkit allows for incremental development. A user can choose to begin and end the design process wherever they choose.

One individual may choose to articulate all of the assessment and feedback activities for a period of study across all the weeks when units, and then to identify their relationship with other elements. Another colleague may choose to focus all their attention on the personal contextual element and identify where the individual students pre-existing knowledge and experience provide a central thread to their design. Yet another colleague may choose to identify their tutor contact time first and all other elements subsequently. Where an individual starts the design process says much about their approach to learning and teaching, their epistemological assumptions, and the relative value they place on learners' ownership of learning.

The toolkit provides the opportunity for students to annotate each spreadsheet with the actual time spent on suggested engagement activities. It also allows students themselves to add comments to individual sheets using the same cell comment facility used to provide pedagogical guidance for faculty. The flexibility of the spreadsheet means that faculty can collate, week by week or at the end of the period of study, a sample or entire cohorts' experiences, and in so doing, modify and develop their design. This signifies the toolkit's evaluative function.

The transparency of the learning design represented by the toolkit provides a powerful diagnostics tool. Student feedback on the quality and value, timing and pace, usefulness or redundancy, or different elements of learning can be easily compared to the intended learning design and assessed for their validity. Beyond simply collecting evaluation data, the data are collected within the context of the learning itself providing an immediate environment for evaluation. Encouraging students to insert cell comments in response to the guidance they have been given, reflecting on the choices they made, the difficulties encountered with particular activities and so on, is also incidentally developing the students' skills in manipulating spreadsheets.

IMPLICATIONS FOR THE NET-GENERATION

The SOLE model and its associated toolkit did not set out to address directly the implications of a supposedly digitally wired and networked generation of students, but it does so. It aims to support the process of learning design in such a way that it is contemporarily relevant, focused on individual students' context, and cognisant of the complexity of students' learning environment. In itself neither model nor toolkit addresses the question of digital literacy or information management skills, but it does provide an organising framework that learning designers can use to identify and anticipate the engagement activities, what the student is being asked to do, across nine distinct but interrelated elements.

If in identifying that the personal context of students is such that they uniformly possess hand-held mobile devices capable of accessing Web content, then a learning designer might choose to provide access to learning materials by this means. Should it be clear that students' social context is one in which active participation in sports is a near certainty, then the course might be designed in such a way so as to use this fact. Attention to the realities of the individual student within a social context, and subsequently within a peer context, allows the learning designer to produce a design relevant and pertinent to the reality of that particular cohort of students. Refreshing these considerations each semester, or each year, ensures that the decisions about how and where to use technology are based on individual student contexts and needs and not on institutional fetishisms dictated by commercial third parties.

Universities must accept that the context of the student now takes precedence over the established 'industrial' context in which our institutions primarily have their foundations. Increasingly, individuals have constructed, through choices made and using personalised tools, unique contexts within which they perceive learning takes place (Luckin, 2010). These 'user-generated contexts' represent new emerging relationships with time, space and sense of place (Pachler, Bachmair, Cook, & Kress, 2010), as well as with notions of belonging, cultural exchange and redefinitions of what Bourdieu describes as habitus, that amalgamation of socially learnt dispositions, that define who were are relative to 'others' (Bourdieu, 1977).

The danger is that current practice in learning design does not challenge the underlying assumptions of the designers themselves. It does not challenge existing attitudes to the established canonical knowledge of disciplines or the priority given to particular learning activities in particular contexts. Instead, there is a tendency for institutions to add rather than review, to impose on academic faculty perceived needs to meet perceived expectations, rather than to facilitate changing patterns of behaviour in response to changing contexts. This is most clearly evidenced by the introduction of the now ubiquitous online environments, variously described as virtual learning environments or collaborative environments, but which often serve little purpose beyond that of a repository. Where practice has evolved towards online dialogue there is the discussion fora, in which staff often find themselves caught between the frustration of establishing enthusiastic participation from students and the fear that wholesale engagement would mean massively increased workloads. Guidance on effective online practice that suggests each student requires personalised, reassuring and motivational support makes large-scale online collaborative discussions impractical, though not impossible. The adoption of technologies for the purpose of supporting established learning patterns has led to cynicism, confusion, and frustration on both the part of students and faculty in many of our institutions. We must deconstruct and reconstruct our practice, challenging our assumptions about how students learn and our roles and responsibilities towards their learning.

Contemporary learners, like contemporary consumers, voters, and audiences, seek to exercise choice. They expect immediacy, responsiveness and feedback on their choices (Jones & Healing, 2010). In the developed world, our lifestyles are characterised by a changing attitude to time, no longer do we rush from work to the post office or bank at lunchtime; instead we use online banking for many of the services we require. We don't rush home to watch our favourite television programmes, but rather we download them or watch them online at the time of our convenience. It is not simply that times have changed but that the very nature of relationship with time has changed. As a consequence, contemporary learners are not limited to the learning experience 'between bells ringing in the schoolyard.' Society has moved past the routines of the agrarian age dictated by the seasons and still further beyond the ticking clock and shift bell of the industrial age. Yet most of our educational institutions remain wedded to a timetable, dictated to by room allocations, and reading lists contingent upon shelf space in the library stacks. Contemporary learners are ill served by the structures of our institutions, not because there isn't enough technology, e-learning, or digital resource, but because the fundamental design of learning itself does not allow them to make choices, utilise responses and provide feedback.

As the head of e-learning in a British university in the mid 2000s I often heard faculty declare confidently 'that cannot be taught online.' The question, of course, was really whether it could be learnt online, whether the student in their virtual engagement with the learning could benefit by the distance, the time to reflect, and the opportunities for considered discussion and repeated review of material. The faculty concerned nonetheless made a valid point. They could not teach that material online and they did not, and could not be expected to, know how to shift their perspective to one that focused entirely on whether the learner could learn in a changed environment. Like many others, I have found the notion of the net generation less than helpful in conversation with faculty. It has seen ill-informed educational leadership scurrying into the arms of self-aggrandising digital advocates, and to commit to massive expenditure on IT systems they did not fully understand. What has been helpful is that the conversations, news reports, conference papers and policy polemics regarding the net generation have served as a disturbing dilemma (Mezirow, 1978), a wake-up call to the industrial educational machine. There is a growing realisation that epistemologies themselves evolve, and that there are new emerging digital epistemologies (Lankshear & Knobel, 2003), complex literacies, unevenly distributed through our societies, which require mature and varied responses (Gee, 2008).

Learning design should be relevant for each cohort of students. To be more explicit, learning design should be relevant for each context, defined by space, time and participants. An effective learning design for a campus-based humanities degree program for full-time undergraduate students, mostly aged under 25, in Vancouver should be expected to look very different from a part-time distance supported public health education programme for practising social workers at a Kenyan regional university. Yet both might be effective, conscientiously tailored to the needs of their cohort. Both are likely to make use of educational technologies appropriate to the intended cohort in their context. The best practice in learning design is the one that is appropriately tailored to the needs of an identified cohort of students.

FUTURE RESEARCH DIRECTIONS

The Student-Owned Learning-Engagement (SOLE) model has already been presented and demonstrated in conferences and workshops in New Zealand, the United Kingdom and United States. The toolkit has been used in whole, or in part, to design or evaluate several university level programmes of study. As the evidence through practice accumulates, it is anticipated that the toolkit will develop to take advantage of the functionality of Microsoft Excel. The embedded guidance in the downloadable toolkit will evolve to reflect the latest literature and shared best practice.

The question of where the individual learning designer chooses to begin the design process is one intended avenue of future research. Simply, the discussion with junior and experienced faculty about the orientation of the model (where the orientation of text does not portray the author's own implicit assumptions) is a fascinating one. Early experience with the model in New Zealand suggested that some colleagues wish to give priority to the social context of learning and would choose to place this element at the 'top' or 'start' of the model. In a workshop with a distance learning course team at the inception of the model, colleagues placed the learning materials element at the 'top.' Since there is no correct orientation of the model, this process of beginning the learning design discussions with the agreed positioning of the elements portrays many assumptions, individual and shared, about the responsibilities for learning placed on faculty and students, and about the relative importance of students' engagement with feedback versus quality learning materials, or tutor contact versus peer support. Future research on the model will, therefore, focus on how faculty use the model to initiate their learning design process (see Figure 4).

Figure 4. SOLE model without a predetermined orientation May 2011

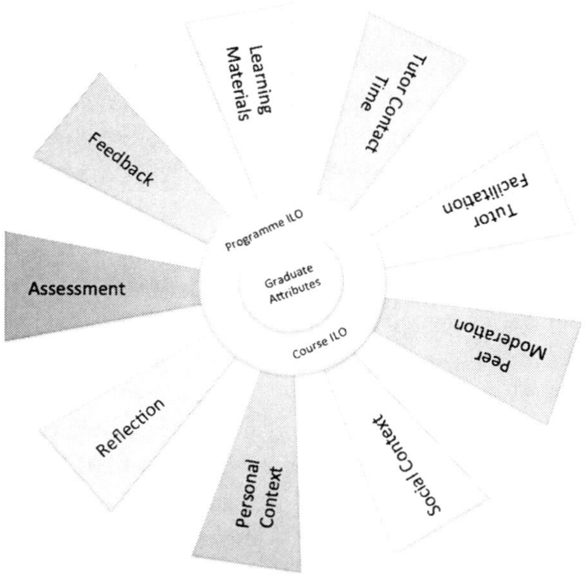

The value of the toolkit, particularly its descriptive, developmental, diagnostic and evaluative dimensions will be borne out in practice. An online community that supports implementation of the model and toolkit, www.solemodel.org, will collate and evaluate user experience in order to refine the toolkit further. The degree to which this particular approach to learning design facilitates a more relevant and tailored learning experience for students, is the focus of this research.

CONCLUSION

Higher Education Institutions are challenged to teach in increasingly diverse ways, to increasingly diverse populations. Established universities find themselves competing with other tertiary providers, professional associations and often more responsive and dynamic private education providers. Senior university leaders must acknowledge that the very nature of knowledge creation, stewardship and propagation has changed. Academics, trained in one epistemological universe must be supported in adapting their skills to a new one. The adoption of the SOLE model of learning design provides the individual teacher with something to work with, or counter to, to improve or adopt. The sensitive introduction of a context aware design process, such as that represented by the SOLE model, customised to each institution is necessary if the challenge of adopting the very best of educational technologies to meet the demands of new emerging generations of learners is to be met.

REFERENCES

Atkinson, S. (2009). *Revolution and pedagogy: Why e-learning can still transform university teaching* (proceedings). EQIBELT Workshop 2007-2008. Zagreb, Croatia: SRCE / University of Zagreb.

Atkinson, S. (2011). Embodied and embedded theory in practice: The student-owned learning-engagement (SOLE) model. *International Review of Research in Open and Distance Learning*, *12*(2), 1–18.

Biggs, J., & Tang, C. (2007). *Teaching for quality learning at university: What the student does* (3rd ed.). Buckingham, UK: Open University Press.

Boud, D. (Ed.). (1993). *Using experience for learning*. Open University Press.

Boud, D., & Prosser, M. (2002). Appraising new technologies for learning: A framework for development. *Educational Media International*, *39*(3), 237. doi:10.1080/09523980210166026

Bourdieu, P. (1977). *Outline of a theory of practice*. Cambridge University Press.

Conole, G., Dyke, M., Oliver, M., & Seale, J. (2004). Mapping pedagogy and tools for effective learning design. *Computers & Education*, *43*(1-2), 17–33. doi:10.1016/j.compedu.2003.12.018

Conole, G., & Fill, K. (2005). A learning design toolkit to create pedagogically effective learning activities. *Journal of Interactive Media in Education*, *1*. Retrieved from http://jime.open.ac.uk/jime/article/viewArticle/104.

Daniel, J. (1996). *Mega-universities and knowledge media: Technology strategies for higher education*. London, UK: Kogan Page.

Davidson, C. (2009). *The future of learning institutions in a digital age*. Cambridge, MA: MIT Press.

De Liddo, A. (2010). From open content to open thinking. *World Conference on Educational Multimedia, Hypermedia and Telecommunications 2010*, (pp. 3178-3183).

Gee, J. P. (2008). *Social linguistics and literacies: Ideology in discourses*. Routledge.

Henkel, M. (2005). Academic identity and autonomy revisited. In Bleiklie, I., & Henkel, M. (Eds.), *Governing knowledge* (*Vol. 9*, pp. 145–165). Berlin, Germany: Springer-Verlag. doi:10.1007/1-4020-3504-7_10

Hung, D. W. L., & Chen, D.-T. (2001). Situated cognition, Vygotskian thought and learning from the communities of practice perspective: Implications for the design of Web-based e-learning. *Educational Media International*, *38*(1), 3.

Jenkins, H. (2009). *Confronting the challenges of participatory culture: Media education for the 21st century*. Cambridge, MA: The MIT Press.

Jones, C., & Healing, G. (2010). Net generation students: Agency and choice and the new technologies. *Journal of Computer Assisted Learning*, *26*(5), 344–356. doi:10.1111/j.1365-2729.2010.00370.x

Jones, C., Ramanau, R., Cross, S., & Healing, G. (2010). Net generation or digital natives: Is there a distinct new generation entering university? *Computers & Education*, *54*(3), 722–732. doi:10.1016/j.compedu.2009.09.022

Lankshear, C., & Knobel, M. (2003). *New literacies: Changing knowledge and classroom learning*. Buckingham, UK: OU Press.

Laurillard, D. (1993). *Rethinking university teaching: A framework for the effective use of educational technology*. London, UK: Routledge.

Luckin, R. (2010). *Re-designing learning contexts: Technology-rich, learner-centred ecologies*. London, UK: Routledge.

Luehmann, A. L., & Tinelli, L. (2008). Teacher professional identity development with social networking technologies: learning reform through blogging. *Educational Media International*, *45*(4), 323. doi:10.1080/09523980802573263

Mezirow, J. (1978). *Perspective transformation. Adult Education Quarterly, 28(2), Pachler, N., Bachmair, B., Cook, J., & Kress, G. (2010). Mobile learning: Structures, agency, practices*. New York, NY: Springer.

ADDITIONAL READING

Antomarchi, C. (2000). Values, public, plurality, what do we teach? How do we learn about it? *ICOM Committee for Conservation. Working Group on Education and Training in Conservation. Newsletter*, (November), 7-8.

Barford, J., & Weston, C. (1997). The use of video as a teaching resource in a new university. *British Journal of Educational Technology*, *28*(1), 40–50. doi:10.1111/1467-8535.00005

Barton, D., & Tusting, K. (2005). *Beyond communities of practice: language, power and social context*. Cambridge University Press. doi:10.1017/CBO9780511610554

Basham, J. D., & Meyer, H. (2010). The Design and Application of the Digital Backpack. *Journal of Research on Technology in Education*, *42*(4), 339–359.

Bawane, J., & Spector, J. M. (2009). Prioritization of online instructor roles: Implications for competency-based teacher education programs. *Distance Education*, *30*(3), 383–397. doi:10.1080/01587910903236536

Bowman, L. L., Levine, L. E., Waite, B. M., & Gendron, M. (2010). Can students really multitask? An experimental study of instant messaging while reading. *Computers & Education*, *54*(4), 927–931. doi:10.1016/j.compedu.2009.09.024

Burden, K., & Atkinson, S. (2009). Personalising teaching and learning with digital resources: DiAL-e Framework case studies. In O'Donoghue, J. (Ed.), *Technology Supported Environment for Personalised Learning: Methods and Case Studies*. Hershey, PA: IGI Global. doi:10.4018/978-1-60566-884-0.ch006

Cronjé, J. C. (2011). Using Hofstede's cultural dimensions to interpret cross-cultural blended teaching and learning. *Computers & Education*, *56*(3), 596–603. doi:10.1016/j.compedu.2010.09.021

Facer, K. (2011). *Learning Futures: Education, Technology and Social Change* (1st ed.). Routledge.

Ferris, S. P., Minelli, M. C., Phillips, K. R., & Leonard, J. G. (2003). *Beyond Survival in the Academy: A Practical Guide for Beginning Academics*. Hampton Press.

García Canclini, N., & Schwartz, translated by M. (2009). How Digital Convergence is Changing Cultural Theory. *Popular Communication: The International Journal of Media and Culture*, *7*(3), 140.

Hatzipanagos, S., & Warburton, S. (2009). Feedback as dialogue: exploring the links between formative assessment and social software in distance learning. *Learning, Media and Technology*, *34*(1), 45–59. doi:10.1080/17439880902759919

JISC. (2006). Design for Learning. Retrieved October 31, 2010, from http://www.jisc.ac.uk/whatwedo/programmes/elearningpedagogy/designlearn.aspx.

Jones, N., Blackey, H., Fitzgibbon, K., & Chew, E. (2010). Get out of MySpace! *Computers & Education*, *54*(3), 776–782. doi:10.1016/j.compedu.2009.07.008

Joy, A., Sherry, J. Jr, Venkatesh, A., & Deschenes, J. (2009). Perceiving images and telling tales: A visual and verbal analysis of the meaning of the internet. *Journal of Consumer Psychology*, *19*(3), 556–566. doi:10.1016/j.jcps.2009.05.013

King, K. P. (2002). *Keeping Pace with Technology: Educational Technology That Transforms: Challenge and Promise for Higher Education Faculty* (*Vol. 2*). Hampton Press.

Kohls, L. R., & Knight, J. M. (1994). *Developing Intercultural Awareness: a Cross-Cultural Training Handbook (Vol. Second)*. Boston, MA and London: Intercultural Press Inc.

Latchem, J. (2006). How does Education Support the Formation and Establishment of Individual Identities? *International Journal of Art & Design Education*, *25*(1), 42–52. doi:10.1111/j.1476-8070.2006.00467.x

Oblinger, D. G., & Oblinger, J. L. (Eds.). (unknown). *Educating the Net Generation* (e-book.). EDUCAUSE. Retrieved from http://www.educause.edu/Resources/EducatingtheNetGeneration/.

Parry, R. (2007). *Recoding the museum: digital heritage and the technologies of change*. Routledge. doi:10.4324/9780203347485

Robinson, K. (2011). *Out of Our Minds: Learning to be Creative* (2nd ed.). Capstone.

Shephard, K. (2003). Questioning, promoting and evaluating the use of streaming video to support student learning. *British Journal of Educational Technology*, *34*(3), 295–308. doi:10.1111/1467-8535.00328

Srinivasan, R., Boast, R., Furner, J., & Becvar, K. M. (2009). Digital Museums and Diverse Cultural Knowledges: Moving Past the Traditional Catalog. *The Information Society*, *25*(4), 265–278. doi:10.1080/01972240903028714

Tight, M. (2002). *Key Concepts in Adult Education and Training* (2nd ed.). Routledge.

Zheng, R., & Ferris, S. P. (2007). *Understanding Online Instructional Modeling Theories and Practices (illustrated edition.)*. Information Science Reference. doi:10.4018/978-1-59904-723-2

KEY TERMS AND DEFINITIONS

Constructive Alignment: Advocated by Professor John Biggs (2007) as the articulation of learning outcomes using active verbs, what the learner should be able to do, which subsequently form the basis of assessment and teaching activity design.

Descriptive: Something which is factually grounded, informative rather than subjective or emotive. A model used to reveal, make transparent, the anticipated learning process.

Developmental: Concerned with supporting development over a defined time period. A model which supports the collaborative development of a learning design.

Diagnostic: Tool, instrument or mechanism used to determine the cause or nature of something. A model used to determine the efficacy in teaching and learning.

Evaluative: Tool, instrument or mechanism for establishing the success or efficacy of intended outcomes. A model used to support the evaluation of a learning design.

Learner-Centered: Concept of the learners' active engagement with learning, cognitive and socio-culturally determined, with respect to learning. Concept providing the focal point, or orientation, for the learning design processes.

Mega-University: Term coined by Professor John Daniels to describe global University with enrolments over 100,000 concurrent students.

Student-Owned Learning-Engagement Model (SOLE): A conceptual model illustrated through a visual representation of nine element of learning engagement activity.

Toolkit: A collection of advice and guidance designed to support the implementation of theoretical principles into practice.

Chapter 2
The Gloss and the Reality of Teaching Digital Natives:
Taking the Long View

Star A. Muir
George Mason University, USA

ABSTRACT

Characterizations of youth growing up with the Internet as Digital Natives have begun a revolution in teaching, but have also been problematized in the literature, opening up significant questions about stereotypical assumptions made by teachers about students in the classroom. Research indicates that a continuing gap exists between "power users" and "digital strangers," which has broad implications for educational priorities and classroom practice. Evidence is also mounting that heavy internet and concurrent media usage impacts both students' ability to focus and their evolving habits of mind as the brain responds to new sources of positive reinforcement. This chapter explores some of these tensions in characterizing and responding to Digital Natives, and seeks to identify a responsive pedagogy of classroom practices that tap into student passions, offer students some techniques to learn focus, attention, and other important skills for both digital and "analog" environments, and address persistent skill gaps between students.

INTRODUCTION

When Marc Prensky (2001) developed the term "Digital Native," he had little idea of the resonance this term would have in our culture. In commerce, entertainment, the workplace, education and numerous other sectors of life, the term has infiltrated society. In usage it has functioned to frame identity, create stereotypes, support grants, sell cell phones, gadgets and lifestyle choices, design curricula, mislead administrators, and inform policymakers, all within a span of about ten years since Prensky's (2001) first writing

DOI: 10.4018/978-1-61350-347-8.ch002

about "Digital Natives, Digital Immigrants." An open Google search of the terms yields 5.89 million results, while linking them together ("digital native") yields roughly 454,000 results. Some of the intensive "cottage industry" that has grown up around the term reflects a high level of "gloss," as multiple different perspectives appear somewhat "polished" and are offered as representative and essentializing descriptors for myriad kinds of people growing up in radically diverse environments. This is at least partly why use of the term "Digital Native" appears at times both glib and perceptive, both laden with misconceptions and full of potential.

This chapter takes a longer view of educating Digital Natives by first discussing some challenges and opportunities outlined for educating students raised with the internet, then problematizing the concept of Digital Native as a hasty generalization, identifying particularly challenging habits of mind emerging from extended internet and multimedia use, and offering a responsive pedagogy that tries to address these challenges through discovery, mindfulness and sharing strategies.

CONTEXTUALIZING THE DIGITAL NATIVE

In the 1990s, the media ecology tradition began identifying an emerging cultural evolutionary shift, which included in part the fall of linear thinking, and the rise of an age of chaos. Rushkoff (2006) describes the rise of holism, animism, consensual hallucination, and distanced participation, and explored myriad ways the "screenagers" embrace chaos, ultimately leading us in adapting to our new cultural milieu. When Prensky introduced the native/immigrant distinction in 2001, he emphasized the need for new learning tools, particularly video games, that would interest as well as inform students. Later, in *Don't Bother Me Now, Mom—I'm Learning* (2006), he extolled the problem-solving and decision-making skills learned using video games. In his most complete work to date on Digital Natives, *Teaching Digital Natives: Partnering for Real Learning*, Prensky (2010) likens his Partnering pedagogy to Problem-, Inquiry-, Challenge-, and Case-based learning, with additional perspectives on the roles of teachers and students in using technology to engage students in ways our current "digital immigrant" designed schools do not. Teachers should avoid the classic "tell and test" in favor of asking probing questions, suggesting challenges, topics and tools, being open to learning about technology from students, supplying context, and evaluating student output for rigor and quality.

Aimed at least in part at reassuring educators uncertain of their new roles, Prensky distinguishes between perennial and relatively unchanging learning Verbs (skills needed to master, like analyzing, evaluating, reflecting, problem-solving, presenting) and rapidly changing Nouns (tools used for developing skills like podcasts, wikis, blogs, brainstorming and game creation tools). In his view, teachers have a responsibility to focus on the selection of Verbs and provide clear quality expectations and feedback, but will often have a learning role because of lack of familiarity with some of the Nouns. Through partnerships, teachers need to tap into student passions to drive learning, and to provide learning that is not just relevant (it relates to something students know) but real (there is a perceived connection between what is learned and doing something useful in the world), while letting students have more control over the Noun (technology) they use.

Focusing on more specific qualities of learners raised in a digital world, Jukes, McCain and Crockett's (2010) underscore the urgency of adapting educational strategies by tracing evolving functional differences in brain structure (neuroplasticity, enhanced visual processing, reading in an "F" pattern, more than 60% are not auditory or text learners) to explain why students are bored in school and have very different learning preferences. To avoid an impending "disconnect tragedy," they advocate educational strategies that feature whole-mind instruction moving away from memorization toward project learning, development of various fluencies (solution, information, collaboration, creativity, media and digital citizenship), and higher order thinking skills (reordering and reframing Bloom's taxonomy to Remembering, Understanding, Applying, Analyzing, Evaluating, and Creating). In their view, teachers show sbecome facilitators and expert problem and question creators, letting students access information "natively," creating opportunities for collaboration, and developing a love for reading while incorporating visual communication within the curriculum.

Among numerous challenge for teachers, Jukes, McCain and Crockett (2010) identify some very deep-seated habits of mind exhibited by digital immigrant educators and administrators (p. 35) (see Table 1).

From this educationally focused perspective, the old framework set by digital immigrants must give way to a new perspective, with a recognition of changing preferences and different roles for the students and the teacher.

Table 1. Educator and digital learner preferences

Digital Learners prefer...	Many Educators prefer...
Information quickly through multiple multimedia sources	Slow and controlled release of information from limited sources
Processing pictures, sounds, color, and video before text	Provide text before pictures, sounds, color, and video
Random access to hyper-linked multimedia information	Provide information linearly, logically, sequentially
Network simultaneously with many others	Students work independently before they network and interact
Learning "just in time"	Teaching "just in case"
Instant gratification with immediate and deferred rewards	Deferred gratification and delayed rewards
Learning that is relevant, active, instantly useful, fun	Memorization for testing.

Research has not, however, focused exclusively on educational and learning characteristics of this new "Net Generation." Tapscott's (2009) team interviewed over 10,000 youth and young adults across twelve countries, and examined several norms of this group at length, including Scrutiny ("trust but verify"), Collaboration, Entertainment (via heavy multitasking), Speed (24X7 Just-in-Time), and Customization. The impact of these norms on educational preferences is notable, Tapscott argues, in that the old model of absorbing vast quantities of information is giving way. "Teachers," Tapscott writes, quoting a high school principal, "are no longer the fountain of knowledge, the Internet is" (p. 126). Now that students can find knowledge in an instant, there is a new focus: "It's not what you know that really counts; it's how you navigate in the digital world and what you do with the information you discover" (p. 134). Discovery, assessment and application become more important for classroom practice, and educators should encourage collaboration but move away from broadcast model to a more personalized, customized model. Students should not be expected to sit quietly and absorb information, but to have a conversation, preferably about something relevant to the real world, interesting, even fun.

Yet not all learning for Digital Natives need necessarily be heavily reliant on technology. Palfrey and Gasser (2008) surveyed evolving notions of identity and privacy, perceptions of risk, degrees of online addiction and activism, and learning styles, concluding that most Digital Natives prefer moderate use of technology, and consider it important not to use technology more but to use it more effectively. Digital Natives can best learn, they claim, through several strategies: (1) fostering learning by doing in digital environments, (2) letting them create their own master work, (3) encouraging team-based learning, and (4) using technology for feedback loops.

Although all these authors provide a compelling image of the Net Generation, based in part on survey work and broad experience, and there are undertones of both urgency and incredible excitement about new possibilities, the phrase Digital Native here becomes a bit shiny and glossy. The barriers to learning, the formatting preferences, the learning styles, the rewritten roles, are all heavily generalized. This shining vision of the educational system responding to the needs of digital learners hides difficulties and some rather challenging implications under the gloss. The following sections will address some of the implications of generalizing about the technical capacities of a generation.

DIGITAL NATIVES AS A HASTY GENERATIONALIZATION

Discussions of Digital Natives and the Net Generation have met with considerable skepticism across an array of theorists, critics, and social scientists. Selwyn (2009) observes that while "the notion of children and young people as confident and often 'expert' computer users has proliferated popular and political rhetoric in Western societies for the past thirty years" (p. 1), the "overall tenor and tone of these discursive constructions of young people and technology tend towards exaggeration and inconsistency" (p. 8). Most of the arguments using these constructions, he concludes, are based on an essentialist biological reading of youth as naturally technically skilled, which "fail to acknowledge the diversity of the lived experience" (Buckingham, 1998, p. 556). Vaidhyanathan (in "Net Generation," 2010) sees this as an "essentially…wrong-headed argument that assumes that our kids have some special path to the witchcraft of 'digital awareness'" (n.p.) This argument has been characterized as "knowledge through anecdote," with highlighted instances of "spectacular" digital practices by some young people, where in the empirical literature a more common picture of less spectacular technology use and engagement emerges (Selwyn, 2009, p. 11).

At a practical and personal level, Michael Wesch, a digital learning innovator, expresses skepticism that his students have more than a superficial familiarity with digital tools they use frequently, particularly related to the social and political potential of these tools (in "Net Generation," 2010, n.p.). This is supported by research in focus groups done with undergraduate freshmen and sophomores, where Burhanna, Seeholzer and Salem (2009) found heavy use of Web 2.0 technologies, but students demonstrated limited knowledge of and interest in specific elements within Web 2.0 technologies. Many were unaware of features like bookmarking and had limited use of more advanced and expressive features. Some were unaware that a "wiki" allows users to change content.

Some of the reality beneath the gloss emerges when reviewing social science research on the generational gap.

A particularly virulent outcry about the empirical basis and application of the term Digital Native has come from Bennett and colleagues in Australia, the United Kingdom, and South Africa. Reviewing debate over the term, Bennett, Maton and Kervin (2008) found that only a minority of students (near 21%) were engaged in creating their own content and multimedia for the web, and that internet use by children depends on the contexts for use, socio-economic status, and family dynamics. Surveying the empirical basis for the Digital Native claims, they conclude that there may be "as much variation *within* the digital native generation as *between* the generations" (p. 779). The very great danger, they argue, is that important variations are overlooked and these generalizations are used as a basis for policy decisions, budget allocations, and educational practice. They conclude by noting that the rhetoric surrounding Digital Natives is based less on clear research evidence, and more on a created and self-sustaining "moral panic" about the state of education and the urgent need for change.

In a special section of the *Journal of Computer Assisted Learning*, these arguments are both developed and heightened. Brown and Czerniewicz (2010b) problematize the commonly used terms ("Net Generation," "Millenials," "i-Generation," and "Digital Natives," among others) as "gross oversimplifications," and question the determinism implicit in these constructions, with the resultant focus on adapting to these technology changes rather than focusing attention on how to shape them. The implications of this deterministic effect of technology on the character and cognitive development of youth and young adults lend new meaning to traditional conceptions of authority "colonizing the natives."

Refocusing attention away from access to technology (a common survey measure) to technology-based activities, Bennett and Maton (2010) find significant variations between age, gender, and socio-economic status. There are of course high level and very low level users, yet even within "moderate use" categories, there is still great variation in the focus and rationale for technology use. They make the important point that many everyday technology activities (e.g., general information-seeking) do not translate particularly well for academic practices or tasks requiring synthesis and critical evaluation, and that educators need to understand and move beyond simple distinctions between "everyday" and "educational" contexts. And they finally comment about the "certainty-complacency" spiral in which the growing use of the term Digital Native amplifies the certainty with which some authors approach the topic, and induces an "intellectual complacency" that continues to offer sensationalist declarations without a strong empirical base.

Looking more deeply at the types of Net Generation students, Kennedy, Judd, Dalgarnot and Waycott (2010) conducted a cluster analysis of over 2000 students at three Australian universities using seven scales of Web 2.0 Publishing, Media Sharing, Advanced Mobile Use, Gaming, Creating and Using Media, Standard Web Use, and Standard Mobile use. Using Multivariate Analysis of Variance, they provide a four-cluster solution that recognizes four types of student technology users (p. 337) (see Table 2).

Ultimately, they conclude, the portion of the population that might fit the descriptions of Digital Natives seem to be the exception rather than the rule. Age, they report, may be "a comparatively weak factor when it comes to explaining variations in students' use of technology" (p. 341). Their clear implication is that whole scale changes in curriculum and/or teaching approaches based on assumptions of Digital Native homogeneity are simply not justified.

The latest 2010 release of the Educause Center for Applied Research (ECAR) longitudinal study of students and information technology (IT) within the United States reveals a similar pattern distin-

Table 2. Types of student technology users

Type	Percentage	Description
Power Users	14%	Wide range of technologies, significantly more frequent use.
Ordinary Users	27%	Regular users of standard web and mobile technologies; use emerging technologies and games on average no more than monthly; generally do not use Web 2.0 publishing and file sharing.
Irregular Users	14%	Ordinary users but engage in technology-based activities less frequently; moderate users of web and mobile technologies, and relatively low users of other technologies except Web 2.0 Publishing.
Basic Users	45%	Extremely infrequent use of new and emerging technologies and less than weekly or monthly use of standard Web technologies; regular users of standard mobile features.

guishing technology access from usage. Whereas nearly all surveyed students (99%) owned at least one computer, roughly 50% agreed they were "adequately prepared to use IT in college," and just around 25% disagreed or strongly agreed with this assessment (Smith and Caruso, 2010, p. 37). In results for use of technology, daily text messaging went from 50% in 2008 to nearly 75% in 2010, and Facebook use increased from 89% to 97% over the same time period. But while 80% rate themselves as expert at using the internet to search for information, fewer than 60% said they were skilled or expert at evaluating reliability and credibility of online information, and less than 50% indicated they were skilled or expert at understanding ethical and legal issues of accessing and using digital information (Smith and Caruso, 2010, p. 55). Even this broad-based survey of a large sample of American college students (almost 37,000), while indicating growing use of specific technologies, yields clear differences in use and in self-reports of IT competence which problematize generalizations about the urgency of evolving educational practices.

Some of the implications of these differences are drawn most strongly in regard to the continuing digital divide, and what Brown and Czerniewicz (2010a) characterize as "digital apartheid." Basing their conclusions on a three phase project that spanned surveys of 6500 South African college students, another of 3500 students, and a final set of thirty-eight interviews and six focus groups, they found that only 26% might properly be termed Digital Natives, with 33% of students having less than 4 years of technology experience, and 17% having fewer than 2 years of experience. The term Digital Native, they argue, really describes a very small elite, and they identified an important group (22%) that lack both experience and opportunities to use technology, which they term "digital strangers." These students, Brown and Czerniewicz write, are part of a widening digital divide:

'Digital strangers'... are not only lagging behind their 'native' counterparts at the start of their university careers but are falling even further behind as they have to prioritize their ICT use, and make hard choices which generally do not include making use of social software and exploiting Web 2.0 opportunities. (2010a, p. 364)

Hargittai (2010) echoes this concern in her survey of over 1,000 first year students in a general education course required of all students:

Considerable variation exists even among fully wired college students when it comes to understanding various aspects of Internet use. Moreover, these differences are not randomly distributed. Students of lower socioeconomic status, women, students of Hispanic origin, and African Americans exhibit lower levels of Web know-how than others. (p. 108)

There are substantive differences in the way people integrate digital media into their life, and these differences hold up even for college students thought to be wired and savvy.

Finally, the myth or reality of Digital Natives is explored by Margaryan, Littlejohn and Vojt (2011) in their review of extant research on variations in technology use, along with a mixed method quantitative and qualitative research approach. They found no evidence for a generation of students adopting radically different learning styles, exhibiting new forms of literacy, or using digital technologies in sophisticated ways. Regardless of age and subject discipline, they conclude, student attitudes toward the learning process appear to be influenced largely by the "teaching approaches" used by lecturers, and students "appear to conform to fairly traditional pedagogies," with some additional use of tools that deliver content (p. 438).

This discussion has important implications for how educators approach the challenges of teaching today's students. On the one hand, the hasty generationalization in much of the Digital

Native literature speaks against the assumption of widespread Information technology (IT) literacy, and cautions about the application of broadscale standardized models for supporting student IT use for learning inside and outside the classroom. On the other hand, rates of technology access and usage still seem to be increasing, and the prevalence of technology as a social environment is certainly expanding. Capitalizing on opportunities for robust engagement within the classroom still merits strong and reasoned consideration of the value of teaching with technology. It is particularly valuable to consider the way in which instructional technology is used and modeled, especially given the other dark side of the Digital Native coin.

A CULTURE OF DISTRACTION

The use of technology in the educational system has a long history of critics and detractors, much of it couched as a choice between clear alternatives. In 2003, Oppenheimer offered an extended critique of technology's role and influence in the educational system. From case studies of school districts run amuck to trenchant observations about industry "partnerships" with educational institutions, Oppenheimer offers this summary of a generation "poised between two possible directions":

In one, today's students have a chance to become confident, creative masters of the modern tools of their day and, subsequently, to move our world a step closer to meeting its growing challenges. They can also, however, become victims of the commercial novelties we are visiting upon them... America's students... have become a distracted lot. Their attention span—one of the most important intellectual capacities anyone can possess—shows numerous signs of diminishing. Their ability to reason, to listen, to feel empathy, among other things, is quite literally flickering. (p. xx)

Detailing similar various impacts of politics and commerce on childhood in the age of the internet, Montgomery (2007) concludes on the need for critical skills (e.g. perspective-taking, principled reasoning, critical information evaluation strategies) to enhance political engagement and avoid the excesses of the new digital marketplace and the dangers of self-obsession, instant gratification, and impulsive behaviors.

Before addressing more specifics about this "culture of distraction," it is important to explain how this might be consonant with the hasty "generationalization" previously noted. Bennett, Selwyn, Wesch and others are most obviously objecting to assumptions of technical skill levels and the allocation of educational resources and priorities based on stereotypes of a younger generation of technical sophisticates. It is noteworthy that every level of User in Kennedy, Judd, Dalgarnot and Waycott (2010), from Power to Basic, regularly engages in mobile communications. It is also hard to ignore the ECAR results that daily text messaging among college students in the U.S. rose from 50% to nearly 75% in two years, and that Facebook use increased from 89% to 97% over the same time period (Smith and Caruso, 2010, p. 55). While many students, including those termed "digital strangers," may be inexperienced or unsophisticated as technology users, it is becoming increasingly evident that this message-saturated environment has effects both on cognitive learning processes and on the learning environment as a whole.

Prensky (2001, 2006, 2010) originally grounds innovative teaching strategies in identifying ways to get beyond the talking head of the digital immigrant classroom and meet students halfway in their media-rich environments; the "disconnect tragedy" his Partnership pedagogy aims to prevent is based in part on evoking information rich simulations, and on stimulating student engagement so that they will pay attention. This is accomplished both through more visually stimulating environments and through multi-tasking. Rosen,

Carrier and Cheever (2010) follow Prensky on why students hate school learning environments, and in particular focus on multi-tasking as an area of mental and cognitive development, challenging conventional wisdom that learning involves uni-tasking. Where Baby-Boomers might report multi-tasking four things at once, Gen-Xers report five, and the Net- and iGeners report handling up to six tasks simultaneously (p. 81). While they acknowledge that some tasks don't go with others that use the same mental resources (i.e., dual-task interference between video-gaming and other problem-solving tasks), some tasks (like listening to music) are carried out with multiple other demands on their attention. The impact of sustained multi-tasking activity, they acknowledge, could "lead to a preference by youths for task switching over sustained attention during cognitive tasks" (p. 85). But their primary recommendation is that student multi-tasking is beneficial because it keeps interest up during the central task at hand. Students studying with other distracting interruptions may take longer to accomplish tasks, but they are more interested and engaged while they work. While they underscore that many of the "iGeneration" actually lack media literacy skills, and need to learn analysis, filtering, evaluation and synthesis skills, parents and educators should consider meeting the need for speed and multi-tasking through the use of mobile technologies, engaging interest and passion via social networking, and consider using video games to motivate learning. Among recent work on multi-tasking, Klingberg (2009) acknowledges the dual-task effect (e.g. driving attention decreases while having a cell phone conversation but not while listening to the radio), but ultimately concludes there is no evidence that more mentally demanding or challenging situations "impairs our powers of concentration" (p. 164). The resulting stress, he argues, is more specific to an individual's sense of control than it is generalizable to an increasingly high stimulus environment.

There is a growing area of research, however, that is not as sanguine about the impact of a media-cluttered environment, which centers largely around three areas of concern: the effects of continuous partial attention, information-seeking habits of mind, and cultural implications of a distracted population.

In *iBrain: Surviving the Technological Alteration of the Modern Mind*, Small and Vorgan (2008) analyze the impact of continuous multi-tasking and distractions on the development of certain areas of the brain. Young Digital Natives, they observe, have become "stimulus junkies," drawn to flashy graphics, color, and "intense, rapidly changing visual stimuli" (p. 38). The essential question, for them, is if "a teenager has the tools and the know-how to gain immediate mental gratification from instant messaging or playing a video game, when will that teen learn to delay satisfying every pressing whim or urge in order to completely finish a tedious project or a dull task?" (p. 33). They note that continuous partial attention places the brain in a heightened state of stress and becomes self-sustaining:

They no longer have time to reflect, contemplate, or make thoughtful decisions. Instead, they exist in a sense of constant crisis—on alert for a new contact or bit of exciting news or information at any moment. Once people get used to this state, they tend to thrive on the perpetual connectivity. It feeds their egos and sense of self-worth, and it becomes irresistible. (2008, p. 18)

One problem of continuous partial attention is that over time, people become spaced out and fatigued, make mistakes, and become irritable and distracted. And over longer periods of time, with constant "wiring up for rapid-fire cyber searches," the brain's neuroplasticity begins to develop neural circuitry that prefers and is customized for "rapid and incisive spurts of directed concentration" and less tolerant of reflective, mindful and other-aware habits of mind. This is closely related to what

Shenk (1997) earlier described as the "fragmentia" of "data smog."

A related impact involves the rise of Attention Deficit Disorder (ADD) and Attention Deficit Hyperactivity Disorder (ADHD). Small and Vorgan (2008) note that a strong and consistent relationship has been established between media use and hyperactivity, such that the American Academy of Pediatrics is now recommending no television for children under two years of age. Adolescents who played console or internet video games for more than an hour a day, Chan and Rabinowitz (2006) report, had more symptoms and more intense symptoms of ADHD. Small and Vorgan (2008) also discuss the incidence of adult ADHD, validated in part by the University of California at Irvine study of distracted work habits among office employees. Mark's research (in "Too Many Interruptions," 2006) on a high tech office setting revealed a general distracted pattern for workers switching among events (the average amount of time that people spent on any single event before being interrupted or before switching was about three minutes), changing devices (the average amount of time that people spent working on a device before switching was 2 minutes and 11 seconds), and shifting between "working spheres" (each person worked on an average of 12.2 different working spheres every day and switched working spheres, on average, every 10 minutes and 29 seconds ("Too many interruptions," 2006, n.p.).

Addressing the implications for information-seeking habits of mind, Carr (2010) traces the history of critical "tools of the mind" like the map and the clock, and argues that every technology has an "intellectual ethic" that has a profound effect on the mind and on culture. Outlining the impact of the computer on writing, books and "deep reading," Carr traces the changing positive reinforcements from internet use that impact the "Juggler's Brain" by reinforcing rapid and scattered patterns of information seeking and retrieval. Several areas of study provide evidence of the impact of heavy internet use on reading retention and habits of mind: comparisons of hyperlinked and linear reading which show less retention and weaker application of hyperlinked text (DeStefano & LeFevre, 2005), assessments of modern office workers flitting from media to media and fragmenting their office experiences (following Mark's work above), internet use studies showing a rising "F" pattern of scanning along with reduced time per web page (Nielsen, 2006), and the impact of such "power-browsing" on distractivity and a loss of problem-solving skills (Liu, 2005). Educators may have already observed the impact of these new information-seeking habits of mind if they have noticed the increasing difficulty students have focusing and reading books and long articles.

A final area of impact concerns the effects such "distractions" have on the transmission and development of culture. Bauerlein (2008) discusses "knowledge deficits" in History (57% of high school seniors scored below basic), Civics (only 1 in 50 college students know the first right guaranteed by the First Amendment, 25% did not know any freedom protected by it), Science and Math (46% didn't reach "basic" levels on the national senior science exam), and Fine Arts (attendance is low and dropping despite more leisure time, more money, and more venues like museums). He argues that this has occurred because the Youth Generation of the 1960s has coddled students and encouraged habits of distraction from important learning (pp. 17-25). Jackson's (2009) vision of the coming dark ages is more nuanced than Bauerlein's approach, and offers some interesting insight into the possibility for a "Renaissance of Attention." The impending dark age is summarized in her chapter on McThinking:

Smitten with the virtual, split-split, and nomadic, we are corroding the three pillars of our attention: focus (orienting), judgment (executive function) and awareness (alerting). The costs are steep: we begin to lose trust, depth, and connection in our relations and our thought. Without a flourishing array of attentional skills, our world flattens and thins. And most alarmingly, we begin to lose our ability to collectively face the challenges of our time. Can a society without deep focus preserve and learn from its past? Does a culture of distraction evolve to meet the needs of its future? These surely are litmus tests of a new dark age and challenges we look perilously at risk of failing. (p. 215)

Jackson ultimately concludes with a focus on the gift of attention, and explores several aspects of learning to pay attention: tracing the efforts of the Buddhism-inspired Shamatha Project to thoroughly test and study three months of intensive cloistered meditation practice on 30 volunteers; identifying software developed by Rueda, Posner and Rothbart (2005) and by Klingberg (2005) to assist in boosting attention; and exploring how assessments like the Attention Network Test can shed light on how focus, judgment and awareness respond to different training strategies.

As we draw a close to the problematization of the characterizations and mental habits of Digital Natives, it seems obvious that concerns about pedagogy and Digital Natives offer refractions that are at once "ways of seeing and ways of not seeing" (Burke, 1935, p.70). A responsive pedagogy, under these swirling circumstances and contradictory prognoses, needs to account for teacher uncertainty about change, to blend student passion and content discovery, to create new pathways to mindfulness that enable positive responses to "fragmentia," and to encourage the kind of sharing that recognizes digital diversity and taps into it as a source of learning.

A RESPONSIVE PEDAGOGY FOR THE LONG VIEW

This section suggests that a responsive pedagogy for Digital Natives should not focus primarily on adopting newer and cooler tools for learning, or necessarily on radical systemic curriculum changes that push faculty farther and farther out of their comfort zones. Such a pedagogy also does not ignore powerful evidence about the effect of extended internet use, and the need, not only for a critical perspective on digital information, but for the identification of and modeling of tools to reassert control over runaway habits of mind. Based on clear evidence of an ongoing skill-and-experience gap among students entering our classrooms, it should look for creative ways to encourage learning across the diversity of experience. My conceptualization of a responsive pedagogy will address short term practices, but will do so with an eye toward the full lifetimes of experiences that await the younger generation. Three areas of exploration begin addressing the implications of passionate co-discovery, contemplative mindfulness, and sharing of informal knowledge.

Blending Passion, Content, and Feedback in Discovery Learning

Personal experience with students and teenagers indicates that when they are passionate about something, it will hold their attention and help anchor abstract information via personal engagement. Discovery learning clearly doesn't have to use technology to engage student interest, but the framing of technology as a distraction or as a resource can create vastly different classroom atmospheres. As a Digital Immigrant struggling not just with course redesign but with conceptual redesign, I offer two examples of modest changes that have great potential to stimulate learning interactions: A technology etiquette and expectations statement for a syllabus, and a playsheet approach that involves both web questing and critical evaluation.

McCain (2005), in his work on *Teaching for Tomorrow*, makes an interesting case for a shift from school skills (memorization, retrieving course material for projects) to emerging real world skills (e.g., collaboration, problem-solving at a distance). He stresses several ways to teach for independent and higher learning: Resist the temptation to "tell," provide context to content, and move to problem solving (shift to discovery and real world role playing). In my class this began with the baby step of reorienting the technology ground rules from exclusionary ("you will not be distracted or connected outside of class during class time") to inclusionary with purpose ("technologies are welcome in service of class learning").

While neither particularly innovative nor exhaustive, Figure 1 is the foundation of my shared attitude about how we are free to use and must also respect limits on use of technology during class time. It likewise creates space around my communication response times and my willingness to share ideas and technical expertise on a level of relative equals. Pausing to ensure understanding and agreement on this aspect of the "contractual" syllabus is well worth the time not only as "rule-setting" but as "attitude-framing" as well.

The latest iteration of my co-discovery process involves "playsheets" which reflect my struggle with deciding which fifteen percent of my lectures and readings I was hoping students would ultimately remember. The charts involve no high technology, but are simply questions and prompts that arise from the material for that unit.

Figure 2 is one example of a playsheet and I usually offer two or three per course module. The playsheets are generally handled in three ways: (1) Handed out in class to work in groups or individually for 20 minutes followed by a clarifying and confirming 15 minute review session to see how well they identified concepts and issues (often followed by several Youtube or media applications); (2) Handed out to groups or individuals with the expectation they will develop an extended application and each make a 90-120 second presentation followed by discussion about the rationale and appropriateness of the applications; and (3) Handed out in advance for individual work with the textbook and the internet that is submitted as a weekly writing exercise. I try and ensure that every group has access to a laptop or wireless

Figure 1. Syllabus statement of technology etiquette and expectations

New Rules:

1) Bring technology to class as needed to surf, research and contribute to classroom learning experiences. Such technologies shall NOT BE USED FOR PERSONAL BUSINESS during class time.

2) Make suggestions and provide support to our class for effective use of new and traditional technologies.

3) <u>Don't disrupt others with your technology.</u> If urgent calls need to be received, please take them out of the classroom into the hallway.

4) I'm available by e-mail and voice-mail, but I generally <u>reserve 48 hours turnaround time on queries</u>, especially over the weekends or breaks. I will communicate occasionally to your GMU e-mail address.

5) Sorry, no technology during quizzes.

6) Do not sell or financially profit from distribution or sale of any notes or images of this class.

7) Submit assignments like this:

***File names have your last name, class number, assignment**
(e.g., Smith300Paper2) NO DASHES OR SPACES
EVERY ASSIGNMENT IN A SINGLE FILE

8) Respect each other and the mission of the institution

internet device, including making available the instructor station, and handle these as zero-history groups that work under time pressure to extract and assess relevant information from their digital environment.

Strategies for Mindfulness, Focus, and Contemplative Pedagogy

There is a growing movement devoted to bringing contemplative practice to increasing numbers of college students, at least in part, Zajonc (2008) writes, because:

attention is one of our most precious abilities and is crucial for successful learning. While few would deny this, conventional pedagogy makes little effort to develop the student's native capacity for attention directly. Yet a long tradition exists within contemplative communities where attention has been highly prized and trained through carefully designed exercises. Contemplative pedagogy draws on this long experience and adapts such exercises for secular college and university settings. (p. 9)

The Center for Contemplative Mind in Society recently published a Handbook of Classroom Practices in contemplative practices. The use of different kinds of meditation, for example, has informed learning and reflective practice in architecture, poetry, writing, law, criminal justice, traditional cultures and a host of other courses. Meditation strategies range from breath-awareness

Figure 2. History and foundations playsheet

Your group has 20 minutes to fill in the answers, after which you will be expected to fill in part of the grid during class discussion.

Who were the Sophists and what did they do that impacted the development of Rhetoric?	
What did Plato think of the Sophists, their occupations, and their relationship to Truth?	
How did Aristotle define Rhetoric? What is an artistic form of proof and what are the three major artistic proofs?	
What three genres, or types of discourse, did Aristotle discuss, and how do they have power in modern times?	
Who was Cicero, and what are the five canons of Rhetoric? Is there an easy way to remember them?	
In what ways does the history of our origins as a discipline continue to impact our understanding of communication and critical analysis today?	

meditation, pebble meditation, mantra meditation, and labyrinth-walking meditation. More courses and degree programs are being focused around certain types of contemplative practices, and there are numerous related centers underway at institutions around the country, including a Contemplative Studies Initiative at Brown University, a Program in Creativity and Consciousness Studies at the University of Michigan, a Contemplative Practice Program at Brooklyn College, a Center for Consciousness Studies at the University of Arizona, Tucson, and more recently a Center for Consciousness and Transformation at George Mason University (Bush, 2008, p. 6). Astin, Astin and Lindholm (2011) directly address the need for higher education to cultivate and enhance students' inner lives. Conducting a 5-year study of the impact of college on spiritual values which flow in part from meditation and self reflection, their findings indicate that "[g]rowth in equanimity enhances students' grade point average, leadership skills, psychological well-being, self-rated ability to get along with other races and cultures, and satisfaction with college" (p. 135). Klingberg (2009), Jackson (2009) and Small and Vorgan (2008) discuss meditation as an antidote to the stress and distraction of a mediated society, and Jackson includes it among the practices that could lead to her "Renaissance of Attention." Recent research indicates that even brief training in meditation has "reduced fatigue, anxiety, and increased mindfulness…, significantly improved visuo-spatial processing, working memory, and executive functioning," and enhanced "the ability to sustain attention" (Zeidan, et. al., 2010, p. 597).

Among a wide variety of mindfulness and meditation exercises that are being applied in classes across the nation, there are three specific practices that do not entail large amounts of class time or assume that an entire course will be focused around contemplative practices. These are aimed, in part, at creating habits of mind that can be useful to students struggling with data smog, fragmentia, and the urge for constant stimulation. First is using guided meditation to bring students to a quiet place in anticipation of a discussion or writing activity.

Figure 3 is a directed mindfulness exercise that seeks to remove students from the hustle and bustle of their lives, find a quiet, safe place, and come from that quiet place to write or enjoy discussion that is more flow and less analytic. There are numerous examples of these kinds of exercises (see Kabat-Zinn (1994) and Small and Vorgan (2008), p. 143) and while they don't take too much class time, they have the added benefit of giving students tools to develop habits of mind that are neither frenzied nor driven.

A second classroom practice is to model relationship to technology, to respect the gifts we receive from technology but to place intentional limits on use. Many people have the experience of getting "sucked into" technology, sitting down for a specific task and looking up hours later and wondering where the time went. This "mindlessness" about technology is particularly difficult to address because students are of necessity tied to their technology for much of their school work. Going "cold turkey" without any technology for a period is another recommended approach (see Shenk (1997) and Powers (2010) on "data-fasting" or taking an "Internet Sabbath"), but one that students have great difficulty with as an absolute solution.

Using the phrases (or at least the ideas) from Figure 4 can help stress intentionality when engaging and disengaging technology in the classroom. It also helps to have something to say when students are distracted by their technology, and clearly not participating or being present in the now. Finally, and importantly, responding to technology glitches in a positive way, by being thankful for a new opportunity, by increasing awareness of the realities of an imperfect world, and by reminding people that we may not control all of what happens with technology, but we certainly control our attitudes about unplanned experiences. Stress in an information overload context, as Klingberg (2009)

Figure 3. Quiet spaces visualization writing prompt

Sit comfortably in your chair, relaxed but not slumped over. Close your eyes, and for a moment, think of all the things that are pressing on you, your list of things to do, your family obligations, your facebook communications, your schoolwork, activities you have committed to, your work schedule, upcoming events... Bring yourself to the center of all of this buzzing, demanding life... Now, let it slip away... Feel yourself sitting, feel the chair, feel people breathing, feel yourself breathing. With each breath in, absorb the peacefulness and quiet... With each breath out, let go of all demands, all obligations, all worries. There will be plenty of time for everything, but right now, be here, be empty... breathe in quiet, breath out worries...

From this relaxed space, remember a place, a place where you could relax, where you felt safe. Perhaps a cubby hole you used to hide in, or a scene of natural beauty, or even drowsing on the couch listening to the rain outside on the window. Find that safe, comfortable place, where you are warm and relaxed. Something tugs at your sleeve, a noise, a message... Let it go... it will be there on your return. A sound like a computer beep tries to get your attention... Let it go... you have plenty of time to relax and come back to it. Relax into this place, a place where all of your worries and distractions are put away for the moment... all the noises are hushed, and you stop doing, and just be for a moment. Remember this place, like an old friend who will welcome you back when you are in need.

As you bring your mind back to this moment, this place, this chair... come back in quiet. Keep a still center, stay relaxed and still apart from all the worries and everything tugging at your attention. Stay in that quiet space for a moment, and open your eyes.

Focus your attention on [topic]... Not on what somebody else has written, or something someone else said, but on your experience, your feelings... in this moment, from this quiet space, you own [the topic]. Still in quiet, take out a sheet of paper and write down two things about how you own or shape [the topic]. Stay relaxed, don't push, and let your own thoughts, free of all other expectations, flow onto the paper.

reminds us, is largely an individual perception about the loss of control.

The third practice has been prevalent for some time, rising in importance as portfolios and electronic portfolios become more prominent in educational practice (see Cambridge, Kahn, Tompkins and Yancey (2001)): Checking in on how particular assignments, courses, or learning programs are working to transform students. These "meta-assignments" require students to stop, reflect, and be mindful of the challenges and accomplishments of their learning process.

Requiring students to reflect on what and how they learned (or didn't!) (see Figure 5) may not always result in more careful planning about their educational choices, but it does offer a consistent opportunity to evaluate strengths and weaknesses in their own learning, and also to pause and articulate a sense of accomplishment before rushing on to the next distraction.

Contemplative pedagogy may not be for everybody, but more and more institutions are recognizing the value of helping students develop their attention skills, and see the value of mindfulness practice on the development of leaders, on encouragement of more positive psychological states, and on meditative "emptiness" that opens up space for creative solutions to a wide array of contemporary problems.

Framing the Rich/Poor Gap as an Engine of Learning

What Bennett and others (Bennett & Maton, 2010; Bennett, Maton &Kervin, 2008) offer in their critique of the Digital Native language is awareness that there remain important differences

Figure 4. Modeling approaches to technology control

To counter habitual and autonomic uses of technology, foster mindfulness about technology use, and model limits on time and intrusion, consider using some of the following phrases or ideas during classroom interactions.

[When turning on or beginning technology use]
We give thanks for the richness technology brings to our lives, and intend to use this technology for [X time] with the purpose of introducing examples that will deepen our discussion and understanding.

[When ending technology use]
Thank the technology and the support we receive for learning resources that have helped make our time more focused and our discussions/activities richer. It is time to leave our tools in gratitude until another day.

[When interrupting student distractive use of technology outside of class purposes]
In this class, we agree to limit outside technology use and minimize distractions to our learning community. Thank you for shutting down and closing your technology to be more fully engaged with what we are doing here now.

[When dealing with technology problems and breakdowns]
We remain thankful to technology for reminding us that we live in an imperfect world, and also for the lesson that we still have control of our attitudes about challenges and frustrations we face.

in technology access, experience, and skill sets across a seemingly monolithic characterization of "young folks these days." Early work by Solomon, Allen and Resta (2002) compiled a variety of perspectives on equipment and resource stratification, with a clear emphasis on strategies within institutions and within classrooms that can help manage the challenge of equitable access to technology. Warschauer (2004) has made remarkable gains moving the discussion of the digital divide away from hardware issues to one of social inclusion. Through case studies around the world, he observes that for many, the ability to use technology as part of a social experience is more important than simply gaining access to the technology. But the evidence from Bennett and Maton (2010), Hargittai (2010), and Kennedy, Judd, Dalgarnot and Waycott (2010) indicate pretty clearly that after decades of the "technology revolution," classrooms still are filled with students that have great variation in their technology skills and comfort levels. Even following the ECAR survey numbers, 25% of students disagreed or strongly disagreed that they were adequately prepared to use the technology available for learning (Smith and Caruso, 2010). Brown and Czerniewicz's (2010a & 2010b) "digital stranger" still has presence and importance in our classroom. So a final component of a responsive pedagogy is to recognize and address continuing gaps between technology skill and comfort levels, not just as a problem to be overcome, but as an opportunity to be realized. This invites a view which is focused not just on overcoming the digital divide, but on using that divide as an "engine of learning," as a

Figure 5. Reflective practice through meta-assignments

Add a final paragraph to your project reflecting on 1) the specific improvements you made during the finalization process, 2) the difficulties and challenges you encountered (and what you did), and 3) How you feel about the project. Finally, identify one thing you learned while creating this assignment.

means of fostering collaborative interaction that "spreads the wealth around."

In a group discovery exercise, one which encourages students to use their mobile technologies in an information gathering and discovery process, an educator can work to ensure that every group has some form of technology. But this is a distribution strategy, only peripherally designed to share technology skills or to use skill gaps to drive transferal of informal knowledge. Among a variety of potential strategies that directly tap this learning "engine," two are worth noting here: The use of learning contracts to individualize skill-building and regularize skill-sharing, and the encouragement of peer tutoring as a mechanism for sharing informal knowledge about how technology works. Figure 6 illustrates one approach to course management that allows students to customize their learning while requiring them to share technology tips and experiences. By framing the class requirements as general categories under which students have choices for specific assignments, students can be encouraged to address gaps in their own skill sets and seek either institutional resources or peer tutoring to develop and then demonstrate their technology skills.

Figure 6 not only sets a habit of mind that may translate to lifelong learning by designing and implementing a learning plan (following Knowles (1986)), but it creates a presentation/demonstration framework that encourages sharing of infor-

Figure 6. Course contract

Course Contract
Preliminary Contract ☐ Final Contract ☐
Student Name/e-Mail:
Please make choices and selections, check appropriate boxes, insert titles/names where appropriate, and total each category.

<u>Category</u>	<u>Percent in Each Category</u>
Class Participation	5%
Reading Comprehension (15%, best 3 of 4 quizzes)	15%
Critical Analysis (10% minimum, 30% maximum)	___
☐ CA1–Critical web page review (10%)	
☐ CA2–Cultural analysis of the role of computers in society (15%)	
☐ CA3–Apply communication theory to computer communication (15%)	
☐ CA4–Rhetorical criticism of artifact about computers (15%)	
☐ CA5–Analyze computerized database for credibility (5%)	
☐ CA6–Critical review of online magazine or journal (5%)	
Computer Skills (10% minimum, 30% maximum)	___
☐ CS1–3 different file types from 3 different countries (5%)	
☐ CS2–Listserv printout (5%)	
☐ CS3–Progressively redefined keyword search (5%)	
☐ CS4–Chat room logon and printout (5%)	
☐ CS5–Develop web page (15%)	
☐ CS6–Web page makeover (10%)	
☐ CS7–Learn new software package (15%)	
☐ CS8–Learn new computer language (15%)	
☐ CS9–Graphics manipulation (5%)	
☐ CS10–Develop agreed upon computer skill (5-15%)	
Presentation/Demonstration (10% minimum, 30% maximum)	___
☐ PD1–FORUM Presentation (5%)	
☐ PD2–PRACTICUM Tidbit (5%)	
☐ PD3–PRACTICUM Chunk (10%)	
☐ PD4–Extended Demonstration (10%)	
☐ PD5–Homepage Tour (5%)	
☐ PD6–Database Tour (10%)	
Collaborative Learning/Group Presentation	___
☐ CL1—Construct a campaign (20%)	
☐ CL2—Present a debate (20%)	
☐ CL3—Informative multimedia presentation (20%)	
☐ CL4—Tutoring option (20%)	
CHECK TOTAL = 100%: ☐	_____

Figure 7. Collaborative tutoring option

CL4 A student who already has some of the computer skills identified above may tutor a classmate on that skill. Tutor may **not** simply complete the assignment for the student, but must convey the skill necessary for the student to carry out the assignment independently. Journal entry required. Tutor must map out and write up objectives and plan of action, and both teacher and learner must also provide an evaluation of the teaching experience. Contract required. Prior approval of tutoring required. (15%)

mal technology knowledge AND sharing of learning struggles and solutions.

Another strategy, which is integrated in the above contract as an option under the Collaborative Learning category, is to create space or optional credit for tutoring among classmates. Spigelman and Grobman (2005) provided much of the theory behind classroom writing tutoring, and offer specific techniques to guide such tutoring. In this instance, however, the tutoring option is flexible and may address a range of technologies or a specific technology that is part of a student's contract goals.

There still needs to be assurances of rigor, of proper planning for the experience, and of reflective evaluation of the tutoring experience, but Figure 7 is one of the most direct ways that a Rich/Poor gap in student skill sets can become a positive force for learning rather than a "problem" for the instructor.

FUTURE RESEARCH DIRECTIONS

These elements of a responsive pedagogy are based on a mixture of empirical work and instructional experience, but there are still obvious knowledge gaps that, if filled, would yield significant benefits for educators in the twenty-first century. Substantial research has been done on multi-tasking and distractedness, but a clear focus for additional research is the modeling and use of mindfulness techniques (contemplative pedagogy) to enhance focus and attention among youth immersed in a heavily mediated environment. Much of the literature about the value of meditation does not address populations of youth who crave constant stimulation, and reviews on the integration of meditation into course practice tend to be anecdotal rather than empirical. Creating awareness of and space for mindfulness and explicit uni-tasking would need to be investigated both for short-term impacts and for longitudinal effects.

Likewise the digital divide has been approached as an economic, a class and a race phenomenon, but only recently as a social issue in itself, and rarely as an opportunity for learning and the sharing of informal technical knowledge. Empirical and comparative assessment of multiple approaches to peer learning and sharing could benefit educators by offering alternative techniques to overcome the persistent problem of the "digital stranger."

CONCLUSION

It becomes evident that there are wonderful opportunities to use technology as a tool for rich learning, and also that there are continual challenges of bypassing generational stereotypes and giving students tools to overcome the "shallows" of developing habits of mind. A responsive pedagogy cannot simply focus on gee whiz technologies that offer positive learning opportunities only for portions of the student body, nor can it retreat from technology or shirk responsibility in light of increasing evidence about stimulus addiction, escalating patterns of "mindless" distractions, and an inability to sustain focus and attention. In short, a responsive pedagogy must look up from the technologies and the distractions of the moment and address challenges and habits of mind that will affect this generation and future generations for decades and perhaps centuries to come. While perhaps not focusing on the "seventh generation" of environmental lore, this perspective seeks understanding beneath the gloss of competing visions of educational technology in the 21st Century, and hopes for willingness to roll up sleeves and grapple with the realities of both the miraculous wonders of learning with technology and the worst nightmares of inequity, selfishness and distraction that are human reflections off of the surface of our shining tools.

REFERENCES

Astin, A., Astin, H., & Lindholm, J. (2011). *Cultivating the spirit: How college can enhance students' inner lives*. San Francisco, CA: Jossey-Bass.

Bauerlein, M. (2008). *The dumbest generation: How the digital age stupefies young Americans and jeopardizes our future*. New York, NY: Penguin.

Bennett, S., & Maton, K. (2010). Beyond the "digital natives" debate: Towards a more nuanced understanding of students' technology experience. *Journal of Computer Assisted Learning, 26*, 321–331. doi:10.1111/j.1365-2729.2010.00360.x

Bennett, S., Maton, K., & Kervin, L. (2008). The "digital natives" debate: A critical review of the evidence. *British Journal of Educational Technology, 39*, 775–786. doi:10.1111/j.1467-8535.2007.00793.x

Brown, C., & Czerniewicz, L. (2010a). Debunking the "digital native": Beyond digital apartheid, towards digital democracy. *Journal of Computer Assisted Learning, 26*, 357–369. doi:10.1111/j.1365-2729.2010.00369.x

Brown, C., & Czerniewicz, L. (2010b). Describing or debunking? The net generation and digital natives. *Journal of Computer Assisted Learning, 26*, 317–320. doi:10.1111/j.1365-2729.2010.00379.x

Buckingham, D. (2007). *Beyond technology*. Cambridge, UK: Polity Press.

Burhanna, K., Seeholzer, J., & Salem, J. Jr. (2009). No natives here: A focus group study of student perceptions of Web 2.0 and the academic library. *Journal of Academic Librarianship, 35*, 523–532. doi:10.1016/j.acalib.2009.08.003

Burke, K. (1935). *Permanence and change*. New York, NY: New Republic.

Bush, M. (2008). What is contemplative pedagogy? In *Contemplative practices in higher education: A handbook of classroom practices* (pp. 5–7). Northhampton, MA: The Center for Contemplative Mind in Society.

Cambridge, B., Kahn, S., Tompkins, D., & Yancey, K. (Eds.). (2001). *Electronic portfolios: Emerging practices in student faculty, and institutional learning*. Washington, DC: American Association for Higher Education.

Carr, N. (2010). *The shallows: What the internet is doing to our brains*. New York, NY: Norton.

Chan, P., & Rabinowitz, T. (2006). A cross-sectional analysis of video games and attention deficit hyperactivity disorders symptoms in adolescents. *Annals of General Psychiatry, 5*. Retrieved from http://www.ncbi.nlm.nih.gov/pmc/articles/PMC1635698/pdf/1744-859X-5-16.pdf. doi:10.1186/1744-859X-5-16

DeStefano, D., & LeFevre, J. (2007, May). Cognitive load in hypertext reading: A review. *Computers in Human Behavior, 23*, 1616–1641. doi:10.1016/j.chb.2005.08.012

Hargittai, E. (2010, February). Digital na(t)ives? Variation in internet skills and uses among members of the "net generation". *Sociological Inquiry, 80*, 92–113. doi:10.1111/j.1475-682X.2009.00317.x

Jackson, M. (2009). *Distracted: The erosion of attention and the coming dark age*. Amherst, NY: Prometheus.

Jukes, I., McCain, T., & Crockett, L. (2010). *Understanding the digital generation: Teaching and learning in the new digital landscape*. Thousand Oaks, CA: Corwin.

Kabat-Zinn, J. (1994). *Wherever you go there you are: Mindfulness meditation in everyday life*. New York, NY: Hyperion.

Kennedy, G., Judd, T., Dalgarnot, B., & Waycott, J. (2010). Beyond natives and immigrants: Exploring types of net generation students. *Journal of Computer Assisted Learning*, *26*, 332–343. doi:10.1111/j.1365-2729.2010.00371.x

Klingberg, T. (2005). Computerized training of working memory in children with ADHD—A randomized, controlled trial. *Journal of the American Academy of Child and Adolescent Psychiatry*, *44*, 177–186. doi:10.1097/00004583-200502000-00010

Klingberg, T. (2009). *The overflowing brain: Information overload and the limits of working memory*. New York, NY: Oxford University Press.

Knowles, M. (1984). *Using learning contracts*. San Francisco, CA: Jossey-Bass.

Liu, Z. (2005). Reading behavior in the digital environment. *The Journal of Documentation*, *61*, 700–712. doi:10.1108/00220410510632040

Margaryan, A., Littlejohn, A., & Vojt, G. (2011). Are digital natives a myth or reality? University students' use of digital technologies. *Computers & Education*, *56*, 429–440. doi:10.1016/j.compedu.2010.09.004

McCain, T. (2005). *Teaching for tomorrow: Teaching content and problem-solving skills*. Thousand Oaks, CA: Corwin Press.

Montgomery, K. (2007). *Generation digital: Politics, commerce, and childhood in the age of the internet*. Cambridge, MA: MIT Press.

Nielsen, J. (2006, April 17). F-shaped pattern for reading web content. *Alertbox*. Retrieved from http://www.useit.com/alertbox/reading_pattern.html.

Oppenheimer, T. (2003). *The flickering mind: Saving education from the false promise of technology*. New York, NY: Random House.

Palfrey, J., & Gasser, U. (2008). *Born digital: Understanding the first generation of digital natives*. New York, NY: Basic Books.

Powers, W. (2010). *Hamlet's BlackBerry: A practical philosophy for building a good life in the digital age*. New York, NY: HarperCollins.

Prensky, M. (2001). Digital natives, digital immigrants. *Horizon*, *9*, 1–6. doi:10.1108/10748120110424816

Prensky, M. (2006). *Don't bother me now, Mom—I'm learning!* St. Paul, MN: Paragon House.

Prensky, M. (2010). *Teaching digital natives: Partnering for real learning*. Thousand Oaks, CA: Corwin.

Rosen, L., Carrier, M., & Cheever, N. (2010). *Rewired: Understanding the iGeneration and the way they learn*. New York, NY: Macmillan.

Rueda, M., Rothbart, M., & Posner, M. (2005). Training, maturation and genetic influences on the development of executive attention. *Proceedings of the National Academy of Sciences of the United States of America*, *102*, 14931–14936. doi:10.1073/pnas.0506897102

Rushkoff, D. (2006). *ScreenAgers: Lessons in chaos from digital kids*. New York, NY: Hampton Press.

Selwyn, N. (2009). *The digital native—myth and reality.* Paper presented at the meeting of the Chartered Institute of Library and Information Professionals, London. Retrieved from http://www.scribd.com/doc/9775892/Digital-Native

Shenk, D. (1997). *Data smog: Surviving the information glut*. New York, NY: HarperOne.

Small, G., & Vorgan, G. (2008). *iBrain: Surviving the technological alteration of the modern mind*. New York, NY: CollinsLiving.

Smith, S., & Caruso, J. (2010). *The ECAR Study of undergraduate students and Information Technology, 2010*. Boulder, CO: Educause.

Solomon, G., Allen, N., & Resta, P. (2002). *Toward digital equity: Bridging the divide in education*. Boston, MA: Allyn & Bacon.

Spigelman, C., & Grobman, L. (Eds.). (2005). *On location: Theory and practice in classroom-based writing tutoring*. Logan, UT: Utah State University Press.

Tapscott, D. (2009). *Grown up digital: How the Net generation is changing your world*. New York, NY: McGraw Hill.

The net generation, unplugged. (2010, March 4). *The Economist,* Retrieved from http://www.economist.com/node/15582279.

Too many interruptions at work? (2006, June). *Gallup Management Journal.* Retrieved from http://gmj.gallup.com/content/23146/too-many-interruptions-at-work.aspx

Warschauer, M. (2004). *Technology and social inclusion: Rethinking the digital divide*. Cambridge, MA: MIT Press.

Zajonc, A. (2008). What is contemplative pedagogy? In *Contemplative practices in higher education: A handbook of classroom practices* (p. 9). Northhampton, MA: The Center for Contemplative Mind in Society.

Zeidan, F., Johnson, S. K., Diamond, B. J., David, Z., & Goolkasian, P. (2010, June). Mindfulness meditation improves cognition: Evidence of brief mental training. *Consciousness and Cognition, 19*(2), 597–605. doi:10.1016/j.concog.2010.03.014

ADDITIONAL READING

Baym, N. (2010). *Personal connections in the digital age*. Boston, MA: Polity.

Bekebrede, G., Warmelink, H. J. G., & Mayer, I. S. (2011, September). Reviewing the need for gaming in education to accommodate the net generation. *Computers & Education, 57*(2), 1521–1529. doi:10.1016/j.compedu.2011.02.010

Chiesa, A., Calati, R., & Serretti, A. (2011, April). Does mindfulness training improve cognitive abilities? A systematic review of neuropsychological findings. *Clinical Psychology Review, 31*(3), 449–464. doi:10.1016/j.cpr.2010.11.003

Clark, L. (2009, June). Digital media and the generation gap. *Information Communication and Society, 12*, 388–407..doi:10.1080/13691180902823845

Corrin, L., Lockyer, L., & Bennett, S. (2010, December). Technological diversity: An investigation of students' technology use in everyday life and academic study. *Learning, Media and Technology, 35*, 387–401..doi:10.1080/17439884.2010.531024

Ebner, M., & Schiefner, M. (Eds.). (2010). *Looking toward the future of technology-enhanced education: Ubiquitous learning and the digital native*. Hershey, PA: Information Science Reference.

Jones, C., Ramanau, R., Cross, S., & Healing, G. (2010, April). Net generation or Digital Natives: Is there a distinct new generation entering university? *Computers & Education, 54*(3), 722–732. doi:10.1016/j.compedu.2009.09.022

Kirschner, P. A., & Karpinski, A. C. (2010, November). Facebook and academic performance. *Computers in Human Behavior*, *26*(6), 1237–1245. doi:10.1016/j.chb.2010.03.024

Klages, M., & Clark, J. (2009, Spring). New worlds of errors and expectations: Basic writers and digital assumptions. *Journal of Basic Writing*, *28*, 32–49.

Kolikant, Y. B. (2010, November). Digital natives, better learners? Students' beliefs about how the Internet influenced their ability to learn. *Computers in Human Behavior*, *26*(6), 1384–1391. doi:10.1016/j.chb.2010.04.012

Krech Thomas, H. (2011, April). Student responses to contemplative practice in a communication course. *Communication Teacher*, *25*(2), 115–126.. doi:10.1080/17404622.2010.527296

Kroll, K. (Ed.). (2010). *Contemplative teaching and learning: New directions for community colleges*. San Francisco, CA: Jossey-Bass.

Manafy, M., & Gautschi, H. (Eds.). (2011). *Dancing with digital natives: Staying in step with the generation that's transforming the way business is done*. Medford, NJ: CyberAge Books.

McArthur, J. (2009, January). Composing podcasts: Engaging digital natives in the communication classroom. *Communication Teacher*, *23*, 15–18. doi:10.1080/17404620802592957

Moore, A., & Malinowski, P. (2009, March). Meditation, mindfulness and cognitive flexibility. *Consciousness and Cognition*, *18*(1), 176–186. doi:10.1016/j.concog.2008.12.008

Nash, G., & Mackey, K. (2007). The digital natives are restless: Using the mobile phone camera creatively in visual arts and media classrooms. *Screen Education*, *47*, 92–97.

Schoeberlein, S., & Sheth, S. (2009). *Mindful teaching and teaching mindfulness: A guide for anyone who teaches anything*. Boston, MA: Wisdom Publications.

Sprenger, M. (2010). *Brain-based teaching in the digital age*. Alexandria, VA: Association for Supervision and Curriculum Development.

Tapscott, D. (1999). *Growing up digital: The rise of the net generation*. New York, NY: McGraw Hill.

Thomas, M. (Ed.). (2011). *Deconstructing digital natives: Young people, technology, and the new literacies*. London: Routledge.

Thornham, H., & McFarlane, A. (2011, March). Discourses of the digital native. *Information Communication and Society*, *14*(2), 258–279..doi:10.1080/1369118X.2010.510199

Turkle, S. (2011). *Alone together: Why we expect more from technology and less from each other*. New York, NY: Basic Books.

Wei, L., & Hindman, D. B. (2011). Does the digital divide matter more? Comparing the effects of new media and old media use on the education-based knowledge gap. *Mass Communication & Society*, *14*(2), 216–235.. doi:10.1080/15205431003642707

Weil, M., & Rosen, L. *Technostress: Coping with technology @ home @ work @ play*. Hoboken, NJ: John Wiley & Sons.

Yaros, R. A. (2008, Winter). Digital natives: Following their lead on a path to a new journalism. *Nieman Reports*, *62*(4), 13–15.

KEY TERMS AND DEFINITIONS

Contemplative Pedagogy: A growing movement in both K-12 and higher education that emphasizes reflection, meditation, and mindfulness as avenues for self-improvement and enhanced learning, and as a means to reduce conflict, violence, and disruptive behavior.

Continuous Partial Attention: A mental state where multiple information streams are maintained such that attention fairly constantly flickers between different stimuli.

Digital Apartheid: Term describing the rich/poor gap implications of focusing educational institution resources on supporting higher-end technology student learning at the expense of those with less digital access and privileges.

Digital Immigrant: An older adult who grew up and was educated in a world before the internet.

Digital Native: A teen or young adult who has spent most of their formative years with access to the internet.

Distracting Work Environment: Research indicating workers switching rapidly between *events*, *devices* and *working spheres* while at work, with impacts on worker productivity.

Habits of Mind: Mental habits created by constant use of media that influence how information is sought and processed, including web page eye scanning patterns, seconds per web page, clicks per web site, and credibility attributed to web sources, as well as difficulty in engaging in sustained reading of one static source.

Mindfulness: A mental state where attention is focused on the here and now, on being present, and on unitasking without continual distractions.

Partnering Pedagogy: Approach advocated by Marc Prensky for teaching Digital Natives which emphasizes discovery- and problem-based learning while empowering students to explore and use different technologies to achieve learning objectives.

Responsive Pedagogy: Teaching of Digital Natives that reflects an appreciation for the value of existing and emerging technologies to stimulate discovery and interest while using strategies that recognize and avoid the dangers of stereotyping all youth as tech-savvy, and employing techniques that help students focus and overcome increasingly ingrained poor habits of mind.

Chapter 3
Personalized Integrated Educational Systems:
Technology for the Information-Age Paradigm of Education in Higher Education

Charles M. Reigeluth
Indiana University, USA

William R. Watson
Purdue University, USA

Sunnie Lee Watson
Ball State University, USA

ABSTRACT

This chapter presents a detailed description of the powerful and necessary role technology can play in higher education in the current information-age. This article calls for a Personalized Integrated Educational System (PIES), a comprehensive and integrated application of technology to the learning process, which will provide four primary roles for student learning: record keeping, planning, instruction, and assessment. Each of these four major roles is described in terms of the functions it provides to support student learning. Finally, secondary roles such as communication and general data administration are described in order to illustrate the systemic nature of PIES technology necessary to fully support the learner-centered approach that is essential in the information-age paradigm of higher education.

INTRODUCTION

Higher education institutions are facing unprecedented pressures for fundamental change. The digital natives or the Net generation think and learn differently than those who grew up without interactive digital technology as an everyday part of life (Prensky, 2006; Beck & Wade, 2004), and they now comprise the student bodies of today's higher education institutions. The manner in which the higher education system will need to reflect the changing cognitive processes of digital natives is critical, and their expectations regarding the learning process reflect this.

DOI: 10.4018/978-1-61350-347-8.ch003

Oblinger and Oblinger (2005) note that the Net Generation has learning preferences that match their general attributes, including preferences for: working in teams, interactive learning experiences supporting inductive discovery and experimentation, visual and kinesthetic rich learning experiences, clear structure and the opportunity for achievement, and the ability to contribute to issues they perceive as important. These preferences call for engaging and personalized instruction and student choice. However, the current approach of most higher education classes focuses on knowledge delivery through lectures rather than learner control, engagement, and skill building. The enrollment attrition of many institutions attests to the disconnect for many Net Generation students entering higher education and how institutions often fail to retain those students who struggle to achieve in a model designed to sort them into those who can and those who cannot, rather than ensure their learning. With institutions under pressure to cut budgets, class sizes can be large and students lack the personalized attention they need to succeed.

The harsh reality is that with faculty attention stretched between teaching and other responsibilities and large class sizes, the personalization of learning processes for higher education students is not feasible without technology. And yet, the needs of the information age demand a transformation to a learner-centered, personalized paradigm of learning, regardless of the degree that students have grown up using technology.

Although members of the Net Generation are often grouped by age (individuals born after the use of Internet and information technology became commonplace), a more accurate grouping is made by grouping those who are heavy technology users (Oblinger & Oblinger, 2005). This has been confirmed by a number of recent empirical studies and reviews that have found that current higher education students have varied experiences, skills, and perspectives on the use of Internet and computer technology (Bennett & Maton, 2010; Jones, Ramanau, Cross, & Healing, 2010; Kennedy, Judd, Dalgarnot & Waycott, 2010). These differences do not alter the fact that modern society is currently in the information age marked by movements towards knowledge economies, easy access to information, and a focus on customization, collaboration, and complex problem solving, among other attributes (Reigeluth, 1994).

The information age, ushered in by information communications technology, has created new educational needs, tools, and realities. Regardless of whether individuals are heavy technology users, given our increasing reliance on information technology and as more and more people are born into and live in this information-technology-rich environment, the distinctions between those who were raised on technology and those who were not will lesson (Prensky, 2009).

Furthermore, with the existing demands of the information age and its knowledge economy, a new paradigm of education is needed that focuses on ensuring student learning, rather than merely sorting learners. This chapter presents a vision for a systemic application of technology to the learning process to support the learner-centered paradigm of learning necessary to meet the needs of the Net Generation and all students in the information-age society.

BACKGROUND

The new educational *needs* include preparing far more students for the information age, versus the industrial age. The information-age economy now requires students to be prepared for knowledge work (which typically entails solving ill-structured problems), collaboration, initiative, self-direction, systems thinking, use of advanced technologies, widely varying skill sets (which requires customization), and much more (Reigeluth, 1994). Recent educational literature by the American Psychological Association, the National Research Council, and others, have called for a shift to the learner-centered paradigm of education (Alexander & Murphy, 1993; APA, 1993; Bradford, Brown & Cocking, 1999; Lambert & McCombs, 1998; McCombs & Whisler, 1997; Ormrod, 2008; Watson & Reigeluth, 2008). Learner-centered instructional approaches stress the importance of individual learners and their backgrounds, talents, and needs, while also integrating the best knowledge about learning and instructional methods. The new educational *tools* include computers, mobile devices, and the Internet. The new educational *realities* include the expense of higher education (which has been growing much faster than the rate of inflation – Trombley, 2003) and the expense of moving to a university (which, for those who already have a full-time job, includes giving up or temporarily leaving that job). Furthermore, today's students and members of the Net Generation can no longer be prepared to do one job for their entire careers as the dynamism of modern society requires workers prepared to solve problems and adapt to varied and complex situations using an ever expanding toolkit of skills and knowledge, much of it self-taught.

In response to these unprecedented pressures, new higher education institutions are emerging that offer Internet-based alternatives (such as Phoenix University, Walden University, and Kaplan University), and existing ones are developing online programs (Rudestam & Schoenholtz-Read, 2002). However, the business model of these new universities is fundamentally different from that of the traditional, brick-and-mortar universities. The latter put a lot of money into teachers (professors) but little into course development, whereas the new online universities invest a lot in course development and spend little on teachers. This new business model promises to be far more cost effective, given the new educational tools and realities. But what about quality? Advances in knowledge about learning and instruction, combined with advances in the affordances or capabilities of technology, now allow high quality learning experiences to be offered through this new business model – if the right tools and methods are utilized.

So what tools and methods are useful to support the needs of Net Generation learners and to maximize the effectiveness of all learners? To answer this question, it is important to recognize that (1) students learn at different rates; (2) students have differing amounts of time per day that they can devote to learning; and (3) students have different needs, interests, and talents that influence what they should or want to learn. The first and second issues lead us to recognize that decisions about when a student moves on to the next topic should be determined by level of learning rather than amount of time – by when mastery is reached rather than when the course calendar says to move on. In other words, the concept of semesters or quarters does not serve students well, as students learn at different rates. The third issue leads us to recognize that decisions about what a student learns next should be allowed to vary from one student to another in order to facilitate growth of individual talents and interests. In other words, the concept of a course with a fixed set of content to be learned by all students does not serve students well. Does this mean that we need to do away with semesters and courses in higher education? Only if there is a better paradigm to take their place. So let's explore a vision of what might be better.

Given the new needs of Net Generation learners and the new educational needs, tools, and realities of the information age just discussed, we envision that in the future the majority of higher education will be offered online using the new business model. This means that powerful technological tools and well designed, interactive, learning resources will be needed. We currently see four major roles and many minor roles for technology, all of which should be seamlessly integrated into a single system. Since there is no existing term that communicates all these roles, we propose a new term, Personalized Integrated Educational System (PIES). The major roles for PIES include *record keeping* for student learning, *planning* for student learning, *instruction* for student learning, and *evaluation* for (and of) student learning. The minor roles include communication, PIES administration, general student data, and personnel information. These major and minor roles will incorporate technology throughout the entire learning process and allow the learner-centered approach necessary to meet the needs of the Net Generation learners.

FUNCTIONS OF PERSONALIZED INTEGRATED EDUCATIONAL SYSTEM (PIES)

As previously discussed, Net Generation learners have particular learning needs and preferences. The new paradigm of higher education must be learner-centered in order to meet the needs of these students as well as the needs of the information-age society. In order to effectively manage and implement a new-paradigm approach to higher education, technology will be needed to support the entire learning process. We call such a system PIES, and this section describes the functions such a system must offer.

1. Record Keeping for Student Learning

The new paradigm of higher education will require the student, mentor-teacher, and parents[1] to be informed of what the student has actually learned at any point in time. This will be necessary to make good decisions about what to learn next and to assure that progress is continuous and personalized. The PIES Record Keeping tool will replace the current transcript. The transcript only serves to compare one student with another and tells you nothing about what a student has actually learned. In contrast, this tool will provide systematic and comprehensive information about what each student has learned. We imagine that this tool will have three components: (1) a general record of what can be learned; (2) a personal record of what has been learned by each student; and (3) a personal record of student characteristics that influence learning for each student.

1.1 Knowledge[2] Inventory

The purpose of this general record is to inform the planning process (role #2) by providing information about all available knowledge, some of which will be required by a higher education institution for specific degrees or certifications. This information will provide the student, mentor-teacher, and parents with a vision of what should be and could be achieved. Furthermore, the knowledge will be organized into maps for each domain of learning based on Domain Theory (Bunderson, Wiley, & McBride, 2009). Each domain map will include (a) major attainments with boundaries showing the easiest and hardest version of each attainment, (b) categories of attainments, where each category represents a pathway for learning, and (c) a difficulty-based sequence of attainments along each pathway. For each attainment in the map, there will be an indication as to whether or not it is required for a given degree or certification, and if so, what level of difficulty is required. In essence, the Knowledge Inventory will present a list of things that should or could be learned, along with levels, standards, and/or criteria at which they should or could be learned.

1.2 Personal Attainments Inventory

The purpose of this personal record is also to inform the planning process (role #2), only it will do so by keeping track of each student's progress in meeting the required and optional standards, and therefore what is within reach for the student to learn next. It will serve as a customized mastery progress report to the student, mentor-teacher, and parents. In this tool, attainments will be checked off as they are reached, and if any are not listed in the Knowledge Inventory, they can be added to the Personal Attainments Inventory. Each attainment will be documented and reported by date attained, and the record will identify any required knowledge (in the Knowledge Inventory) that is overdue and what knowledge is due next in each domain. Each attainment will also be linked to evidence of its accomplishment, ranging from original artifacts with a formal evaluation, to summary data from a simulation-based performance test. Given this information, the student will be able to easily generate different kinds of portfolios for different purposes by pulling out selected attainments and artifacts. All the information recorded, including the attainments and evidence, will have flexibly controlled access to protect the learner's privacy.

1.3 Personal Characteristics Inventory

This personal record is intended to inform both the planning process (role #2) and the instructional process (role #3). It will keep track of each student's characteristics that influence learning, such as learning styles, profile of multiple intelligences, student interests, major life events, and so forth. These data will be convenient to refer to when major decisions about learning objectives and goals are to be made by/for the student and will be especially useful for teachers who are not familiar with the student. They will help mentor-teachers to customize each student's learning plan to best suit his or her interests, learning styles, life experiences, and educational experiences. But the Personal Characteristics Inventory will also be an effective tool to customize the instruction itself. The student data will be fed into computer-based tutorials, simulations, and other computer-based learning tools to automatically tailor appropriate parameters of the instruction for each student. And the teachers will refer to these data to improve the way they coach and advise the student during projects and other instructional events.

Clearly, a customized paradigm of education requires keeping a lot of records. Technology can tremendously alleviate the time, drudgery, and expense of maintaining and accessing those records. The record-keeping tool will provide systematic and comprehensive information for customizing the learning process, including the Knowledge Inventory (what is to be learned), the Personal Attainments Inventory (what the student has learned), and the Personal Characteristics Inventory (the student's characteristics that influence instruction). It will facilitate collaborative efforts among students, teachers, the community, the state, and the nation to ensure that appropriate standards are being met while customized attainments are achieved by each student. And it will facilitate customizing the instruction to each student's individual needs.

2. Planning for Student Learning

If Net Generation students are educated in a paradigm suitable to meet their needs, instruction must be customized for each individual learner, an approach that is necessary not only for attainment-based learning, but also to meet the preferences of Net Generation learners (Oblinger & Oblinger, 2005). Customized instruction requires a personal learning plan (PLP). Assisting with development of that plan is the second major role for PIES. This planning will usually be done in a meeting (virtual or face-to-face) between the student and his or her mentor-teacher, while using the planning tool.

This planning tool will have many functions. It will help the student and mentor-teacher to (1) decide on *long-term goals*; (2) identify the full range of attainments (*current options*) that are presently within reach for the student that could help meet those long-term goals; (3) select from those options the attainments that they want to pursue now (*short-term goals*), based on requirements, long-term goals, interests, opportunities, etc.; (4) identify *projects* (or other means) for attaining the short-term goals; (5) identify *other students* who are interested in doing the same projects (if desired); (6) specify the *roles* that the mentor-teacher, parent, and any others might play in supporting the student in learning from the project; and (7) develop a *contract* that specifies goals, projects, teams, roles, deadlines, and milestones.

2.1 Long-Term Goals

Many students graduate from higher education not knowing what they want to do with their lives. We propose that students should be encouraged to think about life goals (not just career goals) from the beginning of post-secondary education (if not earlier) and should be encouraged to be constantly on the lookout for better goals. Given the Net Generation's desire for personally meaningful and structured learning (Oblinger & Oblinger, 2005), this function is not only necessary for effective learning, but will also help Net Generation students understand what they must learn and why. A study by Harackiewicz, Barron, Tauer, Carter and Elliott (2000) found that setting achievement goals has a positive effect on how students approach, experience, and perform in class. Setting of goals – a means to building self-efficacy – proves to be a highly effective method for encouraging self-regulated learning (Schunk, 1990, 1991; Zimmerman, 1990). Long-term goals can help students pick motivating topics to study and give instrumental value for much of what they study. Therefore, the planning tool will help a student and mentor-teacher to develop and revise, in a collaborative fashion, the student's long-term goals. It will include access to motivating, informational, interactive multimedia programs about different careers and ways of life.

2.2 Current Options

Another important function in educational planning is to know what attainments are within reach, given what the student has already learned. The planning tool, therefore, will access the student's Personal Attainment Inventory and compare it to the general Knowledge Inventory to automatically identify the full range of attainments that are current options for the student. This will be the student's world of possibilities for her or his next PLP.

2.3 Short-Term Goals

The student's PLP will specify what learning goals the student will accomplish during the next contract period (variable, but typically about three months). Thus, the planning tool will help the student and mentor-teacher to select from the current options the attainments to pursue now, based on requirements, long-term goals, interests, opportunities, and so forth, providing the structure desired by Net Generation learners (Oblinger & Oblinger, 2005). These goals typically will come from many different competency areas or subject areas. This is a crucial function of the planning tool because it will set the goals for the next learning contract, or PLP.

2.4 Projects

Having identified the ends for the PLP, the next step will be to identify the means, so this is another function for the planning tool. Typically, projects will be used as the means, an active form of instruction preferred by the Net Generation (Oblinger & Oblinger, 2005), but other options will sometimes be available (e.g., readings with discussions, or tutorials). The tool will help the student and mentor-teacher to identify projects or other means available in the college or community or online that will enable the student to attain the short-term goals. This tool will identify, say, a dozen projects rank ordered by the number of short-term goals (attainments) that each addresses. The student will then select the projects that are most related to their interests and long-term goals and cover all the short-term goals. Depending on the scope of each project, a student will undertake from one to about five projects during a single contract period. Finally, this tool will also have a feature that allows teachers and community people – and even students – to post projects that they have developed or are sponsoring.

2.5 Teams

"The unfolding of the self always grows out of interaction with each other" (Ranson, Martin, Nixon, & McKeown, 1996, p. 14). Collaborative learning is a powerful form of learning (Gokhale, 1995), and a form preferred by the Net Generation (Oblinger & Oblinger, 2005). Thus, in most cases, students will work together in small teams on their projects (virtually or face-to-face). This means that another important function for the planning tool is to identify other students who are interested in working on the same project at the same time. Friends will sometimes choose projects so that they can work together, but mentor-teachers will only allow so much of that and will also require their students to work with students they do not know, seeking to create teams that are highly diverse (age, race, gender, socio-economic status). The planning tool will also use personality inventories (e.g., Myers-Briggs) to help students understand why their teammates may behave quite differently and how to deal with that.

2.6 Roles

In addition to collaborating with peers, students will receive support from their teacher, their mentor-teacher, and perhaps various others (like community members or task experts). Therefore, another function for the planning tool is to help the teacher and mentor-teacher to define what they will do to support the student's learning on each project. Roles of the students and others who are not present in the planning meeting between the student, teacher, and mentor-teacher will be determined with help from the contract-planning tool.

2.7 Contracts

The final step of the planning process will be to create the contract that contains the PLP. These contracts provide the structure many Net Generation learners crave (Oblinger & Oblinger, 2005). Reigeluth and Garfinkle (1994) identify learning contracts as a written agreement that "will serve a planning and monitoring function" (p. 64). A learning contract will essentially be an agreement between a student, teacher, and mentor-teacher that specifies the goals that the student wishes to achieve, the means (primarily projects) that will be used to achieve them, the teacher's and mentor-teachers' roles in supporting the student, and the deadline for completing each project (negotiated with the teammates for each project). Students and mentor-teachers, as Reigeluth and Garfinkle note, will meet once every contract period (three months or so) to review the results of the previous contract and plan a new contract for the next period. Typically there will be a separate contract for each project during the period.

Clearly, the planning tool will be crucial to the instructional process in an information-age educational system. It would likely be impossible to customize the learning experience for each student without it. It will specify what the student, teacher, and mentor-teacher will do, and it will be instrumental for monitoring the student's progress.

3. Instruction for Student Learning

Net Generation learners prefer engaging, collaborative, customized, and meaningful instruction (Oblinger & Oblinger, 2005). In a learner-centered paradigm, all learners should be given choice in their learning process, and therefore, an important role of PIES is managing learners' instruction.

Once a contract has been developed and signed, the projects need to be conducted. This is when instruction, broadly defined as "anything that is done purposely to facilitate learning" (Reigeluth & Carr-Chellman, 2009), will take place. To implement the kind of learner-centered instruction required for the information age (S. L. Watson & Reigeluth, 2008), the teacher will not be able to do all the teaching. The teacher's role will change to selecting or designing mostly Web-based instructional tools for students to use and coaching students during their use of those tools. So what functions need to be performed in this third major role for PIES? We see four functions: (1) project initiation; (2) instruction; (3) project support; and (4) instructional development. Combined, these four functions will ensure that PIES truly supports learner-centered instruction in the information-age paradigm of education.

3.1 Project Initiation

The project initiation tool will help the teacher and students to get started on each project. Depending on the age of the students, this tool will be used by the student, teacher, or both. The primary functions it serves will be to introduce the students to the project or problem to be solved (its goals and initial conditions) and help them get organized. They will already know a little about the project from the planning tool, and they will have already set a deadline for completing the project with their teammates. This Project Initiation tool will provide access to more information about the project (or problem) and will help the teammates identify tasks to perform, how they will work together on each task (collaboratively on the same tasks, or cooperatively on different tasks), the resources they will need, and milestones for different tasks during the project (time management). This information about the project will often be provided in a multimedia simulation such as Bransford's STAR LEGACY, which provides (a) "look ahead and reflect back binoculars," (b) an inquiry cycle that involves presenting a challenge, generating ideas, exploring multiple perspectives, researching and revising, testing your mettle (formative assessment), and going public, (c) additional inquiry cycles for "progressive deepening," (d) general reflection and decisions about legacies, and (e) assessment (see Schwartz, Lin, Brophy, & Bransford, 1999).

3.2 Instruction

Once the students get organized on a project, they will begin working on it. As they work on it, they will encounter (identify) attainments they need in order to be successful. These will include such attainments or components of an attainment as: information that needs to be memorized, understandings that need to be acquired, skills that need to be developed, and various kinds of affective development. Some of these attainments and components will be developed by leaving the "project space" (which often occurs in a computer-based simulation) and entering the "instructional space" comprised of customizable learning objects of various kinds (Gibbons, Nelson, & Richards, 2002; Hodgins, 2002; Wiley, 2002), including mini-simulations, tutorials, Webquests, and drill-and-practice (some in the form of educational games), that allow full development of an individual attainment or component, complete with its "automatization" (Anderson, 1983; Salisbury, 1990), if appropriate for mastery of it. Some attainments and components will also be acquired by using research (information-access) tools on PIES. Most, but not all, such attainments and components will be developed in PIES. Some may exist as resources offered by businesses and other community organizations, but those resources will be located primarily through PIES. Once those attainments and/or components have been mastered, the student will reenter the project space and continue work on the project, cooperating or collaborating with teammates, as appropriate. Debriefing and reflection on the project activities at the end of the project – and periodically during the project – will also be important to the learning process and will be facilitated by the instructional tool.

3.3 Project Support

This function of the instructional tool has two purposes: helping the students to manage the project and helping the teacher and mentor-teacher to monitor and support the students' work on the project. Students will review project planning materials and check off project milestones and goals as they are completed. The system will alert teachers and mentor-teachers to student progress on the project, such as notifying teachers of the submission of project deliverables or the completion of project milestones, in order to encourage and guide the student's progress, make recommendations, and facilitate the completion of the project. The teacher will also suggest resources or provide comments on submitted project deliverables to guide the student while he or she continues to work on the project.

3.4 Instructional Development

The final function for the instructional tool is to support teachers, staff, mentor-teachers, and even students in the development of new instruction – projects, learning objects, and other instructional tools. PIES will contain a large repository of instructional tools that provide varied approaches to instruction. However, it seems that there will never be enough powerful instruction for all learners in all contexts. Therefore, an important feature for PIES will be to support the development of new instructional tools, which will often serve as learning objects, and will then be added to the repository and evaluated for effectiveness (see next section), ensuring that instruction continually improves. A powerful authoring system will support the creation of these new instructional tools by providing instructional guidance and even automatic development and programming of the instruction, similar to Merrill's (M. David Merrill & ID2 Research Group, 1998) ID Expert. User-created content is an everyday reality in today's information age, with popular video games including "modding" toolkits to allow players to create their own versions of games, and Internet users developing their own content in the form of wikis and blogs, as well as videos and podcasts which they upload to share with others and continue the cycle of development and modification (Brown & Adler, 2008). This instructional development tool will provide similar support in customizing and creating customized instruction and projects. Furthermore, the easy and efficient application of learning object standards to created instruction will be a necessity in order to better share learning objects and evaluate their suitability and interoperability for different platforms (Connolly, 2001).

This section has highlighted the instructional functions that PIES should provide. These include (a) introducing the project to a learner (or small team), (b) providing instructional tools (simulations, tutorials, drill & practice, Webquests, research tools, communication tools, and learning objects) to support learning during the project, (c) providing tools for monitoring and supporting student progress on the project, and (d) providing tools to help teachers and others develop new projects and instructional tools.

4. Assessment for (and of) Student Learning

The assessment tool will be integrated with the instructional tool, so that teaching and testing will be fully integrated (Mitchell, 1992; Wiggins, 1998). To accomplish this, we envision the assessment tool fulfilling six functions: (1) presenting authentic tasks for student assessment; (2) evaluating student performances on those tasks; (3) providing immediate feedback to the student on the performances; (4) assessing whether or not an attainment has been reached; (5) developing student assessments; and (6) improving instruction and assessment.

4.1 Presenting Authentic Tasks

The same authentic tasks that are used during instruction will be used for student assessment. The project itself will be an authentic task. And so will the instances (or cases) used in the "instructional space," where much of the learning occurs. Those instances, however, will not be restricted to the project that motivates the learner to master the attainments. To truly master an attainment, the learner must be able to use it in the full variety of situations for which it is appropriate. Those authentic situations will be used as the instances for the demonstrations (or examples) and applications (practice) of the attainment. There will be a large pool of authentic instances to draw from that will include all the types of instances. And the learner will continue to work on the instances until an established criterion is met across all the desired types of instances. In this manner, the applications will serve a dual role of instruction and assessment (both formative and summative). Simulations will often be used to enhance authenticity. Authenticity of applications will enhance transfer to real situations in which the attainments are needed. Authenticity will also help students understand *why* they are learning a particular attainment, and how it could be useful to them. This will help students become and stay motivated to learn (Frederickson & Collins, 1989).

4.2 Evaluating Student Performances

Whether in a simulation or a tutorial or drill and practice, the assessment tool will be designed to evaluate whether or not the criterion was met on each performance of the authentic task on PIES. If the performance is not done on PIES, then a teacher or other trained observer (who could even be a more advanced student) will have a handheld computer with a rubric for evaluating success on each criterion, and that information will be uploaded into PIES.

4.3 Feedback

Research has shown that frequency of *formative assessments* is positively related to student achievement (see, e.g., Marzano, 2006). Thus, based on the evaluation of student performance, the learner will be provided immediate feedback of either a confirmatory or corrective nature. This immediate feedback will often even be given during the performance for the greatest effect on learning, in which case it will be similar to coaching, scaffolding, or guiding the learner's performance, or it could be given at the end of the performance. This will be most cost-effective if done by a computer system online, which requires the kind of up-front investment in instructional development that is characterized by the new business model for online universities.

4.4 Certification

When the criterion for successful performance has been met on x out of the last y unassisted performances, the *summative assessment* will be complete and the corresponding attainment will be automatically checked off in the student's personal inventory of attainments, and a link will be provided to the evidence for that attainment (e.g., in the form of test results or artifacts produced). This avoids the problem so prevalent in collaborative problem-based learning – that a group product is not a good measure of the learning of each individual member of the group, for it is common that different students contribute different skills to the overall performance. Also, in cases where feedback is given during a performance, successful performance will not count toward the criterion. To count, the student's performance must be unassisted.

4.5 Test Development

The assessment tool will also serve the function of supporting teachers and others in the development of formative and summative assessments for new instruction. Due to the integration of instruction and assessment in PIES, the test development tools will also be integrated with the instructional development tools, which will deal with feedback. For certification, the major function will be to help the developer identify the criterion for attainment and develop any necessary rubrics, so the tool will tap into information in the Knowledge Inventory described earlier and will help the test developer link the rubrics to the knowledge standards.

4.6 Improvement of Instruction and Assessment

The final function of the assessment tool will be to formatively assess the instruction and assessments in PIES. It will do so by automatically identifying areas in which students are having difficulties, and it will even have diagnostic tools that offer a menu of suggestions for overcoming those problems. Those diagnostic tools will include proven principles of instruction, such as those represented by Merrill's (2009) "First Principles of Instruction."

INTEGRATION OF THE FOUR ROLES

These four roles for student learning will be seamlessly integrated. The record-keeping tool will provide information automatically for the planning tool, which will identify instructional tools that are available. The assessment tool will be integrated into the instructional tool as well. In addition, the assessment tool will feed information automatically into the record keeping tool. Finally, there will be many other secondary roles or functions for PIES that will support these four major roles for student learning, as explained in the following section.

5. Secondary Roles

The final set of roles necessary for PIES will encompass secondary roles, or functions, which are not necessarily directly related to student learning; although some, such as communication functions, can be used for learning. These functions are organized into four kinds: (1) communication; (2) general student data; (3) personnel information; and (4) PIES administration. While these functions will not always directly deal with student learning, they will nevertheless be necessary functions for PIES to be truly systemic in nature and provide the functionality needed to manage the entire learning process for a higher education institution.

5.1 Communication

Communication functions are essential in supporting a learner-centered environment, as they allow teachers to communicate and collaborate with other teachers and staff, with their students, with their students' parents, and with members of the community and other stakeholders in the learning process. Students will communicate and collaborate with each other and will contact their teachers for help, and parents will be able to check on their children's progress and be more involved in their learning. Being able to communicate remotely via Internet technologies will allow education to extend beyond the walls of the classroom. Therefore, PIES will support Web communication technologies such as these. Furthermore, Web 2.0 technologies that allow for user-created content have become increasingly popular, and the Web has become a participatory social space to such a degree that *Time Magazine* named their person of the year for 2007 as "You" (Grossman, 2006). Furthermore, these Web 2.0 technologies such as wikis, blogs, and podcasts, and video sharing sites such as YouTube have helped to increase the participatory nature of learning (Brown & Adler, 2008). Additionally, PIES support for such additional Internet technologies as Webpage creation, discussion boards, and whiteboards will provide valuable tools for collaboration and communication. The inclusion of RSS feed support (Duffy & Bruns, 2006), which allows users to subscribe to favorite Websites and be notified of updated content, will put further power for communicating and organizing information into the hands of all users and stakeholders. While the use of these Web technologies will not always be applied directly to the learning process, more and more researchers are discussing the application of wikis (Augar, Raiman, & Zhou, 2004; Duffy & Bruns, 2006; Lamb, 2004), blogs (Duffy & Bruns, 2006; Williams & Jacobs, 2004), podcasts (Lum, 2006), and video-sharing sites such as YouTube (Bonk, 2008) to education, so these Web 2.0 technologies will certainly be powerful tools for instruction as well as communication.

5.2 General Student Data

One type of data PIES will be responsible for handling is student data (aside from data related to student learning). These data will include the student's name, address, birth date, parent information, health information, attendance, and so forth. However, in supporting the learner-centered paradigm of education, PIES will also handle student information necessary for supporting information-age higher education, which has moved beyond the current constraints of grade levels, class periods, and so forth. Therefore, PIES will also manage such student data as who the student's mentor-teacher is, records of major life events (which may be important for the mentor-teacher to have knowledge of), work experience, current employer (if any), what learning community the student belongs to, and community organizations he or she is involved with. PIES will protect and restrict access to private information based on the user's role in order to adhere to FERPA and other regulations and ensure appropriate user privacy. In sum, the management of student data will be a key function of PIES. PIES will gather, secure, and allow easy management of data such as those described above in order to effectively support the truly learner-centered environment necessary to meet the needs of today's learners.

5.3 Personnel Information

The third secondary function is the management of information about personnel in the post-secondary institution. As PIES will be systemic in nature (Watson, Lee, & Reigeluth, 2007; Watson & Watson, 2007) and responsible for managing the entire learning process of a learning organization (Szabo & Flesher, 2002), it needs to be capable of managing *all* of the data related to learning, including those of the personnel. These data will include general information, such as name and address, but also data related to learner-centered instruction, such as assigned students, certifications and awards received, and professional development plan and progress. These data will also serve the teacher in providing evidence of excellence by identifying awards and recognitions received by students and storing samples of exemplary student work and evidence of learning. Additional information will be tied directly to the teacher's instructional activities and will include learning objects, other instructional components, and assessments developed by the teacher, as well as records of student evaluations performed by the teacher. Proper management of this information by PIES will support the new role of teachers as facilitators, coaches, and mentors that is required in a learner-centered environment (McCombs & Whisler, 1997).

5.4 LMS Administration

Another secondary function focuses on administration of PIES itself. As software that manages the entire learning process, PIES will necessarily gather and store a great deal of data, including some that is sensitive. An important feature of PIES will therefore be supporting the administration of these data and providing and restricting access to them. While it will be extremely important that data such as medical records and social security numbers be kept secure by PIES, it will also be important that proper access to data and PIES' reporting features be handled in a consistent and efficient manner. The ability to input, retrieve, and update data will be managed by user role. Therefore, some teachers will have access to some of a student's personal information, such as attendance records, parents' names and contact information, and so forth; and some support personnel, such as a health professional and a guidance counselor, will have access to other personal information, such as physical and mental health records. Furthermore, data will be kept not only on students, but also on teachers and staff. It is therefore very important that PIES will offer strict security while still providing appropriate access to data in order to effectively support the information needs of the institution and its personnel.

This section has highlighted some secondary functions that PIES will provide. These include functions related to communication, general student information, personnel information, and PIES administration, and there are certainly others that we have not mentioned here that could be included. However, it is not appropriate for PIES to address administrative functions, such as budgeting, payroll, and purchasing, as those are not directly related to the student learning process.

ARCHITECTURE AND INTERFACE

An important aspect of PIES will be its open architecture and customizable user interface. PIES, as we have described it, will serve a number of roles and must incorporate features to suit each role. Rather than a mammoth, static application, the quality, effectiveness, and development cost of PIES will best be served through a focus on openness, modularity, interoperability, and customization. These traits, demonstrated by popular Web 2.0 tools (in contrast with institution-centric and course-focused traditional technologies, such as Course Management Systems), have resulted in increasing calls for similar educational tools that also share these attributes.

Open technology is defined as "tools, processes, and frameworks that interoperate in an open fashion to create and deliver content that is itself accessible, flexible, and repurposable" (Bush & Mott, 2009, p. 3). Openness can have different meanings when referring to technology, from being free to the user like open educational resources, or providing access to view and modify source code, like open source programming; however, the key concept is the focus on modularity, customization, and interoperability (Bush & Mott, 2009). Ideally, PIES will be open source, allowing institutions to customize and modify it to best suit their specific needs. Furthermore, by being open source, PIES will be developed by a community rather than a single institution, spreading development costs, promoting innovation, and allowing it to be offered for free or at a reasonable cost.

Customization will not be limited to developers customizing PIES to suit their own needs, but will also entail support of user customization. Web 2.0 tools, such as iGoogle and Facebook, serve as good models for how, even if not offering full access to source code, Web applications can be interoperable through proprietary Web Application Programming Interfaces, which allow developers to develop new modules or add-ons to existing programs. As PIES has a wide range of necessary features, by taking a modular approach with a focus on interoperability, developers will contribute modules that together combine to form PIES as a whole. This approach can be seen in the variety of Web apps available for iGoogle or Facebook, allowing users to customize both the interface and the available features to suit their specific needs.

By allowing users to customize their own use of PIES, it will promote ease of use and effectiveness by allowing user control. Just as a user in iGoogle can drag in news subscriptions from various sites, their local weather report, daily quotations, email, and even documents they are sharing and editing, a student in PIES will be able to customize it by managing its layout, projects she is currently working on, resources she is currently using, a portfolio of her completed work, her personal learning plan, a list of her targeted learning attainments, messages, alerts, and other forms of communication, and application modules she is using for the various group and individual projects she is working on.

PIES will not only offer a significant change in how technology can be used for instructional and administrative functional purposes in higher education, but will also offer an extensive move away from current educational software to an open and modular architecture and customizable interface that will result in an efficient, effective and innovative system that fully meets all of its users' educational needs.

The learner-centered paradigm of education focuses on developing learners who are self-directed, critical thinkers, with strongly developed communication, collaboration, and problem-solving skills. The instruction function supports tailoring the instruction to the ways that digital natives think. Also, the evaluation function supports the attainment of whatever outcomes the professor and student believe are important. By supporting, and indeed making possible this sort of environment, PIES lays the foundation for a system of education that meets the needs of the modern global society and its digital native learners.

FUTURE RESEARCH DIRECTIONS

Higher education is already in a significant state of change due to the influx of Net Generation learners, and trends reflect this. Most institutions now offer online or blended courses, and the use of course management systems (CMSs) such as Blackboard, Moodle, and Sakai is common practice. These technologies seek to help students and instructors manage the learning process within the course. However, the course-centric nature of these technologies not only breaks student learning into courses but also remains largely teacher and institution-focused (Attwell, 2007; Bush & Mott, 2009; Weller, 2009).

Recent trends show a rejection of this model and the call for customizable and personalized approaches to learning management, such as the use of personal learning environments (PLEs) that better suit the needs and expectations of Net Generation learners (Mott & Wiley, 2009; Wilson et al., 2006). PIES reflects this trend towards customizing and personalizing the learning process for each learner and granting more self-directed learning (learner control).

Significant challenges remain, and future research is needed to realize PIES and adopt a new paradigm of higher education that meets the needs of the Net Generation and the information-age society. First, significant research and development will need to be done in order to understand how to best develop PIES. Given the potential costs and complexity of such a systemic technology, we recommend a focus on modular and open-source architecture, allowing for the development to be spread out among developers and over time. We stress the need for funding to support such an effort.

Research is also needed on the design of the instructional component of PIES. Research on how to best design the project space and instructional space will help ensure that instruction facilitated through PIES is of high quality. Furthermore, research on the design and development of an avatar to seamlessly integrate the project and instructional spaces will be needed. Research is also needed on how the teacher's role should change to support Net Generation students' learning through PIES.

Finally, for PIES to support the learner-centered paradigm of education so important for the information age and Net Generation learners, higher education institutions will need to transform their organizational structures and stakeholder roles. Research will be needed on how to support higher education institutions as they transform from their current systems focused on comparing and sorting students through time-based student progress to a mastery-focused paradigm that more clearly defines what skills and knowledge will be gained and focuses on helping students gain and demonstrate mastery of them. Considerable research is needed on professional development for the new teacher roles, including helping faculty to evolve their mindsets about education and using PIES to support the management of the entire learning process.

CONCLUSION

It should be apparent that technology will play a crucial role in the success of higher education institutions in the information-age, particularly given the needs and preferences of the Net Generation. It will enable a quantum improvement in student learning, and likely at a lower cost per student per year than in the current industrial-age paradigm. Just as the electronic spreadsheet made the accountant's job quicker, easier, and less expensive, the kind of PIES described here will make the teacher's job quicker, easier, and less expensive.

PIES fills a primary necessity for truly learner-centered instruction by freeing teachers to take on their new roles in a learner-centered environment: facilitators, counselors, and coaches, rather than being the main source of instructional content (McCombs & Whisler, 1997). In order to support this, PIES will provide a variety of instructional features that allow teachers to truly customize learning for each learner, and to facilitate choice and control for the learners as they work towards mastery of required attainments and deep knowledge of all standard subjects and skills. PIES will support students directly in their new roles, as active agents of their own learning (Schlechty, 2002).

However, such dramatic changes in the roles of teachers, students, and technology are not easy to navigate. They will be easier for online universities using the new business model. Traditional higher education institutions will require dramatic changes in mindsets about education for all their teachers, administrators, and staff, and this will require a systemic transformation process that is carefully conceived and executed. The problem is that paradigm change is a time-intensive and therefore expensive process that requires considerable resources as well as considerable expertise in the transformation process. Higher education institutions are indeed facing unprecedented pressures for fundamental change, and those that have sufficient vision and agility will make the necessary investment to transform themselves and their business model, while many others will likely become obsolete.

ACKNOWLEDGMENT

This chapter is an adapted version of the article, "Roles for technology in the information-age paradigm of education: Learning Management Systems," authored by Reigeluth, C.M., Watson, W.R., Watson, S.L., Dutta, P., Chen, Z., & Powell, N.D.P. and published in 2008 in *Educational Technology, 48*(6), 32-39. It has been adapted to focus on higher education.

REFERENCES

Alexander, P. A., & Murphy, P. K. (1993). *The research base for APA's learner-centered psychological principals. Taking research on learning seriously: Implications for teacher education.* Paper presented at the Annual Meeting of the American Psychological Association, New Orleans.

American Psychological Association Presidential Task Force on Psychology in Education. (1993). *Learner-centered psychological principles: Guidelines for school redesign and reform.* Washington, DC: American Psychological Association and the Mid-Continent Regional Educational Laboratory.

Anderson, J. R. (1983). *The architecture of cognition*. Cambridge, MA: Harvard University Press.

Attwell, G. (2007). E-portfolio: The DNA of the personal learning environment. *Journal of E-learning and Knowledge Society, 3*(2).

Augar, N., Raiman, R., & Zhou, W. (2004). *Teaching and learning online with wikis*. Paper presented at the Australian Society for Computers in Learning in Tertiary Education Conference, Perth, Australia.

Bennett, S., & Maton, K. (2010). Beyond the digital natives debate: Towards a more nuanced understanding of students' technology experiences. *Journal of Computer Assisted Learning, 26*, 321–331. doi:10.1111/j.1365-2729.2010.00360.x

Bonk, C. J. (2008). *YouTube anchors and enders: The use of shared online video content as a macrocontext for learning*. Paper presented at the American Educational Research Association Annual Meeting.

Brown, J. S., & Adler, R. P. (2008). Minds on fire: Open education, the long tail, and learning 2.0. *EDUCAUSE Review, 43*(1), 16–32. Retrieved from http://connect.educause.edu/Library/EDUCAUSE+Review/MindsonFireOpenEducationt/45823.

Bunderson, C. V., Wiley, D. A., & McBride, R. (2009). Domain theory for instruction: Mapping attainments to enable learner-centered education. In Reigeluth, C. M., & Carr-Chellman, A. A. (Eds.), *Instructional-design theories and models: Building a common knowledge base* (*Vol. III*, pp. 327–347). New York, NY: Routledge.

Bush, M. D., & Mott, J. D. (2009). The transformation of learning with technology. *Educational Technology Magazine, 49*(March-April), 3–20.

Connolly, P. J. (2001). A standard for success. *InfoWorld, 23*(42), 57–58.

Duffy, P., & Bruns, A. (2006). *The use of blogs, wikis and RSS in education: A conversation of possibilities*. Paper presented at the Online Learning and Teaching Conference, Brisbane.

Frederickson, J. R., & Collins, A. (1989). A systems approach to educational testing. *Educational Researcher, 18*(9), 27–32.

Gibbons, A. S., Nelson, J. M., & Richards, R. (2002). The nature and origin of instructional objects. In Wiley, D. A. (Ed.), *The instructional use of learning objects: Online version*.

Gokhale, A. A. (1995). Colaborative learning enhances critical thinking. *Journal of Technology Education, 7*(1), 22–77.

Grossman, L. (2006). *Time's person of the year: You*. Retrieved May 5, 2008, from http://www.time.com/time/magazine/article/0,9171,1569514,00.html?aid=434.

Harackiewicz, J. M., Barron, K. E., Tauer, J. M., Carter, S. M., & Elliot, A. J. (2000). Short-term and long-term consequences of achievement goals: Predicting interest and performance over time. *Journal of Educational Psychology, 92*(2), 316–330. doi:10.1037/0022-0663.92.2.316

Hodgins, H. W. (2002). The future of learning objects. In Wiley, D. A. (Ed.), *The instructional use of learning objects: Online version*.

Jones, C., Ramanau, R., Cross, S., & Healing, G. (2010). Net generation or digital natives: Is there a distinct new generation entering university? *Computers & Education, 54*(3), 722–732. doi:10.1016/j.compedu.2009.09.022

Kennedy, G., Judd, T., Dalgarnot, B., & Waycott, J. (2010). Beyond natives and immigrants: Exploring types of net generation students. *Journal of Computer Assisted Learning, 26*, 332–343. doi:10.1111/j.1365-2729.2010.00371.x

Lamb, B. (2004). Wide open spaces: Wikis, ready or not. *EDUCAUSE Review, 39*(5), 36–48.

Lum, L. (2006). The power of podcasting. *Diverse Issues in Higher Education, 23*(2), 32–35.

Marzano, R. J. (2006). *Classroom assessment and grading practices that work.* Alexandria, VA: Association for Supervision and Curriculum Development.

McCombs, B., & Whisler, J. (1997). *The learner-centered classroom and school.* San Francisco, CA: Jossey-Bass.

Merrill, M. D., & ID2 Research Group. (1998). ID Expert: A second generation instructional development system. *Instructional Science, 26*(3-4), 242–262.

Merrill, M. D. (2009). First principles of instruction. In Reigeluth, C. M., & Carr-Chellman, A. A. (Eds.), *Instructional-design theories and models: Building a common knowledge base* (*Vol. III*). New York, NY: Routledge.

Mitchell, R. (1992). *Testing for learning.* New York, NY: The Free Press.

Prensky, M. (2009). H. sapiens digital: From digital immigrants and digital natives to digital wisdom. *Innovate 5*(3). Retrieved February 9, 2009, from http://innovateonline.info/index.php?view=article&id=705.

Ranson, S., Martin, J., Nixon, J., & McKeown, P. (1996). Towards a theory of learning. *British Journal of Educational Studies, 44*(1), 9–26. doi:10.1080/00071005.1996.9974055

Reigeluth, C. M., & Carr-Chellman, A. A. (Eds.). (2009). *Instructional-design theories and models: Building a common knowledge base* (*Vol. III*). New York, NY: Routledge.

Reigeluth, C. M., & Garfinkle, R. J. (1994). Envisioning a new system of education. In Reigeluth, C. M., & Garfinkle, R. J. (Eds.), *Systemic change in education* (pp. 59–70). Englewood Cliffs, NJ: Educational Technology Publications.

Salisbury, D. F. (1990). Cognitive psychology and Its implications for designing drill and practice programs for computers. *Journal of Computer-Based Instruction, 17*(1), 23–30.

Schlechty, P. (2002). *Working on the work.* New York, NY: John Wiley & Sons.

Schunk, D. H. (1990). Goal setting and self-efficacy during self-regulated learning. *Educational Psychologist, 25*(1), 71–86. doi:10.1207/s15326985ep2501_6

Schunk, D. H. (1991). Self-efficacy and academic motivation. *Educational Psychologist, 26*(3), 207–231. doi:10.1207/s15326985ep2603&4_2

Schwartz, D. L., Lin, X., Brophy, S., & Bransford, J. D. (1999). Toward the development of flexibly adaptive instructional designs. In Reigeluth, C. M. (Ed.), *Instructional-design theories and models: A new paradigm of instructional theory* (*Vol. II*, pp. 183–213). Mahwah, NJ: Lawrence Erlbaum.

Szabo, M., & Flesher, K. (2002). *CMI theory and practice: Historical roots of learning managment systems.* Paper presented at the E-Learn 2002 World Conference on E-Learning in Corporate, Government, Healthcare, & Higher Education, Montreal, Canada.

Watson, W. R., Lee, S., & Reigeluth, C. M. (2007). Learning management systems: An overview and roadmap of the systemic application of computers to education. In Neto, F. M. M., & Brasileiro, F. V. (Eds.), *Advances in computer-supported learning* (pp. 66–96). London, UK: Information Science Publishing.

Watson, W. R., & Watson, S. L. (2007). An argument for clarity: What are learning management systems, what are they not, and what should they become? *TechTrends, 51*(2), 28–34. doi:10.1007/s11528-007-0023-y

Weller, M. (2009). Using learning environments as a metaphor for educational change. *Horizon*, *17*(3), 181–189. doi:10.1108/10748120910993204

Wiggins, G. (1998). *Educative assessment: Designing assessments to inform and improve student performance*. San Francisco, CA: Jossey-Bass Publishers.

Wiley, D. (2002). Connecting learning objects to instructional design theory: A definition, a metaphor, and a taxonomy. In Wiley, D. A. (Ed.), *The instructional use of learning objects: Online version*.

Williams, J. B., & Jacobs, J. (2004). Exploring the use of blogs as learning spaces in the higher education sector. *Australasian Journal of Educational Technology*, *20*(2), 232-247. Retrieved from http://www.ascilite.org.au/ajet/ajet20/williams.html.

Wilson, S., Liber, O., Johnson, M., Beauvior, P., Sharples, P., & Milligan, C. (2006). *Personal learning environments: Challenging the dominant design of educational systems.* Paper presented at the ECTEL Workshop on Learner-Oriented Knowledge Management and Knowledge Management-Oriented Learning, Heraklion, Crete.

Zimmerman, B. J. (1990). Self-regulated learning and academic achievement: An overview. *Educational Psychologist*, *25*(1), 3–17. doi:10.1207/s15326985ep2501_2

ADDITIONAL READING

Anderson, T. (2006). PLE's versus LMS: Are PLEs ready for Prime time? Retrieved April 19, 2011, from http://terrya.edublogs.org/2006/01/09/ples-versus-lms-are-ples-ready-for-prime-time/.

Attwell, G. (2007a). E-portfolio: The DNA of the personal learning environment. *Journal of E-learning and Knowledge Society*, *3*(2).

Attwell, G. (2007b). Personal learning environments - The future of eLearning? *E-Learning Papers*, *2*(1), 1–8.

Bailey, G. D. (1993). Wanted: A roadmap for understanding integrated learning systems. In Bailey, G. D. (Ed.), *Computer-based integrated learning systems* (pp. 3–10). Englewood Cliffs, New Jersey: Education Technology Publications, Inc.

Cifuentes, L., Mercer, R., Alverez, O., & Bettati, R. (2010). An architecture for case-based learning. *TechTrends*, *54*(6), 44–50. doi:10.1007/s11528-010-0453-9

Ellis, R. K. (2009). A field guide to learning management systems, *ASTD Learning Circuits.* Retrieved April 19, 2011, from http://www.astd.org/NR/rdonlyres/12ECDB99-3B91-403E-9B15-7E597444645D/23395/LMS_fieldguide_20091.pdf.

Finke, W. F. (2004). Basic LMS architecture for learner-centric learnflows or how reusable learning objects fit into co-constructivist learning processes. *Wissen in Aktion-Der Primat der Pragmatik als Motto der Konstanzer Informationswissenschaft, Festschrift für Rainer Kuhlen*. *Schriften zur Informationswissenschaft*, *41*, 309–328.

Fletcher, J. D., Tobias, S., & Wisher, R. A. (2007). Learning anytime, anywhere: Advanced distributed learning and the changing face of education. *Educational Researcher*, *36*(2), 96–102. doi:10.3102/0013189X07300034

Foreman, S., & Davis, R. (2005). Learning management system report and recommendations: Analysis and recommendations: Eaton University.

Fritzberg, G. J. (2001). From rhetoric to reality: Opportunity-to-learn standards and the integrity of American public school reform. *Teacher Education Quarterly*, *28*(1), 752–758.

Johnston, K., & Ross, H. (2001). Teaching to higher standards-from managing to imagining the purposes of education. *Teachers College Record*. Retrieved from http://www.tcrecord.org/Content.asp?ContentID=10804.

Martindale, T., & Dowdy, M. (2009). Personal Learning Environments Retrieved March 14, 2010, from http://teachable.org/papers/2009_ple.pdf.

Mott, J., & Wiley, D. (2009). Open for learning: The CMS and the open learning network. *Education*, *15*(2). Retrieved from http://www.ineducation.ca/article/open-learning-cms-and-open-learning-network.

Rengarajan, R. (2001). LCMS and LMS: Taking advantage of tight integration. *RetrievedFebruary*, 2010, from http://www.e-learn.cz/soubory/lcms_and_lms.pdf.

Schneider, D. K. (2007, October 7th, 2010). Personal learning environment, from http://edutechwiki.unige.ch/en/Personal_learning_environment.

Sclater, N. (2008). Web 2.0, personal learning environments, and the future of learning management systems. *EDUCAUSE Center for Applied Research Research Bulletin, 2008*(13). Retrieved from http://ccblog.typepad.com/weblog/files/ERB0813.pdf.

Smith, M. S., & Casserly, C. M. (2006). The promise of open educational resources. *Change*, *38*(5), 8–17. doi:10.3200/CHNG.38.5.8-17

Watson, S. L., & Watson, W. R. (2011). 'The Role of Technology and Computer-Based Instruction in a Disadvantaged Alternative School's Culture of Learning'. *Computers in the Schools*, *28*(1), 39–55. doi:10.1080/07380569.2011.552042

Weller, M. (2009). Using learning environments as a metaphor for educational change. *Horizon*, *17*(3), 181–189. doi:10.1108/10748120910993204

Wiley, D. (2006). RIP-ping on Learning Objects Retrieved May 14, 2010, from http://opencontent.org/blog/archives/230.

Wiley, D. (2007). *On the sustainability of open educational resource initiatives in higher education*. Retrieved from http://www.oecd.org/dataoecd/33/9/38645447.pdf.

Wilson, S., Liber, O., Johnson, M., Beauvior, P., Sharples, P., & Milligan, C. (2006). *Personal Learning Environments: Challenging the dominant design of educational systems.* Paper presented at the ECTEL Workshop on Learner-Oriented Knowledge Management and Knowledge Management-Oriented Learning, Heraklion, Crete.

KEY TERMS AND DEFINITIONS

Educational Technology: The application of soft processes and hard products, including but not limited to computer technology, for educational purposes.

Educational Software: Computer software for education.

Information Age Society: A knowledge and information based society.

Learner Centered Paradigm of Education: An approach to education that places the learner as the focus of the educational process and mission, supporting customized and personalized approaches to learning and involving the learner as a co-collaborator in the learning process.

Learning Management Systems: Educational software that manages the entire learning process.

Personalized Integrated Educational Systems: A proposed new technology that is open, customizable and systemically integrates into the entire learning organization and all learning processes, including the record keeping, planning, instruction, and assessment for student learning as well as secondary functions for managing the entire learning process.

Systemic Change: The approach to change that seeks to utilize systems thinking to design a new system rather than merely alter an existing one.

ENDNOTES

1 Parents are included throughout this chapter if certain conditions are met, such as the student is being claimed as a dependent on income tax returns, the parents are paying for the student's education, and/or the student wants the parents involved.

2 Knowledge is used in the most generic meaning of all that one can learn. It includes everything in the cognitive, psychomotor, and affective domains (skills, understandings, information, attitudes, values, etc.).

Chapter 4
Frustration Vaccination?
Inoculation Theory and Digital Learning

Josh Compton
Dartmouth College, USA

ABSTRACT

Inoculation theory is a classic theory of social influence, describing how exposure to weakened versions of challenges motivates a process of resistance to protect against future, stronger challenges. Inoculation theory can offer useful guidance to teachers as they talk with Net Generational students about digital learning projects. Discussions guided by inoculation theory raise and refute potential challenges students may have in the process of completing their digital learning projects, helping to protect students against discouraging frustration, but also, encouraging a more thoughtful, nuanced consideration of the use of technology in meeting learning objectives. Inoculation theory-guided discussions will not only impact what students are thinking about, but even how they are thinking—bolstering digital learning project objectives.

INTRODUCTION

Digital learning can be a healthy part of Net Generational students' education regimens; projects that incorporate collaborative engagements with peers and with technology reflect a dynamic approach to knowledge (see Barnes, Marateo, & Ferris, 2007, for a review). Students can learn from creating original public service videos to educate and advocate, from recording pod-casts that share their literary analyses with a wider audience, from creating online how-to-guides for scientific experiments, and from consulting and analyzing digital resources to prepare speeches that help address pressing global problems. Technology and learning objectives can combine in ways that are dynamic and effective, with digital learning as part of a robust, nourishing curriculum.

DOI: 10.4018/978-1-61350-347-8.ch004

We should also consider, however, the other side of the medical analogy: While digital learning can be part of a healthy education regimen, digital learning also risks unique complications and side effects. For one thing, incorporating technology into classroom projects introduces potential problems with technology, from faulty equipment to confusing instructions, and these problems can distract from key learning goals and erode students' (and teachers') enthusiasm. Frustrations with technology become frustrations with projects, and frustrations with projects become frustrations with failing to meet learning objectives.

The analogy to medical treatment can be extended further: Digital learning can have adverse side effects, as digital learning processes can reinforce potentially unhealthy learning practices. Without thoughtful preparation and consideration, technology can move students toward "the habits of instant gratification and shallow thinking" (Barnes, Marateo, & Ferris, 2007, para. 20). Efficiency of information retrieval from technology can overshadow other learning processes that are more deliberate and careful. In pursuit of pragmatic benefits, pedagogical objectives can be slighted.

Fortunately, the medical analogy allows us to consider a remedy: inoculation. The premise of this chapter is that inoculation theory—a theory of resistance to influence (see McGuire, 1964; Compton & Pfau, 2005)—may provide an antidote to help teachers address complications and negative side effects of digital learning projects. Inoculation theory offers guidance as we consider best teaching practices using digital learning projects with Net Generational students.

Inoculation theory may offer benefits both practical and heuristic. When guiding discussions with students about digital learning projects, inoculation theory impacts *what* students are thinking about during digital learning projects and also *how* they are thinking about projects. Inoculation may help reflect something Barnes, Marateo, and Ferris (2007) observed of computer and digital technology: ways "to teach Net Geners not just what to learn but how to learn" (para. 20). Indeed, we may find that inoculation theory secures some of the pragmatic benefits of digital learning (e.g., efficiency) while simultaneously protecting pedagogical aims (e.g., thinking more critically). Inoculation helps prepare students to meet expected challenges during digital learning projects and, in the process, models a more robust, more deliberate way of thinking.

The case for inoculation theory-based discussions about digital learning classroom projects with Net Generational students is built on three ideas explored in this chapter: (1) Even if teachers and students have favorable attitudes toward and beliefs about digital learning projects (see Liaw, Huang, & Chen, 2007), such positions can be eroded by technology problems and other frustrations; (2) Some complications can be preempted, or at least lessened, by using fundamental components of inoculation theory to raise and refute challenges before they occur; and (3) Inoculating against specific complications, like frustration with technology problems, also fosters more nuanced ways of thinking.

Before considering a potential antidote to digital learning project side effects, it is important to note how inoculation theory fits within a conversation about Net Generational learning styles. Perhaps most importantly, inoculation-based communication does not merely tell an audience something. Inoculation models a deliberate, thorough analytical process, and its success is based more on active, dynamic thinking than on passive recall of information. By promoting active thinking, inoculation reflects Net Generational learning on a conceptual level. As Oblinger and Oblinger (2005) succinctly put it: "Students do best when they actively construct their own knowledge" (p. 2.13).

Inoculation also provides applied, practical benefits that are consistent with Net Generational learning styles. For example, Net Generational learners expect immediacy, but immediacy is not always feasible (Oblinger & Oblinger, 2005). Nevertheless, teachers should be aware of this expectation, and inoculation provides a method for addressing it. For example, in light of the expediency offered by email, Net Generational students often expect quick response times from teachers when answering their emailed inquiries (Oblinger & Oblinger, 2005). Faculty may want to clearly communicate anticipations of their response times, and inoculation provides a framework for this type of communication—a way to preempt avoidable, unhelpful frustrations with digital learning by raising and responding to challenges before they occur. Inoculation is an exciting perspective from which to consider Net Generational learning—both on conceptual and applied levels.

BACKGROUND

William McGuire's approach with inoculation theory in the early 1960s was, in many ways, novel. Instead of exploring ways of making messages more persuasive, he turned his research toward making people more resistant to persuasion and influence (see Compton & Pfau, 2005; McGuire, 1964).

The distinction seems simple—between exploring ways of enhancing persuasion and ways of instilling resistance to persuasion—yet the distinction has significant implications. With inoculation theory, the goal is not to persuade people to change their minds about something, but instead, to protect their existing positions against future challenges to the position. The comparison to medical treatments is illustrative. Doctors can treat conditions after patients are sick, but they can also prepare patients for future threats that have yet to occur (see McGuire, 1964). But how can a model of communication take an existing position (attitude, value, belief, opinion) and strengthen it so that it remains robust in the face of future challenges and attacks?

Inoculation theory's namesake does a nice job of explaining how the process of attitudinal inoculation works (McGuire, 1964). A conventional medical inoculation occurs through exposure to a weakened version of an offending agent, such as a virus. The virus is weakened enough so that the person does not get sick but strong enough so that it motivates a process of protection, such as the production of antibodies. Upon encountering a stronger offending agent, such as a stronger (or non-weakened) virus, those inoculated are less likely to get sick when compared to those who were not exposed to the weakened virus. Perhaps one of the most familiar examples of such an inoculation is an annual flu shot. Weakened versions of the influenza virus prompt a strengthening process in healthy patients, whereby exposure to weaker flu ultimately results in resistance to stronger flu. Medical inoculation is a type of training for disease resistance—a way to start small to build the process of resistance against stronger future attacks. We can consider similar processes from other contexts, such as singers warming up with scales before tackling more demanding performances, or an athlete stretching muscles before putting their bodies through more arduous tasks. Jumping into the more challenging tasks—unprepared without preparation—often leads to failure. But beginning with smaller challenges prepares for stronger challenges that could otherwise overwhelm.

Similar processes are at work with attitudinal inoculation. Attitudinal inoculation occurs through exposure to weakened versions of challenges—attempts at persuasion, or challenges to an existing way of thinking about something. The weakened challenges presented during attitudinal inoculation are diluted enough so that they do not convince the person to change position, but the weakened challenges are strong enough to motivate a process of resistance, or a bolstering of that position. Then, upon encountering future stronger challenges, those inoculated are more likely to hold their positions and resist influence (see McGuire, 1964; Compton & Pfau, 2005). In short, inoculation protects by preempting future challenges. The medical analogy offers a clear explanation for how attitudinal inoculation can confer resistance to future challenges. But what would a message guided by inoculation theory look like?

The standard inoculation message is a two-sided message. That is, counterarguments (or, challenges to an existing position) are raised in a message, but refutations of the counterarguments are also provided. The refutations weaken the counterarguments (see Lumsdaine & Janis, 1953). In other words, challenges are presented, and weakened, in an inoculation message. In a standard inoculation message used in resistance research, two or three counterarguments are raised, followed by refutations of those counterarguments, for a simple pattern of counterargument-refutation, counterargument-refutation.

But this component—preemptive refutations of counterarguments—is only part of the process of how inoculation-based messages strengthen positions. Threat is the other part. Inoculation researchers have conceptualized threat as the recognition of a position's vulnerability (see, for example, Pfau et al., 2009). People experience threat when they realize that a position that they hold (e.g., attitude, belief, opinion) may not be as secure as they had originally thought. This recognition—this acknowledgement of vulnerability—triggers a strengthening process, presumably the consideration of additional counterarguments and refutations of those counterarguments. Without this acknowledgement of a position's vulnerability—of the risk of possibly changing one's stance—there is little motivation to engage in more active consideration of the issue (Compton & Pfau, 2005).

It is important to clarify that threat in inoculation is a specific kind of threat, a conceptualization of threat that may not match more common ways of thinking about it. Threat in inoculation is not a warning of punishment; threat in inoculation is not intimidation, nor is it a matter of scaring people into doing something differently (see Pfau, 1995). Instead, threat in inoculation is an acknowledgement that a currently held position could change under the pressure of future challenges. That is, the standard for threat in inoculation is not that people believe they *will* change their minds or *must* change their minds; the standard for threat is the belief they *might* change their minds. In inoculation, threat is vulnerability, and this vulnerability motivates more deliberation about the position. A person experiencing threat in the inoculation process might think something like: "Maybe I haven't fully considered my position on this issue. I'd better give this some more thought and attention."

These two processes—threat and counterarguing—ultimately lead to resistance during the process of attitudinal inoculation: Inoculation messages lead people to acknowledge the vulnerability of a current position (or attitude, or belief), which is called *threat*, and then they think through counterarguments and refutations of counterarguments, which is called *counterarguing*. These two processes work together, with threat providing the motivation for robust preemptive refutation through counterarguing (see Compton & Pfau, 2005; McGuire, 1964).

One of the features of inoculation that makes it a particularly attractive framework for communication strategies is that raising and refuting *some* counterarguments confers protection against *multiple* counterarguments (see Pfau & Kenski, 1990). That is, an inoculation message does not need to raise and refute *every* potential counterargument, or *every* potential challenge, to a position in order to confer resistance to future influence. Instead, the process of resistance unleashed by raising and refuting a few counterarguments protects against a range of challenges—including challenges not even mentioned in the inoculation message (McGuire, 1964). Here we find a power of attitudinal inoculation that we do not always find with medical inoculations. A flu inoculation, for example, protects against a specific type of flu virus. Flu shots change each year to target the strongest variants of the flu. But an attitudinal inoculation—by raising and refuting a few challenges to a position—protects against a wide range of challenges to a position. This attribute of inoculation is particularly important in the context of ever-changing technology—and ever-changing technology challenges.

While the format of an inoculation message is clear-cut—raising and refuting challenges, usually in a two-sided message format—the resulting thinking triggered by inoculation messages is more complex. By presenting multiple considerations, inoculation messages offer richer, more nuanced treatments of issues—which consequently lead to richer, more nuanced thinking about issues. It is not just that inoculation messages are memorable; inoculation messages also change how people think about issues.

This attribute—inoculation-based messages leading to more thinking about an issue—provides one of the strongest arguments for inoculation's potential in improving digital learning projects with Net Generational students. Scholars have warned of the risks of "the habits of instant gratification and shallow thinking" (Barnes, Marateo, & Ferris, 2007, para. 20). For example, students may overestimate the relevance of the first articles retrieved through a Google search and apply superficial standards for assessing a source's credibility (Combes, 2008). Likewise, in her review of Internet literacy, Coiro (2003) warns of "shallow, random, and often passive interactions with text" (p. 458) that can characterize students' Internet use. Inoculation may address such potential problems by generating more thinking about an issue (e.g., Pfau et al., 2004) and thinking that endures (e.g., Pfau et al., 2004).

To encourage students to engage in richer, more nuanced thinking about digital learning projects, we may find inoculation theory to be a valuable tool. It can guide how we engage our students in digital learning activities, and this is the argument that we consider next.

THE CASE FOR APPLYING INOCULATION THEORY TO DIGITAL LEARNING

For much of inoculation theory's development, resistance has been conferred to explicit, distinct attack messages, such as political attack advertisements (e.g., Pfau & Burgoon, 1988) and peer pressure to smoke cigarettes (e.g., Pfau & Van Bockern, 1994). In most cases, inoculation's application has reflected a "fight fire with fire" approach—to protect against an explicit persuasive challenge, offer an explicit preemption of that challenge through inoculation.

Inoculation's efficacy against explicit attack messages has an impressive track record in persuasion literature, with successful applications in health, politics, and commerce (see Banas & Rains, 2010; Compton & Pfau, 2005). However, to my knowledge, researchers have not yet explored inoculation's efficacy as an applied classroom teaching strategy—although it has been assessed with educational issues (e.g., plagiarism, Compton & Pfau, 2008) and with students as study participants (e.g., elementary, Pfau & Van Bockern, 1994; e.g., college, Pfau et al., 2009).

Although inoculation in an educational setting has not been thoroughly studied, its success is theoretically consistent. Indeed, Compton and Pfau (2005) proposed extending inoculation to other forms of influence. The theoretical case for extending inoculation to less conventional attack messages is strong: Inoculation should be able to confer resistance to *any* challenge to an attitude or belief, not just conventional, explicit persuasive messages (see Compton & Pfau, 2005; McGuire, 1964). A few contemporary inoculation researchers have tested this idea, moving from inoculating against specific persuasive messages toward types of influence that occur in more subtle, less identifiable ways. For example, Haigh and Pfau (2006) wondered if inoculation treatments could help boost employee morale in the workplace. Their findings suggested that raising and then refuting potential challenges to employee commitment—prior to employees experiencing such challenges—could lead employees to demonstrate more positive attitudes toward their employer and have better morale. Applying inoculation to less tangible influences expands its utility—from explicit forms of persuasive attack to more abstract challenges to existing attitudes, beliefs, and opinions.

New insight into inoculation—new applications (e.g., Haigh & Pfau, 2006) and new theorizing (e.g., Compton & Pfau, 2005)—suggests that inoculation may help Net Generational students and their teachers as they engage in digital learning projects. Simply adding technology to class projects and instruction without careful analysis does not protect against less effective ways of thinking, such as "the habits of instant gratification and shallow thinking" (Barnes, Marateo, & Ferris, 2007, para. 20). But inoculation theory can offer such protection: It can preempt specific technology problems and unleash thinking that is more robust, more complex.

For an inoculation-based message to inoculate, the "right" attitude must first be in place (see Compton & Pfau, 2005; McGuire, 1964). That is, inoculation takes an existing position and makes it stronger, protecting it against future challenges. But one study found that even if the "right" attitude is not in place inoculation can still be an effective persuasive strategy, moving positions toward the points advocated in the inoculation-based message (Wood, 2007).

In the context of the Net Generation's experiences with digital learning, the pertinent attitude would be students' attitudes toward digital learning technology, or the use of digital learning technology for a specific course project. Some data suggests that students have confidence in their technology knowledge (e.g., McEuen, 2001); students also have favorable attitudes toward technology (e.g., Havelka, 2003), as do their instructors (e.g., Liaw, Huang, & Chen, 2007).

Protecting students' favorable positions on potential benefits of digital learning technology is important. When frustration leads to resistance, technology use can suffer (see Smart & Desouza, 2007, for a treatment of technology resistance in a business context), and "no matter how advanced or capable the technology is, its effective implementation depends upon users having a positive attitude toward it" (Liaw, Huang, & Chen, 2007, p. 1069).

I pause here to clarify my main argument. I am not advocating the elimination of all struggles during digital learning projects. As many education theorists have pointed out, students (and teachers) learn from challenges. Inoculation is not a cure-all; complications will still arise, problems will emerge, and projects will not always go smoothly. The difference—and this is an important difference—is that, with the aid of inoculation theory, students may be better equipped to interpret and think through the challenges, shifting their focus from their frustration to ways of working through the complications. This is an important distinction in my argument: It's not just that inoculation will prepare students for ways of addressing specific technology complications (e.g., a blog post won't post, so what can I do about this?), but more importantly, that inoculation will help students to think more carefully, more critically about the use of technology (e.g., I wonder what other problems I might face when using this technology? What are some other impacts of using this specific technology to meet this specific goal?). More robust thinking can help students to interpret the challenges in ways that are more productive to learning.

Applying inoculation theory to digital learning challenges answers a call for thinking more broadly about Net Generational learning. As Mishra, Koehler, and Kereluik (2009) put it, a "focus on specific technologies instead of broader, generative frameworks of thought will always be limited, preventing us from keeping up with the rapid pace of change of technology and ultimately make us fall behind" (p. 50). It also offers a more nuanced perspective of technology—not only its benefits, but also its costs—which helps us better understand how Net Generational students learn. As Hartman, Moskal, and Dziuban (2005) summarized: "To a great extent, the behaviors of the Net Gen are an enactment of the capabilities afforded by modern digital technologies" (p. 6.3).

I contend that inoculation theory provides a particularly enlightening "framework of thought"—for teachers and Net Generational students using digital learning technologies. Besides the practical implications of approaching digital learning from an inoculation theory perspective, we also gain pedagogical insight by looking at a bigger picture—a theory-guided perspective of the benefits and drawbacks of approaches that characterize Net Generational learning.

RECOMMENDATIONS

Applying inoculation theory to the development and communication of digital learning projects can help to prevent, or at least lessen, two potential adverse effects of digital learning: (1) frustration caused by technological problems such as failed equipment or unclear instructions (see Sang, Valcke, van Braak, & Tondeur, 2010) or not knowing how to use a specific type of technology (see Kvavik, 2005, McNeely, 2005); and (2) an overemphasis on quick information retrieval (see Barnes, Marateo, & Ferris, 2007) and risks of superficial knowledge engagement, or "shallow thinking" (Barnes, Marateo, & Ferris, 2007, para. 20). Raising and refuting potential challenges before beginning a digital learning project may gain both of these benefits. We consider these two areas next, beginning with the pragmatic benefit of preparing students for potential technology problems.

Inoculation can lessen to-be-expected complications with technology. Of course, technology can help students learn (e.g., Blumenfeld et al., 1991). But technology can also be frustrating—for students and for teachers. If the frustration affects attitudes and/or perceptions of efficacy (self-efficacy or technology-specific efficacy), this can discourage the use of technology for learning (Sang, Valcke, van Braak, & Tondeur, 2010). For students, the frustrations may come from a number of barriers, including perceptions that technology is "of limited usefulness or too difficult to learn" (Blumenfeld et al., 1991, p. 378) or when students have not been taught a specific skill needed to use the technology (Kvavik, 2005; McNeely, 2005). Similarly, teachers can experience frustration with technology, for example, when technology does not work properly (Woelk, 2008) or when institutional support is limited (Woelk, 2008). One principal summarized teacher frustrations toward technology: "If you are pushing yourself to really learn stuff…you're going to have technical problems. It's going to be frustrating, and you'll want to take an ax to things" (Bryson & de Castell, 1998, p. 552). But there may be another option besides an ax—something that offers more precision and is proactive instead of reactive: inoculation.

Following the tenets of inoculation theory, teachers can predict and share potential digital learning challenges with their students—and solutions (or refutations) of these challenges—before they happen, possibly preempting some of the frustration when the obstacles are eventually confronted. By talking with students about possible or probable complications, these influences are raised and refuted before they occur—a format that reflects inoculation theory. It is not that challenges won't occur, but instead, that students are better prepared for the challenges when they do.

In my own courses, prior to extensive use of the Blackboard Learning System (an online-based education system, see www.blackboard.com), I talk about some challenges students—and teachers—have had in the past, and then ways we have worked through the challenges. For example, I offer some hypothetical situations about students who have posted work to Blackboard only to discover later that the post did not upload. I show them a simple way to double-check that assignments have been posted. This simple example offers a counterattitudinal argument ("Online blogging isn't reliable because work sometimes doesn't post when students think that it has") and a refutation of that argument ("We can confirm and prevent misunderstandings about whether our work has been posted"). This raises and refutes a potential—and common—challenge before it occurs. And as we learn from nearly fifty years of inoculation scholarship, inoculation does more than teach specific refutations (e.g., how to confirm that a blog post is actually posted); inoculation also motivates more robust, more nuanced, and longer-lasting thinking about the issue (Compton & Pfau, 2005). Considering one potential complication leads to thinking about other complications—and how to overcome other complications.

This is one approach teachers can use to utilize inoculation theory in introducing and describing digital learning projects: pointing toward specific problems that might arise during the course of the project and offering ways to overcome such challenges. Additionally, teachers can use a more generic counterargument-refutation message strategy when introducing digital learning projects. As an example of this inoculation strategy, a teacher can mention, in general, that students will likely experience technological difficulties with digital learning projects, and then provide different ways of interpreting or reframing technological challenges. For example, students can be encouraged to consider struggles that occur during projects "as attempts to make meaning and to solve difficult and demanding problems" (Blumenfeld et al., 1991, p. 379). I use a similar approach when I describe the Blackboard component of my speech courses on my syllabus, beginning with: "We will frequently use online blogging to facilitate our goals in the course. Some characteristics of online blogging can be frustrating, so let me share some thinking about why I use it so much in this course." I then describe my aims with the use of technology in my course, a discussion that takes place in the context of potential frustrations with the technology. This approach, while more generic than a point-by-point analysis of specific challenges (e.g., confusions about whether an assignment has posted), reflects the framework of inoculation theory: counterarguments ("Digital learning projects can be frustrating") and refutation(s) ("Despite frustrations, digital learning projects offer a number of benefits").

The key, whether offering specific two-sided messages or more generic ones, is to raise and refute digital learning complications *before* the challenges arise. Teachers can include this information in early-in-the-term course overviews and/or the syllabus, or teachers can tailor an approach to each digital learning project as it is assigned. Inoculation-informed communication about digital learning projects reflects a deeper approach of integrating digital learning projects into classroom curriculum—an approach that not only considers potential challenges, but also includes acknowledgements of challenges in the design and communication of digital learning projects. The goal is not to avoid the complications, but instead, to help students begin thinking more carefully and critically about technology as the project progresses.

BENEFITS

In the process of preparing such inoculation-based messages, teachers benefit by looking ahead and thinking through potential complications. Teachers get a better understanding of the potential problems, helping them make more informed decisions about how (or whether) to use digital learning technology for each particular project. Inoculation-based messages educate recipients of the messages as well as the creators of the messages.

We find clear practical benefits of digital learning project discussions guided by inoculation theory. But other benefits move beyond overcoming technological problems by influencing how students understand pedagogical considerations that inform digital learning projects.

Inoculation effects endure. Like the medical vaccine that gave inoculation its name, inoculation needs time to confer resistance (see McGuire, 1964). In a medical inoculation, this time is needed for the body to develop antibodies in protection against a future virus. In an attitudinal inoculation, time is needed for those inoculated to think more about the issues, to raise and refute additional counterarguments, a process that bolsters the position or attitude (Compton & Pfau, 2005). One study found that inoculation messages motivate active thinking about an issue that endures for at least 44 days (Pfau et al., 2004). Another found some attitudinal effects of inoculation lasting for several months (Pfau & Van Bockern, 1994). Talking about digital learning projects using a two-sided message format—raising and refuting potential challenges before they occur—unleashes a process that keeps students thinking about the issues. An inoculation-informed message gives students something to think about—and the motivation to keep thinking. Notably, the type of thinking unleashed by inoculation includes multiple perspectives on an issue—a possible antidote to hasty generalizations and superficial thinking (Barnes, Marateo, & Ferris, 2007).

For example, telling students at the start of a project that they will be blogging may provide the basic details of the project, but it does little to motivate—let alone sustain—student interest in the technology and the implications of the technology on their learning. However, an inoculation-informed description of the assignment would raise and refute potential challenges with using blogging as a learning project. Students could be encouraged to consider, for example, how writing for a general audience will create limitations on their use of more specialized terminology. Or, students could consider how audience expectations for frequent postings may impact how, what, and when they write. Inoculation scholarship suggests that raising and then responding to these challenges—prior to the actual challenges—motivates a process of thinking that continues for days—and even months (Pfau & Van Bockern, 1994).

Consequently, with longer periods of contemplation and information processing, inoculation promotes deeper, more careful thinking about issues, and this can deepen students' understandings and attitudes about connections between technology and learning—a goal with digital learning (see Mishra, Koehler, & Kereluik, 2009). As Brown (2005) points out, "In 1900, learning consisted largely of memorization; today it relies chiefly on understanding" (p. 12.4). Inoculation, in contrast to other message strategies, not only provides more complex information (e.g., two or more sides of issues), but also serves as a catalyst for more thinking about the issue, beyond what is included in the message (Compton & Pfau, 2005; McGuire, 1964) and this may lead to deeper understanding.

Furthermore, inviting students to think through the project—before the project begins—involves them more deeply in the projects, and "[a]ctively involving the end user in the design process can break down some…barriers" that lead to technology resistance (Joseph, 2010, p. 146). Teachers can work with their students to generate a list of potential challenges they may face when working with a specific technology, or with technology in general. For example, I use video recording technology in several of my courses, and my students have been among my most valuable resources for information about how video files are best viewed on the campus network (practical implications) as well as how video technology has affected how they assess their work (pedagogical implications). Teachers are not restricted to a linear, lecture format when talking with their students about potential or probable technology complications; instead, the requisite counterarguments and refutations can—and in most cases, should—emerge through dialogue with students.

These characteristics of inoculation theory-motivated thinking help to alleviate potential side effects of digital learning: "the habits of instant gratification and shallow thinking" (Barnes, Marateo, & Ferris, 2007, para. 20). By prolonging thinking about the issues, inoculation theory protects against hasty generalizations; by motivating a consideration of counterarguments and refutations, inoculation theory protects against shallow thinking. We may find that inoculation not only helps Net Generational students to work through technological problems, but also, helps Net Generational students to think more carefully and deliberately about technology as a part of learning.

FUTURE RESEARCH DIRECTIONS

While I am an advocate for raising and refuting potential challenges to digital learning project success prior to the start of a project, a number of questions continue to motivate my own thinking, practice, and research. These areas warrant future study as we continue considering ways that inoculation theory can guide discussions with Net Generational students about digital learning projects in the classroom.

Some technology barriers are there for a reason or reasons, and it is worth noting that some complications or frustrations with technology shouldn't be inoculated against. A specific project design may not be the best way to meet a course objective, or the technology may not be used effectively for the needs of the project. Just as students should be prepared to confront and overcome some barriers to digital learning projects, teachers should also be prepared—and open toward—reconsidering the aims of the projects themselves. Teachers should not merely collect potential counterarguments against a project to design inoculation messages; each potential counterargument should be given fair hearing. Otherwise, there is a chance that we could inoculate against barriers that are there for a reason.

On a related note, future research should also consider whether inoculation-based messages help to define frustrations or challenges as problems to be confronted rather than simply ignored. Under some conditions, students may not become frustrated when using technology (see Combes, 2008), and instead of working through a problem, they may simply stop and try something else. Holman (2011) found that students are not always able to identify problems when using online searches, for example. Future research may find that inoculation helps to identify challenges as problems that can be overcome instead of problems to be ignored.

Effectiveness of inoculation theory-based discussions needs empirical testing in the context of classroom digital learning projects. Just as continual assessment is important for us to consider (and reconsider) the effectiveness of digital learning projects in the classroom, we should continue to assess the effectiveness of inoculation theory as a guide for digital learning project discussions. Inoculation boasts an impressive track record of success in conferring resistance to influence—with an impressive amount of empirical support for its ability to affect responses to challenges (Banas & Rains, 2010; Compton & Pfau, 2005). But we need more investigations of inoculation as a classroom communication approach. As part of this needed research, scholars should also consider any potential "side effects" of inoculation treatments. For example, the process of inoculation can elicit affect responses (e.g., anger, see Pfau et al., 2009), and research should consider whether any of these emotional responses could serve as distractions.

The focus of this chapter was on considering inoculation theory applications in talking about digital learning projects in a traditional classroom setting. However, one may also be able to apply aspects of inoculation theory to communication and project design in an online course. Teachers of online courses could turn to inoculation theory to help preempt specific technology complications and promote the type of active thinking that we have explored in this chapter.

CONCLUSION

Talking about projects—at length and in depth—does not need to be a dilatory phase of course instruction; if such discussions are thoughtful and strategic, such discussions become vibrant parts of instruction and of learning. This chapter proposed that turning to inoculation theory is one way to improve our discussions with Net Generational students about digital learning projects. As Oblinger and Oblinger (2005) remind us: "It isn't the technology per se that makes learning engaging for the Net Gen; it is the learning activity" (p. 2.16). Inoculation may function as a strategy for preempting frustrations with technology that turns focus away from the learning activity—distractions that can impede learning.

By raising and refuting potential challenges, inoculation theory can guide discussions about digital learning projects, transforming linear descriptions (e.g., telling students about the project) into descriptions that are more complex and more interesting. Discussions with Net Generational students about digital learning projects should be as dynamic and active as the projects themselves, and inoculation adds a layer of complexity that enhances student learning. It is appropriate that conversations about digital learning are dynamic, thought provoking, and robust—all characteristics that we can also apply to inoculation theory.

REFERENCES

Banas, J. A., & Raines, S. A. (2010). A meta-analysis of research on inoculation theory. *Communication Monographs*, *77*(3), 281–311. doi:10.1080/03637751003758193

Barnes, K., Marateo, R. C., & Ferris, S. P. (2007). Teaching and learning with the net generation. *Innovate, 3*(4).

Blumenfeld, P. C., Soloway, E., Marx, R. W., Krajcik, J. S., Guzdial, M., & Palincsar, A. (1991). Motivating project-based learning: Sustaining the doing, supporting the learning. *Educational Psychology*, *26*(3 & 4), 369–398.

Brown, M. (2005). In Oblinger, D., & Oblinger, J. (Eds.), *Educating the net generation* (pp. 12.1–12.22). Boulder, CO: EDUCAUSE.

Bryson, M., & de Castell, S. (1998). New technologies and the cultural ecology of primary schooling: Imagining teachers as Luddites in/deed. *Educational Policy*, *12*(5), 542–567. doi:10.1177/0895904898012005005

Coiro, J. (2003). Exploring literacy on the Internet: Reading comprehension on the Internet: Expanding our understanding of reading comprehension to encompass new literacies. *The Reading Teacher*, *56*(5), 458–464.

Combes, B. (2008). *The Net generation: Tech-savvy or lost in virtual space?* Paper presented at the IASL Conference: World Class Learning and Literacy through School Libraries.

Compton, J., & Pfau, M. (2005). Inoculation theory of resistance to influence at maturity: Recent progress in theory development and application and suggestions for future research. In Kalbfleisch, P. (Ed.), *Communication yearbook 29* (pp. 97–145). Mahwah, NJ: Lawrence Erlbaum.

Compton, J., & Pfau, M. (2008). Inoculating against pro-plagiarism justifications: Rational and affective strategies. *Journal of Applied Communication Research*, *36*(1), 98–119. doi:10.1080/00909880701799329

Haigh, M. M., & Pfau, M. (2006). Bolstering organizational identity, commitment, and citizenship behaviors through the process of inoculation. *The International Journal of Organizational Analysis*, *14*(4), 295–316. doi:10.1108/19348830610849718

Hartman, J., Moskal, P., & Dziuban, C. (2005). Preparing the academy of today for the learner of tomorrow. In Oblinger, D., & Oblinger, J. (Eds.), *Educating the net generation* (pp. 6.1–6.14). Boulder, CO: EDUCAUSE.

Havelka, D. (2003). Students beliefs and attitudes toward information technology. *Information Systems Education Journal, 1*(4), 3–9.

Holman, L. (2011). Millennial students' mental modes of search: Implications for academic librarians and database developers. *Journal of Academic Librarianship, 37*(1), 19–27. doi:10.1016/j.acalib.2010.10.003

Joseph, R. C. (2010). Individual resistance to IT innovations. *Communications of the ACM, 53*(4), 144–146. doi:10.1145/1721654.1721693

Kvavik, R. B. (2005). Convenience, communications, and control: How students use technology. In Oblinger, D., & Oblinger, J. (Eds.), *Educating the net generation* (pp. 7.1–7.20). Boulder, CO: EDUCAUSE.

Liaw, S.-S., Huang, H.-M., & Chen, G.-D. (2007). Surveying instructor and learner attitudes toward e-learning. *Computers & Education, 49*, 1066–1080. doi:10.1016/j.compedu.2006.01.001

Lumsdaine, A. A., & Janis, I. L. (1953). Resistance to counterpropaganda produced by one-sided and two-sided propaganda presentations. *Public Opinion Quarterly, 17*, 311–318. doi:10.1086/266464

McEuen, S. F. (2001). How fluent with information technology are our students? *EDUCAUSE Quarterly, 4*, 8–17.

McGuire, W. J. (1964). Inducing resistance to persuasion: Some contemporary approaches. In Berkowitz, L. (Ed.), *Advances in experimental social psychology* (*Vol. 1*, pp. 191–229). New York, NY: Academic Press. doi:10.1016/S0065-2601(08)60052-0

McNeely, B. (2005). Using technology as a learning tool, not just the cool new thing. In Oblinger, D., & Oblinger, J. (Eds.), *Educating the net generation* (pp. 4.1–4.10). Boulder, CO: EDUCAUSE.

Mishra, P., Koehler, M. J., & Kereluik, K. (2009). The song remains the same: Looking back to the future of educational technology. *TechTrends, 53*(5), 48–53. doi:10.1007/s11528-009-0325-3

Oblinger, D., & Oblinger, J. (2005). Is it age or IT? First steps toward understanding the Net Generation. In Oblinger, D., & Oblinger, J. (Eds.), *Educating the net generation* (pp. 2.1–2.20). Boulder, CO: EDUCAUSE.

Pfau, M. (1995). Designing messages for behavioral inoculation. In Maibach, E., & Parrott, R. L. (Eds.), *Designing health messages: Approaches from communication theory and public health practice* (pp. 99–113). Newbury Park, CA: Sage Publications.

Pfau, M., & Burgoon, M. (1988). Inoculation in political campaign communication. *Human Communication Research, 15*(1), 91–111. doi:10.1111/j.1468-2958.1988.tb00172.x

Pfau, M., Compton, J., Parker, K. A., Wittenberg, E. M., An, C., & Ferguson, M. (2004). The traditional explanation for resistance based on the core elements of threat and counterarguing and an alternative rationale based on attitude accessibility: Do these mechanisms trigger distinct or overlapping process of resistance? *Human Communication Research, 30*, 329–360. doi:10.1093/hcr/30.3.329

Pfau, M., & Kenski, H. C. (1990). *Attack politics: Strategy and defense*. New York, NY: Praeger.

Pfau, M., Semmler, S. M., Deatrick, L., Mason, A., Nisbett, G., & Lane, L. (2009). Nuances about the role and impact of affect in inoculation. *Communication Monographs, 76*(1), 73–98. doi:10.1080/03637750802378807

Pfau, M., & Van Bockern, S. (1994). The persistence of inoculation in conferring resistance to smoking initiation among adolescents: The second year. *Human Communication Research*, *20*, 413–430. doi:10.1111/j.1468-2958.1994.tb00329.x

Sang, G., Valcke, M., van Braak, J., & Tondeur, J. (2010). Student teachers' thinking processes and ICT integration: Predictors of prospective teaching behaviors with educational technology. *Computers & Education*, *54*, 103–112. doi:10.1016/j.compedu.2009.07.010

Smart, B., & Desouza, K. (2007). Overcoming technology resistance. *Business Strategy Review*, 25-28.

Woelk, K. (2008). Optimizing the use of personal response devices (clickers) in large-enrollment introductory courses. *Journal of Chemical Education*, *85*(10), 1400–1405. doi:10.1021/ed085p1400

Wood, M. L. M. (2007). Rethinking the inoculation analogy: Effects on subjects with differing preexisting attitudes. *Human Communication Research*, *33*, 357–378. doi:10.1111/j.1468-2958.2007.00303.x

KEY TERMS AND DEFINITIONS

Counterarguing: A process of raising and refuting challenges to a current position; reflects an active way of thinking about a position which can involve more critical thinking.

Inoculation Effects: Changes to attitudes, affect, behaviors and/or thinking following exposure to an inoculation pretreatment message; the primary goal of inoculation is to confer resistance, or protection of a position, attitude, and/or belief.

Inoculation Pretreatment Message: A message that raises and refutes challenges to a position, attitude, or belief before stronger challenges occur.

Inoculation Theory: A theory first introduced by William McGuire that explains how resistance to future challenges can be conferred through preemptive exposure to weakened versions of future challenges.

Threat: Recognition of vulnerability of an existing position; motivates more thinking about a position.

Chapter 5
Face-to-Face Communication outside the Digital Realm to Foster Student Growth and Development

Charles F. Aust
Kennesaw State University, USA

ABSTRACT

Benefits of college go beyond acquisition of skills and knowledge to include understanding, effective decision-making, personal growth, and maturation. While online courses and online social interactions grow, the benefits of and preference for face-to-face interaction remain important. Digital learners are human beings, so non-digital ways of fostering their development remain relevant. Face-to-face interactions of significance occur in the classroom, and the real physical presence of each other cannot always be replaced by digital tools and delivery, nor should it be. While not downplaying online and digital technologies' role in advancing academic progress online, in-person face-to-face learning experiences contribute in important ways to students' growth and adaptation. Each time instructors and students communicate, they co-construct their evolving social reality. Face-to-face interactions provide unique capabilities and benefits in that transformational process, as this chapter explores.

INTRODUCTION

As digital capabilities rapidly develop and are applied to education, concerns are being raised and some soul-searching is going on about the quality and direction of American higher education in general (e.g., Arum & Roksa, 2011; Bok, 2006; Harris & Cullen, 2010; Hersh & Merrow, 2006; Menand, 2010; O'Brien, 2009; Zemsky, 2009).

In addition, scholars are asking what our increasing reliance on and heavy use of digital technology and online activity are doing to us socially and intellectually. Experts raise questions about the isolating effects of digital devices (e.g.

DOI: 10.4018/978-1-61350-347-8.ch005

Turkle, 2011) and express concerns about diminished intellectual abilities and intelligence (e.g., Bauerlein, 2008). Others assert that digital technology is diminishing our ability to think deeply and is eroding academic standards (e.g., Jacoby, 2008). The balance between digital connection with others and contemplative time alone with one's thoughts and feelings is deemed important but is getting more and more out of balance (e.g., Powers, 2010). There are concerns that digital technology is affecting our relationships and social life (Baym, 2010).

This is compounded by increasing concerns about online learning, which is growing. More than 20% (3.9 million) of all students in American colleges and universities (18 million) were taking at least one online course in the fall of 2007 (Allen & Seaman, 2008). That number jumped to 5.6 million by fall 2009 (Kaya, 2010). Online enrollment and the number of institutions offering online courses have steadily grown in number and this growth is seen across almost every discipline. Approximately one-third of baccalaureate institutions consider online delivery to be a critical component of their long-term strategy (Allen & Seaman, 2008).

Financial pressures make online delivery more and more attractive to institutions. For example, at the University of Florida, which was hard-hit by a 25% cutback in state funding over three years, 12 percent of credit hours were being earned online in the fall of 2010. The administration expects that to increase to 25 percent by 2015 (Gabriel, 2010).

Whether the concerns are about the quality of higher education, the diminishment in social relationships or intellectual ability, or the reasons driving increased enrollment and availability of online courses, it is worthwhile to consider whether something is lost when there is limited or no face-to-face interaction of instructor with students and of students with each other. Likewise, it may be useful to ponder the possibility that there are some compelling reasons to retain and promote in-person, face-to-face experience in the learning process in the midst of increasing online delivery of courses. To the extent that face-to-face communication contributes to the effectiveness of education, it is a significant variable not to be lost in the expanding flurry of new applications and digital devices (e.g., the iPad) that are electronic and digital technologies and mobile learning experiences available to more and more of the net generation. So, while technology will continue to impact teaching methods, we also need to keep in mind the important benefits of and the preference for face-to-face interaction in the developmental process for college students.

One of the most impactive decisions students make about college is the major they will select and study in depth. Another impactive but not mindful decision they will make on a daily basis, concerns their use of technology in lieu of face-to-face communication, not just in their learning but in their social interactions. Most students are heavy users of online technology and social media. But for us, the overarching question is what leads to a more memorable and meaningful college experience. Although students rarely consider these issues, I contend that there may be obvious and subtle but significant benefits in the long run by choosing to include face-to-face experience with instructors and fellow students. It is worthwhile to ponder what is gained by obtaining at least some face-to-face experience in this life-changing process of earning a college degree. The remainder of this chapter will examine some of these considerations.

But first, a word about what this chapter is not, and a few details about my background related to this topic. This chapter does not intend to "take sides." It is not meant to argue whether online or in-person learning is better. Both have their strengths and weaknesses. Rather, it explores the benefits of actions and conditions that occur either best or only in face-to-face communication, when people are physically present to one another, and reasons why that adds value to the developmental journey for college students as well as instructors. At the same time, I also acknowledge appreciation for online tools and processes that computer-mediated-communication affords students and instructors.

Why does in-person face-to-face experience in the educational process matter enough to me to write this chapter? Before I became a professor of communication I was a family and children's services caseworker and had training as a counselor. I also have studied recovery support groups, where being in the presence of one another is vital to mutual support and recovery efforts. I share these details about myself only to explain to the reader that I come to this interesting educational matter with a deep appreciation for the efficacy and importance of face-to-face interaction as a transformational force. I also have a keen interest in ways we help one another journey through life, especially with education.

COLLEGE EXPERIENCE AS A DEVELOPMENTAL, THERAPEUTIC JOURNEY

Teachers are change agents. Students finish our courses different than they started, perhaps just from learning course content, but maybe sometimes by gaining insights that contribute to their personal growth and development. Each time our lives intersect with our students in communication, we and our students co-construct our social reality (Blumer, 1969; Goffman, 1959). We both come out of the interaction changed, experiencing a new social reality.

Digital learners are human beings, not electronic devices, so no matter how much they utilize technology and social media for social interaction and learning, non-digital ways of communicating and development are still important. The effects of real physical presence of each other cannot always be replicated or replaced by digital delivery, nor should they be, for a variety of reasons. (Levy, Nardick, Turner & McWatters, 2011). Some learning is better achieved by face-to-face interaction. Some human interactions of value cannot be delivered or replicated in digital form, and indeed, have their value because humans are physically present to one another in those interactions.

Education is a developmental journey of change and growth. Students are still maturing when they come to college (Astin, Astin, & Lindholm, 2011; Kloss, 1994; Palmer, 1998, Weimer, 2002). In fact, the act of obtaining an education is a change process. Students are seekers. On their quest for meaning and understanding, they wonder what is important to them, what to do with their lives and their energy, and what sort of world they want to help create. They may face choices about letting go and revising parts of their identity. Then again, we are all continually changing and growing. Indeed, we are all on that journey, instructors as well as students.

Communication in educational contexts can serve a therapeutic function for students. Any action or process can be therapeutic when it facilitates adjustment or adaptation and contributes to well-being. Barnlund (1968) considers communication therapeutic when it helps bring about personal insight or reorientation. Another conception of therapy is helping a person to "achieve better self-understanding, thereby aiding that individual in deciding how to direct behaviors to best satisfy personal needs and accomplish personal goals" (Kreps, 1986, p. 190).

These conceptions can apply to the developmental process of college students. One could hope that the efforts of instructors facilitate such understanding, insight, decisions, and goal achievement. The benefits of earning a college degree can go beyond knowledge and skill acquisition to the overall well-being of the student as a person who functions more effectively and fully in his or her social world. So when we help students understand themselves better, and help them decide how to direct their actions in ways that allow them to accomplish their goals for personal as well as academic and professional growth, we have been therapeutic.

Digital technologies can contribute to this development but in-person face-to-face interaction with no intervening electronic process is useful and uniquely suited for some situations (more about this later). Face-to-face interaction can, at times, be just as powerful, if not more so, in the experiences students and professors have with each other in the classroom, a place of development, growth, and co-construction of social reality. These interactions have important implications for students and the world they are making. They come to understand themselves better and grow in their personal and professional dealings with others in their expanding social world, a larger world that, in the long run, is not solely nor mainly experienced in digital form.

EMBODIMENT, INVOLVEMENT, AND MOOD: THEORETICAL EXPLORATION

This section examines a special set of ideas about why in-person presence and face-to-face interaction are needed and valuable in the educational process. It is influenced by the writing of Hubert L. Dreyfus whose book *On the Internet* (2009) provides the following key insights into why bodily presence matters in the learning process.

Dreyfus (2009) asks what our bodies mean to us. And what does the experience of our bodies in relation to other bodies that share physical space with us mean to us? In short, our bodies make things matter. However, our physical engagement with the world of people and objects is so woven into our sensate being that its pervasiveness becomes assumed, seemingly imperceptible, unless we intentionally think about it. That is, we become oblivious to it. And it is our tendency to be oblivious to it unless we are restricted or unable to bring our bodies to a desired location. Despite this taken-for-granted tendency, bringing our bodies materially to a setting has such a profound role and effect on our experience. Our ability to take our bodies to locations and perceive people and things and have cognitive and emotional responses to them – all of this occurring over and over again – are what make things matter to us.

Dreyfus (2009) implicates the sense of involvement we have through our bodily presence with one another as an important element in development of proficiency, an advanced stage in the learning process. As one wishes to advance in the learning process, embodiment is eventually necessary. Dreyfus (2009) argues that to go from the level of competence to proficiency the content must matter to the student. For the content to matter, the student must become emotionally involved. The way to do this, he proposes, is to link the physically experienced real world with abstract theoretical understanding. And that linking eventually has to involve bodily presence, or embodiment. "At every stage of skill acquisition beyond the first three, involvement and mattering are essential... Only emotional, involved, embodied human beings can become proficient and expert" (p. 46-47).

Being physically present increases the available sensory information with which to perceive similarities with others and the conditions being shared in that physical space and time, such as mood. But how is mood relevant? Heidegger (1995) talked of local worlds, gatherings of people who share friendship, celebratory purpose, and a sense that they are somehow blessed. Borgmann (1984) had a similar conception of such an experience which he called focal practices. People are drawn together by some kind of common ground and come together to share in that experience of common ground. Some details about the gathering, such as how and when, may vary but the coming together is based on a commitment shared by the participants which motivates them to collectively make this experience happen. A sense of sharing ensues in various ways, including shared mood (Dreyfus, 2009).

I don't wish to put too fine a point on the comparison, but the classroom could be considered not unlike a local world, a focal practice, to use Heidegger's (1995) and Borgmann's (1984) terms, respectively. Perhaps not friendship (although that can emerge among students who take classes together), but a common ground of purposes draw students and instructor together for learning, development, progress.

Dreyfus (2009) asserts that focal occasions require a shared mood. He also asserts that all the participants share that mood. Can students at a computer screen experience a shared mood? Does a shared mood even exist for online students at a computer screen? Can a podcast draw them in? Or a YouTube video or a tweet or a videoconference? Even if a mood can be conveyed electronically, is it fully the experience one would have if in person and physically present to all the others in the group and physically experiencing the environmental conditions all others in the group are feeling with their five senses?

One cannot fully grasp the mood of a situation via telepresence, if, indeed, a mood has been engendered at all, in the same way one can grasp and experience the mood of a group gathering in person. Being physically present allows us to fully sense the mood and share in that mood. And Dreyfus (2009) argues that mood contributes significantly to our ability to make sense of what we are experiencing, and making sense is essential to the learning process.

The mood of a group is not generated by one individual alone, is not under the control of a single individual, according to Heidegger (1995). One cannot control the mood of a group. But a mood can pervade a group, can become a significant determinant of the shared experience. "Moods are powerful in that they are not under our control, and yet they determine what matters in our interactions with others and so govern our social behavior" (Dreyfus, 2009, p. 117). It makes what happens in a face-to-face situation such as the classroom matter. Dreyfus puts it this way: "...there is always some shared mood in the classroom and it determines what matters..." (page 59).

The above can be illustrated with a phenomenon that happens on occasion in my courses. Sometimes I experience an all-at-onceness, a unity, so to speak, with what I call the "constellation" of students, these particular students involved and developing a relationship with each other in this particular context with this particular focus (the nature of the course and its content) and in relation to me as their facilitator and as part of the experience we are all having at the moment. I liken this to a *gestalt*. There is a sense of sudden melding into an emotional whole, a collective mood, which is greater than the sum of the parts (the individuals in the room with their own personal experience). My sense is that a majority, if not all, experience this unique chemistry of melding together in spirit, in mood, at this moment in the class meeting.

Such an awareness of the mood and awareness that the mood is shared among the group members is part of what makes experience of mood meaningful and hedonically impactive. Each one senses that all are sharing in the experience at that moment. I sense the chemistry that develops among them that occurs by them being physically and uniquely present to one another and interacting with each other. Mood is part of this momentary phenomenon. But it could also extend to the entire semester in a unified way that brings a special gratification of connection, inspiration, and fellowship. I propose this because on occasion I actually hear students in a class say at the end of the semester that they are sorry the course is ending. They seem to wish the shared experience and the mood it produces could continue. Dreyfus (2009) explains:

When a focal event is working to the point where it has its particular integrity, one feels extraordinarily in tune with all that is happening, a special graceful ease takes over, and events seem to unfold on their own. This makes the moment an all-the-more enchanting and unforgettable gift. (p. 109)

Embodiment, involvement and mood are essential to the learning process and an in-person educational experience contains these key elements, which facilitate learning.

I add one more idea to Dreyfus's (2009) thinking about embodiment that relates to in-person participation in the classroom. Making the effort and taking the time to travel in order to be with others physically is a form of nonverbal communication. That act conveys meaning. The physical act of travel communicates that the person and/or the purpose are important enough in some way that makes being physically present matter. It communicates in a unique way a level of interest, caring and commitment that an electronic process does not convey. While we might take nonverbal actions for granted, their importance, their meaning and impact can be quite significant. It is another reason why our bodies make things matter.

Now let us turn to other considerations about the nonverbal.

Nonverbal Cues and Impact on Communication

Elements of nonverbal communication, such as tone of voice, volume, pace, eye contact, posture, physical distance, walking around the room, and gestures all have communication value because they convey meaning. Online methods such as podcasts and videos are able to capture and convey some of these elements, while e-mail and text messaging are lacking in these qualities (Adler & Rodman, 2009). When sender and receiver are face-to-face, all of these nonverbal elements are available to perceive and use in the interaction and they add to the richness and impact of the exchange.

Meaning and intent might not be effectively communicated without nonverbal cues. Two examples are when humor and irony are employed. In the absence of nonverbal facial cues and vocal tone, the use of humor and irony online will likely have limited impact or unintended consequences which could cause misunderstandings and conflict (McKeachie & Svinicki, 2006).

Attentiveness in the Classroom

As students use mobile digital technologies in an online world, many sources of experience are readily available. Some of those sources can add to the learning experiences in a course, such as a relevant Web site or database. But sources irrelevant to the learning material are easily accessible and attractive, such as Facebook or texting. Irrelevant, distracting paths that could fully engage the attention of students are a click or a text away. Granted, distractions also are possible in the physical classroom, such as coughing or whispered side conversations, but not the alluring and vivid Web-based content that could divert the full attention of students away from the classroom activity. Yes, a classroom full of students also contains distractions, but no fully engrossing alternatives like Web-based content are readily available in class to draw the full attention of students completely away from the learning situation. So another benefit of in-person learning in which electronic devices are set aside, at least temporarily, is less difficulty maintaining the attention level of students and the minimizing of fully engrossing irrelevant digital diversions.

Group Silence in the Room

Another value of face-to-face communication comes from silence. There is educational value in being in a room with others and all are observing moments of silence for reflection and learning.

For a large number of students to be in a room together and to maintain silence can be an unusual experience that could be dramatic and provocative, in part because it is rare and novel. Kloss (1994) writes about the "creative silence" he promotes by talking less in class and allowing extended periods of silence so that students have quiet time in which to think and formulate ideas. Palmer (1998) advocates the use of silence in class as a chance to reflect. Silence can invite insight and awareness that fosters discussion (Brooks, 2011) and can make the ensuing discussion powerful (Gravois, 2005). Clarity of thought and understanding the significance of contemplated experience are also benefits of using silence in the classroom (Hart, 2004; Reda, 2010).

The value of silence cannot be replicated online or digitally. Although students can gather together in real-time digital and online environments, attempting the simultaneous experience of silence in those situation is quite a challenge. If all students are assembled together in the classroom the environment is uniform for all present and thus achieving a period of silence for all is more feasible.

The Risks of Communication and Teaching

Face-to-face presence also promotes learning through risk. All communication involves risk in that we are not in control of outcomes. Also, we don't know everything. Yet we as instructors are willing to make ourselves vulnerable in our role as educators for the good of our students. Attempting to foster change is risky. It makes us vulnerable to failure and embarrassment. But there is value and potential positive impact in risking success or failure in the presence of others (Palmer, 1998).

Likewise, for students there is a risk. The response of the professor and other students can have a significant impact on their learning and sense of self. The student might experience the anticipation of those responses from others as motivation that inspires and challenges the student. Then, after the student acts, the resulting responses that are elicited from instructor and peers could serve to validate, teach, encourage, correct and motivate change in behavior. The real possibility of vulnerability enhances and intensifies the experience when the student is physically present to other students and to the instructor. The experience is cognitively and affectively different when experienced in person. More kinds of sensory inputs are entering the brain than text or images on a screen. Effects are immediate. And the temptation to hide is not an option. Blending into the background is not so easy.

Witnessing such acts of daring and willingness to be vulnerable and extend oneself for some worthwhile goal (to learn or to teach) can be dramatic, vivid, memorable and formative. Dreyfus (2009) considers this to be a powerful aspect of embodiment. The student is fully experiencing a situation, grasping the situation and what it means, what its value is, what the consequences are for those involved in the interaction. The moment matters, sometimes profoundly.

Paradoxically, vulnerability can create a safe space for participants. When one allows oneself to be vulnerable and open, it models courage and openness that encourages others to open up. When others see that the consequences are meted out in respectful ways, and they see that the instructor is also willing to be vulnerable and open in the situation, it fosters security and willingness to risk (Palmer, 1998). Students want to know they will be respected despite their weaknesses or insecurities. We create a safe space in which to be human, imperfect, accepted as we are, if we, as instructors, are willing to be vulnerable for the benefit of our students and respond respectfully to students when they make mistakes (Palmer, 1998).

Another way we make ourselves vulnerable is sharing personal experiences at appropriate times for appropriate reasons. This can inspire and move students in ways that are supportive and enhancing of their well-being. Kochersberger (2008) in an article called "The Healing Power of a Class," shares a touching story about how he eventually came to the difficult decision to tell his classes, at the end of the semester in December, about the suicide of his son in July. He says he was very careful to discern that he was not telling them for his own benefit, but he decided there might be some benefit to his students if they were told. But he did it at a carefully chosen time-on the very last day of class. "I wanted those students to understand the incredible healing role they played for me. I had a sharp realization just then that they had, in a way, saved me. Without their clear-eyed hopefulness…I might have sunk under the weight of my sorrow" (p. B28). The powerful, face-to-face sharing that he did resulted in a healing, edifying effect on one of his students.

Ultimately, instructor and student are evolving as we navigate our shared social reality in the classroom. We exist in that moment as real, flesh-and-blood, vulnerable social beings. This unique intersection of lives – students with teacher and students with students – imbues this social exchange with transformational potential as each of us knows and is known by others.

CLASS MEETING AS A SOURCE OF SUPPORT

Face-to-face presence has other learning benefits. On those occasions when a class meets after a traumatic event that disturbs the sense of safety and order of the campus, community or the nation, convening the class and gathering together physically can offer a palpable sense of shared support and reinforcement of order. It offers a predictable routine, something tangible, clear-cut and anchoring, symbolizing a comforting, reassuring purpose that all can embrace cognitively and emotionally in the midst of the unexpected event that makes life suddenly seem ambiguous and out of control. There is a unique value for participants in the room that is not likely to be experienced as fully or as effectively online or digitally.

It may be that students beset by chaos and trauma also find it a welcome diversion to attend class. The class may be a place to come to that is orderly, focused, intended to promote their progress, and gets them in touch with a larger world and a process that is hopeful, psychically nourishing, and positive. Can they experience that on a screen in the form of text or computer-delivered video or in audio via podcasts? Yes, but not in the same way and perhaps not in as rich and supportive a way as actually physically leaving the home or apartment and moving through the wider physical surroundings to a campus, a building, a classroom, a process full of stimuli that can divert from thoughts and emotions that hover over them if they are physically alone while interacting virtually with others. IThe class experience can be so different and so constructive that it provides at least temporary relief, or perhaps even healing, maybe in small, gradual doses, but healing just the same.

We physically take our bodies to a place where our brains can dwell on entirely different stimuli. It's not a geographic "cure" but perhaps helpful as part of a coping strategy. The classroom experience could be for some a respite of diversion that gets their minds off of problems and diverts their attention to actions that imply a better future is possible. A sense of hope might be felt or renewed.

Making face-to-face connections of a sustained and supportive nature can benefit vulnerable students with emotional and mental health difficulties. College populations contain students who struggle with such difficulties. Incoming first-year students are reporting record-low levels of emotional health, according to the latest annual survey of freshmen by the Higher Education Research Institute at UCLA's Graduate School of Education & Information Studies (Klein, 2011). Directors of college health centers have reported an increase in the number of students who come to college with psychological problems. Up to 85 percent of counseling centers reported an increase in the number of students coming to their centers with significant mental health problems (Farrell,

2008). Suicide is the third leading cause of death among those 15 to 24 years old (American Foundation for Suicide Prevention, 2011). Pavela (2006, cited in Hoover, 2006), in an interview with *The Chronicle of Higher Education* (Hoover, 2006), links suicide with depression, and sees isolation as one of the triggering factors. He stressed the need for feeling a part of a community, not as the total answer to depression and suicide but as one component of prevention.

Ontological Value of Memory-Making

Face-to-face interaction can also promote a meaningful sense of self. Ontological might not be a word that pops into a student's mind if asked to sum up college in one word. Yet college experiences can be associated with efforts to search for actions and meanings in order to make sense of college and life in general, not unlike ontology, that branch of philosophy that deals with questions about being. And in that searching and sense-making, a phenomenon can occur that the humanistic psychologist Abraham Maslow (1970) calls a peak experience, that is, actions and perceptions marked by insight and ecstasy. In-class interactions can contribute to relationships between people that sustain themselves in the form of vivid memories. One's own reflections about self in relation to others in the form of knowledge, insight, memories, and emotion can trigger sudden exhilaration. And for that fleeting period of time everything seems to make sense. It is a perception of harmony of self with the world, of being an integrated part of everything in an all-at-onceness not unlike the *gestalt* experience I referred to previously.

While this kind of rapturous event might or might not occur in a classroom, memories of in-person interactions in the classroom could play a role. We might savor details about when we had that face-to-face experience, who was involved, the context in which it occurred, the knowledge and insight grasped at that moment, all contributing to that "ah-ha! moment" of insight and intense pleasure. There may be great joy and gratitude in pondering and savoring the in-person experiences that contributed to this momentous cluster of thoughts and feelings that suddenly coalesce in such a peak experience.

Some Instructor Perspectives

Instructors who have experience utilizing digital and computer technologies in their teaching also value face-to-face interaction. Kennelly teaches an online course in geography-information-systems project management every semester for Pennsylvania State University from his home campus, Long Island University, and describes the experience as very positive. His online students, who tend to be older than his face-to-face students, tend to be more motivated and engaged. But he says he also wishes he could have what he calls face time. "The important thing is to establish a connection between the instructor and the students," he says (cited in Keller, 2010, p. B16).

It is because faculty value in-person interaction with their students that they might also see online tools as important. Mark David Milliron (2010), deputy director of postsecondary improvement at the Bill & Melinda Gates Foundation, in a commentary in *The Chronicle of Higher Education*, urges educators to use *online* delivery so that, among other reasons, they are able to maximize the value of the *face time* they have with those students. Khan (2010) predicts that *face time* will remain valuable and be enhanced as a result of the implementation and enhancement of online methods.

Marshall's view (2011) reflects the desire of many instructors to maintain a sense of community while also utilizing digital technology so that students can have the best experience with both. She wants to embrace technology without compromising a sense of community in her classes. She poses the challenge this way: "How can I learn to teach with technology in a way that doesn't compromise the feeling of community, engagement, focused attention, and sense of personal responsibility that I value so much and want my students to value, too?" (online-no page number)

Lang (2010) writes about ways to care about our students and care about teaching. He places great emphasis on this caring as an important variable in one's effectiveness as a change agent with students. And he echoes the advice of Perlmutter (2010) who proposes that a way to be an effective teacher is to care about students and care about teaching. He advocates face-to-face interactions as a way to care about and help students through the learning process. Both writers count it an immense privilege to have an edifying impact on the lives of students, and deem face-to-face contact as one of the conduits through which this can occur.

If we instructors need inspiring moments and gratifying evidence that we have made a difference in the lives of our students in order to reinvigorate our love of teaching and strengthen our motivation to again and again engage with students in the arduous intellectual process of facilitating their knowledge gains and intellectual insights, or as an antidote to burnout (Kolowich, 2011), and if the preferred way for an instructor to obtain that renewed motivation is with face-to-face interactions, then that is an important realization and value upon which to act in the span of a semester and in the long arc of one's career.

Soul Presence

Metaphysics is that branch of philosophy that ponders what exists in reality and what is the nature of what exists (Thiroux & Krasemann, 2009). It includes questions such as "what is the nature of the physical world, and is there anything other than the physical, such as the mental or spiritual" (page 2).

How does this relate to the topic of face-to-face classroom experience? One way it relates is regarding the question of the soul. Does each human being have a soul? If so, can one person be truly in the presence of the other's soul via electronic means? Perhaps a time will come when technology provides a simulated presence of another that is experienced as life-like. Yet as long as a person knows that the other's presence is technologically simulated, no matter how closely it resembles real, physical presence, in at least some peoples' estimations, it will still not satisfactorily replace the physical presence of a person. In their estimation a soul-presence is necessary and that can only be possible in the physical presence of one another. Perhaps based on course content, learning objectives, or their philosophical or pedagogical beliefs and values, instructors may wish to have the sense of soul presence as part of the educational experience with their students, and wish for students to have that with each other in the class. To them, sensing the soul of the other is vital to the kinds of interpersonal communication connections they wish to have in the class.

FUTURE RESEARCH DIRECTIONS

Numerous questions continue to be asked about online courses: how much work is involved to teach them, how effective they are, how rigorous they are for students, and how commonplace they will become in American higher education (e.g., Clift, 2009; Digital Campus, 2011; Greco, 2009; Parry, 2009; Parry, 2010; Seaman, 2009, Shieh, 2009). Answers to these questions will better inform the efficacy and the role of face-to-face interaction in the learning process.

Also, it will be important to continue to measure student attitudes and preferences as more of them become familiar with online and hybrid courses and experience their benefits and effects, in comparison to participating in the learning process face-to-face. In preliminary research with 300 students at six colleges, Levy, et. al. (2011) found that, while students are aware of and appreciate the power and convenience of digital technologies, they also express concerns and confusion about the use of these technologies in education. A majority expressed a variety of reservations about use of digital technology and how it was affecting their lives. These researchers argue that student attitudes and preferences need to be investigated on a large scale. Furthermore, students need to be "given permission to express opinions they may tacitly assume are not welcome" (p. B28) by faculty and administrators. For example, are more students taking online courses because they like them and want them or out of expediency? Must they enroll in them because their choices are limited? Should we assume that, because students register for online courses, they prefer them to courses requiring classroom attendance? It might be for some not a preference but a resignation to having no other choice if online delivery is the only choice offered or one of a very restricted set of choices for a specific course. Student voices need to be a part of the ongoing conversation regarding the crucial place of digital technology in their education.

CONCLUSION

The ideas explored in this chapter assist the reader in thinking about what might be gained if students experience meaningful in-person, face-to-face classroom interactions while in college. I believe it is worthwhile to ponder what is gained and what is lost when we accept the digital and de-emphasize embodied face-to-face presence with one another in learning environments. And likewise, it is useful to ask what is gained and what is lost when we emphasize embodied face-to-face presence and de-emphasize digital methods in those learning environments.

Dreyfus (2009) draws a conclusion about Second Life that could also apply to college. "For the time being, if we want to live life at its best, we will have to embrace our embodied involvement in the risky, moody, real world" (p. 120). Perhaps we can say something similar about college, in that the best experiences of that developmental journey will require our embodied selves to engage in the risky, moody, real world of the classroom.

While we help our students accomplish learning objectives and advance their academic progress through electronic and digital means, we can, by the ways we communicate and co-construct our social realities in each other's physical presence, also foster growth and adaptation on the journey toward a fuller and more satisfying life. Students need to experience each other and the professor in real time in each other's physical presence, not just in digital form. Digital delivery can provide many benefits but the in-person, face-to-face experience offers vital opportunities for growth and development that are difficult if not impossible for students to experience the same way in digital form.

As education and technology continue to evolve it is likely that aspects of digital delivery will continue to be valued and new teaching methods and capabilities will be added. Still, qualities and aspects of the experience of being physically present will also continue to offer benefits that both students and professors will value and seek as part of the developmental process of education. Digital technologies are useful and important, but being in each other's real presence and interacting in person are also rich and valuable components of this evolving formative journey as students make their educational way.

REFERENCES

Adler, R. B., & Rodman, G. (2009). *Understanding human communication*. New York, NY: Oxford.

Allen, I. E., & Seaman, J. (2008). *Staying the course: Online education in the United States, 2008*. Retrieved from http://sloanconsortium.org/sites/default/files/staying_the_course-2.pdf.

American Foundation for Suicide Prevention. (2011). Facts and figures: National statistics. Retrieved from http://www.afsp.org/index.cfm?fuseaction=home.viewPage&page_id=050FEA9F-B064-4092-B1135C3A70DE1FDA.

Arum, R., & Roksa, J. (2011). *Academically adrift: Limited learning on college campuses*. Chicago, IL: University of Chicago Press.

Astin, A. W., Astin, H. S., & Lindholm, J. A. (2011). *Cultivating the spirit: How college can enhance students' inner lives*. San Francisco, CA: Josey-Bass.

Barnlund, D. C. (1968). Therapeutic communication. In Barnlund, D. C. (Ed.), *Interpersonal communication: Survey and studies* (pp. 613–645). Boston, MA: Houghton Mifflin.

Bauerlein, M. (2008). *The dumbest generation: How the digital age stupefies young Americans and jeopardizes our future*. New York, NY: Penguin.

Baym, N. K. (2010). *Personal connections in the digital age*. Malden, MA: Polity Press.

Blumer, H. (1969). *Symbolic interactionism*. Englewood Cliffs, NJ: Prentice-Hall.

Bok, D. C. (2006). *Our underachieving colleges: A candid look at how much students learn and why they should be learning more*. Princeton, NJ: Princeton University Press.

Borgmann, A. (1984). *Technology and the character of contemporary life: A philosophical inquiry*. Chicago, IL: University of Chicago Press.

Brooks, D. (2011, March 21). Getting students to talk. *The Chronicle of Higher Education*. Retrieved from http://chronicle.com/article/Getting-Students-to-Talk/126826.

Clift, E. (2009, May 21). I'll never do it again. *The Chronicle of Higher Education*. Retrieved from http://chronicle.com/article/Ill-Never-Do-It-Again/44250/.

Digital Campus. (2010, May 8). *The Chronicle of Higher Education*. Retrieved from http://chronicle.com/section/The-Digital-Campus/529/.

Dreyfus, H. L. (2009). *On the Internet*. New York, NY: Routledge.

Farrell, E. F. (2008, February 29). Counseling centers lack resources to help troubled students. *The Chronicle of Higher Education*. Retrieved from http://chronicle.com/article/Counseling-Centers-Lack/33930/.

Gabriel, T. (2010, November 4). Learning in dorm, because class is on the Web. *The New York Times*. Retrieved from http://www.nytimes.com/2010/11/05/us/05college.html.

Goffman, E. (1959). *The presentation of self in everyday life*. Garden City, NY: Doubleday.

Gravois, J. (2005, October 21). Meditate on it. *The Chronicle of Higher Education*, A10–A12.

Greco, G. (2009, May 21). A reaffirmation of why I became an educator. *The Chronicle of Higher Education*. Retrieved from http://chronicle.com/article/A-Reaffirmation-of-Why-I/44254/.

Harris, M., & Cullen, R. (2010). *Leading the learner-centered campus: An administrator's framework for improving student learning outcomes*. San Francisco, CA: Jossey-Bass.

Hart, T. (2004). Opening the contemplative mind in the classroom. *Journal of Transformative Education*, *2*, 28–46. doi:10.1177/1541344603259311

Heidegger, M. (1995). *The fundamental concepts of metaphysics*. Bloomington, IN: Indiana University Press.

Hersh, R. H., & Merrow, J. (2006). *Declining by degrees: Higher education at risk*. New York, NY: Palgrave Macmillan.

Hoover, E. (2006, May 19). Giving them the help they need. *The Chronicle of Higher Education*. Retrieved from http://chronicle.com/article/Giving-Them-the-Help-They/25347/.

Jacoby, S. (2008). *The age of American unreason: Dumbing down and the future of democracy.* London, UK: Old Street.

Kaya, T. (2010, November 16). Enrollment in online courses increases at the highest rate ever. *The Chronicle of Higher Education.* Retrieved May 16, 2011, from http://chronicle.com/blogs/wiredcampus/enrollment-in-online-courses-increases-at-the-highest-rate-ever/28204.

Keller, J. (2010, November 5). Mapping a virtual future at Penn State. *The Chronicle of Higher Education*, B16.

Khan, S. (2010, November 5). YouTube U. beats YouSnooze U. *The Chronicle of Higher Education*, B36–B38.

Klein, A. (2011, Jan. 26). Incoming college students rate emotional health at record low, annual survey finds. *UCLA News.* Retrieved from http://www.heri.ucla.edu/PDFs/press/2010CIRPpressrelease.pdf.

Kloss, R. J. (1994). A nudge is best: Helping students through the Perry Scheme of Intellectual Development. *College Teaching*, *42*, 151–158. doi:10.1080/87567555.1994.9926847

Kochersberger, B. (2008, June 20). The healing power of a class. *The Chronicle of Higher Education*, B28.

Kolowich, S. (2011, May 16). Built for distance. *Inside Higher Ed.* Retrieved from http://www.insidehighered.com/layout/set/print/news/2011/05/16/online_faculty_burnout.

Kreps, G. (1986). *Organizational communication.* White Plains, NY: Longman.

Lang, J. M. (2010, November 2). The invisible curriculum. *The Chronicle of Higher Education.* Retrieved from http://chronicle.com/article/the-invisible-curriculum/125197/.

Levy, D. M., Nardick, D. L., Turner, J. W., & McWatters, L. (2011, May 8). No cellphone? No Internet? So much less stress. *The Chronicle of Higher Education*, B27–B28.

Marshall, S. (2011, February 3). More face-to-face, less face-to-screen. *The Chronicle of Higher Education.* Retrieved February 19, 2011, from http://chronicle.com/article/More-Face-to-Face-Less/126163.

Maslow, A. H. (1970). *Motivation and personality* (2nd ed.). New York, NY: Harper & Row.

McKeachie, W. J., & Svinicki, M. (2006). *McKeachie's teaching tips: Strategies, research and theory for college and university teachers.* New York, NY: Houghton Mifflin.

Menand, L. (2010). *The marketplace of ideas: Reform and resistance in the American university.* New York, NY: W.W. Norton.

Milliron, M. D. (2010, November 5). 2010). Online education vs. traditional learning: Time to end the family feud. *The Chronicle of Higher Education*, B31–B32.

O'Brien, P. M. (2009). *Accreditation: Assuring and enhancing quality, new directions for higher education.* San Francisco, CA: Jossey-Bass.

Palmer, P. J. (1998). *The courage to teach: Exploring the inner landscape of a teacher's life.* San Francisco, CA: Jossey-Bass.

Parry, M. (2009, August 31). Professors embrace online courses despite qualms about quality. *The Chronicle of Higher Education.* Retrieved from http://chronicle.com/article/Professors-Embrace-Online/48235.

Parry, M. (2010, July 4). Linked in with: A writer who questions the wisdom of teaching with technology. *The Chronicle of Higher Education.* Retrieved from http://chronicle.com/article/Is-Technology-Making-Your/66128/.

Pavela, G. (2006). *Questions and answers on college student suicide: A law and policy perspective*. Asheville, NC: College Administration Publications.

Perlmutter, D. D. (2010). *Promotion and tenure confidential*. Cambridge, MA: Harvard University Press.

Powers, W. (2010). *Hamlet's Blackberry: A practical philosophy for building a good life in the digital age*. New York, NY: Harper Collins.

Reda, M. M. (2010, September 5). What's the problem with quiet students? Anyone? Anyone? *The Chronicle of Higher Education*. Retrieved from http://chronicle.com.

Seaman, J. (2009). Online learning as a strategic asset, volume II: The paradox of faculty voices. Retrieved from http://www.aplu.org/NetCommunity/Document.Doc?id=1879.

Shieh, D. (2009, February 10). Professors regard online instruction as less effective than classroom learning. *The Chronicle of Higher Education*. Retrieved from http://chronicle.com/article/Professors-Regard-Online/1519/.

Thiroux, J. P., & Krasemann, K. W. (2009). *Ethics: Theory and practice*. Upper Saddle River, NJ: Pearson.

Turkle, S. (2011). *Alone together: Why we expect more from technology and less from each other*. New York, NY: Basic Books.

Weimer, M. (2002). *Learner-centered teaching*. San Francisco, CA: Jossey-Bass.

Zemsky, R. (2009). *Making reform work: The case for transforming American higher education*. Piscataway, NJ: Rutgers University Press.

ADDITIONAL READING

Abelson, H., Ledeen, K., & Lewis, H. (2008). *Blown to bits: Your life, liberty and happiness after the digital explosion*. Boston: Pearson Education.

Bonk, C. J., & Graham, C. R. (2006). *The handbook of blended Learning: Global perspectives, local designs*. San Francisco: Pfeiffer.

Carr, N. (2010). *The Shallows: What the Internet is doing to our brains*. New York: Norton.

Ess, C. (2003). Liberal arts and distance education: Can Socratic virtue (arête) and Confucius' exemplary person (junzi) be taught online? *Arts and Humanities in Higher Education*, *2*, 117–137.. doi:10.1177/1474022203002002002

Evans, N. J., Forney, D. S., Guido, F. M., Patton, L. D., & Renn, K. A. (2009). *Student Development in College: Theory, Research and Practice*. San Francisco: Jossey-Bass.

Jackson, M. (2008). *Distracted: The erosion of attention and the coming Dark Age*. Amherst, NY: Prometheus.

Lanier, J. (2010). *You are not a gadget: A manifesto*. New York: Knopf.

Maushart, S. (2011). *The winter of our disconnect: How three totally wired teenagers (and a mother who slept with her iPhone) pulled the plug on their technology and lived to tell the tale*. New York: Penguin.

Means, B., Toyama, Y., Murphy, R., Bakia, M., & Jones, K. (2010). Evaluation of evidence-based practices in online learning: A meta-analysis and review of online learning studies. Washington, DC: U.S. Department of Education. Retrieved from http://www2.ed.gov/rschstat/eval/tech/evidence-based-practices/finalreport.pdf.

Nye, D. E. (2006). *Technology matters: Questions to live with*. Cambridge, MA: MIT Press.

Palmer, P., & Zajonc, A. (2010). *The heart of higher education: A call to renewal.* San Francisco: Jossey-Bass.

Parry, M. (2010, October 31). Tomorrow's college. *The Chronicle of Higher Education.* Retrieved from http://chronicle.com/article/Tomorrows-College/125120/.

Shirky, C. (2010). *Cognitive Surplus: Creativity and generosity in a connected age.* New York: Penguin.

Tapscott, D. (2009). *Growing up digital: How the net generation is changing your world.* New York: McGraw-Hill.

KEY TERMS AND DEFINITIONS

Embodiment: Physical presence that permits direct perception of and interactions with people, objects and environment and the concomitant cognitive and emotional responses evoked by those perceptions and actions.

Face-to-Face: Experience that occurs when people are physically present to one another with no intervening electronic or mechanical process involved.

Gestalt: A perceptual phenomenon integrating parts into a whole and experienced as a unified sensation greater than the sum of the individual parts.

Hybrid Course (also referred to as Blended Learning): A course in which some learning activities and reading materials exist online, and classroom activity is reduced but not eliminated.

Metaphysics: That branch of philosophy that ponders what exists in reality and what is the nature of what exists.

Online: Accessible in digital form on the Internet using computer equipment.

Ontology: That branch of philosophy concerned with questions of being; ontological-adjective form of ontology.

Peak Experience: Actions and perceptions marked by insight and ecstasy. A concept created by the humanistic psychologist Abraham Maslow.

Self-Actualization: A state in which one realizes one's fullest potential. A concept created by the humanistic psychologist Abraham Maslow.

Therapeutic: Used here in relation to communication, an actions or process that facilitates adjustment or adaptation and contributes to well-being.

Section 2
Theory and Practice

There is nothing so practical as a good theory (Kurt Lewin).

The previous section established the value of theory to advance our understanding of pedagogy. The theories, concepts, and models discussed in Section One help us both understand our teaching, and how learning is affected by different factors. But without linking them to classroom practice, theories do not achieve their potential.

The chapters in this section demonstrate the effectiveness of developing theory through empirical research. Using research methods that included surveys and experiments, the researchers significantly add to pedagogical literature. Robert Zheng and Jim Gleason use experimental methods. Zheng examines the influence of multi-modal presentation and multi-tasking on Net Generation students' performance in complex problem solving. Gleason explores the impact of interactivity on measurable student knowledge acquisition.

The other authors in this chapter used survey methods or triangulated their research. D'Urso and Scott examine technology-enhanced classroom education and technology-enhanced online education, comparing the learning environments. They investigated the role of communication technologies in predicting the importance of various technologies, satisfaction with key course elements, perceived learning outcomes, and objective measures of classroom performance. Ben DaCosta, Carolyn Kinsell, and Angelique Nasah's survey research questions the concept of digital propensity applied to the Net Generation. They surveyed 580 postsecondary students to investigate the differences between digital natives and digital immigrants.

While findings of the research in this section vary in significance, the empirical research can help educators improve teaching and learning by linking sound practice with theory.

Chapter 6
Millennials are Digital Natives?
An Investigation into Digital Propensity and Age

Boaventura DaCosta
Solers Research Group, USA

Carolyn Kinsell
Solers Research Group, USA

Angelique Nasah
Solers Research Group, USA

ABSTRACT

The abundance of opinions about Millennials has made it very difficult to separate reality from conjecture, especially with regard to the suppositions made about their propensity towards technology. Labeled as digital natives, Millennials are thought to possess learning traits never before seen as a result of growing up in the digital information age. In this chapter, we present the findings of a study in which postsecondary students (N = 580) were surveyed to quantitatively investigate the differences between digital natives and digital immigrants. Findings revealed that of the ten traits investigated, only two showed significant difference, and of these two traits, only one favored the digital native notion, shedding doubt on the strong digital propensity claims made about today's Millennials. Although differences were found, we cannot say with any certainty that there is an unambiguous delineation that merits the digital native and digital immigrant labels. The findings raise a variety of implications for institutions training pre-service teachers; educators interested in using digital media, devices, and social networks in their classroom; curriculum developers designing instructional material; educational leaders developing information and communication technology policy for school; and researchers investigating digital propensity with today's youth.

DOI: 10.4018/978-1-61350-347-8.ch006

INTRODUCTION

The Millennial Generation (Howe & Strauss, 2000), Generation M (Roberts, Foehr, & Rideout, 2005), the Net Generation (Tapscott, 1998), Digital Natives (Prensky, 2001a), or whatever you choose to call today's generation of tech-savvy students, they are by far the most investigated, most marketed to, and most captivating generation to date (Cone, Inc., 2006).

To most of you, this should not come as much of a surprise. Considered to have been "born digital" (Palfrey & Gasser, 2008) into the late twentieth and early twenty-first centuries (actual dates are in question; see Kelan & Lehnert, 2009), rough estimates place Millennials at over 80 million in the U.S. alone (Howe & Strauss, 2003). And while Americans have always had an enormous interest with the notion of generational change, which has been traditionally discernable by specific events, famous individuals and/or products, and character traits of the people found during a specific era (Fishman, 2004), the "contagious" (Hoover, 2009) nature of Millennials has turned them into an industry.

There have been countless articles and books written about Millennials in the past decade. They have found their way into primetime television, when the CBS news show, 60 Minutes, originally broadcast *The Age of the Millennials* in November of 2007 (Safer, 2007). There are even individuals who regard themselves as subject matter experts, and consult for huge fees to large companies (Hoover, 2009), such as Merrill Lynch and Ernst & Young (Safer, 2007), as well as universities and colleges, to help these institutions understand how to keep this generation happy, motivated, and productive.

Yet, even with the big business this age bracket has generated and all the information that has been made available, our understanding of Millennials is, by and large, muddled (Hoover, 2009). Granted, understanding each new generation of young people has always appeared to be a lesson in futility, with every older generation looking unfavorably on the new. However, other than a number of popular books, whose theories are considered to be largely based on anecdotal evidence, there is scant empirical data to support many of the assumptions put forth about Millennials (studentPOLL, 2010).

Take for instance the widely cited theories by Howe and Strauss (2000). As strong as many of their arguments appear to be on the surface, they are fueled by an assortment of questionable research. Hoover (2009) explains that the presumptions made by Howe and Strauss (2000) "were based on a hodgepodge of anecdotes, statistics, and pop-culture references, as well as on surveys of teachers and about 600 high-school seniors in Fairfax County, Va., which in 2007 became the first county in the nation to have a median household income of more than $100,000, about twice the national average" (¶ 9).

It goes without saying that the abundance of opinions about Millennials has made it very difficult to separate reality from conjecture. Regrettably, as one delves deeper into specific aspects of this generation, the subject becomes no less jumbled, but is instead filled with even more contradictions and bafflement. In fact, one does not need to go any further than the suppositions made about their propensity toward technology to find contradictions and disagreement.

DIGITAL PROPENSITY

Those holding a sympathetic and optimistic view of this generation insist that Millennials are native speakers of the digital age—that is to say, *Millennials are Digital Natives*. They do not have to translate or learn technology, but instead merely experience it. They have spent their entire lives so immersed in a digital culture that it has fundamentally changed the way in which they process information (Prensky 2001a; 2001b), resulting in learning styles and preference never before seen.

It has been suggested that this generation is so drastically different that our educational system is unable to keep pace (Oblinger & Oblinger, 2005; Prensky, 2001a; Tapscott, 1998). Pundits such as Prenky (2001a), for example, have stressed, "Our students have changed radically. Today's students are no longer the people our educational system was designed to teach" (p. 1). Rationale such as this is generally attributed to the belief that our educational system is predominately comprised of teachers from the analog age (Jones, Harmon, & O'Grady-Jones, 2005), also commonly called *digital immigrants* (Prensky, 2001a), who will never be as fluent with technology as their students because they will always retain, to some degree, a foothold in, or "accents" from, their analog past (Prensky, 2001a).

Prensky (2001a; 2001b) contends that although these teachers are fully capable of learning new technologies and adapting to their new digitally rich environment, they are at a disadvantage because they were socialized differently from the students they serve. Examples of these accents include editing a document originally authored on a computer in hard copy or calling a person to discuss an email. Altogether, Prensky (see 1998, 2001a, 2001b) has identified ten core differences he believes exist between digital natives and digital immigrants. These propositions are summarized in Table 1.

Prensky (2001a) has argued that these digital immigrant accents are a serious problem because "our Digital Immigrant instructors, who speak an outdated language (that of the pre-digital age), are struggling to teach a population that speaks an entirely new language" (p. 2). These educators have made the assumption that their students learn the same way they did when they were students. An invalid assumption, Prensky (2001a) has pointed out, because it is unlikely that today's students can learn the old ways—"their brains may already be different" (p.3). Consequently, Prensky (2001a) has proposed that educators need to rethink how they teach this new generation, which does not necessarily mean starting over from scratch, but instead presenting the material in a way that today's students more readily understand.

As expected, such blanket claims have not been accepted without scrutiny. Those who hold these Millennials in a less favorable light see these claims as nothing more than an overly simplified characterization of an entire generation and the tech-savvy qualities argued to be found are not universally shared among all young people. In other words, *not all Millennials are Digital Natives*. In fact, some have argued that much of the commentary on the digital native premise is anecdotal at best. For example, Pivec and Pivec (2008) concluded that the theories proposed by Prensky are severely flawed. They assert that the Prensky publications are predominately opinion papers, not peer-reviewed studies, offering little with regard to empirical support for his claims.

Others have been more blatant in their skepticism. Bauerlein (2008), for example, quotes President Randy Bomer of the National Council of Teachers of English, who stated that teens are "drowning in their own ignorance and a-literacy" (p. 65). Bauerlein (2008) has argued that while this generation has been blessed with limitless high-tech wonders, they have squandered these technologies, using computers mostly for self-absorbed entertainment purposes, and socially-networking on the Internet instead of pursuing civic, historical, and cultural awareness. And then there are those who have suggested that the premise of the digital native is a "misleading and deceptive title that dissuades educators from looking at the intricacies of how individuals engage digital media" (Guo, Dobson, & Petrina, 2008, p. 237).

Empirical Support

Unfortunately, empirical evidence on the matter is as mixed as the opinions themselves. Some researchers, for example, are very optimistic, such as Conole, Laat, Dillon, and Darby (2006),

Table 1. Digital native differences (Derived fromPrensky, 1998,2001a,2001b)

Difference	Description
Twitch Speed vs. Conventional Speed	Prensky (2001a, 2001b) has suggested that digital natives can gather information, figuratively speaking, at the same speed as playing a twitch game. Prensky (1998) has contended that humans have always been capable of processing information at faster speeds. This ability, however, has been typically seen in only a small percentage of the population, such as with jet pilots and race car drivers. Today's students, however, are showing signs of this ability in large numbers, which Prensky (1998) has pointed out may be in part due to their digital game play. This is a departure from their digital immigrant counterparts, who prefer to gather information at a slower, more traditional pace.
Parallel Processing vs. Linear Processing	Prensky (2001a, 2001b) has suggested that digital natives have become extremely good at multitasking. Today's students are much more willing and adept at the parallel processing of information. Examples include watching TV while doing homework or listening to music while interacting with a computer. This is a departure from their digital immigrant counterparts, who are not as adept at multi-tasking and are more comfortable with the linear processing of information.
Random Access vs. Step-by-Step	We have discussed how Prensky (2001a, 2001b) has proposed that digital natives work at twitch speed. Thus it only makes sense that he has taken this idea one step further contending that today's students prefer to gather information using random access practices rather than step-by-step approaches. This should not come as much of a surprise given how integral the Internet has become in our everyday lives. Prensky (1998) has suggested that technologies, such as hyper linking, "has increased their [digital natives] awareness and ability to make connections, has freed them from the constraint of a single path of thought, and is generally an extremely positive development" (¶ 12). This is a departure from their digital immigrant counterparts, who prefer a more procedural approach.
Graphics First vs. Text First	Prensky (2001a, 2001b) has suggested that digital natives prefer graphics over text. Today's students have had so much exposure to mediums (such as multimedia) which use high-quality graphics with little or no accompanying text that their visual sensitivity has sharpened dramatically. For example, digital natives might be much more interested in reading a story presented as an online graphic novel than a traditional printed book predominately comprised of text. This is a departure from their digital immigrant counterparts, who prefer text before graphics.
Connected vs. Stand-alone	Prensky (2001a, 2001b) has suggested that digital natives want to be connected or networked. Today's students are equally comfortable with synchronous and asynchronous forms of communication, allowing them to communicate in technological ways never before seen. For example, digital natives know when it is more prudent to leave a message on a social networking website rather than voice-mail in terms of getting a timely reply. This is a departure from their digital immigrant counterparts.
Active vs. Passive	Prensky (2001a, 2001b) has suggested that digital natives are proactive in their learning. Today's students are not interested in the traditional teacher-centered models commonly used in classrooms, but instead prefer a hands-on approach, such as learning by doing. For example, digital natives would rather figure things out through trial and error rather than read a manual. This is a departure from their digital immigrant counterparts, who were limited to the methods of a more traditional teacher-centered approach.
Play vs. Work	Prensky (2001a, 2001b) has suggested that digital natives enjoy learning through play, an idea in step with his stance on digital game-based learning and an idea shared by others in which games are seen as a "natural education technology" (Stapleton, 2004, p. 1). Today's students believe that learning can take place through play and that learning does not have to be a laborious, work-related activity. This is a departure from their digital immigrant counterparts, who see learning as a task, which involves effort and work.
Payoff vs. Patience	Prensky (2001a, 2001b) has suggested that digital natives are willing to put in the effort if they see value in the payoff. Essentially, "what you determine what you get, and what you get is worth the effort you put in" (Prensky, 1998, ¶ 26). Today's students expect immediate feedback and payoff for their efforts, at times lacking the patience that are sometimes attributed to age and experience. This is a departure from their digital immigrant counterparts, who show much more patience and willingness to wait for the payoff.
Fantasy vs. Reality	Prensky (2001a, 2001b) has suggested that digital natives indulge in fantasy play, which pervades into their everyday lives. Today's students have embraced computers and the Internet as a vehicle to make fantasy play easier and more realistic. This may in part explain the popularity behind some online virtual environments, such as SecondLife®. This is a departure from their digital immigrant counterparts in which these types of technological applications for indulging in fantasy were not available and reality was more the norm.
Technology as Friendly vs. Technology as Foe	Prensky (2001a, 2001b) has suggested that digital natives have wholeheartedly embraced technology, incorporating it as part of their everyday lives. For example, today's students see having a computer and being connected as an absolute necessity as opposed to a want. This is a departure from their digital immigrant counterparts, who may fear it, tolerate it, or will never trust it.

who in surveying UK undergraduate students (*N*= 427), found that students were using technologies in "pervasive," "integrated," "personalized," "social," and "interactive" ways (p. 6). Students made wide-ranging use of personal technology (e.g., mobile phones and laptops), as well as software packages (e.g., MS Office) in working with information. These students used these technologies for their own needs, intermingling general technology and resources with institutional or course tools and resources. Based on their findings, Conole et al. (2006) concluded that "there is a shift in the nature of the basic skills with a shift from lower to higher levels of Bloom's taxonomy, necessary to make sense of their complex technologically enriched learning environment" (p. 6).

Then there are those who have shown discouraging results, such as Margaryan and Littlejohn (2008), who in surveying undergraduate Social Work and Engineering students in two UK universities (*N*= 160), did not find evidence in support of the claims that students were using a wide range of technology for learning and socialization. On the contrary, students in their study made limited, recreational use of social networking sites. The students showed little knowledge about the use of authoring tools, virtual worlds, web publishing, or other emergent social technologies.

To compound matters, some have indicated that the excessive use of technology may be a factor in the development of poor health and health-related choices. Frank, Dahler, Santurri, and Knight (2010), who in surveying 4,257 students in an urban Midwestern school district, found that those involved in excessive texting (i.e., *hyper-texting*; more 120 times a day) and networking on social websites (i.e., *hyper-networking*; more than 3 or 4 hours a day) were more likely to engage in risky behaviors, like smoking, drinking, and were more sexually active with more sex partners. They also found that this group was more at a risk of being obese and developing eating disorders.

Contradictory findings such as these have led many to strongly caution that our understanding of this generation's use of technology is far from clear (Bennett, Maton, & Kervin, 2008). In fact, some empirical evidence has suggested that the actual uses of technology by this generation are much more limited in scope than what has been proposed (Selwyn, 2009). According to Lohnes and Kinzer (2007), recent studies have suggested that Millennials do not expect or want to use technology in educational settings in the same way they do at home or in the community. Actually, there is little empirical support to suggest that this generation wants more technology integration in the classroom (McWilliam, 2002). According to Keen (2007), students are much more interested in using technology for social-networking purposes than for learning.

All things considered, these arguments have left many conflicted between being suspicious of the strong claims favoring a generation of radically different learners from that of past generations, but at the same time, conceding to the fact that this generation has been exposed to technological advancements never before seen. This balance between unreserved accord and skepticism may be best summed up by Selwyn (2009) who asserted:

Whilst there is a clear need to remain mindful of the changing information and technological needs of children and young people it is clear that we do well to avoid the excesses of the digital native debate and instead concentrate on enhancing our understandings of the realities of technology use in contemporary society. (p. 12)

Purpose of Study

Erring on the side of caution, we contend that further empirically-based study is needed to examine the digital propensity preferences of Millennials in order to promote a healthier understanding of their technology use as it relates to learning. In other words, does the research substantiate the strong digital native claims that have been permeating into the public, political, and academic landscape throughout the late twentieth and early twenty-first century?

The findings presented herein of a 2006 study focus on just this, by exploring the digital native traits proposed by Prensky (see 1998, 2001a, 2001b). We used age as the discriminatory factor because of the generational arguments discussed thus far and because prior research suggests that age is one of the factors that plays a significant role in explaining why people use information and communication technology (ICT) to varying degrees (Kennedy, Krause, Judd, Churchward, & Gray, 2008; Kvavik, Caruso, & Morgan, 2004; Livingstone & Bober, 2004; see Selwyn, 2009).

Based on our discussion and the work of Prensky (see 1998, 2001a, 2001b), we test the research hypothesis that digital native differences exist between individuals based on age. To be more specific, we test the belief that Millennials (those younger than 30 years of age, as derived from Prensky [2001a, 2001b], and thus used for the purpose of the presented study) will exhibit the characteristics of digital natives, whereas those over 30 years of age will exhibit the characteristics of digital immigrants.

We anticipate that the findings herein will be of assistance to educators, educational policymakers and researchers in separating reality from conjecture with regard to the digital native debate and lead to a better understanding of Millennials' digital propensity and the role ICT plays in their education.

METHOD

Participants

The study was carried out in 2006 at a large metropolitan university in the southeastern part of the United States. From a population of 38,045 undergraduate and 6,608 graduate students, all graduate students and 1,890 undergraduate students were selected. Of this group, 580 responded (graduate, $n = 395$; undergraduate $n = 185$).

Although we focused solely on age, a number of other demographic variables were collected, including gender, socioeconomic status (measured as family annual income), and the number of computers in the household. For example, participants chose from "less than \$9,999," "\$10,000-19,999," "\$20,000-39,999," "\$40,000-59,999," or "\$60,000 or more" when asked "My family's annual gross income is." When asked "My gender is," participants chose from "male," "female," or "transgender;" and in response to the statement "I have the following number of computers in my home," participants chose from "none at all," "1," "2," "3," or "4 or more." Demographic information was self-reported.

From the 580 postsecondary students who participated, 45% of the participants reported being female ($n = 262$), whereas 37% reported being male ($n = 212$); a 52% majority of the participants reported an age range of 20-29 ($n = 212$); a 41% majority reported a family annual income at \$60,000 or more ($n = 212$); and 30% of the participants reported having at least two computers in the home ($n = 157$), with 36% of participants reporting that at least two people were living in the home ($n = 192$). These demographics are shown in Table 2.

Measures

A fifty-item questionnaire was used which was designed to measure the frequency with which individuals use various forms of ICT in their everyday lives (K. Henderson, personal communication, 2005; 2006). Since the study was conducted in 2006, the instrument focused on technologies commonplace at the time. Examples of technologies incorporated into the instrument included mobile devices, email, two-way instant messaging, chat rooms, blogs, and personal web pages, to name a few. Of the fifty items in the questionnaire, 6 were demographic in nature; 10

Table 2. Participant demographics

Demographic	Number	Levels	Frequency	Percent	Median Response
Family Annual Income	523	$0-$9,999 $10,000-$19,999 $20,000-$39,999 $40,000-$59,999 $60,000 or more Missing Response/%Total	76 53 93 89 212 57	14.5 10.1 17.8 17.0 40.5 100.0	$40,000-$59,999
Number of Computers in Home	531	None at all 1 2 3 4 or more Missing Response/%Total	10 132 157 113 119 49	1.7 24.9 29.6 21.3 22.4 100.0	3
Number of People in Home	535	1 2 3 4 5 or more Missing Response/%Total	81 192 121 89 52 45	15.1 35.9 22.6 16.6 9.7 100.0	2
Respondent Age	538	50 and over 40-49 30-39 20-29 18-19 Missing Response/%Total	60 49 90 279 60 42	11.2 9.1 16.7 51.9 11.2 100.0	20-29
Respondent Gender	476	Male Female Transgender Missing Response %Total	212 262 2 104	36.6 45.2 3.0 14.3 100.0	Female
Graduate or Undergraduate	580	Graduate Undergraduate Missing Response/%Total	395 185 0	68.1 31.9 100.0	Graduate

Participants were at least 18 years of age, were not paid for their participation, and were treated in accordance with the American Psychological Association's (APA) Ethics in Research with Human Participants (APA, 2002).

focused specifically on the propositions put forward by Prensky (see 1998, 2001a, 2001b), which were intended to measure the differences between digital natives and digital immigrants (see Table 1); the remaining thirty-four items measured the frequency of general ICT usage. Data collected during the 2006 study were intended to analyze ICT usage on a large and broad scale. This chapter focuses on a subset of this dataset. Namely, the findings presented in this chapter focus specifically on the 10 items investigating the Prensky (see 1998, 2001a, 2001b) propositions. Again, we do this against the age demographic item. These 10 items are described in Table 3.

With regard to the reliability of the questionnaire, two pilot studies were conducted (Norman, 2008). In the first, 2005, pilot, graduate students in an Instructional Technology program at a large metropolitan university in the southeastern part of the United States were solicited through email. Based on their responses, questionnaire items were removed that were negatively correlated or which had low correlations. Scores from the questionnaire were deemed reliable with a Cronbach alpha of 0.858.

In the second 2006 pilot, a random sampling of undergraduate and graduate students was taken at the same university. Like the first pilot, these

Table 3. Ten questionnaire items investigatingPrensky (1998,2001a,2001b) propositions

Differences / Item	Reponses
Twitch Speed vs. Conventional Speed	
I use handheld game devices.	Not at all Weekly 2-3 days per week Daily More than 3 times per day
Rationale: We chose these devices for the simple fact that game availability is typically limited on this platform as compared to that of computer and console based games. And of the games available, focus is generally placed on games that leverage reaction time and precision.	
Parallel Processing vs. Linear Processing	
I prefer to complete multiple tasks (e.g. Instant Messaging, alternative activities, watching TV) rather than one task at a time while I'm learning.	Strongly agree Agree Neutral Disagree Strongly disagree
Random Access vs. Step-by-Step	
I prefer training and/or education that allows me to randomly access various components of a lesson, rather than materials that step me through a lesson one component at a time.	Strongly agree Agree Neutral Disagree Strongly disagree
Graphics First vs. Text First	
I prefer training and/or educational materials that present graphics, rather than text first.	Strongly agree Agree Neutral Disagree Strongly disagree
Connected vs. Stand-alone	
I use a portable digital assistant (PDA) (e.g. PocketPC, PalmPilot, Blackberry).	Not at all 1-5 times per day 6-10 times per day 11-15 times per day 16 or more times per day
Rationale: We chose these types of devices over a computer or other types of Internet-ready products because these assistants are small, portable, are typically always within reach of their users, and are constantly connected to a network.	
Active vs. Passive	
I prefer training and/or education that encourages me to communicate and learn with others rather learning by myself.	Strongly agree Agree Neutral Disagree Strongly disagree
Rationale: We asked this question based on research that has been conducted on active learning and the benefits behind activities such as classroom discussion and learning groups. We understand that there has been substantial debate and controversy surrounding the topic, but feel that these types of activities speak to the digital native notion.	
Play vs. Work	
I prefer training and/or education that is play oriented, rather than work oriented.	Strongly agree Agree Neutral Disagree Strongly disagree
Payoff vs. Patience	

Continued on following page

Table 3. Continued

Differences / Item	Reponses
I have downloaded movies from the Internet.	At no time during the week Weekly 2-3 times per week Daily More than 3 times daily
Rationale: We wanted to see if participants were willing to put in the time and know how to download movies for immediate payoff than say, more time consuming means, such as the use of online/postal services (e.g., NetFlix®; our study pre-dates streaming availability, our focus was on postal delivery), or by visiting a brick and mortar rental store.	
Fantasy vs. Reality	
I participate in group games (MMORPGS).	Not at all Weekly 2-3 days per week Daily More than three times per day
Rationale: We chose these types of games because they fall into the genre of role-playing where a very large number of players interact with one another in what is typically a Tolkien-ish fantasy-themed virtual game world. In these environments, players assume the role of characters, many times customizing the character traits to resemble themselves or their alter-ego. The more popular examples include EverQuest® and World of Warcraft®.	
Technology as Friendly vs. Technology as Foe	
I use email or the Internet to complete group assignments for school and/or work.	Not at all Weekly 2-3 days per week Daily More than 3 times per day
Rationale: We wanted to see if participants would embrace the use of ICT as part of their learning in completing tasks.	

scores were also determined to be reliable with a Cronbach alpha of 0.851 ($N = 580$). To further examine the trustworthiness of the questionnaire, a reliability analysis was carried out, which were determined to be reliable with a coefficient of 0.882 (n = 284; Norman, 2008). A correlations analysis of the correlated item-total resulted in the removal of two questions, which resulted in a reliability coefficient of 0.885.

Procedure

Participants were invited to complete the online questionnaire by email. Participants were instructed to "Give the answer that truly applies to you and not what you would like to be true, or what you think others want to hear" and to "Think about each statement by itself and indicate how true it is. Do not be influenced by your answers to other statements." Questionnaire items could be answered in any order and could be skipped. Participants could also withdraw from the study at any time.

RESULTS

To investigate the digital native notion proposed by Prensky (see 1998, 2001a, 2001b), a data analysis strategy composed of the Kruskal-Wallis H test was employed. The test was conducted to evaluate whether the population medians on the dependent variables, that is the aforementioned propositions (see Table 1), were the same across the independent factor, age (see Table 2). This test was performed in lieu of a one-way analysis of variance (ANOVA) due to the controversial use of ANOVA for Likert scale items, and thus, to avoid any unnecessary criticism. First, we examined aggregated age groups, those 29 years of age and younger and those 30 years of age and older. If overall significance was found, we then examined all the levels of the independent factor, conducting a Mann-Whitney *U* test as a follow-up for pairwise comparisons when overall significance was found while comparing the individual age levels. A critical value of.05 was used to determine statistical significance.

For the purpose of our statistical analysis, we tested the following hypotheses:

- **H_0:** *There are no differences between age groups (those 29 years of age and younger and those 30 years of age and older) and the theorized digital native traits.*
- **H_1:** *There are differences between age groups (those 29 years of age and younger and those 30 years of age and older) and the theorized digital native traits.*

General Findings

Findings revealed that of the ten traits investigated, only the two—connected versus stand-alone and play versus work—showed statistically significant differences between digital natives (those 18 to 29 years of age) and digital immigrants (those 30 years of age and older).

Connected vs. Stand-Alone

A Kruskal-Wallis test was conducted to evaluate the differences among the aggregate 18-29 and 30 and over age groups on median change in the frequency with which participants used portable digital assistants. The test, which was correlated for tied ranks, was statistically significant, $\chi^2(1, N = 531) = 24.87$, $p < .01$. Thus, we reject the null hypothesis; there are differences between the age groups and the frequency with which they use portable digital assistants. However, further analysis revealed that the 30 and over age group used portable digital assistants more frequently (25.8%) than the 18-29 age group (9.9%). While differences exist between the age groups, this analysis, in part, does not support the overarching research hypothesis.

A Kruskal-Wallis test was next conducted to evaluate the differences among the five age groups (18-19, 20-29, 30-39, 40-49, and 50 and over; see Table 2) on median change in the frequency with which participants used portable digital assistants. The test, which was correlated for tied ranks, was statistically significant, $\chi^2(4, N = 531) = 28.49$, $p < .01$. Again we reject the null hypothesis; there are differences between the age groups and the frequency with which they use portable digital assistants.

Mann-Whitney *U* follow-up tests were conducted to evaluate pairwise differences among the five age groups, controlling for Type I error across tests by using the Holm's sequential Bonferroni approach. The results of the tests indicated a significant difference between four of the ten pairwise groups: the 18-19 and 20-29 age groups, the 20-29 and 30-39 age groups, the 20-29 and 40-49 age groups, and the 20-29 and 50 and over age groups. The 30-39 age group used portable digital assistants the most (27%), followed by the 40-49 age group (26.5%), and the 50 and over age group (23.3%), with the 18-19 (18.3%) and 20-29 (8.4%) age groups using portal digital assistance the least. Although significant differences were found, they were not what we expected.

Play vs. Work

A Kruskal-Wallis test was conducted to evaluate the differences among the 18-29 and 30 and over age groups on median change in the preference for educational material that is play versus work oriented. The test, which was correlated for tied ranks, was statistically significant, $\chi^2(1, N=532) = 10.14$, $p < .01$. Thus, we reject the null hypothesis; there are differences between the age groups and the preference for educational material that is play versus work oriented. Further analysis revealed that the 18-29 age group had a larger preference for play oriented education material (48.3%) than the 30 and over age group (36.9%). This analysis, in part, supports the overall research hypothesis.

A Kruskal-Wallis test was next conducted to evaluate the differences among the five age groups (18-19, 20-29, 30-39, 40-49, and 50 and over) on median change in the preference for educational material that is play versus work oriented. The test, which was correlated for tied ranks, was statistically significant, $\chi^2(4, N = 532) = 11.42, p = .02$. Again, we reject the null hypothesis; there are differences between the age groups and the preference for educational material that is play versus work oriented.

Mann-Whitney *U* follow-up tests were conducted to evaluate pairwise differences among the five age groups, controlling for Type I error across tests by using the Holm's sequential Bonferroni approach. The results of the tests indicated a significant difference between only one of the pairwise groups: the 18-19 and 30-39 age groups. The 18-19 age group preferred play oriented educational material (49.1%) more so than the 30-39 (40.5%) age group.

The Remaining Eight Differences

The Kruskal-Wallis tests, which were correlated for tied ranks, were not statistically significant for the remaining eight traits (Twitch speed vs. conventional speed, $\chi^2(1, N = 531) = .08, p = .78$; Parallel processing vs. linear processing, $\chi^2(1, N = 532) = .44, p = .51$; Random access vs. step-by-step, $\chi^2(1, N = 532) = 2.2, p = .14$; Graphics first vs. text first, $\chi^2(1, N = 535) = .35, p = .55$; Active vs. passive, $\chi^2(1, N = 532) = 1.76, p = .18$; Payoff vs. patience, $\chi^2(1, N = 537) = 1.11, p = .29$; Fantasy vs. reality, $\chi^2(1, N = 538) = 2.68, p = .1$; and Technology as friendly vs. technology as foe, $\chi^2(1, N = 534) = 1.9, p = .17$)), revealing no differences between the two age groups, thus failing to reject the null hypothesis in each case.

DISCUSSION

In the case of connected versus stand-alone, our analysis revealed a statistically significant difference, but not in the manner which was expected. Digital immigrants reported a higher frequency of use with regard to portable digital devices (25.8%) than digital natives (9.9%). A closer examination looking within each age group revealed that there were significant differences between digital natives (i.e., 18-19 and 20-29 age groups) and between digital natives and digital immigrants (i.e., 20-29 and the 30-39, 40-49, and 50 and over age groups). However, the digital immigrants still reported a higher frequency of use with regard to portable digital devices (30-39, 27%; 40-49, 26.5%; 50 and over, 23.3%) than digital natives (18-19, 18.3%; 20-29, 8.4%). Based on proposition by Prensky (see 1998, 2001a, 2001b), we would have expected to see the difference in favor of digital natives. Meaning, reported frequency would have been higher with the digital native group opposed to the digital immigrant. This finding may be explained, in part, by the fact that most of the digital immigrants were graduate students (30-39, 90%; 40-49, 77.6%; 50 and over 48.3%) and thus may have used such technologies in their professional lives. Furthermore, bear in mind that our study was conducted prior to the 2007 unveiling of the iPhone®, which in itself launched a new breed and popularity for portable mobile digital devices. And so our study does not account for this.

In the case of play versus work, our analysis revealed a statistically significant difference. Digital natives reported a larger preference for play oriented education material (48.3%) than digital immigrants (36.9%). A closer examination within each age group revealed similar results; there were differences between digital native and digital immigrants. The 18-19 age group preferred play oriented educational material (49.1%) more so than the 30-39 (40.5%) age group. These findings appear to substantiate at least one of the claims made by Prensky (see 1998, 2001a, 2001b).

The remaining eight traits (twitch speed versus conventional speed, parallel processing versus linear processing, random access versus step-by-step, graphics first versus text first, active versus passive, payoff versus patience, fantasy versus reality, and technology as friend versus technology as foe) did not show statistically significant differences between the two age groups. These findings put into question the eight remaining differences proposed by Prensky (see 1998, 2001a, 2001b).

In conclusion, the findings reported herein do not substantiate the strong digital native claims made in past years about today's Millennials. While differences do appear to exist, we cannot say with any clarity that there is an unambiguous delineation that merits the digital native and digital immigrant labels. At least not when examined solely from the standpoint of age. Pre-service teachers, educators, curriculum developers, policy-makers, and the like should, therefore, be wary of the digital propensity claims made about Millennials. This is not to say that such claims should be entirely dismissed. Instead, we simply suggest that caution be exercised when implementing the recommendations provided by commentators in recent years about teaching today's so-called tech-savvy students.

Limitations

First and foremost, the study presented herein was conducted in 2006, before much of the technology that is common today had become widely available. For instance, Facebook® did not expand its membership to the general public until late 2006, Twitter® did not begin to gain popularity until 2007, and Apple® did not unveil the iPhone® to the public until early 2007. Consequently, the findings presented herein are an accurate representation of the differences and similarities between digital natives and digital immigrants with regard to the technologies commonplace at the time this study was conducted, but not at the time this chapter was published. And although we agree that this study be best repeated today, we point out that the notion itself of the digital native and associated debate has existed for at least a decade before many of today's technologies came to be. Thus, while we point to the age of the study presented herein as a concern, the findings still put into question the claims made in past years about Millennials' propensity towards technology.

The reliability and validity of the instrument may also be in question. The reliability of the questionnaire was examined in pilot studies; however, the questionnaire may not accurately reflect an individual's propensity towards general ICT usage. In other words, some of the items may not have accurately measured the traits proposed by Prensky (see 1998, 2001a, 2001b). For example, the item "I use handheld game devices," may not have been a good measure in which to examine the trait, twitch speed vs. conventional speed. We chose to use handheld game devices as the measure for this trait based on the Prensky (2001a, 2001b) proposition that digital natives gather information at the same speed as playing a twitch game and that the games typically available on these types of devices predominately leverage reaction time and precision in their game play. We understand, however, that there is the risk that the item measured the frequency with which participants used handheld game devices, not the actual rate of information gathering or information processing. Other items we understand may be questionable include, "I have downloaded movies from the Internet," as a measure in which to examine the trait, payoff versus patience, and the item "I use email or the Internet to complete group assignments for school and/or work," to examine the trait, technology as friendly vs. technology as foe. Consequently, further examination of the questionnaire is warranted. This may entail the review of other instruments designated to measure digital propensity or which better distinguish between digital natives and digital immigrants, such as the instrument developed by Guo, Dobson, and Petrina (2008) which is founded on studies and theories (see Gable & Wolf, 1993; Gibson & Nocente, 1998; ISTE NETS, 2000; Scheffler & Logan, 1999) focused on ICT aptitude.

Furthermore, the internal validity of the instrument may have been threatened by the email-based recruitment strategy employed. That is, only those who use email would have received the invite to participate in the study, excluding participants who may communicate through other digital or analog means. Then there is the online nature of the questionnaire itself, which may have discouraged those with low digital propensity from participating.

There are also concerns with regard to the population sampled. From the total population, participants composed only 5% of graduate students and less than 1% (or approximately 10% sampled) of undergraduate students, resulting in a low response rate. Furthermore, the population was restricted to postsecondary students from a single university. At the same time, most reported being female, and therefore generalizations outside of this population are difficult.

Finally, it is unknown if responses were skewed as a result of outside influences to each participant's environment or if participants focused on socially desirable answers.

FUTURE RESEARCH DIRECTIONS

The study presented herein arose from the philosophy that we need to be mindful of the excesses of the digital native debate and instead concentrate on a healthier understanding of the realities behind technology use with today's youth. While we believe that students' use of ICT is more a matter of digital literacy and access rather than a generational trait (see Nasah, DaCosta, Kinsell, & Seok, 2010), we admit that the limitations noted warrant further study. Consequently, we recommend that subsequent investigations include a more diverse sampling of participants, to include K-12 as well as postsecondary students, adults in the workforce, and military personnel, especially new recruits. That is to say, a study of this nature presents opportunities to investigate how the use of ICT may impact other areas of contemporary society, such as employability of today's students entering the workforce for the first time, and college and military recruitment. Educators, educational policy makers, practitioners, researchers, and instructional technologists would benefit from such insights when placed in appropriate contexts. These findings also lend themselves to subsequent longitudinal studies related to the reality that as we move further into the new millennia and our youth begins to age, the distinctions of the past will become less relevant, if not moot—an idea that appears to be gaining ground.

CONCLUSION

Prensky (2009) has begun to move away from the terminology that has made him synonymous with today's tech-savvy students. In recent years, he has begun to propose other distinctions, steering clear of the topic of age and generational differences. In one of his latest articles, Prensky (2009) concluded that "although many have found the terms useful, as we move further into the 21st century when all will have grown up in the era of digital technology, the distinction between digital natives and digital immigrants will become less relevant." (p. 1). In light of this, he has suggested that we need to focus on a new set of differences, thinking in terms of *digital wisdom*—a twofold concept referring "both to wisdom arising from the use of digital technology to access cognitive power beyond our innate capacity and to wisdom in the prudent use of technology to enhance our capabilities" (p. 1). In doing so, Prensky (2009) maintains that we will transcend the digital native debate, putting an end to the native/immigrant generational distinctions.

By thinking in terms of this new set of differences, Prensky has eliminated the age factor, which has been a serious point of contention by many with regard to his theory. Instead, his digital wisdom concept lends itself more closely to the concept of a natural advancement. As to whether this new concept takes root as ferociously as his digital native concept, only time will tell.

REFERENCES

American Psychological Association. (2002). Ethical principles of psychologists and code of conduct. *APA Online*. Retrieved from http://www.apa.org/ethics/code/code-1992.aspx.

Bauerlein, M. (2008). *The dumbest generation: How the digital age stupefies young Americans and jeopardizes our future (or, don't trust anyone under 30)*. New York, NY: Penguin Books.

Bennett, S., Maton, K., & Kervin, L. (2008). The digital natives debate: A critical review of the evidence. *British Journal of Educational Technology*, *39*(5), 775–786. doi:10.1111/j.1467-8535.2007.00793.x

Cone Inc. in collaboration with AMP Agency (2006). *The 2006 Cone millennial cause study. The millennial generation: Pro-social and empowered to change the world.* Retrieved from http://www.greenbook.org/Content/AMP/Cause_AMPlified.pdf.

Conole, G., Laat, M. D., Dillon, T., & Darby, J. (2006). *JISC LXP student experiences of technologies: Final report*. Joint Information Systems Committee. Retrieved from http://www.jisc.ac.uk/media/documents/programmes/elearningpedagogy/lxpprojectfinalreportdec06.pdf.

Fishman, A. (2004). Understanding generational differences. *National Underwriter / Life & Health Financial Services, 108*(2), 4-5.

Frank, S., Dahler, L., Santurri, L. E., & Knight, K. (2010, November 9). *Hyper-texting and hyper-networking: A new health risk category for teens?* [Multimedia recording] Retrieved from http://apha.confex.com/apha/138am/webprogram/Paper224927.html.

Gable, R. K., & Wolf, M. B. (1993). *Instrument development in the affective domain: Measuring attitudes and values in corporate and school settings* (2nd ed.). Boston, MA: Kluwer Academic Publishers.

Gibson, S., & Nocente, N. (1998). Addressing instructional technology needs in faculties of education. *Alberta Journal of Educational Research Edmonton*, *44*(3), 320–333.

Guo, R. X., Dobson, T., & Petrina, S. (2008). Digital natives, digital immigrants: An analysis of age and ICT competency in teacher education. *Journal of Educational Computing Research*, *38*(3), 235–254. doi:10.2190/EC.38.3.a

Hoover, E. (2009, Oct. 11). The millennial muddle. How stereotyping students became a thriving industry and a bundle of contradictions. *The Chronicle of Higher Education*. Retrieved from http://chronicle.com/article/The-Millennial-Muddle-How/48772/.

Howe, N., & Strauss. W. (2003). *Millennials go to college*. American Association of College Registrars and Admissions Officers & LifeCourse Associates.

Howe, N., & Strauss, W. (2000). *Millennials rising: The next great generation*. New York, NY: Vintage Books.

ISTE NETS. (2000). *Educational technology standards and performance indicators for all teachers*. Retrieved from http://www.iste.org/standards.aspx.

Jones, M. G. (1997). *Learning to play, playing to learn: Lessons learned from computer games*. Retrieved April 29, 2010, from http://www2.gsu.edu/~wwwitr/docs/mjgames/index.html.

Jones, M. G., Harmon, S. W., & O'Grady-Jones, M. (2005). Developing the digital mind: Challenges and solutions in teaching and learning. *Teacher Education Journal of South Carolina, 2004-2005*, 17–24.

Keen, A. (2007). *The cult of the amateur: How today's Internet is killing our culture*. London, UK: Broadway Business.

Kelan, E., & Lehnert, M. (2009, Feb.). The millennial generation: Generation Y and the opportunities for a globalised, networked educational system. *Beyond Current Horizons*. Retrieved from http://www.beyondcurrenthorizons.org.uk/the-millennial-generation-generation-y-and-the-opportunities-for-a-globalised-networked-educational-system/.

Kennedy, G., Krause, K.-L., Judd, T., Churchward, A., & Gray, K. (2008). First year students' experiences with technology: Are they really digital natives? *Australasian Journal of Educational Technology, 24*(1), 108–122.

Kvavik, R. B., Caruso, J. B., & Morgan, G. (2004). *ECAR study of students and information technology, 2004: Convenience, connection, and control*, (p. 5). Retrieved from http://net.educause.edu/ir/library/pdf/ers0405/rs/ers0405w.pdf.

Livingstone, S., & Bober, M. (2004). Taking up online opportunities? Children's use of the Internet for education, communication and participation. *E-learning, 1*(3), 395–419. doi:10.2304/elea.2004.1.3.5

Lohnes, S., & Kinzer, C. (2007). Questioning assumptions about students' expectations for technology in college classrooms. *Innovate, 3*. Retrieved from http://innovateonline.info/index.php?view=article&id=431&action=article.

Margaryan, A., & Littlejohn, A. (2008). *Are digital natives a myth or reality? Students' use of technologies for learning.* Unpublished manuscript, Glasgow Caledonian University.

McWilliam, E. L. (2002). Against professional development. *Educational Philosophy and Theory, 34*(3), 289–300. doi:10.1080/00131850220150246

Nasah, A., DaCosta, B., Kinsell, C., & Seok, S. (2010). The digital literacy debate: An investigation of digital propensity and information and communication technology. *Educational Technology Research and Development, 58*(5), 531–555. doi:10.1007/s11423-010-9151-8

Norman, D. K. (2008). *Predicting the performance of interpreting instruction based on digital propensity index score in text and graphic formats*. Unpublished dissertation, University of Central Florida.

Oblinger, D. G., & Oblinger, J. L. (Eds.). (2005). *Educating the Net generation*. Boulder, CO: EDUCAUSE.

Palfrey, J., & Gasser, U. (2008). *Born digital: Understanding the first generation of digital natives*. New York, NY: Basic Books.

Pivec, M., & Pivec, P. (2008). *Games in schools: Executive summary.* Retrieved fromhttp://www.paulpivec.com/Games_in_Schools.pdf.

Prensky, M. (1998). *Twitch speed: Keeping up with young workers*. Retrieved from http://www.twitchspeed.com/site/article.html#twitch.

Prensky, M. (2001a). Digital natives, digital immigrants. *Horizon, 9*, 1–6. Retrieved from http://www.marcprensky.com/writing/default.asp. doi:10.1108/10748120110424816

Prensky, M. (2001b). Digital natives, digital immigrants, part II: Do they really think differently? *Horizon, 9*, 1–6. Retrieved from http://www.marcprensky.com/writing/default.asp. doi:10.1108/10748120110424843

Prensky, M. (2009). H. sapiens digital: From digital immigrants and digital natives to digital wisdom. *Innovate, 5*(3). Retrieved from http://www.innovateonline.info/index.php?view=article&id=705.

Roberts, D. F., Foehr, U. G., & Rideout, V. (2005). *Generation M: Media in the lives of 8-18 year-olds*, (pp. 1-145). Retrieved from http://www.kff.org/entmedia/upload/Generation-M-Media-in-the-Lives-of-8-18-Year-olds-Report.pdf.

Safer, M. (2007, May 25). The "millennials" are coming. *CBS News.com: 60 Minutes*. Retrieved from http://www.cbsnews.com/stories/2007/11/08/60minutes/main3475200.shtml.

Scheffler, F. L., & Logan, J. P. (1999). Computer technology in schools: What teachers should know and be able to do. *Journal of Research on Computing in Education*, *31*, 305–326.

Selwyn, N. (2009). *The digital native - Myth and reality*. Paper presented at the CILIP (Chartered Institute of Library and Information Professionals) London seminar series. Retrieved from http://www.scribd.com/doc/9775892/Digital-Native.

Stapleton, A. J. (2004). *Beyond entertainment: Games as learning technologies*. Paper presented at the AIMIA Game Based-Learning Seminar, Melbourne, VIC.

Student Poll. (2010). Research dispels Millennial theories: Millennials appear more like than different from their parents' generation. *The CollegeBoard*. Retrieved from http://professionals.collegeboard.com/data-reports-research/trends/studentpoll/millennial.

Tapscott, D. (1998). *Growing up digital: The rise of the Net generation*. New York, NY: McGraw-Hill Companies.

ADDITIONAL READING

Bennett, S., Maton, K., & Kervin, L. (2008). The 'digital natives' debate: A critical review of the evidence. *British Journal of Educational Technology*, *39*(5), 775–786. doi:10.1111/j.1467-8535.2007.00793.x

Hoover, E. (2009, Oct. 11). The millennial muddle. How stereotyping students became a thriving industry and a bundle of contradictions. *The Chronicle of Higher Education*. Retrieved from http://chronicle.com/article/The-Millennial-Muddle-How/48772/.

Howe, N. & Strauss. W. (2003). *Millennials go to college*. American Association of College Registrars and Admissions Officers & LifeCourse Associates.

Howe, N., & Strauss, W. (2000). *Millennials rising: The next great generation*. New York: Vintage Books.

Prensky, M. (1998). *Twitch speed: Keeping up with young workers*. Retrieved from http://www.twitchspeed.com/site/article.html#twitch.

Prensky, M. (2001a). Digital natives, digital immigrants. *Horizon*, *9*, 1–6. Retrieved from http://www.marcprensky.com/writing/default.asp. doi:10.1108/10748120110424816

Prensky, M. (2001b). Digital natives, digital immigrants, part II: Do they really think differently? *Horizon*, *9*, 1–6. Retrieved from http://www.marcprensky.com/writing/default.asp. doi:10.1108/10748120110424843

Prensky, M. (2009). H. sapiens digital: From digital immigrants and digital natives to digital wisdom. *Innovate*, *5*(3). Retrieved from http://www.innovateonline.info/index.php?view=article&id=705.

KEY TERMS AND DEFINITIONS

Digital Immigrant: Describes generation(s) of individuals born prior to the mass availability of digital technology, who have adopted such technologies in limited capacities later in life.

Digital Native: Describes the generation of students born into the digital age, who are much more adept at using ICT than their counterparts from prior generations.

Digital Propensity: The degree or frequency with which individuals use various forms of information and communication technology in their everyday lives.

Information and Communication Technology (ICT): Any digital product that can be used to store, retrieve, manipulate, transmit, or receive electronic information, such as mobile devices, email, two-way instant messaging, chat rooms, blogs, personal web pages, and so on.

Marc Prensky: An American-born author and lecturer of education and learning, known best for his controversial "digital native" and "digital immigrant" notions as well as his contributions on the topic of game-based learning.

Millennial Generation: A demographic group of individuals, typically seen as the generation following Generation X, who have been asserted to depict unique characteristics influenced by their upbringing and lifelong exposure to digital technologies.

Twitch Games: A type of game that requires the player to react quickly to circumstances in order to continue playing (Jones, 1997), such as the game © *Tetris*.

Chapter 7
Net Geners' Multi-Modal and Multi-Tasking Performance in Complex Problem Solving

Robert Z. Zheng
University of Utah, USA

ABSTRACT

This chapter examines the influence of multi-modal presentation and multi-tasking on Net Generation students' performance in complex problem solving. The goals of the chapter are to examine (a) the differences between multi-modal presentation/multi-tasking and non multi-modal presentation/multi-tasking, (b) the influence of visual cognitive style on both types of performances, and (c) the relationship among the variables under study. The findings of the study showed that participants performed best with multi-modal presentation as evidenced in their reduced cognitive load, and their improved self-efficacy and performance in multiple rule-based problem solving. The findings also revealed that multi-tasking could block learners' learning pathway due to an increase in cognitive load. Discussion on the significance of the findings and their implication for educational community is made with suggestions for future research.

INTRODUCTION

Traditionally, learning is delivered through one mode, that is, either in the form of visual presentation using text (e.g., textbook) or with pictures (e.g., diagrams, photos). An implicit assumption associated with above instructional practice is that learners would become more focused and therefore more efficient in learning when distractions are minimized during the learning process (Swenson, 1980). Nonetheless, with the increasing presence of web technology and multimedia in education, a new generation of learners who are digital-tech savvy and often

DOI: 10.4018/978-1-61350-347-8.ch007

called the Net-Generation (Net Geners) or digital natives, have adapted themselves to multi-modal learning and multi-tasking. Multi-modal learning is typically characterized by processing information through multiple sensory stimuli including auditory, visual, and manipulative resources. Net Geners have consistently used multiple visuals such as images, animation, and videos as source of information search. Meanwhile, they have also displayed an inclination toward working on multiple tasks simultaneously as opposed to one task at a time. Some describe this new phenomenon as Net-Generation phenomenon (Feiertag & Berge, 2008; Jones, Ramanau, & Cross, 2010). Critics attribute the Net-Generation phenomenon to the fast pace of social life, the advancement of new digital technologies, and the exponential increase of new information in the modern society (Jones & Healing, 2010).

Controversy exists concerning multi-modal presentation and multi-tasking (Gonzalez, Jover, & Cobo, 2010; Martin, 2008; Skylar, 2009). Some asserted that multi-modal presentation and multi-tasking improve information processing, thus enhancing efficiency in learning (Kennedy, Judd, Dalgarno, & Waycott, 2010). Others contended that the access of information through multiple sensory stimuli and working with multiple tasks simultaneously can short change the quality of deep learning. Critics of this camp (e.g., Bennett, Maton, & Kervin, 2008) complained about the reduced abilities of Net Geners in writing, spelling, grammar, etc. showing that the writing norm of the Net Geners is represented by "email and texting" styles. They thus concluded that Net Geners may gain breadth in learning, but such knowledge is acquired at the sacrifice of depth in thinking.

Evidently, improving critical thinking of Net Geners has become an issue of central concern for researchers. Meanwhile, researchers become aware that Net Geners' multi-modal and multi-task performance can be mediated by such factors as visual cognitive style and self-efficacy in learning. The goals of this chapter are to explore (1) the cognitive and affective aspects related to multi-modal presentation and multi-taking; and (2) the influence of visual cognitive style on learners' performance where multi-modal presentation and multi-tasking were implemented.

WHO ARE THE NET GENERATIONS?

The Net Generation, also known as the Millennial Generation (or Millennials), represent a new generation after Generation X who, as Barnes, Marateo and Ferris (2007) pointed out, are independent and self-autonomous learners, actively seeking information using new technologies, and engaged in social interaction with others online or offline. According to Barnes et al., Net Geners prefer interactive environment with multiple forms of feedback and are interested in assignments that provide different resources where personally meaningful learning experiences can be derived. They are habituated users of new technologies including multimedia, mobile technologies, the web, and other forms of advanced technologies. They tend to multi-task when learning, using the Internet, mobile devices and playing video games at the same time. Net Geners are avid users of online social communication tools such as Facebook, twitter, MySpace, etc. More importantly, they display a social communication pattern that goes beyond time and space boundaries. Kennedy et al. (2010) agree, "Net Generation students demand instant access to information and expect technology to be an integral part of their educational experience" (p. 332).

For many, Net Geners are young people who develop a natural aptitude and high skill level in new technologies (Tapscott, 2009; Winter, Cotton, & Gavin, 2010). Kramer and Bernhardt (1999) noted that new digital technologies like Internet, online gaming, simulations, etc. can significantly influence learners' behavior, particularly that of Net-Generation. They pointed out that the affordances of new digital technologies such as anonymity, asynchronous/synchronous communication, anytime/anywhere learning, etc. have changed people's way of information processing and learning. However, this rhetoric about Net Generation, that is, technology determinism, has been challenged by a growing body of literature which seeks an alternative explanation for the Net Generation phenomenon (Bennett et al., 2008; Jone & Czerniewicz, 2010; Jones & Healing, 2010). For example, Jones and Healing (2010) attempted to explain the Net Geners' learning phenomenon from the perspective of agency and activity. The authors demonstrated that Net Geners' interaction with technology is mediated by activity and structural conditions, that is, agencies—departments, schools and universities—design and redesign courses in relation to available technologies. While there is a clear strength in this approach, in particular, by focusing on the interaction of activity and agency rather than on technology determinism as a way to explain Net Geners' use of digital and network technologies, the Net Geners' behavior can be better understood from the cognitive, psychological, and affective aspects in learning.

FACTORS INFLUENCING MULTI-MODAL PRESENTATION AND MULTI-TASKING

As discussed previously, one of the salient characteristics pertinent to Net Geners' learning is multi-modal presentation and multi-tasking. The questions related to this phenomenon would be: What are the pros and cons associated with multi-modal presentation and multi-tasking? What are the possible cognitive constraints associated with the information processing habit(s) mentioned above? How do multi-modal presentation and multi-tasking influence Net Geners' affective aspects in learning such as attitude, motivation, and so forth? The following section attempts to address the above questions by identifying the factors that influence multi-modal presentation and multi-tasking in learning.

Cognitive and Affect Factors

Starting from early 90s, Mayer and his colleagues (Mayer & Anderson, 1991; Mayer & Moreno, 2003; Mayer & Sims, 1994) have conducted a series of studies to examine the cognitive role of different sensory inputs in relation to comprehension and transfer in learning. Based on Paivio's (1986) Dual Coding Theory, Mayer and his colleagues asserted that incoming information can be encoded differently depending on the types of sensory inputs. For example, visual information is coded differently than that of auditory information. As we all know it, learners learn differently. Some learn visually, others learn auditorily. Mayer (2001) thus pointed out that multimedia should be designed in a way that best meets the needs of learners. Mayer and his colleagues (Mayer, 2001; Mayer & Moreno, 2003; Mayer & Sims, 1994) studied the effects of different multimedia designs on learners' information processing. They found that when information is presented through well-coordinated multiple sensory inputs such as placing the pictures and text on the same display (i.e., special continuity principle), the learner's ability to form a mental representation of the incoming information improves, hence the improvement in comprehension, retention, and transfer of knowledge. In contrast, when multimedia is designed in violation of the principles of multimedia learning (e.g. spatial contiguity, coherence, etc.), learning suffers (Doolittle, Terry, & Mariano, 2009). Mayer (2001) thus concluded that multi-modal presentation (e.g., multimedia) only becomes beneficial when it is designed in such a way that minimizes the cognitive costs associated with learning.

Related to Mayer's cognitive theory of multimedia learning, the Cognitive Load Theory (CLT) proposed by John Sweller (Sweller & Chandler,

1991, 1994) aims to explain the mental effort involved in learning and why some materials are more difficult to learn than others. Drawing from working memory research (Baddeley, 1986, 1999), Sweller and his colleagues found that learning became difficult if (1) the content was complex enough to induce high mental load and (2) the design of the content delivery (i.e., content presentation) became so complex that required extra cognitive resources to coordinate different sources of information. Sweller and Chandler (1991) called the mental load imposed upon by the first type of learning *intrinsic load*. The intrinsic load is induced by the structure and complexity of the instructional material. Usually, teachers or instructional designers can do little to influence the intrinsic cognitive load. The mental load induced by the second type of learning is called *extraneous load*. The extraneous load is caused by the format and manner in which information is presented. For example, teachers may unwittingly increase learners' extraneous cognitive load by presenting materials that "require students to mentally integrate mutually referring, disparate sources of information" (Sweller & Chandler, 1991, p.353). Consider the task presented in Figure 1. The learner would have to expend extra cognitive resources coordinating the information between the text and the image, which may overtax the working memory resources allocated to the processing of visual information. Instruction like this would be likely to induce a high level of extraneous cognitive load.

Both intrinsic and extraneous cognitive loads can be detrimental to learning. This is because our ability to process information is limited by our working memory (WM) capacity (Baddeley, 1999; Baddeley & Logie, 1992). When intrinsic or extraneous load increases, the cognitive resources in our WM will decrease. Limited cognitive resources mean a reduced WM capacity in information processing which can further affect our cognitive information processes such as comprehension, analysis, synthesis, and so forth.

Research on multi-tasking suggests that multi-tasking can overtax cognitive resources and increase cognitive load during performance. Drews, Yazdani, Godfrey, Cooper, and Strayer (2009) studied the effects of multi-tasking on individual performance when driving. They compared the single task (driving) and dual-task (driving + texting) in a simulation environment and found that participants in the dual-task condition responded more slowly to the onset of braking lights and showed impairments in forward and lateral control compared with a driving-only condition. Similar findings were obtained by Hosking and Young (2009) who concluded that multi-tasking in driving (driving + texting) reduced individual primary attention on the road condition as evidence by a substantial increase in drivers' variability in lane position and missing of lane changes. The above research has pointed to the detrimental effect of multi-tasking on primary task performance. However, the majority of the research in this area is focused on driving related behavior. Few studies have addressed the effect of multi-tasking on learning behavior pertaining to Net Geners. The

Figure 1. An example of instruction that may induce high extraneous load

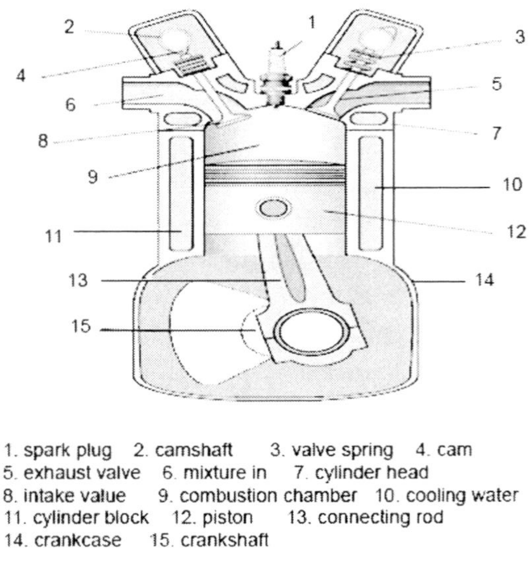

current study aimed to fill this gap by examining the cognitive constraints in multi-tasking related to problem solving by Net Geners.

In addition to the cognitive factors discussed above, the affective factor can significantly influence individual's task performance. Of particular interest to researchers is the role of self-efficacy in learning. Research has shown that self-efficacy is the most central or pervasive variable that influences learners' learning behavior and performance (Bandura, 1993; Lodewyk & Winne, 2005). Self-efficacy is defined as a belief that an individual has about his or her capabilities to execute the courses of actions required to manage prospective situations. Unlike efficacy which is often referred to the power to produce an effect, self-efficacy is the individual's self-perception of his or her power to produce that effect (Bleicher & Lindgren, 2005; Lodewyk & Winne, 2005). Recently, researchers become interested in the relationship between self-efficacy and online learning. They found that self-efficacy is closely related to learners' performance in online learning and social communication (Eastin, 2005; Lin, 2006, Lin & Overbaugh, 2009; Livingstone, Bober, & Helsper, 2005). Lin and Overbaugh (2009) studied the role of self-efficacy in learners' involvement in an online discussion forum. The results revealed that learners' involvement in online discussion, that is, number of postings and responses to postings was positively related to how learners perceived themselves as a learner. In a separate study, Zheng, McAlack, Wilmes, Kohler-Evans, and Williamson (2009b) investigated the relationship among multimedia, self-efficacy and performance and found that self-efficacy significantly mediated learners' use of multimedia as well as their performance in learning. Zheng et al. (2009b) noted that learners who were self-confident were often more motivated and therefore were more effortful in learning. They concluded that improved self-efficacy would positively affect learners' motivation, effort, and their performance in learning.

In short, the existing research suggests that multi-modal presentation facilitates learner's information processing when it is optimally designed to help generate mental representation of incoming information (see Mayer, 2001; Moreno & Mayer, 1999; Mousavi, Low, & Sweller, 1995). Multitasking, on the contrary, can impede learning due to attention distraction on the primary task. Since working memory resources are limited, presenting mutually competing tasks (e.g., multi-tasking) can significantly affect the allocation of limited cognitive resources in working memory resulting in an increase in cognitive load associated with task performance.

The above research in cognitive effects of multi-modal presentation and multi-tasking is further complemented by the findings in affective domain which have shown that self-efficacy can significantly mediate the use of technology and performance. Based on the literature which has identified the differences between single vs. dual tasks (e.g., Drew et al., 2009) and in modalities (Mayer, 2001), as well as the mediating role of affective factor in learning (e.g., self-efficacy), it is hypothesized that there would be a difference between multi-modal presentation/multi-tasking and non multi-modal presentation/multi-tasking in terms of cognitive load, self-efficacy and performance.

- **Hypothesis 1:** *There would be a difference between multi-modal presentation/multi-tasking and non multi-modal presentation/multi-tasking in terms of cognitive load, self-efficacy and performance.*

Visual Cognitive Style

Although the theories discussed above provide robust explanations to the Net Geners' learning, the phenomenon related to Net Geners' learning is much more complex than what we have yet seen. In addition to modality and working memory capacity issues, factors like cognitive style can significantly influence learners' information processing.

Before discussing further the relationship between cognitive styles and learning, it would be helpful to distinguish between learning styles and cognitive styles since they are often used interchangeably in various occasions. A clarification on the terms would aid our understanding of the functional role of cognitive styles in learning. Learning styles describe the conditions (i.e., auditory, visual, haptic, etc.) under which we best learn, whereas cognitive styles are about how we perceive and think (Lever-Duffy, McDonald, & Mizell, 2003). The construct of cognitive style is considered to be a consistent, stable variable in learning. Keefe (1982) stated that cognitive styles are "the cognitive, affective, and physiological traits that serve as relatively stable indicators of how learners perceive, interact with, and respond to the learning environment" (p. 1). This view is shared by Smith and Ragan (2005), who propose a framework of learner characteristics in which cognitive styles are subsumed under the category of stable-differences. While we can adapt or change our learning styles to improve the conditions under which we learn, it is difficult to change our cognitive styles, which determine the way we process information. Because of its stableness in predicting learners' behavior, the cognitive style has been widely used to explain variables in learning like performance and achievements.

There are different types of cognitive styles in learning. In an early study Kirby (1979) provided a comprehensive summary of 19 cognitive styles and concluded that all learners learn differently. Kirby believed that cognitive styles constitute important dimensions of individual differences in learning (see also Mayer & Massa, 2003). One cognitive style particularly relevant to multimedia learning is visualization which indicates that some people are better at processing information visually than others (Zheng, Flygare, Dahl, 2009a). In psychology, the former is defined as high visual learners and the latter as low visual learners. High visual learners can significantly benefit from visuals which help them bridge the internal and external worlds (Zheng, Miller, Snelbecker, & Cohen, 2006). High visual learners prefer using graphics, pictures, diagram, etc. to form the mental representation of the incoming information. In education, visuals such as images, videos, and multimedia have been widely used to support visual learners' learning.

Because of the difference in information processing between high and low visual learners, visualization has been identified as an important cognitive style to explicate learners' behavior associated with visually related learning (Plass, Homer, & Haywood, 2009). For example, Zheng et al. (2006) studied the impact of multimedia on learners' problem solving skills by examining whether visual ability would influence learners' problem solving. They found a significant correlation between media and visualization. George-Palilonis and Filak (2010) investigated the effects of interactive information graphics on student enjoyment, engagement, and perceptions of learning and found that visuals including both interactive and non-interactive can significantly enhance learners' comprehension, knowledge retention and application in learning, especially for high visual learners. Similar findings were obtained by Hoffler, Prechtl and Nerdel (2010), who identified the influence of visual cognitive style on learners' information process when learning with animations and static pictures.

In summary, research has provided the evidence that learners' performance in multi-modal learning can be significantly affected by their visual cognitive style. It is important to put in perspective learners' visual ability when studying the phenomenon of, for instance, multi-modal learning. Based on the above literature, we further hypothesized that visual cognitive style can influence individual's performance in multi-modal tasks.

- **Hypothesis 2:** *Visual cognitive style would influence individual's performance in multi-modal tasks.*

Although the existing research has identified the role of individual variables (e.g., cognitive load, self-efficacy, cognitive style) in multi-modal and multi-task related performance (Drew et al., 2009; Mayer & Moreno, 2003; Zheng et al., 2006), it is still unclear to what extent those variables are related to each other to influence Net Geners' ability to process multi-modal presentation and multi-tasking. Zheng (2010) points out that "Relationship identification is important because identifying the relationship of the variable under study would help develop effective modules for learning" (p. 436). Given that the existing research has showed some interesting results on the relationship among media, self-efficacy and performance (e.g., Zheng et al., 2009b, the current study aimed to explore the relationship among cognitive load, self-efficacy, cognitive style and performance in relation to Net Geners' multi-modal presentation and multi-tasking.

- **Hypothesis 3:** *There would be some correlations among cognitive load, self-efficacy, cognitive style, and performance.*

THE STUDY

The study consisted of two sub-studies. The first study examined the difference between multi-modal presentation/multi-tasking and non multi-modal presentation/multi-tasking in terms of cognitive load, self-efficacy, cognitive styles, and achievement performance. A correlation analysis was conducted to understand the relationship among cognitive load, self-efficacy, cognitive styles, and performance. The second study focused on the impact of multimedia design on cognitive load. The purpose of the second study was to find out whether it was the multi-modal presentation alone or the combination of multi-modal presentation and multi-tasking that influenced the cognitive load in task performance. For both studies, a total of 84 college students were recruited (Study 1, $n = 43$; Study 2, $n = 41$). Of 84 participants, 53 were females and 31 were males. Majority of the participants were born between 1990 and 1991 and were defined as Net Geners. Most of them (65%) began accessing computers in elementary school, some (15%) started as early as kindergarten. The participants' average age was 20.14 ($SD = 2.44$).

Study 1

Forty-three participants (females = 25, males = 18) were recruited. Participants first signed the consent form and were asked to fill out demographic information. Then they took a spatial visualization test and a pretest in self-efficacy. The study consisted of two experimental conditions: multi-modal presentation/multi-tasking (experiment group) and non multi-modal presentation/multi-tasking (control group). Participants were randomly assigned to the groups based on the results of randomization. Participants in each group were then given a URL to the study webpage where they performed problem solving tasks based on the group to which they were assigned. After the problem-solving tasks, the participants were asked to complete a cognitive load questionnaire and a post test in self-efficacy. The entire study took about 90 minutes.

Problem Solving Tasks (PSTs)

The PSTs consisted of two multiple rule-based problems. They were *Tower of Hanoi* and *Seating Arrangement*. The tasks were counter-balanced to off-set the item carry-over effect in the experiment.

Differing from single rule-based problems which require a straightforward deductive thinking such as applying the rule of card sorting to the action of sorting a deck of cards, a multiple rule-based problem involves a complex, nonlinear thinking where the learner reaches a solution by engaging in a series of cognitive activities such as analyzing, synthesizing, and evaluating while holding several conditions and rules in mind within a short time framework, thus it would induce high cognitive load in task performance (Zheng et al, 2006, 2009b). Figure 2 shows an example of multiple rule-based problem.

Multi-Modal Presentation

The PST tasks included both graphics (visual) and manipulation (haptic) stimuli. Participants first read the text and looked at the graphics and then moved the disks around the pegs while solving the problem (Figure 2). It was believed that participants would be more effective in solving multiple rule-based problems with manipulation because this would assist them in simulating possible solutions before they made their final decision.

Multi-Tasking

The multi-tasking involved a dual task situation. The two tasks included (1) solving the multiple rule-based problem and (2) keeping track of the changing number at the upper right corner of the web page. The number at the upper right corner changed every two seconds (Figure 2).

Two versions of problem-solving tasks were created. The first version was multi-modal presentation/multi-tasking as shown in Figure 2 in which the participant used two modalities, that is, visual (graphics) and manipulative (moving the disks around) modes to solve the problem. They were also assigned a dual task which required them to solve the problem while counting the number in the circle at upper right corner of the

Figure 2. An example of multiple rule-based problem

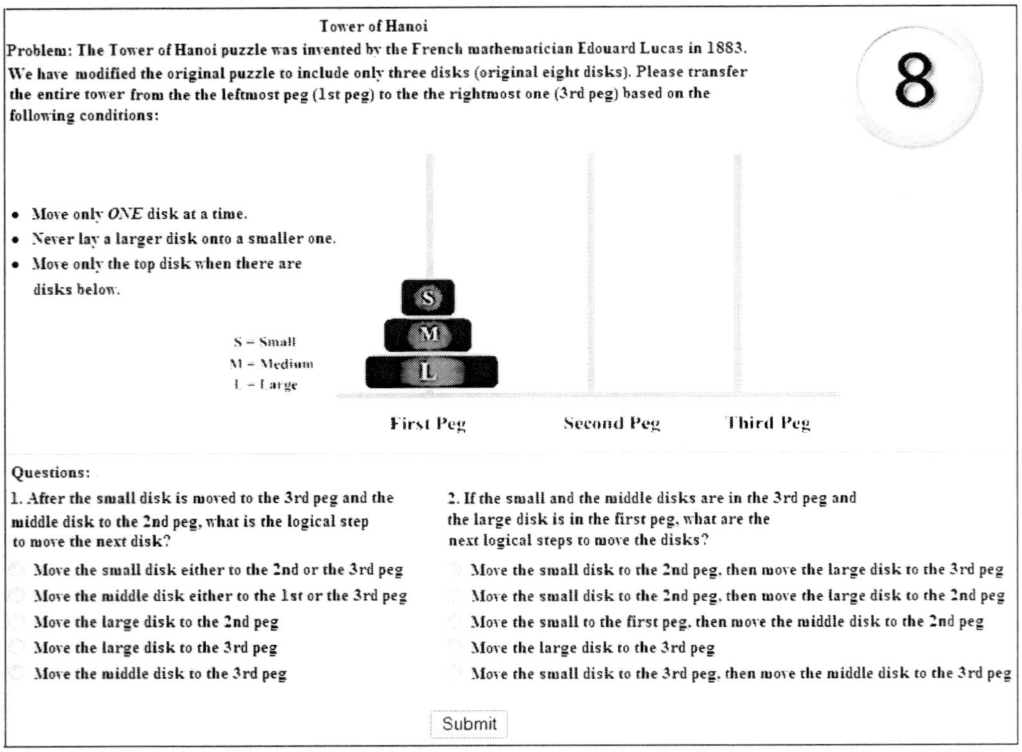

page. This version was used for the experiment condition. The second version was non multi-modal presentation/multi-tasking, meaning there was only one mode (static graphics). Participants could not move the images around in this version. There was only one task which involved solving multiple rule-based problems without counting the number at the upper right corner. The circle with the changing numbers was removed in this version. This version was used for the control condition. At the end of the task, participants were required to answer two questions at the bottom of the page and click the submit button when they were ready. The total possible score one could obtain on PSTs was 4 points.

Measures

Visual Spatial Test

The spatial visual test was adopted from VZ(2) of Kit of Factor-Referenced Cognitive Tests (Ekstrom, French, Harman, with Derman, 1976). The VZ(2) has 20 problems. In each problem there are some figures drawn at the left of a vertical line and there are five figures drawn at the right of the line. The figures at the left represent a square piece of paper being folded, and the last of these figures has one or two small circles drawn on it to show where the paper has been punched. The participant was required to identify which of those figures on the right is the correct one to the left. The test took about 7 minutes. The total possible score one could obtain on the test was 20 points. The test reported a reliability of.75 for males and.77 for females, and an overall reliability of.84 for college students.

Cognitive Load Questionnaire

The measure of cognitive load was adopted with the author's permission from an instrument called Cognitive Load Questionnaire developed by Paas (1992). The original questionnaire contains three questions that measure three different constructs related to cognitive load. The first question asks how much mental effort one has invested in learning, the second question is about the difficulty of the content, and the third question queries how difficult it is to understand the content. Since each question measures a different construct in cognitive load, the cognitive load is calculated based on each question rather than adding the scores of three questions together. That is, depending on the focus and the nature of the research, the researcher often uses one question to measure the cognitive load in his/her study. For example, Ayres (2006) selected one question from Paas's instrument: "I experienced the foregoing problem solving as: (1-not difficult at all to 9-very difficult)" to measure the cognitive load associated with content difficulty of the math problem. In another study, Kalyuga (2006) adopted one cognitive load question "How easy or difficult was the problem solving to understand? (1- very easy to 9-very difficult)" as a measurement of participants' cognitive load on understanding the math problem. In a cross-validation study by Windell and Wieber (2007), the authors compared NASA Task Load IndeX with Short Self-report Instrument (SSI; Paas, Renkl, & Sweller, 2003) which contained a single question derived from Paas's questionnaire. Evidently, it is generally acceptable both in practice and theory to adapt one question to measure a particular aspect of cognitive load involved in the study. For the purpose of this study, we took the first question which tapped into participants' overall cognitive effort in problem solving: In solving the preceding problems, I invested: (1-very low cognitive effort to 9-high cognitive effort)

Self-Efficacy Measure

The self-efficacy measure was adopted with authors' permission from an instrument called Self- and Task-Perception Questionnaire (STPQ) developed by Lodywyk and Winne (2005). The instrument used a 5-point Likert scale to measure participants' perception of self-efficacy in learning and learners' perception of self-efficacy in performance. The instrument contained 7 items with a total possible score of 35 points. The instrument reported a reliability of.72 to.92.

Results

Table 1 shows the means and standard deviations for problem-solving, cognitive load, changed self-efficacy (Self-efficacy $_{post}$ – Self-efficacy $_{pre}$) and spatial visual scores between experiment and control groups. The changed self-efficacy score was calculated by subtracting pre self-efficacy scores from the post self-efficacy scores. A t-test was performed for the visual-spatial between experiment and control groups. Results showed no significant difference between the groups, $t(2, 41) = .798, p = .429$ (2-tailed). The following discussion will focus on the hypotheses proposed.

- **Hypothesis 1:** *There would be a difference between multi-modal presentation/multi-tasking and non multi-modal presentation/ multi-tasking in terms of cognitive load, self-efficacy and performance.*

A t-test was used to compare the two groups in terms of their cognitive load, problem solving performance, and self-efficacy scores. The results showed significant differences for problem solving performance, $t(2, 41) = 4.714, p < .001$ (2-tailed); and self-efficacy, $t(2, 41) = 2.906, p < .01$ (2-tailed). No significance was found for cognitive load, $t(2, 41) = -.149, p = .882$ (2-tailed). The results partially rejected hypothesis 1 with cognitive load showing no significant difference between the groups.

- **Hypothesis 2:** *Visual cognitive style would influence individual's performance in multi-modal tasks.*

A Multivariate Analysis of Covariance (MANCOVA) was performed with visual-spatial scores as covariate. Results showed that spatial-visual ability was not a significant covariate for cognitive load, $F(1, 40) = .069, p = .794$; problem solving performance, $F(1, 40) = .082, p = .776$; and self-efficacy, $F(1, 40) = .808, p = .374$. Thus, the hypothesis 2 was rejected.

- **Hypothesis 3:** *There would be some correlations among cognitive load, self-efficacy, cognitive style, and performance.*

A correlation analysis was run to determine if the variables under study had significant correlations among them. Findings indicated that self-

Table 1. The descriptive statistics for problem-solving test, cognitive load, visual-spatial between experiment and control groups (n=43)

	Problem Solving		Cognitive Load		Spatial-Visual		Self-Efficacy	
	M	SD	M	SD	M	SD	M	SD
Experiment Group	3.00	0.54	6.81	1.24	10.76	0.53	26.71	1.87
Control Group	2.18	0.58	6.86	1.12	10.63	0.49	24.50	2.97
	Problem Solving		Cognitive Load		Apatial-Visual		Self-Efficacy	
Problem Solving	-							
Cognitive Load	-.363*		-					
Spatial-Visual	0.37		-.044		-			
Self-Efficacy	.333*		-.641**		-.076		-	

*. Correlation is significant at the 0.05 level (2-tailed)
**. Correlation is significant at the 0.01 level (2-tailed)

efficacy was significantly correlated with problem solving performance (r =.333), indicating the higher the performance scores on problem solving, the better the self-efficacy of the participant. Self-efficacy was also negatively correlated with cognitive load (r = -.641), showing the higher the cognitive load, the lower the self-efficacy of the participant. Finally, problem-solving performance was negatively correlated with cognitive load (r = -.363), meaning the better the problem-solving performance of the participant, the lower the cognitive load. The results of correlation analysis confirmed our prediction that there were correlations among cognitive load, self-efficacy, cognitive style, and performance.

Discussion

Firstly, the findings of the study confirmed the prediction that there were differences between multi-modal presentation/multi-tasking group and non multi-modal presentation/multi-tasking group in terms of self-efficacy and problem-solving performance. Secondly, the findings indicated significant correlations among the variables under study which suggest that researchers and practitioners need to put in perspective the relationship among those variable when researching or designing multi-modal presentation and multiple tasks for Net Geners. Thirdly, it was found that visual cognitive style had no significant influence on participants' performance, self-efficacy and cognitive load. This finding is surprising because the literature has shown that spatial-visual ability is significantly correlated with multimedia learning (Mayer & Sims, 1994). One possible explanation is that the current finding was probably confounded in that the dual task, which imposed a high cognitive burden on the leaner, could wash away some of the benefits the spatial-visual ability brought to task performance. In general, participants with high spatial-visual ability usually perform well with multimedia because the visuals in multimedia enhance their cognitive information processes. However, if the learner experiences a high cognitive load, in this case high extraneous cognitive load as induced by dual tasks, his/her performance could be seriously affected regardless of the visual benefits the multimedia has brought to him/her. This was supported by the fact that the interactive multimedia (i.e., manipulating the images to solve problems) showed no benefits in load reduction which contradicted findings in previously studies (Zheng et al., 2006, 2009b). One explanation could be since this study added a dual task component in the experiment design, participants probably experienced a higher cognitive load than those in our previous studies. To find out if this was the case, we conducted a follow-up study by removing the counting-the-number task from the problem solving tasks.

Study 2

Forty-one college students (females = 28, males = 13) were recruited. The procedure was similar to Study 1. Participants completed their consent form, filled out demographic information, took pre self-efficacy and spatial visual tests, then started working on problems, followed by post self-efficacy test and a cognitive load questionnaire. The same PSTs were used in the second study except that the counting number task was removed. Participants need only to focus on their problem solving tasks. The study took about 90 minutes. The participants were randomly assigned to the experiment group (n = 21) and the control group (n = 20) based on the results of randomization.

Results

Analysis on descriptive data was performed. The results were presented in Table 2. Next, we performed a t-test to see if there was a difference in participants' spatial-visual abilities between the groups. The result was consistent with Study 1, showing no significant difference for the groups, $t(1, 39)$ =.474, p = 638 (2-tailed). Like Study 1, statistical analyses were performed based on the hypotheses. Please note that the hypothesis 1 in the second study was slightly adjusted due to the removal of dual task.

- **Hypothesis 1:** *There would be a difference between multi-modal presentation and non multi-modal presentation in terms of cognitive load, self-efficacy and performance.*

A series of t-tests were conducted to compare the differences between the experiment and control groups with respect to cognitive load, self-efficacy, and performance. The results showed significance for all three variables with cognitive load, $t(1, 39) = -6.402, p < .001$ (2-tailed); self-efficacy, $t(1, 39) = 3.527$, $p < .001$ (2-tailed); and performance, $t(1, 39) = 3.649$, $p < .001$ (2-tailed). The results confirmed the hypothesis 1 that there was a difference between multi-modal presentation and non multi-modal presentation in terms of cognitive load, self-efficacy and performance.

- **Hypothesis 2:** *Visual cognitive style would influence individual's performance in multi-modal tasks.*

The MANCOVA was run with spatial-visual as covariate. Results showed that spatial-visual ability was marginally significant for cognitive load, $F(1, 38) = 3.627$, $p = .064$ and problem solving performance, $F(1, 38) = 4.138$, $p = .051$; but not for self-efficacy, $F(1, 38) = .255$, $p = .616$. Unlike Study 1, the results partially confirmed hypothesis 2. This could be the result of the removal of dual task.

- **Hypothesis 3:** *There would be some correlations among cognitive load, self-efficacy, cognitive style, and performance.*

The results of correlation analysis revealed that self-efficacy was significantly correlated with problem solving performance ($r = .361$) and it was negatively correlated with cognitive load ($r = -.422$). Problem-solving performance was negatively correlated with cognitive load ($r = -.352$). All above were consistent with the findings of Study 1. However, a new finding from Study 2 was that there was a significant correlation between spatial-visual ability and problem-solving performance ($r = .354$).

Table 2. The descriptive statistics for problem-solving test, cognitive load, visual-spatial between experiment and control groups (n=41)

	Problem Solving		Cognitive Load		Spatial-Visual		Self-Efficacy	
	M	**SD**	**M**	**SD**	**M**	**SD**	**M**	**SD**
Experiment Group	3.00	0.54	5.42	0.67	11.76	0.99	25.95	2.01
Control Group	2.40	0.50	6.85	0.74	11.60	1.18	23.60	2.25
	Problem Solving		**Cognitive Load**		**Spatial-Visual**		**Self-Efficacy**	
Problem Solving	-							
Cognitive Load	-.352*		-					
Spatial-Visual	.345*		-.074		-			
Self-Efficacy	.361*		-.422**		-.036		-	

*. Correlation is significant at the 0.05 level (2-tailed)
**. Correlation is significant at the 0.01 level (2-tailed)

Discussion

The findings from Study 2 were significant in the following two aspects. First, it provided preliminary evidence that multi-tasking did not benefit participants when involving deep level thinking such as multiple rule-based problem solving. This was shown by the findings of Study 2 in which the dual-task was moved and an immediate improvement in task performance was found in terms of reduced load, improved self-efficacy and performance in problem solving (Table 2). The results support the findings in the literature which showed that multi-tasking could do more harm to individuals than what the public has known (Watson & Strayer, 2010; Winter, Cotton & Gavin, 2010). Second, it confirmed the findings in previous studies that multi-modal (Zheng et al., 2006, 2009b), not the combination of multi-modal presentation and multi-tasks, improved individuals' performance in problem solving which consequently enhanced their self-efficacy. An improved self-efficacy then was helpful because it motivated participants to become more engaged in problem solving and make greater effort in solving the problems. This type of mental effort, according to Sweller and his colleagues (van Merrienboer & Sweller, 2005; Low, Jin, & Sweller, 2009), increased the germane cognitive load which was essential for the success of complex problem solving.

GENERAL DISCUSSION

Research on Net Geners with respect to their behavior such as multi-modal presentation and multi-tasking is still in its infancy. Few studies have explored the impact of multi-modal presentation and multi-tasking on Net Geners' performance, self-efficacy, cognitive styles, and mental effort involved in problem solving. The current study therefore investigated the potential benefits associated with multi-modal presentation and multi-tasking. The study generated several important findings. The following discussions thus focus on the findings.

Differences between Multi-Modal Presentation / Multi-Tasking and Non Multi-Modal Presentation / Multi-Tasking

Significant differences were detected between multi-modal presentation /multi-tasking and non multi-modal presentation /multi-tasking. Findings from both studies consistently showed that participants in the experimental group performed better than those in the control group (see Tables 1 and 2). This is because in complex tasks like multiple rule-based problem solving, participants need to externalize their thoughts/ideas through some form of visualization. For example, to be able to physically move the disks of different sizes across the pegs (Tower of Hanoi) on a computer screen would externalize participants' abstract thinking and visually simulate multiple solutions while solving the problems. In contrast, the non multi-modal presentation consumed much of the cognitive resources as the participants worked through the problems. This is because they had to mentally go through various solutions and at the same time memorized the rules, steps, etc. It goes without saying that such mental process would impose a huge cognitive load on the participant.

While recognizing the learning benefits of multi-modal presentation/multi-tasking, it should be noted that multi-modal presentation and multi-task combined may not produce the best results in problem solving as indicated by the high cognitive load the participants experienced with multi-tasking. The follow-up study confirmed the prediction when multiple tasks were changed to a single task in problem solving. This indicates that the design of digital materials including multimedia and other types of technology should be based on our knowledge of human cognitive architecture and our understanding of human information processing capacity, just as when educators develop their instruction they need to take participants' developmental level into account, without which, we could do a disservice to our students.

A unique approach of this study in terms of identifying the differences between multi-modal presentation and multi-tasking and non multi-modal presentation and non multi-tasking is to examine the cognitive load, cognitive styles, self-efficacy and learner performance and to explicate from cognitive and affective aspects which design approach works and which does not. Findings suggest that self-efficacy can affect performance in problem solving and can be affected by cognitive load which is related to the design of digital materials. For example, a big difference occurred between adding multi-task and removing such task when participants reported their cognitive load related to the complex problem solving. It was shown that removal of the dual task helped reduce extraneous load and improved participants' self-efficacy in complex problem solving.

Influence of Visual Cognitive Style on Problem-Solving Performance

As discussed early in the literature review, visual cognitive styles such as spatiality and visualization can significantly influence the way people process visual information. Visuals including graphics, animation, simulation, etc. can enhance learners' information process as well as their formation of mental representation of incoming information. The findings of current study have contributed to this literature by not only recognizing the benefits of spatial-visual cognitive style in multimedia learning but also pointing to the fact that such benefits can be compromised if there is a high cognitive load involved. For example, in the first study, it was found that the visual cognitive style was not significant between the experiment and control groups. Also, it was not significant as a covariate for cognitive load, performance and self-efficacy. In other words, it did not produce any learning benefits in terms of reducing the load, increasing performance and enhancing self-efficacy in task performance. It was not until the multi-task was removed in the experiment group in Study 2 then did a marginal significance occur in visual cognitive style on cognitive load and performance. It can thus safely be concluded that the benefits of visual cognitive style are dependent on the design of the learning material itself. Increasing extraneous cognitive load such as multi-tasking would wash out the visual benefits.

Correlations among Cognitive Load, Self-Efficacy, Visual Cognitive Style, and Performance

The correlation analyses have generated some interesting findings (see Figure 3). All three variables—cognitive load, self-efficacy, and visual cognitive style—have significant correlations with performance. Of particular interest is that cognitive load has a negative correlation with performance which proves again that the design including multi-modal presentation and multi-tasking should take into consideration the influence of cognitive load on performance. Next, there is a significant negative correlation between self-efficacy and cognitive load. This suggests that improving self-efficacy in a technology-rich environment can be challenged by the amount of cognitive load the learner experiences in learning. Low cognitive load can potentially contribute to positive learning including motivation and positive self-perception.

In addition to the significant correlations discussed above, there are two correlations that are worth mentioning. One is the correlation between cognitive load and visual cognitive style and the other is self-efficacy and visual cognitive style. It is interesting that both have shown negative correlations. For the former, the results suggest

Figure 3. Correlation analysis for performance, cognitive load, cognitive styles, and self-efficacy

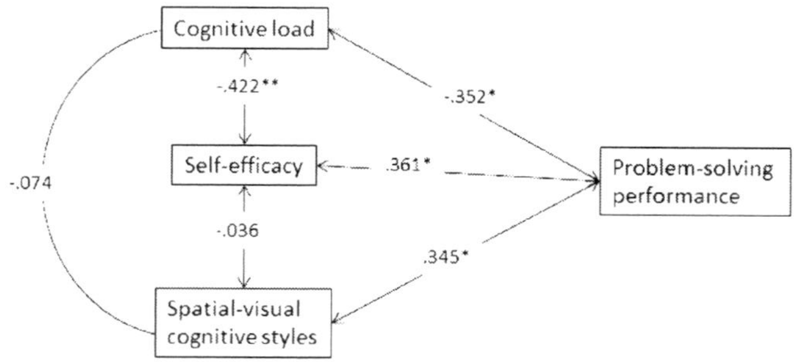

that the higher the learner's spatial-visual ability, the lower the cognitive load he/she may experience in multi-modal presentation (Please note that this is the correlation results from the second study where the multi-task was removed). Whether this means the spatial-visual learner may learn more effectively with multimedia is yet unknown. However, this can be an interesting hypothesis for future research although the current results were not significant. The second correlation suggests that people with high self-efficacy pertaining to their learning and performance were less influenced by visual cognitive style. As it was mentioned above, the results for both correlations were insignificant. Any discussion surrounding that can only be considered hypothetical which requires further studies to understand the cause and effect of such phenomenon.

FUTURE RESEARCH DIRECTIONS

This explorative study zeroed in on key issues pertinent to Net Geners' problem solving ability. The findings revealed cognitive and affective dimensions in multi-modal presentation and multi-tasking. Future research should be directed toward an understanding of the relationship between spatial-visual cognitive styles and cognitive load by identifying the impact of the cognitive load on spatial-visual cognitive style and vice versa. More research should be conducted to unveil the causal relationship between spatial-visual cognitive styles and self-efficacy. The research in this area is significant at both practical and theoretical levels. At practical level, the findings can guide the educators including school counselors and curriculum specialists to leverage Net Geners' learning behavior (e.g., multi-tasking) to develop curricula that would meet the learning needs of this new generation. At the theoretical level, the findings could aid our knowledge of the relationship between cognitive and affective aspects in Net Geners' performance.

Future research should include a larger sample size with diverse ethnic background and use more robust methodology like path analysis or structural equation modeling (SEM) to identify the relationships and the trend of the variables under study. It is suggested that future studies should examine at a greater depth of the impact of multi-tasking and its cognitive and affective implications on learning, and explore from a design perspective (e.g., coactive media) the ecological factors that may influence multi-tasking.

CONCLUSION

Research on Net Geners' multi-modal presentation and multi-tasking is far and few between. The current study reflects the imminent needs of the field to understand Net Geners' cognitive and affective aspects related to multi-modal presentation and multi-tasking. This study focused on three important aspects: (a) the differences between multi-modal presentation /multi-tasking and non multi-modal presentation/multi-tasking, (b) the influence of visual cognitive styles on both types of performances, and (c) the relationship among the variables under study. To achieve these goals, the following variables were examined that related to Net Geners' multi-modal presentation and multi-tasking. They included cognitive load, visual cognitive styles, self-efficacy, and performance.

The findings of the study revealed that participants performed best with multi-modal presentation as shown in their reduced cognitive load, improved self-efficacy and performance in multiple rule-based problem solving. The findings also revealed that there was an increase in cognitive load when involving multi-tasking. Overall, multi-modal presentation was shown to be superior over the non multi-modal presentation when participants were engaged in complex problem solving like multiple rule-based problems. Even with the addition of multi-tasking, the above advantage still remained.

This supports the findings in previous research that multi-modal presentation enhances learners' cognitive information processing in learning (Reed, 2006; Zheng, 2007, 2009; Zheng, Yang, Garcia, & McCadden, 2008). Although previous research suggests that multimedia learning is closely related to spatial-visual cognitive style (Mayer & Sims, 1994), the current study did not find significant results for such relationship. However, what has been found was that the relationship turned from non-significant to marginally significant as the multi-task learning was removed in Study 2 (see discussions in Study 1 and 2). This finding pointed to a promising direction in future research in multi-modal presentation and multi-tasking. It revealed an important relationship among multi-modal presentation, multi-tasking and spatial-visual cognitive style. Finally, the correlation analyses not only lent support to the above finding but also revealed the important relationship between variables such as the negative and positive relationships among the variables.

In conclusion, the current study has provided preliminary findings about Net Geners' multi-modal presentation and multi-tasking. It revealed the benefits and at the same time the limitations associated with multi-modal presentation and multi-tasking. The study is exploratory. Further research is needed to verify and confirm the findings of this study. Research on Net Geners' multi-modal presentation and multi-tasking is interdisciplinary. It involves neurosciences, developmental, cognitive and psychological research, as well as research in social behaviors. Therefore, a research agenda that integrates above multiple areas should be developed for future research.

REFERENCES

Ayres, P. (2006). Impact of reducing intrinsic cognitive load on learning in a mathematical domain. *Applied Cognitive Psychology*, *20*, 287–298. doi:10.1002/acp.1245

Baddeley, A. D. (1986). *Working memory*. Oxford, UK: Oxford University Press.

Baddeley, A. D. (1999). *Essentials of human memory*. Hove, UK: Psychology Press.

Baddeley, A. D., & Logie, R. H. (1992). Auditory imagery and working memory. In Reisberg, D. (Ed.), *Auditory imagery* (pp. 179–197). Hillsdale, NJ: Lawrence Erlbaum Associates.

Bandura, A. (1993). Perceived self-efficacy in cognitive development and functioning. *Educational Psychologist*, *28*, 117–148. doi:10.1207/s15326985ep2802_3

Barnes, K., Marateo, R. C., & Ferris, S. P. (2007). Teaching and e-learning with the net generation. *Innovative, 4*. Retrieved on January 9th, 2011, from http://www.innovateonline.info/index.php?view=article&id=382.

Bennett, S., Maton, K., & Kervin, L. (2008). The digital natives debate: A critical review of the evidence. *British Journal of Educational Technology, 39*, 775–786. doi:10.1111/j.1467-8535.2007.00793.x

Bleicher, R. E., & Lindgren, J. (2005). Success in science learning and preservice science teaching self-efficacy. *Journal of Science Teacher Education, 16*, 205–225. doi:10.1007/s10972-005-4861-1

Doolittle, P., Terry, K., & Mariano, G. (2009). Multimedia learning and working memory capacity. In Zheng, R. (Ed.), *Cognitive effects of multimedia learning* (pp. 17–33). Hershey, PA: Information Science Reference/IGI Global Publishing.

Drews, F. A., Yazdani, H., Godfrey, C. N., Cooper, J. M., & Strayer, D. L. (2009). Text messaging during simulated driving. *Human Factors, 51*, 762–770. doi:10.1177/0018720809353319

Eastin, M. S. (2005). Teen Internet use: Relating social perceptions and cognitive models to behavior. *Cyberpsychology & Behavior, 8*(1), 62–75. doi:10.1089/cpb.2005.8.62

Ekstrom, R. B., French, J. W., & Harman, H. H. with Derman, D. (1976). *Kit of factor-referenced cognitive tests.* Princeton, NJ: Educational Testing Service.

Feiertag, J., & Berge, Z. L. (2008). Training Generation N: How educators should approach the Net generation. *Education + Training, 50*(6), 457–464. doi:10.1108/00400910810901782

George-Palilonis, J., & Filak, V. (2010). Visuals, path control, and knowledge gain: Variables that affect students' approval and enjoyment of a multimedia text as a learning tool. *International Journal on E-Learning, 9*(4), 463–480.

Gonzalez, J. A., Jover, L., & Cobo, E. (2010). A web-based learning tool improves student performance in statistics: a randomized masked trial. *Computers & Education, 55*(2), 704–713. doi:10.1016/j.compedu.2010.03.003

Hoffler, T. N., Prechtl, H., & Nerdel, C. (2010). The influence of visual cognitive style when learning from instructional animations and static pictures. *Learning and Individual Differences, 20*(5), 479–483. doi:10.1016/j.lindif.2010.03.001

Hosking, S. G., & Young, K. L. (2009). The effects of text messaging on young drivers. *Human Factors, 51*, 582–592. doi:10.1177/0018720809341575

Jone, C., & Czerniewicz, L. (2010). Describing or debunking? The Net generation and digital natives. *Journal of Computer Assisted Learning, 26*(5), 317–320. doi:10.1111/j.1365-2729.2010.00379.x

Jones, C., & Healing, G. (2010). Net generation students: Agency and choice and the new technologies. *Journal of Computer Assisted Learning, 26*(5), 344–356. doi:10.1111/j.1365-2729.2010.00370.x

Jones, C., Ramanau, R., & Cross, S. (2010). Net generation or digital natives: Is there a distinct new generation entering university? *Computers & Education, 54*(3), 722–732. doi:10.1016/j.compedu.2009.09.022

Kalyuga, S. (2006). Assessment of learners' organized knowledge structures in adaptive learning environments. *Applied Cognitive Psychology, 20*, 333–342. doi:10.1002/acp.1249

Keefe, J. W. (1982). Assessing student learning styles: An overview. In Keefe, J. W. (Ed.), *Student learning styles and brain behavior* (pp. 1–17). Reston, VA: National Association of Secondary School Principals.

Kennedy, G., Judd, T., Dalgarno, B., & Waycott, J. (2010). Beyong natives and immigrants: Exploring types of net generation students. *Journal of Computer Assisted Learning, 26*, 332–343. doi:10.1111/j.1365-2729.2010.00371.x

Kirby, P. (1979). *Cognitive style, learning style and transfer skill acquisition*. Columbus, OH: The National Center for Research in Vocational Education, The Ohio State University.

Kramer, R., & Bernhardt, S. A. (1999). Moving instruction to the web: Writing as multi-tasking. *Technical Communication Quarterly*, *8*(3), 319–336. doi:10.1080/10572259909364671

Lever-Duffy, J., McDonald, J. B., & Mizell, A. P. (2003). *Teaching and learning with technology*. Boston, MA: Allyn & Bacon/Pearson.

Lin, H. F. (2006). Understanding behavioral intention to participate in virtual communities. *Cyberpsychology & Behavior*, *9*(5), 540–547. doi:10.1089/cpb.2006.9.540

Lin, S. Y., & Overbaugh, R. C. (2009). Computer-mediated discussion, self-efficacy and gender. *British Journal of Educational Technology*, *40*(6), 999–1013. doi:10.1111/j.1467-8535.2008.00889.x

Livingstone, S., Bober, M., & Helsper, E. J. (2005). Active participation or just more information? Young peoples' take up of opportunities to act and interact on the internet. *Information Communication and Society*, *8*(3), 287–314. doi:10.1080/13691180500259103

Lodewyk, K. R., & Winne, P. H. (2005). Relations among the structure of learning tasks, achievement, and changes in self-efficacy in secondary students. *Journal of Educational Psychology*, *97*, 1, 3–12. doi:10.1037/0022-0663.97.1.3

Low, R., Jin, P. T., & Sweller, J. (2009). Cognitive architecture and instructional design in a multimedia context. In Zheng, R. (Ed.), *Cognitive effects of multimedia learning* (pp. 1–16). Hershey, PA: IGI Global.

Martin, F. (2008). Effects of practice in a linear and non-linear web-based learning environment. *Journal of Educational Technology & Society*, *11*(4), 81–93.

Mayer, R. E. (2001). *Multimedia learning*. Cambridge, UK: Cambridge University Press.

Mayer, R. E., & Anderson, R. (1991). Animations and narrations: An experimental test of a dual-coding hypothesis. *Journal of Educational Psychology*, *83*, 484–490. doi:10.1037/0022-0663.83.4.484

Mayer, R. E., & Massa, L. J. (2003). Three facets of visual and verbal learners: Cognitive ability, cognitive style, and learning preference. *Journal of Educational Psychology*, *95*, 833–846. doi:10.1037/0022-0663.95.4.833

Mayer, R. E., & Moreno, R. (1998). A split attention effect in multimedia learning: Evidence for dual processing systems in working memory. *Journal of Educational Psychology*, *90*, 312–320. doi:10.1037/0022-0663.90.2.312

Mayer, R. E., & Moreno, R. (2000). A coherence effect in multimedia learning: The case for minimizing irrelevant sounds in the design of multimedia instructional messages. *Journal of Educational Psychology*, *92*, 117–125. doi:10.1037/0022-0663.92.1.117

Mayer, R. E., & Moreno, R. (2003). Nine ways to reduce cognitive load in multimedia learning. *Educational Psychologist*, *38*(1), 43–52. doi:10.1207/S15326985EP3801_6

Mayer, R. E., & Sims, V. K. (1994). For whom is a picture worth a thousand words? Extensions of a dual-coding theory of multimedia learning. *Journal of Educational Psychology*, *86*(3), 389–401. doi:10.1037/0022-0663.86.3.389

Moreno, R., & Mayer, R. E. (1999). Cognitive principles of multimedia learning: The role of modality and contiguity. *Journal of Educational Psychology*, *91*, 358–368. doi:10.1037/0022-0663.91.2.358

Mousavi, S. Y., Low, R., & Sweller, J. (1995). Reducing cognitive load by missing auditory and visual presentation modes. *Journal of Educational Psychology*, *87*, 319–334. doi:10.1037/0022-0663.87.2.319

Paas, F. (1992). Training strategies for attaining transfer of problem-solving skill in statistics: A cognitive load approach. *Journal of Educational Psychology*, *84*, 429–434. doi:10.1037/0022-0663.84.4.429

Paas, F., Renkl, A., & Sweller, J. (2003). Cognitive load theory and instructional design: Recent developments. *Educational Psychologist*, *38*, 1–4. doi:10.1207/S15326985EP3801_1

Paivio, A. (1986). *Mental representations: A dual coding approach*. Oxford, UK: Oxford University Press.

Plass, J., Homer, B., & Haywood, E. (2009). Design factors for educationally effective animations and simulations. *Journal of Computing in Higher Education*, *21*, 31–61. doi:10.1007/s12528-009-9011-x

Reed, S. (2006). Cognitive architectures for multimedia learning. *Educational Psychologist*, *41*, 87–98. doi:10.1207/s15326985ep4102_2

Skylar, A. (2009). A comparison of asynchronous online text-based lectures and synchronous interactive web conferencing lectures. *Issues in Teacher Education*, *18*(2), 69–84.

Smith, P. L., & Ragan, T. J. (2005). *Instructional design* (3rd ed.). Hoboken, NJ: John Wiley & Sons.

Sweller, J., & Chandler, P. (1991). Evidence for cognitive load theory. *Cognition and Instruction*, *8*(4), 351–362. doi:10.1207/s1532690xci0804_5

Sweller, J., & Chandler, P. (1994). Why some material is difficult to learn. *Cognition and Instruction*, *12*(3), 185–233. doi:10.1207/s1532690xci1203_1

Swenson, L. C. (1980). *Theories of learning: Traditional perspectives/contemporary developments*. Belmont, CA: Wadsworth.

Tapscott, D. (2009). *Growing up digital: The rise of the net generation*. New York, NY: McGraw-Hill.

van Merrienboer, J. J. G., & Sweller, J. (2005). Cognitive load theory and complex learning: Recent developments and future directions. *Educational Psychology Review*, *17*, 147–177. doi:10.1007/s10648-005-3951-0

Watson, J. M., & Strayer, D. L. (2010). Supertaskers: Profiles in extraordinary multi-tasking ability. *Psychonomic Bulletin & Review*, *17*, 479–485. doi:10.3758/PBR.17.4.479

Windell, D., & Wieber, E. N. (2007). *Measuring cognitive load in multimedia instruction: A comparison of two instruments*. Paper presented at American Educational Research Association Annual Conference, Chicago, IL.

Winter, J., Cotton, D., & Gavin, J. (2010). Effective e-learning? multi-tasking, distractions and boundary management by graduate students in an online environment. *ALT-J: Research in Learning Technology*, *18*(1), 71–83. doi:10.1080/09687761003657598

Zheng, R. (2007). Cognitive functionality of multimedia in problem solving. In Kidd, T., & Song, H. (Eds.), *Handbook of research on instructional systems and technology* (pp. 230–246). Hershey, PA: Information Science Reference/IGI Global Publishing. doi:10.4018/978-1-59904-865-9.ch017

Zheng, R. (Ed.). (2009). *Cognitive effects of multimedia learning*. Hershey, PA: Information Science Reference/IGI Global Publishing.

Zheng, R. (2010). Effects of situated learning on students' knowledge acquisition: An individual differences perspective. *Journal of Educational Computing Research*, *43*(4), 463–483. doi:10.2190/EC.43.4.c

Zheng, R., Flygare, J., & Dahl, L. (2009a). Style matching or ability building? An empirical study on FDI learners' learning in well-structured and ill-structured asynchronous online learning environments. *Journal of Educational Computing Research, 41*(2), 195–226. doi:10.2190/EC.41.2.d

Zheng, R., McAlack, M., Wilmes, B., Kohler-Evans, P., & Williamson, J. (2009b). Effects of multimedia on cognitive load, self-efficacy, and multiple rule-based problem solving. *British Journal of Educational Technology, 40*(5), 790–803. doi:10.1111/j.1467-8535.2008.00859.x

Zheng, R., Miller, S., Snelbecker, G., & Cohen, I. (2006). Use of multimedia for problem-solving tasks. *Journal of Technology, Instruction. Cognition and Learning, 3*(1-2), 135–143.

Zheng, R., Yang, W., Garcia, D., & McCadden, B. P. (2008). Effects of multimedia on schema induced analogical reasoning in science learning. *Journal of Computer Assisted Learning, 24*, 474–482. doi:10.1111/j.1365-2729.2008.00282.x

ADDITIONAL READING

Cheung, W., Li, E. Y., & Yee, L. W. (2003). Multimedia learning system and its effect on self-efficacy in database modeling and design: An exploratory study. *Computers & Education, 41*(3), 249–270. doi:10.1016/S0360-1315(03)00048-4

Cho, M. H., Demei, S., & Laffey, J. (2010). Relationships between Self-Regulation and Social Experiences in Asynchronous Online Learning Environments. *Journal of Interactive Learning Research, 21*(3), 297–316.

Hodges, C. B. (2008). Self-Efficacy in the Context of Online Learning Environments: A Review of the Literature and Directions for Research. *Performance Improvement Quarterly, 20*(3-4), 7–25. doi:10.1002/piq.20001

Ikegulu, P. R., & Ikegulu, T. N. (1999). *The effectiveness of window presentation strategy and cognitive style of field dependence status on learning from mediated instructions*. Ruston, LA: Center for Statistical Consulting (ERIC Document Reproduction Service No. ED428758).

Liu, M., & Reed, W. M. (1994). The relationship between the learning strategies and learning styles in a hypermedia environment. *Computers in Human Behavior, 10*(4), 419–434. doi:10.1016/0747-5632(94)90038-8

Liu, X. J., Magjuka, R. J., & Lee, S. H. (2008). The effects of cognitive thinking styles, trust, conflict management on online students' learning and virtual team performance. *British Journal of Educational Technology, 39*(5), 829–846. doi:10.1111/j.1467-8535.2007.00775.x

Lloyd, B. T. (2002). A conceptual framework for examining adolescent identity, media influence, and social development. *Review of General Psychology, 6*, 73–91. doi:10.1037/1089-2680.6.1.73

MacNeil, R. (1980). The relationship of cognitive style and instructional style to the learning performance of undergraduate students. *The Journal of Educational Research, 73*(6), 354–359.

Madell, D., & Muncer, S. J. (2007). Internet communication: An activity that appeals to shy and socially phobic people? *Cyberpsychology & Behavior, 9*(5), 618–622. doi:10.1089/cpb.2006.9.618

Moallem, M. (2008). Accommodating individual differences in the design of online learning environments: A comparative study. *Journal of Research on Technology in Education, 40*(2), 217–245.

Puzziferro, M. (2008). Online Technologies Self-Efficacy and Self-Regulated Learning as Predictors of Final Grade and Satisfaction in College-Level Online Courses. *American Journal of Distance Education, 22*, 72–89. doi:10.1080/08923640802039024

Raghubar, K. P., Barnes, M. A., & Hecht, S. A. (2010). Working memory and mathematics: A review of developmental, individual difference, and cognitive approaches. *Learning and Individual Differences, 20*(2), 110–122. doi:10.1016/j.lindif.2009.10.005

Scheiter, K., & Eitel, A. (2010). *How to foster the integration of text and diagrams: An eye tracking study on the use of signals in multimedia learning*. Poster presented at the 32nd Annual Meeting of the Cognitive Science Society. Portland, OR.

Sheeks, M. S., & Birchmeier, Z. P. (2007). Shyness, sociability, and the use of computer-mediated communication in relationship development. *Cyberpsychology & Behavior, 10*(1), 64–70. doi:10.1089/cpb.2006.9991

Thro, M. P. (1978). *Individual differences among college students in cognitive structure and physics performance*. Paper presented at the annual meeting of the American Educational Research Association. Toronto, Canada.

Witkin, H. A., & Goodenough, D. R. (1977). Field dependence and interpersonal behavior. *Psychological Bulletin, 84*, 661–689. doi:10.1037/0033-2909.84.4.661

Witkin, H. A., Moore, C. A., Goodenough, D. R., & Cox, P. W. (1977). Field dependent and field independent cognitive styles and their educational implications. *Review of Educational Research, 47*(1), 1–64.

KEY TERMS AND DEFINITIONS

Cognitive Load: According to cognitive load theory (CLT), three types of cognitive load exist: *intrinsic load*, *extraneous* or *ineffective load*, and *germane* or *effective load*. The *intrinsic cognitive load* refers to cognitive load that is induced by the structure and complexity of the instructional material. Usually, teachers or instructional designers can do little to influence the intrinsic cognitive load. The *extraneous cognitive load* refers to the cognitive load caused by the format and manner in which information is presented. For example, teachers may unwittingly increase learner's extraneous cognitive load by presenting materials that "require students to mentally integrate mutually referring, disparate sources of information" (Sweller et al., 1991, p. 353). Finally, the *germane cognitive load* refers to cognitive load that is induced by learners' efforts to process and comprehend the material. The goal of CLT is to increase this type of cognitive load so that the learner can have more cognitive resources available to solve problems.

Cognitive Style: Cognitive styles are about how we perceive and think which is different from learning styles that describe the conditions (i.e., auditory, visual, haptic, etc.) under which we best learn. The construct of cognitive style is considered to be a consistent, stable variable in learning. Keefe (1982) stated that cognitive styles are "the cognitive, affective, and physiological traits that serve as relatively stable indicators of how learners perceive, interact with, and respond to the learning environment" (p. 1). Research shows all learners learn differently. Therefore, there are different types of cognitive styles in learning. It is widely recognized that cognitive styles constitute important dimensions of individual differences in learning.

Extraneous Cognitive Load: The extraneous load is caused by the format and manner in which information is presented. For example, teachers may unwittingly increase learners' extraneous cognitive load by presenting materials that "require students to mentally integrate mutually referring, disparate sources of information" (Sweller & Chandler, 1991, p.353). Suppose we see a heart circulation image with annotated texts right next to the relevant parts of the heart. This would help the learner immediately identify the meaning of the components in the heart circulation. If the texts are separated from the image and listed on a separate page or below the image, the learner would have to expend extra cognitive resources coordinating the information between the text and the image, which may overtax the working memory resources allocated to the processing of visual information. Instruction like this would be likely to induce a high level of extraneous cognitive load.

Intrinsic Cognitive Load: The intrinsic cognitive load refers the load induced by the structure and complexity of the instructional material. Usually, teachers or instructional designers can do little to influence the intrinsic cognitive load. The common practice to reduce or bypass intrinsic cognitive load is to build prior knowledge (e.g., scheme) using pre-training, or develop skills for knowledge automaticity.

Multi-Tasking: It refers to the performance by an individual of appearing to handle more than one task at the same time. The term has been applied to Net Generation who simultaneously multiple media to engage in multiple tasks. Much of this multitasking is not inherently coupled or coordinated except by the user. For example a user may be browsing the Web, using e-mail, or talking on the phone while watching TV. More directly coordinated forms of media multitasking are emerging in the form of "coactive media."

Multi-Modal Presentation: Multi-modal presentation refers to learn with multiple modalities including visual, auditory, haptic and other forms of modality. A common form of applying modalities to learning is multimedia learning where instructors and learners engaged in various instructional and learning activities using multiple sensory inputs to facilitate cognitive information processes.

Net Generation: Net Generation, also known as Millennial Generation (or Millennials), represent a new generation after Generation X who are independent and self-autonomous learners, actively seeking information using new technologies, and engaged in social interaction with others online or offline. Net Geners prefer interactive environment with multiple forms of feedback and are interested in assignments that provide different resources where personally meaningful learning experiences can be derived. They are habituated users of new technologies including multimedia, mobile technologies, the web, and other forms of advanced technologies. They tend to multi-task when learning, using the Internet, mobile devices and playing video games at the same time. Net Geners are avid users of online social communication tools such as Facebook, twitter, MySpace, etc. and display a social communication pattern that goes beyond time and space boundaries.

Self-Efficacy: Self-efficacy is believed to be the most central or pervasive variable that influences learners' learning behavior and performance. Self-efficacy is defined as a belief that an individual has about his or her capabilities to execute the coruses of actions required to manage prospective situations. Unlike efficacy which is often referred to the power to produce an effect, self-efficacy is the individual's self-perception of his or her power to produce that effect.

Chapter 8
Interactivity and Its Effect on Student Learning Outcomes

James P. Gleason
Eastern Kentucky University, USA

Laura Beth Daws
Georgia Highlands College, USA

ABSTRACT

As members of the Net Generation embrace digital communication and interactive technology, educators have increasingly integrated them into the classroom in an effort to attract and motivate digital learners, but often without considering how these approaches affect the learning process. This chapter examines the nature and impact of interactivity as a discrete element within an instructional setting. It explores whether the recognition of interactivity by students measurably contributes to actual cognitive learning and, more importantly, how. If the positive impact of interactivity within the teaching process is to be replicated and exploited, instructors must understand which elements contribute to online student learning, in what ways, and to what degree.

Outcome Interactivity Theory is used as a framework to test the impact of interactive functionality in instructional content on knowledge acquisition and satisfaction learning outcomes for students. Results are described, and limitations and practical implications are discussed.

INTRODUCTION

The old joke about our parents "walking to school every day through the snow, uphill *both* ways" is obviously an exaggeration, but it's undeniable that today's students—the Net Generation students—live in a world vastly different from that of prior generations. Their educational environment is shaped by virtually unlimited information access and a wide range of communication technologies at their fingertips. More importantly, these "digital natives" (Bennett, Maton & Kervin, 2008) have grown up with advanced technologies, accustomed to using them as learning aids in the classroom and expectant that their instructors will be adept at successfully integrating them into the curriculum.

DOI: 10.4018/978-1-61350-347-8.ch008

Members of the Net Generation display a comfort level with digital communication and technology that is at once inspiring and daunting. They effortlessly embrace opportunities for multitasking, vigorously use social media (to excess, some would argue), and casually expect instant gratification from the digital world. On the other hand, they often show less tolerance for traditional media and teaching approaches. For example, few students in my recent upper division communication classes got their news through old media sources such as television news. Not one read a newspaper on a daily basis!

Educators have increasingly integrated interactive digital technologies and applications into the classroom in an effort to attract and motivate these digital learners, but often without due consideration to the impact these approaches have on the learning process. While it's clear that students like these more interactive approaches to instruction, collaboration and even advising, what is less obvious is the manner in which these approaches affect both the learning process and the learning outcomes they yield. An aspect that demands great scrutiny is the *measurable* value delivered by these interactive technology applications.

In this chapter, we take a fresh look at this critical aspect of teaching and learning by examining the nature and impact of *interactivity* as a discrete element within an instructional setting. We explore whether the recognition of interactivity by students measurably contributes to actual cognitive learning and, more importantly, how. In addition, as interactivity itself is generally considered to be a multidimensional construct, instructors must understand which elements of the construct contribute to online student learning, in what ways, and to what degree. In this way they can apply the positive impact of interactivity in a meaningful way within the teaching process.

As a framework for this discussion, the chapter presents *Outcome Interactivity Theory* (Gleason & Lane, 2009) as a theory-based conceptualization of the interactivity construct, one that encourages empirical testing and generalization. In addition, it describes a study that stands out from earlier scholarship by examining interactivity's role as a receiver-based construct and measuring its contribution to *outcomes* for participants in a communication event. This study operationalizes interactivity as a positive learning outcome (in this case, knowledge acquisition), and tests several hypotheses regarding interactivity's contribution under experimental conditions. Also of particular value, a set of original and highly reliable measurement scales were applied for the first time, and quantify the influence of specific individual dimensions and elements on interactivity as defined by the Outcome Interactivity Theory model.

BACKGROUND

The Net Generation as Learners

A stroll around any campus confirms that online communication among adolescents and young adults, and among traditional college age students in particular, is prevalent (Zickuhr, 2010). According to a recent Pew Research Center report about generational usage of the Internet, 90-100% of people aged 18-33 use email, 80-89% use social media, and 60-69% use instant message clients. Students of the Net Generation, or people born between 1980 – 1994 (Tapscott, 1998), are surrounded by and immersed in new media and new technologies, and not just in their personal lives. Instructors of Net Generation students often struggle with how to best reach this unique population. Instructors wonder whether to embrace online and interactive approaches to instruction as a means of best serving a cadre of students that have "grown up digital" (Tapscott, 1998). It is thus important to consider the impact of new technologies on learning outcomes and the learning process.

Instructors are often "digital immigrants" (Prensky, 2001) to this new, uncharted territory where life is as much online as it is in person. Current trends indicate they are adding the use of new technologies to their regular classroom instruction and assuming the outcomes will be positive. As colleges across the United States offer more online classes and degree programs than ever before, instructors are using online teaching tools to reach a new generation of students in innovative ways.

This move toward increased online offerings is motivated by a number of factors, one of which may be a desire to accommodate Net Generation students' desire and preference for technology in everyday life. In some institutions the impetus is the increasing cost of traditional classroom-based instruction, Others find online classes an effective means of reaching out to rural, non-traditional or military students for whom daily campus visits are problematic (Eastern Kentucky University has been particularly successful in this regard). Still others look at the growing success of online institutions such as the University of Phoenix and Strayer University and don't want to be left behind. Regardless, online instruction is here to stay, and experienced instructors must learn and embrace its nuances to maintain the quality and effectiveness of their teaching in this environment.

The positive impact of instructor/student interactions is well-established (Nadler & Nadler, 2001), particularly for out-of-class communications as they relate to both teacher efficacy and student achievement. Even with online classes, when the instructor and student may never meet in person, it is still possible to facilitate positive instructor/student interactions with a range of new media tools. To date, however, little attention has been paid to the manner in which email, social media applications (such as Facebook, Twitter, Google Chat and other instant messaging clients) and other interactive communication channels have altered the manner in which instructors and students interact, not only in the online instruction setting but for students who are still taking traditional, in-person classes. Many instructors now supplement or replace traditional, face-to-face office hours with availability on social media outlets or other means of virtual availability, enhancing student/faculty communication and even calling to question the practice of providing traditional office hours at all (Daws & Gleason, 2011).

While the effectiveness of technology in the classroom is generally accepted, the presumption is that the technology itself is a substantial contributor to positive learning outcomes. Yet this assumption discounts the potential positive impact of such contributors as teacher efficacy, student motivation, and technological skill level, reflecting a critical gap in the research. To date, research findings in this area are mixed. Twenge (2009) suggests that the generational differences found in the Net Generation learner are so considerable compared to previous generations that instructors should adjust teaching style and use of technology in order to reach the younger students. However, one cannot assume that all Net Generation learners learn in the same way, given varying levels of online access or skill sets with technology (Bennett, Maton & Kervin, 2008). In investigating how the use of digital technology contributes to learning among Net Generation students, scholarship surrounding the interactivity construct suggests answers about whether some technological characteristics are more helpful to learning outcomes than others.

Interactivity

Over the past several decades, many scholars have examined various dimensions of interactivity in an attempt to articulate a comprehensive definition. However, these models fail to capture the full range and complexity associated the construct. Further, to date researchers had failed to produce a theory-driven model that can be measured in an experimental setting.

These efforts have borne little fruit in yielding a theory-driven model of how interactivity affects the process and impact of communication (Bucy, 2004; Sundar, 2004). Without such a model, the construct proved difficult to operationalize and apply in a predictable and *measurable* manner.

It appears that little effort had been directed toward theorizing how interactivity affects the process and impact of communication (Sundar, 2004; Bucy, 2004). A more balanced and theory-based model of interactivity was needed, one that incorporates a variety of elements within a wider unifying construct that ultimately predicts the influence of interactivity on user behaviors.

The continued study of interactivity is important because the construct can play a central role in influencing the *success* of a mediated communication exchange. However, while its pan-contextual nature enables interactivity to find application across a range of communication contexts (including instructional ones), its breadth has made the construct difficult to corral.

Interactivity had typically been measured by relating it directly to the presence of a technological feature, a user's perception or a combination of both. In each case, interactivity was generally framed as something driving the communication process from within. Much ambiguity falls away when interactivity is viewed instead as an outcome state, or something that occurs *as a result* of the mutual influence of a number of contributing dimensions within the communication event, including both technology and user perception.

It matters how interactivity is conceptualized because it can play a central role in influencing both the outcome and perceived success of a communication exchange such as an online lesson. A longstanding problem in defining the interactivity construct is that it has frequently been forced to fit a variety of condition states and conflicting models, particularly as new Web-based technologies have continued to emerge over the past 20 years. Some early models (Rafaeli, 1988; Heeter, 1989; Neuman, 1991; Steuer, 1992) emphasized its roots in technology and the various features and functions at play. Later, more user-centered models (Laurel, 1986; Ha & James, 1998) described interactivity as a piece of a communication process rather than something resulting from it.

These categories are broad and loosely defined groupings and, in fact, some scholars combine elements of two or even all three in their models. For example, Bucy (2004) describes interactivity as being operationally composed of three principal elements: properties of technology, attributes of communication contexts and user perceptions. Similarly, Yoo (2007) summarizes prior conceptualization efforts into three principal areas: feature-, process-, and perception-oriented interactivity.

From a feature-based orientation, Steuer (1992) defined interactivity as the extent to which the medium allows the participant to modify the content or form of a mediated environment in real time. Similar conceptualizations of interactivity (Heeter, 1989; Ha & James, 1998) often relied heavily on lists of individual technology functions or features viewed to facilitate two-way communication in a manner emulating face-to-face exchanges.

From a process-oriented perspective, scholars focused on exchanges and message responsiveness in a communication setting. Rafaeli & Sudweeks (1997, Interactivity section, para. 2) defined interactivity as "the extent to which messages in a sequence relate to each other and especially the extent to which later messages recount the relatedness of earlier messages."

Historically, this variety of incomplete (and sometimes conflicting) conceptualizations tended to yield inexact or unsatisfying operationalizations of the interactivity construct (Bucy, 2004). In some ways, even the inexact use of some terminology has contributed to the confusion.

Though obviously related, the words interactive and interactivity each describe something quite distinct from one another. While the terms are often applied interchangeably in casual usage, the roles these terms play and the elements they describe within the communication process differ in important ways. The distinction between the two is important.

The term *interactive* refers to technological channel features or content elements that *facilitate* a communication event in which these elements act upon or with other technologies and technological features to obtain data or commands, and in response give immediate results or updated information. Such an entity might be said to possess some level of "interactive functionality."

Interactivity, on the other hand, describes a summative perception of the degree to which a user (the interactant) participates (interacts) in a communication process (the interaction) with substantive interactive features of a technology or content. From this perspective, interactivity is an individual's perception of a positive outcome state *resulting* from the integration of a number of distinct contributing dimensions during mutual and reciprocal message exchanges.

A more balanced definition was needed, one that incorporates a variety of elements within a wider unifying construct to ultimately predict and measure the influence of interactivity on user behaviors. Such a definition must also address three limitations in extant interactivity literature.

First, the importance of interactivity is more completely realized (and more easily operationalized) when interactivity is viewed as an outcome and the *result* of the mutual influence of a number of contributing elements within the event. Each participant individually recognizes the extent of the resulting interactivity at play, and this level varies from user to user.

This outcome-based conceptualization of interactivity is ultimately central to a participant's perceived satisfaction with the communication event itself. Only the individual receiver can recognize the extent of the perceived interactivity at play, and this varies from user to user. It is rarely a case of whether "interactivity" is or is not perceived. Rather, the question is one of *degree*—the extent to which the individual interactive elements or dimensions are apparent in the mediated communication, the degree to which they influence each other, and the perceived level of interactivity that results.

As an outcome state perceived by an individual user, interactivity is shaped by three predictive dimensions: *technological features*, *relevant user experiences*, and reactive communicated *content*. Each of these dimensions is described, in turn, below.

It's clear that the use of technology can have an influence on the communication process. However, technology does not inherently foster or constitute interactivity by nature, and a feature can possess interactive functionality without necessarily eliciting the perception of interactivity. Rather, *technological features* and interactive functionality hold the *potential* to yield the perception of interactivity for individual users under certain circumstances. The degree to which a technology enables this perception is determined by the degree to which a particular user takes advantage of its available interactive elements or dimensions (Bucy, 2004). Thus, the level of interactivity elicited by a particular product or technology can and will be perceived differently from user to user. In short, technology matters, but there's more going on.

Technology-focused models are limited in recognizing the importance of this user influence within the process. This focus on the *what* at the expense of the *why* oversimplifies the complex nature of the intersecting human influences at play, and fails to take into account the variable nature of interactivity in its perception by users (Massey & Levy, 1999; Lee, 2000; McMillan, 2002; Stromer-Galley, 2004; Wu, 2005).

Not surprisingly, the notion of interactivity as a variable can be troublesome to technology-centered models. Certainly some technology aspects are unvarying. For example, a computer keyboard has a finite and generally consistent number of keys, and a given cell phone may or may not be capable of receiving and displaying email messages. However, an individual's use of a particular technology defines *both* the medium and the message for that user in terms of their value. Symbols are meaningless until interpreted by a user, and how each interprets them is influenced by a wide range of reactions and behaviors.

Essentially, interactivity must be conceptionally and operationally defined as a receiver-oriented construct. Considerable scholarship has already made a strong case for the central role of *user perception* as it relates to user experience, interactivity and the communication process (Laurel, 1986, 1991; Massey & Levy, 1999; Heeter, 1989; Stromer-Galley, 2000; Downes and McMillan, 2000). In defining interactivity as a perceptual variable, the user must actively *recognize* the presence of interactivity, which Wu (2005) defines as a "psychological state experienced by [the] site-visitor." While the *potential* for interactivity can reside in some technology, interactivity itself does not. In other words, the recognition of interactivity just doesn't *happen*, but is initiated by each user's (receiver's) actions or involvement.

In every exchange, something must be communicated, and this communicated content illustrates a second limitation in interactivity literature. The reactive impact of *content*, a previously underrecognized contributor to the mediated communication experience, is determined by the *opportunity* for interaction provided specifically by the communicated content. Importantly, it does so in a unique manner independent of the technology or medium used to communicate it, and the perception of interactivity is directly influenced by the receiver's interaction with this content. Surprisingly, the role of content is rarely addressed in the interactivity literature.

Although clearly technology enabled, even Web page hotlinks might reasonably be considered as interactive *content* elements. While it is true that technology offers the opportunity for perceptions of interactivity by delivering the content, it is the content *itself* and not the technology that directly solicits the response or action from the user. Much as creativity or writing skill determine a reader's interest in or satisfaction with a book or magazine article, it is creative judgment that determines where, how frequently and with what wording specific hotlinks are integrated into a Web page's content. These subjective decisions directly affect audience perceptions of the effectiveness of the site. To be clear, the technology only provides the opportunity to include these hotlinks, while the specific links are *content* elements that contribute to the *perception* of increased interactivity.

By examining the interactivity construct and these three predictive dimensions (technological features, relevant user experiences and content), a more meaningful definition of the interactivity construct emerges:

Interactivity is an observable feature of a communication event that reflects the degree to which interactive technology and content elements are influenced by relevant experiences to empower a participant to achieve a desired communication goal or outcome.

Thus, it is *the user's* recognition and application of interactive functionality in the technology or communicated content (embodying the potential for interactivity) as intended by the sender. It might be thought of as the realization of *interactivity potential* (a sender-based perspective) as *interactivity recognized* (a user-based perspective).

Outcome Interactivity Theory (OIT) (see Figure 1) differs from these earlier conceptualizations by examining interactivity's role in contributing to *outcomes* for participants in a communication event (Gleason, 2007). According to OIT, an individual's recognition of interactivity requires the integration and mutual influence of three separate and distinct dimensions—actual interactive features and functions of the *technology* employed, the presence of similarly reactive elements in the *content* being communicated, and the relevant individual user experiences and specific context shaping how a user encounters this technology and content. It is the user experiences and context that empower the participant to employ and apply these interactive elements within the communication event toward a desirable outcome.

From this outcome-based perspective, neither technology nor content inherently foster or constitute interactivity by nature. Either can exhibit considerable interactive functionality (or the *potential* for interactivity) without actually eliciting the recognition of interactivity by a given participant. This view is in sharp contrast to models that consider interactivity to be akin to a technological attribute, as though interactivity can simply be "added" to a product or process. This new conceptualization has implications for instructional design, in that one cannot add interactivity into a design plan beyond encouraging its potential. Rather, one would design specific interactive elements into a lesson or presentation such that the potential for interactivity is present, and therefore the resulting perception of interactivity would act as a mediating variable that would contribute positively toward the planned and desired learning outcomes (see Figure 2).

As described above, interactivity is a multidimensional construct, and the OIT theoretical model integrates a number of relevant sub-dimensions for each predicting dimension (see Figure 2).

The *technological features* dimension considers the capacity of individual technologies and media, including specific actual features, functions, attributes or applications, to influence the recognition of interactivity by a participant as a result of a communication event. The technological features dimension of OIT is shaped by four specific elements: *user control*, *directionality*, the actual *communication speed* and the *sensory complexity* of the communication.

The *relevant user experiences* dimension addresses how an individual responds to one or more elements of interactive functionality and the opportunity for the potential increases in perceived interactivity they present. These user experiences are shaped, and the resulting outcome enabled, by two contributing sub-dimensions: *context* and *user perception*.

Context describes a participant's readiness and receptivity to respond to an element within the communication event, and is shaped by the environment, both physical and virtual, in which the communication occurs (Kiousis, 2002). The manner in which a user comes into contact with computer-mediated content will have either a positive or negative impact on how it is received. This impact will be present regardless of whether the contact involves a technology, medium, ap-

Figure 1. Outcome interactivity theory

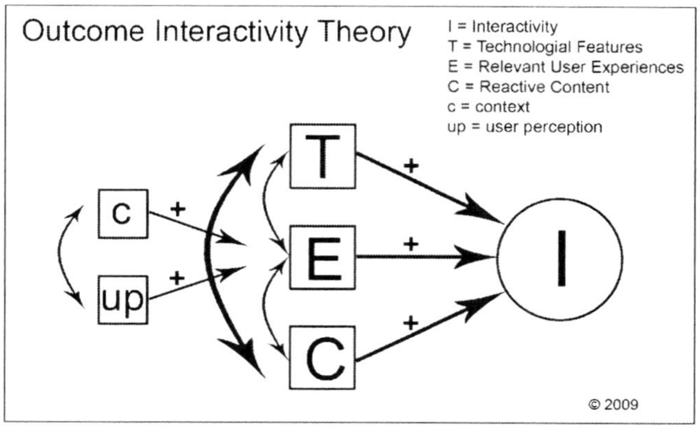

Figure 2. OIT predicting dimensions and contributing sub-dimensions

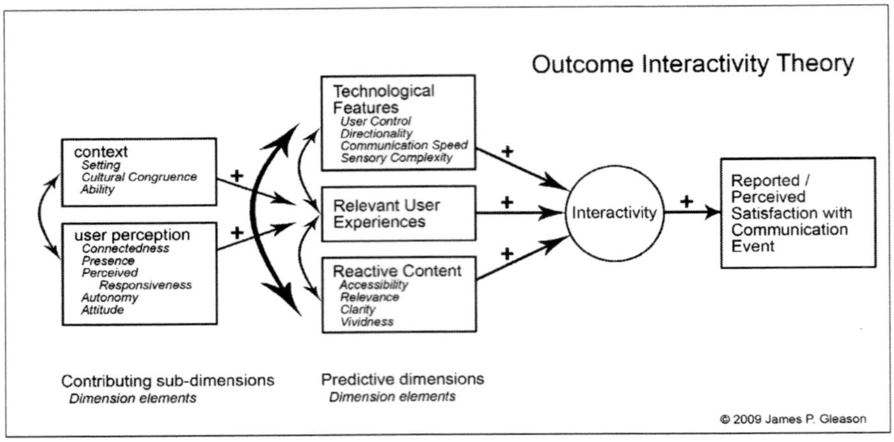

plication, message or other form of communication content.

Interestingly, new media formats may not always or uniformly be *perceived* by individual users as affording opportunities to interact or participate, though they may actually possess features associated with interactivity by researchers. In fact, depending on skill level, experience or even mood, different users may perceive a different range of options or level of interactivity that are possible for the same medium, application or content.

The literature describes a number of elements that contribute to this contextual influence. For example, the environment in which the communication event takes place, familiarity and comfort level with technology features, message content, process or even other participants, and even responsiveness, user feedback and sense of place may contribute to increased levels of comfort (Lee, 2000; McMillan, 2002).

User perception is defined by individual differences that shape each individual user's receptivity to interactive features or content. Again, the literature describes a number of such elements that can have a positive influence. Perceived speed is how fast users *think* the system allows participants to react to one another's transmissions. Presence is the degree to which the communication event emulates direct or face-to-face communication or an immersive environment (Kiousis, 2002). Choice is the availability to select content options and of unrestrained (Ha & James, 1998). Proximity is the degree to which a respondent feels he or she is *near* other subjects when engaging with the system or participating in the event (Kiousis, 2002). Connectedness is the feeling of being able to link to the outside world and to interact with content as if physically present in a natural environment (Steuer, 1992; Ha & James, 1998). Finally, the perceived purpose and the level of synergy with the actual event also contribute (McMillan, 2002). Each of these elements can play a substantial role in enhancing user perception of interactivity.

Finally, the *reactive content* dimension considers the capacity of interactive functionality within the communicated content to influence the recognition of interactivity. The reactive content dimension includes four dimension elements: *accessibility*, *clarity*, *relevance* and *vividness*.

Accessibility describes the manner in which online content is structured, delivered and presented, including how it is written, designed or organized. This presentation enables each user to select and display this content in its most (personally) desirable form and sequence (McMillan, 2002). High levels of accessibility would be expected to positively influence the recognition of interactivity. A higher value would be indicated by a greater number of desirable options or a higher degree of flexibility in the ways in which the content could be modified or an interaction with another participant could occur (when compared to another sample).

Clarity describes the degree to which sought-after content is displayed with appropriate or expected visual and conceptual organization (logical placement, sequence, etc.), and with a generally acceptable level of accuracy, clear writing style and grammatical, spelling and punctuation standards. Content with a high level of clarity is easy to read, without obvious factual errors, and free from grammatical errors and other similar distractions, and would be expected to be positively correlated with high levels of interactivity.

Relevance describes the degree to which available content is desirable and consistent with a user's goals for the communication event. Relevance is influenced by the communicated content's intuitiveness, appropriateness and congruity. At issue is whether the available content is the *right* content—that is, more or less desirable for that participant in that particular communication event. This outcome-oriented and user-centered variable is determined by the needs of the user rather than the intentions of the content producer, and therefore is consistent with both Uses and Gratifications Theory (Katz, Blumler, & Gurevitch, 1974) and Expectancy-Value Theory (Palmgreen & Rayburn, 1985). Highly relevant content would be expected to be more engaging and to be positively correlated with the recognition of interactivity.

Vividness describes the degree to which available content is displayed using high levels of graphic richness, animation and audio/visual elements (when compared to traditional media). New media content is noteworthy for its typically higher level of vividness, which sets it apart by making the content presentation more appealing and engaging. Moderate to high levels of vividness would be expected to positively influence the recognition of interactivity, although extreme levels of visual richness would be more likely to be viewed negatively as noise and interfere with desired outcomes.

Thus, Outcome Interactivity Theory provides a roadmap for communicators in disciplines as diverse as instructional design, online marketing and advertising, digital entertainment and politics. It can enable communicators to more effectively apply interactive functionality as a constructive element within the development process as a means toward enhancing desired outcomes for a wide range of audiences.

The next section explores how Outcome Interactivity Theory can be applied in an instructional context.

THE RELEVANCE OF INTERACTIVITY IN THE INSTRUCTIONAL CONTEXT

Without a theory-driven model to operationalize the construct, the task of *applying* interactivity in some meaningful way becomes that much more difficult. If one believes interactivity contributes to communication outcomes in a positive way (and the authors do), it's imperative to operationalize the interactivity construct in a concrete and generalizable way that can be applied and *tested* across in a variety of contexts including instructional design.

Interactivity is relevant to educators to the degree that it positively contributes to a desirable outcome for the user in an individual communication exchange. In the study described here, this positive outcome is operationalized as knowledge acquisition and satisfaction as demonstrated by students as a result of participation in an online instructional module.

Similarly, interactivity is also relevant to the Net Generation learner. Net Generation students, as already noted, are growing up with technology in their personal lives and are accustomed to its presence in the classroom from very early on in their educational careers. Teachers in grades K-12 rely on interactive technology to achieve curriculum outcomes more than ever; even pre-school children play with interactive toys and robots for both educational and entertainment purposes. When Net Generation students go to college, it would not be unreasonable for them to expect their instructors to demonstrate at least basic competency with the effective use of interactive teaching methods. The study here offers some support to the idea that Net Generation students may learn better with interactive instructional approaches presented by instructors.

Online instructional modules are graphically rich, offer considerable interactive functionality, and are widely used to facilitate student achievement and the resulting positive learning outcomes. The study posits that, in an instructional context, both interactivity and positive student outcomes are facilitated by the use of interactive functionality embodied in the technology and communicated content of the lesson.

For example, while teachers and students alike enjoy Web-based instruction, it is not clear whether, how and to what degree these efforts lead to actual *cognitive* learning by students when tested under experimental conditions. The empirical study here operationalizes interactivity as a positive learning outcome, and tested several hypotheses regarding interactivity's contribution under experimental conditions. This study tested the impact of interactive functionality in instructional content on student learning outcomes, specifically knowledge acquisition (or actual cognitive learning) and satisfaction (affective learning).

The experiment manipulated individual elements of the reactive content dimension of the OIT model—accessibility, clarity, relevance and vividness—to determine whether perceived interactivity contributed to these student learning outcomes.

The specific question driving this research is whether the incorporation of interactive functionality into online instructional modules offers improvements in student knowledge acquisition and satisfaction when compared to traditional static instructional modules.

The results are surprising.

STUDY DESCRIPTION AND RESEARCH METHODS

The study used *Outcome Interactivity Theory* as a framework to measure the degree to which high levels of interactive functionality (as a component of online instructional content) contribute to increased student cognitive and affective learning. Variables were measured using a pre-test and post-test control group full experimental model (Bailey, 1994) comparing two groups of subjects participating in one of two equivalent online lessons. One lesson sample used content presented as text only (in the form of a simple HTML document), while the other sample used content displaying considerably greater interactive functionality and graphic richness.

The study hypothesized that lesson content displaying high levels of interactive functionality will positively influence student learning outcomes when compared to more static lesson content (low interactive functionality). It was expected that subjects using the more interactive lesson sample would report a higher level of knowledge acquisition as indicated by higher quiz scores (cognition) and satisfaction with the lesson (affect) when compared to the less interactive lesson.

The following hypotheses were tested as repeated measures of group differences using an independent samples t-test.

- **H1a:** *Students participating in the treatment group (online instructional modules with high potential interactivity) will dis-*

play a higher level of knowledge acquisition (cognitive learning) after exposure to the online content than students in the comparison (low potential interactivity) group.

- **H1b:** *Students participating in the treatment group (online instructional modules with high potential interactivity) will display a higher level of satisfaction with the lesson content (as a measure of affective learning) after exposure to the online content than students in the comparison (low potential interactivity) group.*

These two hypotheses were measured by eliciting responses to an online survey tool after participating in an online instructional module.

In addition, the Outcome Interactivity Theory model was tested by measuring whether interactivity predicts knowledge acquisition and satisfaction using a linear regression. The following hypotheses were tested:

- **H2a:** *A high level of interactivity in online content will predict a high level of student knowledge acquisition after exposure to the content.*
- **H2b:** *A high level of interactivity in online content will predict a high level of student satisfaction after exposure to the content.*

Students using online instructional modules with a high degree of interactive functionality were expected to demonstrate higher levels of knowledge acquisition and satisfaction with the lesson content than for those using content presented in a less interactive manner. Student knowledge acquisition was operationalized as positive variance in post-test scores between comparison and treatment groups. The impact of interactivity on student affect was operationalized as a positive variance in satisfaction or content preference between groups as measured by a content preference measurement scale.

The study hypothesized that lesson content displaying high levels of interactive functionality (reflected as high levels of accessibility, clarity, relevance and vividness) would positively influence student learning outcomes.

Content with a high degree of *accessibility* was displayed in the treatment sample in the following manner: pop-up links were available to provide additional information; if selected, an animated graphic could be displayed and manipulated by the subject; and a menu of selectable content display preferences was presented. The *clarity* variable was measured but not expressly manipulated. High *relevance* was displayed in the treatment sample by an introductory overview provided to indicate relevant topics within lesson content. High *vividness* was displayed in the treatment sample in the following manner: hotlinks displayed as buttons; bold, underlined and red used to indicate pop-up text links; the use of an appealing color layout; and an available animated graphic that presented content in alternative form.

The amount of interactive functionality displayed by the comparison and treatment online instructional module samples (as an indication of interactivity) was manipulated as the independent variable and was expected to positively affect the subject's knowledge acquisition score and level of preference with the content as an outcome of the lesson.

Study Population

Study participants (n=311) were recruited from a population of undergraduate students at a large Midwestern university, of which 114 (36.7%) were male and 197 (63.3%) were female. A Pearson chi-square test [χ^2 (1) = 2.650, p >.05] indicated no significant difference in gender across the two experimental conditions. Similarly, subjects in the control and treatment groups showed no significant differences in terms of class rank, ethnicity, major, age and level of comfort with math or statistics coursework.

More than 98% of the subjects had been using the Internet for four years or more, indicating (an anticipated) substantial level of experience. A Pearson chi-square test [χ^2 (4) = 3.368, $p > .05$] indicated no significant difference in the amount of subject Internet experience across the two experimental conditions.

In addition, subjects' need for cognition (Cacioppo et al., 1984) was measured to ensure the degree to which any variance between the comparison and treatment subject groups might be due to reluctance or discomfort with technical or complex lesson content was not different between groups. A chi-square test [χ^2 (29) = 27.180, $p > .05$] indicated no significant difference in subject need for cognition across the two experimental conditions.

Two groups of participants were used in the study, and used the same lesson content presented in one of two experimental conditions: the comparison sample as static HTML text files with minimal interactive functionality, and the treatment sample as more interactive and graphically rich content. A comparison of scores for a pre-test of initial knowledge of lesson content was also used to further ensure equivalency between subject groups.

Research Procedures and Measures

The study was conducted entirely online. This approach was both efficient and consistent with the subject matter and the Web-based tools used in the study. In order to limit the likelihood of prior familiarity, the researcher selected a statistics lesson as content used in the study, expecting that most students in these introductory communication classes would not yet have encountered this subject matter.

The study activity included three parts. Part One consisted of taking a brief pre-test assessment. Part Two consisted of reading or interacting with the lesson content in the online instructional module. Part Three involved a post-test assessment and measurement survey.

The identical pre-test and post-test assessments consisted of ten questions relating to the content subject matter. The level of subject knowledge acquisition for each experimental condition was measured as the difference between pre-test and post-test scores.

Each subject also completed a post-test survey to measure preference for the lesson content, perception of interactivity, and levels of accessibility, relevance, clarity and vividness of the sample content.

With the exception of the pre-test and post-test assessments and demographic data, each survey question collected data using a five-point Likert-type scale.

The newly developed research scales were informed and influenced by elements of a number of other existing scales (Bunz, 2001, 2003; Palmgreen, Wenner & Rayburn, 1980; Zaichkowsky, 1986). However, they were adjusted by the researcher to specifically examine and test the influence of dimensions in the Outcome Interactivity Theory model, and were unique to this study. (The exception was Need For Cognition, which was measured using a scale developed by Cacioppo et al. (1984)).

The ten measurement scales used in this study employed a total of 66 separate questions and showed a high overall level of reliability ranging from α=.692 to α=.876. Overall reliability across all ten composite scales was α=.756 (n=311). For the purposes of most analyses, a composite scale was created from multidimensional scales and each was treated as a unidimensional scale.

Satisfaction was operationalized as the subjects' preference for the content. Content preference employed an eight-item multidimensional scale (α=.862, n=311) to explain 64.85% of the variance (51.57% and 13.28% respectively).

Table 1 is a descriptive statistics chart for content preference.

Table 1. Descriptive statistics for content preference scale (n=311)

	Mean	Std. Deviation	N
This Web site made me feel like I was communicating with someone.	2.38	1.037	311
Overall, the Web site was easy to use.	3.94	.888	311
This Web site helped me do well in this lesson.	3.06	1.018	311
This Web site made me want to learn more about statistics.	2.17	1.058	311
I was able to find the information I was looking for on this Web site.	3.58	.926	311
This Web site made learning about statistics more enjoyable.	2.44	.985	311
I would recommend this Web site to a friend.	2.71	1.089	311
I think my friends would enjoy visiting this Web site.	2.23	.962	311

Interactivity, conceptualized by OIT as an outcome of the communication event, was measured using a nine-item multidimensional scale (α=.876, n=311) to explain 64.19% of the variance (38.46% and 25.73% respectively). The four questions in the first factor considered the appearance of the content, while the remaining five dealt more with navigation. The researcher considered both appearance and navigation to be contributors to the vividness of the content, and therefore a composite multidimensional scale reflecting both elements is an appropriate measure of vividness

Table 2. Descriptive statistics for original ten-item interactivity scale (n=311)

	N	Mean	Std. Deviation
To what degree does this Web site possess or contain interactivity?	311	3.62	1.377
To what degree did this Web site react to your direction or influence?	311	3.58	1.293
How important to you is the amount of interactivity on this Web site?	311	4.00	1.491
To what degree did the amount of interactivity on this Web site affect how you used it?	311	3.81	1.400
To what degree did the amount of interactivity on this Web site make it seem more appealing?	311	3.67	1.476
To what degree did the amount of interactivity on this Web site affect how interesting the content was?	311	3.70	1.528
To what degree did your experience help you appreciate any interactive features of this Web site?	311	3.74	1.415
To what degree did the technological features on this Web site affect how interactive it was?	311	3.71	1.388
To what degree did the content on this Web site affect how interactive it was?	311	3.87	1.421
How important is it to you that a Web site contains a lot of interactivity?	311	4.71	1.522
Valid N (listwise)	311		

in this experiment. Table 2 is a descriptive statistics chart for the original ten-item scale for interactivity.

Results

The first set of hypotheses tested group mean differences between the treatment and comparison groups for student learning outcomes (knowledge acquisition and satisfaction).

Hypothesis 1a tested whether students participating in the treatment group (online instructional modules with high interactive functionality) would display a higher level of knowledge acquisition after exposure to the online content than students in the comparison (low interactive functionality) group. Results of the independent samples t-test revealed higher post-test means for the treatment group (M = 5.3101, S.D. = 2.31281) than for the comparison group (M = 5.1242, S.D. = 2.41247). However, the differences were not statistically significant [t (309) = -.694, p >.05], and Hypothesis 1a was not supported.

Hypothesis 1b tested whether students participating in the treatment (high interactive functionality) group would display a higher level of satisfaction after exposure to the online content than students in the comparison (low interactive functionality) group. Results of the independent samples t-test revealed higher means for satisfaction for the treatment group (M = 2.9241, S.D. =.74224) than for the comparison group (M = 2.6985, S.D. =.66121), and the differences were statistically significant [t(309) = -2.826, p <.005]. Therefore, Hypothesis 1b was supported.

The regression analysis for Hypothesis 2a revealed that interactivity sufficiently predicted knowledge acquisition: R^2 =.019, F(1) = 5.871, p =.016. Interactivity [t = 2.423, p =.016, β =.137] significantly predicted knowledge acquisition (see Table 3), and Hypothesis 2a was supported. However, interactivity only accounted for 1.6% of the variance with regards to knowledge acquisition.

The regression analysis for Hypothesis 2b revealed that interactivity sufficiently predicted satisfaction: R^2 =.293, F (1) = 127.794, p <.001. Interactivity predicted satisfaction [t = 11.305, p <.001, β =.541] at a statistically significant level (see Table 4). Hypothesis 2b was strongly supported, and interactivity accounted for 29% of the variance with regards to satisfaction.

DISCUSSION

Does interactive online instruction produce different results from traditional static instructional modules? Conventional wisdom seems to suggest all technology is good, and since Net Generation students like it, it *must* play a positive role in student cognitive learning.

Surprisingly, study results did *not* support the positive impact of interactivity (as embodied by a high level of interactive functionality in online lesson content) on measurable student knowledge acquisition between treatment and comparison groups. Although a direct link between the percep-

Table 3. Regression model for interactivity and knowledge acquisition

Model		Unstandardized Coefficients		Standardized Coefficients	t	Sig.
		B	Std. Error	Beta		
1	(Constant)	3.998	.521		7.677	.000
	INTERACTIVITY	.317	.131	.137	2.423	.016
Dependent Variable: KNOWLEDGE_ACQ *Note: Adj.* R^2 =.015						

Table 4. Regression model for interactivity and satisfaction

Model		Unstandardized Coefficients		Standardized Coefficients	t	Sig.
		B	Std. Error	Beta		
1	(Constant)	1.356	.133		10.176	.000
	INTERACTIVITY	.378	.033	.541	11.305	.000
a. Dependent Variable: SATISFACTION *Note: Adj.* R^2 =.290						

tion of interactivity and actual student knowledge acquisition was expected, such a link has not been supported by this study. It's worth noting that the failure to yield statistically significant increases in *cognitive* student learning outcomes finds some consonance in Instructional Design literature. Richard Mayer's *static-media hypothesis* (Mayer, 2009) is particularly relevant in this regard.

In contrast, however, students *did* display a significantly higher level of satisfaction (or affective learning) in the treatment group than in the comparison group. In interpreting the results, the recognition of interactivity clearly influences *satisfaction* positively. Thus, the skillful application of interactive functionality in an instructional context *can* have a positive effect on student attitudes toward lesson content, which in turn could lead to decreased resistance and increased attention to lessons and online assignments. This finding suggests introducing interactive functionality in instructional technology and lesson content (and thereby increasing resulting interactivity) may encourage students to pay closer attention, work harder and study longer.

The implications of such findings (and the obvious need for additional research in this area) are considerable in light of the rapid growth of (and accelerated momentum toward) distance learning and other online instruction. As the example of the Net Generation makes plain, the need for improved instructional tools, techniques and strategies in the digital domain becomes manifest.

The idea that students like and readily embrace technology in an instructional context is parsimonious. What these results do *not* suggest, however, is that extending this affective outcome to more cognitive results is automatically successful. What *is* supported, however, is that the application of interactivity results in increased student satisfaction and leads to substantial motivational and self-esteem benefits. And increased student satisfaction is, in and of itself, a worthy and useful goal.

Also of particular value in this study, a set of original and highly reliable measurement scales were applied for the first time, and *quantify* the influence of specific individual dimensions and elements on interactivity as defined by OIT. Although informed and influenced by elements of a number of other existing scales, they were adjusted by the researcher to specifically examine and test the influence of dimensions in the Outcome Interactivity Theory model, and were unique to this study.

FUTURE RESEARCH DIRECTIONS

The researcher selected a statistics lesson as content used in the study, expecting that most students in these introductory communication classes would not yet have encountered this subject matter (which, indeed, they had not). However, without a direct connection to any class curriculum for which the participants would be held accountable, participants may have found the content uninteresting and therefore failed to give the lesson sufficient attention—regardless of the level of interactivity—to achieve more representative results. Alternately, participants may have found the content to be too long or too difficult. In either case, the impact of subject motivation was not measured.

Since the study sample was selected for practical purposes from only one university, it may reflect the cultural identity of that community alone. Since the sample population was largely made up of members of the Net Generation, it came as no surprise that subjects reported substantial technological experience going into the study. In fact, 98% had used the Internet for four years or more, suggesting subjects displayed a high level of confidence with interactive tools and applications atypical of the general population. Using subjects from a broader population would help ensure a more normal distribution of Internet skills and experience, and potentially increase the generalizability of the results. Additional research into the ways a variety of demographic and psychographic groups perceive and embrace interactivity could prove particularly valuable to product designers and content developers. Further, testing different subject groups would allow tests for group differences of cognitive load using a variety of content approaches, topics, amounts and levels of complexity when measured under time constraints.

This study measured the technological features and relevant user experiences dimensions of the OIT model as global constructs without either manipulating them or measuring their individual elements. The researcher opted to focus on the content dimension of the OIT model since it has received far less scholarly scrutiny, and leave the detailed study of the technological features and user experiences dimensions for future studies.

Another potentially fruitful avenue for researchers involves expanding future studies within the instructional design context, and exploring additional applications and communication contexts in which to apply the interactivity construct, such as the impact of interactivity on mediated out-of-class communication, impact of interactivity on perceived levels of immediacy, and the importance of interactivity in facilitating instructor/student communication.

CONCLUSION

The study described above tested the influence of interactive functionality in the content dimension of the Outcome Interactivity Theory model and, with the exception of those hypotheses relating directly to knowledge acquisition, all other results were statistically significant and, in the case of several, at the $p < .001$ level. Taken together, these results reinforce the integrity of Outcome Interactivity Theory and the dimensions and elements it describes.

This chapter argues that, despite the vigorous embrace of interactive digital technology by the Net Generation, its successful use in an instructional environment is perhaps more complex and nuanced that might be apparent at a glance. While not *directly* leading to improve cognitive learning, the skillful application of interactive functionality *can* positively affect student attitudes toward lesson content. As this study indicates, the Net Generation student embraces interactivity for educational purposes, not just for personal or social uses. Thus, the inclusion of interactive technology and approaches in the classroom might suggest to the Net Generation student that their instructors not recognize this new learning style preference, but are also making a conscious effort to apply it toward a more positive learning experience for the classroom as a whole.

In particular, interactivity was found to have a pronounced effect on student satisfaction, meaning students should enjoy learning from instructors who strategically include interactive instructional approaches in their classroom communications. Thus, introducing interactive functionality in instructional technology and lesson content may encourage a student to pay closer attention, work harder and study longer. Net Generation students seem to be motivated to learn when the instructor is motivated to reach them on their level by facilitating positive, meaningful learning experiences. While acknowledging a need for additional research in this area, it is clear Outlook Interactivity Theory can provide a useful framework to measurably refine and improve the application of technology in an instructional setting.

Improving student satisfaction is a good first step in the application of Outlook Interactivity Theory and, from this new perspective, its further application within an instructional environment can provide a useful new tool for educators to engage members of the Net Generation.

REFERENCES

Bailey, K. D. (1994). *Methods of social research* (4th ed.). New York, NY: Free Press.

Bennett, S., Maton, K., & Kervin, L. (2008). The "digital natives" debate: A critical review of the evidence. *British Journal of Educational Technology*, *39*(5), 775–786..doi:10.1111/j.1467-8535.2007.00793.x

Bucy, E. (2004). Interactivity in society: Locating an elusive concept. *The Information Society*, *20*(5), 373–383..doi:10.1080/01972240490508063

Bunz, U. (2001). *Usability and gratifications—Towards a website analysis model.* Paper presented at the 87th Annual Meeting of the National Communication Association.

Bunz, U. (2003). Growing from computer literacy towards computer-mediated communication competence: Evolution of a field and evaluation of a new measurement instrument. *Information Technology. Education et Sociétés*, *4*(2), 53–84.

Cacioppo, J. T., Petty, R. E., & Kao, C. F. (1984). The efficient assessment of need for cognition. *Journal of Personality Assessment*, *48*(3), 306–307. doi:10.1207/s15327752jpa4803_13

Daws, L. B., & Gleason, J. P. (2011). *Instructor perceptions of online office hours: Helping or hurting?* Paper presented at the 2011 Kentucky Conference on Converging Trends in Teaching & Learning, Erlanger, KY.

Downes, E., & McMillan, S. (2000). Defining interactivity: A qualitative identification of key dimensions. *New Media & Society*, *6*(2), 157–179. doi:10.1177/1461444002225751

Gleason, J. P. (2007). More than the medium: The unique role of content in user perception of interactivity. *International Journal of the Book*, *5*(1), 77–84.

Gleason, J. P., & Lane, D. R. (2009). *Interactivity redefined: A first look at outcome interactivity theory.* Paper presented at the Annual Meeting of the National Communication Association.

Ha, L., & James, E. L. (1998). Interactivity reexamined: A baseline analysis of early business Web sites. *Journal of Broadcasting & Electronic Media*, *42*(4), 457–474.. doi:10.1080/08838159809364462

Heeter, C. (1989). Implications of new interactive technologies for conceptualizing communication. In Salvaggio, J. L., & Bryant, J. (Eds.), *Media use in the information age* (pp. 217–235). Hillsdale, NJ: Lawrence Erlbaum.

Katz, E., Blumler, J., & Gurevitch, M. (1974). Uses of mass communication by the individual. In Davidson, W. P., & Yu, F. (Eds.), *Mass communication research* (pp. 11–35). New York, NY: Praeger.

Kiousis, S. (2002). Interactivity: A concept explication. *New Media & Society*, *4*(3), 355–383.

Laurel, B. (1986). *Toward the design of a computer-based interactive fantasy system.* Unpublished doctoral dissertation, The Ohio State University.

Laurel, B. (1991). *Computers as theater.* Reading, MA: Addison-Wesley Publishing Company.

Lee, J.-S. (2000, August 9-12). *Interactivity: A new approach.* Paper presented at the AEJMC Annual Conference, Communication Technology & Policy Division, Phoenix.

Massey, B. L., & Levy, M. L. (1999). Interactivity, online journalism, and English-language Web newspapers in Asia. *Journalism & Mass Communication Quarterly*, *76*(1), 138–151.

Mayer, R. E. (2009). *Multimedia learning* (2nd ed.). New York, NY: Cambridge University Press.

McMillan, S. J. (2002). A four-part model of cyber-interactivity: Some cyber-places are more interactive than others. *New Media & Society*, *6*(2), 271–291. doi:.doi:10.1177/146144480200400208

Nadler, M. K., & Nadler, L. B. (2000). Out of class communication between faculty and students: A faculty perspective. *Communication Studies*, *51*(2), 176–188..doi:10.1080/10510970009388517

Neuman, W. R. (1991). *The future of the mass audience*. Cambridge University Press.

Palmgreen, P., & Rayburn, J. D. (1985). An expectancy-value approach to media gratifications. In Rosengren, K. E., Wenner, L. A., & Palmgreen, P. (Eds.), *Media gratifications research* (pp. 61–72). Beverly Hills, CA: Sage.

Palmgreen, P., Wenner, L. A., & Rayburn, J. D. (1980). Relations between gratifications sought and obtained: A study of television news. *Communication Research*, *7*, 161–192.. doi:10.1177/009365028000700202

Prenksy, M. (2001). Digital natives, digital immigrants. *Horizon*, *9*(5), 1–6.. doi:10.1108/10748120110424816

Rafaeli, S. (1988). Interactivity: From new media to communication. In *Sage Annual Review of Communication Research: Advancing Communication Science* (*Vol. 16*, pp. 110–134). Beverly Hills, CA: Sage.

Rafaeli, S., & Sudweeks, F. (1997). Networked interactivity. *Journal of Computer-Mediated Communication*, *2*(4).

Steuer, J. (1992). Defining virtual reality: Dimensions determining telepresence. *The Journal of Communication*, *42*(4), 73–93.. doi:10.1111/j.1460-2466.1992.tb00812.x

Stromer-Galley, J. (2004). Interactivity-as-product and interactivity-as-process. *The Information Society*, *20*(5), 391–394. doi:10.1080/01972240490508081

Sundar, S. S. (2004). Theorizing interactivity's effects. *The Information Society*, *20*(5), 385–389.. doi:10.1080/01972240490508072

Tapscott, D. (1998). *Growing up digital: The rise of the Net generation*. New York, NY: McGraw-Hill.

Twenge, J. M. (2009). Generational changes and their impact in the classroom: Teaching generation me. *Medical Education*, *43*(5), 398–405.. doi:10.1111/j.1365-2923.2009.03310.x

Wu, G. (2005). The mediating role of perceived interactivity in the effect of actual interactivity on attitude toward the Website. *Journal of Interactive Advertising*, *5*(2).

Yoo, C. Y. (2007). Implicit memory measures for Web advertising effectiveness. *Journalism & Mass Communication Quarterly*, *84*(1), 7–23.

Zaichkowsky, J. L. (1985). Measuring the involvement construct. *The Journal of Consumer Research*, *12*, 341–352. doi:10.1086/208520

Zickuhr, K. (2010). [Report from the Pew Internet and American Life Project.]. *Generations (San Francisco, Calif.)*, 2010.

ADDITIONAL READING

Baringer, D., & McCroskey, J. C. (2000). Immediacy in the classroom: Student immediacy. *Communication Education*, *49*, 178–186.. doi:10.1080/03634520009379204

Blankenship, K. L., & Craig, T. Y. (2006). Rhetorical question use and resistance to persuasion: An attitude strength analysis. *Journal of Language and Social Psychology*, *25*(2), 111–128.. doi:10.1177/0261927X06286380

Bucy, E. P., & Tao, C. C. (2007). The mediated moderation model of interactivity. *Media Psychology*, *9*(3), 647–672..doi:10.1080/15213260701283269

Chesebro, J., & McCroskey, J. C. (1998). The development of the teacher clarity short inventory (TCSI) to measure clear teaching in the classroom. *Communication Research Reports*, *15*(3), 262–266..doi:10.1080/08824099809362122

Chesebro, J., & Wanzer, M. B. (2006). Instructional message variables. In Mottet, T., Richmond, V., & McCroskey, J. (Eds.), *Handbook of instructional communication: Rhetorical and relational perspectives* (pp. 89–116). Boston, MA: Pearson/ Allyn & Bacon.

Dick, W., & Carey, L. (1996). *The Systematic Design of Instruction* (4th ed.). New York: Harper Collins College Publishers.

Downs, C. W., & Hazen, M. (1977). A factor analytic study of communication satisfaction. *Journal of Business Communication*, *14*(3), 63–73.. doi:10.1177/002194367701400306

Groeling, J. P. (2004). *Does technology make a difference in the classroom? A comparison of online and traditional courses employing models of competence and uses and gratifications.* University of Kentucky.

Infante, D. A., Rancer, A. S., & Womack, D. F. (2003). *Building communication theory* (4th ed.). Prospect Heights, IL: Waveland.

Jensen, J. F. (1998). Interactivity: Tracking a new concept in media and communication studies. *Nordicom Review*, *1*, 185–204.

Kearney, P., Plax, T. G., Richmond, V. P., & McCroskey, J. C. (1985). Power in the classroom III: Teacher communication techniques and messages. *Communication Education*, *34*, 19–28.. doi:10.1080/03634528509378579

Keller, J. M. (1983). Motivational design of instruction. In Reighluth, C. M. (Ed.), *Instructional design theories: An overview of their current status* (pp. 383–434). Hillsdale, NJ: Lawrence Erlbaum.

Martin, M. M., Chesebro, J. L., & Mottet, T. P. (1997). Students' perceptions of instructors' socio-communicative style and the influence on instructor credibility and situational motivation. *Communication Research Reports*, *14*(4), 431–440..doi:10.1080/08824099709388686

Mayer, R. E., Hegarty, M., Mayer, S., & Campbell, J. (2005). When static media promote active learning: Annotated illustrations versus narrated animations in multimedia instruction. *Journal of Experimental Psychology. Applied*, *11*(4), 256–265..doi:10.1037/1076-898X.11.4.256

McCroskey, J., & McCroskey, L. (2006). Instructional communication: The historical perspective. In Mottet, T., Richmond, V., & McCroskey, J. (Eds.), *Handbook of instructional communication: Rhetorical and relational perspectives* (pp. 33–47). Boston, MA: Pearson/Allyn & Bacon.

McMillan, S. J., & Hwang, J. S. (2002). Measures of perceived interactivity: An exploration of the role of direction of communication, user control, and time in shaping perceptions of interactivity. *Journal of Advertising Research*, *31*(3), 29–42.

Plax, T. G., & Kearney, P. (1992). Teacher power in the classroom: Defining and advancing a program of research. In Richmond, V. P., & McCroskey, J. C. (Eds.), *Power in the classroom: Communication, control and concern* (pp. 67–84). Hillsdale, NJ: Lawrence Erlbaum.

Ramirez, A., Walther, J. B., Burgoon, J. K., & Sunnafrank, M. (2002). Information-seeking strategies, uncertainty, and computer-mediated communication: Toward a conceptual model. *Human Communication Research, 28*(2), 213–228. doi:.doi:10.1111/j.1468-2958.2002.tb00804.x

Rayburn, J. D., & Palmgreen, P. (1984). Merging uses and gratifications and expectancy-value theory. *Communication Research, 11*(4), 537–562.. doi:10.1177/009365084011004005

Richmond, V. P., Gorham, J. S., & McCroskey, J. C. (1987). The relationship between selected immediacy behaviors and cognitive learning. In McLaughlin, M. L. (Ed.), *Communication Yearbook 10* (pp. 574–590). Newbury Park, CA: Sage.

Richmond, V. P., & McCroskey, J. C. (1992). Increasing teacher influence through immediacy. In Richmond, V. P., & McCroskey, J. C. (Eds.), *Power in the classroom: Communication, control and concern*. Hillsdale, NJ: Lawrence Erlbaum.

Stephens, K. K., & Mottet, T. P. (2008). Interactivity in a web conference training context: Effects on trainers and trainees. *Communication Education, 57*(1), 88–104..doi:10.1080/03634520701573284

Stokes, D. (1997). *Pasteur's quadrant: Basic science and technological innovation* (pp. 58–89). Washington, DC: Brookings.

Tevin, J. J., & McCroskey, J. C. (1997). The relationship of perceived teacher caring with student learning and teacher evaluation. *Communication Education, 46*(1), 1–9.. doi:10.1080/03634529709379069

Wanzer, M. B. (1995). Student affinity-seeking messages and teacher liking: Subordinate initiated relationship building in superior-subordinate dyads. Unpublished doctoral dissertation. West Virginia University.

KEY TERMS AND DEFINITIONS

Accessibility: Part of the Reactive Content dimension of Outcome Interactivity Theory, it describes the manner in which communicated online content is structured, delivered and presented, including how it is written, designed or organized, enabling each user to select and display this content in its most (personally) desirable form and sequence.

Clarity: Part of the Reactive Content dimension of OIT, it describes the degree to which sought-after content is displayed with appropriate or expected visual and conceptual organization (logical placement, sequence, etc.), and with a generally acceptable level of accuracy, clear writing style and grammatical, spelling and punctuation standards.

Instructional Design: A systematic approach to designing and creating effective instruction that incorporates learning theories, information technology, systematic analysis, educational research and management methods.

Interactivity: An observable feature of a communication event that reflects the degree to which interactive technology and content elements are influenced by relevant experiences to empower a participant to achieve a desired communication goal or outcome.

Knowledge Acquisition: A student learning outcome reflecting observable and measurable cognitive learning.

New Media: Digital, interactive or online channels of communication such as the Internet and related applications such as email, online chat and social media.

Outcome Interactivity Theory: Considers interactivity to be the result of a communication event involving the successful integration of three *predictive dimensions*: the presence of actual interactive technological features, the presence of similarly reactive content elements, and relevant user experiences that empower the user to employ these interactive elements within the communication event toward a desirable outcome.

Relevance: Part of the Reactive Content dimension of OIT, it describes the degree to which available content is desirable and consistent with a user's goals for the communication event.

Student Learning Outcomes: Cognitive, affective or behavioral changes elicited in a student as a result of an instructional event or activity.

Vividness: Part of the Reactive Content dimension of OIT, it describes the degree to which available content is displayed using high levels of graphic richness, animation and audio/visual elements (when compared to traditional media).

Chapter 9
Engaging the Digitally Engaged Student:
Comparing Technology-Mediated Communication Use and Effects on Student Learning

Scott C. D'Urso
Marquette University, USA

Craig R. Scott
Rutgers University, USA

ABSTRACT

The role of communication technologies in the learning process is both a dynamic and complex issue. Yet, we know surprisingly little about how the use of specific communication technologies may influence classroom performance, key learning outcomes, and other measures of course satisfaction. The research reported here attempts to add to our knowledge about the role of communication in the technology-enhanced classroom (TEC) education and in technology-enhanced online (TEO) education through a direct comparison of two courses. Our findings indicate additional support for "The No Significant Difference Phenomenon." Furthermore, we found that prior experiences lead students to gravitate towards their preferred learning environments, and that basic website elements are required in any learning environment to enhance student outcomes. Finally, we found that when used appropriately, the benefits of communication technology use in education outweigh many of the drawbacks.

INTRODUCTION

There are few educational settings in much of today's world without some form of advanced technology being used. From the introduction of the personal computer in some classrooms in the early and mid-1980s, to today's students carrying around laptop and tablet computers wirelessly accessing the ever-expanding virtual universe of the Internet, students and teachers are faced with many decisions regarding the use of technology in and out of the classroom. Although technology is ubiquitous in face to face (FtF) as well as

DOI: 10.4018/978-1-61350-347-8.ch009

online education, when the role of communication technology is discussed in relation to education, most of us initially think of distance education or distance learning. The United States Distance Learning Association (n.d.) defines distance learning on their website as "the acquisition of knowledge and skills through mediated information and instruction, encompassing all technologies and other forms of learning at a distance" (www.usdla.org). In such a definition, mediated information and various technologies are clearly highlighted. Over 4.6 millions students were enrolled in at least one online course in 2008, up 17% from the previous year (Allen & Seaman, 2010). With the USDLA (http://www.dltoday.net) reporting that the majority of post-secondary students in the U.S. will participate in online virtual learning at some level by 2011, our understanding of this learning environment, and the technologies that make it possible, is especially important.

The use of computer-based technologies is not only relevant to distance learning, but also has become an important part of traditional education (see Sherblom, 2010). In some instances the same technologies that may be used to deliver instruction in a distance education course today, can be used to enhance the traditional classroom environment. For example, in large classes where face-to-face (FtF) exchanges are limited, technology may provide a means for sharing information and facilitating communication between instructors, students, and others. Computer-mediated communication (CMC) use in the classroom has become a prevalent fixture in education today, according to Thompson (2008). Bejerano's (2008) research also parallels this changing environment, noting that collegiate classrooms are viewing the Internet as the new medium for instruction.

Many of the technologies used in distance learning and enhanced traditional classrooms are primarily *communication* technologies. Examples include chat rooms (Kirkpatrick, 2005), virtual worlds (Nesson & Nesson, 2008), discussion boards (Levine, 2007), and videoconferencing (Umphrey, Wickersham & Sherblom, 2008). This communication technology use is consistent with a clear desire for quality interactions in any learning environment. For example, the research indicates the most successful online courses allow for increased access to the instructors and feature more democratic discussions (Swan, 2001). And, among the 10 concepts Janicki and Liegle (2001) associate with effective web-based instruction are a variety of presentation styles, clear feedback, consistent layout, clear navigation, and available online help.

Despite this recognition of the importance of interaction and communication technologies to facilitate such exchanges, we know surprisingly little about how the use of specific communication technologies may influence classroom performance, key learning outcomes, and other measures of course satisfaction. Furthermore, while "*The No Significant Difference Phenomenon*" would suggest similarities between traditional and distance learning environments (Russell, 1999), the exact role of communication technology in classroom and dispersed settings that both make use of such tools remains unclear. The research reported here attempts to add to our knowledge about the role of communication in the technology-enhanced classroom (TEC) environment and in the technology-enhanced online (TEO) environment. We begin with a review of relevant literature leading up to our three research questions. From there we describe our research, which compares the two learning environments directly. Next we present findings, and then conclude with a discussion, limitations, and directions for continued work in this area.

BACKGROUND

Before we address the literature specific to our research, we are first compelled to clarify terms. One of the real challenges in this literature is the diverse vocabulary used to describe various learning environments. As we alluded to in our introduction, *traditional* typically, but not always, refers to classrooms largely unsupported by computer-based technology. Of course, today, a number of traditional classrooms might use technology to supplement and enhance learning. These arrangements can be labeled web- (or technology- or computer-) supported or web- (or technology- or computer-) enhanced. *Distance education* has historically included very traditional channels (e.g., audiocassettes, mailing printed papers) (see Lease & Brown, 2009). Today, the term *distance education* has become limited in its scope as more and more students enroll in online courses while enrolled in *traditional* courses at the same time and at the same institution. Distance education models may use a number of online and other computer-based technologies, much in the same way the TEO classes do. These contexts can and have been termed web-based, online, and e-learning. The term *hybrid* has more recently been used to describe courses with features of both traditional classrooms and technology-enhanced learning or even distance education (see Berger & Topol, 2001).

To hopefully clarify rather than add to the terms used, we see key differences between the location of students relative to the instructor and to one another (co-located in class versus dispersed across time/space) and the level of computer-based technology used to support the learning experience. Table 1 attempts to display these simple, but crucial differences, because the specifics regarding media attributes of a study are key to understanding the context and results of the research. Though our goal is to not to create or even elaborate on such a taxonomy, it does help illustrate our focus on what we see as two increasingly common learning environments: TEC (technology-enhanced classrooms where students are co-located with one another and the instructor on regular basis, but with use of computer-based technology in the class) and TEO (technology-enhanced online education where students are rarely, if ever, co-located with one another or the instructor for class purposes, but are connected with use of computer-based technology as a primary tool in the course). We wish to emphasize that computer-based technology is present in both of these learning environments (though not necessarily the same exact tools), but they differ primarily in terms of location of students/instructors. Although most previous literature has tended not to directly compare these two learning environments in this manner, we see them in need of this type of assessment given changes in education. Thus, the point of comparison is not about whether one has computer-based technologies, it is about the use of technologies as they support interaction (and other educational processes) and facilitate learning goals in both classroom and distance learning environments.

General Comparisons of Learning Environments

In general, the bulk of the previous literature has offered conclusions supporting the idea that learn-

Table 1. Learning contexts based on location and use of computer-based technology

		Computer-Based Technology Use	
		Non Computer-Based (Traditional)	**Computer-Based (Technology-Enhanced)**
Location of Learners Relative to Instructor and One Another	Co-located in Time/Space (Classroom)	*Traditional Classroom*	*Technology-Enhanced Classroom (TEC)*
	Dispersed Across Time/Space (Distance Learning)	*Traditional Distance Learning*	*Technology-Enhanced Online (TEO) Learning*

ers in a TEO scenario perform as effectively as students in TEC, furthering Russell's (1999) "*The No Significant Difference Phenomenon*" claim. Today there is a growing body of research on the comparison of traditional and Web-based learning indicating similar results (see White, 1999). In fact, research of this nature has become such a frequent focus of scholars examining educational environments that a website (http://www.nosignificantdifference.org/) has been created to document this research as it becomes available. As an example, Thirunaryanan and Perez-Prado (2001-2002) found that, in a comparison of pre- and post-test data on course material, there was no significant difference in the overall achievement from the students in the traditional versus the online version of the course. Furthermore, Carswell, Thomas, Petre, Price and Richards (2000) found no significant differences in learning outcomes of students enrolled in an entirely web-based computer science course as compared to their traditional course counterparts. Also, Long and Javidi (2001) found similar results in a comparison of two communication courses taught in traditional and online formats.

A comprehensive examination of comparisons of the two learning environments can be found in a report by Benoit, Benoit, Milyo, and Hansen (2006). The report concludes that, as both students and instructors become more experienced and adept with distance learning venues and related technology, learning and satisfaction with distance learning could increase. Similarly, even though Zhao, Lei, Kai & Tan's (2005) review found support for "*The No Significant Difference Phenomenon,*" there were significant differences in the research studies themselves. In particular, they note that in studies prior to 1998, there were no reported differences, however; in studies published after 1998, distance learning environments were more effective than FtF education. In particular, the studies by Benoit et al. (2006) and Zhao et al. (2005) may indicate that a transition is occurring in the learning environment, where both the *Net Generation* students and instructors are becoming more adept in maximizing the benefits of distance learning.

Other examples of differences can still be found in several studies. For example, Maki, Maki, Patterson, and Whittaker (2000) found that students in a web-based course learned more, performed better, but liked the course less than traditional ones. When the study was replicated, similar results were found (Maki & Maki, 2002). Faux and Black-Hughes (2000) found differences as well, but in the other direction. Students in their traditional course showed the most improvement between pre- and post-tests as opposed to two other courses, one an Internet-based version and the other utilizing a combination of traditional and Internet-based learning. Timmerman and Kruepke (2005) found in their meta-analysis of computer-assisted instruction (CAI) studies that a higher level of performance existed in the CAI environments. They also note that there is a great deal of ambiguity when it comes to defining 'traditional instruction' as learning technologies have become pervasive in education. They suggest that this should be recognized when evaluating studies between CAI and traditional learning environments. Whether differences exist or not, it is very difficult to compare learning environments in general without knowing more about them. We suggest one critical difference relates to the nature of the interaction in the learning context. This in turn suggests the role of communication technologies may influence various outcomes.

Importance of Interaction

Even with online courses, many students may assume a level of interaction that resembles the experience of FtF classes. It is this interaction that can often be the difference between a successful and a failed course. Moore (1993) suggested that for a successful online course there are three essential types of interaction: (a) learner-content interaction, (b) learner-learner interaction, and

(c) learner-instructor interaction. Such claims have been echoed and supported regularly in the literature. For example, Palloff and Pratt (1999) stated that key to the overall process of learning in the online environment are the interactions among the students, the interactions between students and faculty, and the opportunities for collaboration that occur as a result of these interactions. Additionally, they posit that a well-delivered course will provide multiple ways for interaction to occur, as this will deepen the learning experience and create a positive learning environment. Similarly, Swan (2001) found that among the general factors that significantly improved student's satisfaction and perceived learning in an online environment were interaction with instructors and active discussion among course participants.

More recent research also supports the need for interaction with and involvement of the instructors. An & Frick (2006) noted that a majority of students preferred FtF discussion to CMC; however, they also felt that they would learn better from instructors who were more involved and enthusiastic about CMC. Additionally, speed and convenience were viewed as more important to students regardless of the format of instruction. Focusing more on the instructor, Umphrey, Wickersham, and Sherblom (2008) found that instructor immediacy and receptivity, classroom communication connectedness/mutuality, satisfaction, quality, and interaction involvement were all viewed more negatively in the CMC environment than those in the FtF context. Both of these studies point to the need for increased instructor involvement in order to have successful CMC-based courses, whether in person or in an online context. This increased involvement is borne out in a study by Worley and Tesdell (2009) who found that instructors spend more time, nearly 20% more, per student when teaching an online course.

However, interaction differences may exist across learning environments. For example, in a study of instructors who teach in online environments, Smith and Ferguson (2003) found that online courses result in greater student-instructor equality, more explicitness in written instructions, larger workloads for the instructor, and deeper thinking in discussions. Conversely, LaRose and Whitten (2000) contend that many web-based courses fail to address the lack of interaction between students and the instructor, often seen as the leading concern of online learners. Furthermore, the interaction matters because it is related to key learning outcomes. When looking at the amount of interaction between students and instructors, Richard and Ting (1999) found that students who learned via written correspondence with their instructors were more concerned with instructor feedback, while students in the online learning environment felt that all interactions with the instructor were important. In a more recent study of online/web-based courses, Gregory (2003) found that students were generally satisfied with the quality of the instruction and education they received—and that assessment was based in large part on having meaningful real-time interaction between students and the instructor. Finally, Huang (2002) found that learner-instructor interaction was positively correlated with learner to content interaction. Hence, the literature overall appears to show that the more student-faculty interaction present in the online environment, the greater the level of student-content interaction.

The Digitally Engaged Student

One of the most significant changes related to the contemporary education scene is the transformation of students from the passive learner of the past to today's *digitally engaged student*. According to a recent report from the Pew Internet & American Life Project (Zickuhr, 2010), millennials, or those 18 - 33 years of age, are the most likely individuals, compared to other generations, to access the Internet wirelessly, use laptops or cell phones, belong to social-networking sites, send instant messages, read blogs, and participate in virtual worlds. This tech-savvy generation appears to crave access to information, using technology in nearly every aspect of life – and the education environment is no different (see Lenhart, Raine & Lewis, 2001; Livingstone, Bober & Helspur, 2005). Levin and Arafeh (2002) noted that this has led to warnings of a 'digital disconnect' between students and their instructors.

Today's *Net Generation* students are not passive in their education, but rather as Dede (2005) noted they are active learners that integrate information from a multitude of sources. More recent statistics show this trends toward greater technology involvement in student learning is not slowing down. Smith and Caruso (2010) found in a large-scale survey that 84% of college students own a laptop, with another 46% owning a desktop computer. Even greater numbers of students, 63%, own an internet-capable mobile device such as a phone or tablet. They also note that beyond the mere presence of technology, 66% of the students used a course management system in at least one of their courses, with 35% of them accessing the system daily. TEC and TEO education environments are a closer match to their non-education lives, which may explain the growing interest in understanding these environments, the students, and the technologies.

Communication Technology

Increasingly, in the context of both the TEC and TEO environments, interaction is facilitated in sizable part by various communication technologies (see Thompson, 2008). Such tools can assist with learner-content, learner-learner, and learner-instructor interactions. Web-based courses that employ multiple technologies, such as video, chat, and discussion boards, can provide students with options for how they learn and interact with others. In addition, these courses are more likely to support student involvement compared to those that rely primarily on text-based interactions.

In general, a number of scholars highlight the value of communication technologies for learning. Freitas, Myers, and Avtgis (1998) point out a number of positive aspects of online learning and the use of computer-mediated interaction, such as: (a) opportunity to participate in online discussion, (b) interaction with the course material, and (c) access to the Internet. In general, faculty typically have a positive attitude towards the use of technology in teaching (Nnazor, 1998). Less common is research on the specifics of which technologies are valuable, for what purposes, and what outcomes; however, there is some evidence of this in the existing literature.

Online discussion tools have been examined more than most technologies. Hiltz and Wellman (1997) found that the use of online discussion led to increased satisfaction, and were also associated with achievement levels that were comparable to traditional FtF classes. Previous research has shown that students perceive online discussions as more equitable and democratic compared to traditional classroom discussions (Harasim, 1990). These discussions give the students time to reflect upon contributions from other students while developing their own. Similarly, the success of online courses can be linked to the value that instructors place on these discussions (Hawisher & Pemberton, 1997). Looking at links between discussion and performance, Jiang and Ting (2000) found a positive link between perceived learning in the online environment and the percentage of course grades based on discussions, and between perceived learning and the specificity of instructors' discussion instructions. Althaus (1997) reported that individuals who were active in both computer-mediated discussions (CMD) and FtF interactions were in a superior learning environment, tended to make higher grades than non-CMD users, and reported learning more than those only using FtF interaction. More recently, Levine (2007) notes that discussion boards provide something unique that is beyond what is possible in a FtF interaction. Levine believes that this tool supports "higher order constructivist learning and the development of a learning community" (p. 68).

Other communication tools are described in the literature as well. Russo and Benson (2005) found that satisfaction with learning was more highly correlated with perceptions of others (i.e., students) than perceptions of the instructor. Additionally, they found that opportunities for students to connect with one another and the instructor, through chat, discussion boards, and interactive sessions were significantly related to the positive evaluations of the course. Wernet, Olliges, and Delicath (2000) found that students reported mixed reactions to the use of course web-tools in more of a traditional class. They perceived the use of online lecture notes as having an impact on their course performance; however, tools such as the discussion board and online grade book had no perceived impact. Other perceived successes included the use of online quizzes and tests. Stith (2000) reported that there appears to be a relationship between students' grades and the number of bulletin board articles read on the web, while visits to the course website alone had no correlation.

Conclusion to Literature Review

Collectively, we suggest that this literature suffers from several challenges. First, it is often difficult to know exactly what is being compared because of the various terms used to describe the learning contexts; furthermore, the comparability of various learning conditions can become a real challenge as well when such comparisons are attempted. Second, there is evidence of "*The No Significant Difference Phenomenon*" with some key outcomes, but other data suggest key differences in learning contexts—and in both cases the explanation for such similarities is often unclear. We suggest that variations and similarities in interaction, especially as facilitated by communication technology, may help in better understanding such findings. This leads to a third challenge in that studies specifically examining various communication technologies and how they might relate to various outcomes of interest remain rather limited.

TWO TECHNOLOGICALLY ENHANCED LEARNING CONTEXTS: STUDY CONTEXT AND RESEARCH QUESTIONS

The current study attempts to tackle the challenges outlined above through a comparison of two courses taught in consecutive semesters utilizing nearly identical course technologies, instructors, and content—but with students in either a technology-enhanced classroom (TEC) education environment or a technology-enhanced online (TEO) education environment. The different locations create potentially different needs and opportunities for how students interact with content (in-person vs. streaming video), interact with one another (mix of offline and online vs. almost completely online), and interact with the instructors (again, mix of offline and online vs. almost completely online). Thus, we are able to examine the role of different communication technologies and their influence on learning outcomes across two distinct but comparable contexts where computer-based technology is widely used in education. While McFarland and Hamilton (2005) had similar goals in their study, the current study examines two much more distinct environments, one in which there was regular FtF interaction in a more traditional manner and another where FtF interaction was nearly non-existent. The conditions in McFarland and Hamilton's study were also significantly different in that neither of the courses were conducted in a lecture format, which contrasts from the lecture format utilized in this study.

For this study, students in the initial semester participated in a classroom lecture and discussion environment, which was enhanced through the use of web-based technology (TEC). The instructor, teaching assistant, and students interacted, both during class time as well as through online synchronous and asynchronous discussions, chat and online office hours. Students also interacted somewhat extensively in online case study teams as a key assignment in the course. Class sessions were filmed showing both the instructor and the attending students. Special effort was made to capture the interactions between the instructor and students rather than simply record the presentation of the instructor. Upon completion of the semester, the video was integrated with PowerPoint slides utilized during lectures to create a series of video lectures. Each recorded lecture reflected the same content and length as the original. The following semester, the same instructor and teaching assistant taught the same course keeping everything associated with the class as similar to the first semester as possible—including assignments such as the online case studies, quizzes and exams. One major difference was the content delivery method; rather than have the students come to a lecture class three times a week for an hour, they would have access to a streaming-video version of the lectures recorded the previous semester. Students in this technology-enhanced online (TEO) education version of the course were able to view the same material and the prior classroom interactions between the instructor and students from the TEC section. A study by Boster, Meyer, Roberto, Inge and Strom (2006) provides support for the use of video-streaming as a delivery method as they note both a higher mean examination performance in both elementary and secondary courses and on average an increase in student learning outcomes. Both courses in the current study utilized web-based courseware to provide a place for additional material, activities and interaction between instructor, teaching assistant and students.

Based upon the existing literature and our goal to address some of the challenges related to the two distinct learning environments, the current research project explores the following primary research questions:

- **RQ_1:** How do the two learning environments compare on (a) the importance of various technologies, (b) satisfaction with key course elements, (c) perceived learning outcomes, and (d) objective measures of classroom performance?
- **RQ_2:** How well does the importance of various communication technologies predict (a) satisfaction with key course elements, (b) perceived learning outcomes, and (c) objective measures of classroom performance? Are there differences between the learning environments in making such predictions?

Finally, to help address the use of technology in the course, we sought to answer the following:

- **RQ_3:** How does the use of technology relate to the student opinions regarding the course?

RESEARCH METHODS

Participants and Procedures

Research participants were students in two sections of an upper division Organizational Communication course at a large public university in the United States. Students enrolled in the two classes were given extra credit in exchange for participation. In addition to completing survey questionnaires, they were told orally, FtF and online through written reminders, that log information from the course website would be used in this research—but they were also assured that none of that information would be examined until after final grades were turned in for the course. In the TEC course, 47 students completed both the pre-and post-course survey, for a response rate of 94%. In the TEO education version of the class, 71 students completed both surveys for a response rate of 81% (plus 11 more who only completed the post-course survey, bringing the partial response rate to 93%). The sample, from both the TEO and TOC sections, was comprised of 73% females and 27% males. Eighty percent of the students owned a computer, which was typically located at their home. Respondents reported taking an average of one previous online course, six courses where course management tools had been used, two where discussion boards were utilized, and 13 courses where e-mail use between students and the instructor/teaching assistant was routine.

Respondents from the two learning groups were similar on a number of the pre-course survey measures. However, there were also several significant differences on some of the 40-items from the pre-course survey. Regarding email use, TEO students reported more expertise, experience, reflection before responding, reading, and frequency of checking their email than did students in the TEC—although TEO students had generally taken fewer previous courses that utilized email. TEO students also tended to use the Internet more and have more positive attitudes about technology use than did TEC students. Finally, motives for taking the course varied significantly: TEO students took their class to avoid work/scheduling conflicts and to gain skill for the future more so than did TEC students; conversely, TEC students were significantly more motivated about engaging in class discussions than were TEO students. Given these differences, we control for key differences in the two learning groups in the statistical tests that follow.

Measures

Data for this research were collected at both the beginning and end of each of the two comparable classes. Except as noted, questionnaires were based on previous published assessments by Berge and Myers (2000) and Long and Javidi (2001), with some modifications. The pre-course survey began with 20 items assessing each student's experience with various communication technologies as well as attitudes about working on computers. We created a 5-item scale (α =.69) out of those email use items indicating differences between the learning groups and used it as a control variable in several analyses. A single item on the questionnaire also assessed level of acquaintance with others taking the class. Eleven items examined goals and motivations for taking the course (e.g., increasing knowledge, avoiding work/schedule conflicts, acquire skills for use in the future, engage in class discussion with others), which were also seen as potential controls given the importance of this individual learner characteristic.

The post-course survey contained 25 items assessing the importance of various classroom tools as they related to success in the class. Principal component analysis with varimax rotation reduced these to seven key factors accounting for 16 items and 67% of the total variance: chat and discussion board (5 items, α =.87), instructor/TA phone/office (4 items, α =.89), website basics (2 items, α =.65), instructor/TA email (2 items, α =.93), and several important one-item measures related to printed readings, in-class conversations, and online quizzes. Additionally, we also examined 11 items asking about specific learning outcomes that were directly tied to the 11 goals/motivations asked about on the pre-course survey (each of which remained its own outcome when data reduction efforts failed to produce clear factor structures).

The post-course questionnaire also measured course difficulty (5 items, α =.74), participation in the class (3 items, α =.71), instructor communication competence (5 items reduced to 4 to improve reliability, α =.68), and teaching assistant communication competence (5 items, α =.84). Additionally, we added a measure of identification with other online case study student team members (4 items, α =.82) based on Cheney's (1982) Organizational Identification Questionnaire. Finally, we included an open-ended question used to answer the final research question. In addition to the survey data, objective performance was based on total points in the course (out of 1000 maximum).

Analysis

To answer $RQ_{1a\text{-}d}$, we used ANOVA and ANCOVA to compare the two learning groups and to control for key differences in the two groups (prior email use, motivation to avoid scheduling conflicts, and motivation to engage others in classroom discussion). $RQ_{2a\text{-}d}$ uses hierarchical regressions, where we entered motivation to engage others in classroom discussion as a key control variable first, followed by the set of technology importance predictors on step 2, followed by the learning group type on a final step; R^2 and R^2_{change}, along with individual beta weights are used to answer the research questions. Given the somewhat exploratory nature of the research, the nonrandom sample, and the relatively small sample size, we use a significance criterion of $p \leq .05$, but provide some key results that approached, but did not achieve significance as one way to evaluate the research.

For the final research question, one author and a trained undergraduate research assistant familiar with the course both coded all the open-ended comments from the questionnaires (44 from the TEC section and 80 from the TEO class). Each entire comment made by a respondent was rated as either positive, negative, mixed positive/negative, or all neutral. Additionally, each comment was coded for the type of technology mentioned, which fell into 12 categories: none/general, announcements, chat, forums/discussion boards, website/WebCT generally, logs/archives, email, quizzes, streaming video/lectures, online notes, other, and multiple above categories. After training together on the first 10 items, the coders then individually coded all remaining comments. Although overall initial agreement was only 68%, we note that disagreements were readily resolved through discussion and the large number of categories (12×4) contributed to the disagreement rate.

RESULTS

Research Question 1

RQ_{1a} asks how the two learning environments compare on the importance of various technologies for success in the course. ANOVA reveals statistically significant differences between TEC (M = 3.28) and TEO (M = 3.83) students in importance of chat/discussion boards, $F(1, 126) = 4.70$, $p = .03$, and importance of in-class conversations with others (M = 4.42 and 3.28, respectively), $F(1, 126) = 6.78$, $p = .01$. Other results approached significance, such as the importance of website basics (M = 6.42 and 6.57, respectively), $F(1, 126) = 3.01$, $p = .09$, and importance of email (M = 5.63 and 6.14, respectively), $F(1, 126) = 3.48$, $p = .06$. When controlling for prior email use and the key motivations related to scheduling conflicts and engaging in classroom discussion, learning type continues to account for statistically significant difference in the importance of chats/discussion boards, $F(1, 111) = 9.33$, $p = .003$, $\eta^2_p = .08$, and email, $F(1, 111) = 2.76$, p = .10, $\eta^2_p = .03$; but not for website basics ($p = .40$) nor in-class conversations ($p = .13$).

RQ_{1b} asks how the two learning environments compare on satisfaction with key course elements. ANOVA reveals only one statistically significant difference between TEC (M = 4.47) and TEO (M = 3.99) students related to course participation, $F(1, 125) = 7.59$, $p = .01$. When key control variables are entered, the effect for learning group type disappears here ($p = .18$). RQ_{1c} compares the two learning environments as they relate to perceived learning outcomes. ANOVA reveals statistically significant differences between TEC (M = 4.93) and TEO (M = 5.78) students related to avoiding work and class scheduling conflicts, $F(1, 126) = 10.72$, $p = .001$, and for contributing to the field of organizational communication (M = 3.53 and 4.21, respectively), $F(1, 126) = 5.45$, $p = .02$. These differences persist even after considering key control variables for both avoiding work and scheduling conflicts, $F(1, 111) = 5.68$, $p = .02$, $\eta^2_p = .05$, and for contributing to the field, $F(1, 111) = 9.45$, $p = .003$, $\eta^2_p = .08$. Finally, in answer to RQ_{1d}, there are no statistically significant differences between the two learning groups in terms of objective measures of classroom performance, $F(1, 127) = .645$, $p = .42$.

Research Question 2

RQ_2 asks how the importance of various technologies predicts other variables and whether there are differences between the learning environments in making such predictions. Based on correlations, we selected only the most relevant technology importance variables (chat/discussion board, website basics, email, and traditional phone/office) and the single most important control variable (motive to engage in classroom discussion) for inclusion in these analyses. Doing so was necessary to limit the number of variables included relative to sample size (Tabachnick & Fidell, 2001). After entering the control initially followed by the four technology importance variables, we entered learning group type on a final step.

Several learning outcomes are predicted by these variables. The control variable predicts the learning outcome related to networking with experts in the communication field, $R = .25$, $R^2_{adjusted} = .05$, $F(1, 109) = 7.07$, $p = .009$. Adding in the technology importance predictors results in a statistically significant improvement to the model, $R = .44$, $R^2_{change} = .13$, $F(4, 105) = 4.27$, $p = .003$. In this equation, the only statistically significant individual predictor is importance of chat/discussion boards for success, $\beta = .34$, $p = .002$. Adding in learning group type to the regression equation did not result in a statistically significant change in R^2. As for the outcome of avoiding work and class scheduling conflicts, neither the control nor the technology importance variables were predictive; however, learning group type resulted in a near statistically significant change in R^2, $R = .33$, $R^2_{change} = .03$, $F(1, 104) = 4.27$, $p = .06$. In addition to the predictive power of learning group type, importance of website basics was also a statistically significant predictor in this model, $\beta = 2.03$, $p = .05$. Regarding the outcome of contributing to the field of organizational communication research, the control variable was not predictive; however, the group learning type, $R = .34$, $R^2_{change} = .03$, $F(1, 104) = 4.02$, $p = .05$, adds a statistically significant explanation. Also, the technology importance variables approached significance, $R = .29$, $R^2_{change} = .08$, $F(4, 105) = 2.28$, $p = .07$. In the final model with all predictors, only group learning type is a statistically significant individual predictor, $\beta = .21$, $p = .05$.

Next, the control variable predicts the learning outcome related to engaging in classroom discussion with others in the course, $R = .29$, $R^2_{adjusted} = .07$, $F(1, 109) = 9.63$, $p = .002$. Adding in the technology importance predictors results in a statistically significant improvement to the model, $R = .43$, $R^2_{change} = .10$, $F(4, 105) = 3.24$, $p = .02$. In that model, not only is the control variable still statistically significant, but so is importance of traditional phone/office, $\beta = .28$, $p = .01$. The importance of website basics also approached significance, $\beta = .18$, $p = .06$. Learning group types does not add statistically significant explanation to the other variables in the model. Finally with respect to learning outcomes, the control variable predicts having acquired skills in occupation/job, $R = .25$, $R^2_{adjusted} = .06$, $F(1, 108) = 7.32$, $p = .008$. Adding in the technology importance predictors results in a statistically significant improvement to the model, $R = .49$, $R^2_{change} = .16$, $F(4, 104) = 5.38$, $p = .001$. In that model, not only is the control variable still statistically significant, but so is importance of chat/discussion board, $\beta = .29$, $p = .007$, and importance of website basics, $\beta = .25$, $p = .006$. Learning group types does not add statistically significant explanation to the other variables in the model.

Regarding other variables, the control variable does not predict course instructor communication competence. Adding in the technology importance predictors results in a statistically significant improvement to the model, $R = .39$, $R^2_{change} = .11$, $F(4, 105) = 4.50$, $p = .002$. The only significant individual predictor is website basics, $\beta = .26$, $p = .007$, and again, learning group type does not add statistically significant explanation to the model. A nearly identical picture emerges for course TA communication competence. The control variable does not predict course TA communication competence, but adding in the technology importance predictors results in a statistically significant improvement to the model, $R = .33$, $R^2_{change} = .06$, $F(4, 105) = 3.02$, $p = .02$. The only statistically significant individual predictor is website basics, $\beta = .28$, $p = .004$, and again, learning group type does not add statistically significant explanation to the model. Finally, the control variable predicts identification with online case study team, $R = .20$, $R^2_{adjusted} = .03$, $F(1, 109) = 4.33$, $p = .04$. Adding in the technology importance predictors results in a statistically significant improvement to the model, $R = .38$, $R^2_{change} = .11$, $F(4, 105) = 3.31$, $p = .01$. The only individual predictor to approach significance is website basics, $\beta = .17$, $p = .08$, and again, learning group type does not add statistically significant explanation to the model.

Research Question 3

RQ_3 was answered with responses to an open-ended survey question: "How did the use of technology and online features of the class impact your opinion/views of the course?" Tables 2 and 3 display representative comments from the two learning environments. In both environments, positive comments are most prevalent, followed by mixed positive/negative, negative, and then neutral. The most common "technologies" referenced in the remarks of students in both learning environments are "general" and those mentioning "multiple technologies." However, we note that the TEC learning environment comments are spread across only four tools, whereas students in the TEO learning environment discuss 10 different technology categories. Beyond the general and multiple technologies discussed, there are a number of comments about the nature of the streaming video/lectures in the online-dispersed learning environment (but no mention of lectures during the traditional environment).

DISCUSSION

This research examines the use and importance of communication technology in two different learning contexts where it is used: TEC and TEO learning environments. Furthermore, it examines how those tools relate to learning and other key outcomes. Based on the findings reported here, we are able to draw several general conclusions.

First, we note that the students who selected these different learning environments were different from one another—especially in terms of prior technology use as well as in general motivation/goals for taking the course. Such differences are consistent with literature suggesting that individual motivations and experience may vary by student (Vonderwell, 2003). It is important to note that in the department where the two courses researched here were taught, students had options for taking other sections of the course where technology would not have been as prominent.

Second, there is substantial evidence of the "*The No Significant Difference Phenomenon.*" None of the course element satisfaction variables, nor the total points in the class, were different across learning contexts. Only a few of the 11 learning outcomes were statistically different, and even most of the technology variables were no longer different after control variables were included to adjust for initial differences in students. Even as we consider the comments from students about the role of technology in their class, the nature of their comments are very similar across learning contexts. Therefore, these findings provide additional support for "*The No Significant Difference Phenomenon*" between the technology-enhanced

Table 2. Positive comments about the role of communication technology as related to class

Course Type	Representative Comments
Technology-Enhanced Classroom Education	"It definitely enhanced the course by organizing all of the thoughts and the events of the class. It was like insurance for students because you could always stay connected to what was going on and the progress you were making in the class." "In respect to the group projects, quizzes, and some participation point activities, I loved the online features. I also liked how grades and comments were done online! In regards to all these things, it made everything convenient...it's easy to do group things online and not have to worry about having to all meet at a certain time." "It made me realize how useful technology and online features could be in helping to teach a class. The use of technology better prepared us for class – through online lecture notes, assignments, and case study requirements. I was very pleased with the use of technology in this course and I believe it really made the course appealing – I would like to see more of this used in future classes."
Technology-Enhanced Online Education	"This course helped me to see just how important technology is and can be in organizations. Taking an online course helped me to feel confident that I can meet the technology demands that I will face in the future. The technology brought a lot to the course; it changed things up a bit and made the class more exciting." "I really enjoyed this course. Everything was well structured and easy to follow. Having the online notes to follow along with videos was very helpful. Since this course was so organized it made it all the technology involved simple with little problems. Questions were responded to immediately (even though asynchronous). The use of technology and online features influenced my opinion greatly. It made the course awesome and ever more interesting." "This was my first online course and I really enjoyed it. It allowed me to schedule lectures into my day at a time that was appropriate for my individual needs. Though some might find it difficult to keep up with this course work, online forums, and chats made retaining the information a lot easier for me."

Table 3. Negative comments about the role of communication technology as related to class

Course Type	Representative Comments
Technology-Enhanced Classroom Education	"I hated doing online case studies as a group. Their inability to get their act together on time deeply hindered our group grade and my overall grade...Doing group work (not online) is easier to set deadlines and to get people to start the ball rolling... Online, people were harder to influence." "To be honest, it was more of a burden than a learning tool, something that I had to get done." "I didn't feel there was worthwhile communication in our online case studies...there was so little communication and motivation to participate...I felt my group members were not discussing the case with the rest of us, but rather writing opinions and not responding to the rest."
Technology-Enhanced Online Education	"I found it difficult to stay motivated for the course material. Going to an actual classroom and experiencing the interaction with a professor is much more valuable in terms of motivation than I thought it would be. In terms of the actual online tools used...there wasn't nearly the sense of community that gets built in a face to face class setting." "The ability to set your own schedule with the technology was helpful, but it increases opportunities for procrastination." "It was not as easy or convenient as I was hoping. The class took up a lot of time and more work than just sitting in the actual classroom for 3 hours a week. The lectures were hard to pay full attention to and a lot of other work was also involved... it took up more work and time then most other classes."

classroom and technology-enhanced online education courses (which we believe have only rarely been compared). At the same time, these results seem to question conventional wisdom about what must surely be differences in two seemingly very distinct ways of teaching.

Third, while there are few statistically significant differences in these learning contexts overall, there are some differences related to the importance of communication technology. In fact, there are more differences related to technology importance than for the various outcome variables; and, in most cases, learning context fails to add additional explanation above and beyond that accounted for by communication technology variables when predicting those outcomes. More specifically, the TEO students viewed the chat/discussion board, website basics, and email as more important than did TEC students. Conversely, the TEC students felt that the in-class conversations were clearly more important than did their TEO counterparts. Additionally, even though students in both learning environments were generally positive about the various technologies we examined in terms of their role in the course, there were comments about a much larger range of technologies from the TEO students. It may be that a student in that setting seeks out technological alternatives for FtF interaction that would normally occur during the classroom setting. This seems consistent with some previous research, including that of Walther and Parks (2002). In short, students adapt to their surroundings by maximizing their communication through available means and channels—and may use a wider range of tools when in-class conversations are not a viable option.

As one final overall conclusion, some communication technology importance variables are predictive of more outcomes than are others. Consistent with existing literature, the use of chat and discussion board technologies were predictive of outcomes such as acquiring skills for work and networking with experts. In these classes we had guest experts speak to the students—and especially in the TEO class students would use discussion boards to post question in advance and the chat tool was used for the actual interaction with the guest. Additionally, students in the TEO class who felt that taking such a course provided them with special technology-related skills may have also been the ones who were actively using and valuing primary interaction tools like discussion boards and chat. However, the most predictive of the technology importance variables were the website basics (which included web page announcements and basic assignment descriptions). The importance of these website basic features positively predicted learning outcomes of engaging in class discussion and acquisition of skill for work. Additionally, the website basics were associated with communication competence of instructor, communication competence of TA, and even identification with student case study team. We suspect that providing useful announcements on the website and providing clear and detailed assignment descriptions helps students in both learning environments by reducing uncertainty. Indeed, the mean technology importance scores for both learning contexts on this factor are well above 6 on a 7-point scale.

Implications

The results reported here have several implications for students and instructors in courses utilizing technology. First, the findings suggest different students—based primarily on prior experience with tools such as email and distinct motivations/goals—gravitate toward either the TEC or TEO settings. Students should therefore think about their prior experiences and their goals when self-selecting into a TEC classroom versus TEO courses. For instructors and academic departments, it may be wise when possible to provide both types of learning environments so students can choose what is most appropriate for them. We had that luxury with this particular course, so students in the TEO course were generally ones who chose to be there rather than in a classroom setting—had that not been the situation, our findings may have differed somewhat.

The findings in support of "*The No Significant Difference Phenomenon*" can be used to support opposing arguments. For some, our results would further confirm claims that there is no real advantage of dispersing students in a distance education course. Even if technology is used in both learning contexts, tools such as streaming video servers are more expensive and the workload is often greater for faculty in distance education contexts. Such views may lead some to suggest that the TEO context has little to offer, but could be used as a last resort in situations where more TEC settings are not possible. Another view on this, and one we subscribe to, is that the results show there is no significant decline in learning. Thus, providing different learning options such as the TEO context may better meet certain students' needs and help them to learn effectively. There may be no difference in learning outcomes, but if students are able to take courses consistent with their own learning abilities and goals, then the overall learning may improve (though we do not have data to directly test that specific claim).

The importance of website basics suggests that even if one does little else with technology, there are some key minimums that will enhance a number of outcomes regardless of learning context. Instructors need to be sure to keep announcements current and helpful. Furthermore, detailed assignment descriptions should be included on the website. Students will find these most useful when they actually check and read them. To a somewhat lesser extent, there are clear positives associated with using tools such as discussion boards and chat. We think the idea of the virtual online guest, which is similar to what Russo and Chadwick (2001; Chadwick & Russo, 2002) call virtual visiting professors, is a wonderful use of these tools to facilitate student interaction with others outside the classroom (in addition to the interaction with one another and with the instructor that is seen as so important to learning).

Finally, the positive views that students in both environments had about technology suggests that when it is used appropriately, its benefits can outweigh any drawbacks. We are as aware as anyone that sometimes technology is used poorly in the classroom. But, in most ways, students perceive a number of positives related to the communication technologies examined here. The nature of our findings may serve to provide guidelines for teachers especially as they decide the extent to which they wish to include technology in their courses. The negative comments and mixed comments also remind us that problems remain and not all students respond in equal ways about the role of technology in education.

FUTURE RESEARCH DIRECTIONS

Future research in this area should begin by addressing some of the key limitations of the research reported here. Although we think the sort of comparison we were able to make with identical content and teachers as well as very similar technologies across two learning environments is valuable, it too has problems. For example, we, as instructors, were more experienced by the time we did the TEO version of the course and the students were clearly not identical—all of which suggests efforts have to be made to find reasonable comparisons to make when examining differences (and similarities) across learning contexts. Another limitation was that we lost some of the log data on usage of various website tools—meaning that we relied heavily on self-reports of usage. Greater use of behavioral and other log data could add additional information.

Now that we have some ideas about the extent to which communication technologies may matter in these learning contexts, and even which ones are key, we need to know more about what was actually communicated using these technologies. What was communicated in the website announcements and assignment descriptions that apparently made them so important? Which uses of the chat and discussion board tools, and what comments on them actually made a difference for students? Future research should begin to focus even more on the actual messages communicated to/from students, instructors, and others.

Finally, future research must continue to be very careful about exactly what is being compared. As we have noted, this is often not clear in the literature when one person's use of the term "*traditional*" classroom includes new communication technologies but another's use of that same terms does not. We think one of the most appropriate points of comparison is to examine differences based on the general location of students and instructors relevant to one another (co-located versus dispersed), recognizing that technology may be used extensively in both settings. Certainly, other work should examine hybrid classes and other variations—while also being sensitive to terminology used and what exactly is being compared or examined.

CONCLUSION

We have little doubt that new communication technologies will continue to be part of most educational settings. We have even less doubt that, when used appropriately, they can serve a vital role in facilitating the sorts of interaction that are so crucial to learning in both traditional classroom and more online settings. As a result, scholarship that continues to examine the role of communication technology in learning must move forward. As it does, researchers would be wise to continue to consider a sizable variety of communication technologies—ranging from very basic one-way information sharing found on course websites to much more interactive technologies such as social media—as all being tools relevant to the *Net Generation* of digitally-engaged students. We hope the research reported here is a useful step in this direction.

REFERENCES

Allen, I. E., & Seaman, J. (2010). *Learning on demand: Online education in the United States, 2009*. Babson Park, MA: Babson Survey Research Group.

Althaus, S. L. (1997). Computer-mediated communication in the university classroom: An experiment with on-line discussions. *Communication Education*, *46*, 158–174. doi:10.1080/03634529709379088

An, Y. J., & Frick, T. (2006). Student perceptions of asynchronous computer-mediated communication in face-to-face courses. *Journal of Computer-Mediated Communication*, *11*(2). Retrieved from http://jcmc.indiana.edu/vol11/issue2/an.html. doi:10.1111/j.1083-6101.2006.00023.x

Bejerano, A. R. (2008). Raising the question #11 – The genesis and evolution of online degree programs: Who are they for and what have we lost along the way? *Communication Education*, *57*, 408–414. doi:10.1080/03634520801993697

Benoit, P. J., Benoit, W. L., Milyo, J., & Hansen, G. J. (2006). *The effects of traditional vs. web-assisted instruction on student learning and satisfaction*. Columbia, MO: University of Missouri.

Berge, Z., & Myers, B. (2000). Evaluating computer mediated communication courses in higher education. *Journal of Educational Computing Research*, *23*, 431–450.

Berger, K. A., & Topol, M. T. (2001). Technology to enhance learning: Use of a web site platform in traditional classes and distance learning. *Marketing Education Review*, *11*, 15–26.

Boster, F. J., Meyer, G. S., Roberto, A. J., Inge, C., & Strom, R. (2006). Some effects of video streaming on educational achievement. *Communication Education*, *55*, 46–62. doi:10.1080/03634520500343392

Carswell, L., Thomas, P., Petre, M., Price, B., & Richards, M. (2000). Distance education via the Internet: The student experience. *British Journal of Educational Technology*, *31*, 29–46. doi:10.1111/1467-8535.00133

Chadwick, S. A., & Russo, T. C. (2002). Virtual visiting professors: Communicative, pedagogical, and technological collaboration. In Comeaux, P. (Ed.), *Communication and collaboration in the online classroom* (pp. 75–91). Bolton, MA: Anker.

Cheney, G. (1982). *Identification as process and product: A field study*. Unpublished master's thesis, Purdue University, West Lafayette, IN.

Dede, C. (2005). Planning for "Neomillenial" learning styles: Shifts in student's learning style will prompt a shift to active construction of knowledge through mediated immersion. *EDUCAUSE Quarterly*, *28*, 7–12.

Faux, T. L., & Black-Hughes, C. (2000). A comparison of using the Internet versus lectures to teach social work history. *Research on Social Work Practice*, *10*, 454–466.

Frietas, F. A., Myers, S. A., & Avtgis, T. A. (1998). Student perceptions of instructor immediacy in conventional and distributed learning classrooms. *Communication Education*, *47*, 366–372. doi:10.1080/03634529809379143

Gregory, V. L. (2003). Student perceptions of the effectiveness of Web-based distance education. *New Library World*, *104*, 426–431. doi:10.1108/03074800310504366

Harasim, L. (1990). *On-line education: Perspectives on a new environment*. New York, NY: Praeger.

Hawisher, G. E., & Pemberton, M. A. (1997). Writing across the curriculum encounters asynchronous learning networks or WAC meets up with ALN. [Online]. *Journal of Asynchronous Learning Networks*, *1*(1).

Hiltz, S. R., & Wellman, B. (1997). Asynchronous learning networks as a virtual classroom. *Communications of the ACM*, *40*, 44–48. doi:10.1145/260750.260764

Huang, H. (2002). Student perceptions in an online mediated environment. *International Journal of Instructional Media*, *29*, 405–422.

Janicki, T., & Liegle, J. O. (2001). Development and evaluation of a framework for creating Web-based learning modules: A pedagogical and systems approach. *Journal of Asynchronous Learning Networks*, *5*(1). Retrieved from http://sloanconsortium.org/sites/default/files/v5n1_janicki_1.pdf.

Jiang, M., & Ting, E. (2000). A study of factors influencing student's perceived learning in a Web-based course environment. *International Journal of Educational Telecommunications*, *6*, 317–338.

Kirkpatrick, G. (2005). Online chat facilities as pedagogic tools: A case study. *Active Learning in Higher Education*, *6*, 145–159. doi:10.1177/1469787405054239

LaRose, R., & Whitten, P. (2000). Re-thinking instructional immediacy for web courses: A social cognitive exploration. *Communication Education*, *48*, 320–338. doi:10.1080/03634520009379221

Lease, A. J., & Brown, T. A. (2009). Distance learning past, present and future. *International Journal of Instructional Media*, *36*, 415–426.

Lenhart, A., Rainie, L., & Lewis, O. (2001). *Teenage life online*. Washington, DC: Pew Internet & American Life Project.

Levin, D., & Arafeh, S. (2002). *The digital disconnect: The widening gap between internet-savvy students and their schools*. Washington, DC: Pew Internet & American Life Project.

Levine, S. J. (2007). The online discussion board as a tool for online learning. *New Directions for Adult and Continuing Education*, *113*, 65–74.

Livingstone, S., Bober, M., & Helsper, E. (2005). *Internet literacy among children and young people*. London, UK: London School of Economics.

Long, L. W., & Javidi, A. (2001). *A comparison of course outcomes: Online distance learning versus traditional classroom settings*. Paper presented at the Annual Conference of the National Communication Association, Atlanta, Georgia.

Maki, R. H., Maki, W. S., Patterson, M., & Whitaker, P. D. (2000). Evaluation of a web-based introductory psychology course: I. Learning and satisfaction in on-line versus lecture courses. *Behavior Research Methods, Instruments, & Computers*, *32*, 230–239. doi:10.3758/BF03207788

Maki, W. S., & Maki, R. H. (2002). Multimedia comprehension skill predicts differential outcomes of web-based and lecture outcomes. *Journal of Experimental Psychology. Applied*, *8*, 85–98. doi:10.1037/1076-898X.8.2.85

McFarland, D., & Hamilton, D. (2005). Factors affecting student performance and satisfaction: Online versus traditional course delivery. *Journal of Computer Information Systems*, *46*(2), 25–32.

Moore, M. (1993). Three types of interaction. In Boyd, R. D., & Apps, J. W. (Eds.), *Redefining the discipline of adult education*. San Francisco, CA: Jossey-Bass.

Nesson, R., & Nesson, C. (2008). The case for education in virtual worlds. *Space and Culture*, *11*, 273–284. doi:10.1177/1206331208319149

Nnazor, R. (1998). *Understanding the advent of information technology in teaching at the university: A case study of the University of British Columbia.* Unpublished Doctoral dissertation, University of British Columbia, BC.

Palloff, R. M., & Pratt, K. (1999). *Building learning communities in cyberspace: Effective strategies for the online classroom*. San Francisco, CA: Jossey-Bass.

Richard, J., & Ting, E. (1999). *Making the most of interaction: What instructors do that most affects students' perceptions of learning.* Paper presented at the 5th International Conference on Asynchronous Learning, College Park, MD.

Russell, T. (1999). *The no significant difference phenomenon*. Chapel Hill, NC: Office of Instructional Telecommunication, North Carolina State University.

Russo, T., & Benson, S. (2005). Learning with invisible others: Perceptions of online presence and their relationship to cognitive and affective learning. *Journal of Educational Technology & Society*, *8*(1), 54–62.

Russo, T. C., & Chadwick, S. A. (2001). Making connections: Enhancing classroom learning with a virtual visiting professor. *Communication Teacher*, *15*, 7–9.

Sherblom, J. C. (2010). The computer-mediated communication (CMC) classroom: A challenge of medium, presence, interaction, identity, and relationship. *Communication Education*, *59*, 497–523. doi:10.1080/03634523.2010.486440

Smith, G. G., & Ferguson, D. (2003). The Web versus the classroom: Instructor experiences in discussion-based and mathematics-based disciplines. *Journal of Educational Computing Research*, *29*, 29–59. doi:10.2190/PEA0-T6N4-PU8D-CFUF

Smith, S. D., & Caruso, J. B. (2010). *The ECAR study of undergraduate students and information technology, 2010*. Boulder, CO: Educause Center for Applied Research.

Stith, B. (2000). Web-enhanced lecture course scores big with students and faculty. *Technology Horizons in Education Journal*, *27*, 20–28.

Swan, K. (2001). Virtual interaction: Design factors affecting student satisfaction and perceived learning in asynchronous online courses. *Distance Education*, *22*, 306–331. doi:10.1080/0158791010220208

Tabachnick, B. G., & Fidell, L. S. (2001). *Using multivariate statistics* (4th ed.). Needham Heights, MA: Allyn & Bacon.

Thirunarayanan, M. O., & Perez-Prado, A. (2001-2002). Comparing Web-based and classroom-based learning: A quantitative study. *Journal of Research on Technology in Education*, *34*, 131–137.

Thompson, B. (2008). Characteristics of parent-teacher e-mail communication. *Communication Education*, *57*, 201–223. doi:10.1080/03634520701852050

Timmerman, C. E., & Kruepke, K. A. (2006). Computer-assisted instruction, media richness, and college student performance. *Communication Education*, *55*, 73–104.

Umphrey, L. R., Wickersham, J. A., & Sherblom, J. C. (2008). Student perceptions of the instructor's relational characteristics, the classroom communication experience, and the interaction involvement in face-to-face versus video conference instruction. *Communication Research Reports*, *25*, 102–114. doi:10.1080/08824090802021954

United States Distance Learning Association. (n.d.) *Definition: Distance learning*. Retrieved January 17, 2007, from http://www.usdla.org.

Vonderwell, S. (2003). An examination of asynchronous communication experience and perspectives of students in an online course: A case study. *The Internet and Higher Education*, *6*, 77–90. doi:10.1016/S1096-7516(02)00164-1

Walther, J. B., & Parks, M. R. (2002). Cues filtered out, cues filtered in: Computer-mediated communication and relationships. In Knapp, M. L., & Daly, J. A. (Eds.), *Handbook of interpersonal communication* (pp. 529–563). Thousand Oaks, CA: Sage.

Wernet, S. P., Olliges, R. H., & Delicath, T. A. (2000). Postcourse evaluations of WebCT (Web Course Tools) classes by social work students. *Research on Social Work Practice*, *10*, 487–504.

White, S. E. (1999). *The effectiveness of Web-based instruction: A case study.* Paper presented at the joint meeting of the Central States Communication Association and the Southern States Communication Association, St Louis, MO.

Worley, W. L., & Tesdell, L. S. (2009). Instructor time and effort in online and face-to-face teaching: Lessons learned. *IEEE Transactions on Professional Communication*, *52*, 138–151. doi:10.1109/TPC.2009.2017990

Zhao, Y., Lei, J., Lai, B. Y. C., & Tan, H. S. (2005). What makes a difference? A practical analysis of research on the effectiveness of distance education. *Teachers College Record*, *107*, 1836–1884. doi:10.1111/j.1467-9620.2005.00544.x

Zickuhr, K. (2010). [Washington, DC: Pew Internet & American Life Project.]. *Generations (San Francisco, Calif.)*, 2010.

ADDITIONAL READING

Bates, A. W. (2005). *Technology, e-learning and distance education*. New York: Routledge.

Bennett, S., Maton, K., & Kervin, L. (2008). The 'digital natives' debate: A critical review of the evidence. *British Journal of Educational Technology*, *39*, 775–786. doi:10.1111/j.1467-8535.2007.00793.x

Boyer, N. R., Maher, P. A., & Kirkman, S. (2006). Transformative Learning in online settings: The use of self-direction, metacognition, and collaborative learning. *Journal of Transformative Education*, *4*, 335–361. doi:10.1177/1541344606295318

Carlson, S. (2005). The Net Generation goes to college. *The Chronicle of Higher Education*, (October): 7. Retrieved from http://chronicle.com/free/v52/i07/07a03401.htm.

Clark, R. C., & Mayer, R. E. (2011). *E-learning and the science of instruction: Proven guidelines for consumers and designers of multimedia learning* (3rd ed.). San Francisco: Pfeiffer.

Conger, S. B. (2005). If there is *No Significant Difference*, why should we care? *Journal of Educators Online, 2*, Retrieved from http://www.thejeo.com/Basu%20Conger%20Final.pdf.

Daymont, T., & Blau, G. (2008, May 1). Student performance in online and traditional sections of an undergraduate management course. *Institute of Behavioral and Applied Management*, 274-294.

Feiertag, J., & Berge, Z. L. (2008). Training generation N: How educators should approach the net generation. *Education + Training, 50*, 457–464.

Garrison, D. R., & Anderson, T. (2003). [st century: A framework for research and practice. New York: Routledge Falmer.]. *E-learning*, 21.

Horton, W. (2011). *E-learning by design* (2nd ed.). San Francisco: Pfeiffer.

Howe, N., & Strauss, W. (2000). *Millennials rising: The next great generation*. New York: Vintage Books.

Kelly, O. (2007). Moving to blended delivery in a polytechnic: Shifting the mindset of faculty and institutions. In Bullen, M., & Janes, D. (Eds.), *Making the transition to e-learning: Strategies and issues* (pp. 35–45). Pennsylvania: Information Science Publishing.

Matheos, K. (2003). *Effective teaching with technology in higher education*. San Francisco: Jossey-Bass.

Maushak, N. J., Chen, H. H., Martin, L., Shaw, B. C. Jr, & Unfred, D. (2001). Distance education: Looking beyond "no significant difference.". *Quarterly Review of Distance Education, 2*(2), 119–140.

Oblinger, D. (2003). Boomers, Gen-Xers and Millennials: understanding the new students. *EDUCAUSE Review*, 38, 4, July/August, 37–47.

Rajasingham, L. (2011). New challenges facing universities in the Internet-driven global environment. European Journal of Open, Distance and E-learning. Retrieved from http://www.eurodl.org/index.php?p=current&article=430.

Sandholtz, J. H., Ringstaff, C., & Dwyer, D. C. (1997). *Teaching with technology: Creating student-centered classrooms*. New York: Teachers College Press.

Schwier, R. A., & Dykes, M. E. (2007). The continuing struggle for community and content in blended technology courses in higher education. In M. Bullen, M., & D. Janes (Eds.), *Making the transition to e-learning: Issues and strategies* (pp. 157-172). Hershey, PA: Idea Group.

Yuen, A., & Ma, W. (2008). Exploring teacher acceptance of e-learning technology. *Asia-Pacific Journal of Teacher Education, 36*, 229–243. doi:10.1080/13598660802232779

Zemke, R. (2001). Here come the Millennials. *Training (New York, N.Y.), 38*, 44–49.

KEY TERMS AND DEFINITIONS

Computer-Mediated Communication (CMC): Communication that is mediated through some form of electronic or computer-based system.

Distance Learning / Education: The acquisition of knowledge and skills through mediated information and instruction, encompassing all technologies and other forms of learning at a distance.

E-Learning: Education environments that are primarily technology- or web-based in nature that allow learning to occur without the instructor and students being co-present in the same physical location.

Face-to-Face Communication (FtF): Communication that occurs between individuals who are co-present in the same location and are able to send and receive both verbal and non-verbal messages without mediation.

Hybrid Learning: Education environments that blend traditional educational methods with those based on technology and/or online tools.

No Significant Difference Phenomenon: Education phenomenon based on a comprehensive research project (Russell, 1999) examining more than 350 studies that document no significant differences in student outcomes between alternate modes of education delivery.

Technology Enhanced Classroom (TEC) Education: Education that occurs in classrooms where students are co-located with one another and the instructor on regular basis, but with use of computer-based technology in the class.

Technology Enhanced Online (TEO) Education: Education that occurs when students are rarely, if ever, co-located with one another or the instructor for class purposes, but are connected with use of computer-based technology as a primary tool in the course.

Traditional Learning: Education environments that require that both instructor and students are co-present, where the majority of instruction occurs through direct interaction between instructor and students, and where little if any modern technology is used.

Section 3
Social Media for Digital Learners

There is nothing wrong with change, if it is in the right direction (Winston Churchill).

If there is one defining characteristic of the Net Generation, it is the use of social media. Social media, in its many forms, is ever growing. Some widely accepted social media forums include blogs and vlogs, microblogs, wikis, podcasts, photo sharing sites, social bookmarking, gaming and virtual worlds (like World of Warcraft), as well as those giants of social media, Facebook, MySpace, and Twitter. Wholeheartedly embraced by many (not just the Net Generation, but as fervently by Gen Xers and some Boomers), social media are only cautiously utilized by educators (Selwyn, 2010).

Utilized effectively, social media offer an additional means of expanding our pedagogical toolbox, as the chapters in this section demonstrate. Maureen Ebben, Russell Kivatisky, and Daniel Panici study wiki use to promote group work and collaboration in the classroom. Susanne Croasdaile, Rachel Angel, Erin Carr, Lucy Hudson, and Carin Ursey examine the use of blogs in the classroom and provide best practices for their use. Hilary Wilder, Geraldine Mongillo, and Carrie Eunyoung Hong consider the use of Twitter to promote traditional writing by first year students. Marsha Huber, Jean Kelly, and Shirine Mafi discuss their use of blogs and wikis into their courses, using assignments based on Fink's Paradigm of Significant Learning. Shannan Butler and Corinne Weisgerber examine ways in which students can use social media technologies, such as Twitter, blogs and social bookmarking and others, to build Personal Learning Networks to support learning goals. Keri Stephens, Melissa Murphy, and Kerk Kee utilize webconferencing to engage disconnected students. Finally, William Gibbs examines current principles of instruction, learning, instructional design, and learning theory, and their relevance to the education of digital learners.

The materials in this section are meant to be descriptive, not prescriptive, to provide ideas for those educators wishing to broaden their teaching repertory. We are not advocating any one best way of using social media in the classroom, but rather providing resources and ideas to engage educators as well as learners.

REFERENCE

Selwyn, N. (2010). Web 2.0 and the school of the future, today. In OECD (Ed.), *Research and innovation inspired by technology, driven by pedagogy: A systemic approach to technology-based school innovations*.

Chapter 10
Critical Insights:
Net Generation, Wikis, and Group Collaboration

Maureen Ebben
University of Southern Maine, USA

Russell Kivatisky
University of Southern Maine, USA

Daniel A. Panici
University of Southern Maine, USA

ABSTRACT

Harnessing the potential of technology for increased student engagement may be a key strategy of teaching and learning successfully with Net Generation students. Interactive technology, such as wikis, may serve to foster student engagement, collaboration, and learning. Yet, relatively little systematic classroom-based research demonstrates the effectiveness of wikis or articulates students' perceptions of its use, especially in the context of higher education. This chapter offers case study experience with wikis to address this gap, and offers critical insights about how Net Generation students perceive and use technology in learning. Three main questions are explored in this chapter: (1) What are students' perceptions of technology in teaching and learning in general? (2) What are students' perceptions of wiki technology in teaching and learning, specifically? and (3) What are students' attitudes about group work and collaboration? Pilot data and post-wiki survey results suggest students have widely varying experiences with technology, and hold strong views about the use of technology in instruction. Five critical insights as to best practices for teaching and learning with wikis are offered. Results from this investigation identified three fascinating contradictions in student behaviors and perceptions regarding group work and collaboration that are ripe for further study.

DOI: 10.4018/978-1-61350-347-8.ch010

INTRODUCTION

"Digital natives," "Millennials," "Neo-millenials," "the Net Generation," these labels mark a generation for whom technology is both vital and invisible. Most student members of the Net Generation grew up experiencing communication as interpersonal, global, networked, and instant. For many, the world and its knowledge have, literally, been at their fingertips. They are a distinctive generation, known for their interest in learning and achievement, autonomy and self-direction, networked lifestyles, predisposition for collaboration and connection, and preference for learning that provides hands-on engagement (Barnes, Marateo Ferris, 2007; Oblinger & Oblinger, 2005).

Technology has afforded many of the Net Generation relative freedom and independence to explore their world and seek information, whether Skyping in real-time with friends from across the planet, trying out new identities in virtual spaces, or searching for answers about interests and passions. Further, some of the Net Generation possess a comfort level with creating and coordinating content, and putting it out into the world for others to view, critique, and share. They maintain YouTube channels, write blogs, moderate online discussions, co-create video animation, hold online contests, and engage in other collaborative activities.

What do these habits of technology use mean for teaching and learning with the Net Generation? While these are social uses of technology, the question becomes, how do Net Generation students use technology in their learning, and how do we, as educators, best use technology to enhance learning for Net Generation students?

Technology, Engagement, and Learning

Harnessing the potential of technology for increased student engagement appears to be a key aspect of teaching and learning successfully with Net Generation students. The National Survey of Student Engagement (2009) reported use of "interactive technologies were positively related to student engagement, self-reported learning outcomes, and deep approaches to learning." Further, the report stated: "Students who use interactive technologies are also more likely to say their campus environment is supportive, and contributes to their knowledge, skills, and personal development" (p. 1).

Interactive technology, such as wikis, may serve as tools to increase student engagement and, hence, learning. When used in instruction, wikis may facilitate student interaction and involvement with course materials, encourage collaboration with others, foster digital literacy skills crucial for the twenty-first century, and help students understand and enact their roles as creators and critical users of knowledge and information (Hamid Chang & Kurnia, 2009; Hargadon, 2010; Shapiro & Gonick 2008). Walsh (2010) suggests there are three frequently ballyhooed benefits of collaborative technologies: improved student collaboration, the deconstruction of the authoritative structure characteristic of the traditional classroom environment, and the building of professional expertise. However, relatively little systematic, classroom-based research demonstrates the effectiveness of wiki technology or articulates clearly students' perceptions of its use, especially in the context of higher education. Walsh (2010) argues that although many educators have been teaching with wikis and other collaborative technologies, "few have reported the results of these efforts" (p. 185). This chapter offers our case study experience with wikis as a way to address this gap in the literature. In addition, this chapter presents insights about how Net Generation students perceive and use technology in learning. Thus, this project explores both sides of technology use: the learning (student) side, and the teaching (instructor) side.

Three main questions served to animate this project: (1) What are students' perceptions of technology in teaching and learning in general?

(2) What are students' perceptions of wiki technology in teaching and learning, specifically? and (3) What are students' attitudes about group work and collaboration?

Engagement Theory, Collaboration, and Wiki

Our approach to these questions is to connect the ideas and practices of engagement theory with collaborative technology to facilitate teaching and learning with the Net Generation. Shneiderman and Kearsley (1999) describe engagement theory as an approach to teaching and learning in which students apply course concepts to actual problems that need solutions in the real world. Students are engaged because the issues are compelling and important. Learning occurs because students must understand key ideas and concepts correctly in order for their work to be successful. Engagement theory informs the creation of student activities that require "cognitive processes such as creating, problem-solving, reasoning, decision-making, and evaluation… Engagement theory is based upon the idea of creating successful collaborative teams that work on ambitious projects that are meaningful" (Shneiderman & Kearsley, 1999, p. 20). Technology can play an important role in collaborative group work:

While in principle, such engagement could occur without the use of technology, we believe that technology can facilitate engagement in ways which are difficult to achieve otherwise. So engagement theory is intended to be a conceptual framework for technology-based learning and teaching (Shneiderman & Kearsley, 1999, p. 20). Engagement theory thus offers a pedagogical conceptualiztion of collaboration, and a framework for technology-based teaching and learning. This would seem to be a promising approach for the Net Generation who possess technological and collaborative fluency and who learn by doing (Prensky 2010; Oblinger & Oblinger, 2005). Our use of wiki technology builds upon and applies these tenets of engagement theory and students and collaboration to teaching and learning.

To explore students' perceptions of wiki technology in teaching and learning, and students' attitudes about group work and collaboration, we incorporated wikis in three face-to-face courses. While there are several technologies that entail collaboration and facilitate group work, we chose wiki for four reasons. First, we wanted to bring technology into students' experiences in learning. Ironically, while Net Generation students arrive at university with technological know-how and often high expectations that technology will play a role in instruction and learning, there is often a "lack of exposure to educational uses of those technologies" (Kumar, 2008, p 2069.). Second, we chose wiki technology because it builds upon the collaborative fluency possessed by many Net Generation students while fostering interactivity and engagement. Third, we chose wiki because of research evidence that suggests many students are unfamiliar with wikis. For example, "Kennedy et al.'s (2008) survey found 81.6% of freshmen respondents reported that they had not contributed to wikis" (in Kumar, 2008). Similarly, when 36,950 undergraduates were surveyed in a 2010 ECAR study only 33.1% reported using a wiki of any sort, including Wikipedia or a course wiki in their education (Smith, Caruso, and Kim, 2010). Our pre-wiki survey (discussed below) of students' perceptions and experiences of technology in teaching and learning yielded similar results. Fourth, while numerous studies have shown Net Generation students to be avid users of technology in their everyday lives, they do not necessarily see an educational role for technology beyond basic uses such as, internet searches, email, word processing, and course management applications. Students seldom think to import technology into their learning, and this may be because many students have had limited experience with technological integration of their curriculum (Kumar,

2008). It may be that students are unaware of the ways in which technology could transform their learning experiences. Thus, our final reason for using wiki technology was to exemplify the connection between learning and technology for the Net Generation.

Wiki Technology

Wiki technology allows group members to collaborate and engage in synchronous and asynchronous communication. It was first created by Ward Cunningham in 1995 as a tool to afford site visitors the opportunity to co-edit a web page in a site called WikiWikiWikiWeb (see "wiki" on Wikipedia). In 2001, what is probably the most highly recognized wiki, Wikipedia, was created by Jimmy Wales and Larry Sanger after their first effort to build an online encyclopedia with paid writers failed (Myers, 2010). As a genre, wikis offer a site to grow collections of information, and co-author and co-edit documents. A key feature of a wiki is that it is an open, participatory and dynamic site—ever changing and evolving as participants submit content toward a shared production of knowledge (Minocha, Schencks, Sclater, Thomas, & Hause, 2007; Myers, 2010). Collaboration is most closely associated with the use of wiki. Walsh (2010) writes that a wiki is not just a collaborative tool, but "an embodied theory about what collaboration looks like and how it should work" (p. 188). Ideally, a wiki is a self-correcting and self-organizing entity, establishing and then enforcing its own codes and norms governing communication and interaction. In addition, wikis possess the potential to flatten traditional social hierarchies and create community across time and space. For teaching and learning, this technology would seem to hold promise, especially for fostering student engagement. As Minocha and Roberts (2008) suggest "[wikis] can address pedagogical objectives such as student involvement, group activity, peer and tutor review, knowledge-sharing and knowledge creation" (p. 301).

Although educational wikis are not yet widely used by educators, Phillipson (2008) offers a taxonomy. The most commonly used types of wikis in education include: (1) the *resource wiki,* like Wikipedia, which is a collection of information used to analyze a particular topic, (2) a *presentation wiki* often used by students to collaboratively create a web site or other document to augment a talk, (3) the *simulation wiki* which involves the creation of an artificial situation to represent real events, devices, or processes and students are encouraged to learn something about a given topic of interest by "playing" with the simulation, and (4) the *illuminated wiki* which "functions as hypermarginalia for texts, which students are invited to annotate, analyze, explore and recreate in associative ways" (Walsh, 2010, p. 188). While the inherent properties of wiki technology enable certain types of communication and interaction, the efficacy of its use in education is far from settled. Systematic research on the use of wikis in higher education is scant.

What research does exist suggests that applying wiki technology to learning is a complicated matter that must be approached carefully and thoughtfully in course design and implementation. Minocha and Roberts' (2008) research on the use of wikis and blogs in their online courses reveals uneven success with the use of these technologies. They discuss several caveats and lessons learned, and conclude by outlining key success criteria that must be identified, addressed and met before using wiki (and blog) technology.

Examples of these criteria include [establishing a] direct link between the learning outcomes and the activities the technology will support on the course; clarifying the role of the technology to students; considering the requirements of tutors and students before and after the implementation... ensuring that the technology is usable... and ensuring that there is a provision for early socialization in collaborative activities (Minocha & Roberts, 2008, pp.11-12).

In other words, serious consideration needs to be given to what the technology can do, what the goals of the instructor are, and, most importantly, what level of comfort, interest and expertise students have with the technology, and whether all of these goals can be carried out and supported with the equipment, time and resources available to both instructor and students. These insights informed our use and exploration of wiki effectiveness in teaching and learning.

QUESTIONS AND FINDINGS

Specifically, this project explored three areas related to technology, engagement, collaboration, and the Net Generation: (1) Student Use and Perceptions of Technology, (2) Student Use and Perceptions of Wikis, and (3) Student Attitudes about Group Work and Collaboration. To address the area we conducted a pilot survey to gain insight into student use and perceptions of technology. Next, drawing upon the tenets of engagement theory, we designed wiki projects for three courses and then conducted a post-wiki project survey that elicited student feedback about wiki technology and group collaboration to address the second and third areas.

Question 1: What are Net Generation Student Use and Perceptions of Technology?

Before embarking on the wiki projects, students (n = 46) in three classes completed a survey that asked about their experiences and perceptions of technology use in teaching and learning in a general sense.

Student Use of Technology in Learning

The participants in this study use a variety of technologies for a variety of reasons. All of the students indicated that they use search engines to conduct research and use email to communicate with instructors and/or classmates about assignments and/or homework. An overwhelming preponderance of students use online applications and software such as Google applications (89%), access and take tests and quizzes online (87%), and share electronic resources or documents with classmates. A majority of students take courses online (78%), participate in course social communication such using Facebook or Twitter (78%), write posts/comments on course blogs (76%), and download podcast lectures (58%).

When asked which technologies are the most helpful in teaching and learning, of the eleven technologies listed, the following were perceived by the respondents as being either very helpful or somewhat helpful: (1) Powerpoint (91.3%), (2) Online links and resources (91.1%), (3) Blackboard (83%), (4) Online discussion boards (71%), (5) Online quizzes (56.5%), and (6) Podcasts (56.5%). The other technologies included: blogs (29% found them very helpful or somewhat helpful), wikis (25%), instant messaging (19%), clicker audience responses (19%), and social networks (12%).

Respondents were also asked to indicate, on a five-point Likert scale, how helpful technology is in the learning process (41.3% felt it was very helpful and 39.1% felt it was somewhat helpful). Analysis of the thirty-two (32) written comments concerning student use of technology revealed two themes. First, *technology is ubiquitous and will be especially important in the professional arena:* "Technology is a significant part not only of society but [in] each of our lives," and "Students are not only expected to use technology in the classroom, but also when they are in the workforce as well." Second, *technology is not as important for the instructor as for the student:* "It is important for the student, but not as important for the instructor, but I believe this because I think that an effective teacher makes students think and want to learn... and he or she doesn't need an abundance of technology in order to do this." This data set suggests that students believe the use of technology in the learning process is more important to students than for instructors.

Student Perceptions of Instructor Use of Technology

A majority of students indicated that the use of technology by the instructor of a course is important in teaching and learning (48% believe that *instructor* use of technology is somewhat important and 19% very important). Analysis of the thirty-seven (37) written comments concerning technology and the learning process revealed two themes. First, *technology is important but the instructor is still the most important variable:* "I think that technology can enhance teaching, no doubt about that. However, I do not think it is vital for teachers to be technologically advanced to be successful educators. I have seen old school teachers that use nothing more than the textbook and chalkboard to teach and were some of the best I've ever had." Second, *technology is important in today's world:* "We exist in a world of changing technology. Being exposed to this technology throughout the education process helps us adapt."

Question 2: What are Net Generation Student Perceptions and Use of Wikis?

To explore this question, students enrolled in Media Criticism and Aesthetics, Business and Professional Communication, and Media Effects were introduced to wiki technology and required to work in small groups using a wiki to produce a collaborative project. While the guidelines and expectations for each wiki project were unique to each course, in general students were encouraged to use the wiki platform as a place to store, organize, and display the evolving project as group members worked together to post, revise, edit and respond on the wiki. Students were also encouraged to use the wiki platform as a medium for group communication, tracking project progress, delegating group responsibilities, and authoring group documents (Duffy & Burns, 2006; Mader, 2006). Due to institutional support, students enrolled in each course utilized Google Sites as their wiki platform.

In the Media Criticism and Aesthetics class, the wiki project focused on exploration of the nexus of media representations and environmental sustainability—that is, the critical exploration of taken-for-granted understandings of the natural and social world depicted in media. Students were to work in small groups to compile examples of green washing in media, and analyze these representations as instances of cultural discourses that that shape public understandings and misunderstandings of environmental stewardship and efforts toward sustainability. Students applied concepts and theories form the course, such as ideology, patterns of production and consumption, ideas about the audience as consumers, in their analyses and offered recommendations for changing these patterns of representation.

In the Business and Professional Communication course, the wiki project was geared toward helping students gain a deeper understanding of group processes. Working in small groups to develop products or services in hope of obtaining a hypothetical grant, students were required to analyze group communication processes including problem solving, leadership, and conflict resolution. It was emphasized that the wiki pages could serve as a data bank for students' group process papers and where students could obtain examples of small group communication behaviors (e.g. when someone kept the group on track, provided tension release or acted as a gatekeeper). These examples could, in turn, could be used to support their analyses.

For students enrolled in the Media Effects class, the wiki project centered on using the technology to create a web site that contained research and information about a media effects topic chosen by group members (e.g., media influence on body image; violence against women in the media; social networking and interpersonal relationships; green washing strategies in media advertising). The only explicit requirement for the Media Effects wiki web page was that it include an academic section. In essence, each small group was asked to collaborate on a presentation wiki.

Students and Wiki Use

One question on the pilot survey asked students if they knew what a wiki would be used for. Fifty-two percent (52%) did not know, thirty-seven percent (37%) were not entirely certain but could take a guess, and thirteen-percent (13%) could think of lots of uses for a wiki. Twenty-three respondents attempted to explain or define a wiki and most of these answers suggested that students thought that a wiki is used for collaboration and organization of information and/or for research (similar to Wikipedia).

After they completed the wiki project, students participated in a second survey, the post-wiki project survey. This survey centered on how and why students used wiki to complete their group projects. A clear majority (67.6%) most often used the wiki as a place for each group member to place their individual work. The wiki was also most often used by groups as a site for collection of information (64.7%), as a medium to write and edit collaboratively (52.9%), and as a medium for class presentations (52.9%). Respondents indicated that they most often used wiki as a place to track progress on the project (48.5%), as a medium to produce one document or web site co-authored by all group members (47.1%), and as a place for discussion among group members (29.4%).

Respondents were asked to rate the effectiveness of wiki for different types of common group work. Wikis were perceived as very effective for the following activities: (1) As a place for each group member to place their individual work (67.6%), (2) As a site for collection of information (52.9%), (3) As a medium to produce one document co-authored by all group members (50%), (4) As a medium to write and edit collaboratively (48.5%), (5) As a place to track progress on the project (45.5%), and (6) As a medium for class presentations (44.1%).

Using their experience with wiki during the semester, respondents were asked a number of questions pertaining to wikis and learning. On a five-point scale of 'strongly agree' to 'strongly disagree' the results indicated that wikis are effective for collaborative learning (67.6% strongly agreed or agreed), students perceive that they were more competent using a wiki after the semester long project (53% strongly agreed or agreed), wikis facilitate group learning (52.9% strongly agreed or agreed), and wiki projects were useful in applying course content (52.9%). With a look to the future, forty-seven percent (47%) of respondents would use wiki again for a group project and a majority (67.6%) would recommend the instructor assign a wiki project the next time the course is taught.

If respondents indicated that they did not utilize wiki to its full potential for their group project, they were asked to respond to a series of questions eliciting reasons why the wiki was not used to it full potential. These data reveal four reasons for the failure of groups to use wiki to its fullest potential: (1) Face-to-face communication met group needs (75% of respondents strongly agreed or agreed), (2) Group members were unaware of all of the functions of a wiki (65% strongly agreed or agreed), (3) Group members did not understand how to use wiki (55% strongly agreed or agreed) and (4) Other technology met group needs (50% strongly agreed or agreed).

Question 3: What Are Net Generation Student Attitudes About Group Work and Collaboration?

Attitudes about Group Work

When asked about their perceptions of group work within the classroom environment, seventy-percent (69.6%) of students responded that they feel group work is very important (34.8%) or somewhat important (34.8%) in the learning process. Thirty-eight respondents took the opportunity to explain why they felt that group work was important for their learning. A deep reading of these responses revealed several themes about group work. Students suggested that *group work will be required in the professional world:* "In the 'real world' you are expected to work in groups efficiently," "You have to be able to work with a group in so many jobs," "It is important to know how to work in a group for future jobs and other possibilities," and "It's good experience working with others, to learn how to cooperate with others, and work as a team, like you might have to do at a job after graduating college." Another theme centered around *group work providing one with multiple perspectives*: "It is always helpful to have multiple ideas on one subject," "It's good to learn to work together with different types of people," "It's good experience working with others, to learn to cooperate with others and work as a team," and "Allows students at the same learning level to bounce ideas and further understand topics where with an individual project you're stuck at your level of [knowledge]." A second theme focused on the notion that *group work is important to the development of social skills*: "Helps in learning communication skills with others and within groups," "The better you are working as a team, not only can you learn more, but also be more productive in reaching goals." *Groups can be frustrating when some members don't do their fair share of the work* constituted a theme: The downside is when the group doesn't work well together (poor communication or lazy members, etc). A final theme acknowledged that *successful group work is course-dependent*: "I believe that group work depends on the course. For example, production courses tend to favor group work, while a writing course may be more personal and independent."

Although respondents articulated that group work is important, when given a preference thirty-seven percent (37%) preferred to work alone on class projects (9% preferred to work in a group and 54% did not have a preference). Thirty-three respondents answered the open-ended question associated with this item and an overwhelming number of respondents who would rather work individually on class projects mentioned that *groups are difficult to coordinate* as the reason for their preference: "It can be problematic to coordinate schedules and work load," "I like group work, but it is often very difficult to get together to work on projects outside of class because of everyone's school and work schedules," and "I like working alone because I am solely responsible for my work progress." Other themes revealed in this question included: *Preference for individual control of one's own grade and the task:* "I don't like being graded or relying on the work of other's because it isn't ever up to my expectations which means I usually do projects designed for a group by myself," *Working in groups is okay, if they are "good" groups:* "I am very torn when it comes to learning in groups. Groups can be positive when you have a good group," and *In a group, you are at the mercy of other group members:* "I have yet to work on a project in a group that I couldn't have done better myself."

Perceptions about Collaboration

When asked to explain what working in a group project involves, ninety-four percent (94%) of the sample either strongly agreed or agreed that working in a group format involves exchanging ideas and resources in an ongoing manner throughout the entire time spent on the project, ninety-one percent (91%) strongly agreed or agreed that a group project dividing up the workload and assigning tasks to each group member to work on individually, and sixty-six percent (66%) strongly agreed or agreed that group work is about writing a document or presentation collaboratively with all group members contributing to all parts of the project.

DISCUSSION

This project began as an exploration of teaching, learning and technology among three colleagues. With the aid of a grant, we were able to better understand Net Generation student perceptions and experiences with wikis in learning. As described in the preceding sections, pilot and post-wiki project surveys were employed to collect student input. This section offers explication of the major findings of these instruments focusing on wikis and the Net Generation, critical insights, and suggestions for further research.

Net Generation Perceptions and Uses of Technology

There was a marked difference in students' perceptions of technology use between students and teachers. This was an unexpected result. It appears students have a keen sense of teacher effectiveness and they believe teacher effectiveness operates independently of technology use. The participants in this project seem to be suggesting that a good teacher is what matters most, rather than technology. This is not a Luddite position. Clearly these Net Generation students are not anti-technology; they are avid users of technologies of all sorts as pilot survey results indicate. But students do seem to be insisting on the preservation of quality teaching and keeping teaching at the center of learning—rather than overly privileging technology. Indeed, their comments can best be read as expressing concern that inappropriate substitution of technology for quality instruction may weaken the educational experience. This finding has enormous import for teachers, especially when considering the Net Generation as they seek meaningful experiences. Technology may have changed the educational landscape, but for students, quality teaching remains key.

Wikis and the Net Generation

The pilot survey confirmed the limited exposure, experience and understanding most students have with wikis. More than half of the students had no idea what a wiki would be used for, and while the guesses put forward by other students were good, they displayed a cursory understanding of wikis. Students did not report possessing a high comfort level or deep familiarity with wiki technology and its potential richness.

These results resonate with a study of secondary school students in the UK that explored students' technology practices and perceptions. In this study, researchers found that while students were avid users of various technologies and social media, the "learners seemed cautious about other values associated with Web 2.0 tools, such as the shared construction of knowledge in a public format. Few learners were familiar with the complete spectrum of Web 2.0 activities and only a small number were engaging in more sophisticated activities such as producing self-created content for wider consumption. As the pilot survey demonstrated, most students functioned at the consumption end of technology use as opposed to the producer end. Many students were unfamiliar and even uncomfortable with deeper and more producer-oriented modes of technology use. This suggests that Net Generation students are not a homogeneous group. While some Net Generation students function at the producer end of technology use, many do not. We suggest it may be useful to conceive of student technology use as occupying various points along a consumer-producer continuum with most students somewhere in the middle.

One implication may be that if we wish to employ technology in instruction, we teach not only the skills to use the technology, but also help students understand and feel comfortable with a relatively new social role for many: media creator and knowledge producer for an audience. After all, the Net Generation is no more monolithic than other generations. Some are ahead of the technological curve while others lag behind. We suggest that teachers starting out with collaborative technologies like wikis discuss the ways in which wikis have been used, and talk about our changing social roles as producers as well as consumers of knowledge.

Our data seems to underscore Palfrey and Gasser's (2008) contention that Net Generation students learn best through a three-step process: grazing, deep-dive, and feedback. For students in this project, who were relatively unfamiliar with wikis, their initial foray into the use of wiki served as the grazing experience. As some students reported, they preferred to use other social media for their group collaboration such as Facebook over wiki technology; this seems to represent a grazing back-and-forth between collaborative technologies. Once students understood the potential for wiki and as their worked progressed throughout the semester, they began to experience the deep-dive phase; a latching on to a new technology. Finally, by participating in the post-wiki survey students were afforded the opportunity to offer feedback about wikis and were thus parceling out their likes and dislikes of wiki.

Although students utilized their wikis in appropriate and diverse manners, underutilized was the group communication and discussion feature of wikis. However, other survey data suggest this may be simply because students used alternative means of communication to interact with each other such as face-to-face communication, social networking sites like Facebook and email. Students' perceptions about wiki technology were favorable as students gave it high ratings for effectiveness in fostering group collaboration. But, on other measures, results were mixed. In terms of proficiency of wiki use, only fifty-three percent (53%) strongly agreed or agreed that they were more competent using a wiki after the class project. In addition, only fifty-three percent (52.9%) strongly agreed or agreed that wikis facilitate group learning, and only fifty-three percent (52.9%) felt wiki projects were useful in applying course content. With a look to the future, only forty-seven percent (47%) of respondents would use wiki again for a group project. While these results are not disturbingly low, they may not be a ringing endorsement either. Curiously, a majority (67.6%) recommended the instructor assign a wiki project the next time the course is taught. Perhaps this suggests that students do not feel competent enough to use the technology on their own, but they believe the wiki was a worthwhile part of the course and should continue to be included in future semesters.

Group Work and Collaboration

Because wiki technology is said to foster student engagement and collaboration, and hence learning, we included survey questions about group work to explore students' perceptions and understandings of groups and the role of groups in learning. Results from group work questions reveal tensions, perhaps contradictions, in students' views. On the one hand, students value group work and understand its importance and benefits, as articulated in their responses (group work is necessary to future professional careers, promotes increased social skill, yields a better outcome, etc.). But, on the other hand, thirty-seven percent (37%) admitted they do not care for group work, while fifty-four percent (54%) had no strong feelings either way, and only nine percent (9%) said they preferred to work in a group. This raises an important issue for teachers as they consider collaboration and group work in their course design, projects and assignments. These results may suggest that intercultural differences could be playing a part in the perception of groups and group work. For example, students in the United States are well aware that their culture, generally, elevates and rewards individual behavior over that of a collective. So, although students value group work superficially, at a deeper level, many disliked the burdens of group membership. Most students preferred having control of their own destiny, especially if grading is linked to group work.

Further tensions-or contradictions-arose in the group process questions in which ninety-four percent (94%) of students said that working in a group involves exchanging ideas and resources with all group members in an ongoing manner, while, similarly, ninety-one percent (91%) said that group work involves dividing up the workload and assigning tasks to each group member to work on individually–implicitly, then, not sharing resources and workload, but rather, dividing up the task. That is, if the workload were divided up, why would I research your section? I wouldn't. You would. We would not collaborate and share resources because we are focused on different things. These are opposite positions. You cannot have both. You cannot have both an ongoing collaboration and simultaneously have division of labor—or can you? Yet the vast majority of students agreed to both methods of group process. It may be that students simply reporting that they have had both types of experiences in groups, even within the same group, but at different times. We wonder if these patterns of responses point to a unique understanding of group work and group processes held by students. While these responses appear paradoxical to us, we wonder why students don't see it that way.

Post-wiki qualitative responses were so few on most questions that thematic clusters could not be found. The only exception to this trend was the last question "In the space below, tell us what you think are the benefits and drawbacks of using wiki." The written responses suggested the major benefits of the wiki were having a place to compile data and coordinate efforts. Several students also noted that using the wiki as a source for electronic brainstorming was a benefit to their group process. The major drawbacks included technical difficulties with the Google wiki and the long waiting time for communication to occur among group members. However, as this quote demonstrates, most groups made the best of the situation:

"At first it was challenging as everyone was getting used to the idea and mechanics of the wiki. Once everyone got the hang of the wiki and felt comfortable using it, it became very easy and sensible to use. We would all post on the wiki and respond to each and get things done from there as if we were in an in-person meeting. I think in this class the group collaboration wiki was easily accessed and we were able to communicate in a somewhat efficient way."

Central Insights

Our use of wikis in each of our three classes revealed five central insights. First, given student comments about wiki being cumbersome and difficult to work with, as instructors we need to be aware that we are actually asking students to learn two things. We need to be certain students are not overwhelmed with both learning a new technology, and at the same time, mastering content. We need to think carefully about how technology can enhance learning subject matter while also cultivating a new technological skill.

Second, given the multiple ways in which most technologies can be used, we might also consider giving students more freedom of choice about how and when to use a new technology beyond the requirement that they use it. Rather than imposing too much on them, we could set broad parameters within which students can creatively experiment with technology. In essence, a good approach may be to require a collaborative project and allow students to determine the best technology to use in the completion of that project.

Third, and this may be unique to the Communication and Media Studies discipline where communication is both the subject and object of study, wiki technology provides a workshop/laboratory environment that allows students to scrutinize and become more aware of their own and each others' communication patters and interactions. This focus may have accentuated students' positive view of wiki. They may have become more aware of how wiki can be useful for understanding human communication processes. This raises an interesting question about training in communication dynamics as a prerequisite to working in groups online. Just as training is valuable to those who meet face-to-face, we see no reason why it wouldn't be as valuable to those working online.

Fourth, a very interesting development occurred in several courses. Each group had a techno-expert or 'wiki master' who set up the wiki and led people along the technological path until they could operate on their own. These individuals were not seen as aggressive or controlling. Rather, their peers treated them with respect as these quotes demonstrate:

"Lauren took the responsibility of creating our group website, and for that I thank her, because she did a great job."

"Emily must get credit for being the one who really jumped forth setting this site up. She was very patient...and tried her best to explain it to the rest of us." "Serena got our group's Wiki up and running."

Other individuals were described as task or social-emotional leaders, but techno-experts emerged as a third category. The techno-experts exhibited a blend of task ("here's how it's done") and social-emotional ("don't worry, I'll help you") behaviors. Perhaps that is why they were well-respected members of their groups. They were friendly and helpful, along with being technologically task oriented. We should also note that a majority of the techno-experts were women. As we assess the deployment of technologies in teaching and learning, our aim should be to develop the role of techno-expert in every student. In this way, each student becomes a technological equal without any dependency on a single individual for support. Just as we promote shared leadership in the task and relational areas of group work, we can also advocate sharing responsibility for learning and using technology.

Finally, we must address two central questions, were course objectives achieved and did the wikis help students as intended? The answer to both questions is yes. While full capacity of wiki may not have been utilized, students did use them effectively and course projects, presentations, research and discussions were largely successful. One unforeseen, but gratifying consequence of this experience was that most groups enjoyed using their wikis as these quotes attest:

"I feel the wiki played a good part in our overall success. I know that the wiki was mandatory and that all groups had to use them, but the way that ours was set up made it clear and easy to know what was expected."

"We had the opportunity to use wikis, which allowed us to work virtually through blogs. Everyone transitioned from in-class to online communication with ease, and after becoming acclimated to the new software and online wiki tools, we are able to successfully collaborate and produce a quality product."

These statements demonstrate that wiki was beneficial to many students. Given these positive reactions, we will most likely continue to experiment with wikis and perhaps expand our usage to other courses.

FUTURE RESEARCH DIRECTIONS

Future research directions are indicated from several results of this project. Results revealed three contradictions in student perceptions that serve as future topics for investigation. The first contradiction focuses on the nature of collaboration and group work. While the majority (70%) of students felt that group work was important for teaching, learning and development of social skills, surprisingly most students also reported that they did not prefer to work in groups. Only 9 percent of students stated they prefer group work. What is behind this contradiction? Do students perceive this position as contradictory? Why? Future research would aim to clarify this complex position held by students, and develop ways to address the lack of enthusiasm for group work held by many students. For example, if a group is reluctant or unable to embrace and enact collective ownership (Grant, 2009; Crook, 2008; Lund & Smørdal, 2006) then our work as educators may be to teach and facilitate this process.

A further dimension of this contradiction is the role of culture in shaping students' preference for group work. Future research could explore the ways in which norms and expectations associated with cultural identity play a part in students' behavior. If students identify themselves with an individualistic culture, will they be less willing to work in groups? If they identify with a collectivistic culture, will they be more willing to work in groups? Using these broad definitions, a working hypothesis would suggest this might be the case, but is there a correlation? In what ways does the dominant culture of a country influence how Net generation groups communicate and perform? What about the role of technology in fostering norms of collaboration? To the extent that some Net generation students are identified as "global citizens," will increased digital connectivity and interaction contribute to the creation of a more collectivist consciousness as they unite around global issues? Will this, in turn, result in a greater willingness to cooperate with others in groups? These questions deserve further investigation.

Future research could also help resolve the second contradiction revealed in this project, relating to wiki use. While only forty-seven percent (47%) of students said they would use a wiki in a future group project, the majority of students, sixty-seven percent (67%), felt the instructor should assign a wiki group project the next time the class is taught. What is behind this apparent contradiction? Why should the instructor use wiki, if roughly half the students report that they would not use wiki again? Similarly, after having been introduced to wiki technology in these classes, why do most students say they would not continue using wiki in future? What factors shape student decisions about technology use? Future research would seek to identify and understand these influences.

Finally, future research could also help resolve in a contradiction in the results which indicate inconsistency between students' perceptions of group work as collaboration (94%) and group work as dividing up the task (91%). Since we place so much emphasis on group work, it would be worthwhile to further investigate this paradox. Do students say group work involves collaboration because they think they should, while in practice, students simply divide up the task? Or, are there times of collaboration and times of dividing up the task? If so, when and why do these times occur? For example, does collaboration function primarily at the beginning and end of a group's project with division of labor occurring in the middle for research and data collection purposes? What about roles played by group members? Our research identified the role of "technological expert" within each group. This role emerged naturally but was key in facilitating the coordination and success of the group. How does technology change group roles and dynamics and alter the ways in which collaboration may be carried out? More specifically, how do Net generation students understand collaboration? How do we, as educators, define collaboration? Further, how do we assess collaboration? What does "good" collaboration look like? How do we teach that? What is the role of technology in facilitating and enabling collaboration? These are key conceptual and practical questions ripe for further investigation and clarification.

As Walsh (2010) notes, "I believe we can conclude that the days of asking *what*, *why* and *whether*, about wiki technology are behind us; the questions that face us now begin with *when* and *how*." (p. 208). Further empirical investigation of these and other questions will help deepen our understanding and practices around teaching, learning, and technology as they relate to the Net generation.

CONCLUSION

This project explored students' perceptions of technology use in teaching and learning, and focused on wikis as a collaborative technology for use in higher education. Three central questions were examined: (1) What are students' perceptions of technology in teaching and learning in general? (2) What are students' perceptions of wiki technology in teaching and learning, specifically? and (3) What are students' attitudes about group work and collaboration? Pilot data and post-wiki project survey results suggested students are avid technology users and hold strong views and preferences regarding the effectiveness of different forms of technology used in education. Content analysis of student responses to open-ended questions revealed several key themes related to teaching and learning and technology use. A central finding was that while students see a role for technology in teaching and learning, they also felt strongly that technology should not be used simply for technology's sake, and it must not replace quality teaching. This project also experimented with the use of wiki technology for group projects in three courses. Post-wiki survey results showed about half of students felt wiki technology was an effective instructional technology, and a positive tool to achieve group goals and learning. In addition, this project uncovered three fascinating contradictions in student perceptions and behaviors regarding group work and collaboration. Based on these results, five critical insights as to best practices for teaching and learning with wikis were offered.

REFERENCES

Barnes, K., Marato, R., & Ferris, S. (2007). Teaching and learning with the Net Generation. *Innovate, 3*(4). Retrieved from http://www.innovateonline.info/index.php?view=article&id=382.

Bruns, A., & Humphreys, S. (2007). *Building collaborative capacities in learners: The M/cyclopedia project revisited.* Paper presented at the International Symposium on Wikis, Montreal, Canada.

Carpenter, P., & Roberts, E. (2007). Going wiki in online technology education courses: Promoting online learning and service learning through wikis. *Technology Education Journal, 9*, 58–64.

Crook, C. (2008). *Web 2.0 technologies for learning: The current landscape – Opportunities, challenges and tensions*. Coventry, UK: BECTA.

Duffy, P., & Burns, A. (September, 2006). The use of blogs, wikis and RSS in education: A conversation of possibilities. *Proceedings of the Online Learning and Teaching Conference*, Brisbane, Australia.

Forte, A., & Bruckman, A. (2007). *Constructing text: Wiki as a toolkit for (collaborative?) learning.* Paper presented at the International Symposium on Wikis, Montreal, Canada.

Grant, L. (2009). "I don't care do ur own page!" A case study of using wikis for collaborative work in a UK secondary school. *Learning, Media and Technology, 34*(2), 105–117. doi:10.1080/17439880902923564

Guth, S. (2007). *Wikis in education: Is public better?* Paper presented at the International Symposium on Wikis, Montreal, Canada.

Hamid, S., Chang, S., & Kurnia, S. (2009). Identifying the use of online social networking in higher education. In *Same Places, Different Spaces: Proceedings Ascilite*, Auckland. Retrieved from http://www.ascilite.org.au/conferences/aucklanc09/procs/hamid-poster.pdf.

Hargadon, S. (2010). *Educational networking: The important role web 2.0 will play in education*. Whitepaper. Scribd Online Journal.

Kumar, S. (2008). Can we model wiki use in technology courses to help teachersuse wikis in their classrooms? In K. McFerrin, et al. (Eds.), *Proceedings of Society for Information Technology & Teacher Education International Conference 2008* (pp. 2068-2071). Chesapeake, VA: AACE. Retrieved from http://www.editlib.org/p/27507.

Lund, A., & Smørdal, O. (2006). *Is there a space for the teacher in a wiki?* Paper presented at the International Symposium on Wikis, Odense, Denmark.

Mader, S. (2006). *Using wiki in education: Case studies from the classroom*. Retrieved from www.wikiineducation.com.

Minocha, S., & Roberts, D. (2008). Social, usability, and pedagogical factors influencing students' learning experiences with wikis and blogs. *Pragmatics & Cognition, 16*(2), 272–306.

Minocha, S., Schencks, M., Sclater, N., Thomas, P., & Hause, M. (2007). Collaborative learning in a wiki environment: Case study of a requirements engineering course. *Proceedings of the European Distance and E-learning Network (EDEN) Annual Conference on New Learning 2.0 Emerging Digital Territories, Developing Continuities, New Divides*, Naples. Retrieved from http://www.eden-online.org/eden.php?menuId=353&contentId=587.

Myers, G. (2010). *Discourse of blogs and wikis*. New York, NY: Continuum.

NSSE. National Survey of Student Engagement. (2009). *NSSE: National Survey of Student Engagement* (Online). Retrieved June 13, 2010, from http://nsse.iub.edu/nsse_2009/in.

Oblinger, D., & Oblinger, J. (2005). Is it age or IT: First steps toward understanding the Net Generation. In D. Oblinger & J. Oblinger (Eds.), *Educating the Net generation*. Retrieved from http://www.educase.edu/educatingthenetgen.

Palfrey, J., & Gasser, U. (2008). *Born digital: Understanding the first generation of digital natives*. New York, NY: Basic Books.

Phillipson, M. (2008). Wikis in the classroom: A taxonomy. In Cummings, R. H., & Barton, M. (Eds.), *Wiki writing: Collaborative learning in the college classroom* (pp. 19–43). Ann Arbor, MI: University of Michigan Press.

Prensky, M. (2010). *Teaching digital natives: Partnering for real learning*. Thousand Oaks, CA: Sage.

Shapiro, W., & Gonick, L. (2008). Learning 2.0: Who's in control now? In *Sparking Innovative Learning and Creativity, Summer Conference at Princeton University Proceedings*, (pp. 64-71).

Shneiderman, B., & Kearsley, G. (1999). Engagement theory: A framework for technology-based teaching and learning. *Journal of Educational Technology, 38*(5), 20–23.

Smith, S., Caruso, J., & Kim, J. (2010). *ECAR study of undergraduate students and information technology*. Retrieved at http://www.educase.edu.edu/Resources/ECARStudyofUndergraduateStuden/217333.

Walsh, L. (2010). Constructive interference: Wikis and service learning in thetechnical communication classroom. *Technical Communication Quarterly, 19*(2), 184–211. doi:10.1080/10572250903559381

ADDITIONAL READING

Bonk, C. J. (2009). *The world is open: How web technology is revolutionizing education*. Jossey-Bass.

Boyd, D. (2008). Why youth heart social network sites: The role of networked publics in teenage social life. In D. Buckingham (Ed.), *Youth, identity, and digital media* (pp. 119-142). Cambridge, MA: The MIT Press. doi: 10.1622/dmal.9780262524834.119.

Boyd, D. (2010). Social network sites as networked publics: Affordances, dynamics, and implications. In Papacharissi, A. (Ed.), *Networked self: Identity, community and culture on social network sites* (pp. 39–58). Routledge.

Buckingham, D. (2008). *Youth, identity, and digital media*. Cambridge, MA: MIT Press.

Buckingham, D. (2011). *The material child: Growing up in consumer culture*. Boston, MA: Polity Press.

Buckingham, D., & Willett, R. (2009). *Video cultures: MediatTechnology and everyday creativity*. New York, NY: Palgrave Macmillan.

Burke, M., Kraut, R., & Joyce, E. (2010). Membership claims and requests: Conversation-level newcomer socialization strategies in online groups. *Small Group Research*, *41*(February), 4–41..doi:10.1177/1046496409351936

Carr, N. (2010). *The shallows: What the Internet is doing to our brains*. W. W. Norton & Company.

Collins, A., & Halverson, R. (2009). *Rethinking education in the age of technology: The digital revolution and schooling in America*. Teacher's College Press.

Cragan, J., Wright, D., & Kasch, C. (2008). *Communication in Small Groups* (7th ed.). Belmont, CA: Wadsworth.

Davidson, C. N., & Goldberg, D. W. (2010). *The future of thinking: learning institutions in a digital age*. Cambridge, MA: MIT Press.

Di Giano, C., Goldman, S., & Chorost, M. (2009). *Educating new learning technology designers*. New York: Routledge.

Drotner, K. (2008). Leisure is hard work: Digital practices and further competencies. In D. Buckingham (Ed.), *Youth, identity, and digital media* (pp. 167-184). Cambridge, MA: The MIT Press. doi: 10.1622/dmal.9780262524834.119.

Elfving, D., & Menchen-Trevino, E. (2008). One wiki, two classrooms. In R.Cummings & M. Barton (Eds.), *Wiki writing: Educators on collaborative writing and learning* (pp. 137-148). Ann Arbor, Michigan: University of M ichigan Press.

Ess, C. (2009). *Digital media ethics*. Boston, MA: Polity Press.

Forsythe, D. (2010). *Group Dynamics* (5th ed.). Belmont, CA: Wadsworth.

Galanes, G. (2009). Dialectical tensions of small group leadership. *Communication Studies*, *60*(1), 409–425. doi:10.1080/10510970903260228

Gershon, I. (2010). *The breakup 2.0: Disconnecting over new media*. Ithaca, NY: Cornell University Press.

Goldman, S., Booker, A., & McDermott, M. (2008). Mixing the digital, social and cultural: Learning, identity, and agency in your participation.

Hargittai, E., Fullerton, L., Menchen-Trevino, E., & Thomas, K. (2010). Trust online: Young adults' evaluation of web content. *International Journal of Communication*, *4*. Retrieved from http://ijoc.org/ojs/index/php/ijoc/article/view/636.

Hargittal, E. (2010). Digital na(t)tives? Variation in internet skills and uses among members of the net generation. *Sociological Inquiry*, *80*(1), 92–113. doi:10.1111/j.1475-682X.2009.00317.x

Herr-Stephenson, B. (2011). *Digital media and technology in afterschool programs, libraries and museums*. Cambridge, MA: MIT.

Herring, S. C. (2008). Questioning the generational divide: Technological exoticism and adult constructions of online youth identity. In D. Buckingham (Ed.), *Youth, identity, and digital media* (pp. 71-92). Cambridge, MA: The MIT Press. doi: 10. 1622/dmal.9780262524834.071.

In, D. Buckingham (Ed.), *Youth, identity, and digital media* (pp. 185-206). Cambridge, MA: The MIT Press. doi: 10. 1622/dmal.9780262524834.185.

Jenkins, H. (2008). *Convergence culture: Where old and new media collide*. New York: New York University.

Jenkins, H. (2009). *Confronting the challenges of participatory culture: Media education for the 21st century*. Cambridge, MA: MIT Press.

Kotter, J. (2010). *Learning group leadership: An experiential approach* (2nd ed.). Thousand Oaks, CA: Sage.

Levi, D. (2011). *Group dynamics for teams*. Thousand Oaks, CA: Sage.

Lira, E., Ripoll, P., Peiro, J., & Zornoza, A. (2008). The role of information and communication technologies in the relationship between group effectiveness and group potency: A longitudinal study. *Small Group Research*, *39*(December), 782–745. doi:.doi:10.1177/1046496408323481

Livingstone, S. (2009). *Children and the Internet: Great expectation, challenging realities*. Boston, MA: Polity Press.

Matzat, U. (2009). A theory of relational signals in online groups. *New Media & Society*, *11*(3), 375–394..doi:10.1177/1461444808101617

Menchen-Trevino, E., & Hargittai, E. (2011). Young adults' credibility assessment of Wikipedia. *Information Communication and Society*, *14*(1), 24–51. doi:10.1080/13691181003695173

Schumann, T., & Lukosch, S. (2007). *Patterns for computer-mediated interaction*. West Sussex, England: John Wiley & Sons.

Way, Z., & Hancock, W. (2009). Social identification and interpersonal communication in computer-mediated communication: What you do versus who you are in virtual groups. *Human Communication Research*, *35*(1), 59–85. doi:10.1111/j.1468-2958.2008.01338.x

West, J., & West, M. (2009). *Using wikis for online collaboration: The power of the read-write web*. San Francisco, CA: Jossey-Bass.

KEY TERMS AND DEFINITIONS

Collaboration: Coordinated interaction and communication between participants toward a shared goal or purpose.

Discussion: Flow of communication and interaction among participants around a common topic or interest.

Engagement Theory: An approach to teaching and learning in which students apply course concepts to actual problems that need solutions in the real world.

Group Dynamics: Patterns and processes of communication and interaction among members of a group.

Media Ecologies: Social, cultural, and technological milieu in which mediated communication is situated and occurs.

Participatory Culture: Social and cultural dynamic enabled by affordances of interactive communication technologies. Users gain increased agency to interact with information, produce content, and communicate with others in new ways.

Social Media: Web 2.0 and Web 3.0 interactive communication technologies that have given rise to new forms of social and communicative practices, conventions, and expectations, e.g., blogs, social networks, wikis, location-based networks, multimedia, photography, art, video and music sharing, livecasting, presentation sharing, etc.

Social Networks: Groupings of people, organizations, and institutions and their associated patterns of interaction and communication, e.g., Facebook, Twitter, MySpace, ASmallWorld, Cyworld, Orkut, Tagged, XING, Hyves, My2i, Plaxo, Ning, Foursquare, etc.

Chapter 11
Using Blogs to Overcome the Challenges of a Research Methods Course

Susanne S. Croasdaile
Virginia Commonwealth University, USA

Rachel Angel
Virginia Commonwealth University, USA

Erin Carr
Virginia Commonwealth University, USA

Lucy Hudson
Virginia Commonwealth University, USA

Carin Usrey
Virginia Commonwealth University, USA

ABSTRACT

This chapter describes blogs created by Net Generation students enrolled in a Master's level Introduction to Research in Education course designed according to the principles of Universal Design for Learning (UDL). UDL is a framework for teaching and learning that highlights the need for multiple, flexible means of representation, expression, and engagement. The case study examples highlighted in this chapter demonstrate the possibilities inherent in the use of flexible digital media such as blogs. The importance of formative assessment, particularly through the use of student self-assessment and instructor feedback to close the gap between current performance and learning goals, is discussed. Examples from course blogs are shared to illustrate key points. Best practices for blog use and implications for future study are included.

DOI: 10.4018/978-1-61350-347-8.ch011

INTRODUCTION

In our university, as in many others, there are some courses that students have made apocryphal: some for positive traits, others for more negative ones. Among our master's level students in the School of Education, the introductory level research course is considered to be quite difficult. The reasons circulated among the student body include challenging content, heavy workload, and lack of real world application.

The first author of this chapter is an instructor of this course; the co-authors are her students. Examples from student course blogs illustrate the application of Universal Design for Learning (UDL) to challenging course content. The principles of UDL encourage course design that separates learner goals from instructional methods (Rose & Meyer, 2002). The result is that learners can use a range of methods and materials to develop understanding and show what they know. The instructor's role becomes one of facilitator, providing feedback to learners to help them demonstrate mastery of course objectives and ultimately achieve course goals.

Application of UDL at the tertiary level demands the use of flexible digital media. In this course, students use blogs to explore new content, demonstrate conceptual understanding, make connections to prior knowledge, and draft parts of a research proposal. Blogs offer students the ability to reflect using text, images, charts, tables, hyperlinks and video. For the Net Generation that thinks in images and sounds as much as words and phrases, the blog medium offers a useful canvas for constructing knowledge in a challenging course.

In this chapter, examples from our course blogs illustrate how this medium can be used to provide students with multiple, flexible forms of expression and engagement; a way to self-assess areas of mastery and improvement; and timely, specific written feedback that closes the gap between current performance and course goals.

BACKGROUND

Universal Design for Learning

Universal Design for Learning (UDL) is a framework for teaching and learning based on brain research (Rose & Meyer, 2002). UDL is a lens through which educators design instruction to consider student needs. An appealing aspect of this framework is its emphasis on separating the goal of learning from the instructional method, often capitalizing on the opportunities presented by flexible digital text.

UDL takes into consideration three things: recognition brain networks, which benefit from multiple, flexible representations of content; strategic brain networks, which benefit from multiple, flexible means of expression and apprenticeship; and affective brain networks, which benefit from multiple, flexible means of engagement. The strategic networks help learners plan and carry out tasks. This includes activities from whipping up a strawberry-banana smoothie in the blender to comparing prices of new cell phones on the internet to writing a formal five-paragraph essay. In each situation, we determine what we want to do (goal), determine how we will do it (plan), get started (execution), and decide how we did (evaluation) (Rose & Meyer, 2002). Affective brain networks support not the planning and execution of tasks, but one's engagement in learning.

The strategic and affective networks are of interest in this discussion—without the former, students could accomplish nothing; without the latter, they would not even try. Recent research has demonstrated how students achieve higher educational outcomes in courses using UDL design principles (Simmons, Willkomm, & Behling, 2010); this area is worthy of further exploration.

Net Generation Learners

The university student population is increasingly comprised of "digital natives" (Prensky,

2001) from an "always-connected" generation born into a world in which personal computers became ubiquitous (Bull, 2010). Many grew up with parents and friends calling on cell phones, surfing TV in their bedrooms, playing music on demand, creating PowerPoint assignments at school, and finding answers to questions (with varying degrees of accuracy) by typing them into a search engine.

Ask a member of the Net Generation what they think and they will tell you: they are willing to voice an opinion on almost anything (Lancaster & Stillman, 2003). Millennial students report preferences for positive environments, opportunities to work with others, clear structures, graphics in addition to text, and active learning experiences (Howe, 2003; Wessels & Steenkamp, 2009). They use communication technologies socially and to access information (Mitchell, 2003), but vary widely in their knowledge of how to apply these technologies for academic and professional purposes (Jones & Healing, 2010; Wessels & Steenkamp, 2009).

Current views maintain that this generation possesses different skills and ways of approaching tasks as a result of their exposure to social and information media (Jonas-Dwyer & Pospisil, 2004; Mitchell, 2003; Wessels & Steenkamp, 2009). Characterized as multi-taskers, they expect instant results from their efforts. Like Generation Xers before them, they seek on-the-fly feedback, are comfortable with more relaxed social communication and, unlike Baby Boomer faculty and employers, are not concerned about formal performance conferences and lengthy written evaluations (Jonas-Dwyer & Pospisil, 2004; Lancaster & Stillman, 2003; Prensky, 2001). Net Generation students see themselves as lifelong learners, looking for feedback and a chance to improve their skills (Lancaster & Stillman, 2003).

Formative Assessment and Feedback

Feedback is an important design component in UDL; feedback is also essential to the Net Generation learner. In this discussion, effective formative feedback is considered to be any communication with students that provides information about their current performance and constructive comments that might help them with future learning (Parboteeah & Anwar, 2009; Parr & Timperley, 2010; Parr & Limbrick, 2010). Once a clear goal has been set (e.g., course goal, performance objective), formative assessment can provide feedback on where the learner stands in relation to that goal, as well as how to get there (Black & Wiliam, 1998; Hattie and Jaeger, 1998; Parr & Timperley, 2010; Yorke, 2003).

Recent studies on the current state of student satisfaction with feedback is mixed. Some report student dissatisfaction with feedback due to a perception that it is irrelevant to future work (Handley & Williams, 2011); others indicate that when feedback is specific, it is thought to be good, but provided globally to the group, it is perceived to be useless. In a surprising third category, students perceive that they are receiving more feedback than their instructors perceive they are providing (Montgomery & Baker, 2007).

Universally, feedback is perceived as necessary to enhance learning and achieve outcomes (Clynes & Raftery, 2008). Instructors voice concern, however, regarding the time commitment and ease with which different methods of providing feedback can be executed. Using student blogs is an efficient and effective way to provide Net Generation learners with opportunities to show what they know and engage in formative assessment of their products.

METHODS

Course context and Participants The context for this exploration was a fall semester course in which all students in the course earned a final grade of A or B; and all student blogs met the grading criteria during the 10 weeks of blogging

Participants were graduate students, chosen by the course instructor as partners in investigating how blogs support student learning. From the students most recently enrolled in the course, she invited four to collaboratively explore the topic. The co-researchers were selected based on two criteria: all had stated a desire to engage in further research and each represented a different style of blogging. The four co-researchers represent four blogging styles: formal voice/text-focused, informal voice/text-focused, formal voice/media-focused, and informal voice/media-focused. Formal voice refers to a traditional, third-person academic writing style; informal voice is a more stream-of-consciousness, first-person style.

This range of blogging styles illustrates the typical student blogging experiences the instructor has observed in four semesters of using course response blogs. Although it limits generalizability to the larger graduate student population, the typical case sampling used here helps others to transfer the findings to other, similar students.

Design

To select examples from our blogs and determine representative themes, the researcher and co-researchers met both in pairs and as a group. Working in pairs, we reviewed each of our blogs in its entirety, looking for critical elements. These examples are illustrated below. As a group, we sought commonalities across our work and developed several overarching themes that represent what we see as the key elements of effective blog use in graduate settings.

MEETING THE NEEDS OF NET GENERATION LEARNERS THROUGH BLOGS

Examples from a Graduate Research Course

Excerpts from four students' Introduction to Research in Education blogs are provided, followed by a discussion of themes across the blogs.

Carin

A millennial in her first semester of a school counseling master's program, Carin adopts a formal writing style in her blog entries. She uses a clear prose to convey her thoughts, with different ideas clearly divided into different paragraphs. Carin's responses to the assignment prompts are clear and well-documented, with a focus on providing a complete answer and obtaining useful instructor feedback.

Carin's blogs reveal her level of confidence with each skill addressed in the course. For example, when analyzing a published study she risks making judgment calls regarding the validity of the authors' conclusions.

...I thought the general conclusions that were drawn concerning the implications of these results were overly optimistic. First of all, the results varied quite widely in terms of predictive validity across the board, none of which was discussed in greater detail. Second of all, even though canonical correlation is designed to predict individual and shared variance in the independent and dependent variables, this research design was nonexperimental and does not indicate causality. Therefore, indicating that each of these skills is critical to positive career outcomes in the conclusion is unfounded. Nevertheless, by emphasizing the result that individual and shared variance

among the skills positively predicted 79% of the variance on five of the six outcomes, I believe that, for what it originally set out to do, this study achieved its purpose.

Carin uses traditional text to share her thoughts; the instructor can then respond immediately to the blog entry to reinforce that confidence with agreement or redirect it with constructive feedback. The comments section of the blog can be used for conversation between instructor and student with minimal risk since both the original text and the comments can be added to, changed, deleted, published, and hidden; the locus of control is always firmly in the hands of the learner.

As a student who uses a fairly formal communication style, Carin supplies a great deal of detail in her blog entries. In this excerpt, she shares her ideas about what to put in her final research project:

As the investigator in this particular phenomenological study, I would need to conduct in-depth interviews with students to understand the role their high school counselors played in influencing their sense of confidence in terms of career direction. Rather than gather specific numerical data, I would be attempting to gain a better understanding of the role counselors play in helping high school seniors develop a clear and confidence sense of career direction by gathering verbal descriptions of their personal experiences and qualifying student-counselor interactions by progress made in career-planning. I might even tweak my research design as I go depending on the amount of valuable information I felt that I was getting from these initial observations. My results would be in the form of field notes as opposed to numerical data with the goal being to understand the student-counselor relationship instead of to statistically describe how data reveals a relationship between variables. Due to the intensive and purposeful nature of this type of observation, I would only be able to work with a small sample, perhaps a single school, where I would develop a close and trusting relationship with the individuals participating.

The level of detail Carin provides allows her instructor to offer specific written feedback. Since the blog entry is constructed of digital text, the instructor is able to copy and paste the student's own words into the comments section. An instructor comment might be, "When you write that your 'results would be in the form of field notes as opposed to numerical data' I thought about how some field notes may consist of numerical data; noting a trend using a numerical chart while you are on site may be a useful method for you to record your observations." By using a student's own words when providing feedback, formative comments are clearly tied to the student's demonstrated knowledge.

In the example above, Carin is sharing her plans for the research proposal, which is a complex assignment assessed by a lengthy rubric. Both student and instructor are aware of the goals of the assignment, and this detailed blog entry helps the instructor to provide the feedback that Carin is on the right track. An instructor comment intended to do this is, "You write, 'I would only be able to work with a small sample, perhaps a single school, where I would develop a close and trusting relationship with the individuals participating.' I agree with this; if you select too many sites and too many participants you are likely to defeat your purpose of getting to know what your participants are thinking. The plan that you have outlined is reasonable and doable—go with it!" As in countless student-teacher conversations held after class or during office hours, students are able to share what they are thinking regularly and without concern that it has to be correct. The instructor is freed from the role of summative evaluator and can work as a "guide on the side," clarifying apparent misconceptions, reinforcing correct notions, and applauding insightful decisions. Of course, this depends on the amount of detail the student provides, but that issue exists for classroom conversation as well.

As an academically gifted millennial, Carin clearly asks for the support that she needs:

...I have done my best to explain what is being measured and how it is being coded, but I need some feedback as to what is missing or still unclear as it is hard to see it from my subjective perspective at this point...Most of all I just want to hear what is still missing from this paper. Although I feel that the majority of it is present, I want to be sure that I have a clear and comprehensive proposal in hand that is realistically possible to follow through with in the near future!

In some instances, she was specific about what she did not want feedback on:

I've been through my paper many times at this point and while I recognize that my literature review is long, I really believe that the content is necessary to describe the conceptualization of this study as it occurred to me, especially because I want to explain its relevance/connection with the phenomenon of emerging adulthood. I've used headers for the relevant sections to help bring <sic> more structured, but still I need some outside feedback to help see what readers find necessary and unnecessary to cover in this section.

The instructor need not provide all of the detailed formative feedback; students can conduct self-analysis in their blogs. When prompted to reflect on the skills she has developed over the course of the semester, Carin clearly details the progress she has made. The reflection is a learning activity for her as much as it is a monitoring tool for her instructor.

My ability to effectively sift through research literature is the direct result of the extensive practice I had in doing so while conducting the literature review for my own research proposal. With the help of Marilyn at the library, I am now confident in my skills to access and review educational literature from texts, journals and computer library databases. Although it took a lot of time and effort, I feel good about my ability to write a coherent synthesis of such literature as it relates to the research problem, even when it requires some creativity to connect previously unconnected ideas.

The formal voice Carin has assumed in her blog echoes the writing style and format of traditional graduate-level student assignments.

Erin

Like Carin, Erin is a graduate student in the area of school counseling. In her blog, Erin uses mostly text with a stream-of-consciousness point of view; she uses headings to signify topic changes. Humor and personal reflection play an important role in her writing.

In this course, the blog entries were intended to serve as stepping-stones to creating a research proposal. Erin used her blog exactly this way. In these excerpts, she is reviewing published research studies:

The researchers gained permission from the faculty to give the survey in the actual classes (which is what I plan to do in mine – captive audience!)

I am especially interested in this study because my own would build onto it and look more specifically into the motivation aspect. The first measurement scale that they used might also work in my study. I would need to look more in depth at the studies that helped create it to see how valid just that section was, and if it would fit my research.

As she makes her thought process known in her blog entries, the instructor has an opportunity to jump in and make it a conversation, reinforcing when she is on the right track and redirecting when guidance is needed.

Erin uses analogy to connect new knowledge to old. In this excerpt, she has just finished explaining the threats to internal validity in great detail. Alongside a digital photo of the board game Mousetrap, she writes:

And since this was more of a snoozer of a blog than normal, here's a picture of one of my favorite board games ever! You wind the crank, which swings the boot, which kicks the bucket, which sends the marble down the zig-zag <sic> into the chute, which hits the pole that knocks the hand that supports the ball, that falls through the hole into the bathtub, and then through another hole, and hits the seesaw, which launches the diver who lands in the barrel, which shakes the pole that supports the cage that falls on the mouse. It's all connected. One little threatening piece can mess up the whole game. However, as long as we're aware of these pieces and can point them out, our studies are still worth it.

The ability to make a connection between existing conceptual knowledge and new information is of a higher cognitive level than simple restating of what a text or lecture has provided (Anderson, et al., 2001). Students who use the images and experiences from their lives to make connections to the unfamiliar and often difficult-to-fathom content of graduate school have a sturdier foundation on which to work.

As with Carin's work, Erin's writing demonstrates a high confidence level. Like other millennials, she is willing to offer an opinion and pose new questions.

The author does a good job telling us about his theoretical viewpoint and backing it up with other research about that theory and the instruments used. However, what if you have a different viewpoint?

Erin's writing remains focused on her goal while remaining informal in voice and tone. In this excerpt, she is both analyzing a published research study and poking fun at her instructor.

Having been trained to skip the beginning and skip right to the research question, regardless of the fact that I actually did plan to read this entire article, I automatically know several variables for this study.

Students can make a classroom response blog more or less formal to meet their needs. Where Carin focuses on clearly laying out her thoughts and presenting them in a way that facilitates discussion with the instructor, Erin's entries hint at an awareness of both her instructor and an unknown, greater audience that can benefit from what she has to say. In reflecting on a published research study, she writes:

Cool! We've determined amazing results that all women value ability more than men and that all high school students see affect for music as a major attribution to success or failure ... and then some! Not so fast there, pal. Here's the problem. You can't determine that for sure. You just can't. Why not!? There were lots of participants and there are correlations all over the place. The results were different based on each variable, so why can we not say that these variables caused the results!? It sure looks that way in the graph! Ok yes, there were a lot of participants; over 1000 actually! However, if the variables do make a difference, than the graphs actually somewhat contradict each other. There are just TOO many variables being studied here.

Erin's informal style of personal reflection allows the instructor an unusual entrée into her strategic processing.

In thinking about my question, I have decided that a more qualitative approach is probably best, al-

lowing for focus groups and deeper conversation with the students. The options below, however, are based on a study that is more quantitative in nature. Considering that I would need to know the results of the Myers-Briggs test, the below tests might not be best because there would be no way to choose equal introverted and extroverted students. Just to humor you, let's see what we'd get anyway.... Ok let's be real. In the type of study I'm suggesting, there's no way to get a perfect probability sample. There might be certain professors of the honors classes that don't want to let me in to work with their students. Plus, there are likely several students who will miss class on the day of the Myers-Briggs test, etc. Plus, probability sampling does not allow me to group students based on the factors that I need to in order to research the students. The following options become slightly more feasible. Let's consider.... I could see where this would work in certain topics, however I think for my study, this could skew the results. I need to have little prior knowledge as to why the chosen students chose their major so I don't mess up any interaction between group members or ask any leading questions, etc.... ***Extreme case sampling:*** *This is the idea of using complete outliers to study a certain category. In my case, I might pick students with really unpopular majors or from crazy unique backgrounds. Clearly this is not what I am going for as they wouldn't represent the rest of the students at all. I am marking this one right off the list of options for me.*

This stream-of-consciousness monologue offers many of the positive aspects of informal face-to-face conversation. Many of the connections that an instructor might tease out in conversation with a student are laid bare in the blog entry, ready for feedback. Erin also uses the blog entries to self-assess her work:

I feel like this question is extremely broad....possibly too broad. However, as a qualitative question, this leaves room for changing course if suddenly all of the students are talking about one specific thing or if different issues entirely are brought up. For instance, above, I have shown interest in decisions regarding major as being something that sounds (just from overheard conversations) like something that this population struggles with based on cultural pressure...I'm not sure yet which route would be better. I almost want to lean shockingly toward the quantitative study because it would produce some down-and-dirty statistics that could be shown to faculty and staff to help them understand students better (and likely faster?). However, I definitely see the value in the qualitative study since, when you're looking at societal pressure, you're looking at feelings and emotions that aren't always clearly expressed through a survey. There is good data there that might come from facial expressions and longer interviews that stem from deeper relationships with the participants.

Carin and Erin use different styles but manage to share similar levels of detail in their blog entries. They represent different millennial learner traits, but are consistent in sharing their thought processes, engaging in self-assessment, and their openness to constructive feedback.

Lucy

On the first day of class, Lucy informed the instructor that she was not feeling confident that she would be successful in this course. As she wrote in her final blog entry,

Before taking this course, I heard so many horror stories of the difficulties of the course:

- *The ability of not comprehending the material;*
- *The impossibility of getting an A or B in the course;*
- *Lastly, the dreaded research paper!*

I was so afraid on the first day of class! I did not what to expect...

Lucy's blog was already up and running as a part of the adult learning master's course of study at the university, and her humorous but fairly formal writing style was established. Her blog entries usually include creative visuals, with embedded video and graphic organizers characteristic of her posts. She organizes her thoughts with headings and bulleted lists. Honesty, personal notes and humor also play occasional roles in her entries:

Laaawwwwd, I have had a time with this research paper! From portions of the blogs not saving or converting...from Microsoft Word freezing up, crashing, and then my entire paper was missing! In my lifetime, I have never been so involved in writing a paper. I felt like Job when God stripped him of everything that he had...his money...his family...everything! However, like, Job...I did not curse God! I stood firm because I knew that it would work itself out because I have faith!

Lucy uses an element of self-talk in her blog. Here she reflects on her own process and includes an affirmation:

The literature review is the most important portion of the paper and I find myself making changes every time I read it. I am finding more articles that can be used as a foundation for the study, and I find myself reading the literature review to find ways to include the articles in the proposal. I am working hard to ensure that the literature review is sound! I can honestly say I slacked a little in the middle weeks...overwhelmed; but, I am back on track and ready to ensure that I produce a piece of work that is solid, passionate, and a document that I can be proud of!

Like Erin, Lucy uses analogy to connect new learning to prior knowledge. In this excerpt, she shares with her audience (the instructor and any other potential readers) her way of understanding the difference between causality and correlation, an important concept in research.

Joey and the Broken Refrigerator ... http://www.youtube.com/watch?v=MTbZoKEOkUg. As portrayed in the clip from the show, Friends, Joey accused Rachel of breaking his refrigerator because it stopped working after she moved in. As portrayed in the clip and in real life, it is human instinct to generalize and draw conclusions based on the evidence presented and your personal view or experiences. In fact, this is a touchy subject because in some cases, your personal generalization can be incorrect. This is causation! Causation is the relationship between conduct and result. It is the belief that a certain outcome is the result of a certain variable...For another example on causation view the YouTube video links below, Independent & Dependent Variables (and causal arguments too) and Causation.

Lucy uses hyperlinks, graphics, and video throughout her blog. Figure 1 illustrates how Lucy ties in videos to her responses to compare and contrast ethnographic and phenomenological research methods.

Figure 2 displays a small part of a blog entry in which she includes headings, a bulleted list, a graphic organizer, textual explanation, and three embedded YouTube videos. Lucy's approach to synthesizing a variety of media epitomizes how Net Generation students perceive that if relevant media is available, it should be incorporated into their creative works.

Rachel

Rachel is a working mother completing a master's degree in school counseling. A veteran blogger, she is comfortable with taking digital pictures and sharing them online. Rachel has crafted her research course blog as a series of cooking analogies, complete with personal stories, recipes, hyperlinks, and dozens of food photos. Rachel's often humorous writing style occasionally refers to her need to multitask and meet her own basic needs as well as complete the assignments.

Figure 1. Students use embedded video to provide detail in their explanations

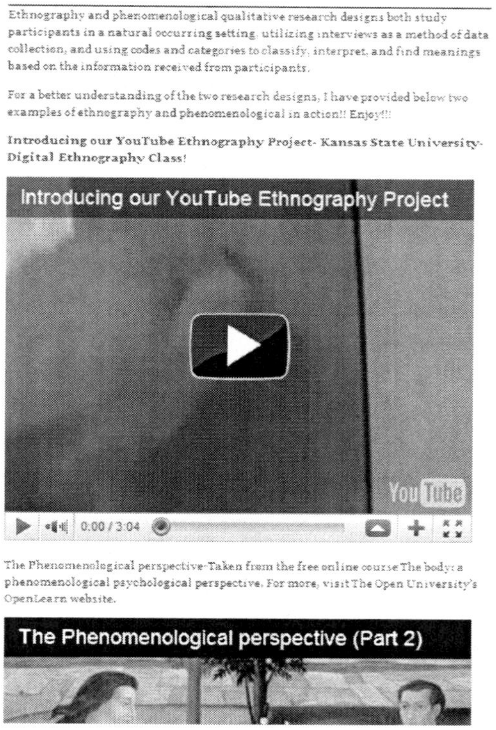

Ethnography and phenomenological qualitative research designs both study participants in a natural occurring setting, utilizing interviews as a method of data collection, and using codes and categories to classify, interpret, and find meanings based on the information received from participants.
For a better understanding of the two research designs, I have provided below two examples of ethnography and phenomenological in action!! Enjoy!!!
Introducing our YouTube Ethnography Project- Kansas State University-Digital Ethnography Class!
Introducing our YouTube Ethnography Project
YouTube
0:00 / 3:04
The Phenomenological perspective-Taken from the free online course The body: a phenomenological psychological perspective. For more, visit The Open University's OpenLearn website.
The Phenomenological perspective (Part 2)

Figure 2. Video, bulleted lists, and traditional text are combined in a blog entry

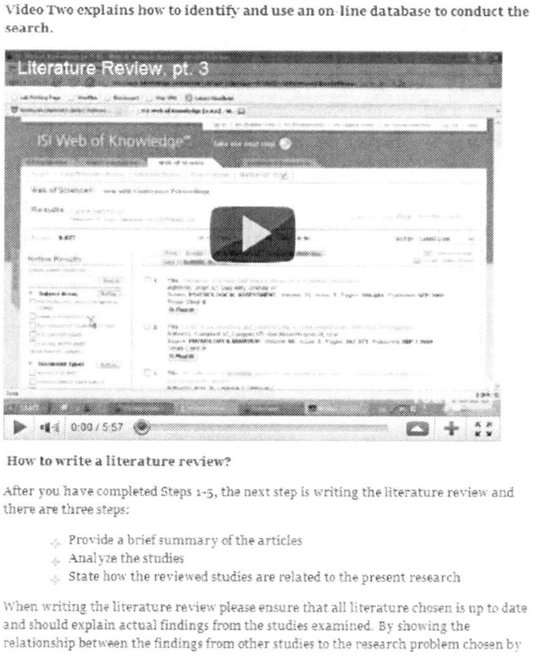

Video Two explains how to identify and use an on-line database to conduct the search.
Literature Review, pt. 3
ISI Web of Knowledge
0:00 / 5:57
How to write a literature review?
After you have completed Steps 1-5, the next step is writing the literature review and there are three steps:
Provide a brief summary of the articles
Analyze the studies
State how the reviewed studies are related to the present research
When writing the literature review please ensure that all literature chosen is up to date and should explain actual findings from the studies examined. By showing the relationship between the findings from other studies to the research problem chosen by

Rachel's use of humor in the blog alerts her instructor to one of two opposite feelings: either confidence in a topic or the lack thereof. In this example, she has the confidence to be playful with the concept of history as a threat to internal validity.

...since the survey is disseminated online, a huge power outage could sweep the eastern seaboard, thus making it impossible to complete. All our computers could blow up. Someone could forget to pay the bill for their internet, forcing them to complete the survey in the library. The library could impose a 10 minute checkout time for all computers. Someone could get in a car accident and break their dominant hand, reducing the likelihood that they could use the computer to do the survey. The researcher could forget to hit the "submit survey" button.

In other situations, she is more tentative, making fewer declarative statements and posing more reflective or tentative ones.

...problem with the survey instrument is including the big 5 assessment, which is crucial to the success of the project. But I cannot honestly give a 120 question online survey, which is what it's turning out to be. I don't want participants who are already pressed for time and stressed about it to spend more than 20 minutes, tops, on completing this. It is a real challenge to know what to leave out and what not to.

Like Erin, Rachel uses humor aimed at a perceived authentic audience, which includes, but is not limited to, the instructor. The conversational tone of her blog is both entertaining and didactic; she intends to teach someone something in an interesting way as opposed to just demonstrating knowledge for a homework assignment. She also uses italics to include "sidebars" related to the cooking theme of her blog, acknowledging that cooking is not the focus of the assignment but is a meaningful topic for her.

It's all about relationship, isn't it? We want to know why things go together and how they affect each other. I've seen it over and over in counseling, because we're trained to look for the small details that draw everything together and present a picture we can work from. Sometimes we made a little leap and make 2+2=5 because we're just trying to find out how to help. We want to fix it. This is very bad when doing a comparative or correlational research study. I'm not quite sure how, but I'm going to attempt to work artichokes into this conversation at some point. Artichokes don't have anything to do with research, but this is a cooking blog and that's what I cooked.

More than just an interest area, cooking is a way for Rachel to make sense of new information by linking it to prior knowledge. She uses analogies to food preparation to think through as well as to present new concepts. In one blog entry (Figure 3), Rachel prepares for the first time Julia Childs' *rix duxelles* and engages in the first refinement of her research question.

Rachel clearly feels comfortable as a blogger and takes control of what she shares in her entries and how she shares it. Some of her entries are quite sophisticated, with careful pre-planning necessary to make a point. In this example, she has shared a lengthy, fairly formal description of the ethical practices necessary in social sciences research, and provides an object lesson.

Now that we've gotten that out of the way, let's make tzatziki! (And I have something that I'll deceptively keep from you until the very end. Tell me if you feel it's unethical, okay?) ...So, do you know what information I didn't disclose? This isn't really tzatziki [hyperlinked to an image of the food], although it's close. It's the only way I can get my son to eat cucumbers. This isn't cucumber dip [hyperlinked to a description of the food], either. It's the red-headed stepchild of two recipes I found and tweaked until I liked it. Will you lose sleep over my deception? Will it make you not want to eat anything out of my kitchen? Did you know I'm bringing this to class so I don't eat it all? Is it unethical to call something by a name because it sounds more interesting and you know people will eat it because they have no idea what's really in it? You tell me.

Rachel, like her peers, conducts self-analysis in her blog entries. She steps back to look at her learning progress by comparing how she engaged in research activities before the course and what she knows how to do now:

I also know how to do a real, live, honest to goodness lit review. I've done them in the past, but admit to overusage of Google. I didn't have a clue about all the databases, google scholar [sic], and other resources available to me.

Figure 3. A personal digital photo and chart are used to support a textual explanation

With a clean towel, take a handful of the chopped mushrooms and slowly, painfully, wring out the moisture. You'll get almost 1/2 cup of moisture from 6 ounces of mushrooms.

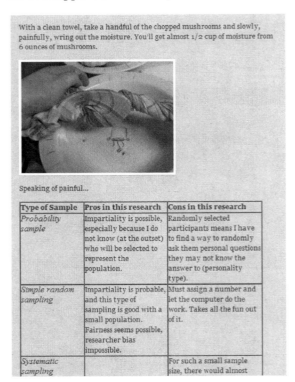

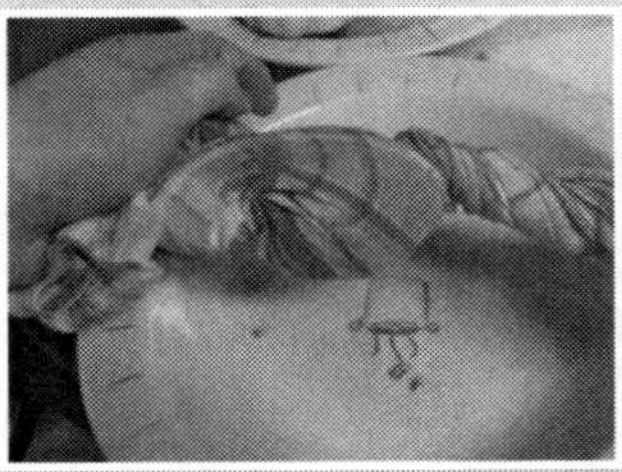

Speaking of painful...

Type of Sample	Pros in this research	Cons in this research
Probability sample	Impartiality is possible, especially because I do not know (at the outset) who will be selected to represent the population.	Randomly selected participants means I have to find a way to randomly ask them personal questions they may not know the answer to (personality type).
Simple random sampling	Impartiality is probable, and this type of sampling is good with a small population. Fairness seems possible, researcher bias impossible.	Must assign a number and let the computer do the work. Takes all the fun out of it.
Systematic sampling		For such a small sample size, there would almost

Rachel also makes clear to the instructor where she is in the learning progression:

...after the bloodbath that was the rough draft, I'm taking one section at a time and really figuring out exactly what to talk about from the lit review. There are so many areas I could go that it's kind of overwhelming but I want a cohesive study, so I'll take each part as a part and then see if that part works as a whole.

Rachel's need for feedback reflects the millennials' desire for multiple needs to be met in a lighthearted way. In this excerpt, she responds to the prompt, "What questions or tasks do you still have in front of you?":

1. is this the right direction? it still seems very broad.
2. can I find out what I want to find out?
3. will I achieve world fame through this project?
4. hours to myself without a child, 140 hours of work/school/work at school, and cakeball making to work on this
5. bringing it all together the way I know I can write it. It's great in my head!

These examples illustrate how Carin, Erin, Lucy, and Rachel, all students in the same research methods course, approach challenging content. This course is known for its heavy workload, yet the tone of the blog entries remains positive and often tempered by humor. The research methods course is disliked by students for its perceived abstractness and lack of real world application, yet here we have seen students make connections to prior knowledge and to resources from the world around them. The difference between previous students' experiences and the experiences illustrated here are due to the application of Universal Design for Learning to the course curriculum.

When instructors apply the principles of UDL to curriculum design, they separate learner goals from instructional methods (Rose & Meyer, 2002). Applying the UDL framework to the research methods course began with setting clear goals that indicate what learners must accomplish while refraining from specifying how they must achieve the goals. This design element avoids the pitfall of confusing the means for achieving the goal with the goal itself—a common source of barriers to effective learning. All four graduate students featured in this chapter use different methods to respond to clearly-focused blog prompts—and all four successfully demonstrate their knowledge of the core concepts of educational research. If the requirement had been to use only traditional prose, those who convey information better through video and graphics would be needlessly marginalized. Conversely, if the instructor had required video compilations, those who prefer text and still images would face a barrier that was inherent in the curriculum—but unrelated to the actual goals of the course.

With flexible digital media (such as blogs) as a canvas, Net Generation learners can use still and moving graphics, sounds, words, and hyperlinks to construct knowledge. As we have seen in these examples, each learner makes her own decisions as to how to construct her knowledge of educational research; as long as multiple, flexible means achieving learner goals are available, adult learners can select their own methods of showing what they know without instructors needing to compromise rigorous course goals.

In the UDL framework, the brain's affective network is supported through the provision of multiple, flexible means of engagement. In the examples above, humor, voice, and the choice of explanatory materials (e.g., images, hyperlinks) illustrate multiple, flexible means of engagement. In addition, as blog posting is an ongoing, topic-focused activity, instructor comments and self-reflection serve as timely, relevant, and continuous feedback—another important design element to support learner engagement.

Exploration of these four graduate students' blogs produces three themes. First, instructors must teach, encourage, and support students as they engage in crafting their own understandings using the media of choice. Second, they must create a positive environment for students to easily convey what they do and do not understand. Finally, instructors must provide timely, relevant, and continuous feedback. Combined, these themes form a call for postsecondary educators to engage in more mindful instructional design using the brain-based UDL framework for teaching and learning.

ANALYSIS

Create a Positive Environment for Formal or Informal Communication

Instructors reconsider their role in teaching and learning when they apply the Universal Design for Learning framework to their courses. One must create meaningful student-centered activities to provide students with multiple, flexible means of expression and engagement. These activities must allow students to convey what they are thinking and why, as well as to ask for guidance when necessary. Instructors must proactively plan for effective communication methods to be part of the course.

Since Net Generation learners prefer positive and relaxed learning environments that offer just-in-time feedback, the traditional formality of university instruction should be reconsidered. Students should be able to engage with instructors at different levels of formality depending on the purpose of the communication.

In the examples above, Carin maintains a level of formality seen in traditional written assignments. She is comfortable working in that register and has no difficulty communicating her ideas using the blog platform. Although she uses a great deal of media in her work, Lucy also communicates with a fairly formal tone, and the blog platform suits her needs equally well.

Erin deviates from that formal tone. Erin uses a stream-of-consciousness style that reveals to the instructor what she is thinking, and why she is thinking it; the online journal format of the blog makes this voice sound natural. These are the reflections of a conversation with a tutor or colleague, the ones that reflect meaning-making. Formal writing assignments might discourage this "thinking aloud" whereas the blog has been an effective medium for Erin's reflections. Since the goal is to process, reflect, and share, her informal communication style is a perfectly appropriate means to achieve that goal.

Rachel uses a similarly informal voice to share her knowledge and understanding in her blog. As a Net Generation multitasker, Rachel approaches new experiences with aplomb, seeking feedback whenever necessary. As informal communicators, Rachel and Erin both use images, stories, and hyperlinks to convey their idea. Later, in writing their research proposals, both switch their tone to a more formal register.

By carefully crafting flexible ways for learners to communicate, instructors create a positive environment for all students to engage and be successful. Since blogs are generally owned and controlled by the writer, students can adopt whatever tone is appropriate to both their learning style and the task.

Support Multimedia Personal Editorship

Digital natives such as Lucy and Rachel think in terms of images as much as words; capitalizing on those preferences in the learning situation makes good sense. Today's students use technology for social communication and can use those same skills and propensities to demonstrate academic mastery if supported in doing so (Jones & Healing, 2010; Mitchell, 2003; Wessels & Steenkamp, 2009).

Blogs allow students to include photos, video, graphic organizers, and hyperlinks to make personal connections to the content. Multimedia personal editorship is a major benefit of using a blog; Chuang (2010) reported 70% of student blogs reviewed included at least one graphic. All of the students whose blogs excerpts are shown here used graphics, including internet memes, personalized photos, cartoons, graphic organizers, and academic video clips. Students use media to clarify points, connect to prior knowledge, provide background information, build relationships with the instructor, and insert humor.

Erin's connection between threats to internal validity and the children's board game Mousetrap, with the photo embedded in the blog entry, is an example of this—a memorable reference is anchored in a single image. Lucy's video clip about Joey from the television program "Friends" is another; she simultaneously illustrates her point, connects it to prior knowledge, and inserts humor. Lucy writes her blog posts from the perspective of teaching the concept to others; now, when facing a situation in which causation is being inferred erroneously, Lucy has an engaging analogy supported through video that explains to others their errors in thinking.

Lucy and Rachel are learners who understand and see value in using multimedia to demonstrate academic mastery. YouTube videos and graphic organizers are an important part of Lucy's learning style; veteran blogger Rachel sees no reason why she should not embed her photos of food into a blog entry if she can use them to prove a point. Their hyperlinked and real-life connections—conveyed through text, sound, and images—are more memorable to them as adult learners than textbook responses. This positive relationship between blogs and student engagement has been discussed in recent literature, with benefits including a sense that assignments are meaningful, increased levels of knowledge, and interest in further learning (Baker, Rozendal, & Whitenack, 2000; Castleberry & Evers, 2010; Ellison & Wu, 2008; Hsu & Wang, 2010; Hsu, Wang, & Comac, 2008; Kaplan, Rupley, Sparks, & Holcomb, 2007; Wang & Hsu, 2008).

For students to make meaningful academic content connections using popular resources such as YouTube, they must have clear goals. Millennial students report that they prefer clear structures and active learning (Howe, 2003; Wessels & Steenkamp, 2009), so instructors are meeting multiple learner needs by setting clear goals but leaving open the means to achieving those goals—a core principle of the UDL framework. Blog assignments in the Research Methods course focused on the goals of the course, with students creating entries that conveyed their understanding of the content and ability to apply it to a specific topic or situation. For example, one course objective requires the student to "Conduct a review of educational literature from texts, journals and computer library databases." As the culminating assignment for the course is a research proposal, summative assessment is taken care of, but the instructor is left to her own devices in supporting students in learning how to conduct the review. To this end, students were given the blog prompt, "Explain how to conduct and write a review of educational literature from texts, journals and computer library databases. Use computer screenshots, flowcharts, narrative description and any other method that might support your response." All students successfully explained the process (a steep learning curve for many beginning graduate students), but they varied in the way they did it.

Rachel, for example, describes the preparation of a roast. She makes connections between her ingredients and the concept of primary and secondary sources. Her reference to Julia Child's recipe oeuvre as "seminal" works conveys the concept of building on important previous research. She chattily tosses in references to Marilyn, a university research librarian, alongside her food references as if she were the star of a cooking show, talking about whatever crosses her mind that is germane to the topic. Lucy, on the other hand, carefully divides the literature review process into stages based on videos that she located (e.g., "Video One explains the purpose of a literature review and the difference between primary and secondary sources," "Video Two explains how to identify and use an on-line database to conduct the search"). She adds in a graphic to illustrate the stages and ties the media together with explanatory text. The important Universal Design for Learning principle for an instructor to note is how the goal is so clear students can use a multitude of methods to achieve it, according to their learning preferences, prior knowledge, and interest areas. If prompts are structured to reflect clear goals, student blogs become a digital portfolio of their personal connections to the course's most important skills and concepts.

When Howe and Strauss write that the millennial generation learner is "special," they note that for instructors "the key is feedback and structure. Constant quizzing and practice, regular instructor review, small projects, and an emphasis upon core skills mastery will be welcome. Large class projects designed to 'spread the class out' and one-time sink-or-swim exams will trigger anxiety, and perhaps resistance, from students and parents" (2003, 73). As blogs are social media intended to be used for an extended period of time (in this course, for approximately 10 weeks), students can use the tool to regularly processing information in any way they desire within a set structure established by the blog prompts. Carin's blog, with its skillful prose, frequently ties her current learning to that which came before. She creates clear statements that summarize concepts and then backs those statements up with examples and explanation. Any purpose a quiz or instructor review might have served has already been handled by her as a reflective adult learner. Erin's detailed stream-of consciousness explanations clearly illustrate her strategic processing. The information gathered from Erin's blog posts about her thought processes is of far greater value to the instructor seeking formative assessment data than any summative assessment such as a "one-time sink-or-swim exam." Of greatest note is that each of these students can identify—on a weekly basis—whether they have mastered the content.

Use Technology to Provide Effective Formative Feedback

Students need to know how their current work compares to their learning goals (Collins & Halverson, 2009). When instructors apply the Universal Design for Learning framework to their curriculum, they set clear goals and make certain that students are aware of what the goals are. As discussed previously, that opens the door for learners to use a range of methods to achieve those goals—reducing unnecessary barriers to learning—but a second, equally important result of conveying clear goals to students is that they can identify what they must do to achieve success.

Students have indicated that they need more than just a "good job" (Hattie & Jaeger, 1998). To improve student goal achievement, instructors must provide specific feedback that shows learners how to close the gap between current performance and the learner goals—or enable the student to self-assess and provide that feedback for themselves (Hattie & Jaeger, 1998; Parr & Timperley, 2010; Yorke, 2003). Learners prefer specific feedback over general feedback or none at all. Once they have experienced effective formative feedback, they are aware that it helps them understand what they need to improve, why it needs to change, and how to do it (Carroll, 1995; Crews & Wilkinson, 2010; Taguchi & Ogawa, 2009; Yorke, 2003). Students also perceive that feedback can help build a relationship with the instructor and be successful in class (Crews & Wilkinson, 2010).

The use of blogs in the Introduction to Research Methods course allowed the instructor to write specific feedback in the comments section of student entries. A couple of examples can illustrate this use of feedback. Early in the semester, Rachel writes:

I choose proportional stratified sampling as my method. And now back to my question. First, we need to define resiliency. Then, we need to define personality. Thirdly, we need to figure out how to identify people's personalities AND their resiliency levels, if we have any hope of making this work. Then, somehow, we have to prove that all of that together makes a beautiful soup of Bachelors, Masters, Doctoral, or other higher-education experience for such people. Here is it (crosses fingers): People with certain personality types evidence more resiliency than other types, no matter their background, gender, or ethnic group, and have better success rates in the realm of higher education. As with all good things…sometimes you just have to throw in a little spice at the end and hope it all works out okay.

Her instructor responds:

Thanks for the veggie slant [smiley-face emoticon acknowledges this week's recipe is meat-free after the student found out the instructor was vegetarian]…Nothing wrong with proportional stratified sampling as long as you can justify the proportions and have a solid sampling frame (a real challenge). Enjoy constructing your operational definitions. Hopefully you find them in your lit review! Once you have, your question will seem less grammatically nightmarish [smiley-face emoticon to soften critical tone].

This brief comment is intended to (1) make a personal connection with Rachel, (2) reinforce that she is headed in the right direction while providing additional advice (i.e., determine on what you are basing the stratification), and (3) show agreement that operational definitions must be determined before continuing on. The emoticons are intended to add tone and soften any harshness that might result from text-only asynchronous communication. Although blog comments are asynchronous, students often respond in person to posted comments during the next class session's break time, indicating that instructor comments are read, digested, and worth discussing during the short period students and faculty are face-to-face.

In her blog, Erin writes:

Even though my study is more qualitative in nature, I still want a bit of randomness to get a variety of backgrounds and personalities…However, as stated, I need to be able to form groups based on certain variables. I think I might start with cluster sampling to narrow down the students, and then take a convenience sample of whoever from this group will actually opt-in to participate.

Her instructor responds, "I agree that you need to be able to form groups based on certain variables, and that cluster sampling is the way to go followed by an opt-in procedure. Nicely done, and not bad for a one-week turnaround in topic focus [smiley-face emoticon]." The comment provides reinforcement that the design decision is a sound one (related to the clear course goal of selecting a sampling method based on an identified research question) and recognizes the effort that Erin put into re-examining her methods based on a revised research question (a common graduate student stumbling block). If Erin's thought process had been flawed, there would have been two options for response: write a comment that poses a constructive question to redirect (e.g., "What might be the challenges posed by that sampling method?") or send the feedback in a private email to avoid publicly redirecting her.

Since it is recognized that instructors cannot realistically provide adequate feedback to students using traditional paper-based methods (Pellegrino & Quellmalz, 2010), it is encouraging that instructors can easily provide timely feedback by using RSS feed readers or other monitoring methods. Coupled with the facility of copying and pasting students' own words into the comments section of blog entries, RSS feed readers make the promise of formative feedback via blogs a reality. In this course, the instructor uses Google Reader to automatically collect blog responses and responds using the "comments" hyperlink at the bottom of each entry. Whereas the details of face-to-face and phone conversations fade, digital comments provide a more permanent record to which students can refer at any time (Li, Moorman, & Dyjur, 2010). Over time, blog feedback can help learners self-assess and build deeper understandings, which can in turn increase self confidence (Li, Moorman, & Dyjur, 2010).

Self-assessment is a valuable skill. When students reflect on their progress in their blog entries, they are noting areas of mastery and confidence as well as uncertainty and confusion. This self assessment demonstrates the sense of awareness necessary for students to generalize skills across settings (Wang, 2010). Blogs are known for fostering this self awareness; the act of reflecting through digital media supports the metacognitive processes of students (Castleberry & Evers, 2010). Rachel's use of humor in her blog posts was noted earlier as alerting her instructor to one of two states of mind: either she is confident in her knowledge and feeling playful, or she is still at the learning stage with a topic and she is using a self-deprecating humor to safely explore it. She is as aware of this as her instructor and takes into consideration her own mental state when approaching learning.

Similarly, Carin tends to make declarative statements when she is confident in her knowledge of topic and pose questions or action steps when she is not. She demonstrates awareness of her own thought processes when she writes:

In terms of coding and analyzing the data, I want to know for sure that I have included the necessary steps and methods of analysis to make my intentions clear in this paper. I have read about the tests of significance, MANOVA and ANOVA, and Cohen's *d* in more detail to help understand how these results will be understood and used to support the 'so what' part of this study, but I feel that I still need outside feedback to feel confident about what is there.

She is focusing on a specific area of a large research proposal (analyzing data), reflecting on her actions thus far (reading up on the topic), and identifying what she still needs (feedback on whether the selected methods of data analysis match the rationale and research questions she has created already). Carin has a strong ability to locate her knowledge of a topic or ability to apply a skill and judge the distance between her current and desired performance. The blog reflections and clear goals enable her to do this. This kind of self-reflection is as valuable to a learner as is external feedback from the instructor.

FUTURE RESEARCH DIRECTIONS

This exploratory study provides several themes to build upon in future research. Each should be examined among different populations of learners. Despite minimum competency requirements, graduate programs enroll students who lack relevant skills and prior knowledge; they often struggle greatly with the content of their selected field. Can blogs, with their opportunities for personal reflection and the provision of formative feedback, be used effectively to close the gap between current understanding and the student's learning goals? At-risk graduate students are not the only population of interest. Are blogs feasible learning tools for undergraduate courses, which often enroll much larger numbers than their graduate counterparts? Do older adult learners benefit from the use of blogs as a learning tool? The amount of technology support available is another path for future research. Does the amount of technology instruction and support relate to students' performance and perceived success with using a blog?

Just as the postsecondary student population is not a homogeneous group, we recognize that not all professors are the same. What characteristics must an instructor possess to make the use of blogs a worthwhile endeavor? RSS feeds assist instructors in providing timely feedback while reducing the amount of time it takes to do so, but many faculty are inexperienced in the effective use of social media. Likewise, postsecondary faculty are not necessarily skilled in how to gauge learner progress and provide effective feedback.

We foresee a need for research into the purpose of student blogging in postsecondary education. Meaningful exploration of the differences between a personal reflection blog (with no instructor-facilitated prompts) and a course reflection blog (in which instructors provide prompts that target critical goals of the course) is necessary to guide faculty as to the effective instructional use of this social media tool.

Peer feedback through blog comments is another area that warrants research. Lundstrom and Baker (2008) are among the few researchers exploring the effects of peer assessment on achievement; the benefits to the individuals providing and receiving feedback is an important area of study.

Finally, we note that much of the existing research is based on satisfaction data. A variety of research methodologies will be necessary to address these topics. Student and instructor perspectives, explored and fleshed out through interviews and document review can provide the depth of understanding we need. Surveys and other methods targeting a larger, more representative sample will help us generalize to a broader group of students and faculty.

CONCLUSION

One limitation of this study was that some of the students in the course may have had more negative experiences than the co-researchers. One of the co-researchers, for example, was contacted by several classmates at the beginning of the semester with questions about how to set up the blog and include multimedia in their entries. She believes that it may be necessary to increase the amount of structure related to the blog assignments for students who are not "tech savvy." For the purposes of this inquiry, however, we limited ourselves to commenting on our own experiences.

Blogs, however, remain a useful pedagogical tool for the Net Generation. The multiple, flexible means of expression and engagement available to students through the use of blogs made a difficult course more manageable. Students process challenging content with the option of using a multimedia approach and can make real world connections rather than traditional academic responses in isolation. The instructor's role of knowledge facilitator on the blog platform is clear as she reinforces their moments of confidence and offers formative feedback in the form of questions and suggestions in the comments area of blog entries. Students' multimedia personal editorship, where they express themselves through the use of self-created and borrowed media (e.g., hyperlinks, embedded video, images), is appropriate for a generation that incorporates images and sounds into their mental models as much as words and phrases. Using multiple media, they construct personal knowledge in a challenging course and self-assess their progress. Embedding blogs into university course designs can offer students multiple, flexible forms of expression and engagement; a way to self-assess areas of mastery and improvement, and timely, specific written feedback that closes the gap between current performance and course goals.

REFERENCES

Anderson, L., Krathwohl, D., Airasian, P., Cruikshank, K., Mayer, R., & Pintrich, P. ... Wittrock, M. (2001). *A taxonomy for learning, teaching, and assessing: A revision of Bloom's taxonomy of educational objectives*. New York, NY: Longman.

Baker, E., Rozendal, M., & Whitenack, J. (2000). Audience awareness in a technology rich elementary classroom. *Journal of Literacy Research, 32*(3), 395–419. doi:10.1080/10862960009548086

Black, P., & Wiliam, D. (1998). Inside the black box: Raising standards through classroom assessment. *Phi Delta Kappan, 80*, 139–148.

Bull, G. (November 2010). The always-connected generation. *Leading and Learning with Technology.* Retrieved January 30, 2011 from http://www.iste.org/learn/publications/learning-and-leading/digital-edition-november.aspx.

Carroll, M. (1995). Formative assessment workshops: Feedback sessions for large classes. *Biochemical Education, 23*, 65–67. doi:10.1016/0307-4412(95)00001-J

Castleberry, G., & Evers, R. (2010). Incorporate technology into the modern language classroom. *Intervention in School and Clinic, 45*(3), 201–205. doi:10.1177/1053451209349535

Chuang, H. (2010). Weblog-based electronic portfolios for student teachers in Taiwan. *Educational Technology Research and Development, 58*(2), 211–227. doi:10.1007/s11423-008-9098-1

Clynes, M., & Raftery, S. (2008). Feedback: An essential element of student learning in clinical practice. *Nurse Education in Practice, 8*(6), 405–411. doi:10.1016/j.nepr.2008.02.003

Collins, A., & Halverson, R. (2009). *Rethinking education in the age of technology: The digital revolution and the schools*. New York, NY: Teachers College Press.

Crews, T., & Wilkinson, K. (2010). Students' perceived preference for visual and auditory assessment with e-handwritten feedback. *Business Communication Quarterly, 73*(4), 399. doi:10.1177/1080569910385566

Ellison, N., & Wu, Y. (2008). Blogging in the classroom: A preliminary exploration of student attitudes and impact on comprehension. *Journal of Educational Multimedia and Hypermedia, 17*(1), 99–122.

Handley, K., & Williams, L. (2011). From copying to learning: Using exemplars to engage students with assessment criteria and feedback. *Assessment & Evaluation in Higher Education, 36*(1), 95–108. doi:10.1080/02602930903201669

Hattie, J., & Jaeger, R. (1998). Assessment and classroom learning: A deductive approach. *Assessment in Education, 5*(1), 111. doi:10.1080/0969595980050107

Howe, N. (2003). *Understanding the Millennial generation*. The Council of Independent Colleges' Presidents' Institute. Retrieved January 30, 2011, from http://www.cic.org/publications/independent/online/archive/winterspring2003/PI2003_millennial.html.

Howe, N., & Strauss, B. (2000). *Millennials rising: The next great generation*. New York, NY: Vintage Books.

Hsu, H., & Wang, S. (2011). The impact of using blogs on college students' reading comprehension and learning motivation. *Literacy Research and Instruction, 50*(1), 68–88. doi:10.1080/19388070903509177

Hsu, H., Wang, S., & Comac, L. (2008). Using audioblogs to assist English-language learning: An investigation into student perception. *Computer Assisted Language Learning, 21*(2), 181–198. doi:10.1080/09588220801943775

Jonas-Dwyer, D., & Pospisil, R. (2004). The Millennial effect: Implications for academic development. *HERDSA 27th Annual Conference Proceedings,* (pp. 194-205).

Jones, C., & Healing, G. (2010). Net generation students: Agency and choice and the new technologies. *Journal of Computer Assisted Learning, 26*(5), 344–356. doi:10.1111/j.1365-2729.2010.00370.x

Kaplan, D., Rupley, W., Sparks, J., & Holcomb, A. (2007). Comparing traditional journal writing with journal writing shared over e-mail list serves as tools for facilitating reflective thinking: A study of preservice teachers. *Journal of Literacy Research, 39*(3), 357–387.

Lancaster, L., & Stillman, D. (2003). *When generations collide: Who they are. Why they clash. How to solve the generational puzzle at work*. New York, NY: HarperCollins.

Li, Q., Moorman, L., & Dyjur, P. (2010). Inquiry-based learning and e-mentoring via videoconferencing: A study of mathematics and science learning of Canadian rural students. *Educational Technology Research and Development, 58*(6), 729–753. doi:10.1007/s11423-010-9156-3

Lundstrom, K., & Baker, W. (2009). To give is better than to receive: The benefits of peer review to the reviewer's own writing. *Journal of Second Language Writing, 18*(1), 30–43. doi:10.1016/j.jslw.2008.06.002

Mitchell, S. (2003). *American generations. Who they are. How they live. What they think*. Ithaca, NY: New Strategist Publications Inc.

Montgomery, J. L., & Baker, W. (2007). Teacher-written feedback: Student perceptions, teacher self-assessment, and actual teacher performance. *Journal of Second Language Writing, 16*(2), 82–99. doi:10.1016/j.jslw.2007.04.002

Parbooteeah, S., & Anwar, M. (2009). Thematic analysis of written assignment feedback: Implications for nurse education. *Nurse Education Today, 29*(7), 753–757. doi:10.1016/j.nedt.2009.02.017

Parr, J., & Timperley, H. (2010). Feedback to writing, assessment for teaching and learning and student progress. *Assessing Writing, 15*(2), 68–85. doi:10.1016/j.asw.2010.05.004

Parr, J. M., & Limbrick, L. (2010). Contextualising practice: Hallmarks of effective teachers of writing. *Teaching and Teacher Education, 26*(3), 583–590. doi:10.1016/j.tate.2009.09.004

Pellegrino, J., & Quellmalz, E. (2010). Perspectives on the integration of technology and assessment. *Journal of Research on Technology in Education, 43*(2), 119–134.

Prensky, M. (2001). Digital natives, digital immigrants. *Horizon, 9*(5), 1–2. doi:10.1108/10748120110424816

Rose, D., & Meyer, A. (2002). *Teaching every student in the digital age: Universal design for learning*. Alexandria, VA: Association for Supervision & Curriculum Development.

Simmons, C. D., Willkomm, T., & Behling, K. (2010). Professional power through education: Universal course design initiatives in occupational therapy curriculum. *Occupational Therapy in Health Care, 24*(1), 86–96. doi:10.3109/07380570903428664

Taguchi, N., & Ogawa, T. (2010). OSCEs in Japanese postgraduate clinical training Hiroshima experience 2000-2009. *European Journal of Dental Education, 14*(4), 203–209. doi:10.1111/j.1600-0579.2009.00610.x

Wang, L. (2010). Integrating communities of practice in e-portfolio assessment: Effects and experiences of mutual assessment in an online course. *The Internet and Higher Education, 13*(4), 267–271. doi:10.1016/j.iheduc.2010.07.002

Wang, S., & Hsu, H. (2008). Reflection from using blogs to expand in-class discussion. *TechTrend, 52*(3), 81–85. doi:10.1007/s11528-008-0160-y

Wessels, P. L., & Steenkamp, L. P. (2009). Generation Y students: Appropriate learning styles and teaching approaches in the economic and management sciences faculty. *South African Journal of Higher Education*, *23*(5), 1039–1058.

Yorke, M. (2003). Formative assessment in higher education: Moves towards theory and the enhancement of pedagogic practice. *Higher Education*, *45*(4), 477–501. doi:10.1023/A:1023967026413

ADDITIONAL READING

Baker, W., & Bricker, R. (2010). The effects of direct and indirect speech acts on native English and ESL speakers' perception of teacher written feedback. *System*, *38*(1), 75–84. doi:10.1016/j.system.2009.12.007

Benner, J., & Kapcsos, K. (2010). From consensus to performance: Formative course assessment in elementary algebra. *Assessment Update*, *22*(6), 8–10.

Boshier, P. (2006). *Perspectives of quality in adult learning*. London: Continuum International Publishing.

Boulton-Lewis, G., Wilss, L., & Mutch, S. (1996). Teachers as adult learners: Their knowledge of their own learning and implications for teaching. *Higher Education*, *32*(1), 89–106. doi:10.1007/BF00139220

Brookes, D., & Lin, Y. (2010). Structuring classroom discourse using formative assessment rubrics. *2010 Physics Education Research Conference-. AIP Conference Proceedings*, *1289*(1), 5–8. doi:10.1063/1.3515248

Brookhart, S. M. (2008). *How to give effective feedback to your students*. Alexandria, VA: Association for Supervision & Curriculum Development.

Carter, S., & Pitcher, R. (2010). Extended metaphors for pedagogy: Using sameness and difference. *Teaching in Higher Education*, *15*(5), 579–589. doi:10.1080/13562517.2010.491904

Di Leo, J. (2010). In praise of tough criticism. *The Chronicle of Higher Education*, *56*(38), B4–B5.

Edyburn, D. (2010). Would you recognize Universal Design for Learning if you saw it? Ten propositions for new directions for the second decade of UDL. *Learning Disability Quarterly*, *33*(1), 33–41.

Ferguson, P. (2011). Student perceptions of quality feedback in teacher education. *Assessment & Evaluation in Higher Education*, *36*(1), 51–62. doi:10.1080/02602930903197883

Geeslin, K. (2003). Student self-assessment in the foreign language classroom: The place of authentic assessment instruments in the Spanish language classroom. *Hispania*, *86*(4), 857–868. doi:10.2307/20062958

Guénette, D. (2007). Is feedback pedagogically correct?: Research design issues in studies of feedback on writing. *Journal of Second Language Writing*, *16*(1), 40–53. doi:10.1016/j.jslw.2007.01.001

Haffling, A., Beckman, A., Pahlmblad, A., & Edgren, G. (2010). Students' reflections in a portfolio pilot: Highlighting professional issues. *Medical Teacher*, *32*(12), e532–e540. doi:10.3109/0142159X.2010.509420

Hampton, S., & Reiser, R. (2004). Effects of a theory-based feedback and consultation process on instruction and learning in college classrooms. *Research in Higher Education*, *45*(5), 497–527. doi:10.1023/B:RIHE.0000032326.00426.d5

Hattie, J., & Timperley, H. (2007). The power of feedback. *Review of Educational Research*, *77*(1), 81–112. doi:10.3102/003465430298487

Hendry, G., Bromberger, N., & Armstrong, S. (2011). Constructive guidance and feedback for learning: The usefulness of exemplars, marking sheets and different types of feedback in a first year law subject. *Assessment & Evaluation in Higher Education*, *36*(1), 1–11. doi:10.1080/02602930903128904

Hourigan, T., & Murray, L. (2010). Using blogs to help language students to develop reflective learning strategies: Towards a pedagogical framework. *Australasian Journal of Educational Technology*, *26*(2), 209–225.

Hyland, F. (2003). Focusing on form: Student engagement with teacher feedback. *System*, *31*(2), 217–230. doi:10.1016/S0346-251X(03)00021-6

Jenkins, A. (2009). Serving millennial first-generation students of color. *Recruitment and Retention in Higher Education*, *23*(2), 1–7.

Jones, E. (2010). Personal theory and reflection in a professional practice portfolio. *Assessment & Evaluation in Higher Education*, *35*(6), 699–710. doi:10.1080/02602930902977731

Kattner, T. (2009). Best practices for working with millennial students. *National On-Campus Report*, *37*(16), 5–5.

Leeder, K. (2008). Meeting millennials on their ground. *College & Research Libraries News*, *69*(8), 455–456.

Luehmann, A., & Frink, J. (2009). How can blogging help teachers realize the goals of reform-based science instruction? A study of nine classroom blogs. *Journal of Science Education and Technology*, *18*(3), 275–290. doi:10.1007/s10956-009-9150-x

Lunt, T., & Curran, J. (2010). 'Are you listening please?' The advantages of electronic audio feedback compared to written feedback. *Assessment & Evaluation in Higher Education*, *35*(7), 759–769. doi:10.1080/02602930902977772

Luschen, K., & Bogad, L. (2010). Youth, new media and education: An introduction. *Educational Studies*, *46*(5), 450–456.

Margolinas, C., Coulange, L., & Bessot, A. (2005). What can the teacher learn in the classroom? *Educational Studies in Mathematics*, *59*(1), 205–234. doi:10.1007/s10649-005-3135-3

Martindale, T., & Wiley, D. (2005). Using weblogs in scholarship and teaching. *TechTrends*, *49*(2), 55–61. doi:10.1007/BF02773972

McIntosh, M. (1997). Formative assessment in mathematics. *Clearing House (Menasha, Wis.)*, *71*(2), 92–96. doi:10.1080/00098659709599333

O'Connor, B., & Cordova, R. (2010). Learning: The experiences of adults who work full-time while attending graduate school part-time. *Journal of Education for Business*, *85*(6), 359–368. doi:10.1080/08832320903449618

Pletka, B. (2007). *Educating the net generation: How to engage students in the 21st century*. Santa Monica, CA: Santa Monica Press.

Ravitz, J. (2002). CILT2000: Using technology to support ongoing formative assessment in the classroom. *Journal of Science Education and Technology*, *11*(3), 293–296. doi:10.1023/A:1016032821506

Ruffo, J. (2008). "Millenial" or "net generation" students and their impact on the development of student- centered facilities. *Planning for Higher Education*, *37*(1), 5–6.

Seale, J. (2010). Doing student voice work in higher education: An exploration of the value of participatory methods. *British Educational Research Journal*, *36*(6), 995–1015. doi:10.1080/01411920903342038

Shabani, K., Khatib, M., & Ebadi, S. (2010). Vygotsky's zone of proximal development: Instructional implications and teachers' professional development. *English Language Teaching*, *3*(4), 237–248.

Shaeiwitz, J. A. (1996). Capstone experiences: Are you doing assessment without realizing it? *Assessment Update*, *8*(4), 4–6. doi:10.1002/au.3650080404

Shalem, Y., & Slonimsky, L. (2010). Seeing epistemic order: Construction and transmission of evaluative criteria. *British Journal of Sociology of Education*, *31*(6), 755–778. doi:10.1080/01425692.2010.515106

Singer, J. (2008). Posting for points: Edublogs in the JMC curriculum. *Journalism Mass Communication Educator*, *63*(1), 10–27.

Su, F., & Beaumont, C. (2010). Evaluating the use of a wiki for collaborative learning. *Innovations in Education and Teaching International*, *47*(4), 417–431. doi:10.1080/14703297.2010.518428

Thein, A., Oldakowski, T., & Sloan, D. (2010). Using blogs to teach strategies for inquiry into the construction of lived and text worlds. *Journal of Media Literacy Education*, *2*(1), 23–36.

Yerbury, H. (2010). Who to be? Generations X and Y in civil society online. *Youth Studies Australia*, *29*(2), 25–32.

Yuksel, G. (2009). Incorporating blogs and the seven principles of good practice into preservice ICT courses: A case study. *The New Educational Review*, *19*(3/4), 29–44.

Zepke, N., & Leach, L. (2010). Improving student engagement: Ten proposals for action. *Active Learning in Higher Education*, *11*(3), 167–177. doi:10.1177/1469787410379680

KEY TERMS AND DEFINITIONS

Affective Networks: Brain networks that benefit from multiple, flexible means of engagement.

Blog: Online time-stamped journal generally used to reflect and share the writer's opinions while offering a method for reader comments on individual entries (contraction of "web log").

Formative Assessment: Feedback provided to a learner regarding their current ability in relation to a learning goal, often includes suggestions of how to close the gap between current performance and mastery.

Multimedia Personal Editorship: Expressing oneself through the use of self-created and borrowed media (e.g., hyperlinks, embedded video, images).

Recognition Networks: Brain networks that benefit from multiple, flexible representations of content.

Strategic Networks: Brain networks that benefit from multiple, flexible means of expression and apprenticeship.

Universal Design for Learning (UDL): A framework for teaching and learning based on brain research.

Chapter 12
Using an Anywhere/ Anytime Technology to Facilitate Student Writing

Hilary Wilder
William Paterson University, USA

Carrie Eunyoung Hong
William Paterson University, USA

Geraldine Mongillo
William Paterson University, USA

ABSTRACT

Can a new technology, widely embraced by today's students, be used to facilitate the traditional writing process? In this chapter, we describe a pilot study which used the social networking tool Twitter to afford anytime/anywhere writing by first-year seminar students at a mid-sized public university in the U.S. Students were expected to post ("tweet") weekly ideas, thoughts, and reflections on their first-year experience throughout the semester; in a sense, using Twitter as an omnipresent notepad for jotting down ideas. At the end of the semester, it was hoped that students would be able to compile all the posts into a formally written text (a "Freshman Survival Guide") to see if they could use a new literacy skill to promote traditional writing.

INTRODUCTION

Today's students are the most wired and connected of any generation. With their facility with technology, can a new technology, widely embraced by today's students, be used to facilitate the traditional writing process? New technologies are not only changing the communication expectations and habits of young people, but they are also changing the literacy requirements that these students will need in their professional and personal lives. Many literacy educators are now looking at ways that these new technologies such as e-mail, cellphone text messages, slideshow presentations, weblog posts, and discussion threads can be used to give students a more compelling purpose and a more valid audience for their writing while using technologies that students prefer.

DOI: 10.4018/978-1-61350-347-8.ch012

BACKGROUND

Many believe that students today learn differently from previous generations (Barnes, Marateo, & Ferris, 2007). They are wired, constantly connected, and expect immediacy in communication, but the Net Generation is not known for their reading or writing skills (Sweeney, 2007). Although many teachers blame the decline in writing skills on the technologies that today's students are immersed in, a recent Stanford Study of Writing (Haven, 2009), reports that the opposite, in fact, is true. Students are writing more than ever, but in a different context and form expected by their college professors. The study finds that students are using technologies such as e-mail, cellphone text messages, slideshow presentations, weblog posts, and discussion threads to write for a compelling purpose and to write for a real audience. Literacy research has demonstrated that students produce better writing products when they have an interest in the subject and feel they are writing for a specific purpose (Alvermann, 2001; Englert, 1992). The Stanford study found that the type of writing students enjoyed most was writing that was performative or "does something" (Lundsford, 2009), like creating a poster or a website related to a social issue in which they had an interest. Similarly, initial findings from the Writing in Digital Environments (WIDE) Research Center show that students find value in writing for personal fulfillment and entertainment, using technologies such as cellphones, Facebook and email (Grabill & Pigg, 2010).

There is little doubt that the composition of traditional academic writing has significantly changed with the advent of new digital literacies, but it is not necessarily bad news. Students' writing scores have steadily improved over the last few years according to the U.S. National Assessment of Educational Progress (National Center for Education Statistics, 2007). Today's students are proficient users of multiple technologies and the use of these technologies requires them to be problem solvers and strategic thinkers (Anstey & Bull, 2006). Turner and Katic (2009) suggest that the non-linear literacy practices that are often engendered by new technologies will help students connect more authentically to the meaning-making processes. Sweeny (2010) suggests that technological literacies are related to writing literacies and should be integrated in teaching the latter. Literacy research (Gee, 2007; Lankshear & Knobel, 2006;New London Group, 2000) obliges us to find a way to bridge the gap between out-of-school (texting, twittering, etc.) and in-school literacy instruction because students see these modalities not only as a social communication tool, but a method to accomplish 'real life' tasks.

New technologies such as smart phones or micro-blogging via common cellphones may afford even greater authentic and meaningful writing for these students, providing an inexpensive, anytime/anywhere technology for communicating their thoughts. Twitter (http://twitter.com/) is an example of a micro-blogging technology that is accessible through computers, smart phones and low-end cellphones. "Twitter is a service for friends, family, and co–workers to communicate and stay connected through the exchange of quick, frequent messages. People write short updates, often called "Tweets" of 140 characters or fewer. These messages are posted to your profile or your blog, sent to your followers, and are searchable on Twitter search…All you need to use Twitter is an internet connection or a mobile phone" (Twitter, 2010). Posted tweets can be read by friends and others who have signed up to "follow" these postings and will appear automatically on their Twitter homepage. Tweets that contain a unique hashtag (e.g. "#obama") can be easily searched for to find ones about a specific topic posted by people you are not following. Tweets that refer to a login name (prefaced with the "@" sign) will automatically appear on that person's Twitter homepage, in the Mention section.

Twitter offers a useful tool for promoting writing among Net Generation students. According to a recent Pew Internet & American Life Project report (Zickuhr, 2010), these students commonly use their cell phones to access the Internet and social-networking sites, and send instant messages. Some professors are already using Twitter to promote writing. For example, Mary Knudson (quoted in Kinzie, 2009) lauds Twitter's suitability for writing assignments, saying that "'Not only does Twitter teach students to write concisely with its strict limit on the length of posts,' she said, 'but it also enables them to share valuable information.'"

PURPOSE OF THIS STUDY

In this pilot study, students used Twitter (accessible via their cellphones or the internet), as part of the traditional writing process. The writing process involves several stages in which students planned, drafted, revised, and edited their work. These stages follow Sandmann's (2006) five parts of the writing process: "prewriting (generating ideas), drafting (getting ideas written down as connected text), revising (refining meaning), editing (focusing on form), and publishing (sharing the completed work)" (p.20). One technique of this traditional process that is often overlooked by students is that of generating ideas or jotting down thoughts before they actually sit down to compose the text. During this pre-writing process, students reflect on and consider what might or might not be of use or interest to their reading audience, and collect bits of information that may or may not be subsequently used. It is a significant step for the remaining process of writing, but often a struggle for students without proper assistance.

It was hypothesized that the use of a familiar, always-available tool (i.e. their cellphones) would promote effective generating of ideas and note-taking, one of the crucial first-steps in the writing process described above. Our study was guided by the following research questions:

1. What technology(ies) do students prefer to write with, and why? Did students take advantage of the anytime/anywhere nature of posting via cellphone text messages?
2. If students use a 'sparse' technology (e.g. 140-character tweets) to record ideas, notes, etc. can they then turn that into a comprehensive (expository) text?
3. What do our students think about the 'new writing literacies' that they are practicing?

Twitter Writing Project

To attempt to answer these questions, in the fall 2009 semester, we asked students in a First Year Seminar course to use Twitter to input their ideas and thoughts each week with the goal of collaboratively combining these into a 'Freshman Survival Guide' at the end of the semester. This study was conducted at a mid-sized public university in northeastern United States, where the majority of students are the first in their families to attend college and many enter without an adequate proficiency in language arts and are required to take a remedial reading course when they start. Most of the students come from the urban/working class communities near the university, and of the 15 students in this particular course, 4 were female and 11 male. Students ranged in age from 18 to 20, and represented Caucasian, Latina/Latino, and African-American ethnic/racial backgrounds.

At the beginning of the semester, students were guided in setting up a Twitter account (only one student in the class had a Twitter account prior to this). They were then instructed, as part of a graded assignment, to submit at least two tweets each week with information which would "help other first-year students at the university survive." Students were reminded of the Twitter assignment each week for the next nine weeks of the semester, with the stated intention of turning the set of tweets into a survival guide at the end of this time. During the last day of class, students were asked to fill out a follow-up survey (Appendix A).

Data collection and analyses incorporated both quantitative and qualitative methods. Quantitative data was gathered and analyzed by examining how and when students submitted their writing samples (as recorded by the Twitter system as part of tweeting or posting). Quantitative and qualitative data were collected and analyzed from the follow-up survey to document students' perceptions and use of new writing technologies in academic context.

Results

Over the nine-week period, 221 tweets were posted by the 14 students. The total number of tweets for a student ranged from 8 to 31, with a class average of 16 tweets (SD= 6.4). Female students posted an average of 15.25 total tweets, while the male students average total tweets was 16.5.

The quantitative results on the follow-up survey are shown in Table 1.

Q1: What Technology(ies) do Students Prefer?

When looking at the technologies that students used to post their tweets (as reported by the Twitter system), the overwhelming choice was via the Twitter website (87%), with only 8% submitted by cellphone texting, and 5% submitted by a mobile web application. When asked on the follow-up survey which technology they used and why, the large majority (70%, in Table 1) responded that they used the Twitter website. Comments added by the students indicated that typing into a keyboard was preferable to typing into a cellphone, in addition to avoiding the extra costs of a text message.

This was a bit surprising, given the amount of text messaging on their cellphones that the students were doing during class, but it is possible that the messages they send to friends are extremely short and require less typing than a 'survival guide tweet.' We then looked at the number of characters per tweet (which Twitter limits to maximum of 140), and saw that these

Table 1. Follow-up survey scores

N=10	Strongly Agree/ Agree	Disagree/ Strongly Disagree	Neutral or Blank
1. Twitter is an easy way to submit my weekly thoughts and suggestions	90%	0%	10%
2. When I did my Twitter posts (tweets), I mostly used ___	**Web**: 70%	**Phone App**: 20%	**Text Msg**: 10%
3. I would have preferred to use Blackboard Discussion Boards to submit my weekly ideas.	40%	50%	10%
4. I would have preferred to use a totally different technology	10%	70%	20%
5. Twitter was hard to use.	0%	90%	10%
6. It is important to be able to write down ideas whenever and wherever they occur to me.	50%	10%	40%
7. Turning Twitter posts into printed text was hard.	10%	40%	50%
8. Using Twitter posts is a good way to get started when writing printed documents.	20%	0%	80%
9. Twitter posts, Facebook updates, emails, SMS messages are all valid "new writing literacies."	40%	10%	50%
10. Teachers should NOT use twitter posts, etc. for school assignments.	10%	50%	40%
11. Schools should teach students how to write using new writing styles and technologies.	40%	20%	40%

ranged from 21 to 91 characters for tweets entered via cellphone texting versus 22 to 131 characters for those entered via the Twitter website, so there was no real difference in message length. There also did not seem to be a difference in writing style or content between texting and website postings, with grammatical and spelling rules only loosely followed in both. For example, the tweet "commuters should get to campus atleast [sic] an hour early because of parking," posted via the website was similar in style to the tweet "sbarro's pepperoni and cheese stromboli is really good" posted via text messaging.

Although it had been hypothesized that students would predominantly use a technology that was always accessible to complete the weekly twitter post assignment, this was not the case in this study, as most used the Twitter website instead. Students seemed reluctant to use a personal technology (their cellphones and text accounts) on a school assignment and instead of making use of an anytime/anywhere technology waited until they were seated at a computer to post their thoughts, much like any other school assignment. However, this may have occurred because students are unaccustomed to using Twitter. The Pew Internet & American Life Project found that only 20% of the 18-35 year age group had tried Twitter (Lenhart & Fox, 2009)

At the same time, when asked hypothetically about using other technologies (questions 3 and 4), 50% did not agree that they would have preferred to use Blackboard (which was used by the course for other assignments) and 70% did not agree that they would have preferred a different technology altogether. For example, one student commented that "[it] Helped communicate w/other students as most would not do so if in the classroom... A Facebook group would have sufficed, but Twitter was not too bad." while another commented "Twitter is a nice change from Blackboard ... I had no problem with Twitter" and a third commented "I probably would not have done it at all.[if it had been on Blackboard]." It should be noted that even though all but one student had never used Twitter before this assignment, it did not appear to be a problem for them, with none reporting that it was hard to use (question 5). One student commented "It was easy. All that needs to be done online is login, type and send." and another noted "easy phone accessible."

When looking at date and time posting data recorded by the Twitter system (Figure 1), it was noticed that students who used the web heavily favored afternoon and late evening hours, whereas students who used their cellphones were more likely to post in the morning and afternoon. Both web and cellphone users were more likely to post on Tuesdays (the day the class met and when students were reminded of the weekly two-tweet assignment), however there were very few cellphone postings made on Sunday (a day that many students typically use to catch up on the week's homework).

We had hoped that the availability and familiarity of cellphone texting would encourage students in their 'spur-of-the-moment note-taking' (as part of the writing process), while they were between classes or participating in on-campus activities (many of our students are commuters). However, the data from this shows that they did not take advantage of this, instead posting at times when they were most likely to be seated at a computer and working on their school assignments. At the same time, it appears that the few students who did post using their cellphones did so during their on-campus hours. These results appear to only partially support the idea that an anytime/anywhere technology would facilitate student writing, at least for academic purposes. This is contrary to the findings in the WIDE report (Grabill & Pigg, 2010) which found that students used cellphones for lecture notes, reading notes, research papers, academic papers and outlines.

Q2: Can Students Turn Tweets Into Formal Text?

When looking at the question of whether students can turn tweets into a comprehensive (expository)

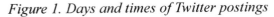

Figure 1. Days and times of Twitter postings

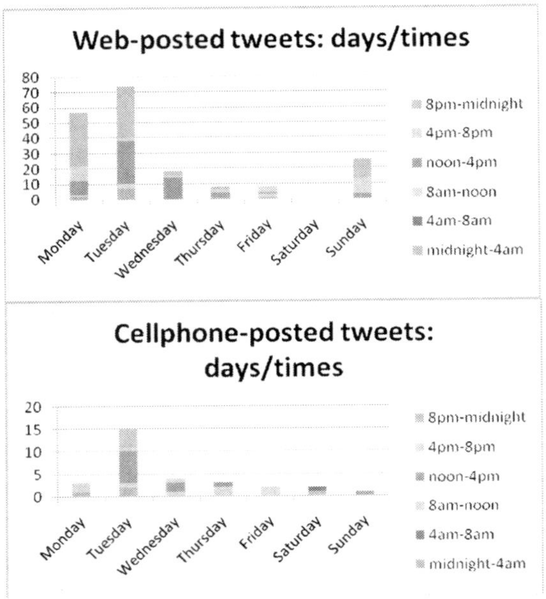

piece of text towards the end of the semester, it became clear to us that there was not enough time left for students to work on this. As a result, the assignment was modified and the students were simply asked to sort the 184 tweets that had been posted thus far (37 of the 221 total were posted after we did this) into the categories. The categories were ones that the class, during a whole-class discussion, had come up with after reviewing the entire set of tweets posted by the class to date. Students were then asked to sort the tweets into bulleted lists under each category and copy them in the Survival Guide. No further attempt was made to turn this into formal, written text, given a lack of time by the end of the semester.

Since students had not had time to produce formally written text for us to analyze, we instead looked at the classification process they used to produce the categorized bullet lists. Appropriate classification of the information by the students indicates an understanding of expository text structure which heavily relies on cognitive classification skills (Williams, 1984). Further, this task is a strong indicator of the students' ability to comprehend the main idea of an expository text. The breakdown of tweets placed in each category is shown in Table 2. It should be noted that not all tweets were placed in a category, and although students derived the categories by reviewing all the tweets, not all categories had tweets placed in them by students.

As noted above, although students came up with the categories of "Extra Curricula" and "Misc.," they did not place any tweets in these categories. At the same time, of the 184 tweets, students decided that 96 (52%) should not be placed in any category. When we looked more carefully at the unused tweets, it appeared that 11 out of the 96 were actually tweets about the student's current status and not really meant for a Survival Guide and therefore appropriately omitted. Examples include "doing laundry at two in the mourning [sic]," "skool [sic] plus about 30+ hrs of work isnt [sic] good.," and "politics exam on November 4th, start studying."

On the other hand, students did not always recognize tweets that might be classified under Extra Curricula, as shown in these unused tweets: "Shea Center has a multitude of events going on all throughout the year. Check out a play or a concert" and "the Rec Center is a great place to work out or play basketball." Similarly, another 21 of the unused tweets could have been put in the Misc. section, for example: "Be careful around kids who seem sick, you never know who has what" and "Having a long distance relationship isn't healthy. Trying to keep up with homework and a companionship, doesn't always work out."

Furthermore, students did not use 24 tweets which could have been chosen for the Study Skills section. A number of these, however, were repetitions of similar suggestions in this category, so their deletion was made sense. At the same time, 11 tweets were placed in more than one category, for example, "do whatever it takes to get a hold of your advisor and talk to him about your options when scheduling." (put in both the Academic and Administration sections), "Use bad rainy days

Table 2. Examples of student-categorized tweets

Category	Examples	Total tweets
Academic	• *Go see your adviser early than later they will be a lot more pleasant* • *The lower level of the Cheng library has a set of PC's. Remember that because the first floor lab is usually filled up!* • *Refer to a syllabus to make sure all your work is on time!* • *Don't be late for class. Wake up a hour and a half to get yourself situated before class starts* • *Read the textbooks even if they don't seem important, trust me they will be.* • *Be sure there is no sign on the door saying your class is cancelled before you go in...* • *MAKE SURE YOU TAKE AT LEAST ONE CLASS THAT INTEREST YOU BESIDES THE G.E. REQUIREMENTS, SO YOU CAN HAVE SOME FORM OF EXCITEMENT*	41
Food	• *Wayne hall has the worst food on campus* • *The cheapest meal on campus is the junior whopper from Burger King* • *The coffe* [sic] *at 7 11 is not good unless it is freshly brewed either go really early or really late*	6
Extra Curricula	------------------------	0
Commuters	• *commuters should get to campus at least an hour early because of parking.* • *if there is no parking in lots 3, 4, or 5 lot 6 is a good last resort.* • *obey speed limits and signs on campus. There are lots of cops.* • *get used to stalking other students for a parking spot*	10
Res. Life	• *Everyone goes home on Friday, so the weekends are quiet if you decide to stay.* • *If you live on campus don't think its okay to leave your door unlocked.*	7
Weather	• *Dress warm due to cold temperatures in the morning on campus* • *Be prepared to walk to class in the rain*	3
Study Skills	• *make sure you proofread papers* • *start assignments early to leave room for problems* • *it is quieter to sit in your car and study* • *looking over notes before a big test helps but only if you PREVIOSLY studied* • *late nite last minute studying is the worst.. ugh*	14
Administr-ation	• *When you register for classes don't over do it and take a lot of credits all at once.* • *follow all directions when registering so that you do not get locked out of your account.* • *don't take online classes your freshman year.* • *schedule your classes wisely. Long breaks in the day can make life boring.*	13
Off-Campus	• *Wayne is considered one of the safest towns in America. I bet WPU didn't tell you that. Check Preakness Shop Centr out if you can.*	1
Email, Blackboard	• *Check your email before class every morning because wpconnect is not always running* • *if you email assignments to your wpconnect email for ease of printing location, also forward a copy to your other email....*	4
Misc.	--	0

to fo [sic] homework."(put in both the Weather and Study Skills sections), and "Make sure you proofread papers" (put in both the Academic and Study Skills sections).

Again, it should be remembered that it turned out that there was not enough time in this study to have students actually turn their tweets into formal text, but we did look at their perceptions of how this might work in questions 6, 7 and 8 of the follow-up survey. In general, a small majority of the students agreed that anywhere/anytime note taking (independent of any particular technology) was important, for example, one student responded, "To not forget valueable [sic] ones [ideas]" while another found note taking unnecessary, "I have a good memory."

Given that students did not go through the tweet to formal text exercise, it is understandable that most students did not give definitive responses on their perceptions of the difficulty of turning tweets into formal text and whether using Twitter was a good way to get started in the writing process. At the same time, students were able to use the technology to produce 'notes' that they then organized into the categories that could be included in a survival guide, so in this sense, the tweets were helpful in getting them started. Clearly more research is needed and future studies should allow time to continue to further steps of the writing process in order to fully understand how the technology can facilitate students' writing.

Q3: What do Our Students Think About the New Writing Literacies?

When looking at the question of students' perceptions of new writing literacies in schools, responses on the follow-up survey (Table 1, above) were conflicting for questions 9, 10 and 11, with many students selecting "Neutral" or leaving the answer blank. Similarly, comments were as varied. Many saw it as a way for teachers to stay in touch with their students, saying, for example:

- "They can be very useful in sharing information"
- "Absolutely! In today's society these social networking services are @ the vanguard of the Internet... It only helps us as most students (and teachers) have accounts."
- "I read them [social network postings] much more than I read books ... I think its a good way to connect to the students... Technology is advancing at a rapid pace and schools should try to keep up with it." and
- "It's a easy way to keep in contact with students ... You [the instructor] should send us tweets also."

However, at least one student noted "Nothing professional about it. (they are already classified as social)... I enjoy [hand] writing more because it gets absorbed into my mind better. [rather than typing]." In addition, another student did not even differentiate between new and traditional literacies, "doesn't matter [whether teachers use social networking tools] ...what new writing styles?" This may suggest that we need to educate/instruct students in ways that help them see the usefulness of new technologies for academic purposes; if students don't see them as appropriate academic tools then teachers will not be able to bridge the gap between these literacies.

Based on these comments, we cannot conclude that the students in our study were overwhelmingly positive about using new technologies in the classroom, but many seemed open to that possibility. Their ambivalence on the survey questions, in conjunction with the fact that many did not use their personal technologies (cellphone texting) to complete the assignment might stem from the fact that this is a new experience, not encouraged (and in many cases, actively discouraged) in previous academic experiences. We anticipate that as greater numbers of older populations use cellphone texting, Facebook, etc. that these forms of writing will gain greater social acceptance and that we are just at the beginning of this phenomenon. Given this trend, we believe that the distinction between writing with new technologies and more traditional ones will begin to disappear.

FUTURE RESEARCH DIRECTIONS

As noted above, more research, and in particular, additional studies which allow time for the continuation of the pre-writing note-taking process into the actual formal writing process, are needed. Subsequent to this pilot study, we will be running this project again in a First Year Seminar class, this time in collaboration with a Basic Reading Skills class. The two courses are run as a cohort, with the same students in both classes. This time, the students will have the benefit of an experienced literacy instructor (the Basic Reading Skills professor) who will be able to work with them and help them turn their tweets into formal text throughout the semester. It is also hoped that explicitly linking a class that covers realistic content (the freshman experience) with a class that provides comprehensive literacy skills will both improve and motivate students' writing, and that they will regard the writing assignment as more authentic and performative, which in turn supports their literacy skills. (e.g. Lundsford 2009; Sweeny 2010).

Students will again have the option of accessing Twitter via their cellphones or the computer in order for us to see if the former technology affords greater spontaneous idea-generation and note-taking. However, even if students do use the computer to post their tweets, they will still need to limit their 'notes' to 140 characters and store/share them in a non-traditional way (posting them to the Twitter website).

This study suggests that educators need to actively work to include new technologies such as Twitter into the curriculum to demonstrate their effectiveness as well as validate them as a legitimate academic tool. Educators must first let students know that they accept these technologies if they are to use them effectively in the classroom.

CONCLUSION

We began this study with the belief that today's students are, in fact, writing and effectively using written communication. However, much of this writing is done outside of the classroom, with new technologies that are still foreign to academic writing. A number of studies are finding that today's students are using text messaging, Facebook, and email to send written communications, in addition to expressing themselves with YouTube videos, Glogster web posters, role-playing and virtual avatars, etc. (Lundsford, 2009; Grabill & Pigg, 2010; Zickuhr, 2010) for many non-academic purposes.

This study represents an attempt to bridge the gap between their out-of- and in-school writing by creating a writing assignment that used a new (but very familiar) technology as part of the formal writing process. What we found was that although our students, by and large, did not take advantage of the anytime/anywhere cellphone texting capabilities of Twitter (preferring instead to access it via computer), they were able to produce a large body of 140-character texting 'notes' for the assigned survival guide. The next step, of turning these notes into a formal text, was not accomplished in this study due to lack of time, so it is not possible to ascertain if this approach would help students link the out-of-school texting with the in-school writing.

However, students demonstrated the ability to classify the information they initially generated as tweets, and then sorted (and in many cases, culled) the tweets into specific categories, suggesting that the use of this technology can facilitate the prewrite stage of the writing process. This stage is an area that students often struggle with. Therefore, using this technology may provide a method to organize information to capture the main ideas and create a structure for producing the final text.

Finally, the survey findings regarding student perceptions of the use of new technologies suggest that the application of these tools in a classroom setting as legitimate learning tools is yet to be fully accepted. The gap between what is considered social versus academic technologies must be specifically addressed in classrooms. If and when these new technologies gain acceptance in facilitating in-school writing, then the use of an anytime/anywhere technology as part of the prewriting process may be significant.

REFERENCES

Alvermann, D. (2001). *Effective literacy instruction for adolescents*. (Executive Summary and Paper). Chicago, IL: National Reading Conference.

Anstey, M., & Bull, G. (2006). *Teaching and learning multiliteracies: Changing times, changing literacies*. Newark, DE: International Reading Association.

Barnes, K., Marateo, R., & Ferris, S. P. (2007, April/May). Teaching and learning with the Net Generation. *Innovate, 3*(4). Retrieved from www.innovateonline.info/.

Englert, C. (1992). Writing instruction from a sociocultural perspective: The holistic, dialogic, and social enterprise of writing. *Journal of Learning Disabilities, 25*(3), 153–172. doi:10.1177/002221949202500303

Gee, J. P. (2007). Affinity spaces. In Gee, J. P. (Ed.), *Good video games + good learning: Collected essays on video games, learning, and literacy* (pp. 87–103). New York, NY: Peter Lang.

Grabill, J., & Pigg, S. (2010). *Revisualizing composition: Mapping the writing lives of first-year college students.* Michigan State University, Writing in Digital Environments (WIDE) Research Center. Retrieved from http://wide.msu.edu/special/writinglives/WIDE_2010_writinglives_whitepaper.pdf.

Haven, C. (2009). *The new literacy: Stanford study finds richness and complexity in students' writing*. Stanford Report, October 12, 2009. Retrieved from http://news.stanford.edu/news/2009/october12/lunsford-writing-research-101209.html.

Kinzie, S. (2009, June 26). Some professors losing their Twitter jitters. *Washington Post.* Retrieved from http://www.washingtonpost.com/wp-dyn/content/article/2009/06/25/AR2009062504027.html.

Lankshear, C., & Knobel, M. (2006). *New literacies: Everyday practices and classroom learning* (2nd ed.). Buckingham, UK: Open Press University.

Lenhart, A., & Fox, S. (2009). *Twitter and status updating*. Pew Internet & American Life Projects. Retrieved July 10, 2010, from http://www.pewinternet.org/~/media//Files/Reports/2009/PIP%20 Twitter%20Memo%20FINAL.pdf.

Lundsford, A. (2009). *The agenda - Andrea Lunsford* [Online video interview]. Retrieved from http://www.tvo.org/TVO/WebObjects/TVO.woa?video?TAWSP_Int_20091001_779626_0.

National Center for Education Statistics. (2007). *National assessment of educational progress, the nation's report card: Writing 2007* (NCES Publication No. 2008468). Retrieved from http://nces.ed.gov/pubsearch/pubsinfo.asp?pubid=2008468.

New London Group. (2000). A pedagogy of multiliteracies: Designing social futures. In Cope, B., & Kalantzis, M. (Eds.), *Multiliteracies: Literacy learning and the design of social futures* (pp. 9–38). London, UK: Routledge.

Sandmann, A. (2006). Nurturing thoughtful revision using the focused question card strategy. *Journal of Adolescent & Adult Literacy, 50*(1), 20–28. doi:10.1598/JAAL.50.1.3

Sweeney, R. (2007, Sep). *Millennial behaviors and higher education focus group results*. Presentation at William Paterson University. Retrieved from http://library1.njit.edu/staff-folders/sweeney/.

Sweeny, S. M. (2010). Writing for the instant messaging and text messaging generation: Using new literacies to support writing instruction. *Journal of Adolescent & Adult Literacy, 54*(2), 121–130. doi:10.1598/JAAL.54.2.4

Turner, K., & Katic, E. (2009). The influence of technological literacy on students' writing. *Journal of Educational Computing Research, 41*(3), 253–270. doi:10.2190/EC.41.3.a

Twitter (2010). *Twitter help center: Frequently asked questions.* Retrieved from http://support.twitter.com/groups/31-twitter-basics/topics/104-welcome-to-twitter-support/articles/13920-frequently-asked-questions.

Williams, J. P. (1984). Categorization, macrostructure, and finding the main idea. *Journal of Educational Psychology*, *76*(5), 874–879. doi:10.1037/0022-0663.76.5.874

Zickuhr, K. (2010). [Washington DC, Pew Internet & American Life Project]. *Generations (San Francisco, Calif.)*, 2010.

ADDITIONAL READING

Alvermann, D. E. (2009). Reaching/teaching adolescents: Literacies with a history. In Hoffman, J. V., & Goodman, Y. M. (Eds.), *Changing literacies for changing times: An historical perspective on the future of reading research, public policy & classroom practices* (pp. 98–107). New York: Routledge/Taylor & Francis Group.

Bennett, S., Maton, K., & Kervin, L. (2008). The "digital natives" debate: A critical review of the evidence. *British Journal of Educational Technology*, *39*(5), 775–786..doi:10.1111/j.1467-8535.2007.00793.x

Clark, J. E. (2010). The digital imperative: Making the case for a 21st-century pedagogy. *Computers and Composition*, *27*(1), 27–35. doi:10.1016/j.compcom.2009.12.004

Dunlap, J. C., & Lowenthal, P. R. (2009). Tweeting the night away: Using twitter to enhance social presence. *Journal of Information Systems Education*, *20*(2), 129–136.

Getto, G., Cushman, E., & Ghosh, S. (2011). Community mediation: Writing in communities and enabling connections through new media. *Computers and Composition*, *28*(2), 160–174. doi:10.1016/j.compcom.2011.04.006

Jenkins, H., Purushotma, R., Clinton, K., Weigel, M., &, Robinson,A.J. (2006). *Confronting the challenges of participatory culture: Media education for the 21st century*. Chicago: The John D. and Catherine T. MacArthur Foundation.

Lankshear, C., & Knobel, M. (2003). *New literacies: Changing knowledge and classroom learning* (2nd ed.). Maidenhead, New York: The Open University Press.

Lankshear, C., & Knobel, M. (2007). Sampling "the New" in new literacies. In M. Knobel & C. Lankshear (Eds.), *A new literacies sampler* (Vol. 29, pp. 1-24). New York: Peter Lang.

Larkin, J. (2011). Twitter views & news. Retrieved July 7, 2011 from http://www.larkin.net.au/blog/2011/03/17/twitter-views-news/.

Lundin, R. W. (2008). Teaching with Wikis: Toward a networked pedagogy. *Computers and Composition*, *25*(4), 432–448. doi:10.1016/j.compcom.2008.06.001

Lytle, R. (2011). 5 unique uses of Twitter in the classroom. Retrieved July 7, 2011 from http://www.usnews.com/education/best-colleges/articles/2011/05/24/5-unique-uses-of-twitter-in-the-classroom.

Manzo, K. K. (2009). Twitter lessons in 140 characters or less. Retrieved July 7, 2011 from http://www.edweek.org/ew/articles/2009/10/21/08twitter_ep.h29.html.

Messner, K. (2009). Pleased to tweet you. *School Library Journal*, *55*(12), 44–47.

Miners, Z. (2010). Twitter goes to college. Retrieved July 7, 2011 from http://www.usnews.com/education/articles/2010/08/16/twitter-goes-to-college.

Online Colleges. (2011). 50 ways to use Twitter in the college classroom. Retrieved July 16, 2001 from http://www.onlinecolleges.net/2009/06/08/50-ways-to-use-twitter-in-the-college-classroom/.

Palmquist, M. (2003). A brief history of computer support for writing centers and writing-across-the-curriculum programs. *Computers and Composition*, *20*(4), 395–413. doi:10.1016/j.compcom.2003.08.013

Raymond, S. (2011). Play and performance: Negotiating new media literacies in academic verses non-academic contexts. In *Proceedings of Society for Information Technology & Teacher Education International Conference 2011* (pp. 3339-3340). Chesapeake, VA: AACE. Retrieved from http://www.editlib.org/p/36834.

Rodrigo, S., & Jolayemi, E. (n.d.) Focused topic: Tweets for surface level tricks & treats. *Kairos: A Journal of Rhetoric, Technology, and Pedagogy*. Retrieved on July 17, 2011 from http://kairos.technorhetoric.net/praxis/index.php/Focused_Topic_Tweets_for_Surface_Level_Tricks_%26_Treats.

Stanford University. (2008). Stanford Study of Writing. Retrieved July 16, 2011 from http://ssw.stanford.edu/index.php.

Thomas, C. (2009, October 24). Clive Thompson on the new literacy. Wired Magazine. Retrieved July 16, 2011 from http://www.wired.com/techbiz/people/magazine/17-09/st_thompson.

Vega, E., Parthasarathy, R., & Torres, J. (2010). Where are my tweeps?: Twitter usage at conferences Retrieved June 2011, from http://www.slideshare.net/ramanuj/twitter-usage-at-conferences.

Young, C., & Kraut, N. (2011). Repurposing social networking tools for the classroom: An examination of Twitter's potential for enhancing ELA content knowledge. In *Proceedings of Society for Information Technology & Teacher Education International Conference 2011* (pp. 3781-3788). Chesapeake, VA: AACE. Retrieved from http://www.editlib.org/p/36916.

Young, J. (2009). 10 high fliers on Twitter. *The Chronicle of Higher Education*, *55*(31), A10.

APPENDIX: FOLLOW-UP SURVEY

Please answer the following 12 questions (front and back) indicating whether you agree or disagree with the statement by marking an "**X**" in the appropriate box and adding your comments.

1. Twitter is an easy way to submit my weekly thoughts and suggestions.

	Strongly Agree		Agree		Neutral		Disagree		Strongly Disagree
Why/Why not?									

2. When I did my Twitter posts (tweets), I mostly used ___

	SMS cell messaging		Smartphone app		Twitter website		Another way (please specify below)
Why did you use this?							

3. I would have preferred to use Blackboard Discussion Boards to submit my weekly ideas.

	Strongly Agree		Agree		Neutral		Disagree		Strongly Disagree
Why/Why not?									

4. I would have preferred to use a totally different technology (please specify below) to submit my weekly ideas.

	Strongly Agree		Agree		Neutral		Disagree		Strongly Disagree
Which technology, and why?									

5. Twitter was hard to use.

	Strongly Agree		Agree		Neutral		Disagree		Strongly Disagree
Why/Why not?									

6. It is important to be able to write down ideas whenever and wherever they occur to me.

	Strongly Agree		Agree		Neutral		Disagree		Strongly Disagree
Why/Why not?									

7. Turning Twitter posts into printed text (e.g. a formal document) was hard.

	Strongly Agree		Agree		Neutral		Disagree		Strongly Disagree
Why/Why not?									

8. Using Twitter posts or something similar is a good way to get started when writing printed documents.

	Strongly Agree		Agree		Neutral		Disagree		Strongly Disagree
Why/Why not?									

9. Twitter posts, Facebook updates, emails, SMS messages are all valid "new writing literacies."

	Strongly Agree		Agree		Neutral		Disagree		Strongly Disagree
Why/Why not?									

10. Teachers should NOT use twitter posts, Facebook updates, emails, SMS messages, etc. for school assignments.

	Strongly Agree		Agree		Neutral		Disagree		Strongly Disagree
Why/Why not?									

11. Schools should teach students how to write using new writing styles and technologies.

	Strongly Agree		Agree		Neutral		Disagree		Strongly Disagree
Why/Why not?									

Any other comments, thoughts, suggestions?

Chapter 13
A Cross-Disciplinary Exploration of Web 2.0 Technologies to Enhance Critical Thinking and Collaboration

Marsha M. Huber
Youngstown State University, USA

Jean P. Kelly
Otterbein University, USA

Shirine Mafi
Otterbein University, USA

ABSTRACT

Social media, offer a means of engaging digital learners in critical thinking and collaborative learning. Interdisciplinary faculty at Otterbein University, a four year comprehensive university in the United States, explored the impact of integrating blogs and wikis into their courses by designing assignments based on Fink's Paradigm of Significant Learning (2003). This chapter presents the collective findings, reflections, and lessons learned from their professional learning community (PLC). First, even though students did improve in organizing and presenting data, their critical thinking skills did not. Second, collaborative learning was enhanced, and Fink's Paradigm of Significant Learning did help faculty integrate blogs and wikis into their courses. Third, student attitudes about using the technology were mostly positive; agreeing that interaction and quality of communication with the professor and other students increased. The authors conclude that even inexperienced faculty should adopt social media tools, as long as there is a clear connection between the courses' learning objectives and the particular technology being used.

DOI: 10.4018/978-1-61350-347-8.ch013

INTRODUCTION

Because preparing students for the workplace is a critical role for universities, a mandate for higher education is to look for ways to converge technology and pedagogy to improve student learning. Moving the learning outside the dimensions of a classroom to the Internet not only provides faculty with new learning tools, but can also impact the learning process itself. Rather than being overwhelmed by these new technologies, we advise faculty, especially the boomer-aged ones, to harness the power of them.

Thus, the purpose of this chapter is to teach faculty how to effectively use two technologies, blog and wikis, in the classroom based on the research and experiences of a cross-disciplinary team of faculty in a Professional Learning Community at Otterbein University. This chapter shares the collective reflections and lessons of the faculty, as well as feedback from student surveys. The chapter concludes with recommendations for implementation and direction for future research.

BACKGROUND

Since the mid-2000s, Web 2.0 technologies, which are also known as "the read/write Web," have been used in higher education in an effort to "take advantage of the benefits of technology to engage NetGeners" (Barnes, Marateo, & Ferris, 2007). Just how much NetGeners are embracing Web 2.0 to enhance their learning, however, is still unclear. For example, a longitudinal survey of college students at forty U.S. higher education institutions found that the number of students who used the Internet for coursework had greatly decreased, but the number who used it for entertainment greatly increased from 2002 to 2009 (Jones, Ramanau, Cross, & Healing, 2010). A study of British college students at five universities found a similar difference between how students used Web 2.0 technologies in particular for social life and study: 78% of those surveyed had never contributed to a blog and 88% had not used a wiki. In fact, over a third reported they were not confident in their skills when using virtual learning environments such as Blackboard (38%) and writing and commenting on blogs and wikis (41%). This prompted researchers to conclude that there was not a "generational homogeneity" of users as predicted by NetGen or digital native inspired literature. Rather they found a "complex picture of minorities...who do not show a strong impulse" towards Web 2.0 participation. (Jones et al., 2010)

In our PLC, we researched whether or not the use of blogs and wikis could improve the learning of the NetGen. For purposes of this paper, we describe blogs and wikis as follows.

Blogs

Introduced in1994 by Justin Hall, Swarthmore student (Thompson, 2006), a blog, short for "weblog," is a website that can be internally or remotely hosted. Many blogs serve as personal diaries or editorials written by a blogger so that they can be read by the public or through private invitation. Blogs have grown in popularity since their introduction. By January 2009, thanks to free blog-creation web host services, 133 million blogs were created (numberof.net, 2010). A survey in 2005 found that 12 million adolescents aged 12-17 maintain their own blogs in the U.S. (Lenhart & Madden, 2005). Today blogs are available as part of course management programs such as Blackboard or are hosted by private companies using open-source software (Zawillinski, 2009).

Blogs are popular because of their ease of use; they can be created in a few minutes and require very little technical expertise. All blogs allow readers to comment on what is written and displays these comments on the page. The blog author has administrative control over the content, giving permission for others to comment, sometimes vetting feedback. A study conducted in 2008 found that many students enjoy blogging and found it beneficial to their educational and social needs (Kerewalla, Minocha, Kirkup, & Conole 2008). They use blogging to build communities, consolidate resources, share ideas, provide and receive emotional support, or use it as a personal journal. An EDUCAUSE report found that about 28% of college students blog, but generally to a small audience known to the blogger such as their friends and family (Salaway & Caruso, 2007; Scaletta, 2006); doubtless the number has grown in the past five years.

The ease of establishing blogs has also made them an attractive tool for education as well. Blogs can prove valuable in two ways – content development and making connections to a larger social network (Nakerud & Scalleta, 2008). Contributions to the blog can include required responses to readings or sustained writing on a particular topic. Scaletta's survey (2006) concluded the real benefits of blogging are gained gradually over time as students find their intellectual voice and become more confident with public writing. Instructors have reported high satisfaction with student interest, learning, and commitment when blogs were used in the classroom (Downes, 2004). Other studies, however, have found problems with blogging such as haphazard contributions to blogs, minimal communication between students, poor quality of course reflection, minimal student engagement, and poor compliance to requirements (Krause, 2004; Hormik & Melis, 2006; Williams & Jacobs, 2004). Some students expressed concern about revealing their perceived academic inadequacies to others in the class, and felt they had nothing to say that would be of interest to other students.

Because of mixed student responses about the utility of blogs, educators need to better understand students' perspective on the use of these technologies (Kerawalla et al., 2008). If they use them mindfully, then blogs can be an effective pedagogical tool. One example of effective classroom blogging is described by Higdon and Topaz (2009). They used a concept called "Just in Time Blogging" (JITB) to promote students' deep understanding of core course materials and their ability to transfer those concepts to other contexts. JITB is an instructional practice where teachers use a series of pre-class assignments to assess students' understanding of the subject. Faculty then alter classroom activities and assignments "just in time" to address specific gaps in students' understanding of the subject matter. Instructors could also provide students with a recommended structure and/or a grading rubric. Kerewella et al. (2008) suggested that blogging activities need to be flexible, voluntary or loosely prescribed, so that students can blog to meet their own needs while also meeting the course requirements (Kerewalla et al., 2008).

Wikis

Created in 1994 by Ward Cunningham, a computer programmer (Cunningham 2010), wikis are web-based tool designed to assist people in working together in a virtual environment. They serve as a collaborative website where all of its authors can edit the pages, and readers leave comments. Although the programming that allows a web page to be edited by a community was first developed in 1994, the web sites did not blossom in popularity until after the introduction of *Wikipedia* in 2001.

Characteristics of wikis make them unique among social media applications and different from blogs. On a wiki, one author at a time can make changes to a given wiki page, locking out other authors until changes have been uploaded. Anyone with a web browser can read and edit a wiki. Wikis can be password protected or public access. Different levels of editing rights can be given to individual contributors such as the ability to edit and delete pages or upload files. A few schools have customized wikis that allow for better security but most institutions rely on external wiki sites or wikis within the course management systems.

Because of wikis editing features, wikis are maximized for sharing and producing content collaboratively while blogs are best for publishing individual writing and comments. (See Figure 1).

Given wikis' later adoption status, much of the research into their effectiveness in higher education has been anecdotal or descriptive (Parker & Chao, 2007). One notable exception found that when students were "neither forced to contribute nor directly rewarded" to participate in a wiki, students did not write new articles or edit existing ones during the semester (Ebner, Kickmeir-Rust & Holzinger, 2008). They concluded that the socio-motivational and psychological aspects of wikis need to be considered if they are to be used on a strictly voluntary basis.

THEORETICAL BACKGROUND

As educators, we wanted to see if blogs and wikis could help NetGen college students improve their critical thinking and collaboration skills, as well as allow faculty to incorporate the six learning goals proposed by Dee Fink (2003). These are: foundational knowledge, application, integration, the human dimension, caring, and learning to learn. Significant learning occurs when learning experiences are developed that exercise those goals. We used this framework as a guide to determine what types of applications we might add to our classes. Two faculty members interested in building critical thinking skills decided to use blogs and wikis to develop those skills. The other faculty members saw blogs and wikis as more of a collaborative tool. The theoretical background supporting our various learning objectives is as follows.

Figure 1. Blogs can be used to distribute required readings and to begin discussion outside of the classroom through comments

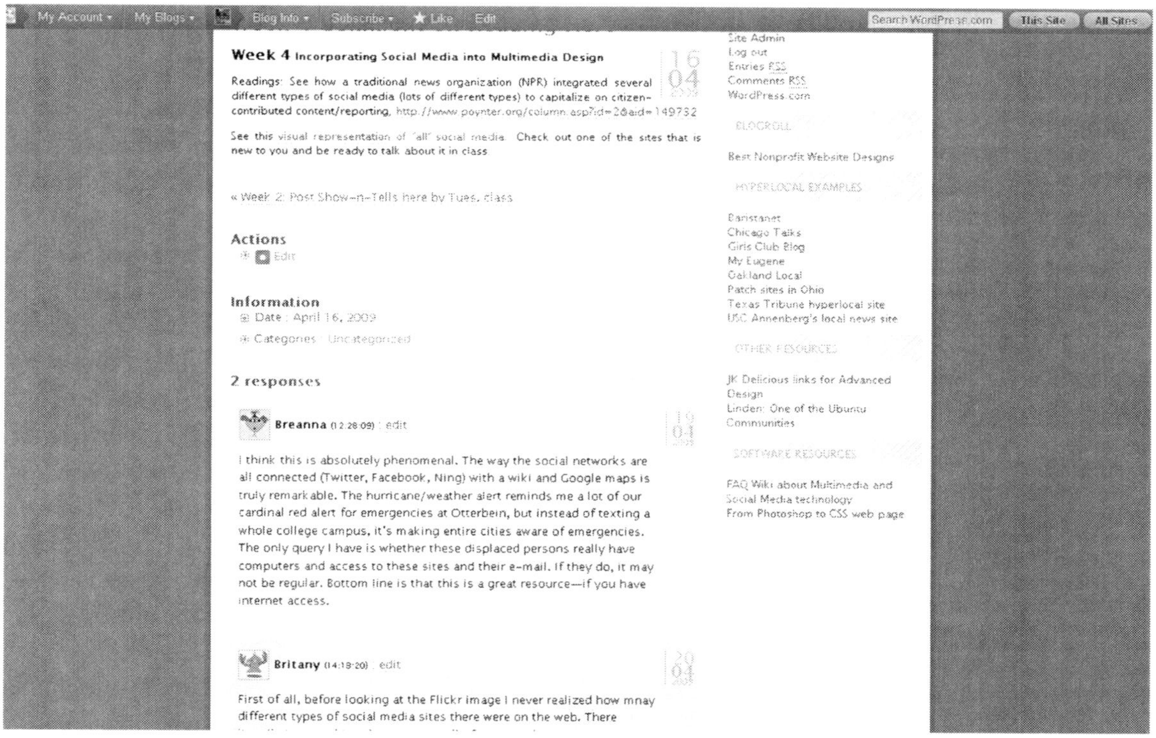

Dee Fink's Paradigm

Fink (2003) asserts that for significant learning to occur, six dimensions of learning as mentioned earlier must happen. In the early stages of the PLC, members brainstormed how social media could be used in conjunction with Fink's learning goals and how to assess it (Table 1). For example, in both the human dimension and caring dimension, Fink implicitly supports the idea of collaborative learning when he observes the reciprocity involved in caring for self and caring for others. Thus, faculty should design learning experiences that develop students' social competence. His advice for designing courses to assure significant learning in the application category includes both analyzing and critiquing issues and situations, another form of critical thinking.

Critical Thinking

A growing body of research has begun to explore how "social media"— wikis, blogs, social networking sites, etc. — might be used in the classroom to improve the ability of NetGen students to think more critically: to identify central issues and assumptions, evaluate evidence, and deduce conclusions. Broadly defined, critical thinking is both a set of cognitive skills and a disposition to apply these skills purposefully (Stupnisky, Renaud, Daniels, Haynes, & Perry, 2008; Scriven & Richard, 2009; Landis, Swain, Friehe, & Coufal, 2007; Ennis, 1987).

Table 1. Learning goals and assessment

Learning Goal	Assessment
Foundational Knowledge – Basic terminology.	Blogs and wikis: How terminology is used.
Application -- Analyzing and critiquing issues and situations; being able to sequence and coordinate multiple tasks in a single project.	Blogs and wikis: evaluate analysis and critiques.
Integration – understand how the subject fits with other disciplines and society.	Wikis: Quality of arguments constructed.
Human Dimension – how does a particular discipline affect others, stakeholders, and what is the influence of the public media.	Wikis: Quality of the communications and links to stakeholder groups.
Caring – develop interest in the topic, using intuition and metaphor to explore the meaning to the person or community.	Blogs: Quality of discussion and reflective comments.
Learning to Learn – taking responsibility for your own learning.	Wikis: Quality of comments and self-reflection.

The disposition to think critically, which has an interdependent relationship to the possession of critical thinking skills, is characterized by a variety of intellectual standards. Studies that have separated the two constructs of disposition and skills suggest that they are related, but not redundant (Stupnisky et al., 2008). Scholars have created a variety of standards to characterize critical thinking. For example, Facione (2011) characterizes it as the tendency to be inquisitive, open-minded, flexible, and self-confident. Facione (2011) identifies six core critical thinking skills, while Paul and Elder (2007), measure seven intellectual standards and Landis et al. (2007) describe ten indicators. While a precise list of critical thinking skills varies across the literature, those abilities can be consolidated to include the ability to identify central issues and assumptions, evaluating evidence, and deducing conclusions (Stupnisky et al., 2008).

Often these lists of critical thinking skills and personal characteristics are used to create rubrics, matrices designed to communicate and measure concise levels of critical thinking accomplishment in written assignments, blog and wiki entries, and classroom discussions (Connors, 2008; Garrison, 1992; Gerlich, Greenlaw, & DeLoach, 2003; Wade, 1995). The rubrics are variously used in classrooms for self-evaluation, assessment, or in scholarship of teaching, as content analysis instruments.

Research results are mixed, however, as to whether or not blogs and wikis can improve critical thinking. Some researchers found that using blogs for reflective writing assignments increased the level and quality of reflective thinking (Bouldin, Homes, & Fortenberry, 2006; Xie, Ke, & Sharma, 2008). Others, like Guiller, Durndell, Ross, and Thomson (2008) found evidence that online discussions increased the critical thinking characteristic of justifying assertions over face-to-face discussion. Their studies led Guiller et al. (2008) to conclude that a blended course design is a "research avenue worthy of exploration" (p. 198). Likewise, MacKnight (2000) concludes that "it is unlikely that students will succeed in substantive, reflective exchanges if they have not learned to carry on similar conversations elsewhere" (p. 39). This suggests that blogs or wikis alone cannot improve a student's critical thinking abilities.

Equally valid, though not explored in the research, is the idea that the ability to think critically does not happen in one term but rather it is a culmination of several terms with different classes. It is a gradual maturing of thought and arguments.

Collaborative Learning

A growing body of research has found that the use of wikis improves student collaboration by moving some authority away from faculty in favor of the students, further empowering them, increasing their self-confidence, and improving their professional development (Evans, 2006; Fountain, 2005; Guzdial, 1999; Martin & Dusenberry, 2007; McCaffrey & Gulbrandsen, 2007; Moxley, 2007; Paretti, McNair, & Holloway-Attway, 2007; Parker & Chao, 2007; Vie & DeWinter, 2008). In addition, Walsh (2010) found that both faculty and students in several communication courses demonstrated improvement in collaboration, but other results were mixed. For example, she did not find evidence of improved student autonomy as reported in earlier research. Walsh's study confirmed an earlier finding by Guzdial (1999) that points to a conflict between the communal role of wiki author and the role of the administrator, who sets the page, the assignments, and grades contributions on the wiki. Finally, faculty members found evidence of student professional development, although the students themselves did not perceive it as such.

This body of research boils down to studies of what type of group learning contributes to collaborative thinking, or "the development of interpersonal skills and other non-cognitive factors that are valued in careers and citizenship" (Barkley, Cross & Major, 2005, p. 16). In one of the earliest experimental studies of collaborative learning in the higher education classroom, Gokhale (1995) concluded that traditional methods (drill and practice) were equally effective in transferring factual knowledge, but that "collaborative learning fosters the development of critical thinking through discussion, clarification of ideas, and evaluation of others' ideas" (p. 5) He also noted the importance of group diversity in knowledge and experience because students are confronted with different interpretations of situations, which improves problem-solving strategies.

The importance of collaboration and social interaction is also discussed by Brookfield in his book Developing Critical Thinkers. He writes, "When we develop critical thinkers, helping them form resource networks with others who are involved in this activity may make a crucial difference. Where such a network does not already exist, one of the most important tasks of those trying to facilitate critical thinking is to encourage its development" (1987, p. 79). Web 2.0 technologies, with their social nature, invite comments and collaboration from a worldwide resource network, therefore offering promise as collaborate learning tools.

Project Outcomes

Given our knowledge of the literature, the research team expected the following outcomes from our various experiments using blogs and wikis to encourage significant learning.

- The students would embrace the technology, adopt it and find new uses, in turn training their instructors at some level.
- The quality of writing and critical thinking would improve because of the public nature of the technologies, which allow others including external experts to see student work even in draft form.
- In-class discussion and preparation would benefit from required out-of-class discussion via these technologies.
- The applications would ease classroom management, especially monitoring of group project work.
- The archiving capabilities of wikis in particular would allow for a new method of assessment of student learning across time. The availability of multiple drafts and revisions of student writing would allow exploration of such variables as improvement of writing skills, depth of reflection, and critical thinking.
- Participation by and collaboration with those outside the university, such as community partners and professionals, would be easier to facilitate.

PROJECT DESIGNS

The Professional Learning Community

The cross-disciplinary team consisted of faculty members at Otterbein University, located in central Ohio. The faculty members were from five different disciplines including: business administration, accounting, life sciences, communication (public relations), and health and physical education. They received a grant from the Ohio Learning Network to form a professional learning community (PLC) where participants agreed to use blogs and/or wikis in their classrooms. The PLC was chosen as a vehicle to bring campus-wide change since the format allows for shared expertise and risk taking. The PLC format proved an effective and efficient way to encourage faculty to embrace new technology. Encouragement, shared expertise, and support of colleagues created a resilient team whose impact as a whole was far greater than one member's individual research or teaching project (Garett, 2010).

The group met every two weeks for one hour for an entire academic year to share their experiences and to learn from each other. With one exception, the participants had no prior experience using Web 2.0 technologies. Thus, each faculty member had to learn the technologies and devise ways to integrate them into their classes. Guided by prior research, theories about critical thinking and collaborative learning, and Dee Fink's guidelines for significant learning (2003), the faculty members developed a wide variety of blog and wiki assignments.

In discussing various uses of blogs and wikis and linking them to Fink's (2003) learning objectives (discussed earlier), some faculty formalized the teaching and learning experimentation, collecting and analyzing data. Other findings were anecdotal. All participants administered an attitudinal survey exploring how Net Generation students felt about the use of wikis and blogs in the classroom. (The blog and wiki applications that faculty members created during the academic year are shown in Table 2.)

The learning objectives for the study were as follows:

- To discuss a variety of approaches for using blogs and wikis in the classroom,
- To share how to use these technologies well,
- To set up realistic expectations for learning outcomes,
- To share if blogs and wikis enhanced collaboration and critical thinking, and
- To present the steps necessary for successfully integrating these technologies in

Table 2. Application on blogs and wikis and related Fink learning goals

Collaborative tool on philanthropy projects	Integration, human dimension
Constructing lesson plans	Integration, learning
Sharing media sources	Integration, caring
Addressing FAQs about software	Learning
Constructing to-do checklists	Learning
Peer editing of writing	Integration
Addressing bi-weekly questions pertaining the discipline	Integration, learning, caring
Writing about the discipline in the media	Integration
Writing about "muddy" points	Learning
Citizen-generated news reporting	Human dimension
Writing lab reports	Integration, learning
Writing case studies	Integration, learning

courses including using professional learning communities.

Following is a more in-depth, discipline-specific discussion of blogs and wikis that were used in our particular classes. The project designs for the different disciplines are discussed below. Discussions reflect that the five professors used wikis and blogs in different ways, and assessed them in different ways.

Management and Accounting

Two faculty members in the Department of Business, Accounting, and Economics used wikis to document, review, and comment on students' philanthropy projects. In this project, students were to collectively select a non-profit agency or agencies to award $4,000 in support of their causes. Student teams created a wiki page on pbworks.com for each non-profit agency that they were studying. Information on the page included a link to the agency's website, the mission statement, press releases and financial statements, and a list of the Board of Trustees (See Figure 2).

Both professors used the wiki as a repository for students to store and manage their work. In the management class, students created an analysis of the agency's environment by identifying strengths, weaknesses, opportunities, and threats as well as a burning issue. Students also posted questions that they had for the agency's staff, and subsequently, shared the answers on the wiki. In the accounting class, students focused on analyzing the financial statements of the organization and evaluating financial risk factors.

Common to both classes was the transparency that the wiki brought to the projects and the real-time feedback the instructor could provide to the students. As the weeks progressed, students could learn from other teams' wiki pages, and pose questions to other groups. For the faculty members, managing the project was easier because they could comment on student work in real-time, meaning as students posted their work, they would add comments. The wiki made it easy for everyone to read the comments from faculty as well as observe issues common to all agencies.

The faculty member in accounting also used the wiki for other applications in her other classes. In all her classes, she added a page where students could write about "muddy" points that she addressed either on the wiki or in the following class lecture. In her Intermediate Accounting class, students constructed self-study chapter guides and to-do checklists to help them better regulate their time. In her Federal Taxation class, she posed questions on the wiki on a bi-weekly basis for the students to address. Different students then organized and categorized the data in a manner presentable to the class. The goal of the assignment was to give students a "take-away" on a variety of relevant career-related topics at the conclusion of the term (See Figure 3).

Anatomy and Physiology

One faculty member in the Department of Biology and Earth Science used blogs in a freshman

Figure 2. Wiki application for a philanthropy project

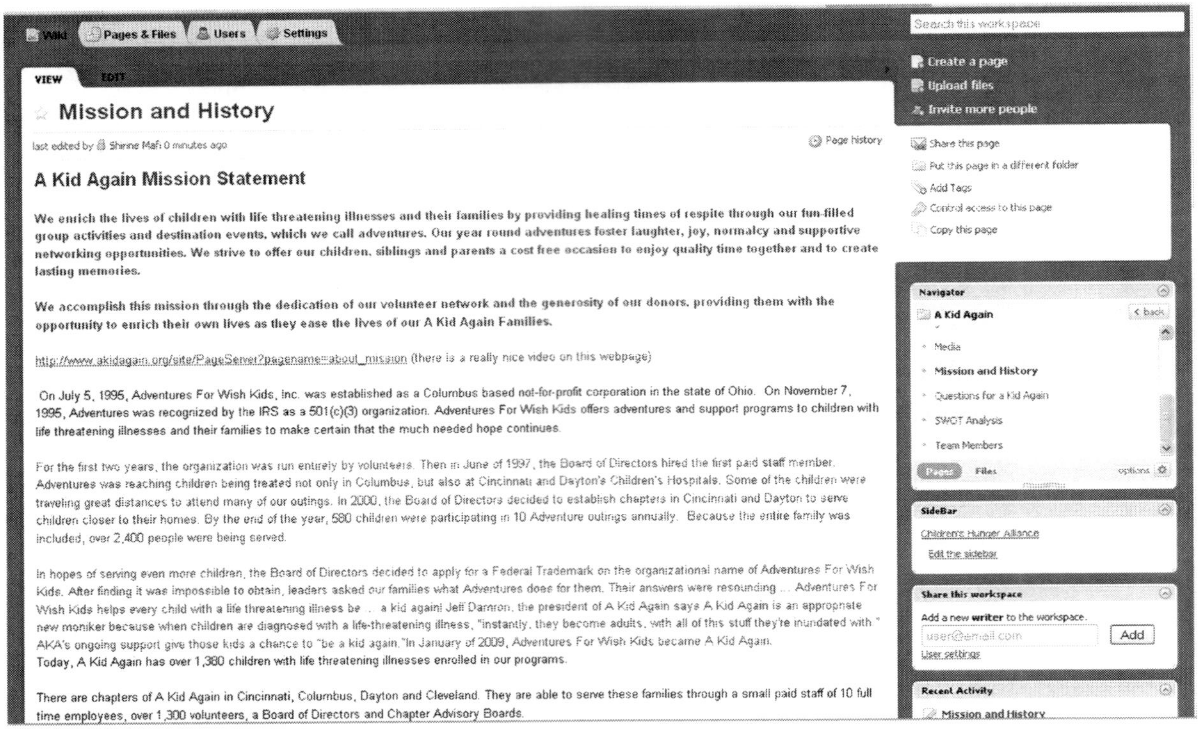

anatomy and physiology course. She formally investigated the question of whether writing and reading blog postings about scientific thinking increased her students' understanding of critical and scientific thinking. The basic aspects of scientific thinking that students were expected to demonstrate were questioning, reasoning, observing, weighing evidence, and explaining.

She used a quasi-experimental design where students in the experimental group were required to write five researched blog postings over a nine-week period on the discussion board area of Blackboard. For each of the postings, a new discussion thread was started, and a description of valued qualities was given. For example, in the fourth week of the term a "basic level" posting would be described as a reflection on a definition from an academic source (books, journals, or websites). An excellent posting was one that "explains, analyzes, and applies a definition posted already" supported by research in academic sources and includes a personal reflection. More-reliable and less-reliable types of Internet sources were discussed, but otherwise students were free to search all electronic and non-electronic sources, and to report any information that held meaning for them.

The faculty member also used the wiki in her upper-level physiology courses for students to write lab reports and address case studies. She chose to use Moodle as her wiki. She also added to her blogs (on Blackboard) and wikis (on Moodle) a place for FAQs about how to use the software.

Health and Physical Education

In a health education course in the Department of Health and Sports Sciences, one faculty member used pbworks.com as the wiki where student teachers were encouraged to share and critique each other's lesson plans. Students designed learning modules for courses as part of their student teaching requirements. As a result, students

Figure 3. Wiki for accounting class

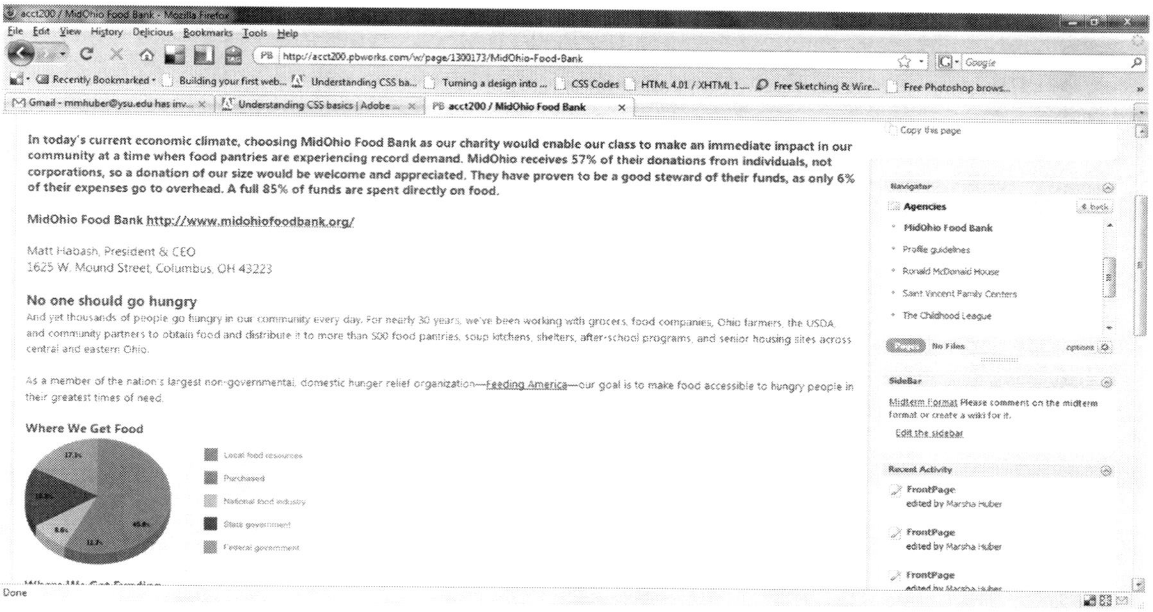

learned from each other's work and improved their own lesson plans week-to-week. In addition, the faculty member could provide real-time feedback to the students as posted to the wikis. This was important because then the students could make immediate changes to their lesson plans.

One of the best aspects of using a wiki was that the supervising teachers could also access the wiki to make comments and add suggestions. By having this professional feedback, students were able to review the comments about their plans and increase their effectiveness based on input from a practicing teacher. This not only helped in the lesson plans for this assignment, but for future lesson plans as well.

Communication

One faculty member in the Department of Communication used a wiki (on pbworks.com) to establish a collaborative learning environment in a junior-level public relations techniques course. The wiki was used for peer and instructor editing of writing assignments (proposals), sharing materials for group projects, communication outside of class, writing, and course management. The course also included a service learning component where brief biographies of students and the faculty member were read by the community partner.

Each student team created public relations materials for a community partner on the wiki, thereby allowing the community partner to comment on the materials in the draft stages. In addition, students edited each other's work, and at the end of the term, several wiki pages were merged into one cohesive document. Most of the course's writing assignments were "turned in" on the wiki, which date-stamped the completion time, thereby allowing for real-time grading. The instructor also taught though the wiki by creating and displaying a press release as an example of how work should be done. It showed the most common errors on one draft, which were corrected in a subsequent draft. The wiki allowed this to be demonstrated via a red-lined page history display (Figure 4).

The faculty member also designed a quasi-experimental study to consider the influence of social media on the ability of NetGen students to

Figure 4. Use of wikis to improve student writing quality

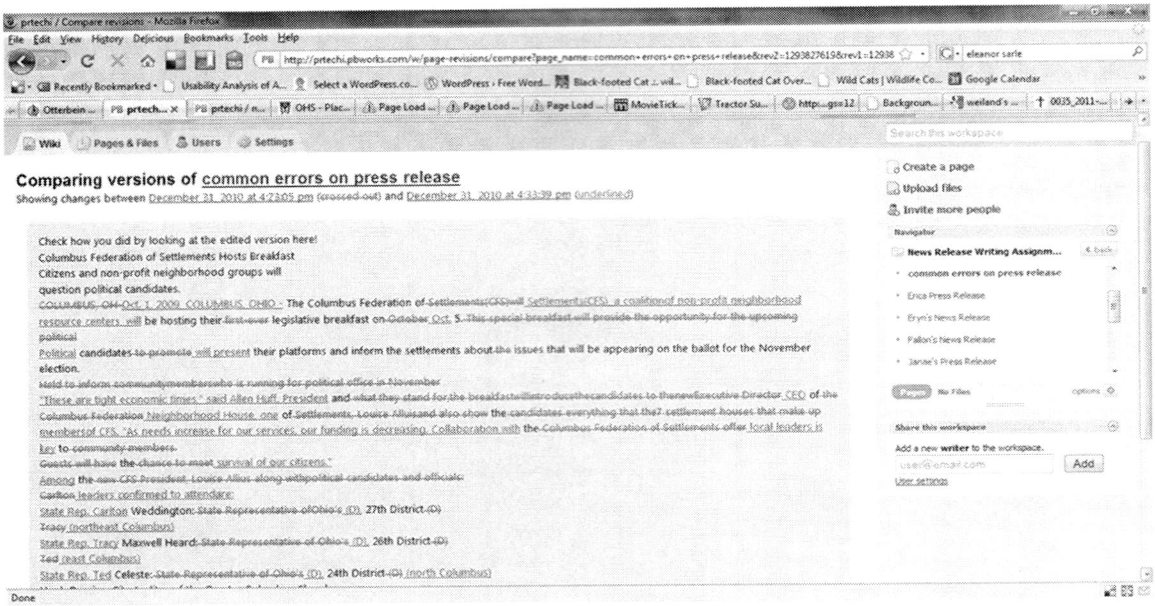

think critically. Using both quantitative and qualitative analyses, the following questions were investigated:

1. Did students' self-reported dispositions toward using critical thinking skills change after participating in a class that used a wiki for collaboration on a service learning project? If so, in what direction and at what level?
2. Did students participating in a service learning class that used a wiki as a collaborative tool demonstrate evidence of a critical thinking perspective in select writing samples? If so, what were the characteristics and themes of that perspective?

To answer these questions, the faculty member employed a multi-stage, quasi-experimental, one-shot, pre- and post-test study design. Students responded to Part B of the Motivated Strategies for Learning Questionnaire (MSLQ), to assess their use of different learning strategies for a college course (Pintrich, McNair, & Holloway-Attaway. 1993). Specifically five items assessed "critical thinking" as the degree to which students report applying previous knowledge to new situations in order to solve problems, reach decisions, or make critical evaluations with respect to standards of excellence. Writing samples – a formal proposal created on the wiki and a final, self-reflective learning journal not on the wiki – were also analyzed using qualitative content analysis. Reviewers evaluated samples for their editing and hyperlinking capacity and whether or not students demonstrated improvements in critical thinking after revision of their wikis. Also explored were how critical thinking in the writing samples compared to students' self-reported disposition.

FINDINGS

One goal of the PLC was to see if we could use blogs and wikis to enhance critical thinking skills and collaboration. Even on a more basic level, however, we were concerned about faculty and students perceptions of ease of use of the technologies. We were also concerned about how our students would react to these new technologies. Although being inexperienced ourselves at using the technologies, we explored whether we could use them effectively in the classroom?

Collaboration and Critical Thinking

Three PLC members used wiki pages as a means of collaboration by providing a central space where students and faculty could contribute to and comment on each other's work. Students could also learn from each other because they could see the work of their classmates. Application of wikis in these classrooms made work progress transparent to the faculty and other members of the class. The research of the PLC members that conducted quasi-experimental research found that the blogs and wikis contributed to collaborative learning, but not necessarily to critical thinking.

Two PLC members, from Anatomy and Physiology and Communications, developed quasi-experimental designs to evaluate if blogs and wikis could develop critical thinking skills. In the Anatomy and Physiology class that utilized blogs, baseline measurements of understanding of critical and scientific thinking were performed in both experimental and control groups in two ways: by analyzing written explanations of scientific and critical thinking; and by scoring a practical task concerning the design of a simple animal nutrition project. The study found that blogging significantly increased the experimental group's ability to explain scientific thinking[1].

In the communication course that that utilized a wiki, conclusions were that self-report of critical thinking dispositions was not an accurate predictor of the ability to apply critical thinking in writing assignments. Change in those dispositions was not statistically significant after participation in a course using a wiki, but students' edits to writing assignments on the wiki did show significant difference in the likelihood to question assumptions and improve support for arguments with evidence, often using hyperlinks.

Student Attitudes

All five PLC participants administered a survey to students in their wiki and blog-enhanced classes (n = 150) which included Introductory Accounting, Intermediate Accounting, Communications, Health Education, Journalism, Management, Federal Taxation, and Nursing. The goal was to gauge student attitudes about the value of using these tools to enhance their learning. The majority of respondents included juniors (44%) or seniors (37%) attending the university either full-time (85%) or part-time (15%). They were of "traditional" age (19 to 22 years old) and predominantly female (66% female, 34% male). The social media tools used in their classes were Wikis (70%), Blogs (9%), or both (21%)

Table 3 and Table 4 show the results related to the amount and quality of interaction of the blogs and wikis. As a whole, students reported that the use of blogs and wikis in the class increased the amount interaction of student with students (53%) and students with the instructor (52%). For about 40% of the students, the use of the new technology made no difference in interaction. Very few students reported that the use of technology decreased interaction (6-7%).

When reporting their perceptions about the quality of interaction, the majority of students were neutral about the influence of wikis and blogs (see Table 4). Forty percent (40%) reported that the quality with other students did increase and 45% reported that the quality increased with the instructor.

When asked about other learning outcomes, 67% percent either agreed or strongly agreed that the technologies were "easy to use" (Table 5). They were split on the question of whether or not they would take another class using blogs or wikis or if it enhanced their learning experience. When asked to describe the relationship of the

Table 3. Student attitudes about the amount of interaction

	Amount of Interaction				
In comparison with the interaction experienced with students and instructors in courses that did not use wikis/blogs, how would you describe the amount of interaction experienced in this class, with:	**Decreased 1**	**Somewhat decreased 2**	**No Difference 3**	**Somewhat increased 4**	**Increased 5**
Other students in your course	2 1%	8 5%	60 40%	57 38%	23 15%
The instructor in your course	2 1%	9 6%	61 41%	59 39%	19 13%

Table 4. Student attitudes about the quality of interaction

	Quality of Instruction				
In comparison to the interaction experienced with students and instructors in other courses that did not use wikis/ blogs, how would you describe the quality of instruction experienced in this class, with:	**Decreased 1**	**Somewhat decreased 2**	**No Difference 3**	**Somewhat increased 4**	**Increased 5**
Other students in the course	4 3%	8 5%	78 52%	46 31%	14 9%
The instructor in the course	6 4%	16 11%	60 40%	53 35%	15 10%

wikis and learning, 29% felt it enhanced their learning, 47% said they were relevant, and 24% did not see any relevancy or relationship. Students were asked if wikis and blogs should stay part of the course design in future offerings of the class. The majority recommended keeping the tools (68%) and 23% said they should not be used in the future; 9% gave conditional responses.

An analysis of written comments indicates that student satisfaction seemed to center around how the wikis/blogs were used. Many students commented that the wikis allowed for more open communication, improved interaction, and helped them learn from each other. Some examples of comments are:

"We were able to communicate with our classmates in a more comfortable arena than the classroom. This made me more comfortable voicing my opinions."

"It provided a space in which we were able to brainstorm and collaborate on a project in a group."

In one class, even though students spent more time preparing the content and assessment on a wiki, they spent less time during the term because the wiki helped them to organize their materials for their projects. Other students liked the fact that they could work on group projects on the wiki anytime. *"It gave me a chance to communicate with my group at home instead of planning meetings with them during our busy schedules."*

On the negative side, some students did not like some of the assignments on the wikis, and thought they were a waste of time. "*I didn't see much relevance in using the wikis for class.*" In some cases, students thought the wikis were "*cluttered*" or complained of other student groups accidentally posting in their folder. Student judgment on ease of use seemed to depend on which wiki system was used – Pbworks was easier to

Table 5. Learning outcomes

Indicate how strongly you agree or disagree with the following statements:	Strongly agree 1	Agree 2	Not sure 3	Disagree 4	Strongly disagree 5
The wikis/blogs were easy to learn how to use.	28 19%	71 48%	14 9%	26 17%	10 7%
The use of wikis/blogs enhanced my learning experience.	7 5%	54 36%	35 23%	38 26%	15 10%
Given the opportunity, I would take another course that used wikis/blogs in the future.	9 6%	45 30%	40 27%	40 27%	15 10%
Overall, I was satisfied with the use of wikis/blogs in this course.	10 7%	54 36%	34 23%	35 24%	15 10%

use than Moodle. In one of the classes, Moodle stopped working during the term. Some students felt that using blogs, wikis, and Blackboard, for example, was technology "*overkill*" and complained about having *"to memorize multiple addresses and htmls."*

Faculty Attitudes

The Otterbein PLC members studied the use of blogs and wikis over one academic year. A key finding was that these technologies enhanced collaborative learning. In addition, it became clear to them that technology should only be used when it is better than traditional teaching tools. In this situation, students embraced the technology and explored how best to use it.

We were surprised by the occasional "push-back" from NetGen students since the literature predicted they would embrace both the technology (Oblinger & Oblinger, 2005). Student questioned the relevancy of blogs and wikis and related assignments describing it as "busy work" or expressing "technophobia" when trying to learn these technologies. We speculated that negative reactions were most common when faculty failed to make a clear connection between the capabilities of the technology and disciplinary learning objectives. Kerawalla's findings confirm what we experienced in our own classroom. Students are often task-focused and outcome-oriented, and find it difficult to understand how new technologies can enhance their learning experience (Kerawalla et al., 2008)

Anecdotal reports from all faculty participants demonstrated that the applications eased classroom management, especially the monitoring of group project work. As a location for all course documents, blog templates offered the most robust organizational hierarchies, while wikis allowed only one level of files in folders. At least one faculty member purchased an augmented account from pbworks.com in order to archive student work, making it visible to her, but invisible to current students. Students continued to build on and use the same blog and wiki sites across terms, deleting and/or saving work by past students as they saw fit.

Faculty participants also felt that wikis in particular seemed best suited for managing and encouraging optimum collaboration on group projects or writing. Wikis allowed for organization of content in folders and supported uploads of a wide variety of files formats including Word, Excel, and PDFs. Student teams also used them to share "to-do lists," and job assignments. Several faculty used wikis to line-edit and comment on student writing, encouraging students to study the "red-lined" version, not just the final draft in order to see what was changed and why. Other faculty paired students or student groups for peer editing, using the draft/redline function to grade the contributions of the editors before the original author turned in a final draft for grading. Other applications included assigning students to create resource wiki pages of FAQs, and/or knowledge banks of collaborative work.

Overall, all the PLC participants felt that the incorporation of wiki and blog technologies into their teaching was worthwhile. The three authors of this paper have continued to use blogs and wikis in their classes as a transparent way to assess group progress and learning outcomes.

Challenges

As with any new technology or application, the adoption of blogs and wikis in the classroom had its challenges. A great deal of thinking and planning was involved on the front end. The faculty had to decide which software package to use and learn how to use it. In addition, members had to teach their students how to use the software. Considering the learning curve and frustration that comes with this, patience is needed when first adopting a new technology. Within one term, however, all the faculty members were comfortable with the use of their chosen blog and/or wiki applications.

One application of wikis that did not meet our expectations was the lack of engagement from the community outside of the classroom in discussion and collaboration. Though the public relations class created wiki pages expressly for the service learning partner to view and edit, such as press release and other drafts, the agency staffs were either too busy to contribute, intimidated by the technology, or felt that they should not step over the teacher-student boundaries. Furthermore, because some of the wikis and blogs were public, professionals had privacy and security concerns regarding information related to their organizations. This was consistent with a finding by Walsh (2010) that password protection and training could relieve anxieties.

Overall, the faculty did not find that the use of blogs and wikis increased the time spent on their classes, except in the beginning of the term. In addition, using blogs and wikis did not seem to increase the time necessary for grading. In fact, because faculty could grade assignments in real-time, the grading load was somewhat relieved. Instead of having all the group projects handed in during one class period, faculty members could grade and comment on assignments throughout the week.

Grading on-line, however, can be problematic if a faculty member does not like "real time" grading. One faculty member voiced her concern when grading student work on wiki pages. The fluid nature of the wiki made it harder for her to assess students' contribution and its value. She found the frequent changes on wiki made this problem more exasperating. Thus, if faculty members do not want to give "real time" feedback to students, then they should probably not use this type of technology in their classes. Research shows that students expect faster feedback on both e-mails and grading of assignments from on-line courses than in traditional courses (Sanders, 2011).

SUGGESTIONS FOR FUTURE RESEARCH

We agree with Walsh (2010) that "based on the proliferation of studies of wikis [and blogs]..., the days of asking what, why, and whether, about wiki pedagogy are behind us; the questions that face us now begin with when and how (p. 25)." Therefore, we recommend that future research operationalize variables that allow direct measurement of learning outcomes across the disciplines. Furthermore, research should determine if the longitudinal advantage of these new technologies over traditional teaching methods. Therefore, we have continued to refine our instruments and collect data about student attitudes regarding the use of blogs and wikis in the classroom across time.

Although this study did not find that the use of blogs and wikis developed critical thinking, we did found that they developed collaborative learning. We discovered that when students create multiple drafts on a wiki, paired with hyperlinks to identify central issues and assumptions, wikis enhanced certain aspects of critical thinking.

We also believe that future studies could address specific research questions regarding Fink's paradigm of significant learning. For example for each of Fink's dimensions, different research questions could be construed as follows in Table 6.

In conclusion, we encourage scholars to work across disciplines to learn how blogs and wikis can enhance teaching and learning. Members of our PLC have continued to collaborate, experiment, and research issues together, inspiring each other and others to use social media as a way to improve teaching and learning.

Step-by-Step Guide

Given our experience with blogs and wikis, here is a guide that can help future scholars adopt blogs and wikis for their classes:

- Research social media applications to determine which method is best for your class. A good source for explanations of blogs and wikis is the web site http://www.commoncraft.com. These videos are also an effective way to introduce a technology to students.
- Decide whether course objectives, content, and student privacy issues are best served by a private or public wiki or blog.
- Communicate to students the relevancy of the technology to the course and their learning.
- Establish ground rules such as the expectations of a collaborative classroom, deadlines, faculty response time, proper tone of comments, and appropriate writing styles for a public space.
- Demonstrate and have students practice using the application. Provide technical support either yourself, student mentors, and/or the IT staff.
- It is okay to start small, using the application in just one or two assignments.
- Have students reflect on their experience with the technology.
- Assess student learning and the use of technology. Possibly provide students with a grading rubric.

Table 6. Research questions based on Fink's paradigm

Learning Goals	Possible Research Questions
Foundational Knowledge	Does the use of blogs and wikis improve student comprehension of terminology?
Application	Does the use of a wiki help students improve their ability to manage a complex project?
Integration	How does a wiki help faculty and students evaluate the quality of arguments constructed?
Caring	Can the use of blogs or wikis increase student interest in the topic?
Human Dimension	Could the public nature of wikis and blogs help students explore this dimension?
Learning to Learn	Do blogs and wikis empower students to direct their own learning?

CONCLUSION

Faculty using blogs and wikis in the classroom should consider its potential implications on teaching and learning. Because blogs and wikis tend to decentralize classroom power dynamics, we recommend that instructors disclose their own level of experience with the technology to their students. They can admit that they don't know all the answers and are willing to abandon a technology if it does not serve learning goals as expected. In a truly collaborative classroom, the instructor is the "Guide on the Side" not the "Sage on the Stage."

Blogs broaden the audience for students' work beyond the instructor to include other stakeholders such as classmates, project partners, and anyone who is permitted to review and comment on its contents. Furthermore, blogs can help faculty better understand what students are learning, allowing faculty to adjust their teaching materials accordingly without sacrificing class time. One faculty commented that reviewing blog entries gave her a sense of who was really engaged with the topic and with the class because she could note the dates and frequency of entries.

Both blogs and wikis can make student work more public, thereby raising the bar for what is considered acceptable quality to outsiders. The projects devised by faculty supported this expectation, especially when multiple drafts of a wiki were graded. Because writing for blogs and wikis made citation of sources immediate and facile through hyperlinks to web pages, it was more likely that students provided support for assertions. Blogs also gave voice to introverted students who otherwise would not have participated in class. Furthermore, blogs allowed students to voice opinions about controversial topics that they might not air in a regular classroom.

ACKNOWLEDGMENT

The authors want to thank the Ohio Learning Network for the grant that made this project possible. In addition, we want to thank Patricia Wilson of Otterbein University for her participation in our PLC and her contributions to this chapter as well as Lois Palau for her editing help.

REFERENCES

Barkley, E. F., Cross, K. P., & Major, C. H. (2005). *Collaborative learning techniques: A handbook for college faculty*. San Francisco, CA: Jossey-Bass.

Barnes, K., Marateo, R., & Ferris, S. (2007). Teaching and learning with the Net Generation. *Innovate, 3,* 1-8. Retrieved from http://www.innovateonline.info/pdf/vol3_issue4/Teaching_and_Learning_with_theNet_Generation.pdf.

Bouldin, A. S., Homes, E. R., & Fortenberry, M. L. (2006). Blogging about course concepts: Using technology for reflective journaling in a communications class. *American Journal of Pharmaceutical Education*, *70*(4), 1–8. doi:10.5688/aj700484

Brookfield, S. D. (1987). *Developing critical thinking*. San Francisco, CA: Jossey-Bass.

Connors, P. (2008). Assessing written evidence of critical thinking using an analytic rubric. *Journal of Nutrition Education and Behavior*, *40*(3), 193–194. doi:10.1016/j.jneb.2008.01.014

Downes, S. (2004). Educational blogging. *EDUCAUSE Review*, *39*(5), 14–26. Retrieved from http://www.educause.edu/pub/er/erm04/erm0450.asp.

Ebner, M., Kickmeier-Rust, M., & Holzinger, A. (2008). Utilizing wiki-systems in higher education classes: A chance for universal access? *Universal Access in the Information Society*, *7*(4), 199–207.. doi:10.1007/s10209-008-0115-2

Ennis, R. H. (1987). A taxonomy of critical thinking dispositions and abilities. In Baron, J. B., & Sternberg, R. J. (Eds.), *Teaching critical thinking skills* (pp. 9–26). New York, NY: Freeman.

Evans, P. (2006, January/February). The wiki factor. *BizEd,* (pp. 28-32).

Facione, P. A. (2011). Critical thinking: What it is and why it counts. *Insight Assessment.* Retrieved from http://www.insightassessment.com/pdf_files/what&why2010.pdf.

Fink, L. D. (2003). *Creating significant learning experiences: An integrated approach to designing college courses*. San Francisco, CA: Jossey-Bass.

Fountain, R. (2005). Wiki pedagogy. *Dossiers Technopedagiques*. Retrieved from http://www.profetic.org/dossiers/rubrique.php3?id_rubrique=110.

Garett, K. (2010). Professional learning communities allow a transformational culture to take root. *Education Digest*, *76*(2), 4–9.

Garrison, D. R. (1992). Critical thinking and self-directed learning in adult education: an analysis of responsibility and control issues. *Adult Education Quarterly*, *42*(3), 136–148.

Gerlich, R. N., Greenlaw, S. A., & DeLoach, S. B. (2003). Teaching critical thinking with electronic discussion. *The Journal of Economic Education*, *34*(1), 36–54. doi:10.1080/00220480309595199

Gokhale, A. (1995). Collaborative learning enhances critical thinking. *Journal of Technology Education*, *7*(1), 1–7. Retrieved from http://scholar.lib.vt.edu/ejournals/JTE/jte-v7n1/gokhale.jte-v7n1.html.

Guiller, J., A., Durndell, A. Ross, A., & Thomson, K. (2008). Peer interaction and critical thinking: face-to-face or online discussion? *Learning and Instruction*, *18*(2), 187–200. doi:10.1016/j.learninstruc.2007.03.001

Guzdial, M. (1999). *Teacher and students authoring on the Web for shifting agency*. Retrieved from http://home.cc.gatech.edu/csl/uploads/6/aera99.html.

Higdon, J., & Topaz, C. (2009). Blogs and wikis as instructional tools. *College Teaching*, *57*(2), 105–109. doi:10.3200/CTCH.57.2.105-110

Homik, M., & Melis, E. (2006). *Using blogs for learning logs*. Oxford, UK: Proceedings of e-Portfolio.

Jones, C., Ramanau, R., Cross, S., & Healing, G. (2010). Net Generation or digital natives: Is there a distinct new generation entering university? *Computers & Education*, *54*, 722–732. Retrieved from http://oro.open.ac.uk/19890/2/8CECE8C9. doi:10.1016/j.compedu.2009.09.022

Kerawalla, L., Minocha, S., Kirkup, G., & Conole, G. (2008). Characterizing the different blogging behaviors of students on an online distance learning course. *Learning, Media and Technology*, *33*(1), 21–33..doi:10.1080/17439880701868838

Krause, S. D. (2004). Blogs as a tool for teaching. *The Chronicle of Higher Education*, *51*(42), 33. Retrieved from http://chronile.com/weekly/v51.i42/42b03301.htm.

Landis, M., Swain, K. D., Friehe, M. J., & Coufal, K. L. (2007). Evaluating critical thinking in class and online: Comparison of the Newman Method and the Facione Rubric. *Communication Disorders Quarterly*, *28*(3), 135–143. doi:10.1177/15257401070280030301

Lenhart, A., & Madden, M. (2005). *Testimony by Amanda Lenhart Senior Research Specialist, Pew Internet & American Life Project*. Testimony to the House Committee on Energy and Commerce.

MacKnight, C. (2000). Teaching critical thinking through online discussions. *EDUCAUSE Quarterly*, *4*, 38–41.

Martin, C., & Dusenberry, L. (2008). Wiki lore and politics in the classroom. In Cummings, R. E., & Barton, M. (Eds.), *Wiki writing: Collaborative learning in the college classroom* (pp. 204–215). Ann Arbor: University of Michigan Press.

McCaffrey, R., & Gulbrandsen, K. (2007, October). *WikiWho? Using wikis to teach audience in the classroom*. Paper presented at the Association for Business Communication Annual Conference. Yosemite, CA.

Moxley, J. (2007). *For teachers new to wikis*. Retrieved from http://writingwiki.org/default.aspx/WritingWiki/For%20Teachers%20New%20to%20Wikis.html.

Nackerud, S. & Scaletta, K. (2008). Blogging in academy. *New Directions for Students Services, 124*. DOI: 10 1002/ss_296.

Numberof.net. (2010). *Number of blogs*. Retrieved from http://www.numberof.net/number-of-blogs/.

Oblinger, D., & Oblinger, J. (2005). Is it age or IT: First steps toward understanding the Net Generation. In Oblinger & Oblinger (Eds.), *Educating the Net Generation*. Boulder, CO: EDUCAUSE. Retrieved from http://www.educause.edu/educatingthenetgen?bhcp=1.

Paretti, M. C., McNair, L. D., & Holloway-Attaway, L. (2007). Teaching technical communication in an era of distributed work: A case study of collaboration between U.S. and Swedish students. *Technical Communication Quarterly, 16*, 327–352. doi:10.1080/10572250701291087

Parker, K. R., & Chao, J. T. (2007). Wiki as a teaching tool. *Interdisciplinary Journal of Knowledge and Learning Objects, 3*, 57–72.

Paul, R., & Elder, L. (2007). *The miniature guide to critical thinking: Concepts & tools*. Dillon Beach, CA: Foundation for Critical Thinking.

Pintrich, P. R., Smith, D. A., Garcia, T., & McKeachie, W. J. (1993). Reliability and predictive validity of the motivated strategies for learning questionnaire (MSLQ). *Educational and Psychological Measurement, 53*(3), 801–813. doi:10.1177/0013164493053003024

Salaway, G., & Caruso, J. B. (2007). *The ECAR study of undergraduate students and information technology*. EDUCAUSE Center for Applied Research. Retrieved from http://connect.educause.edu/library/abstract/TheECARStudyofUnderg/45075.

Sanders, S. (2011, January). *Investigating learning in sciences and professions*. Powerpoint presentation at Better Learning through Technology Institute, Youngstown, OH.

Scaletta, K. R. (2006). *To whom are these texts valuable? An inquiry into student blogging*. Master's project, University of Minnesota. Retrieved from http://inms.umn.edu/events/past/newresearch_2006/scaletta.html.

Scriven, M., & Richard, P. (2009). Defining critical thinking. Retrieved January 29, 2009, from http://www.criticalthinking.org/page.cfm?PageID=410HYPERLINK.

Stupnisky, R. H., Renaud, R. D., Daniels, L. M., Haynes, T. L., & Perry, R. P. (2008). The interrelation of first-year college students' critical thinking disposition, perceived academic control, and academic achievement. *Research in Higher Education, 49*, 513–530. doi:10.1007/s11162-008-9093-8

Subcommitteeon Telecommunications and the Internet hearing on H.R. 5319, The Deleting On-line Predators Act of 2006. Retrieved from http://www.pewinternet.org/~/media//Files/Presentations/2006/2006%20-%207.11.06%20-%20Testimony%20by%20Amanda%20Lenhart.pdf.

Thompson, C. (2006). The early years. *New York Magazine*. February. Retrieved from http://nymag.com/news/media/15971/.

Vie, S., & DeWinter, J. (2008). Disrupting intellectual property: Collaboration and resistance in wikis. In Cummings, R. E., & Barton, M. (Eds.), *Wiki writing: Collaborative learning in the college classroom* (pp. 109–122). Ann Arbor, MI: University of Michigan Press.

Wade, C. (1995). Using writing to develop and assess critical thinking. *Teaching of Psychology, 22*(1), 24–28. doi:10.1207/s15328023top2201_8

Walsh, L. (2010). Constructive interference: Wikis and service learning in the technical communication classroom. *Technical Communication Quarterly*, *19*(2), 184–211. doi:10.1080/10572250903559381

Williams, J. B., & Jacobs, J. (2004). Exploring the use of blogs as learning spaces in the higher education sector *Australasian Journal of Education Technology, 20*(2), 232-247. Retrieved from http://www.ascilite.org.au/ajet/ajet20/williams.html.

Xie, Y., Ke, F., & Sharma, P. (2008). The effect of peer feedback for blogging on college students' reflective learning processes. *The Internet and Higher Education*, *11*(1), 18–25. doi:10.1016/j.iheduc.2007.11.001

Zawillinski, L. (2009). Hot blogging: A framework for blogging to promote higher order thinking. *The Reading Teacher*, *62*(8), 650–651. doi:10.1598/RT.62.8.3

ADDITIONAL READING

Blan, I., Mor, N., & Neuthal, T. (2009). Open the windows of communication: Promoting interpersonal and group interactions using blogs in higher education. *Interdisciplinary Journal of E-Learning and Learning Objects*, *5*, 233–246.

Broussard, C. (2008). Teaching with technology: Is the pedagogical fulerum shifting? *New York Law School Law Review. New York Law School*, *53*, 903–915. Retrieved from http://a.nyls.edu/user_files/1/3/4/17/49/195/256/9Broussard534.pdf.

Burgess, J. (2006). Blogging to learn, learning to blog. In Bruns, A., & Jacobs, J. (Eds.), *Uses of Blogs* (pp. 105–114). New York: Peter Lang.

Butcher, H. K., & Taylor, J. Y. (2008). Using a wiki to enhance knowing participation in change in the teaching-learning process. *Visions*, *15*(1), 30–43.

Cunningham, W. (2010). WikiHistory. Retrieved from http://c2.com/cgi/wiki?WikiHistory.

Dickey, M. (2004). The impact of web-logs (blogs) on student perceptions of isolation and alienation in a web-based distance learning environment. *Open Learning*, *19*(3), 279–291. doi:10.1080/0268051042000280138

Duda, G., & Garrett, K. (2008). Blogging in the physics classroom: A research-based approach to shaping students' attitudes toward physics. *American Journal of Physics*, *76*(11), 1054–1065. doi:10.1119/1.2967707

Ellison, N. B., & Wu, Y. (2008). Blogging in the classroom: A preliminary exploration of student attitudes and impact on comprehension. *Journal of Educational Multimedia and Hypermedia*, *17*(1), 99–122.

Farmer, J. (2006). Blogging to basics: How blogs are bringing online learning back from the brink. In Bruns, A., & Jacobs, J. (Eds.), *Uses of Blog* (pp. 91–103). New York: Peter Lang.

Ferriter, B. (2009). Learning with Blogs and Wikis. *Educational Leadership*, *66*(5), 00131784.

Folley, D. (2010). The lecture is deal long live the e-lecture. *Electronic Journal of e-Learning, 8* (2), 93 – 100.

Freeman, M. (2004). Team-based learning in a course combining in-class and online interaction. In Michaelsen, L. K., Knight, A. B., & Fink, L. D. (Eds.), *Team-based learning: A Transformative use of small groups* (pp. 157–172). Sterling, VA: Stylus.

Frye, E. M., Trathen, W., & Keppenhaver, D. A. (2010). Internet workshop and blog publishing: Meeting student (and teacher) learning needs to achieve best practice in the twenty-first-century social studies classroom. *Social Studies*, *101*, 46–53. doi:10.1080/00377990903284070

Gahbauer, M. (2009). Blogging as a tool for cultivating scientific thinking in non-majors. *International Journal of Science in Society*, *1*(3), 123–135.

Garrison, D. R., & Vaughan, N. D. (2008). *Blended learning in higher education*. San Francisco, CA: Jossey Bass.

Goldman, R. H., Cohen, A. P., & Sheahan, F. (2008). Using seminar blogs to enhance student participation in learning in public health school classes. *American Journal of Public Health*, *98*(9), 1658–1663..doi:10.2105/AJPH.2008.133694

Huann, T., John, O., & Yuen, J. (2005). *Weblogs in education, a literature review*. Retrieved from http://edublog.net/astinus/mt/2005/09/weblogs in educ.html.

King, P. M., & Kitchener, K. S. (1994). *Developing reflection judgment*. San Francisco, CA: Jossey-Bass.

Ko, S., & Rossen, S. (2004). *Teaching on-line* (2nd ed.). Boston, MA: Houghton Mifflin.

Majchrzak, A. (2009). Comment: Where is the theory in wikis? *Management Information Systems Quarterly*, *33*(1), 18–20.

Palsole, S., & Awalt, C. (2008). Team-based learning in asynchronous online settings. *New Directions for Teaching and Learning*, *116*, 87–95. doi:10.1002/tl.336

Phillipson, M. (2008). Wikis in the classroom: A taxonomy. In Cummings, R. E., & Barton, M. (Eds.), *Wiki Writing: Collaborative Learning in the College Classroom* (pp. 19–43). Ann Arbor: University of Michigan Press.

Ramaswami, R. (2008). The prose (and a few cons, too) of blogging. *T.H.E. Journal*, *35*(11). Retrieved from http://www.thejournal.com/articles/23562.

Richardson, W. (2009). *Blogs, wikis, podcasts, and other powerful web tools for classrooms* (2nd ed.). Thousand Oaks, CA: Corwin Press.

Uang, S. (2009). Using blogs to enhance critical reflection and community of practice. *Journal of Educational Technology & Society*, *12*(2), 11–21.

KEY TERMS AND DEFINITIONS

Blended Learning: Learning that involves both on-line and face to face *activities.*

Blogs: Web-based tool designed to provide a virtual forum for discussion.

Collaborative Learning: A methodology in which learners engage in a common task where each individual depends on and is accountable.

Critical Thinking: One's ability to identify central issues and assumptions, evaluating evidence and deducing conclusions.

NetGen: Students that consider computers part of their natural environment.

On-Line Learning: Education that happens on-line via computer.

Professional Learning Community (PLC): A community of practice to enhance learning, teaching and professional development for its members.

Significant Learning: A relational, interactive learning that causes a lasting change in learner's life.

Web 2.0: Read/write web platform to enable people to network and collaborate in online communities.

Wiki: Web-based tool designed to assist people in working together in virtual environment.

ENDNOTE

1 For more information about this study: Gahbauer, M. (2009). Blogging as a tool for cultivating scientific thinking in non-majors. *International Journal of Science in Society*, *1*(3), 123-135.

Chapter 14

Empowering 21st Century Learners through Personal Learning Networks

Shannan H. Butler
St. Edward's University, USA

Corinne Weisgerber
St. Edward's University, USA

ABSTRACT

The discourse surrounding digital natives and their learning needs often presupposes a level of social media knowledge or savviness that is equal, if not superior, to that of any other generation, including that of their teachers. Although it is undeniable that this new breed of students feels comfortable using social media as an integral part of their wired lives, the assumption that digital immersion results in digital literacy may end up preventing a whole generation of students from learning how to take full advantage of the digital tools they grew up with. As long as this assumption goes unchallenged, the net generation may very well continue navigating this digitally mediated world without ever truly understanding the strategic uses of social media technologies. If we are to prepare 21st century students for today's highly competitive global marketplace and rapidly changing world, we need to teach them how to direct their own learning. Fortunately, today's social media technologies make it easier than ever for students to develop independent learning skills. In this chapter we discuss how students can use various social media platforms to identify and connect to communities of experts capable of supporting their learning needs and how to incorporate these personal learning networks into everyday pedagogical practice.

DOI: 10.4018/978-1-61350-347-8.ch014

INTRODUCTION

"The summation of human experience is being expanded at a prodigious rate, and the means we use for threading through the consequent maze to the momentarily important item is the same as was used in the days of square-rigged ships" (Bush, 1945, para. 8).

Hearing Vannevar Bush lament modern society's struggle to keep up with the ever-accelerating pace of knowledge creation, it is important to remember that this statement was made over half a century ago. It is hard to imagine how Bush might react to today's world of networked computers, search engines, and social networks. The sheer quantity of information available to us and the speed at which that information is being disseminated might not only feel overwhelming to some, but it also calls into question the adequacy of our current methods of education and is forcing us to rethink the ways in which we engage 21st century students. As Gonzalez (2004) points out, "half of what is known today was not known 10 years ago. The amount of knowledge in the world has doubled in the past 10 years and is doubling every 18 months according to the American Society of Training and Documentation. To combat the shrinking half-life of knowledge, organizations have been forced to develop new methods of deploying instruction" (para. 1). With the volume of knowledge exponentially increasing, our ability to acquire the knowledge we need for tomorrow is more important than what we already know today (Siemens 2005. In light of these developments it is likely that we will do a great disservice to coming generations of learners if we do not change our current pedagogical approaches.

Personal Learning Networks

One of the ways that may allow us to handle the onslaught of information and prepare our students for living in such a rapidly changing world is through the development of personal learning networks (PLNs). We define PLNs as deliberately formed networks of people and resources capable of guiding our independent learning goals and professional development needs (Weisgerber & Butler, 2011). By fostering collaboration between educators, professionals, and students, many teachers have already taken the opportunity to break down the metaphorical classroom walls (Parry, 2010). The new generation of digital natives, which now occupies our classrooms, offers an interesting opportunity and conversely poses an equally troubling problem. The discourse surrounding these digital natives and their learning needs often presupposes a level of social media knowledge or savviness that is equal, if not superior, to that of any other generation, including that of their teachers. Although it is undeniable that this new breed of students feels comfortable using social media as an integral part of their wired lives, the assumption that digital immersion results in digital literacy may prevent a whole generation of students from learning how to take advantage of the digital tools they grew up with. As long as this assumption goes unchallenged, the net generation may very well continue navigating this digitally mediated world without ever truly understanding the strategic uses of social media technologies.

The Independent Learner

When personal learning networks are discussed in the popular press they are invariably equated with one or more of autodidactical terms: independent learning, lifelong learning, self-regulated learning, or self-directed learning. The prefacing terms independent, auto and self would lead one to believe that PLNs are constructed only by the learner and with only their immediate need for information in mind. Although there are clearly components of self-initiation at work in these labels, the concepts themselves derive primarily from the field of androgogy. Androgogy, the field of adult education, has grown up around the practical challenge of developing educational environments that meet the needs of adult learners. Until recently the field of teaching teachers how to teach was referred to as pedagogy, deriving from the Greek, "to lead the child." The growing population of returning adult students coupled with technological advances allowing for distance education has created an important shift in educational thinking. Androgogy has even begun to shift the field of pedagogy itself away from its traditional moorings.

Self-Regulated Learning

We believe it is useful to examine two of the terms used to describe personal learning networks: self-regulated learning which comes from the traditional field of pedagogy, and self-directed learning which comes from the field of androgogy. By comparing these two terms, we may get a sense of what is required to foster a successful personal learning environment. Laskey and Hetzel (2010) in their discussion of self-regulated learning and self-directed learning have established clear differences between these two often-conflated concepts. According to Zimmerman (2002) self-regulated learners possess specific goals, develop appropriate strategies for accomplishing these goals, manage their time well, monitor and evaluate their performance, and seamlessly navigate both social and physical contexts. Zimmerman (1998) clarifies that "academic self-regulation is not a mental ability, such as intelligence, or an academic skill, such as reading proficiency; rather it is the self-directive process through which learners transform their mental abilities into academic skills." (pp. 1-2) These types of self-regulated learners are also aware of their academic strengths and weaknesses and will choose from an appropriate array of strategies and skills to solve problems (Perry, Phillips, & Hutchinson, 2006). Self-regulation, then, seems to be a personal characteristic more in line with a true autodidact—a characteristic that enables one to learn and solve problems independently. Of course this is not one characteristic but a whole constellation of qualities that seem to promote independent learning. And, if Zimmerman (2002) is correct, these characteristics are not inherent to the individual and not even really characteristics at all as much as they are an embodied process. If self-regulated learning is a favorable personal learning process then that process can be fostered in those who may not already possess it.

Self-Directed Learning

Androgogy's answer to this problem has been the process of developing environments that nurture individuals to become more self-regulated. Within adult education literature this process is referred to as self-directed learning. According to Loyens, Magda, and Rikers (2008), "SDL environments are designed to foster self-direction that students will carry into subsequent learning situations" (p. 418). As discussed in the previous section, the process of self-regulated learning is a characteristic or process observed within some individuals in the classroom setting of traditional pedagogy. These desirable characteristics have been sought by educators, who hope to empower their students to conduct research and problem solving in distance education environments. The structured nature of self-directed learning encourages the continuation of this process beyond the physical classroom or through the electronic one (Candy, 1991). Metacognition is one of the cornerstones of both self-regulated learning and self-directed learning. The term refers to our ability to know what we need to know, our realization that we don't know it now, and our means to acquiring that knowledge (Cao & Nietfield, 2007). Metacognition is not an automatic process and although many learners are not well equipped in this area, Zimmerman (2002) believes it to be a teachable skill. Independent learning then, at least in this context, is far from autonomous. Rather it is a highly structured, goal driven, strategy based, evaluative process. Knowles (1975), one of the fathers of the field of androgogy, established self-direction to be the creation of an environment "in which individuals take the initiative with or without the help of others, in diagnosing their learning needs, formulating learning goals, identifying human and material resources for learning, choosing and implementing appropriate learning strategies, and evaluating outcomes" (p. 18). When we discuss developing PLNs in the classroom setting, it will be from the informed position of self-directed learning with the goal of helping individuals to develop strong self-regulated learning skills.

Although one of the strengths of the Internet is its looseness, we rely on the educational literature that suggests that a true self-directed learning environment must set goals, implement strategies, and provide for evaluation and revision of the environment (Loyens et al., 2008, p. 417). One of the seeming downfalls of the field of adult education has been its dependence on distance education and therefore its frequent embracing of the newest technologies. Many of these decisions, especially early on, led to leading edge technology being placed in the service of a model that lacked sound educational theory. The same reliance on technology as savior has been adapted for the Net Generation. Many educators assume that the Net Generation is made up of self-regulated learners who are comfortable in a technology-based, self-directed learning environment. But Richardson (2006), asserts that, "When people talk about kids being 'digital natives,' it's a real disservice—because it suggests that kids are just somehow born with these abilities to use these technologies well. And that's not the case" (para. 11). Kramarski and Michalsky (2009) suggest that although the "e-learning environment seems to inherently promote the application of self-regulating capabilities, most studies have shown that it often leads to little study because learners do not know how to direct themselves to effectively take advantage of what the environment has to offer" (p. 163). Bujega (2008) also questions the current trend of throwing new technologies at students in hopes that they will embrace and learn from them. He contests the assumption that students want to learn from the same devices that both "amuse and distract" them. It should be clear then that although adult educators have often quickly embraced new technologies for distance learning, those technological choices alone have not necessarily led to better learning environments nor have they necessarily fostered an increase in self-directed learners. Kramarski and Michalsky (2009) suggest that it is the qualities of self-metacognition that is lacking from these loose implementations of technology and further see the structure of the self-directed model as essential to enable them to become beneficial for the learner.

Moving from a Teacher-Centered to a Student-Centered Model of Education

Pintrich (1995) stresses the importance for faculty to model self-regulated learning in the classroom. Other scholars have explored how PLNs are not just useful for students, but are indispensable for allowing teachers to keep current within their fields (Weisgerber & Butler, 2011). A personal learning network can provide additional networking beyond the classroom, colleagues, conferences, and development hours. We find that they often provide lecture and research material as well as offering new pedagogical insights. For Net Generational students to grasp the importance of self-directed learning it is imperative that faculty make self-regulated learning a part of their own professional habits. In order to achieve this, teachers must move from the traditional Cartesian vessel model of knowledge to a more modern networked one. As Adler and Brown (2008) note:

The emphasis on social learning stands in sharp contrast to the traditional Cartesian view of knowledge and learning—a view that has largely dominated the way education has been structured for over one hundred years. The Cartesian perspective assumes that knowledge is a kind of substance and that pedagogy concerns the best way to transfer this substance from teachers to students. By contrast, instead of starting from the Cartesian premise of 'I think, therefore I am,' and from the assumption that knowledge is something that is transferred to the student via various pedagogical strategies, the social view of learning says, 'We participate, therefore we are.' (p.18)

Many teachers especially those new to the profession still see teaching as a teacher-centered activity and fail to see learning as a process between teacher and student as well as various other streams of information and experience (Kramarski & Michalsky, 2009). Teachers wishing to develop self-regulated learning skills should provide student-centered classrooms where Net Generational students have leeway to formulate their learning aims, conceptualize their own problems, and design ways they can address the problems (Perry et al., 2006). Pintrich (1988) agrees, suggesting that allowing students to help decide what they will learn strengthens their self-regulating strategies.

If our understanding of knowledge's fleeting nature and of the benefits of self-directed learning are correct, then teachers must move from their position as knowledge holders to facilitators of knowledge gathering. Kuo's (2010) discussion of competence and self-efficacy brings questions of what it means to have a student-centered education to the fore. Again, the concept of the independent learner with no direction or guidelines is wholly inadequate. Instead, educators must create an environment full of challenges and goals in order to foster independent learning. Interestingly, Locke and Latham (1990) argue that the more challenging the goal, the better the student performance. Having easy goals or no goals at all lends itself to poor student performance. Students must, however, believe that the goals, which have been set, are indeed ones that they can actually reach. Self-efficacy is an important component of self-regulated learning. If students do not believe that they can organize their behavior to achieve the set goal, they are far less likely to be successful (Bandura 1986). A delicate balance between the teacher's scaffolding of the process with formalized goals, strategies, and evaluation and the learner's personal interests, aptitude, efficacy, and skills is required for self-directed learning to take root.

Connectivism and Fostering a Community of Practice

Once the classroom scaffolding (discussed later in this chapter) has been implemented, students are likely to begin gleaning information specifically targeted to their interests and needs. The personal learning network they create allows them to connect to what has been termed a community of learners or a community of practice. Various learning communities may be combined to create a personal learning environment addressing a diversity of knowledge. This section is informed by one such community of writers and digital technology theorists including George Siemens, Stephen Downes, and Howard Rheingold who have broken the boundaries of the academy to directly address Net Generational learners. Siemens (2005) has called the process of becoming a member of such a learning community, Connectivism. "The field of education has been slow to recognize both the impact of new learning tools and the environmental changes in what it means to learn. Connectivism provides insight into learning skills and tasks needed for learners to flourish in a digital era" (Siemens, 2005, para 24). Siemens, his frequent collaborator Stephen Downes (2009), and digital theorist Howard Rheingold (2008) have been among the first academics to often ditch the classroom in favor of social media. This allows them to break out of the old pedagogical model and offer content and courses directly to interested learners through the Internet. Rheingold (2008) goes further and champions the civic involvement offered to Net Generational students who provide their own content directly to the public by advocating for their positions and organizing action around their interests. This kind of "participatory media education" he believes will not only make for empowered learners but also empowered citizens. People like Rheingold and Siemens are oftentimes affectionately referred to as gurus or network Sherpas—guides for those seeking direction in their particular fields of study.

The efficiency, efficacy, and cost effectiveness of these loosely designed networks of professionals and laypersons has not escaped the eye of administrators in Washington D.C. In a climate of budget cuts, these networks seem to be practical ways to continue to foster research and education. According to Tackett and Cator (2011) the Department of Education is currently actively exploring the development of "promise neighborhoods," or communities of practice. These communities can be seen as "groups of people who share a concern or a passion for something they do and learn how to do it better as they interact regularly" (para. 3). These types of networks may well be the future of our educational system but for now, they help those aligned with similar interests to pool their resources and explore new perspectives.

In a speech delivered on the occasion of his inauguration as rector of Glasgow University, Jimmy Reid (1972) passionately argued that "the whole object [of education] must be to equip and educate people for life, not solely for work or a profession" (p. 11) and that "to unleash the latent potential of people" they needed to be given responsibility (p. 10). In a world marked by uncertainty and technological change, we think Reid's advice is even more poignant today than it was in 1972 when he delivered his now famous address. We view personal learning networks as an attempt to live up to Reid's vision of education. By emphasizing students' personal responsibility in the learning process and teaching them how to direct their own learning, PLNs attempt to prepare students for life after college in an ever more rapidly changing world.

While the concept of independent learning itself isn't new, the advent of the social web has extended our personal learning opportunities beyond our immediate network of friends, family and colleagues (Warlick, 2010 and has created countless new ways for students to connect with people and resources from around the world. Indeed, "never before in the history of the planet have so many people—on their own—had the ability to find so much information about so many things and about so many other people" (Friedman, 2006, p. 177). What matters is that students learn to take advantage of this networked society in order to stay abreast of changes in their chosen field, and that they understand how to filter the vast amounts of information available to them. Knowing how to successfully locate high quality resources that can help them stay relevant in a world where knowledge has an ever shorter shelf life is an indispensable skill for the 21st century learner (Rheingold, 2009). Fortunately, today's social media technologies make it easier than ever for Net Generation students to accomplish those goals by building PLNs capable of guiding their learning long after they graduate. In the following sections, we will describe how to use social networking platforms such as blogs, micro-blogs, social bookmarks and other emerging technologies to connect students to a geographically dispersed community of experts. Following that discussion, we will provide a general framework for incorporating PLNs into a variety of classrooms regardless of discipline.

Using PLNs to Turn Students into Networked Learners

Although most social technologies could be used to support self-directed learning initiatives, for space reasons, we will focus on the more common social media platforms in this discussion. The Net Generation is a socially networked generation, but they are not as networked as learners. They need to learn the basic steps involved in creating a PLN, so they can easily repeat the process with other social media tools in an effort to further expand their network. According to Yucht (2009) the first step in building a PLN should consist of "seeking out gurus" (p. 11). While some people may object to the term guru, the general idea of needing to identify experts nonetheless remains paramount. In the realm of social learning, experts refer to Internet users who possess knowledge of value to a learner and who are willing to share that information. In other words, experts are people who can add value to a student's network. Most Net Generational students are familiar with social media for social purposes, but they need to be trained in locating these experts, and may also need to learn to subscribe to their information streams. We will discuss how to accomplish these two steps on various social media platforms next. We will begin with the micro-blogging service Twitter.

Identifying and Following Experts on Twitter

Twitter is a "social networking and micro-blogging service that enables users to send and read short messages (a maximum of 140 characters) known as tweets" (Moody, 2010, p. 3). Although Twitter may not enjoy the same popularity among college students as Facebook (Moody, 2010) – only 18% of college students who go online use Twitter (Young, 2010) – the service boasts 175 million registered users worldwide and facilitates the exchange of 95 million tweets each day ("A few Twitter facts," 2010). Among those millions of users are innumerable thought leaders who use the service daily to share their knowledge and to disseminate the latest information from their field of expertise. In order to reap the pedagogical benefits of Twitter, all students have to do is tap into this steady stream of freely shared resources and ideas. Of course not everything that circulates on Twitter is worthy of inclusion into a network whose primary purpose it is to support a student's particular learning needs. Because of that, students need to be taught to isolate the signal from the noise.

One way to do so is to start with established experts in the field. These could be activists and/or legislators who champion a particular issue of interest to the class, authors who have written books on the topic, professional speakers, bloggers, nonprofit and for profit organizations, etc. While not all of the experts identified in this manner will have a Twitter presence, some of them undoubtedly will. To find out whether a particular person actually tweets, students should log on to the service and use Twitter's built-in search engine to run a query on the person's name. The results from that search will be displayed on a page, which is currently comprised of four tabs ("tweets," "tweets with links," "tweets near you," and "people"). In case the query returns a match, the person's Twitter handle – their unique username -- will show up under the "people" tab. We suggest that students click through to users' Twitter profiles and browse through their latest tweets to get both a sense of what they tend to tweet about and how recently they last used the service. While the first recommendation ensures topic relevance, the latter one is a safeguard against adding people to one's PLN who stopped using Twitter altogether or who use it only very sporadically. If the Twitter user passes those two tests, we recommend that s/he be added to the student's PLN. On Twitter, this is done through "following" the other person, which refers to the act of subscribing to their tweets or updates and which ensures that their updates will appear in the student's timeline ("What is following?," n.d.).

This initial Twitter network building activity may only yield a few leads though. To expand this fledgling network of experts, students should be encouraged to take full advantage of the social nature of Twitter and to explore the list of people who follow, or are followed by the experts they just identified in the previous step. Chances are that quite a few of the users on either one of those lists may share similar interests, have similar backgrounds, or tweet about similar issues. Indeed, each Twitter user's profile page publicly displays the number of people s/he follows and is followed by, and with the click of a button, allows anyone to generate a list of those users complete with a Twitter handle and brief biography. To determine whether any of the listed users should be added to a PLN, we again encourage students to sample some recent tweets in order to determine whether that person could bring value to the network and whether s/he actively uses the service.

Another way to build out a Twitter PLN is through the use of Twitter lists. Twitter recently started providing its own suggestions for who to follow and offers up these recommendations in a number of places, such as (a) a person's homepage, (b) next to another user's profile page, and (c) on a person's own profile page. Suggestions on a person's homepage reflect accounts Twitter thinks you might find interesting "based on the types of accounts you're already following and who those people follow" ("How to use Twitter's suggestions," n.d.). Recommendations beside another user's profile page suggest other registered users like that person, while recommendations on who to follow on a person's own profile page simply suggest users who are similar to that person. In addition to providing these suggestions, Twitter also allows users to build their own lists of people they recommend by organizing others into groups. To view those user-generated lists, students need to pull up a user's profile page and click the "lists" tab right below the biography. That tab features three types of lists: (a) lists created by the user,(b) lists the user follows, and (c) lists following the user. Clicking on a list displays "a stream of tweets from all the users included in that group" ("How to use Twitter lists," n.d.) and provides a good starting point for students interested in expanding their Twitter PLN. "What makes this method of discovery even more worthwhile, is the fact that those Twitter users have already been vetted" by people they trust, and "that it tends to diversify the emerging network" (citation removed for blind review). Before Twitter introduced its own list feature, there were a number of third-party applications such as TweepML (http://tweepml.org/), which offered a very similar service. Using the same process described above, students can use these services' built-in "find a list" search features to locate even more experts to add to their Twitter stream.

Although the steps described thus far should lead to a sizable Twitter PLN, there are a number of other ways to discover expert voices on Twitter. Every Friday thousands of people use the hashtag #followfriday, or #ff to recommend some of their favorite Twitter users to their own network of followers (Baldwin, 2009). We ask students to be on the lookout for those recommendations and to consider adding them to their PLN if they meet the relevancy criteria. Another easy way to identify experts outside one's immediate network is to check out RTs, or re-tweets. Re-tweets refer to Twitter messages that were picked up by a user other than the original author of the message and then re-circulated on Twitter. If a re-tweet shows up in a student's Twitter stream, we encourage that student to look up the person who originally sent out the tweet and to determine whether that person might be worth following.

It is important to note in this regard that the type of network building activity described here should be understood as a dynamic process which needs to be tweaked and revisited from time to time. Students should be encouraged to re-evaluate their network every so often and to delete (or unfollow) voices which do not add any value. Similarly, students should occasionally repeat the discovery methods described above to grow and diversify their PLN. As the observant reader will have noted, so far we have focused entirely on message reception in our discussion of Twitter. Although it is possible to use Twitter more as a customized news service than a personal broadcasting medium, we do encourage students to engage their Twitter network and give back to it by sharing the information they find online. Doing so not only exemplifies the spirit of openness so essential to the concept of PLNs, but it also helps establish students as thought leaders in their own right. Becoming a thought leader requires sustained engagement within the discourse of a specific discipline for an extended period both as consumers and as producers of content. By not only gathering information from your PLN but also giving back to the community which is generating the information, Net Generation students will find themselves immersed in the concepts and language of the field and may well construct themselves as indispensable experts in a particular area. By establishing themselves as thought leaders while still students, they may also be marketing themselves and their personal brand to future potential employers.

Identifying and Following Expert Bloggers

Most of the strategies regarding the identification and validation of experts on Twitter apply to bloggers as well. The first step in adding relevant bloggers to a PLN again begins with a few established experts on the topic of interest to the learner. Although search engines such as Google's blog search (blogsearch.google.com) should suffice to locate the URL of a known expert's blog, discovering unknown voices amidst the estimated 150 million blogs scattered all over the Internet (BlogPulse Stats, n.d.) often requires a more sophisticated approach. Since at this point Net Generation students already have established a fairly extensive Twitter PLN, we recommend checking whether the Twitter users inside that network keep a blog. While some people might argue that such an approach would only duplicate voices inside a student's PLN, we argue that the content produced and shared on blogs differs enough from the type of content shared via Twitter that it merits being included in its own right. To find out whether a particular Twitter users also blogs, students need only check that user's Twitter biography and visit the link listed beneath the bio. Another strategy for expanding the blogging component of a PLN consists of checking a trusted blogger's blog roll. A blog roll is similar to a Twitter list in that it provides a list of blogs endorsed by the blogger. In most cases this endorsement acts as a quality control mechanism certifying the value of the listed blog. Once students have located a number of useful blogs, we suggest that they read through some of the posts and follow back any link contained in those posts. The point of this practice is to determine whether the author or the blog post may have linked to another blog of interest to the student's learning needs.

In order to keep track of the information that flows through the blogs identified in this manner, we introduce students to an RSS aggregator or feed reader – an application "which makes it possible for readers to 'subscribe' to the content that is created on a particular Weblog so they no longer have to visit the blog itself to get it" (Richardson, 2006, p. 75). Feed readers such as Google Reader (www.google.com/reader) or NewsGator (www.newsgator.com/rss-readers.aspx) regularly check a user's subscriptions, gather any new content detected, and then display that content in one window in order to allow the user to "consume massive amounts of information in a structured and organized way" (Briggs, 2010, p. 14). Net Generation learners are already comfortable checking their personal feeds through various channels such as Facebook and text messages. We strongly encourage students to develop a daily habit of checking their RSS feeds as well. Doing so not only allows them to keep up with the information stream they have subscribed to, but as Briggs (2010) argues, it also provides the best way for students to increase their knowledge of a particular subject.

Identifying and Following Social Bookmarking Users

Setting up a feed reader to serve as an aggregator for the content shared by one's blogging network is not the only use of a feed reader though. Once students have created the blog component of their PLN and subscribed to the blogs' RSS feeds, we introduce them to the concept of social bookmarks. Social bookmarking refers to the practice of saving online content in a public database hosted by one of the many social bookmarking services available for free on the Internet. Social bookmarking sites such as Diigo, Delicious, and Furl allow users to save bookmarks to their respective sites and to describe the saved content with user-generated keywords, commonly referred to as tags. "Because social bookmarking services indicate who created each bookmark and provide access to that person's other bookmarked resources, users can easily make social connections with other individuals interested in just about any topic. Users can also see how many people have used a tag and search for all resources that have been assigned that tag" (EduCause, 2005, p. 1). The social nature of this type of bookmarking practice is what renders it so attractive from a pedagogical perspective and why it should be readily embraced by Net Generation learners. It also explains why students should incorporate a social bookmarking element into their PLNs.

In order to do so, students simply need to identify specific tags or users to follow, and then use their feed reader to subscribe to those tags or users. In the first scenario, anytime an Internet user were to save an online resource using the tag a student subscribed to, that resource would be displayed in our student's feed reader. Similarly, if a student were to subscribe to a social bookmarking user, every new resource saved by that user would show up in the student's feed reader. While identifying tags to subscribe to is as easy as determining the keywords one is interested in, discovering users worth following is a bit more complicated. Although some Internet users list their bookmarking usernames on their blogs or Google profiles (www.google.com/profiles), most don't. As a result, students will need to discover those users on their own. We tell students that one way to do so is to start by bookmarking an online resource related to the student's particular interest and to find out what other Internet users bookmarked the same resource. The idea is that if they bookmarked that resource, they must have found it valuable in some way. In this case, the act of bookmarking could indicate their interest in the topic. To verify that this is not an isolated incidence of interest, we show students how to access a list of all of a user's tags. Most social bookmarking sites will display these tags along with a count of how many resources a particular user has tagged with the same keywords. By checking this list, students will get a quick sense for the type of resources a user tends to bookmark – usually enough to determine whether or not that user would be worth adding to a feed reader. Besides examining the most commonly used tags as a criterion for inclusion in a PLN, students should also browse through a user's bookmarks to make sure there are several (and not just a few) resources of value to their learning needs. If a social bookmarking user meets those criteria, all a student has to do is add the user's feed to their feed reader. Since GoogleReader automatically detects feeds, this would be as simple as grabbing the URL (i.e. www.digo.com/users/USERNAME; or www.delicious.com/USERNAME), and cut and pasting it into the "add a subscription" field on the feed reader. Of course, should this user later turn out not to provide any real value to the network, s/he can be removed with the click of a button and replaced by a more appropriate information source. As we mentioned in the previous section, Net Generational students should be quite comfortable checking their feeds. Most Internet users already bookmark sites in their own browsers and with only a few more clicks they can categorize, search, and share them with others. The social aspect of bookmarking will bring a wealth of useful information directly to students without the need to search for it.

Extending the PLN Creation Process to Other Social Media Platforms

As mentioned before, the real power of a PLN lies in the people that comprise the network and not in the technologies that make these connections possible. The rapid proliferation of the social web has no doubt created an unprecedented technological infrastructure capable of fueling these connections, but it is important to remember that at the heart of it all there will always be the human relationships. Because of that, PLNs shouldn't be restricted to any particular social media platform. We chose to describe some of the more popular, and maybe more established ones in this chapter, but we would like to stress that blogs, microblogs and social bookmarking sites aren't the only technologies suitable for incorporation into a PLN. Any technology that is social in nature and brings people together has the potential to serve as the basis of a PLN. By way of example, take Quora (www.quora.com), a new social networking site built around a question and answer format. According to its developers, Quora is "a continually improving collection of questions and answers created, edited, and organized by everyone who uses it" ("About Quora, n.d.). Quora allows any user to post a question to the service and wait for other users to provide the answer. If, and when, Quora reaches critical mass, it could become "a useful crowd-sourcing tool, provided the right people find your questions" (Sledzick, 2011, para. 9). If Quora reaches that milestone, it could become a sort of human Google and the pedagogical implications of having a network of experts devoted entirely to answering questions would be tremendous. At that point, Quora should definitely be considered a viable component of any student's PLN.

Incorporating PLNs across the Curriculum

In order to get students, particularly Net Generational ones, from any academic discipline to realize the benefits of a personal learning network, we suggest designing an independent learning project that gives students an opportunity to tailor a class assignment to their own learning needs and course-related interests. The project should ask students to (1) identify an area of study pertaining to class which they would like to learn more about, (2) outline a plan of study or personal learning contract, and (3) decide on appropriate learning deliverables to demonstrate their mastery of the material. Students should then have to (4) submit this plan to the instructor for approval, (5) create a network of experts that could mentor them and help them complete their chosen project and (6) review and evaluate their network adjusting it for optimal performance. This 6-step process is closely modeled after Knowles (1975) view of self-direction. As we have noted in previous sections, although Net Generation learners may be familiar with many types of digital technology and social media, they may not have the structure they need to adequately learn from it. Knowles' 6-step process addresses this need. Step 1 of our project refers to the process in which individuals diagnose their learning needs, steps 2 and 3 require students to "formulate learning goals "and steps 5 and 6 illustrate what Knowles called the need to identify "human and material resources for learning, choosing and implementing appropriate learning strategies, and evaluating outcomes" (Knowles, 1975, p. 18).

Once all the study plans have been approved, the instructor should introduce the class to the concept of personal learning networks. We suggest spending at least one class period discussing the steps involved in building and growing online connections made possible entirely through new social media technologies. We intentionally start that class session with a conceptual discussion of PLNs, before moving into the more technical aspects involved in building such a network of experts. The second part of the class period should be devoted to a discussion of how to set up a PLN using blogs, micro-blogs (i.e. Twitter), and social bookmarks (i.e. Delicious, Diigo). Students learn that the first order of business is to identify people who could bring value to their network. In order to do so, we discuss a list of strategies for locating relevant blogs, Twitter and social bookmarking site users. Having discussed how to identify experts, students then learn how to subscribe to these blogs, Twitter and social bookmarking users in order to receive automatic notifications when their chosen experts share new resources or information. At the end of that class period, students are asked to use what they have learned to create a PLN capable of helping them complete their project. Since building a PLN is a semester-long project, one issue that tends to arise is the problem of students slacking off and waiting until the end of the semester when the project is due, to start the process of identifying and connecting to a community of learners. This approach is of course diametrically opposed to the very idea of building, growing, and maintaining a PLN and learning from it. In order to prevent students from slacking off, we suggest dividing the project into smaller parts due at separate times throughout the semester.

Part 1: The Personal Learning Contract

For the first part of the assignment, students need to identify an area of study pertaining to the overall topic of the class and draft a personal learning contract – "an explication of purposes that drive one's project and that describe what one wants to achieve"; a statement on strategies which "explicates what activities one intends to carry out and what resources might be used; and a statement regarding the desired or expected outcomes" which "describes some criteria that would allow evaluating if or how successful a project was" (Väljataga & Fiedler, 2009, p. 60). This is the type of information that would generally be covered in a course syllabus under assignments, course objectives, and requirements. Since students will ostensibly be creating their own research agenda in the class, it is important that they construct a Personal Learning Contract that explains in detail what they will attempt to accomplish and how they think that they will go about it. According to Põldoja & Väljataga,(2010), "personal learning contracts allow individuals to describe their objectives, (preferably set up by themselves), explicate the design and formation of their learning experiences as well as selection (perception) of potential resources according to a particular project. However, such an explication is often hard to achieve unguided" (para. 5). We offer students guidance on developing their Personal Learning Contract. One way we do this is to give students an idea of the types of projects that might be suitable for this assignment, we recommend listing a few sample project ideas on the assignment description. For instance, in our Social Media for Public Relations class we suggested that a group of students could research social media applications for nonprofits and design a social media training session (the deliverable) for a local nonprofit interested in learning how to engage its stakeholders via social media. It is important to note that these are just sample projects and to encourage students to design their own assignments tailored to their personal interests and learning needs.

Part 2: The Personal Learning Network

This part of the assignment evaluates the depth and breadth of the actual network students built over the course of the semester. At a minimum, all PLNs should include a Twitter, blog, and social bookmarking component. At the end of the semester, students are asked to hand in a description of their PLN along with the deliverables specified in the personal learning contract. In order to hand this in, students are told to create a list of people they follow on:

- **Twitter:** list the people in your Twitter PLN with their Twitter UserId. Only list people that pertain to your project (i.e. don't list your friends here)
- **Blogs:** list the bloggers you followed for this project. Identify them by (a) name, (b) blog URL, and (c) blog name.
- **Social bookmarking sites:** list the people you follow on Delicious or any other social bookmarking site. Again, only list people you followed for this particular project. List them with their social bookmarking URL.

Part 3: The PLN Presentation

Four weeks after officially assigning the project, students are asked to give a four-minute presentation in which they present the learning network they have created thus far. The point of that presentation is to gauge their progress in setting up a viable PLN, provide feedback so that they can tweak their PLN as needed, and discourage slacking off during the early part of the semester which can severely hamper their success later in the semester. These presentations provide instructors with an excellent opportunity to assess the students' understanding of the concept of a PLN and allow them to intervene in case a student didn't identify suitable experts for inclusion in his/her network. Students are encouraged to start off with a brief description of the project they've picked for their personal learning project before presenting their network. They are asked to create a separate slide for their Twitter, social bookmarking, and blogging network and include the information listed below on their slides.

- **Twitter network slide:** How many experts on your project's topic area are you following? List at least 5 of those experts by their Twitter handle and give an example of useful information (related to your project's topic) each of them has tweeted about.
- **Social Bookmarking network slide:** How many experts on your project's topic area are you following on Delicious or another social bookmarking service? List at least 5 of those experts by their Social Bookmarking UserID and give an example of useful info each of them has bookmarked.
- **Blogging network slide:** How many bloggers who are experts on your project's topic area are you subscribing to with your feedreader? List at least 5 of those bloggers (name the title of their blog) and give an example of useful info each of them has blogged about.

During the presentations, students will not only learn from feedback given by their instructor but will also learn from peer feedback and through watching their peers' presentations. Students may find that they are having similar problems or that some students have come up with solutions to problems that they have yet to figure out. They may also find that they are following some of the same people or are involved in projects that overlap. Through this exchange of information, they may garner new communities to follow and to be followed by. For those of the Net Generation who are not quite up to speed, this is an opportunity to see what their peers have accomplished and learn from their presentation of best practices. For those who have excelled, it is a time for sharing what they have learned with their immediate learning community.

Part 4: Project Deliverables

The project deliverables are identified in the student's personal learning contract and approved in consultation with the course instructor. Deliverables are due by the date specified on each student's personal learning contract. Students are evaluated based on the quality of their final product as well as on the criteria listed on the contract. The grading of the students' final project typically provides the instructor with a good sense for how much they learned from their PLN.

Part 5: Project Presentation

At the end of the semester each student is asked to present his/her personal learning project deliverables to the class. For this assignment, students create a professional 4-5 minute presentation in which they introduce the project they worked on, explain the process involved in creating the deliverable, discuss how the PLN helped them accomplish that process, and showcase the final project. Students are evaluated based on the extent to which they address those 4 areas and on the level of professionalism displayed in their presentation.

This semester-long project is perfectly geared to the needs of the Net Generation. The self-directed approach allows students the autonomy to choose their projects and discern the experts that they will learn from. Through the development of their Personal Learning Contracts, the implementation of their Personal Learning Networks, the presentation of their working processes, experiences, and findings, and finally the production of their deliverables, students engage in a full circle exploration of the development and implementation of a PLN. This extended emersion in social media and the self-directed structure of the environment should provide students with a significant advantage in a competitive technocentric global economy.

FUTURE RESEARCH DIRECTIONS

To date, very little research has been conducted on the merits of PLNs as learning tools for Net Generational students. The purpose of this chapter is to provide a conceptual discussion of PLNs and offer a framework for the design and incorporation of such networks into everyday pedagogical practice. While this chapter doesn't seek to present any empirical research findings on the effects of PLNs, future studies are needed to establish how the creation of learning networks and how participation in them affects various educational outcomes such as academic performance, student engagement, and motivation levels. Beyond the immediate question of the pedagogical benefits, other areas to investigate include the long-term impact of PLNs on self-regulated learning. Do PLN building activities such as the one described in this chapter help students develop new learning processes and are students able to subsequently apply these processes in other classes, or later on in their professional development endeavors? If we want social learning pedagogies based on PLNs to become more widely adopted in college classrooms, it is important that these questions be addressed.

Even if future studies end up affirming the educational merits of networked learning, PLNs are likely to face an uphill battle towards full adoption in the classroom. As Will Richardson, an educational technology consultant and expert on the topic, has pointed out, in order to teach students how to create, maintain and grow a personal learning network, instructors first need to learn how to do so themselves so they can act as models to their students (Rebora, 2010). According to Richardson, this means instructors have to actively participate on the social web and establish a visible online presence. "The people I learn from on a day-to-day basis," he says are Googleable. "They're findable, they have a presence, they're participating, they're transparent. That's what makes them a part of my learning network. If you're not out there—if you're not transparent or findable in that way—I can't learn with you." However, learning to do so requires a much more involved process than attending an occasional teacher workshop. Richardson argues that "teachers need to have a very fundamental understanding of what these digital interactions look like, and the only way that you can do that is to pretty much immerse them in these types of learning environments over the long term. You can't workshop it." (Rebora, 2010, para. 21). And herein lies a major implementation issue—some college professors may be hesitant to join the social web and share their work online, others may resist devoting that much time to establishing an online presence, especially considering that many may not be allowed to count their participation in online forums as scholarly activity for tenure purposes.

CONCLUSION

While the idea of lifelong learning may not be new, most students tend to be unfamiliar with the concept of using social media technologies to deliberately build PLNs capable of supporting their learning goals. This project takes technologies that students are familiar with (primarily for personal entertainment reasons) and teaches them to use them strategically in order to meet their learning needs – not only in this class but also in their other classes as well as in their future jobs. In our experience students approach the project with a healthy dose of skepticism, afraid of having to acquire a new set of skills and knowledge without receiving the typical instructor-led guidance our current education system has led them to expect. Once they get over their initial fears though, we think many of them perceive the project as an empowering experience, showing them that learning can, and does, indeed take place outside the classroom. The sense of empowerment students experience after successfully completing their projects is one of the most powerful outcomes of this assignment and will hopefully convince them to make PLNs a part of their lifelong learning. After all, what better way to demonstrate to students the need for lifelong learning than to let them experience first hand the power of connecting with experts from all over the globe?

REFERENCES

A few Twitter facts. (September 14, 2010). Retrieved November 2, 2010 from http://twitter.com/about#about.

About Quora. (n.d.). Retrieved February 12, 2011, from http://www.quora.com/about.

Adler, R., & Brown, J. (2008). Minds on fire: Open education, the long tail, and learning 2.0. *EDUCAUSE Review*, *43*, 6–32.

Baldwin, M. (2009, March 6). #FollowFriday: The anatomy of a Twitter trend. *Mashable*. Retrieved May 8, 2010, from http://mashable.com/2009/03/06/twitter-followfriday.

Bandura, A. (1986). *Social foundations of thought and action: A social cognitive theory*. Englewood Cliffs, NJ: Prentice-Hall.

BlogPulse. (n.d.). *Stats*. Retrieved November 2, 2010, from http://www.blogpulse.com/.

Briggs, M. (2010). *Journalism next*. Washington, DC: CQ Press.

Bugeja, M. J. (2008). Harsh realities about virtual ones. *Inside Higher Ed*. Retrieved June 9, 2009, from http://m.insidehighered.com/views/2008/03/11/bugeja.

Bush, V. (1945). As we may think. *The Atlantic*. Retrieved February 12, 2011 from http://www.theatlantic.com/magazine/archive/1945/07/as-we-may-think/3881/.

Candy, P. C. (1991). *Self-direction for lifelong learning*. San Francisco, CA: Jossey-Bass.

Cao, L., & Nietfeld, J. L. (2007). College students' metacognitive awareness of difficulties in learning the class content does not automatically lead to adjustment of study strategies. *Australian Journal of Educational and Developmental Psychology*, *7*, 31–46.

Downes, S. (2009, October 5). *Origins of the term "personal learning network."* Retrieved May 10, 2010, from http://halfanhour.blogspot.com/2009/10/origins-of-term-personal-learning.html.

Duxbury, L., Dyke, L., & Lam, N. (2000, April 8). *Career development in the federal public service - Building a world-class workforce*. Treasury Board of Canada Secretariat. Retrieved from http://www.tbs-sct.gc.ca/pubs_pol/partners/workreport-PR-eng.asp?printable=True.

EduCause Learning Initiative. (2005, May). *7 things you should know about ... social bookmarking*. Retrieved February 10, 2010 from http://net.educause.edu/ir/library/ pdf/ELI7001.pdf.

Friedman, T. L. (2006). *The world is flat - Updated and expanded: A brief history of the 21st century*. New York, NY: Farrar, Straus & Giroux.

Gonzalez, C. (2004). *The role of blended learning in the world of technology*. Retrieved from http://www.unt.edu/benchmarks/archives/2004/september04/eis.htm.

How to Use. (n.d.). *Twitter lists*. Retrieved February 10, 2010, from http://support.twitter.com/articles/76460-how-to-use-twitter-lists.

How to Use. (n.d.). *Twitter's suggestions for who to follow*. Retrieved February 10, 2010, from http://support.twitter.com/groups/31-twitter-basics/topics/108-finding-following-people/articles/227220-how-to-use-twitter-s-suggestions-for-who-to-follow.

Johnson, L. Smith, R., Willis, H., Levine, A., & Haywood, K., (2011). *The 2011 horizon report*. Austin, TX: The New Media Consortium.

Knowles, M. (1975). *Self-directed learning: A guide for learners and teachers*. New York, NY: Cambridge.

Kramarski, B., & Michalsky, T. (2009). Investigating preservice teacher's professional growth in self-regulated learning environments. *Journal of Educational Psychology*, *101*(1), 161–175. doi:10.1037/a0013101

Kuo, Y. H. (2010). *Self-regulated learning: From theory to practice*. Kaohsiung, Taiwan: Wenzao Ursuline College of Languages (ERIC Document Reproduction Service No. ED 510 995).

Laskey, M. L., & Hetzel, C. J. (2010). *Self-regulated learning, metacognition, and soft skills: The 21st century learner*. Milwaukee, WI: Cardinal Stritch University (ERIC Document Reproduction Service No. ED 511 589).

Locke, E. A., & Latham, G. P. (1990). *A theory of goal setting and task performance*. Englewood Cliffs, NJ: Prentice Hall.

Loyens, S. M. M., Magda, J., & Rikers, R. M. J. P. (2008). Self-directed learning in problem-based learning and its relationship with self-regulated learning. *Educational Psychology Review*, *20*, 411–427. doi:10.1007/s10648-008-9082-7

Moody, M. (2010). Teaching Twitter and beyond: Tips for incorporating social media in traditional courses. *Journal of Magazine & New Media Research*, *3*(11), 1–9.

Parry, M. (2010, May 4). Most professors use social media. *The Chronicle of Higher Education*. Retrieved May 8, 2010, from http://chronicle.com/blogPost/Most-Professors-Use-Social/23716.

Perry, N. E., Phillips, L., & Hutchinson, L. (2006). Mentoring student teachers to support self-regulated learning. *The Elementary School Journal*, *106*(3), 237–254. doi:10.1086/501485

Pintrich, P. R. (1988). A process-oriented view of student motivation and cognition. In Stark, J. S., & Mets, L. A. (Eds.), *New directions for institutional research, no. 57: Improving teaching and learning through research* (pp. 65–79). San Francisco, CA: Jossey-Bass.

Pintrich, P. R. (1995). Understanding self-regulated learning. [San Francisco, CA: Jossey-Bass.]. *New Directions for Teaching and Learning, 63*, 3–12. doi:10.1002/tl.37219956304

Põldoja, H., & Väljataga, T. (2010). *Externalization of a PLE: Conceptual design of LeContract.* The PLE Conference. ISSN 2077-9119. Retrieved July 24, 2011, from http://pleconference.citilab.eu/cas/wp-content/uploads/2010/06/ple2010_submission_68.pdf.

Rebora, A. (2010, October 11). Change agent. *Education Week Teacher Professional Development Sourcebook.* Retrieved July 26, 2011, from http://www.edweek.org/tsb/articles/2010/10/12/01richardson.h04.html.

Reid, J. (1972). *Alienation.* Speech delivered at the University of Glasgow, U.K. Retrieved February 8, 2011, from http://www.gla.ac.uk/media/media_167194_en.pdf.

Rheingold, H. (2008). Using social media to teach social media. *New England Journal of Higher Education*, (Summer): 25–26.

Rheingold, H. (2009, June 30). Crap detection 101. *San Francisco Gate.* Retrieved February 8, 2011 from http://www.sfgate.com/cgi-bin/blogs/rheingold/detail? entry_id=42805.

Richardson, W. (2006). *Blogs, wikis, podcasts, and other powerful web tools for classrooms.* Thousand Oaks, CA: Corwin Press.

Siemens, G. (2005). Connectivism: A learning theory for the digital age. *International Journal of Instructional Technology and Distance Learning, 2*(1). Retrieved from http://www.itdl.org/Journal/Jan_05/article01.htm.

Siemens, G. (2008). *Learning and knowing in networks: Changing roles for educators and designers.* Paper presented at the University of Georgia IT Forum. Retrieved from http://it.coe.uga.edu/itforum/Paper105/Siemens.pdf.

Sledzik, B. (2011, February 2). Trying to figure out Quora? Me, too! *ToughSledding* [Blog]. Retrieved February 10, 2011, from http://et.kent.edu/toughsledding/?p=6696.

Tackett, L., & Cator, K. (2011). *The promise of communities of practice.* ED.gov. Retrieved from: http://www.ed.gov/oii-news/promise-communities-practice.

Väljataga, T., & Fiedler, S. (2009). Supporting students to self-direct intentional learning projects with social media. *Journal of Educational Technology & Society, 12*(3), 58–69.

Warlick, D. (2009). Grow your personal learning network: New technologies can keep you connected and help you manage information overload. *Learning and Leading with Technology, 36*(6), 12–16.

Warlick, D. (2010). *The art & technique of personal learning networks or: A gardener's approach to learning.* Retrieved from http://davidwarlick.com/wiki/pmwiki.php/ Main/TheArtAmpTechniqueOfCultivatingYourPersonalLearningNetwork.

Weisgerber, C., & Butler, S. (2011). Social media as a professional development tool: Using blogs, microblogs and social bookmarks to create personal learning networks. In Wankel, C. (Ed.), *Teaching arts & science with social media.* Bingley, UK: Emerald. doi:10.1108/S2044-9968(2011)0000003020

What is following? (n.d.). Retrieved February 10, 2011 from http://support.twitter.com/articles/14019-what-is-following.

Young, J. (2010, December 9). 18 percent of college students who go online use Twitter. *The Chronicle of Higher Education*. Retrieved February 8, 2011, from http://chronicle.com/blogs/wiredcampus/18-percent-of-college-students-use-twitter/28642.

Yucht, A. (2009). Building your personal learning network. *Information Searcher*, *19*(1), 11–14.

Zimmerman, B. J. (1998). Academic studying and the development of personal skills: A self-regulatory perspective. *Educational Psychologist*, *33*(2/3), 73–86.

Zimmerman, B. J. (2002). Becoming a self-regulated learner: An overview. *Theory into Practice*, *41*(2), 64–70. doi:10.1207/s15430421tip4102_2

ADDITIONAL READING

Anderson, T. (2006). *PLE's versus LMS: Are PLE's Ready for Prime Time?* Retrieved July 24, 2011 from: http://terrya.edublogs.org/2006/01/09/ples-versus-lms-are-ples-ready-for-prime-time/.

Bellanca, J., & Brandt, R. (2010). *21st Century Skills: Rethinking How Students Learn*. Bloomington, IN: Solution Tree.

Bingham, T., & Conner, M. (2010). *The New Social Learning: A Guide to Transforming Organizations Through Social Media*. San Francisco, CA: ASTD & Berrett-Koehler.

Collins, A., & Halverson, R. (2009). *Rethinking Education in the Age of Technology: The Digital Revolution and Schooling in America*. New York, NY: Teachers College Press.

Costa, F. A., Cruz, E., & Viana, J. (2010). Managing personal learning environments: the voice of the students. *The PLE Conference, ISSN 2077-9119*. Retrieved July 24, 2011 from: http://pleconference.citilab.eu/wp-content/uploads/2010/06/ple2010_submission_9.pdf.

Drexler, W. (2010). The networked student model for construction of personal learning environments: Balancing teacher control and student autonomy. *Australasian Journal of Educational Technology, 26(3)*, 369-385. Retrieved from: http://www.ascilite.org.au/ajet/ajet26/drexler.html.

Fiedler, S., & Väljataga, T. (2010). Personal learning environments: concept or technology? *The PLE Conference, ISSN 2077-9119*. Retrieved July 24, 2011 from: http://pleconference.citilab.eu/wp-content/uploads/2010/07/ple2010_submission_45.pdf.

Fournier, H., & Kop, R. (2010). Researching the design and development of a Personal Learning Environment. *The PLE Conference, ISSN 2077-9119*. Retrieved July 24, 2011 from:http://pleconference.citilab.eu/cas/wp-content/uploads/2010/06/ple2010_submission_88.pdf.

Hill, J. R., Song, L., & West, R. E. (2009). Social Learning Theory and Web-Based Learning Environments: A Review of Research and Discussion of Implications. *American Journal of Distance Education*, *23*(2), 88–103. doi:10.1080/08923640902857713

Huang, J. S., Yang, S. H., Yueh-Min, H., & Hsiao, I. T. (2010). Social Learning Networks: Build Mobile Learning Networks Based on Collaborative Services. *Journal of Educational Technology & Society*, *13*(3), 78–92.

Lenhart, A., Purcell, K., Smith, A., & Zickuhr, K. (2010). Social media and young adults. Washington, D.C.: *Pew Research Center.* Retrieved July 24, 2011 from: http://www.pewinternet.org/Reports/2010/Social-Media-and-Young-Adults.aspx.

Matthews, K. E., Andrews, V., & Adams, P. (2011). Social learning spaces and student engagement. *Higher Education Research & Development*, *30*(2), 105–120. doi:10.1080/07294360.2010.512629

McElvaney, J., & Berge, Z. (2009). Weaving a Personal Web: Using online technologies to create customized, connected, and dynamic learning environments. *Canadian Journal of Learning and Technology, 35(2).* Retrieved July 24, 2011 from: http://www.cjlt.ca/index.php/cjlt/article/viewArticle/524/257.

Pettenati, M. C., & Cigognini, M. E. (2007). Social networking theories and tools to support connectivist learning activities. *International Journal of Web-Based Learning and Teaching Technologies, 2*(3), 42–60. doi:10.4018/jwltt.2007070103

Põldoja, H., & Väljataga, T. (2010). Externalization of a PLE: Conceptual Design of LeContract. *The PLE Conference, ISSN 2077-9119*. Retrieved July 24, 2011 from: http://pleconference.citilab.eu/cas/wp-content/uploads/2010/06/ple2010_submission_68.pdf.

Rebora, A. (2010, October 11). Change agent. *Education Week Teacher Professional Development Sourcebook.* Retrieved July 26, 2011 from: http://www.edweek.org/tsb/articles/2010/10/12/01richardson.h04.html.

Rendell, L., Fogarty, L., Hoppitt, W. E., Morgan, T. H., Webster, M. M., & Laland, K. N. (2011). Cognitive culture: Theoretical and empirical insights into social learning strategies. *Trends in Cognitive Sciences, 15*(2), 68–76. doi:10.1016/j.tics.2010.12.002

Richardson, W., & Mancabelli, R. (2011). *Personal Learning Networks: Using the Power of Connections to Transform Education*. Bloomington, IN: Solution Tree.

Thomas, D., & Brown, J. S. (2011). *A New Culture of Learning: Cultivating the Imagination for a World of Constant Change*. Lexington, KY: CreateSpace.

Thomas, M. (2011). *Digital Education: Opportunities for Social Collaboration*. Houndsmills, U.K.: Palgrave Macmillan.

Tian, S., Yu, A., Vogel, D., & Kwok, R. (2011). The impact of online social networking on learning: a social integration perspective. *International Journal of Networking & Virtual Organisations, 8*(3), 264–280. doi:10.1504/IJNVO.2011.039999

KEY TERMS AND DEFINITIONS

Androgogy: The field of adult education, built around the practical challenge of developing educational environments that meet the needs of adult learners.

Connectivism: "A learning theory for the digital age" (Siemens, 2005) which views learning as a process of building connections and creating a learning community or network.

Personal Learning Contract: "An explication of *purposes* that drive one's project and that describe what one wants to achieve"; a statement on *strategies* which "explicates what activities one intends to carry out and what resources might be used; and a statement regarding the desired or expected *outcomes"* which "describes some criteria that would allow evaluating if or how successful a project was" (Väljataga & Fiedler, 2009, p. 60[1]).

Personal Learning Networks: Deliberately formed networks of people and resources capable of guiding our independent learning goals and professional development needs.

RSS Aggregator or Feed Reader: An application "which makes it possible for readers to 'subscribe' to the content that is created on a particular Weblog so they no longer have to visit the blog itself to get it" (Richardson, 2006, p. 75).

Self-Directed Learning: A highly structured learning environment developed to foster self-regulated learners. Self-Directed environments are goal driven, strategy based, and evaluative.

Self-Regulated Learning: A favorable learning process where independent learners set goals, develop strategies for accomplishing these goals, manage their time, monitor and evaluate their performance, and navigate both the social and physical environment.

Social Bookmarks: Social bookmarking refers to the practice of saving online content in a public database hosted by one of the many social bookmarking services available for free on the Internet. Social bookmarking sites such as Diigo, Delicious, and Furl allow users to save bookmarks to their respective sites and to describe the saved content with user-generated keywords, commonly referred to as tags.

ENDNOTE

1 Väljataga, T., & Fiedler, S. (2009). Supporting students to self-direct intentional learning projects with social media. *Educational Technology & Society, 12 (3),* 58–69.

Chapter 15
Leveraging Multicommunication in the Classroom:
Implications for Participation and Engagement

Keri K. Stephens
University of Texas at Austin, USA

Melissa Murphy
University of Texas at Austin, USA

Kerk F. Kee
Chapman University, USA

ABSTRACT

Computer-mediated classrooms are proliferating and instructors are finding creative ways to reach the digital learners of today. But with all these technology tools, making decisions that are guided by solid pedagogical practices are vital. This study relies on instructional communication, multicommunication practices, and interactivity research and how they play key roles when creating a participatory classroom environment. The tool used to address the problems outlined in this case study is webconferencing—a synchronous Web-based platform that allows the instructor to share slides, create real-time surveys (polls), and provide text chat opportunities for students who are co-located or dispersed. By leveraging the webconferencing tools and the desires of the Net Generation, the classroom in this study became more inclusive, communicative, and interactive.

INTRODUCTION

Technology has infused the contemporary classroom. Whether the instructor chooses to incorporate technology as *part* of the physical learning environment, as the *conduit for* computer-mediated instruction, or if the *students* bring their technology into the classroom, teaching is a different experience than it was five years ago. Many scholars have raised concerns about communication issues that have become more relevant in a computer-mediated communication (CMC) classroom environment (Allen, 2006; Patterson & Gojdyez, 2000; Mathiasen & Schrum, 2010;

DOI: 10.4018/978-1-61350-347-8.ch015

Schwier & Balbar, 2008; Sherblom, 2010; Spector, 2001). Yet there are also several key learning areas where CMC classrooms might enhance learning including improved interactivity, team-based and collaborative problem-solving, and engaging with the content more completely (Anderson et al., 2007; Bernard et al., 2009; Schrire, 2004; Stephens & Mottet, 2008; Vess, 2005; Vogel et al., 2006; Wood & Fassett; 2003). But so far, there is little agreement on whether there are any significant differences between courses using technology and those in a traditional instructional classroom environment (Benoit, Benoit, Milyo, & Hansen, 2006). This study adds to the literature by investigating multicommunication and student learning

In this study, the technology medium used to deliver the educational experience is webconferencing. Relying on rhetorical and relational goal theory (Mottet, Frymier, & Beebe, 2006) the case study and survey findings are used to illustrate how instructors can use webconferencing to improve attendance and participation and harness the current multicommunication behaviors of students into learning practices. To accomplish these goals, first the guiding theoretical perspective is introduced. Next, the background elaborates on the role of the Net Generation learner and the changing needs in contemporary classrooms. The problem and solutions illustrate how technology can be used as a classroom extension without compromising the instructor-student relationship. We end with directions for future research.

BACKGROUND

Theoretical Rationale

Regardless of whether instructors are in a traditional or CMC classroom, the relationship they have with their students is an important component of the learning environment (Frymier & Houser, 2000; Pogue & Ahyun, 2006; Witt, Wheeless, & Allen, 2004). Rhetorical and relational goal theory (Mottet et al., 2006) provides a theoretical reason to have instructors carefully consider the rhetorical and relationship strategies they use in a classroom. *Students* have multiple needs which rhetorical and relational goal theory groups into two areas: academic and relational needs. For example, students can have different learning objectives; some of which are grade-related and others are interpersonal in nature. Furthermore, students differ in the weight they place on these different types of needs. When the students' needs are met, many positive outcomes result including increased student learning, motivation, and more satisfaction with the classroom experience.

In the model depicting the interplay between the student and instructor needs, Mottet and colleagues (2006) provide a framework and suggest that there are many opportunities to expand this perspective and elaborate on the specific strategies used by students and instructors. Past research using webconferencing as the CMC classroom medium has found that interactivity plays a key role and influences the perceived credibility of the instructor (Stephens & Mottet, 2008). Yet this evolving theory highlights an important dilemma for instructors trying to incorporate technology into their classrooms: will using technology influence the instructor-student relationship and can technology be used to accomplish the rhetorical—or compliance-gaining—goals of the instructors? Mottet and colleagues (2006) claim that instructors who are able to use both persuasion and relationship building activities—e.g., compliance-gaining and immediate behaviors, are more likely to meet the needs of more of their students. The current study focuses specifically on these two types of instructor goals—rhetorical and relationship—and offers elaboration and additional contributions to this theory. To understand the particular needs of contemporary college students, we turn our attention to the literature on Net Generation students' expectations.

Net Generation Students' Expectations in a CMC Learning Environment

Prensky (2001) coined the terms 'digital natives' and 'digital immigrants' to describe the students who grew up with computer technologies and the faculty and adults that did not. Given a distinction in their digital cultures and technology behaviors, it is important to understand how these digitally wired Net Generation students want to learn. There are five major expectations that the popular press and scholarly literature suggest are important to help us understand how a CMC learning environment might mesh well with their needs: preference for a blended classroom, technology that adapts to them, quick interaction with instructors, tendency to actively seek information, and a desire for fun learning.

Net Generation college students expect faculty to be experts in their fields but also want teachers who use technology to deliver knowledge (Roberts, 2005). Although there is an expectation of using technologies, Net Generation students generally prefer a balanced use of technology in their learning environment (Roberts, 2005) when technology is used to support traditional instruction (Belal, 2011). In other words, many of them like a blended combination of face-to-face interactions and mediated communication. They also expect technology to conform to their needs and situations 'as adaptive technologies' (Shute & Torreano, 2003; Shute & Towle, 2003; Shute & Zapata-Rivera, 2008), instead of technological structures that require the students to change. The design and use of technologies should be learner-centered (McCombs & Vakili, 2005; Schiller, 2009; Soloway, Guzdial, & Hay, 1994).

Third, students expect speed in interacting with faculty. Net Generation students were raised in a technologically saturated environment, and while there is a debate concerning whether they can actually multitask (e.g., Ophir, Nass & Wagner, 2009 demonstrate they cannot), many reports claim that they expect to be allowed to continue their multitasking practices well into the future (Connaway, Radford, Dickey, Williams, & Confer, 2008; Kofman & Eckler, 2005; Mason, Barzilai-Nahon, & Lou, 2003; Rainie, 2006). Their practices may have contributed to a relatively short attention span (Brown, 2005) and as a result, they are used to receiving fast information (McNeely, 2005), expect rapid responses, and instant gratification (Oblinger & Oblinger, 2005).

There is also evidence that Net Generation students are active searchers of information because of their need for instant gratification (Windham, 2005). It is likely that this need translates into the classroom as well. However, there is sometimes a gap in terms of how fast digital natives like to get information and the speed at which traditional classrooms are providing information (Palfrey & Gasser, 2008; Waycott et al., 2010). If there were ways to allow students to seek information during class without interfering with their attention to the lecture, this could be highly valuable.

Finally, like many young people before, this generation likes learning to be fun. They prefer games to 'serious' work (Prensky, 2001). This could be something more relevant for Net Generation students because they grew up playing many more computer games than prior generations (Lippincott, 2005). This tendency suggests that Net Generation students would enjoy a creative approach to teaching.

Need for Interactive Learning Environments

Oblinger and Oblinger (2005) used focus groups and found that Net Generation students are intuitive visual communicators, can shift their attention easily from one thing to another, have a fast response time, and demand fast turnaround time as well. Their learning styles include a preference for working in teams, interactivity at a rapid pace, as well as preference for visuals over text. Similarly, from an organizational perspective, Net Generation students' positive attributes are such that they are more accepting of diversity, have the ability to see problems and opportunities from fresh perspectives and, not surprisingly, are more comfortable working in teams than past generations (Howe & Strauss 2000; Gorman, Nelson, & Glassman, 2004; Tapscott 1998; Zemke, Raines, & Filipczak, 2000). It is the characteristics, desires and needs such as these that demand experimental, dynamic and interactive learning for the Net Generation students. Moreover, recent emphasis for studying in higher education (e.g., Virtual University) and working in companies (e.g., distributed global teamwork) set clear demands for developing pedagogical models, tools and practices to support collaborative learning in virtual environments (DeCorte, Verschaffel, Entwistle, & Van Merrieboer, 2003; Evans & Gibbons, 2008).

Unfortunately, scholars have discovered that the level of interactivity in a traditional lecture is low. Estimates are that students ask.1 questions per hour in a traditional class; faculty ask.3 per hour (Fletcher, 2003). Technology, like webconferencing, makes it possible to provide learners with anytime, anywhere content and interactions. Computer-based instruction, however, increases the number of questions posed from less than 1 per hour to 180-600 per hour (Fletcher, 2003). This dilemma poses challenges for many educators who do not use technology tools to reach the Net Generation learners.

Re-Conceptualizing Classrooms as Learning Spaces

Given all the expectations discussed above, how should we re-conceptualize the classroom for these Net Generation students and digital natives? Brown (2005) argues that the notion of classrooms needs to be expanded and re-conceptualized as 'learning spaces.' More specifically, "[l]earning spaces encompass the full range of places in which learning occurs, from real to virtual, from classroom to chat room" (p. 12.4). Hartman, Moskal, and Dziuban (2005) concur and argue:

The mobility enabled by wireless communication, combined with an expanding class of wireless-equipped portable computers and PDAs, is leading to new instructional and social patterns. No longer do students need to go to a specific place, or even be seated, to use a computer. An array of multifunctional PDAs capable of wireless communication is allowing such devices to follow their users wherever they go... This is challenging the very definition of learning spaces because learning can now occur both in and out of the classroom, in both formal and informal settings, and by lone scholars or among groups. (p. 6.4)

These arguments are compelling, and with the proliferation of mobile computing devices, learning spaces beyond the physical classroom are increasingly becoming reality. Re-conceptualizing classrooms as learning spaces that can be enabled by technologies expand how faculty and students can participate in teaching and learning in the 21st century. Digital natives and Net Generation students have been networked most, if not all, of their lives. Prensky (2001) describes, "They are used to the instantaneity of hypertext, downloaded music, phones in their pockets, a library on their laptops, beamed messages and instant messaging" (p. 3). His argument provides a strong rationale for the need and timeliness of studying interactivity in this study.

More recently, Prensky (2009) talks about becoming 'digitally wise.' He explains, "Digital wisdom is a twofold concept, referring both to wisdom arising *from* the use of digital technology to access cognitive power beyond our innate capacity and to wisdom *in* the prudent use of technology to enhance our capabilities" (italics original, p. 2). In this study, we explore ways to promote teaching and learning in a blended classroom that demonstrate both types of digital wisdom. Furthermore, Brown (2005) suggests, "Wireless networking...

makes real-time or synchronous interaction (such as real-time polling) among all class participants a very real (and increasingly practical) possibility. Videoconferencing makes it feasible for an invited expert from a remote institution to join a class session" (p. 12.2). Brown's (2005) argument prompted us to study a webconference tool that allows synchronous chats, real-time polling, and expert remote visits as strategies for a blended classroom.

PROBLEMS IN THE 2010 CLASSROOM AND BEYOND

This study uses a case study method (Yin, 2009) to depict the rich details associated with how decisions to implement webconferencing in a novel way were made. This detail is important since CMC learning tools are still emerging and there are so many divergent approaches using the exact same technology tools. There are elements of a narrative analysis (Fisher, 1987) present in this case, as well as analysis of survey data that reflects the perspectives of the students.

Case Study Context

The situation chosen for this analysis is intended to meet the narrative fidelity and probability (Fisher, 1987) needs of many college instructors. The year of the case is 2010. The subjects are college students who carry mobile devices to class and capturing their attention is requiring new educational tactics. This particular case occurred in a large state university, where 30 students were taking an upper-division elective course on technology use at work. The first author of this case study was the instructor of the course, the second author was the teaching assistant, and the third author provided an additional non-co-located classroom to further compare the case study findings. The description that follows explains the case in more detail.

The Problem: Disconnected Students

Teaching a technology theory class on every Monday, Wednesday, and Friday from 2pm to 3pm during football season can be challenging. Not only did attendance drop off on Friday, but discussions were anemic and the students seemed ready to be finished with their day. When these students attended class, they were often using their smart phone and laptop computers and it is doubtful that this use was course-relevant. The primary instructor had taught this course three previous times and never encountered such an apathetic group. Historically she has never had systematic problems with attendance, so she does not have an attendance policy. But this group, meeting from 2pm to 3pm three days a week, caused her to question the decision to have no attendance policy. Eight weeks into the semester she decided to gather feedback from the teaching assistant (TA) and the students to confirm her sinking feelings about the overall engagement of this class.

The TA was a first semester MA student who was new to academia, but had several years of work experience behind her. Her employment assignment time was split between two of the primary instructor's courses, so she got to see the drastic difference between one course taught earlier in the day and the course of growing concern. Both courses were held in the exact same room and there were seven students (out of 40) who were in both classes. The course taught earlier in the afternoon was alive in every way possible. There were never more than one to two students absent, everyone participated, and quite often the conversations continued into the hallway long after class had officially ended. In her own words, the TA said:

Having witnessed students from the teaching perspective for the first time, it was amazing how clearly you can get a read on the students' attitudes and willingness to engage in just a few lectures.

The technology class was so lackadaisical and unmotivated. Very few students took notes and asked questions. You could tell they were paying more attention to their devices, not doing the assigned reading and not willing to share or engage in discussion. It was such an unfortunate difference compared to the other class. I never knew that professors had to take responsibility for poor work ethic and overcome challenges such as this.

To gather the mid-semester feedback, the instructor asked students to take a note card and write three things that were working on one side of the card, and three things needing improvement on the other. She then did a quick content analysis and grouped the comments. She was concerned, but, following past procedure, she shared all the comments with the class and asked for their input in how to address these issues. In the discussion that followed, it became obvious that the students were disconnected from the course. In one specific example, students expected reminders for assignments even if they did not attend class. Only half the class attended on one Friday (the day the instructor reminded the students to look on Blackboard for their assignment due on Monday) and then almost a third of the class did not bring their assignment due on Monday. During the feedback session, the students attributed that to an instructor issue. One student said, “If you would send us an email reminding us of the assignment, we would remember it.” That was not the way this instructor taught. Her philosophy was to develop her students into responsible learners who want to participate in her classes. Despite the harsh realities learned in the student’s feedback the instructor and TA took immediate action and attempted to change the dynamic of the classroom by using technology tools. They hoped that they could increase attendance and improve the relationship they had with the students.

The Solution: Embrace Multicommuncation to Improve Participation

Rather than introduce strict policies banning the use of technology in the classroom, or punishing students for not attending class, the instructor took a more collaborative, less coercive approach and considered how to leverage technology to solve the problems. She decided to use webconferencing to address the issues discussed earlier.

The Technology

Webconferencing is a technology medium most often used to connect participants from multiple geographic locations (Stephens & Mottet, 2008). In this situation, the instructor used webconferencing to provide distance participation opportunities, but she also actively sought ways to use the interactive features of webconferencing—chat and polling functions—to increase the students’ voices in the classroom. Multicommunicating (Reinsch, Turner, & Tinsley, 2008) describes the growing practice of carrying on multiple conversations simultaneously. This practice has exploded with the proliferation of mobile devices that facilitate these types of conversations while students attend classes. This type of communicating in class can be facilitated by using webconferencing tools. For a summary of how the specific components of webconferencing functioned in this study, see Table 1.

Webconferencing Environment

To accomplish the classroom interactivity objectives, the instructor used Adobe Connect webconferencing software. Because course flexibility is a key factor in learners’ perceived satisfaction (Sun, Tsai, Finger, Chen, & Yeh, 2008), this web-based product allows students to participate virtually and there is a mobile phone application that facilitates participation from anywhere. The instructor used

Table 1. Learning options in webconferencing

Learning Option	Advantages	Disadvantages
Virtual Participation Option	Increase participation from students who might not attend in person. Allows for "guest speakers" who are not local	Encourages students to prioritize other activities over class
Rolling Chat – displayed to physically present and virtual participants	Students asked more questions Student-to-student interaction Variety in questions Used students' technology Often viewed as fun	Distracting Students purely in class and students purely online do not directly interact with each other.
Polling students	Provided anonymous forum for participation Normed responses Instructor gets feedback	Students purely in class cannot participate anonymously unless they log into the Internet. Difficult to track if students in the group that is both online and offline repeat their 'votes' when asked to show hands in class as well.

several key features of the webconferencing software to encourage interactivity and learning while controlling some of the potentially more complex features. For example, the only audio channel used was that of the instructor and video was not used at all. This was a conscious decision made to decrease the likelihood that students would have connection issues. Past research suggests that students must have early success with CMC classroom technologies to participate and be satisfied with the experience (Benoit et al., 2006). Webconferences also allow an instructor to project slides, share screens, and respond to questions raised in the chat or the classroom. In this case, certain interactivity features were used that would best facilitate student participation.

Key Decisions Surrounding the Use of Webconferencing

There were several key decisions made in how the webconferencing tool was launched. First, the instructor decided to allow students to provide text-based chat comments during the lecture and that chat was publicly displayed, as an integral part of the class lecture and discussion. The text chat tool in the webconferencing system was an optional tool, but in this class, the Windows were re-sized to make the conversation readable and it was prominently displayed next to the more static, lecture slides. Regardless of their location, students who had logged into the webconferencing system could type and respond to others' comments. This activity occurred simultaneously with the instructor's verbal lecture.

A second key decision, to address the attendance issue, was to provide a mix of three different participation opportunities: (1) Students could come to class and use no technology, yet still respond verbally to questions. These students could also view the chat and were able to comment on their peers' contributions. (2) A second participation option was that students could be physically present in class and use their laptops or mobile devices to connect to the webconference and participate via chat or make verbal comments during class. (3) Finally students could log onto the webconference remotely and participate using the chat function. This collaborative environment was prominently displayed on the large projection screen at the front of the classroom for all the physically-present class attendees to view.

A third key decision was that there needed to be controlled anonymous participation opportunities as well as the public chat; therefore polls were used to show aggregate responses. It is important to note that students who were physically present and did not have laptops or mobile devices could not participate anonymously. This is a limitation of allowing participation in a physical classroom in addition to online participation options. The physically present students had to respond by showing their hands and their responses were added to those participating online. It was important to limit the anonymous participation to poll-type and practice quiz-type activities and make the text-chat identifiable. This limited potentially problematic online behavior because every comment was directly linked to an individual with a real name.

The final decision was to expand the webconference class concept beyond the blended situation (designed to address the problems mounting in this classroom) and include an additional class taught entirely virtually. This class functioned as a source of additional information on the perceived interactivity of the text-chat, the polling, and the usability of webconferencing when the instructor was not co-located. The instructor worked with an instructor located in another state to deliver a webconference-based lecture in this comparison format. There were many similarities between these slightly different formats and they will be further discussed.

To compare the students' opinions across participation options, the study also incorporated an anonymous survey. This instrument was designed with multiple item measures, used published scales for all variables except one (the instrument details are available from the first author), and was administered to the problematic class (N = 22, a 76% response rate) and the additional class where the instructor was not co-located (N = 14, a 71% response rate). The resulting sample was 60.6% (N= 20) female and the majority of the students 73.5% (N = 25) were seniors in their retrospective universities. They rated themselves as fairly strong users of online technology tools such as Skype and instant messaging N = 34, M = 4.62, SD =.78 (on a scale of 1-7) and no one rated themself as a poor or novice user. Because there were differences in participation options, a series of t-tests confirmed that there were no significant differences between the samples in the two locations for any of the reported variables, thus they were combined for analyses.

ANALYSIS OF THE SOLUTION

Meeting Instructor Goals

A primary rhetorical goal (also known as a task goal, Mottet, Frymier, & Beebe, 2006). of the instructor in this case was to increase attendance and provide opportunities for students to actively engage with course content. She sought to expand these opportunities to allow students to connect to class remotely. During every class where webconferencing was offered, attendance increased between 10 and 25 percent. In addition to attendance improvement, only two assignments were turned in late during the second half of the semester. While it could be argued that the improvement in assignments was at least partially due to the mid-course feedback conversation, the increased attendance is likely due, we believe, to webconferencing. These results suggest that the incorporation of webconferencing into the classroom may have helped the instructor meet her rhetorical goals.

This instructor also had relationship goals concerning her students and her TA. In many ways, having students willingly attend class is a type of instructor relational goal in addition to a rhetorical goal. There was an increase in the number of emails and after class conversations that resulted after the implementation of webconferencing. It is difficult to say that these changes were caused by the use of webconferencing, but considering that no other significant course changes were made, it is likely due to this new classroom experience. This is an instructor who also values how the students evaluate her performance in the classroom. She had never seen mid-semester evaluations and student behavior as troubling as they were this semester. At the end the semester, the students rated the course and the instructor as highly as they had in prior semesters. One interpretation is that the relationship was re-built and webconferencing played a role in that process.

Students' Reactions to the Webconferencing Format

Students appeared to be making connections between the course content, and those connections were visible to the other students through the use of public text chat. This egalitarian environment gave the students permission to participate in ways that would not be enabled in a traditional classroom. One open-ended comment from the student survey explains this situation well, "It was great being able to type and send a question during the presentation or make a comment, rather than interrupt the presentation or waiting and allowing it to become irrelevant. It made conversation easier and greatly successful."

Other quotes from the open-ended responses reflect the students' opinions on variety and how they link that to a fun learning environment. One student remarked, "I think it was a great way to add variety to the monotonous routine of attending class in a room." Another student said, "I felt like the novelty of the conference made class extra interesting. I really enjoyed this." In the class where only a single webconference was conducted, the students openly requested that webconferencing be used again because they thought it was an effective way to engage students and promote learning. Using a webconferencing tool to bring a virtual speaker into the classroom also promoted the sense of variety in addition to the new technology.

Interactivity and Perceived Learning

We further tested the students' perceptions that the interactive environment influenced their learning perceptions. Using hierarchical regression equations, in the first step we entered technology problems and webconference satisfaction, and in the second step we entered interactivity. Technology problems were insignificant, so they were removed as a predictor. Webconference satisfaction explained 33 percent of the variance in perceived learning ($\beta = .70, p < .001$). The second step of the regression represented the test of our prediction because we introduced the variable of interactivity into the equation. It accounted for an additional 14.8 percent (R^2 change $= .148$) of the variance ($\beta = .44, p < .01$). The overall model explained 48 percent of the variance in perceived learning. The survey results supported what we had observed in both of the classrooms. Interactivity plays a key role, even beyond the satisfaction they felt with experience, in the Net Generations' perceptions that they are learning.

Bringing the Backchannel Communication to the Forefront

In many traditional lecture classrooms students sit quietly, listen, and a select few students ask questions. In this case, the instructor openly displayed the backchannel communication via a chat log rolling behind her on a large screen while she stood in front of the classroom lecturing and periodically monitoring the rolling chat. She admitted that this was very nerve racking at first because she had no idea how the students would respond and if their behavior would be productive. The result was one of giving voice to students often unheard. The students communicated with one another by actively participating in the live chat instead of simply responding to the instructor's questions. Learning seemed to occur *student to student* in addition to instructor to student. Whether participating virtually or in class, there were options that addressed multiple learning styles and the voices of completely different students emerged through chat.

This case represents an example of how multicommunication can be used productively in the classroom. Thus far, multicommunicating has been explored predominantly in a workplace context and while some studies have shown it to be beneficial, especially in the case of instant messaging (e.g., Reinsch et al., 2008; Rennecker, Dennis, & Hansen, 2006), other research has demonstrated that it can be perceived as uncivil (Cameron & Webster, 2010) and can cause disruptions to practices like organizational meetings (Stephens & Davis, 2009; Turner, & Reinsch, 2010).

Issue-Relevant Backchannel Multicommunicating

The instructor was pleasantly surprised at the high degree of issue-relevant chat conversation that emerged. Less than 5% of the comments were off topic and those could be viewed as rapport building chat. The chat had a fun tone (e.g., references to popular TV shows), but the comments were still issue-relevant. The instructor and her TA believed they had channeled the students' desires to multicommunicate and engaged them in the course content.

Mentally Finishing Class Early

While the text-based conversations were generally on-topic, students appeared to drift off-topic in the last five minutes of class. For example, during one class, a student typed the text: "What is your favorite cereal?" Other students responded and there was laughter in the classroom when the instructor turned around to see that the students were debating the value of Captain Crunch versus Frosted Flakes. These types of off-topic behavior were observed in each of the five classes where webconferencing was conducted and at first, the instructor did not recognize what was happening. Essentially, the students were using their conversations to disconnect mentally from the current class, and prepare to transition for their next activity. This is very common in traditional classrooms and typically takes the form of students putting away their notepads and making noise as they pack up their backpacks and prepare to leave class.

This is obviously a very distracting behavior and when the text is displayed for the class, it is vitally important for the instructor to recognize the behavior and re-direct the students quickly. In a traditional classroom, an instructor might say, "I know you are all anxious to get to your next class, but remember that I always let you out on time, so you can wait to put your books away and still not be rushed." In this case when there was a visual display of off-topic behavior, the instructor laughed with the class, looked at the clock, and reminded the class that they really needed to wrap up this final topic and do a preview for the next class. In one case, the off-topic conversation continued and it was likely distracting to the class. In retrospect, the instructor probably should have quickly clicked a button on the chat feature and disallowed it. Another option would be for the instructor to join the chat, and type in the preview for the next class, while verbally stating the same content. We make these recommendations based on observations that when the instructor joined the virtual chat, it seemed to re-focus the group. This was different from simply stating a verbal comment. This will be further addressed in the directions for future research.

Trends in Participation

When observing the students engaged in this webconference, there were several main trends. First, students who typically did not speak in class participated in the chat, and many of their comments are equally insightful as those shared verbally in class. For example in one lecture on the implications of culture and information and communication technology use, two different students mentioned theories that were discussed in the class over a month earlier in the semester. In the case of the other university included as a comparison in this study, that instructor taught the same course and used a common textbook, but supplemented it with additional materials. During the webconference, this group also raised questions and used key terms that connected to the common textbook. That instructor also noticed that the students integrated that lecture content with his supplemental materials. In both classes, students were making connections between the course content and those connections were visible through text chat and verbal questions asked.

A second trend was that the students seemed to enjoy the lectures and each other more. Not only were quiet students participating for the first time but there was more discussion overall. Some students sat in the back of the traditional classroom and participated exclusively via their laptops and some of those students seemed to enjoy the novelty of their comments being displayed on the "big screen." Students at the comparison university also demonstrated a high degree of participation. Perhaps the mediated dimension of a webconference made the discussion more fun because the instructor observed that a usually quiet student came to the front of the classroom to ask the virtual instructor a question via the audio feature of the webconferening system. The instructor also noticed that one student logged out and logged back in with a new and more creative username for the rest of the chat session. These learners not only felt motivated to perform tasks, but they possessed a level of control over those tasks, key components to learning components learning (Frymier, Shulman, & Houser, 1996). Empowered students should be more likely to see the meaningfulness of course content and activities, feel a greater sense of self-efficacy in performing classroom tasks, and be more likely to perceive that learning course content can have an impact (Schrodt et al., 2008). The novelty of incorporating webconferencing into a traditional classroom created new rhetorical and relational dynamics that were generally quite positive.

In addition, students thrived on the quick, threaded discussion in the chat. Despite being short-lived, the comments were interpersonally significant and allowed the students to connect to one another. The format also added additional visual communication; thus displaying course content in line with students' preferences. When students' brief comments were displayed on the big screen, some students simply expressed agreement with their peers, in the form of "I agree with so and so about..." Although one can argue that these kinds of statements do not fully constitute unique intellectual contributions, a balanced amount of simple agreement from peers can psychologically motivate the students whose comments appeared to represent their peers' opinions. The relational dynamic can also encourage more students to share their opinions online in future sessions.

Expanding Learning Spaces to Include More Students

It is clear in both the scholarly literature and the popular press that the traditional classroom-style lecture format does not provide students with the new learning spaces that some desire and expect. This phenomenon has called instructor training into question and adds uncertainty to the classroom in regards to instructor and student rhetorical and relational goals. However, to overcome the challenges faced in the present case study, the three participation options allowed the instructor to tap into the needs of nearly every student's ideal 'learning space.' This freedom of choice flexibility enhanced the relational goals of both the students and instructors to connect in fresh ways. In addition, this newly created learning space environment set the stage for 'sharing the podium' where new voices emerged and empowered learning occurred among the professor, teaching assistant, distance guest lecturers, and students. Furthermore, empowering students to co-produce a blended classroom learning environment generated an environment of mutual respect which, in turn, created an informal setting where students became more comfortable speaking up in class discussion whether that was through chat or verbal comments.

In sum, the webconferencing format dovetailed with subject matter, students' interests, and communication workplace technologies in more ways than one. It provided a co-created learning space, freedom of choice in participation, experience and practice with interactive technologies, opportunity for informal and yet productive discussion, engagement and empowered learning in the Net Generation's preferred ways, and influenced the instructor-student relationship in a positive light.

FUTURE RESEARCH DIRECTIONS

Limitations of Current Study

It is important to consider the findings from this study in light of the small sample and limited number of locations. It is difficult to say if the classroom in this case could have been turned around using other techniques, but it appears that webconferencing offers one viable option. Another consideration in this study is to understand and listen to a range of voices and opinions because incorporating technology into the classroom will not be helpful to all students. For example, one student said, "It was easy to get distracted if you were connected online, self discipline is needed." It is important to listen to the potential pitfalls associated with webconferencing and continue to incorporate solid pedagogy and technology use practices into our CMC learning spaces.

This study leads to several promising areas for future research. First, as educators of the Net Generation, we need to be leading the field with our use and research in CMC learning environments. To accomplish this task, we must carefully define our CMC tools, design robust studies using a variety of methods, and incorporate our expertise in pedagogy into our research. It is important for our studies to focus less on the specific technology used (other than to define and limit the scope of possibilities), and more on how the technology is used. For example, researchers are beginning to understand how interactivity can play a role in learning when CMC technologies are used. We should further explore these and make sure that what we are observing are not novelties that will fade away as students become accustomed to CMC use.

Understanding How to Use Multiple Modes to Re-Direct Classroom Learning

In the case presented, the instructor noticed that students would use text chat to visually display their mental disconnection from course content during the last five minutes of class. This observation provides the stimulus for a range of future research that focuses on how instructors use multiple modes to re-direct classroom learning. Experienced instructors use related techniques in a traditional classroom and these include, stopping lecture and asking the class to write a minute paper reflecting on the topic, or asking students to share a question they have with the person sitting next to them.

In a CMC classroom, there is very little research into strategies for how instructors can use technology tools to provide a different type of learning stimulus for students. It is possible that by joining the disruptive students in their modality of choice (text chat in this particular case), changes the dynamic of the CMC classroom and the off-topic conversation dissipates. Studies of this nature should go beyond a survey design, because students may not be aware of how this modality matching behavior affects them. Carefully designed experiments could likely capture actual behavior and provide considerable guidance for instructors in a CMC classroom.

This concept extends beyond the situation in the current case and into basic classroom management issues. If the Net Generation students really do crave diversity of experiences, simply moving a lecture on-line will not be sufficient to engage these students. The interactivity tools in webconferencing offer simple, fairly spontaneous opportunities to ask for anonymous aggregated feedback through polling. If all students have access to the Internet-portion of the webconference, they can participate frequently and there is a natural social pressure to respond because the results are displayed with only a couple of second delay. It is even possible to use the polling to create an end to an unproductive line of text-based conversation. For example, the instructor could have created a poll asking about favorite cereal, had everyone vote, and reported a result all within two minutes. That creates a natural way to move on to the next topic.

Cyberlearning Opportunities

Given the availability of and accessibility to information, knowledge, datasets, and experts online, it is likely that teaching and learning will further move away from the traditional model. Earlier in the chapter we argued that a bold attempt would be to support traditional instruction by letting students explore these resources online. Future research could further explore strategies for promoting interactivity with remote information sources and datasets to create engaging virtual learning beyond the classroom. In a National Science Foundation report on 'cyberlearning,' Borgman and colleagues (2008) argue, "Content is no longer limited to the books, filmstrips, and videos associated with classroom instruction; networked content today provides a rich immersive learning environment incorporating accessible data using colorful visualizations, animated graphics, and interactive applications" (p. 5). Strategies discussed in this chapter and similar webconferencing tools can help facilitate cyberlearning, a model that involves "the use of networked computing and commuications technologies to support learning" (Borgman et al., 2008, p. 5).

Classroom Multitasking

This case has danced around the issue of whether instructors should be encouraging students to use technology tools to actively participate in class. It is possible that some of these tools are disruptive for students who prefer to give their undivided attention to the instructor. Past research on multitasking paints a gloomy picture of any human's ability (including the Net Generation) to carry out two cognitive tasks at the exact same time without a decline in performance (Lin, 2009; Ophir, Nass, & Wagner, 2009; Rogers & Monsell, 1995; Stroop, 1935).

However, in a classroom context, if the two tasks are actually more of a multi-channel presentation of similar content, using webconferencing in class might enhance learning. Information theory scholars have explained that bisensory modalities (referred to as between channel redundancy) can be helpful (Broadbent, 1958). Several educational scholars have also relied on the concept of dual coding (Paivo, 1990) to demonstrate that when teachers want to improve retention, using different sensory modes can be highly productive (Kalyuga, Chandler, & Sweller, 2000; Mayer, 1997; Mayer & Moreno, 1998; Mousavi, Low, & Sweller, 1995; Paivo, 1990). Essentially, the webconferencing used in this study, provides visual stimuli in the form of text, in addition to an auditory channel. Prior research suggests that when the content is similar, the channels reinforce one another. Yet, as demonstrated in this case study, sometimes the content is not similar. It is important for future scholarship to examine exactly how these mixed modes contribute to learning and identify points where distraction is detrimental to learning.

Responsiveness to Questions and Needs

The text-based chat used in this study is very similar to instant messaging and prior research on this technology tool also provides guidance for future research. In this case study, students commented that access to others and receiving responses to questions more quickly made them enjoy the experience. While the research regarding instant messaging is mixed in terms of whether it is helpful or interruptive (Stephens, 2008), some research claims that instant messaging can be used to manage interruptions (Garrett & Danziger, 2007; Nardi & Whittaker, 2002). Their research supports the findings here that senders and receivers can interact when it is convenient for them and in the workplace, people tend to have shorter, more frequent interactions that result in little disruption (Garrett & Danziger, 2007). There are considerable research opportunities to explore how these timely, yet potentially interruptive conversations affect classroom learning. Research has established that Net Generation students use instant messaging to interact and manage activities (Baron, 2008; 2010) outside of the classroom, but knowing more about how they use these tools in the classroom can provide guidance as we implement tools like webconferencing into our classrooms.

These are just a few of the more promising areas for future research on webconferencing. In addition, the mobile device application use of webconferencing is virtually unexplored in the literature. In this study, one student reported that the polling function did not work on her smartphone, but she could access everything else. By linking the CMC classroom literature with knowledge gained from what scholars have learned about mobility and mobile device use, a CMC classroom approach could significantly impact the classrooms of the future.

CONCLUSION

Multicommunicating is quickly becoming the norm whether people are at work or trying to learn in the classroom. Webconferencing offers one way to leverage multicommunication for learning and engaging students by embracing digital learning options. If we can balance the use of these interactive classroom tools with the concern of overloading and distracting students, the potential for increasing meaningful classroom participation expands. The Net Generation learners want interactivity and they can be active participants if we think creatively about engaging them.

As instructors consider CMC classroom tools, this case offers a rationale for using webconferencing, advice on how to use this tool productively, and ideas for how we might study these growing trends in the classroom. The instructors in this case study learned that by listening to the concerns and desires of the Net Generation and by leveraging our knowledge of how they use technology, a classroom environment can be transformed. In the process, we did not compromise our learning objectives and we did not use coercive power in the classroom. This case provides a solid example of how we can use technology tools to reach digital learners.

REFERENCES

Allen, T. H. (2006). Is the rush to provide online instruction setting our students up for failure? *Communication Education*, *55*, 122–126.. doi:10.1080/03634520500343418

Anderson, R., Davis, P., Linnell, N., Prince, C., Razmo, V., & Videon, F. (2007). Classroom presenter: Enhancing interactive education with digital ink. *Computer*, *40*(9), 56–61..doi:10.1109/MC.2007.307

Baron, N. S. (2008). Adjusting the volume: Technology and multitasking in discourse control. In Katz, J. E. (Ed.), *Mobile communication and social change in a global context* (pp. 117–194). Cambridge, MA: The MIT Press.

Baron, N. S. (2010). *Always on: Language in an online and mobile world*. Oxford, UK: Oxford University Press.

Belal, A. R. (2011). Students perceptions of computer assisted learning: An empirical study. *International Journal of Management in Education, 5*(1), 63–78..doi:10.1504/IJMIE.2011.037755

Benoit, P. J., Benoit, W. L., Milyo, J., & Hansen, G. J. (2006). *The effects of traditional vs. web-assisted instruction on student learning and satisfaction*. Columbia, MO: The Graduate School, University of Missouri.

Bernard, R. M., Abrami, P. C., Borokhovski, E., Wade, C. A., Tamim, R. M., Surkes, M. A., et al. (2009). A meta-analysis of three types of interaction treatments in distance education. *Review of Educational Research, 79*(3), 1243-1289. doi:1210.3102/0034654309333844.

Borgman, C. L., Abelson, H., Dirks, L., Johnson, R., Koedinger, K. R., Linn, M. C., et al. (2008). *Fostering learning in the networked world: The cyberlearning opportunity and challenge*. Report of the NSF Task Force on Cyberlearning. Retrieved October 15, 2009, from http://www.nsf.gov/pubs/2008/nsf08204/nsf08204.pdf.

Broadbent, D. E. (1958). *Perception and communication*. London, UK: Pergamon Press. doi:10.1037/10037-000

Brown, M. (2005). Learning spaces. In D. G. Oblinger, & J. L. Oblinger (Eds.), *Educating the Net Generation* (pp. 12.1-12.22). Washington, DC: EDUCAUSE. Retrieved from http://www.educause.edu/educatingthenetgen.

Cameron, A. F., & Webster, J. (2010). Relational outcomes of multicommunicating: Integrating incivility and social exchange perspectives. *Organization Science, Articles in Advance*, 1-18. doi:10.1287/orsc.1100.0540.

Connaway, L. S., Radford, M., Williams, J. D. A., & Confer, P. (2008). Sense-making and synchronicity: Information-seeking behaviors of millennials and baby boomers. *International Journal of Libraries and Information Services, 58*, 123–135.

De Corte, E., & Verschaffel, L. Entwistle, & Van Merriëboer, J. (Eds.). (2003). *Unravelling basic components and dimensions of powerful learning environments*. Amsterdam, The Netherlands: Elsevier.

Evans, C., & Gibbons, N. J. (2007). The interactivity effect in multimedia learning. *Computers & Education, 49*(4), 1147-1160. doi:1110.1016/j.compedu.2006.1101.1008.

Fisher, W. R. (1987). *Human communication as narration: Toward a philosophy of reason, value and action*. Columbia, SC: University of South Carolina Press.

Fletcher, D. (2003, September). *Unlocking the potential of gaming technology*. Higher Education Leaders Symposium. Symposium conducted at the Microsoft Corporation, Redmond, Washington.

Frymier, A. B., & Houser, M. L. (2000). The teacher-student relationship as an interpersonal relationship. *Communication Education, 49*, 207–219. doi:10.1080/03634520009379209

Frymier, A. B., Shulman, G. M., & Houser, M. (1996). The development of a learner empowerment measure. *Communication Education, 45*(3), 181–199. doi:10.1080/03634529609379048

Garrett, R. K., & Danziger, J. N. (2007). IM=Interruption management? Instant messaging and disruption in the workplace. *Journal of Computer-Mediated Communication, 13*, 23–42.. doi:10.1111/j.1083-6101.2007.00384.x

Gorman, P., Nelson, T., & Glassman, A. (2004). The Millennial generation: A strategic opportunity. *Organizational Analysis*, *12*(3), 255–270.

Hartman, J., Moskal, P., & Dziuban, C. (2005). Preparing the academy of today for the learner of tomorrow. In D. G. Oblinger, & J. L. Oblinger (Eds.), *Educating the Net Generation* (pp. 6.1-6.15). Washington, DC: EDUCAUSE. Retrieved from http://www.educause.edu/educatingthenetgen.

Howe, N., & Strauss, W. (2000). *Millennials rising*. New York, NY: Vintage Books.

Kalyuga, S., Chandler, P., & Sweller, J. (2000). Incorporating learner experience into the design of multi-media instruction. *Journal of Educational Psychology*, *92*, 126–136. doi:10.1037/0022-0663.92.1.126

Kofman, B., & Eckler, K. (2005). They are your future: Attracting and retaining Generation Y. *Canadian HR Reporter*, *18*, 8. Retrieved from http://www.hrreporter.com/.

Lin, L. (2009). Breadth-biased versus focused cognitive control in media multitasking behaviors. *Proceedings of the National Academy of Sciences of the United States of America*, *106*, 15521–15522..doi:10.1073/pnas.0908642106

Lippincott, J. K. (2005). Net Generation students and libraries. In D. G. Oblinger, & J. L. Oblinger (Eds.), *Educating the Net Generation* (pp. 13.1-13.15), Washington, DC: EDUCAUSE. Retrieved from http://www.educause.edu/educatingthenetgen.

Mason, R. M., Barzilai-Nahon, K., & Lou, N. (2008). The organizational impact of digital natives: How organizations are responding to the next generation of knowledge workers. *Proceedings of the 17th Dubai International Conference on Management of Technology.* doi:10.1109/HICSS.2006.411.

Mayer, R. E. (1997). Multimedia learning: Are we asking the right questions? *Educational Psychologist*, *32*, 1–19. doi:10.1207/s15326985ep3201_1

Mayer, R. E., & Moreno, R. (1998). A split-attention effect in multimedia learning evidence for dual processing systems in working memory. *Journal of Educational Psychology*, *90*, 312–320. doi:10.1037/0022-0663.90.2.312

McCombs, B. L., & Vakili, D. (2005). A learner-centered framework for e-learning. *Teachers College Record*, *107*(8), 1582–1600. doi:10.1111/j.1467-9620.2005.00534.x

McNeely, B. (2005). Using technology as a learning tool, not just the cool thing. In D. G. Oblinger, & J. L. Oblinger (Eds.), *Educating the Net Generation* (pp. 4.1-4.10). Washington, DC: EDUCAUSE. Retrieved http://www.educause.edu/educatingthenetgen.

Mottet, T. P., Frymier, A. B., & Beebe, S. A. (2006). Theorizing about instructional communication. In Mottet, T. P., Richmond, V. P., & McCroskey, J. C. (Eds.), *Handbook of instructional communication: Rhetorical and relational perspectives* (pp. 255–282). Boston, MA: Allyn and Bacon.

Mousavi, S. Y., Low, R., & Sweller, J. (1995). Reducing cognitive leads by mixing auditory and visual presentation modes. *Journal of Educational Psychology*, *92*, 724–733.

Nardi, B., Whittaker, S., & Bradner, E. (2000). Interaction and outeraction: Instant messaging in action. In *CSCW '00: Proceedings of the 2000 ACM Conference on Computer Supported Cooperative Work* (pp. 79-88). Philadelphia, PA: ACM Press.

Oblinger, D., & Oblinger, J. (2005). Is it age or IT: First steps towards understanding the Net Generation. In D. G. Oblinger, & J. L. Oblinger (Eds.), *Educating the Net Generation* (pp. 2.1-2.20). Washington, DC: EDUCAUSE. Retrieved from http://www.educause.edu/educatingthenetgen.

Ophir, E., Nass, C., & Wagner, A. D. (2009). Cognitive control in media multitaskers. *Proceedings of the National Academy of Sciences of the United States of America, 106*, 15583–15587.. doi:10.1073/pnas.0903620106

Paivo, A. (1990). *Mental representations: A dual coding approach*. New York, NY: Oxford University Press.

Palfrey, J., & Gasser, U. (2008). *Born digital: Understanding the first generation of digital natives*. New York, NY: Basic Books.

Patterson, B. R., & Gojdycz, T. K. (2000). The relationship between computer-mediated communication and communication related anxieties. *Communication Research Reports, 17*(3), 278–287. doi:10.1080/08824090009388775

Pogue, L., & Ahyun, K. (2006). The effect of teacher nonverbal immediacy and credibility on student motivation and affective learning. *Communication Education, 55*, 331–344. doi:10.1080/03634520600748623

Prensky, M. (2001). Digital natives, digital immigrants, part 1. *Horizon, 9*(5), 1–6. doi:10.1108/10748120110424816

Prensky, M. (2009). H. Sapiens Digital: From digital immigrants and digital natives to digital wisdom. *Innovate, 5*(3). Retrieved from http://innovateonline.info/pdf/vol5_issue3/H._Sapiens_Digital-__From_Digital_Immigrants_and_Digital_Natives_to_Digital_Wisdom.pdf.

Rainie, L. (2006). *Americans and their cell phones*. Washington, DC: Pew Research Center. Retrieved from http://www.pewinternet.org/~/media//Files/Reports/2006/PIP_Cell_phone_study.pdf.pdf.

Reinsch, N. L., Turner, J. W., & Tinsley, C. H. (2008). Multicommunicating: A practice whose time has come? *Academy of Management Review, 33*, 391–403. doi:10.5465/AMR.2008.31193450

Rennecker, J., Dennis, A. R., & Hansen, S. (2006). Reconstructing the stage: The use of instant messaging to restructure meeting boundaries. *Proceedings of the 39th Hawaii International Conference on System Sciences.* doi: 10.1109/HICSS.2006.411.

Roberts, G. (2005). Technology and learning expectations of the Net Generation. In D. G. Oblinger, & J. L. Oblinger (Eds.), *Educating the Net Generation* (pp. 3.1-3.7). Washington, DC: EDUCAUSE. Retrieved from http://www.educause.edu/educatingthenetgen.

Rogers, R. D., & Monsell, S. (1995). Costs of a predictable switch between simple cognitive tasks. *Journal of Experimental Psychology, 124*, 207–231.

Schiller, S. Z. (2009). Practicing learner-centered teaching: Pedagogical design and assessment of a Second Life project. *Journal of Information Systems Education, 20*(3), 369–381.

Schrire, S. (2004). Interaction and cognition in asynchronous computer conferencing. *Instructional Science, 32*, 475–502..doi:10.1007/s11251-004-2518-7

Schrodt, P., Witt, P. L., Myers, S. A., Turman, P. D., Barton, M. H., & Jernberg, K. A. (2008). Learner empowerment and teacher evaluations as functions of teacher power use in the college classroom. *Communication Education, 57*(2), 180–200.. doi:10.1080/03634520701840303

Sherblom, J. C. (2010). The computer-mediated communication (CMC) classroom: A challenge of medium, presence, interaction, identity, and relationship. *Communication Education, 59*, 497–523.. doi:10.1080/03634523.2010.486440

Shute, V. J., & Torreano, L. A. (2003). Formative evaluation of an automated knowledge elicitation and organization tool. In Murray, T., Ainsworth, S., & Blessing, S. (Eds.), *Authoring tools for advanced technology learning environments: Toward cost-effective adaptive, interactive, and intelligent educational software* (pp. 149–180). The Netherlands: Kluwer Academic Publishers.

Shute, V. J., & Towle, B. (2003). Adaptive e-learning. *Educational Psychologist, 38*(2), 105–114. doi:10.1207/S15326985EP3802_5

Shute, V. J., & Zapata-Rivera, D. (2008). Adaptive technologies. In Spector, J. M., Merrill, D., van Merrienboer, J., & Driscoll, M. (Eds.), *Handbook of research on educational communications and technology* (3rd ed., pp. 277–294). New York, NY: Lawrence Erlbaum Associates, Taylor & Francis Group.

Soloway, E., Guzdial, M., & Hay, K. E. (1994). Learner-centered design: The challenge for HCI in the 21st century. *Interaction, 1*(2), 36–48. doi:10.1145/174809.174813

Spector, J. M. (2001). An overview of progress and problems in educational technology. *Interactive Educational Multimedia, 3*, 27–37.

Stephens, K. K. (2008). Optimizing costs in workplace instant messaging use. *IEEE Transactions on Professional Communication, 51*, 369–380.. doi:10.1109/TPC.2008.2007864

Stephens, K. K., & Davis, J. D. (2009). The social influences on electronic multitasking in organizational meetings. *Management Communication Quarterly, 23*, 63–83.. doi:10.1177/0893318909335417

Stephens, K. K., & Mottet, T. M. (2008). Interactivity in a Web conferencing training context: Effects on trainers & trainees. *Communication Education, 57*, 88–104..doi:10.1080/03634520701573284

Stroop, J. R. (1935). Studies of interference in serial verbal reactions. *Journal of Experimental Psychology, 18*, 643–662. doi:10.1037/h0054651

Sun, P. C., Tsai, R. J., Finger, G., Chen, Y. Y., & Yeh, D. (2008). What drives a successful e-Learning? An empirical investigation of the critical factors influencing learner satisfaction. *Computers & Education, 50*(4), 1183-1202. doi:1110.1016/j.compedu.2006.1111.1007.

Tapscott, D. (1998). *Growing up digital: The rise of the Net Generation*. New York, NY: McGraw-Hill.

Turner, J. W., & Reinsch, N. L. (2010). Successful and unsuccessful multicommunication episodes: Engaging in dialogue or juggling messages? *Information Systems Frontiers, 12*, 277–285.. doi:10.1007/s10796-009-9175-y

Vess, D. (2005). Asynchronous discussion and communication patterns in online and hybrid history courses. *Communication Education, 54*, 355–364..doi:10.1080/03634520500442210

Vogel, J. J., Vogel, D. S., Cannon-Bowers, J., Bowers, C. A., Muse, K., & Wright, M. (2006). Computer gaming and interactive simulations for learning: A meta-analysis. *Journal of Educational Computing Research, 34*(3), 229–243. doi:10.2190/FLHV-K4WA-WPVQ-H0YM

Waycott, J., Bennett, S., Kennedy, G., Dalgarno, B., & Gray, K. (2010). Digital divides? Student and staff perceptions of information and communication technologies. *Computers & Education, 54*(4), 1202-1211. doi:1210.1016/j.compedu.2009.1211.1006.

Windham, C. (2005). The student's perspective. In D. G. Oblinger, & J. L. Oblinger (Eds.), *Educating the Net Generation* (pp. 5.1-5.16). Washington, DC: EDUCAUSE. Retrieved from http://www.educause.edu/educatingthenetgen.

Witt, P. L., Wheeless, L. R., & Allen, M. (2004). A meta-analytical review of the relationship between teacher immediacy and student learning. *Communication Monographs, 71*, 184–207.. doi:10.1080/036452042000228054

Wood, A. F., & Fassett, D. L. (2003). Remote control: Identity, power, and technology in the communication classroom. *Communication Education, 52*, 286–296..doi:10.1080/0363452032000156253

Yin, R. K. (2009). *Case study research: Design and methods* (4th ed.). Thousand Oaks, CA: Sage Publications.

Zemke, R., Raines, C., & Filipczak, B. (2000). *Generations at work: Managing the clash of veterans, Boomers, Xers, and Nexters in your workplace*. New York, NY: AMACOM American Management Association.

ADDITIONAL READING

Baron, N. S. (2010). *Always on: Language in an online and mobile world*. Oxford: Oxford University Press.

Bradford, P., Porciello, M., Balkon, N., & Backus, D. (2007). The Blackboard Learning System: The Be All and End All in Educational Instruction? *Journal of Educational Technology Systems*, *35*(3), 301–314. doi:10.2190/X137-X73L-5261-5656

Descy, D.E. (2008). Second Life. *TechTrends: Linking research & practice to improve learning, 52*(1), 5-6.

Eppler, M. J., & Mengis, J. (2004). The concept of information overload: A review of literature from organization science, accounting, marketing, MIS, and related disciplines. *The Information Society*, *20*, 325–344. doi:10.1080/01972240490507974

Glass, R., & Spiegelman, M. (2008). Incorporating blogs into the syllabus: Making their space a learning space. *Journal of Educational Technology Systems*, *36*(2), 145–155. doi:10.2190/ET.36.2.c

Goodrich, C. (2008). Using web-based software to enhance student learning of analytical and critical skills. *Journal of Educational Technology Systems*, *36*(3), 247–253. doi:10.2190/ET.36.3.b

Hwang, J.-S., & McMillan, S. J. (2002). The role of interactivity and involvement in attitude toward the web site. In A. Abernathy (Ed.) Proceedings of the 2002 Conference of the American Academy of Advertising, (pp. 10-17). Auburn, AL: Auburn University.

Jarmon, L., Traphagan, T., & Mayrath, M. (2008). Understanding project-based learning in Second Life with a pedagogy, training, and assessment trio. *Educational Media International*, *45*(3), 153–171. doi:10.1080/09523980802283889

Jarvenpaa, S. L., & Lang, K. R. (2005). Managing the paradoxes of mobile technology. *Information Systems Management*, (Fall): 7–23. doi:10.1201/1078.10580530/45520.22.4.20050901/90026.2

Lancaster, L. C., & Stillman, D. (2002). *When generations collide: Who they are, why they clash, how to solve the generational puzzle at work*. New York, NY: HarperCollins.

Lawler, C., Rossett, A., & Hoffman, R. (1998). Using supportive planning software to help teachers integrate technology into teaching. *Educational Technology*, *38*(5), 29–34.

Pittinsky, M. S. (2003). *The wired tower: Perspectives on the impact of the Internet on higher education*. Upper Saddle River, NJ: Prentice Hall.

Prensky, M. (2001). Digital natives, digital immigrants, part 2: Do they really think differently? *On the Horizon, 9* (6), 1-6. Rossett, A. (Ed.), *The ASTD e-Learning handbook* (pp. 357-364). New York: McGraw-Hill.

Rossett, A. & Marshall, James. (January, 2010). E-learning. What's old is new again. *Training & Development*. Retrieved from http://www.astd.org/TD/Archives/2010/Jan/Free/1001_eLearning_Whats_Old.htm.

Stephens, K. K., Houser, M. L., & Cowan, R. L. (2009). R U able to meat me: The impact of students' overly casual email messages to instructors. *Communication Education*, *58*, 303–326. doi:10.1080/03634520802582598

Waldeck, J. H. (2006). What does "personalized education" mean for faculty, and how should it serve our students? *Communication Education*, *55*(3), 345–352..doi:10.1080/03634520600748649

Waldeck, J. H. (2007). Answering the question: Student perceptions of personalized education and the construct's relationship to learning outcomes. *Communication Education*, *56*(4), 409–432.. doi:10.1080/03634520701400090

KEY TERMS AND DEFINITIONS

Backchannel Communication: Conversations occurring behind the main, often verbal, channel. This type of communication often occurs through mobile devices or instant messaging systems.

Blended Classroom: A classroom that utilizes face-to-face (FTF) interactions and computer mediated communication (CMC) to enable teaching and learning. In a blended classroom FTF and CMC interactions complement each other instead of serving as a replacement for one another.

Computer-Mediated Classroom: Any class where at least part of the instruction is delivered or enhanced through computer, mobile device, or web-based tool.

Cyberlearning: The of use of a combination of emerging communication technologies, advanced computing/computational technologies (i.e., cyberinfrastructure tools), and digital datasets/information to allow students to share, collaborate, observe, manipulate, and model existing public datasets for educational simulations and research visualizations.

Learning Spaces: A range of physical, social, and virtual spaces where students can interact with instructors, peers, information, and other experts to achieve different learning goals, objectives, and outcomes. Learning spaces expands teaching and learning to anytime, anywhere.

Multicommunication: A communication practice where people carry on multiple conversations, often using different modalities, almost simultaneously.

Webconferencing: A web-based technology tool that allows a teacher or presenter to show PowerPoint slides, provide auditory explanations, and incorporate interactive tools such as text chat, polling (surveys) and whiteboard sharing.

Chapter 16
New Media and Digital Learners: An Examination of Teaching and Learning

William J. Gibbs
Duquesne University, USA

ABSTRACT

The proliferation of digital technologies coupled with technically sophisticated students with high educational expectations requires media educators to rethink conventional teaching and learning practices. Students enter the college experience with a wealth of background knowledge and experience that instructors must take into account when designing new/digital media courses. In this chapter, I examine current principles of instruction, learning, instructional design, and learning theory and their relevance to the education of digital learners. In addition, I outline the development of a digital media course premised on these teaching and learning precepts. Finally, I review some of the challenges faced when instituting innovative instructional practices.

INTRODUCTION

Innovations in broadband, broadcasting, and information technologies now allow media organizations to deliver multimedia content (voice, imagery, text, and video) and to support multimodal human-computer interactions (e.g., touch, speech) across many different types of computing devices. Digital interfaces have evolved enabling people to easily navigate digital spaces to connect with content, services, and other people in unprecedented ways. People can engage in worldwide conversations on just about any topic of interest because network connectivity and digital media support two-way communication. This has led to a proliferation of social media-type sites that deliver news and information more interactively, permitting social relations and virtual communities to evolve.

DOI: 10.4018/978-1-61350-347-8.ch016

These innovations coincide with increased access to and use of digital communication devices (e. g., computer, cell phone). "Thirty-seven percent of people today, including more than half of Internet users, obtain news online whereas ten years ago only 13% of the public and 35% of Internet users went online for news" (Kohut, 2008, p.21). In another study, 44% of respondents reported using one or more Internet or mobile digital sources (cell phones, email, social networks and podcasts) to get news (Pew Research Center, 2010). Digital devices not only enable people to receive information but to be active in gathering and disseminating it.

Technological innovation and ubiquitous digital devices create significant challenges for educators who teach communication media courses. From automobiles, mobile phones, to desktop computers, today's students constantly interact with computational devices. Many begin to use computers at a very young age. Lenhart (2009) points out that social network use is in the domain of young people as are many new and emerging forms of media and computing devices. A majority (75%) of young people between the ages of 12 and 17 have cell phones, now thought to be integral in teen communication (Lenhart, Ling, Campbell & Purcell, 2010). Children use Game Boy, Nintendo, and other gaming systems to play games individually and collectively with friends. By the time they reach a college level course, they will have logged hundreds of hours navigating digital interfaces. This wired generation poses special challenges to educators.

FOUNDATIONS OF LEARNING: STUDENT BACKGROUND

Today's students have become highly sophisticated digital media consumers, and in some cases, producers. They are exceedingly adept at navigating digital interfaces. Nowadays, interfaces represent a dominant means through which students interact with others, shop, take educational courses, play games, and otherwise conduct their lives. While many interfaces are complex, their fundamental purpose is to minimize technical burdens and allow people to access information and/or complete tasks. With them, people perform complex tasks with relative ease. For example, many students effortlessly produce media content by capturing and editing images, words, video and audio with portable recording devices and publishing the content on the web. With minimal mental concentration or physical exertion, they instantly communicate with peers by texting, sending Tweets, or using social networking sites like Facebook. In many ways, interfaces conceal the technical complexities that make these interactions possible. Because interfaces allow students to perform many complex tasks almost effortlessly and because students use technology extensively, they bring unique competencies and expectations to the college classroom. Some enter college with much technical and digital media expertise. Others, despite their extensive use of technology, possess high expectations about developing media content but lack a full appreciation of the underlying technologies, processes, or procedures required to do so professionally. This has profound implications for the communication media educators.

Prior Knowledge and Experience

Current research in teaching and learning strongly emphasizes the need for educators to ascertain what students already know about a topic prior to instruction, especially because students use their background knowledge to form new understandings (Dick, Carey, & Carey, 2008). Students' prior knowledge and experience influence the educational process in many ways, three of which are considered here. First, prior knowledge is a critical factor that impacts learning (Zhu & Grabowski, 2006) and when taken into account, it can."..enhance the student's learning process and lead to better instructional support" (Hailikari, Nevgi

& Lindblom-Ylänne, 2007, p.321). Second, it provides instructors important information about students that they can use to refine teaching and learning practices (Hailikari, Nevgi & Lindblom-Ylänne, 2007). Third, in terms of digital media, the type and amount of prior computing experience shape student expectations about media design and development. A person's past knowledge and experience provides vital information about self-efficacy, one's belief about his/her ability or skill to achieve a level of performance that will in some way lead to desired outcomes (Bandura, 1977, 1994). People who have high self-efficacy express higher outcome expectations than those with low self-efficacy (King & Xia, 1997). Computer self-efficacy has been shown to influence the outcomes one expects when using computers and computer use (Compeau & Higgins, 1995a, 1995b). An individual who has been successful and has had positive prior media experiences is likely to have higher outcome expectations of media use in the future (King & Xia, 1997). This can be especially important in entry level courses. A student could have extensive experience using media and navigating a plethora of interfaces. Because of this experience, the individual may possess high self-efficacy and associated expectations about his/her ability to develop media projects. Assuming competency, the individual might decide to study a more advanced topic over one that is rudimentary. However, one's proficiency at consuming media (i.e., web browsing, social networking) is not an assurance that the individual is familiar with fundamentals of digital media nor the methods, time, effort, and resources needed for media development. It is often difficult for students to make such determinations.

Prior Education

Many students enrolling in bachelor degree programs have had secondary educational experiences that emphasize learner-centeredness, problem-solving, critical thinking, and collaboration. Those inclined to study digital media have likely taken high school courses grounded in these principles. They often possess experience in using media to investigate and solve real-world problems, conduct research, create works of art, and express feelings and ideas. This is also true of many students outside the digital media field. However, it is especially relevant to communication media students because the nature of their courses lends itself to problem-based, life-like projects. Current educational research espouses problem-based learning, cases, real-world projects and associated teaching and learning methods. Merrill (2002) points out that effective learning approaches are problem-centered. They stimulate students' prior knowledge and experience, cause them to demonstrate and apply what they've learned, and to integrate new knowledge and skills in real-world applications. Despite this, some instructors adhere to instructivist teaching practices (e.g., lecture) that may not fully account for students' prior knowledge or the learning expectations they bring to the classroom. In a review of dimensions of objectivism and constructivism, Cronjé (2006, p. 391) reviewed primary characteristics of the instructivist philosophy, some of which include: (a) objectivist epistemology; (b) underlying psychology is behavioral; (c) reductionist sequencing; (d) authoritarian-didactic instructor role; (e) abstract experiential orientation; and (e) highly structured, with little or no accommodation for individual differences. Typically, an instructivist approach compartmentalizes content into small instructional units (reductionist sequencing), removing it from a real-world context. In this approach, teaching and learning are content-centric and teacher-directed rather than learner-centered. It is a transmission pedagogy premised on the belief that students learn by grasping the content of the instructor's explanations or lectures (Ravitz, Becker & Wong, 2000). Regarding multimedia learning, Mayer (2009) discussed transfer-centered approaches that spotlight technological capabilities rather than learner needs whereby learners adapt to the attributes of the technology rather than the technologies conforming to the needs of learners. He contends that such approaches generally do not promote enduring educational improvements.

Teacher-directed pedagogy is inadequate to prepare many Net Generation students. In many ways, it is incompatible with the experiences of digital learners who are often technically savvy and for whom problem-solving, real-world learning, and other innovative pedagogical approaches may be customary. Thus, a digital learner's assimilation into college-level courses may be greatly influenced by the pedagogy or educational philosophy adopted by the instructor. Students may find courses grounded in instructivist approaches (e.g., lecture, memorization) to be divergent from their experience, and possibly more challenging.

FOUNDATIONS OF TEACHING AND LEARNING: THEORY AND INSTRUCTIONAL DESIGN

Pervasive developments in digital technologies impact the knowledge, skills, and expectations students bring to the educational experience. Accordingly, recent developments in teaching and learning afford educators new ways to approach educational processes to better address the needs of digital learners. In this section, I provide an overview of instruction, instructional design, and theories of instruction and learning. This review is fundamental to discourse on teaching and learning, and especially relevant to the education of digital learners. These principles can inform our efforts to educate students for whom networked and digital technologies have become an integral part of daily life.

Instruction and Instructional Theory

Instruction is the preparation of activities and materials to achieve specific learning goals (Driscoll, 2000; Smith & Ragan, 2005). It involves arranging a set of events or external conditions (e.g., activities, procedures, and materials) to support learners' internal mental processing (internal conditions) (Gagne & Dick, 1983). Instruction takes into account learner characteristics (e.g., interests, needs, prior knowledge and experience); task(s) to be learned; the learning environment; media; and the circumstances in which learning is to take place.

Instructional theories attempt to explain the causal link between specific pedagogical events (e.g., instructional activities, procedures, and materials) and improvements in human learning and performance (Gagne & Dick, 1983). According to Gagne and Dick (1983,),."..theories of instruction attempt to relate specified events comprising instruction to learning processes and learning outcomes, drawing upon knowledge generated by learning research and theory" (p. 264). Instructional theories are prescriptive. They help educators develop more effective instruction by providing them a researched and theoretical basis to guide the design and development of instruction. Gagne's theory of instruction, for example, defines (a) a taxonomy of learning outcomes (verbal information, intellectual skills, cognitive strategies, attitudes, and motor skills), to differentiate types of capabilities learners can acquire, (b) learning hierarchies, the notion that for specific learning tasks, learners must acquire elemental skills prior to learning complex skills; (c) events of instruction, a sequence of events that lessons should follow for optimal learning; and (d) conditions of learning, determining the unique conditions necessary for the learner to acquire skills, knowledge or attitudes (Driscoll, 2000, p. 347). An understanding of such concepts provides educators and instructional developers a means to establish the conditions for learning, develop effective instruction, and ultimately enhance learning outcomes.

Learning Theory

Learning is a change in an individual's knowledge, attitude, behavior, beliefs, or capabilities resulting from his/her experience in the environment rather than other conditions, such as drugs or physiological intervention (Mayer, 2009; Mayer, 1982). In the 1950s, behaviorism was the accepted view of learning in American psychological science (Bruer, 1997). In the behaviorist view, an external environment can be arranged so that when stimuli get presented to a subject, a desired response ensues. Behaviorist precepts of learning stress observable changes in performance through teacher-initiated, stimulus-response approaches. Behaviorism is an elegant theory. Many current instructional practices are based on it. However, detractors claim, among other things, that deconstructing content into small manageable chucks de-contextualizes it, masking relationships among concepts. Moreover, behaviorism does not explain internal mental processes (Magliaro, Lockee, & Burton, 2005). It evokes the idea that instruction is something that is done to students without them engaging in their own deep mental processing. If instructors arrange the right external conditions, they can map what they know onto students' minds.

Cognitive science is the study of how the human mind works, how people think, remember, and learn. Studies in cognitive science, unlike behaviorism, explore internal mental processes. Cognitive information processing is an information processing perspective of cognition, advocated by most cognitive learning theorists (Smith & Ragan, 2005). Cognition is characterized by transformation of information from stimuli in the environment, to internal mental processes, to a response by the learner. Key stages of cognitive information processing include."..attention, selective (feature) perception, short-term memory, rehearsal, long-term memory storage, and retrieval" (Gagne & Dick, 1983, p. 266). Understanding the information processing stages can help instructors arrange instructional events (external conditions) to support internal mental operations at each stage of processing. For instance, learners' prior knowledge and experience are integral to helping them encode new information with existing knowledge. As new information is attended to, learners try to relate it to what they already know. When learners relate new information to existing knowledge, information becomes memorable. Suppose, for example, learners are studying new and somewhat abstract topics about atoms and electrons. When studying electrons orbiting the nucleus, the lesson might include a description of the solar system. The solar system depiction helps make the information more memorable as learners associate the new information (i.e., electrons orbiting the nucleus) with something already familiar, planet rotations around the sun in our solar system.

Constructivism is an educational philosophy that asserts learners construct their own reality, meaning, and knowledge from their experiences (Smith & Ragan, 2005; Jonassen, 2000). Learning is an active process in which meaning-making is an individualized, idiosyncratic process. Knowledge cannot be instructed by teachers nor can they map their reality on to the minds of learners. Teaching is viewed as a process of helping learners construct meaning by providing them authentic learning experiences and guiding them through the meaning-making process. Characteristics of constructivist learning, as described by Jonassen, Peck, and Wilson (1999) and cited in Partlow and Gibbs (2003, p. 70) include:

a. learning is active. Learners integrate new information and experiences with existing knowledge and mental models. They create their own knowledge and meaning and do not passively receive information from the instructor;
b. multiple perspectives are valued and necessary;
c. rather than competitive, learning is collaborative and cooperative;

d. learners are given control and responsibility for learning. Learning should be student-centered and the instructor adjusts her or his role from that of instructor to that of learning guide, facilitator, and coach;
e. learning is authentic and real-world based. Learners should be provided complex, authentic, and relevant problems (Driscoll, 2000).

When characteristics of constructivism manifest themselves in the classroom, they can be observed as specific student behaviors and teaching practices. Ravitz et al. (2000) state that indicators of constructivist practices can be grouped in the following categories: (a) project-based learning; (b) group work; (c) problem-solving; and (d) reflective thought. Additional components of constructivist pedagogy include an emphasis on active engagement in learning characterized by student projects and limited direct instructional (instructivist) activities (Becker & Riel, 2000).

Instructional Design

Because of the complexity of developing effective instruction, educators follow instructional design (ID) processes. ID is a systems approach to the design and development of instructional materials, activities, information resources, and evaluation that is guided by theories of instruction and learning (Smith & Ragan, 2005). The ID process helps instructors to first understand student interests, experiences, and learning needs and from this information to develop strategies, materials, and assessments aimed at helping students attain course objectives. Inherent in the process is continual evaluation and revision. Moreover, ID helps to ensure that instruction is developed methodically. The main components of ID models typically include analysis, design, development and evaluation. ID models serve to identify efficient and effective procedures for the design of instruction. For example, Dick, Carey, and Carey (2008, pp. 6-8) present a model that embodies theories, procedures, and techniques for instructional designers. It includes the following components:

1. identify instructional/learning goals
2. conduct instructional analysis
3. analyze learners and contexts
4. write performance objectives
5. develop assessment instruments
6. develop instructional strategy
7. develop and select instructional materials
8. design and conduct formative evaluation
9. revise instruction
10. design and conduct summative evaluation

These processes will be discussed further in the case study presented later in the chapter. Even when they are used informally, they can lead to more effective and efficient instruction and ultimately improved learning. While some instructional systems require teams of designers and developers that implement these processes in a highly formalized manner, individual instructors can used them informally in their courses with positive results.

CASE STUDY

The proliferation of digital technologies, coupled with an increasing number of technically sophisticated students with high educational expectations, requires media educators to rethink conventional teaching and learning. In 2005 another faculty member and I developed a technology intensive core course in digital media for the Journalism and Multimedia Arts (JMA) program. The course helps students develop technical proficiency in industry standard development technologies (software and hardware) and broaden their conceptual knowledge of digital technologies (e.g., formats, applications, industry uses, terms, people). To account for the needs of digital learners in the

JMA program and engage them meaningfully, we predicated our curriculum development on current principles of teaching and learning; based on the premise that knowledge is not transmitted from teacher to student but rather individually constructed by the learner. Here I will utilize a course-based case study to:

1. examine precepts of instruction, learning, instructional design, and learning theory and their relevance to teaching and learning in a digital age;
2. examine how these teaching and learning precepts were implemented; and
3. describe challenges when instituting new instructional practices and provide related recommendations.

Rationale for Case Study

Based on work in cognitive psychology, it is generally agreed that learning is enhanced when students engage in problem-solving (Mayer, 1992). According to Merrill (2002),

"Many current instructional models suggest that the most effective learning products or environments are those that are problem-centered and involve the student in four distinct phases of learning: (a) activation of prior experience, (b) demonstration of skills, (c) application of skills, and (d) integration of these skills into real-world activities." (p. 44)

This is relevant to the education of digital learners for three primary reasons. First, as mentioned earlier, students, particularly those entering communication media programs, have likely had exposure to new innovations in teaching and learning that were problem-based and espoused constructivist precepts. For many years, learners have met in classrooms with teachers who take the role of lecturer (Bork, 1996) and minimal interaction occurs. Recent advances in teaching and learning endeavor to promote student engagement, critical thinking, problem-solving, and collaboration, which ultimately prepares students to be productive citizens in a technologically sophisticated world. Second, in media programs, course outcomes, specifically in design and development classes, lend themselves to problem-based learning approaches that involve life-like projects. Huang (2009, p. 264) reports that a project approach to learning,

... requires a great depth of planning and persuasion based on research and reading. It mandates students to have a solid grasp of hands-on skills and to learn more if necessary; especially when they have made mistakes...[it] embodies all the integration endeavors in the balancing game and truly reflects the full spectrum of Bloom's Taxonomy. (p. 246)

Third, digital learners live in a world inundated with computing devices and associated interfaces that afford new modes of interaction, communication and ways to solve problems. Not only do media graduates need proficiency in software, hardware and programming, but they need problem-solving and analytical skills. Ubiquitous technology necessitates that digital learners and future professionals and leaders in their fields are proficient in using technology to solve problems in creative ways. Graduates of media programs should possess skills in the following areas: software and hardware, programming, creativity and innovation, problem-solving, and analytical skills (Haung, 2009).

The course considered in the following section is used as a case to explore issues faced by educators who teach courses in communication media, to increasing populations of digital learners. An overview of the course is followed by examples of my efforts to premise teaching practices on principles of instruction and learning, specifically problem-based learning and constructivism. The aforementioned topics of instructional and learning theory and instructional design are considered as they guide the curriculum design and teaching approaches.

Course Description

Duquesne University's department of Journalism and Multimedia Arts (JMA) provides students a unique educational experience that blends journalism, media, digital design, and computing. The curriculum prepares students to become effective and thoughtful civic communicators and media developers who are versed in: (a) the complex role media play in society; (b) media operations; (c) digital multimedia design and development; and (d) media regulation and ethics. Graduates go to work for newspapers, magazines, television and radio stations, public relations and advertising agencies, and web and multimedia design and development industries.

Like the majority of new media educational programs, JMA endeavors to balance conceptual and technological skill learning (Huang, 2009; Ryan & Switzer, 2001). Dennis et al. (2003, p. 297) noted that, "No other field takes emerging communication technologies as seriously as journalism and mass communication." Correspondingly, the JMA curriculum is suffused with technology. It must be responsive to tectonic technological shifts that have instigated changes in, among other things, human communication behavior, news reporting, and media preparation and distribution.

The digital media course is introductory. It takes an integrative approach to communication (digital) media by combining principles of communication, art, design, and technology. Students work on projects that engage them in media design activities aimed to enrich professional communication. In addition, they demonstrate skill in using industry standard software to create digital media content. There are several sections of the course, all of which are taught in a computer laboratory. The course has several goals that can be categorized as conceptual-theoretical, technical, and design and development. This categorization defines the overall foundations of the course but is not meant to be absolute for there is certainly overlap among them. Conceptual-theoretical relates to educating students in essential design precepts, including, among others, color, typography, document design and layout, information architecture, graphic formats, digital imaging, and video and sound editing. The Technical aspects pertain to rudimentary computing concepts and networking fundamentals. Instructors review concepts such as domain name, IP address, uniform resources locator, Internet protocols (FTP, HTTP), file management, and network drive configurations. Additionally, students are versed in hardware operations (e.g., scanners, cameras). For the Design and Development component, students study how to design and development content for multiple media distribution outlets. They develop skills and knowledge in web publishing, print document design, illustration, video and sound recording. Through these activities, students gain proficiency in industry software.

Students

Most students who enroll in the course are freshman and sophomore, primarily journalism and digital media majors. However, a substantial portion of them are from outside the JMA major enrolling from disciplines such as business, pharmacy, computer science, and music. The course is popular with a total of five sections being offer each semester. Students who enroll are intelligent, hardworking, and motivated by a desire to learn the topics presented in the syllabus. The majority of them are representative of their generation: extremely proficient digital media consumers who navigate most interfaces with ease. Many are avid users of social networking sites, blogs, website, games, and mobile device applications.

Instructional Apprcaches

Analysis

As mentioned, the Dick, Carey, and Carey (2008) instructional design model includes ten components that we (course instructors) adhered to, even if only informally. The analysis described in this section corresponds to the first four components of the model: (a) instructional/learning goals; (b) instructional analysis; (c) learners and contexts; and (d) performance objectives. To solidify instructional goals, we consulted with industry leaders, internal and external (to the university) educators, and local businesses and industries to evaluate emerging trends, processes, and technologies. We asked these individuals, among other things, what topics should the course cover and what should our graduates know and be able to do in order to be competent professionals. From this, we compiled a list of goals or course topics. Next, we conducted an instructional analysis by identifying the steps or processes one must perform to achieve each goal, which helped us determined the skills and knowledge required for goal attainment. In some cases, we outlined detailed steps that later served as a foundation for course lessons. For the learner and context analysis, although we were quite familiar with our students and the environment, we made class observations, conducted formal and informal analyses (e.g., surveys, interviews) to ascertain students' knowledge and interests, and we reviewed student work from other courses. This provided us information about student preferences as well as entry-level knowledge and skills. Finally, based on the aforementioned steps, we wrote detailed performance objectives for each course goal. Individual instructors wrote their own objectives. While we established course goals for all sections, each instructor determined his/her objectives for reaching those goals.

In the following paragraphs, I elaborate further on this analysis by providing specific examples related to its outcomes. The analysis was essential to our work. Among other things, it helped us learn a great deal about students' background, which informed course development and enabled us to acquire technologies to better support students.

A multitude of factors affect the education of college students, one of which is student background knowledge and experience. What students bring to the classroom, in many ways, influences the pace of a course; the depth of ancillary topics covered; temporal patterns, when topics get presented; class interactions, amount of questions and remediation; peer and instructor tutoring, among other things. Each semester on the first day of class, instructors survey students to collect information about their knowledge and experience with digital media, the goals they want to accomplish in the course, and their familiarity with computing hardware and software. The compilation of data over the past several years provides a unique profile of students. These data are essential to media educators because they help them gauge student competencies and learning needs. With this information, instructors can more effectively establish course goals, objectives and corresponding assessments (i.e., tests that measure whether or not students achieved the objectives). For instance, we have observed that students bring to the classroom a wealth of experience with digital media and technology. Their ability to operate interfaces is extremely high, which can be emboldening. However, there is often an inclination among students that given one's proficiency at using interfaces and manipulating digital media, the transition to a larger scale client-base project is negligible. We find that many are unaware of the development time require for media projects, conceptual design and planning, technical requirements, media formats, coding, and time management. Some entry-level students experience difficulty with factors such as file and time management, which become critical in major course projects. Running out of disk space, inability to locate files, problems encountered when moving linked media, and attempting to complete a semester project in a week's time are common issues for beginning students. Moreover, some students are not aware of what they need to know. A student who has previously created a website may believe that he/she is proficient in web development and thus perceive some course topics as too elemental. Often these individuals find the demands of developing a website for a client far exceed their current proficiency level. Therefore, it is incumbent upon instructors to provide students, despite their proficiency at media consumption or their perceived technical proficiency, a sound foundation is the rudiments of technology, as well as design and development processes. Instructors realize, however, that some students enter the course with high technology skills. In such cases, the instructors individually assess the student's competency and then, when appropriate, modify course projects to encourage the individual to challenge and further develop his/her skills.

When the course was initially developed, goals and objectives were established based on feedback collected from industry leaders in the communication media fields. Each semester those goals are reconciled with data obtained from students as instructors attempt to address student needs without comprising course goals. For example, students are often interested in learning new and poplar software applications and thus may request instruction on a software program. If the program is within the purview of the course capstone project, instructors will consider adding it. At the same time, students consistently request that instructors make technical notes (i.e., class notes, slides) available for review. Such requests have been met. All sections of the course have websites, where students can access class notes, slides, project assets files, the syllabus, and assignments. Each instructor has notes about how to perform specific software tasks, the purpose of which is to support self-directed learning. Notes include tutorials on software operations needed to complete projects. They are tailored by each instructor. In addition, one instructor developed detail instructor notes that are available to students in all sections. These are comprehensive tutorials on digital media topics such image optimization and video compression as well as step-by-step instructions for software operations. In addition to websites, all course sections have Blackboard sites that are primarily used for the posting of grades.

An outcome based on student feedback, industry leader feedback, and class observations was the adoption of Sonic Foundry's Mediasite. This system video records classes and broadcasts them over the Internet. Available live or in archived fashion, students can see the instructor teaching, any graphical support materials shown to the class, and the output from computers and DVDs. Students can view the materials on or off campus. Virtually all the course content is accessible and searchable, over the Web. Students who miss class due to illness can review the recordings.

Mediasite and detailed instructor notes are two examples of course components that espouse constructivist's precepts. A characteristic of constructivist learning is providing learners control and responsibility for learning (Jonassen, Peck, & Wilson, 1999). Recorded classes accompanied by detailed notes allow students to reflect on content in a way that suits their learning needs. Students control the content. They access it any time and organize it in ways that makes sense to them. During a lecture, the instructor controls the pace and sequence of topics, which may be contrary to how students learn best. These two components allow students to manage the pace and sequence of instruction by accessing only the content they need at that moment. Additionally, Mediasite enables instructors to evaluate their own teaching. By reviewing the videos of classes, instructors can assess their teaching methods and style in great detail, which enables them to make refinements.

Another benefit of Mediasite and instructor notes is that they free students from note-taking during class demonstrations. Students often want to take notes to remember information and ultimately enhance their learning. However, excessive note-taking or trying to represent complex computing operations in written form may be too cognitively demanding. When students write or type notes during technology demonstrations, they shift attention between the instructor, typing, and note-taking, which invariably causes them to miss steps. Many students fall behind because they are unable to take notes and follow a demonstration. Note-taking is a complex activity that requires much cognitive effort. As Piolat, Olive and Kellogg (2005, p. 306), note, "It is a unique kind of written activity that cumulates both the inherent difficulties of comprehending a message and of producing a new written product." Mediasite and instructor notes allow students to select and attend to the information that is most relevant at a specific moment. Students can follow demonstrations without their attention being diverted by the complexity of note-taking. Those who benefit from written notes can write them as they study the materials outside of class.

Design and Development

In this section, I discussed design and development as encapsulated by the three stages of the Dick, Carey, and Carey (2008) ID model: (a) develop assessment instruments; (b) develop instructional strategy; and (c) develop and select instructional materials. Based the goals and objectives outlined in the analysis, we identified assessment instruments that corresponded to the type of knowledge and skills that characterized the course objectives and were capable of measuring relevant student performance. For instance, if the goal was for students to be proficient in web technologies, then assessing their knowledge about the origins of the Internet would be insufficient. It would be more congruous to use a combination of assessments such as objective tests that measure one's conceptual knowledge of web technologies (e.g., key facts, terms, and developments) and multiple performance/skill-based tests that measure one's ability to develop for the web. The assessment instruments that we eventually created included objective tests, design rubrics, performance tests (e.g., creating small projects while being observed), live demonstrations/critiques, and work portfolios.

Guided by the analysis we devised strategies to help students achieve course learning goals and objectives. Strategies include activities to motivate and engage students and/or methods of presenting new content that include examples, demonstrations, and opportunities for student participation (Dick, Carey & Carey, 2008). For example, one goal gleaned from the analysis was that students should recognize various forms of branding and thus be capable of developing logos for print and digital formats. This goal necessitates a number of sub-skills and knowledge to accomplish. Table 1 presents an instructional strategy approach for this goal, specifically tailored to logo design. It illustrates how the strategy could be implemented during class. In Table 1, the phases represent the core components of the strategy. The events are the activities that occur during each phase.

After identifying instructional strategies, instructors developed and/or produce materials, such as learning guides, class notes, presentation slides, and case studies. They continually observe students to evaluate their success and to determine how effective their methods and materials were in supporting learning. Based on these observations, they may refine their strategies and materials. These processes are highly iterative whereby methods and materials get implemented, evaluated, and refined on an ongoing basis. Central to this process and to the views of all instructors is the idea that pedagogy is designed to accommodate students. It is grounded in or reflects student needs, and is not solely prescribed by the instructor.

As mentioned, the course design is premised on cognitive learning principles and constructivism. This is not to say that there are no behavioral or instructivist pedagogical aspects. Instructors often

Table 1. Implementation of instructional strategy

Phase of instruction	Instructional strategy - Events
Instructional orientation	Provide overview of topic, brand creation, logo design.
	Gain student attention by introducing relevant and familiar examples.
	Discuss topic (branding) importance and relevance to previous topics and student learning.
Content presentation	Review foundational precepts such as customer needs, information and logo design (e.g., conveying meaning, graphical elements, lines, prominence, color, type).
	Demonstrate design with examples and non-examples (e.g., logos that do not represent specific precepts).
Practice	Ask students to identify and discuss branding and logo designs based on specific information and graphical design precepts. Provide feedback.
Content presentation	Demonstrate/draw a prototype logo design for students.
	Provide students a short case summary of a company or organization that requires branding, logo design services.
Practice	Ask students to design (draw) a print logo based on the case summary using design precepts. Provide feedback.
Content presentation	Demonstrate for students how to create a digital rendering of a logo with software program.
Practice	Ask students to create a digital rendering of the printed logo they made previously. Provide feedback.
Feedback/Evaluation Evaluation	Monitor student work and provide coaching.
	Ask students to evaluate their own work using design rubrics and then provide the instructor a summary of the evaluation.
	Ask students to collect feedback from fellow students.
	Evaluate student works and provide feedback.

deconstruct content in to small manageable bits of information (Cronjé, 2006) that they present to students. They give practice exercises or assessments for which they provide reinforcement so that appropriate responses become conditioned (Bruer, 1997). Quizzes are assigned that assess factual knowledge. For instance, during web development lessons, instructors may segment html coding elements, Cascading Style Sheets (CSS), and programming into manageable chucks to prevent cognitive overload. They may require students to submit segments of code that get progressively refined through instructor feedback so that specific coding practices, rules, and style become routine.

Typically, classes include a presentation of core concepts as well as a demonstration or modeling of how those concepts apply to real-world situations. Students receive projects that require them to analyze problems (or needs), define and design solutions, and then develop technology-based applications that address those problems (or needs). Students receive problem cases and scenarios and instructors coach them as they develop technical solutions. Engaging students in projects involves all the elements that characterize competence in media program graduates (Huang, 2009).

Assignments are structured so that each new project escalates in complexity, challenging students' core proficiency. As mentioned, assignment sequence and topic segmentation initially follows a behavioral orientation to reduce complexity. However, as the course progresses, exposing students to more complex problems and the relationships among concepts are important and characteristic of a cognitive constructivist orientation. As an example, for one assignment students develop a communication campaign that requires them to conduct audience and informational analyses and from which they design and develop a digital media campaign comprised of a website, video commercial, informational brochure or poster, business cards, and logo. Each component of the campaign is reduced to small units of instruction such as coding, image optimization, video editing, design and layout. Students must apply these foundational precepts in the development of the campaign. While they may understand image optimization, for example, using optimization techniques to meet client needs adds new levels of complexity and opportunities for deep learning.

For the campaign, each student must first identify a client with whom to work during the semester. Students interact with their clients to learn about their needs. Clients evaluate and approve designs prototypes. Project types must fall in to one of the following categories:

- **Category 1:** Develop a campaign to promote a professional business or organization. The intent of this type of campaign would be to develop materials for a business or organization that does not currently have the media to disseminate information about its services.
- **Category 2:** Develop a campaign to foster awareness of an important social, humanitarian, environmental, political, or health cause/issue. The intent of this type of campaign would be to make people aware of an important issue such as conditions of the homeless, global warming, world hunger, energy conservation, human rights, or animal rights, among others.

After students identify a client, they must write a project proposal and specifications document that outlines the creative approach to develop the media campaign, including: (a) a rationale for the project; (b) analysis of need; (c) description of the intended audience for whom the project is being created; (d) technical and media requirements; and (e) implementation and dissemination plan, including timeline and budget; (f) formative evaluation.

This communication campaign project includes specific media elements:

- **Illustration:** This is an exercise in color, illustration, and design. Using precepts of color and design, students study and analyze the professional illustrations from ten companies or organizations. They summarize their findings. Based on the analysis, students use a digital illustration program to create an illustration for the media campaign. The illustration (e.g., logo) must be prepared for a variety of media outlets (e.g., television/video, print, Web).
- **Print design and layout:** Part A: This is a creative exercise in typography, print and page layout design, and image manipulation. Students create the following: (1) business card; (2) trifold brochure. Part B: Students work in teams, to develop a newsletter for a client.
- **Motion and sound:** Students study and analyze five television commercials (2 local, 2 national, and 1 international). Based on this analysis, they use images, composited video, and visual and sound effects to create a commercial. The final commercial is deployed on a DVD and the Web.
- **Web publishing:** Students identify and analyze websites that may relate to their topic. They write a design document that communicates the purpose of the site, its design and layout as well as specific technical features that enhance aesthetics and usability. Based on precepts of color, typography, design, layout and usability, students create a website to support their media campaign. According to Merrill

(2002), learning is facilitated by engaging students in solving problems, using their prior knowledge as a foundation for new learning, and having students apply and integrate new knowledge. What follows is a common example of how we endeavor to reflect these principles as well as constructivist practices (Ravitz et al., 2000; Jonassen, Peck, & Wilson, 1999) in course instruction:

- **Real problems and active learning:** Students are assigned a real-world problem to solve (develop a media campaign for a real client). It is important that the project reflect the complexity of what media professionals encounter in the real world. The media campaign project example has multiple dimensions of complexity, including information gathering, design and layout, collaboration, time and personnel management, file management, software skills, and interpersonal skills.
- **Prior knowledge:** Developing a media campaign is a new experience for most students. To activate prior knowledge, we discuss the activity in the context of something with which students are already familiar, such as writing a story or a research paper. We provide examples as well as probing questions about how to collect information, how to understand what the message is, how to convey the message, and how to ensure one fully understands the client's needs. Students are then assigned to collect information from the client and to clearly define the client's message.
- **Multiple perspectives:** After students have defined the message and the content, they must share it with others to get a multi-perspective assessment of its clarity and the related content. Students must also explain the message from the client's perspective and from the customer's perspective. A multiple perspective view of the information allows students to identify ambiguity. For instance, while the message may be clear to the client or manager it may not be understood by the people who will actually need the information (i.e., customers).
- **Apply and integrate:** Students layout their message and content for specific media, such as print, web, and video. For example, if a portion of the media campaign is a print brochure, poster, or flyer, students would draw it out on paper and ask the instructor, client, and other students to provide them feedback and then revise accordingly.
- **Learner control:** Instructors might then demonstrate how students could develop the media elements using a particular software application and then ask students to apply what has been demonstrated. Instructors provide scaffolding or interim support to students to help reduce the disparity between what they can do and what they need to accomplish in order to successfully complete the task. As student proficiency increases, instructors reduce scaffolding but provide individual coaching as needed. Throughout the course, the instructor's role alters from teacher, to facilitator, to coach who helps individual students.
- **Collaboration:** Throughout the activity, students work with others and in groups to practice, assess each others' work, and to brainstorm ideas. Students who are proficient in particular areas help others with their projects.
- **Evaluation:** The ultimate assessment of student work is the client's review and acceptance of the project. Here again, the evaluation is authentic and allows students to determine if they met the client's needs.

The media campaign project engages students in solving real-world problems, similar to the challenges encountered by media professionals. At the same time, it involves learning on multiple dimensions. It requires knowledge of design theory and development process, technical proficiency as well as skill in planning, time management, and collaboration.

Evaluation

The evaluation described in this section corresponds to the two components of the Dick, Carey, and Carey (2008) ID model: (a) design and conduct formative evaluation; and (b) revise instruction. Their model also includes summative evaluation. However, because summative evaluation is usually a formal form of evaluation performed by independent evaluators is beyond the scope of this chapter.

On an ongoing basis, we employ several course evaluation methods. First, each semester students critique classes and provide instructors feedback. In addition, we survey students to assess the positive and negative aspects of the course. Feedback is reviewed and discussed and, where appropriate, modifications to the course are made. Second, because the course is rooted in technology and digital media, it is subject to continuous updates, review, and revisions. Software updates, new emergent technologies and design approaches warrant continual modifications. For example, software updates are persistent. As new versions get released, class notes must be revised; procedures for accomplishing design and development tasks must also get amended. Additionally, we continue to consult industry professionals who provide input regarding course topics and direction. Third, instructors provide each other feedback about course modifications and emergent trends in new media design and development.

Recommendations

In the following paragraphs, I provide several additional observations and recommendations regarding the teaching and learning of digital learners.

Instructors must encourage students to plan prior to developing digitals materials and to adhere to iterative design-development processes. Often students attempt to move from the onset of a problem directly to digital design, at times without full conceptualization of the problem. As a result, after an artifact has been constructed, the individual realizes that the design was erroneous. For instance, a student may develop a media campaign for a client who has a small business. He/she is required to meet with the client who provides the student with a need or a problem (e.g., we need to promote our business but do not have the resources to do so). Subsequent to the initial meeting, students have exhibited a tendency to begin making digital creations/designs. There is often the perception that after the initial meeting with the client, one can build from start to finish. Moreover, because some students are proficient in digital media, they tend to be more inclined to begin digital development, prior to conceptual design. In some cases, students construct the media campaign with minimal input from the client, only to learn that they did not adequately address the problem or the client's need. Some students seemingly have the perception that conceptual design can be circumvented by digital creation.

Implementing new teaching and learning methods can be challenging. Some students have the expectation that instructors lecture, and they listen and respond to questions. When instructors implement alternatives instructional methods, students may perceive that something is wrong or that the quality of instruction is lower, even though the outcome may be higher. Often when students engage in problem-solving or constructivist approaches, the classroom changes from a lecture with periodic questions to an open environment where students are talking, walking around, and interacting. At the onset, this may appears unorganized or unstructured. Thus, is it important to inform students about the plan prior to the class, provide a clear rational for the activity, and propose a sequence of events or timeline, and described intended outcomes.

A challenge with respect to the education of digital learners is managing diverse skill levels in the classroom. While most students are proficient consumers of digital media like the web, social networking, and texting, some are less familiar with web (e.g., XHTML, CSS, XML, PHP) and multimedia (e.g., audio/video software tools, compression) development technologies. When there is a diverse skill level among students, team mentoring projects can be used, whereby a senior more experience student partners with a novice. The team is given cases for which they develop digital artifacts. A benefit of the approach is that both students (experts and novice) work through project specifications, design, development, and usability while learning from the class and each other. Teaching the novices helps the more experience student solidified what he/she knows about the topic. It also gives them valuable teaching/mentoring practice. The approach aids the novice who learns the technical aspects of the project from a more senior/experience students. A disadvantage of this approach is when students mismanage their time. They tend to allocate responsibility for specific portions of the project, with the senior member usually taking on the development components. This serves as a disadvantage to the novice because she/he doesn't learn the development aspect of the project. This can be easily circumvented by requiring students to make a plan, and meeting periodically with them to ensure they are on task.

Another challenge for communication media educators is to keep pace not only with recent teaching and learning methods but also rapidly changing technologies and preparing associated instructional materials. Because many students are accustomed to digital technologies and associated interfaces, they are highly capable and possess high educational expectations. While young people become increasingly proficient in using digital technologies, many educators, besieged by a proliferation of computing devices and software, struggle to stay current and are perplexed about ways to meaningfully infuse technologies in teaching and learning. Updating skills and learning current technologies continuously is expected of all educators (Ružić-Dimitrijević & Maja Dimitrijević, 2010; Turner, 2005) but it is especially true of those who teach communication media to digital learners.

FUTURE RESEARCH DIRECTIONS

In this chapter, I examined the education of digital learners by reviewing foundational precepts of instruction and learning and by making observations pertaining to the development and subsequent teaching of a communication media course. I discussed several general observations about the background experience today's students bring to the classroom. For example, because digital interfaces are ubiquitous in society making many complex media development tasks easier, students enter media communications programs with unique technical skills as well as expectations about media development. Interfaces have gotten easier to use but the complexity of many underlying technologies has actually increased. This can have profound educational implications. Have students become highly skilled at navigating interfaces to accomplish their tasks but less cognizant of technological foundations? Future research could investigate the extent to which pervasive easy-to-use- interfaces shape media students': (a) expectations about media use and development, (b) awareness or comprehension of core technologies, and (c) ability to develop digital media products.

Instructional theory, learning theory, and instructional design are fundamental to the development of effective learning programs. However, in technology intensive fields such as journalism and media communications, instructors may be disinclined to embrace these precepts in favor of transfer-centered pedagogical approaches that emphasize technological capabilities. Rather than grounding teaching and learning first and foremost on these elemental principles, instructors develop and implement instruction based largely on the technical characteristics of media, which usually impedes lasting learning improvements (Mayer, 2009). This is perpetuated by many factors including time demands on instructors, continual technical advancement, and by the fact that the aforementioned theoretical precepts are often tangential to instructors' educational training. Instructors may feel that there is simply insufficient time to stay current, maintain technical proficiency and, at the same time, prepare curricula based on theoretical and instructional design principles with which they are only marginally familiar. Future research is needed that investigates new methodologies and models for rapid instructional development that is specifically attuned to the communications media field and the challenges these educators face due to constant technological change.

CONCLUSION

Digital devices and associated interfaces are commonplace today, which is a key factor in why so many young people are highly proficient digital media consumers. Some are also keen media developers. The knowledge and experience they bring to the college classroom has profound implications for teaching and for how educators design educational courses. Technological advances have been pervasive and recurring, instigating tectonic shifts in human communication. The rate of technological change is unprecedented. Software and devices rapidly transform as new technologies get introduce while others become obsolete. This poses daunting challenges for educators who endeavor to keep pace and/or who strive to find constancy in the subject matter taught in courses comprised of digital learners. In many cases, these factors contribute to educators employing transfer-centric pedagogy whereby they focus mainly on technological capabilities while adhering to instructivist practices.

Media educators face many challenges and opportunities teaching technology intensive courses to digitally competent students who are accustomed to ubiquitous technological innovation. Current theories of learning and instruction can and should guide them when developing and teaching courses. Adhering to sound instructional and learning precepts such as understanding students' prior knowledge, focusing on authentic problems, affording learners control over their own learning, have great potential for engaging today's digital learners in meaningful learning experiences.

REFERENCES

Bandura, A. (1977). Self-efficacy: Toward a unifying theory of behavioral change. *Psychological Review*, *84*, 191–215. doi:10.1037/0033-295X.84.2.191

Bandura, A. (1994). Self-efficacy. In Ramachaudran, V. S. (Ed.), *Encyclopedia of human behavior* (*Vol. 4*, pp. 71–81). New York, NY: Academic Press.

Becker, H. J., & Riel, M. (2000, December). *Teacher professional engagement and constructivist-compatible computer use*. Retrieved April 23, 2011, from http://www.crito.uci.edu/tlc/findings/report_7/.

Bork, A. (1996). Highly interactive multimedia technology and future learning. *Journal of Computing in Higher Education, 8*(1), 3–28. doi:10.1007/BF02942393

Bruer, J. T. (1997). *Schools for thought: A science of learning in the classroom.* Cambridge, MA: The MIT Press.

Compeau, D. R., & Higgins, C. A. (1995a). Application of social cognitive theory to training for computer skills. *Information Systems Research, 6*(2), 118–143. doi:10.1287/isre.6.2.118

Compeau, D. R., & Higgins, C. A. (1995b). Computer self-efficacy: Development of a measure and initial test. *Management Information Systems Quarterly, 19*(2), 189–211. doi:10.2307/249688

Cronjé, J. (2006). Paradigms regained: Toward integrating objectivism and constructivism in instructional design and the learning sciences. *Educational Technology Research and Development, 54*(4), 387–416. doi:10.1007/s11423-006-9605-1

Dennis, E. E., Meyer, P., Sundar, S. S., & Pryor, L., Rogers, Everett M., Pavlik, J. (2003). Learning reconsidered: Education in the digital age. *Journalism & Mass Communication Educator, 57*(4), 292–317.

Dick, W., Carey, L., & Carey, J. O. (2008). *The systematic design of instruction.* Boston, MA: Allyn & Bacon.

Driscoll, M. P. (2000). *Psychology of learning for instruction.* Needham, MA: Allyn & Bacon.

Gagne, R. M., & Dick, W. (1983). Instructional psychology. *Annual Review of Psychology, 34,* 261–295. doi:10.1146/annurev.ps.34.020183.001401

Hailikari, T., Nevgi, A., & Lindblom-Ylänne, S. (2007). Exploring alternative ways of assessing prior knowledge, its components and their relation to student achievement: A mathematics based case study. *Studies in Educational Evaluation, 33*(3-4), 320–337. doi:10.1016/j.stueduc.2007.07.007

Huang, E. (2009). Teaching button-pushing versus teaching thinking the state of new media education in US universities. *Convergence: The International Journal of Research into New Media Technologies, 15*(2), 233–247. doi:10.1177/1354856508101584

Jonassen, D. H. (2000). *Computers as mindtools for schools.* Upper Saddle River, NJ: Merrill Prentice Hall.

Jonassen, D. H., Peck, K. L., & Wilson, B. G. (1999). *Learning with technology.* Columbus, OH: Prentice Hall.

King, R. C., & Xia, W. D. (1997). Media appropriateness: Effects of experience on communication media choice. *Decision Sciences, 28*(4), 877–910. doi:10.1111/j.1540-5915.1997.tb01335.x

Kohut, A. (2008). *Audience segments in a changing news environment: Key news audiences now blend online and traditional sources.* Pew Research Center Biennial News Consumption Survey. The Pew Research Center for the People & Press.

Lenhart, A. (2009). *Adults and social network websites.* Pew Internet & American Life Project. Retrieved December 23, 2010, from http://www.pewinternet.org/Reports/2009/Adults-and-Social-Network-Websites.aspx.

Lenhart, L. R., Campbell, S. & Purcell, K. (2010). *Teens and mobile phones.* Pew Internet & American Life Project. Retrieved April 23, 2011, from http://pewinternet.org/Reports/2010/Teens-and-Mobile-Phones.aspx.

Magliaro, S. G., Lockee, B. B., & Burton, J. K. (2005). Direct instruction revisited: A key model for instructional technology. *Educational Technology Research and Development, 53*(4), 41–55. doi:10.1007/BF02504684

Mayer, R. E. (1982). Learning. In Mitzel, H. E. (Ed.), *Encyclopedia of educational research* (pp. 1040–1058). New York, NY: Free Press.

Mayer, R. E. (1992). *Thinking, problem solving, cognition* (2nd ed.). New York, NY: W.H. Freeman.

Mayer, R. E. (2009). *Multi-media learning*. New York, NY: Cambridge University Press.

Merrill, D. M. (2002). First principles of instruction. *Educational Technology Research and Development, 50*(3), 43–59. doi:10.1007/BF02505024

Partlow, K. M., & Gibbs, W. J. (2003). Indicators of constructivist principles in Internet-based courses. *Journal of Computing in Higher Education, 14*(2), 66–95. doi:10.1007/BF02940939

Pew Research Center. (2010). *Americans spending more time following the news*. Pew Research Center. Retrieved May 18, 2011, from http://people-press.org/http://people-press.org/files/legacy-pdf/652.pdf.

Piolat, A., Olive, T., & Kellogg, R. T. (2005). Cognitive effort during note taking. *Applied Cognitive Psychology, 19*(3), 291–312. doi:10.1002/acp.1086

Ravitz, J. L., Becker, H. J., & Wong, Y.-T. (2000). *Constructivist compatible beliefs and practices among US teachers*. (Teaching, Learning & Computing Report 4.) Irvine, CA: Center for Research on Information Technology and Organizations, University of California. Retrieved May 18, 2011, from http://www.crito.uci.edu/TLC/findings/report4/.

Ružić-Dimitrijević, L., & Maja Dimitrijević, M. (2010). Challenges IT instructors face in the self-education process. *Journal of Information Technology Education, 9*, 35–48.

Ryan, M., & Switzer, L. (2001). Balancing arts and sciences, skills, and conceptual content. *Journalism & Mass Communication Educator, 56*(2), 55–68.

Smith, P. L., & Ragan, T. J. (2005). *Instructional design*. Danver, MA: John Wiley & Sons, Inc.

Turner, L. (2005). 20 technology skills every educator should have. *THE Journal*. Retrieved January 4, 2011, from http://thejournal.com/articles/17325_1.

Zhu, L., & Grabowski, B. L. (2006). Web-based animation or static graphics: Is the extra cost of animation worth it? *Journal of Educational Multimedia and Hypermedia, 15*(3), 329–347.

ADDITIONAL READING

Bloom, B. (Ed.). (1956). *Taxonomy of educational objectives: Handbook I: Cognitive domain*. New York: David McKay Co.

Boot, E. W., van Merrienboer, J. G., & Veerman, A. L. (2007). Novice and experienced instructional software developers: effects on materials created with instructional software templates. *Educational Technology Research and Development, 55*(6), 647–666. doi:10.1007/s11423-006-9002-9

Bostock, S. J. (1998). Constructivism in mass higher education: A case study. *British Journal of Educational Technology, 29*(3), 225–240. doi:10.1111/1467-8535.00066

Campbell, K., Schwier, R. A., & Kenny, R. F. (2009). The critical, relational practice of instructional design in higher education: an emerging model of change agency. *Educational Technology Research and Development, 57*(5), 645–663. doi:10.1007/s11423-007-9061-6

Clark, R. (1994). Media will never influence learning. *Educational Technology Research and Development, 42*(2), 21–29. doi:10.1007/BF02299088

Coberna, W. W., Schuster, D., Adamsa, B., Applegatea, B., Skjolda, B., & Undreiub, A. (2010). Experimental comparison of inquiry and direct instruction in science. *Research in Science & Technological Education, 28*(1), 81–96. doi:10.1080/02635140903513599

Fleishmann, K. (2010). The POOL model: Foregrounding an alternative learning and teaching approach for digital media design in higher education. *Art. Design & Communication in Higher Education*, *9*(1), 57–73. doi:10.1386/adch.9.1.57_1

Gerber, S., & Scott, L. (2007). Designing a learning curriculum and technology's role in it. *Educational Technology Research and Development*, *55*(5), 461–478. doi:10.1007/s11423-006-9005-6

Hill, J. R., & Hannafin, M. J. (2001). Teaching and learning in digital environments: The resurgence of resource-based learning. *Educational Technology Research and Development*, *49*(3), 37–52. doi:10.1007/BF02504914

Jonassen, D. H. (2006). On the role of concepts in learning and instructional design. *Educational Technology Research and Development*, *54*(2), 177–196. doi:10.1007/s11423-006-8253-9

Juniu, S. (2006). Use of technology for constructivist learning in a performance assessment class. *Measurement in Physical Education and Exercise Science*, *10*(1), 67–79. doi:10.1207/s15327841mpee1001_5

Kolb, D. (1985). *Learning style inventory*. Boston, MA: McBer and Company.

Kozma, R. B. (1994). Will media influence learning? Reframing the debate. *Educational Technology Research and Development*, *42*(2), 7–19. doi:10.1007/BF02299087

Mayer, R. E., Moreno, R., Boire, M., & Vagge, S. (1999). Maximizing constructivist learning from multimedia communications by minimizing cognitive load. *Journal of Educational Psychology*, *91*(4), 638–643. doi:10.1037/0022-0663.91.4.638

Mayer, R. E., & Sims, V. K. (1994). For whom is a picture worth a thousand words? Extensions of a dual-coding theory of multimedia learning. *Journal of Educational Psychology*, *86*(3), 389–401. doi:10.1037/0022-0663.86.3.389

Neo, M., & Neo, T. K. (2009). Engaging students in multimedia-mediated constructivist learning – Students' perceptions. *Journal of Educational Technology & Society*, *12*(2), 254–266.

Overbaya, A., Pattersonb, A. S., Vasua, E. S., & Grablec, L. L. (2010). Constructivism and technology use: Findings from the IMPACTing leadership project. *Educational Media International*, *47*(2), 103–120. doi:10.1080/09523987.2010.492675

Reigeluth, C. M. (1995). Educational systems development and its relationship to ISD. In Anglin, G. J. (Ed.), *Instructional Technology: Past, Present, and Future* (2nd ed., pp. 84–92). Englewood, CO: Libraries Unlimited, Inc.

Ryberg, T., & Dirckinck-Holmfeld, L. (2008). Power users and patchworking: An analytical approach to critical studies of young people's learning with digital media. *Educational Media International*, *45*(3), 143–156. doi:10.1080/09523980802283608

Yanchar, S. C., South, J. B., Williams, D. D., Allen, S., & Wilson, B. G. (2010). Struggling with theory? A qualitative investigation of conceptual tool use in instructional design. *Educational Technology Research and Development*, *58*(1), 39–60. doi:10.1007/s11423-009-9129-6

Zheng, R., McAlack, M., Wilmes, B., Kohler-Evans, P., & Williamson, J. (2009). Effects of multimedia on cognitive load, self-efficacy, and multiple rule-based problem solving. *British Journal of Educational Technology*, *40*(5), 790–803. doi:10.1111/j.1467-8535.2008.00859.x

KEY TERMS AND DEFINITIONS

Constructivism: An educational philosophy in which learning is viewed as an active process. Learners construct their own reality. Instructors cannot impart their knowledge onto learners. They can provide experiences that support a learner's own construction of knowledge.

Digital Interface: A digital interface is the medium through which humans interact with computers. Interfaces represent an amalgamation of visual, auditory, and functional components that people see, hear, touch, or talk to as they interact with computers (digital devices).

Digital Teaching and Learning: Encompasses the utilization of new media in activities and processes related to instruction and learning.

Human-Computer Interaction and Learning: Refers to interactional processes between learners and computational devices and the extent to which that interaction supports or impedes learning.

Instructional Design: A systematic approach that educators and instructional developers use to guide the design and development of instructional materials, activities, information resources, and evaluation. Following instructional design processes helps ensure effective and efficient instruction and learning experiences. Major phase of instructional design include analysis, design, development, and evaluation.

Instructivism: A form of instruction characterized by focused teaching and teacher-directed approaches. Content is broken down into its elemental parts and sequence accordingly, usually from low to higher complexity. Hierarchical learning or sequence learning is emphasized over life-like situations or complexity. Learners adapt to the instruction rather than accommodations being made for learner needs and preferences.

New Media: A broad term that usually refers to emergent forms of digital multimedia content accessible on various computing platforms and devices. It consists of digital images, video, audio, interactivity, or combinations of these media.

Pedagogy: Generally refers to the practice of teaching including the strategies that are used for instruction and intended to promote learning.

Section 4
Pedagogy and Technology for the Net Generational Classroom

I never teach my pupils; I only attempt to provide the conditions in which they can learn (Albert Einstein).

The classroom of today is radically different from the classroom of the last century, and the differences arise only in part because of our students. The past decade has seen increasing legislation directed at higher education, intensifying demands for accountability from both the general public and legislators, and cost-cutting measures imposed by cash-strapped institutions. These changes take place hand-in-hand with unprepared students, demands for graduates with better skills and knowledge than their predecessors, a rapidly changing workplace, and a rising faculty work load. In these circumstances, pedagogy often takes a back seat. But it is at just such times that pedagogy should assume greater importance.

Pedagogy is important because it "draws attention to the process through which knowledge is produced." (Lusted, 1986, p. 2). What teachers do and how they do it is critically important, to us, to our students, and to society. The chapters in this section provide a wide pedagogical repertory. Scott Roberts and Steven Buzinksi discuss Action Learning assignments as a way to help Net Generation students learn by engaging relevant material using familiar media. Rachel Ellaway and Janet Tworek examine the influences of the Net Generation meme on professional education, and present a digital professionalism framework that not only works within medical education, but can be effective in any applied field. Jessica Fargnoli discusses the rationale and benefits for the use of audio and video capture as a pedagogical tool for engaging and instructing the Net Generation. Sally Blomstrom focuses on service learning as a pedagogical approach for Net Generation learners, and presents a case study as an example. Chris Gurrie and Brandy Fair highlight best practices of teaching and engagement while implementing PowerPoint, as a way to help today's learners better retain course materials. Rukhsana Ahmed examines how technology-enhanced experiential learning methods can enhance Net Generation student learning.

The range of ideas and pedagogies in this chapter offer inspiration in improving teaching and learning. However, it's important to realize that the materials in this section (as in the previous section) are meant to be descriptive, not prescriptive, to provide ideas for those educators wishing to broaden their teaching repertory. There is no one best way to teach, just as there's no one best way to learn.

REFERENCE

Lusted, D. (1986). Why pedagogy? *Screen*, *27*(5), 2–16.

Chapter 17
Action Learning:
Inspire Lasting Learning through Truly Applied Projects

Scott P. Roberts
University of Maryland, USA

Steven G. Buzinski
University of Maryland, USA

ABSTRACT

Students, and in particular those that have come to be known as members of the Net Generation, learn best when they are presented with the opportunity to engage relevant material using media which they perceive to be familiar and effective. Going beyond academic exercises, Action Learning assignments cater to the generational expectation that their actions have immediate and meaningful social implications. Through five component steps, Action Learning projects guide students through identifying, implementing, and evaluating an informed attempt to make a measurable impact on the world beyond their academic buildings. In doing so we create purposeful scholarship, move beyond basic demonstrations of learning, and enhance information encoding for future utilization.

INTRODUCTION

The fundamental aim of an instructor could be defined as having clear goals (outcomes), evidence-based approaches for achieving those goals (means), and a way to objectively measure progress towards them (assessment). The means used to guide students toward this end may vary widely, but the end itself should always be to effectively and efficiently support learning beyond the perfunctory memorization of facts and concepts. The problem we wish to address here is what happens when we restrict our scope to a back and forth exchange of knowledge, when students perform well on assessments but soon thereafter cannot reproduce this initial demonstration of expertise.

DOI: 10.4018/978-1-61350-347-8.ch017

Research in pedagogy and the cognitive sciences suggests that some approaches might be better suited than others to ultimately facilitate advanced and lasting learning. Specifically, the use of pedagogies that move student learning beyond discrete principles and towards integration and application to real-world challenges are positively correlated with information learning, memory, and recall (McDaniel & Fisher, 1991; Bjork, 1988). Action Learning, as we refer to it here, is exactly that; presenting students with an opportunity to demonstrate their learning by taking course content from the classroom and putting it to real use in campus, local, national, and even international communities. The framework described here is focused on creating high-impact, action-focused coursework that integrates contemporary learning theory with modern mechanisms of communication, outreach, and activism.

This level of engagement plays a particularly important role in motivating and inspiring a generation of students that are accustomed to immediate and unbounded access to the internet generally, and social networking technologies specifically, which transcend the traditional boundaries of information discovery and dissemination. Much has been made about the divide between the "Net Generation" (Tapscott, 2009) and previous generations of learners, with some arguments going as far as positing a fundamental shift in the basic cognition of the Net Generation, arguing that their brains are "wired" differently (Matulich, Papp, & Haytko, 2008) and therefore process information in a qualitatively unique way. There is, however, limited research supporting a profound cognitive shift beyond that based on personal observation and intuition (Jones & Healing, 2010). While compelling evidence to support such a radical difference in the basic cognitive processes of Net Generation learners is currently unavailable, there is a burgeoning field of work demonstrating that this group generally has a high level of technology use before college (Eynon, 2009), confidence in using basic computing technologies (Jones, Ramanau, Cross, & Healing, 2010), preferences for internet based-access to content (Kennedy, Judd, Dalgarnot, & Waycott, 2010), and uses computers to support social and educational activities on a daily basis (Kenedy, Judd, Churchward, Gray, & Krause, 2008). These differences suggest that the Net Generation will profit both from the cognitive benefits of the Action Learning approach common to all learners and from the technology-empowered applications specific to their self-identified learning preferences.

In this chapter we first review some of the underlying theoretical and empirical support for engaging students with truly applied assignments. We then outline the essential components of an Action Learning project and present a case study from a senior-level university course. Finally, we discuss some of the challenges of implementing Action Learning coursework and the pedagogical benefits to students, instructors, and the broader campus community.

PEDAGOGICAL MODELS

Perhaps the most widely referenced model for conceptualizing gradations of learning is Bloom's Taxonomy (1956). Bloom's model, which Anderson made minor revisions to (Pohl, 2000), eloquently lays out a continuum of assessment. At the more basic levels a student has demonstrated learning by simply memorizing a fact (remembering) or explaining a concept (understanding). Deeper learning, however, is demonstrated when students use a concept in a novel context (applying), think critically about the validity of the concept and its application (analyzing), defend their analysis (evaluating), and ultimately act upon that analysis and evaluation to develop something meaningful (creating). The essential point here is that instructors must structure assignments and assessments that build on the core knowledge in a meaningful, productive way. Students, regardless of their generational preferences or dispositions, must be engaged and challenged with the opportunity to demonstrate learning at the most advanced levels. However, for students accustomed to creating and sharing information through technology-oriented media among both immediate peers (e.g., Facebook) and the global community (e.g., YouTube comments), it is particularly beneficial to use these tools as the mechanism for housing their learning.

Bloom's taxonomy has served as a conceptual foundation for the contemporary emphasis on problem-based learning, emphasizing cooperative application, analysis, and evaluation in a realistic context. A good deal of scholarly work has demonstrated the effectiveness of engaging students in learning vis-à-vis problem-solving (see Hmelo-Silver, Duncan, & Chinn, 2007) rather than instructor-focused lectures. Indeed the current generation of students is well practiced at solving problems by seeking information from digital resources (Kenedy et al., 2008) in addition to epistemic authorities. Additional support for the efficacy of application models is found in the cognitive sciences, specifically research on information encoding, storage and retrieval (Glass & Holyoak, 1986).

COGNITIVE MODELS

Learning begins with properly encoding information. Regardless of the course topic, encoding involves attending to environmental stimuli (e.g., class discussion), transforming stimuli into usable mental representations, and storing those representations in memory (Glass & Holyoak, 1986). The extent that information is processed will determine the completeness of one's mental representation (Craik & Lockheart, 1972). If information is processed peripherally, that is, if a student thinks about it only briefly, it will result in a partially encoded mental representation. If information is processed for a longer period and with greater scrutiny, a more complete mental representation will be encoded. With extended practice using information (e.g., thinking about how it applies to various scenarios), mental representations become more enriched. The encoding process is important because when students ultimately wish to use stored information, they will only be able to recall it to the extent that it was encoded in the first place (Anderson, 1983b).

The encoding process continues with transferring mental representations to a storage system, often referred to as long-term memory (Baddeley, 1986). Information in long-term memory is stored in groups, connected together through three different types of cognitive link: semantic, affective, and associative (Tulving, 1972; 1983). A semantic link adjoins information that shares a similar conceptual meaning, usually derived from one's language. For example, one might have thoughts of a desk semantically linked to thoughts of an office chair. An affective link adjoins information that one feels equally positively or negatively about. Bargh (1990) demonstrated that if a person is exposed to a positively valenced word (puppies) other positively valenced concepts (party) become activated. Finally, an associative link adjoins information that has been repeatedly paired together. Pavlov famously created an associative link in the minds of his dogs by repeatedly pairing a bell and food. When one piece of information in long-term memory is activated, all the information cognitively linked to it becomes more likely to be activated as well.

After information is encoded and stored in long-term memory, it must be retrieved in order to actually be used (Glass & Holyoak, 1986). When one searches for information, a search cue or "echo" is sent through long-term memory, and information that is cognitively associated with it will become more cognitively accessible (Hintzman, 1990). Pedagogies, then, that force students to apply concepts to a true real-world problem will result in the elaboration of existing echo traces and of the echo-target relationship (McDaniel & Fisher, 1991).

Applied, problem-based pedagogy ultimately produces more extensive (storage) and enriched (encoding) cognitive networks, which increase the likelihood that students will be able to activate (retrieval) the appropriate information upon demand, as well as generate more enriched cognitive representations. This combination of factors, largely absent in non-applied models of learning, produces the cognitive foundation necessary for students to move beyond the lower levels of information mastery and toward such higher levels of expertise as evaluation and creation (Bloom, 1956). If in fact there are qualitative differences in the cognitive processes of the Net Generation (Matulich, Papp & Haytko, 2008) then we would expect encoding and retrieval to be most effective when it takes place within a technology-oriented framework.

SO WHAT MAKES IT ACTION LEARNING?

Action Learning, as we have conceptualized it here, is a full-circle approach for engaging students with the challenge of applying course content and advancing the scholarly progress towards solving real-world problems. As such, the Action Learning process provides benefits to student learners (i.e., mastery of pertinent course information) as well as the broader community (i.e., advancement of a social cause). Through the six component steps listed below, we guide students through identifying, implementing and evaluating an informed attempt to make a measurable impact on the world beyond their academic buildings.

- **Assess:** Students begin by assessing the state of a social problem. What is the scope of the problem? What to date has been done to address it? What factors contribute to its prevalence? What segments of the population might be most important to target with focused interventions? Who are the stakeholders?
- **Conceptualize:** Students then conceptualize what a solution to this problem might look like. That is, what would the specific goal be? Can progress be made simply by raising awareness? Are there facts that a target audience needs? What forms might an intervention take? What would make an intervention particularly effective at accomplishing its goal within the confines of the available time and resources? What evidence supports this approach?
- **Tackle:** Once an evidence-based approach is refined, the students then set out to tackle the problem hands-on by producing a tangible product. Examples could include online public service videos, social networking campaigns, informational resources, or organized events.
- **Instigate:** To put their product to work students must then instigate the desired behavior that will lead their target audience towards change. For example, in the case of a persuasive or informational online video this might take the form of launching a marketing campaign to connect the target audience with the product via social networks, outreach to stakeholders, or motivating viral growth with direct appeals to popular websites, listserves and the media.
- **Operationalize:** Students must next implement a strategy to operationalize the success of their efforts. Surveys, direct feedback from the target audience, commitments from stakeholders, and target audience behavior (e.g., hits on a link for more information, online pledges signed, observed seat belt use leaving campus) may provide objective measures of the campaign's success.

- **Notify:** Finally, students should be tasked with notifying others about their effort. This may take the form of a formal presentation or academic paper posted online, outlining their effort, its rationale, and the evidence of its success that future interventions can build on.

A CASE STUDY IN ACTION LEARNING

To illustrate the evolution of an Action Learning approach, consider a senior-level course on the Psychology of Communication and Persuasion at the University of Maryland. The course was initially designed and taught as a traditional lecture course by Dr. Judson Mills, one of the most prolific Social Psychologists in the classic attitude change literature. Dr. Jarrod Hyman, at the time a graduate student of Dr. Mills, took over the course in 2004 and incorporated a group project. His students were randomly assigned an existing brand (e.g., Gatorade) and a target audience (e.g., senior citizens) and asked to apply specific course concepts towards the development of a fictional marketing campaign. To add a level of realism and intensity the groups were then asked to present and defend their campaigns to graduate students acting as the company's board of directors.

Since both authors have served on the board for these presentations it was clear to us that the students could not help but learn from preparing and defending their campaigns, and from listening to those of their peers. Dr. Hyman established advanced learning outcomes and the students took pride in the realization that they had succeeded in integrating and applying what they had learned. It was remarkable how engaged and invested students were in applying their knowledge and creative skills, and some of the campaigns were as ingenious as they were entertaining. Unfortunately, the product of their learning was relegated to a filing cabinet at the close of the semester.

We inherited the course in 2007 (Dr. Scott Roberts) and 2009 (Steven Buzinski) respectively, and developed the group projects into Action Learning assignments. Rather than develop fictional campaigns, groups of ten students are each tasked with developing a public service announcement and marketing campaign to address a social cause of their choice. They began by doing background research on the issue and presenting their findings on the nature, cause, and scope of the problem. Each group then worked closely with the instructor to identify the specific goals of their intervention and refine their strategic application of course concepts in creating the desired attitudinal, behavioral, or cognitive change in the target audience.

Once a storyboard was approved the groups produced their videos (not to exceed two minutes in length) and which were posted by the instructors on YouTube. Throughout the semesters students in this course have produced over two dozen public service campaigns addressing a wide range of social issues, including topics relating to health (e.g., nutrition, sexuality, body image, exercise, mental health), safety (e.g., impaired and distracted driving, assault prevention, emergency preparedness) and social justice (e.g., human trafficking, credit card debt, mental health stigma, academic integrity). Most of the videos, which have garnered a combined 92,000 views at the time this chapter was written, can be viewed online at http://www.youtube.com/adoptinitiativeUMD.

The student groups had two weeks to implement their marketing strategy before preparing a final paper and delivering a formal defense of their project to a board of up to ten social psychologists and university administrators. A fifteen-minute presentation was followed by up to twenty minutes of questions from the board. The intensity of the defense allowed the students an opportunity to demonstrate Bloom's (1956) evaluation-level learning and to develop professional presentation skills.

During the final two weeks of the semester, the University of Maryland administers a standard course evaluation survey. The survey, which includes both likert scale items and free-response text, is completed online and deindividuated results are made available at the close of the administration period. Mean responses on the Likert items are compared to the college mean for courses of a similar level. Results from the University of Maryland's standardized course evaluation survey collected in the spring of 2009, when we co-taught the course, are presented in Table 1.

Even more telling in our opinion, are some of the free response comments left on the evaluation survey:

"A LOT of work but very worth it. It really helped me learn the course material and is all very applicable to the real world."

"Having to recall information from class and apply it to our PSA made it more personal and made us re-process the information. I picked up experience working in large groups, experience marketing, and experience presenting. This project also helped improve my skills at formulating arguments."

"It was like we were 'living' the material through our group projects. I had no choice but to remember the material because even when we got to the fun part of recording the PSA, the concepts were still being applied."

Table 1. Student responses to Likert scale items

<table>
<tr><th>Likert Scale Item (0-4)</th><th colspan="2">Action Learning Course</th><th>College Mean (400-level)</th></tr>
<tr><td>The course was intellectually challenging</td><td colspan="2">3.88</td><td>3.22</td></tr>
<tr><td>I learned a lot from this course</td><td colspan="2">3.92</td><td>3.17</td></tr>
<tr><td>The instructor was well-prepared for class</td><td colspan="2">4.00</td><td>3.44</td></tr>
<tr><td>This instructor was an effective teacher</td><td colspan="2">3.83</td><td>3.15</td></tr>
<tr><td>The instructor was effective in communication course content</td><td colspan="2">4.00</td><td>3.19</td></tr>
<tr><td>The instructor helped create an atmosphere that kept me engaged in course content</td><td colspan="2">4.00</td><td>3.07</td></tr>
<tr><td>I gained a good understanding of the concepts/principles in this field</td><td colspan="3">100% Strongly Agree</td></tr>
<tr><td>The teaching methods in this course helped me learn the material</td><td colspan="2">4% Strongly Disagree</td><td>92% Agree or Strongly Agree</td></tr>
<tr><td>Given the course level and number of credits, the workload was...</td><td>0%
Too Low</td><td>54% Appropriate</td><td>46%
Too High</td></tr>
<tr><td>How much effort did you put into the course</td><td>0%
Little</td><td>0%
Moderate</td><td>100% Considerable</td></tr>
</table>

THE CHALLENGES OF ACTION LEARNING ASSIGNMENTS

It is worth noting that implementing Action Learning assignments poses some challenges for both instructors and students. Though by no means insurmountable, it is nonetheless important to consider the obstacles and pitfalls of engaging students in real-world problem solving before committing yourself.

Ideas

Perhaps the largest challenge most instructors face is in identifying opportunities for Action Learning in their course. While a course on persuasion intuitively lends itself to public service campaigns, other disciplines may require a bit more creativity. For example:

- Students in a philosophy course might design online videos that demonstrate challenging concepts and seek commitments from instructors at other institutions to offer the link as supplemental resources for their students.
- Students in a history course might develop engaging and relevant websites that promote majoring in the field and supply them to local high school guidance offices.
- Students in a computer science course might consult with local service organizations (e.g., a domestic violence shelter) and develop online training resources to aid clientele in developing workplace skills.
- Students in a dance class might organize a local community event via social networking technologies (e.g., Twitter) to promote dancing of any type as a fun and social form of exercise and creative expression.
- Students in a marketing course might team up with small non-profit organizations to provide technical support for expanding their online presence, developing proposals and implementing solutions.

Time

There is no question that organizing and supporting Action Learning assignments requires an additional investment of time for instructors, and it may seem as though the curriculum is too tight to add in another major assignment. Additionally, many instructors perceive an obligation to present content during class meetings and are concerned with the expectation that "anything we have to know should be covered in lecture." However, it has been our experience that structuring coursework around active out-of-class learning (rather than just passively reading a chapter) frees up the necessary time needed to focus on application, group work, and problem solving.

Pushback

It is not uncommon to experience pushback from the students themselves, as many in their later years have grown quite accustom to, and comfortable with, a more traditional lecture-and-test format. Adding to the out-of-class demands and requiring work that isn't directly related to the course curriculum (e.g., editing a video) may seem, from their perspective, to be unfair. That said, the key to obtaining buy-in from the students is to engage them in a discussion of pedagogy. Too often we, as the instructors, assert our status in designed a course without taking a moment to ensure that the students understand our intention and our approach as well as they understand specific assignment requirements or grading criteria. Presenting not only the learning objectives, but also the evidence-based teaching strategy that underlines the assignments, allows students to become surprisingly receptive to unconventional and challenging work.

Resources

Another challenge that both the instructor and students face is the lack of resources to implement Action Learning projects. In assigning random groups of ten students to produce public service videos, it quickly became apparent that there were inequities in access to resources; some groups had high-definition video cameras and personal computers with video editing software while had neither. The instructor's challenge is to support these projects without creating undue burdens or disadvantages. Not only may students have difficulty securing the resources they need when it comes to technology-oriented products (e.g., software to make a functional website, edit a digital video, or manipulating a digital image), students may also not have the training and experience to do it well. In orienting ourselves towards Millennial learners, we have to be sensitive to the distinction between being surrounded by technology and being tech-savvy. Just because Net Generation learners may be dispositionally oriented towards using technology does not mean they are experts in all facets, and learning new skills can be as frustrating for them as it is for their parents.

In many cases the resources and training problem can be solved on campus, and most students may not even be aware of what additional equipment, software, and training is available to them. Further, small grants at the departmental, college, or university level may be available to help purchase instructional equipment. Another approach would be to partner with local businesses and organizations that might sponsor the projects, allowing students to borrow donated video cameras or provide them with subscriptions to online training resources. Finally, there may be courses or student organizations with expertise in these skills that can provide technical assistance as part of their own coursework or community service initiatives. Social loafing is a pervasive problem in any college classroom that utilizes group projects. It becomes an especially problematic issue when projects are the size of those advocated by Action Learning. Over several semesters of conducting Action Learning projects, we have come up with several solutions, based on social psychological research, that minimize the occurrence of social loafing.

Social Loafing is the conscious or non-conscious reduction of effort that individuals exhibit when working on collective tasks (Karau & Williams, 1993). It has been shown to cause reduced effort on physical, cognitive, evaluative, creative, and work-related tasks (Karau & Williams, 2001). Latane, Williams, & Harkins (1979) even went so far as to label this phenomenon a "social disease," with negative consequences for almost all areas of social life. Social Loafing is not inevitable, though, as many interventions have been found to attenuate its prevalence.

The Collective Effort Model (CEM), a theory of individual motivation in groups, integrates much of the past 100 years of research on social loafing, and serves as a means to predict and eliminate its antecedents (Karau & Williams, 1993). The CEM proposes nine specific variables that determine the level of social loafing expected in group work. These variables are listed in Table 2.

Based on the CEM, we have developed several suggestions for minimizing the problem of social loafing in Action Learning courses. Because of the intensive nature of Action Learning, it was impossible for us to utilize smaller groups, so we focused on the issues of accountability and work differentiation. First, rather than assign a term paper, we have utilized a team wiki document. Each team member is tasked to make one or more edits to the document each week. The use of a wiki allows both group members and the instructor to see exactly what each member of the team is contributing as the semester progresses, eliminating the sense of anonymity that students often develop in group work.

Second, we administer quarterly intra-team evaluations in their virtual learning environment on which students anonymously rate the level

Table 2. The collective effort model (Karau & Williams, 1993)

Individuals are *less likely* to loaf when they:
1. Work in smaller groups
2. Believe their performance can be evaluated
3. Perceive their contributions to group work as unique
4. Are provided with a standard to compare their performance
5. Work on tasks that are intrinsically interesting to the self
6. Work in a situation that activates a salient group identity
7. View favorable collective outcomes as important
8. Have feelings of high self and group-efficacy
9. Expect their co-workers to perform poorly

of participation of all team members (including themselves). We have found that using quarterly, rather than post-project evaluations produces a greater sense of responsibility for one's portion of the work. If, however, a student is evaluated by his/her teammates as contributing significantly less than others, a private meeting is scheduled with the student to talk about the issue. This meeting is often enough to motivate loafers to start contributing more to the project.

Third, we developed a system of job titles that each team member volunteers for at the beginning of the semester. Every job title has a different focus and different duties. We also encourage teams to divide work and task it to sub-groups within the team. The combination of these factors allows team members to feel that they are contributing something unique to the overall project, which increases motivation to perform and decreases social loafing.

Finally, we develop a series of deadlines for the projects throughout the semester. With each successive deadline that is met, teams develop an increased sense of group efficacy. This increases the belief that their team can accomplish the overall goal of the Action Learning project, which in turn motivates them to work hard rather than loaf.

The Added Benefit

An added benefit of integrating Action Learning projects into the classroom is the opportunity for instructors and departments to stand out as leaders in answering the call for service learning and civic engagement. Universities are increasingly emphasizing the importance of building bridges between classroom and the community and are eager to showcase exemplary teaching that empowers students to make an impact on their campus, community, and world at large. Action Learning is exactly that, and there is no limit to the influence of creative, informed and engaged students of the Net Generation.

FUTURE RESEARCH DIRECTIONS

Expanding on case studies and anecdotal accounts, future research can empirically test the pedagogical benefits of Action Learning and specifically assess which components of the approach are instrumental in engaging Net Generation learners. For example, if in fact there are qualitative differences in the cognitive processes of these students (e.g., Matulich, Papp, & Haytko, 2008) then we would expect encoding and retrieval to be most effective when it takes place within a technology-oriented framework. Designing rigorous and well-controlled experiments to test this hypothesis is a challenging but necessary next step in clarifying the role of generational disposition on the underlying cognitive processes that support learning and memory.

Separate from investigating the cognitive aspects of Action Learning, further research is also needed on the determinants of student engagement. More work can be done to elucidate whether it is the integration of social technology with their coursework that uniquely draws Net Generation students to Action Learning assignments. Would similar assignments that engage students with the opportunity to apply their scholarly work towards a social cause be as effective if they were not supported by the technology this generation is accustomed to using? Or is the technology just one (albeit effective) way of engaging them with the sense that their academic efforts are as socially relevant and as impactful as their other exploits? Well-designed studies on engagement can parse out the benefits of integrating technology from the sense of social empowerment those technologies support.

CONCLUSION

This chapter has provided an integrative pedagogical approach to enhance student engagement and mastery of information through truly applied projects. Referred to hear as Action Learning, instructors can guide students through *assessing* the state of a social problem, *conceptualizing* what a solution might look like, *tackling* the problem by producing a tangible product, *instigating* their target audience towards change, *operationalizing* the success of their efforts and *notifying* others about their effort. In doing so, instructors can move student scholarship beyond the academic treadmill and cater towards a generational expectation that their efforts should have substantial social implications.

REFERENCES

Anderson, J. R. (1983b). Retrieval of information from long-term memory. *Science*, *220*, 25–30. doi:10.1126/science.6828877

Baddeley, A. D. (1986). *Working memory*. New York, NY: Oxford University Press.

Bargh, J. A. (1990). Auto-motives: Preconscious determinants of social interaction. In Higgins, E. T., & Sorrentino, R. M. (Eds.), *Handbook of motivation and cognition* (*Vol. 2*, pp. 93–130). New York, NY: Guilford.

Bjork, R. A. (1988). Retrieval practice and the maintenance of knowledge. In Gruneberg, M. M., Morris, P. E., & Sykes, R. N. (Eds.), *Practical aspects of memory: Current research and issues* (*Vol. 1*, pp. 396–401). New York, NY: Wiley.

Bloom, B. S. (1956). *Taxonomy of educational objectives, handbook I: The cognitive domain*. New York, NY: David McKay Co Inc.

Craik, F. I. M., & Lockheart, R. S. (1972). Levels of processing: A framework for memory research. *Journal of Verbal Learning and Verbal Behavior*, *11*, 671–684. doi:10.1016/S0022-5371(72)80001-X

Eynon, R. (2009). *Harnessing technology: The learner and their context. How young people use technologies outside formal education. Survey Report*. Coventry, UK: Becta.

Glass, A. L., & Holyoak, K. J. (1986). *Cognition* (2nd ed.). New York, NY: Random House.

Hintzman, D. L. (1990). Human learning and memory: Connections and dissociations. *Annual Review of Psychology*, *41*, 109–139. doi:10.1146/annurev.ps.41.020190.000545

Hmelo-Silver, C. E., Duncan, R. G., & Chinn, C. A. (2007). Scaffolding and achievement in problem-based and inquiry learning: A response to Kirschner, Sweller, and Clark (2006). *Educational Psychologist*, *42*, 99–107. doi:10.1080/00461520701263368

Jones, C., & Healing, G. (2010). Net generation students: Agency and choice and the new technologies. *Journal of Computer Assisted Learning*, *26*, 344–356. doi:10.1111/j.1365-2729.2010.00370.x

Jones, C., Ramanau, R., Cross, S. J., & Healing, G. (2010). Net generation or digital natives: Is there a distinct new generation entering university? *Computers & Education*, *54*, 722–732. doi:10.1016/j.compedu.2009.09.022

Karau, S. J., & Williams, K. D. (1993). Social loafing: A meta-analytic review and theoretical integration. *Journal of Personality and Social Psychology*, *65*, 681–706. doi:10.1037/0022-3514.65.4.681

Karau, S. J., & Williams, K. D. (2001). Understanding individual motivation in groups: The collective effort model. In Turner, M. E. (Ed.), *Groups at work: Theory and research* (pp. 113–141). Mahwah, NJ: Lawrence Erlbaum Associates Publishers.

Kennedy, G., Judd, T., Churchward, A., Gray, K., & Krause, K.-L. (2008). First year students' experience with technology: Are they really digital natives? *Australasian Journal of Educational Technology*, *24*, 108–122.

Kennedy, G., Judd, T., Dalgarnot, B., & Waycott, J. (2010). Beyond natives and immigrants: Exploring types of net generation students. *Journal of Computer Assisted Learning*, *26*, 332–343. doi:10.1111/j.1365-2729.2010.00371.x

Kirschner, P. A., Sweller, J., & Clark, R. E. (2006). Why minimal guidance during instruction does not work: An analysis of the failure of constructivist, discovery, problem-based, experiential, and inquiry-based teaching. *Educational Psychologist*, *41*, 75–86. doi:10.1207/s15326985ep4102_1

Latane, B., Williams, K., & Harkins, S. (1979). Many hands make light the work: The causes and consequences of social loafing. *Journal of Personality and Social Psychology*, *44*, 78–94.

Matulich, E., Papp, R., & Haytko, D. L. (2008). Continuous improvement through teaching innovations: A requirement for today's learners. *Marketing Education Review*, *18*, 1–7.

McDaniel, M. A., & Fisher, R. P. (1991). Tests and test feedback as learning sources. *Contemporary Educational Psychology*, *16*, 192–201. doi:10.1016/0361-476X(91)90037-L

Pohl, M. (2000). *Learning to think, thinking to learn: Models and strategies to develop a classroom culture of thinking*. Cheltenham, UK: Hawker Brownlow.

Sweller, J. (2006). The worked example effect and human cognition. *Learning and Instruction*, *16*, 165–169. doi:10.1016/j.learninstruc.2006.02.005

Tapscott, D. (2009). *Grown up digital: How the Net Generation is changing your world*. New York, NY: McGraw-Hill.

Tulving, E. (1972). Episodic and semantic memory. In Tulving, E., & Donaldson, W. (Eds.), *Organization of memory* (pp. 381–403). New York, NY: Academic Press.

Tulving, E. (1983). *Elements of episodic memory*. Oxford, UK: Clarendon Press.

ADDITIONAL READING

Aggarwal, P., & O'Brien, C. L. (2008). Social loafing on group projects: Structural antecedents and effect on student satisfaction. *Journal of Marketing Education*, *30*, 255–264. doi:10.1177/0273475308322283

Bolkan, S., & Goodboy, A. K. (2010). Transformational leadership in the classroom: The development and validation of the student intellectual stimulation scale. *Communication Reports*, *23*, 91–105. doi:10.1080/08934215.2010.511399

Clark, S. E., & Gronlund, S. D. (1996). Global matching models of recognition memory: How the models match the data. *Psychonomic Bulletin & Review*, *3*, 37–60. doi:10.3758/BF03210740

Foushee, R. D., & Sleigh, M. J. (2004). Going the extra mile: Identifying and assisting struggling students. In B. Perlman, L. I. McCann, & S. H. McFadden (Eds.), *Lessons learned: Vol. 2. Practical advice for teaching of psychology* (pp. 303-311). Washington, DC: American Psychological Society.

George, J. M. (1992). Extrinsic and intrinsic origins of perceived social loafing in organizations. *Academy of Management Journal, 35*, 191–202. doi:10.2307/256478

Glover, J. A. (1989). The "testing" phenomenon: Not gone but nearly forgotten. *Journal of Educational Psychology, 81*, 392–399. doi:10.1037/0022-0663.81.3.392

Golding, J. M. (2011). The role of attendance in lecture classes: You can lead a horse to water.... *Teaching of Psychology, 38*, 40–42.

Hintzman, D. (1990). Human learning and memory: connections and dissociations. *Annual Review of Psychology, 41*, 109–139. doi:10.1146/annurev.ps.41.020190.000545

Horstmanshof, L., & Zimitat, C. (2007). Future time orientation predicts academic engagement among first-year university students. *The British Journal of Educational Psychology, 77*, 703–718. doi:10.1348/000709906X160778

Jassawalla, A., Sashittal, H., & Malshe, A. (2009). Students' perceptions of social loafing: Its antecedents and consequences in undergraduate business classroom teams. *Academy of Management Learning & Education, 81*, 42–54. doi:10.5465/AMLE.2009.37012178

Liazos, A., & Liss, J. R. (2009). Civic engagement in the classroom: Strategies for incorporating education for civic and social responsibility in the undergraduate curriculum. *A Project Pericles® white paper.*

Liss, J. R., & Liazos, A. (2010). Incorporating education for civic and social responsibility. *Changemag.org.*

McKeachie, W. J., & Svinicki, M. (2006). *McKeachie's Teaching tips: Strategies, research, and theory for college and university teachers*. Boston: Houghton Mifflin.

Naveh-Benjamin, M., Craik, F. I. M., Guez, J., & Dori, H. (1998). Effects of divided attention on encoding and retrieval processes in human memory: Further support for asymmetry. *Journal of Experimental Psychology, 24*, 1091–1104.

Richlin, L. (2006). *Blueprint for learning: Constructing college courses to facilitate, assess, and document learning.* Sterling: Stylus

Roediger, H. L., & Karpicke, J. D. (2006). Test-enhanced learning: Taking memory tests improves long-term retention. *Psychological Science, 17*, 249–255. doi:10.1111/j.1467-9280.2006.01693.x

Rotgans, J. I., & Schmidt, H. G. (2011). The role of teachers in facilitating situational interest in an active-learning classroom. *Teaching and Teacher Education, 27*, 37–42. doi:10.1016/j.tate.2010.06.025

Shiue, Y. C., Chiu, C. M., & Chang, C. C. (2010). Exploring and mitigating social loafing in online communities. *Computers in Human Behavior, 26*, 768–777. doi:10.1016/j.chb.2010.01.014

Unsworth, N., & Engle, R. W. (2007). The Nature of Individual Differences in Working Memory Capacity: Active Maintenance in Primary Memory and Controlled Search From Secondary Memory. *Psychological Review, 114*, 104–132. doi:10.1037/0033-295X.114.1.104

KEY TERMS AND DEFINITIONS

Action Learning: Presenting students with an opportunity to demonstrate their learning by taking course content from the classroom and putting it to real use in campus, local, national and even international communities.

Bloom's Taxonomy: A classification system that posits six levels of learning, which gradually increase in cognitive complexity. The levels, from lowest to highest, are: remembering, understanding, applying, analyzing, evaluating, and creating.

The Collective Effort Model (CEM): An empirically supported theory that identifies nine specific variables predictive of social loafing in group work.

Encoding: Attending to environmental stimuli (e.g., class discussion), transforming stimuli into usable mental representations, and storing those representations in memory (Glass & Holyoak, 1986).

Problem Based Learning: A pedagogy wherein students learn about a subject vis-à-vis solving a complex, often real-world, problem that is based on the interested topic.

Retrieval: Accessing a stored mental representation for use in accomplishing some cognitive task.

Social Loafing: The conscious or non-conscious reduction of effort that individuals exhibit when working on collective tasks (Karau & Williams, 1993).

Storage: Accurately maintaining the encoded mental representations over some span of time.

Chapter 18
The Net Generation Illusion:
Challenging Conformance to Social Expectations

Rachel Ellaway
Northern Ontario School of Medicine, Canada

Janet Tworek
University of Calgary, Canada

ABSTRACT

The thesis of this chapter is that the Net Generation concept has become a powerful meme that influences professional education in ways that can be both distracting and disruptive. We explore the interactions between the Net Generation meme and medical education and identify points of consonance and dissonance between them. In doing so we present a critical response to the idea of a Net Generation, as well as its specific manifestations and impacts on the development of healthcare professionals. A digital professionalism framework is presented as a way to restore balance within medical education, as well as situating it within an increasingly digital social milieu.

INTRODUCTION

This book is predicated on the idea of contemporary youth functioning as a Net Generation (NetGen) that is somehow distinct from their predecessors due to their exposure to and facility with digital technologies. However, the ubiquity and validity of this model may not be as wide as it might seem. This chapter challenges the validity of this model applied to contemporary learners in health professional education. Although the contemporary learning environment for health professionals has undeniably changed following the uptake of digital media (both within professional practice and in its wider social contexts), we suggest that not only can the NetGen meme fail to represent the lived reality of many current learners, it can actively interfere with their education and professional development.

DOI: 10.4018/978-1-61350-347-8.ch018

Our position is not to reject the digital, but rather to find a positive accommodation and balance between the necessary aspects of professional education and the realities of life and practice in a digital society. This chapter is organized in three sections. The first appraises the evidence behind different NetGen models. The second considers the influence of the NetGen meme on learner and faculty habits and beliefs in health professional education, and it proposes a model of digital professionalism to help to address these challenges. We close with an exploration of how we can both improve learning and build better relationships with our technologies through critical appraisal of technological competences and their alignment with the needs of the educational and practice ecologies in which they are expressed.

THE NetGen MEME

We use Dawkins' concept of a 'meme' (1976) as representing cognitive concepts and models that are transferred between minds and adapted across sociocultural contexts. The idea of the Net Generation has taken on memetic qualities; a complex mix of beliefs, interpretations and frames regarding generational capabilities associated with using digital media. More specifically, the NetGen meme is founded on a binary differentiation between a 'digital native' youth who are intrinsically able to function in new media environments and their 'digital immigrant' seniors who can only aspire to the same levels of ability. The analysis of a literature review for "Net Generation" (using ERIC, PsycINFO, and Academic Search Complete) returned multiple texts that, upon review, cited the same core references (Tworek, 2007). Table 1 summarizes the key texts that created the grounding for the NetGen meme along with more recent publications (Ito, Baumer, Bittanti, Boyd, Cody & Herr, 2009; Rideout, Foehr & Roberts, 2010).

According to this review, the Net Generation idea is based on a mixture of research studies (e.g. Kent & Facer, 2004; Rideout, Foehr & Roberts, 2005, 2010 and Foehr; Howe & Strauss, 2005; Ito et al., 2009) and theoretical models (e.g. Prensky, 2001; Dede, 2005; Oblinger &and Oblinger, 2005). Whilst the theoretical works propose and perpetuate the Net Gen meme, the empirical studies, particularly Rideout et al (1999; 2005; 2010), indicate that although youth are spending more and more time with digital technologies, this is largely for entertainment and social purposes. Youth are not as a result intrinsically "media-savvy" and exposure to media does not necessarily equate with generative, creative or constructive learning outcomes. There are rich media ecologies among some (but not all) youth that cross home and school (work) environments (Kent & Facer, 2004; Ito et al., 2009). The subset of younger generation members who do develop some degree of expertise follows from particular areas of interest (such as photography, astronomy or car repair), where expertise is defined by an increase in technical competence with the tools of the domain (such as programming, audio editing or multimedia design). Considered thus, the NetGen meme is based on limited evidence.

Issues such as diversity of access, equity, attitudes, and depth of media use are obscured if the academic discussion is based on digital natives being intrinsically "able" and the digital immigrants "not able" to thrive in digital environments. There are other contributing factors beyond that of age. For instance, economic factors separate those with access to digital media from those who do not (Grant, 2007). While recent statistics show the economic gap between digital 'haves' and the 'have nots' is narrowing, it remains a concern (Statistics Canada, 2009; United States Census Bureau, 2010).

Attitudes towards technology do not fall along generational lines (Parasuraman, 2000; Caison, Bulmna, Pai & Neville, 2008). There are many youth who approach technology with discomfort and insecurity, and there are many seniors who are both capable and confident in digital environ-

Table 1. Principal published works that establish the Net Generation meme

Author	Generation Birth Years	Name	Evidence
Tapscott (1997)	1977-1997	*Media Generation*	Online chat with 28 teens
Rideout et al, 1999, Rideout, Foehr and Roberts (2005), Rideout, Foehr and Roberts (2010)	"young people aged 8 to 18"	*Gen M*	1999 report: 2,065 children aged 8-18 2004 report: 2,032 students ages 8-18 2009 report: 2002 students ages 8–18
Howe and Strauss (2000)	1982 - 2000	*Millenials*	500 high school seniors in southeastern U.S.
Prensky (2001)	unspecified	*Digital Natives*	Exposure to media
Beck and Wade (2004)	1975 - 2004	*Gaming Generation*	Playing video games Survey business leaders
Kent and Facer (2004)	"young people ages 9 – 18"	*Young people*	Survey in 2001: n=1818 Survey in 2003: n= 1471 Group semi-structured interviews: n=192 Family interviews: n=19 (representing 11 families)
Dede (2005)	unspecified	*Neomillenials*	Exposure to media
Oblinger and Oblinger (2005)	1982–1991	*Net Generation*	Exposure to media
Ito, et al. (2009)	"Under the age of 25" in 2005	*Digital Youth*	659 semi-structured interviews, 28 diary studies, focus group interviews with 67 participants; 78 interviews; 363 survey respondents; 5,194 observation hours; 10,468 profiles on social sites; 15 online discussion group forums, and more than 389 videos.

ments (Meng, Eliot & Hall, 2010). In a study of teachers in a large urban school board in Canada, Slater, Crichton and Pegler (2010) concluded that career cycle is more important than generation in an individual's use of technology in teaching. Gender, education achievement, and geographic location have also been identified as variables that frequently reflect differences in using digital tools and learning resources (Barron, 2004; Commerce, 2010; Hargittai, 2008; Warschauer, 2000; DiMaggio, Hargittai, Celeste, & Shafer, 2004).

Clearly the NetGen meme proves less convincing under scrutiny. It overlooks learner diversity, it overemphasizes students' roles around digital media, and it oversimplifies the ways in which new media are utilized. The next section considers how the NetGen meme can be disruptive to education and training.

NetGen AND MEDICAL EDUCATION

Preparing doctors for practice takes many years. Even when fully qualified their training continues throughout their careers as they maintain their skills and keep up to date with new developments in their field. Although the cost of training doctors varies for learners (depending on national or institutional funding models), society's investment is consistently high, largely stemming from its dependence on the continuity and quality of this process. Anything that disrupts or otherwise reduces the efficiency of medical education must therefore be considered with particular concern.

The NetGen effect is somewhat obscured in medical education due to the limited attention paid to technological competence as opposed to more traditional clinical competencies (Krause, Roulette, Papp & Kaelber, 2006). As an example, an internal survey at the University of Edinburgh that tracked incoming medical students' experience and attitudes to information technologies. While there was a rise in computer ownership from 55% of learners in 2001 to more than 90% by 2005, the level of self-defined competence remained constant with 53% of learners considering themselves of average ability, 33% above average and 14% below. The number who had received formal training in using computers remained constant at around 65%. When they were set a series of basic computing tasks (as a way of triaging those who actually needed additional training) more than a third were unable to complete them without additional support and training. This was a repeated pattern over a number of years. This demonstrates a fairly constant deficit between higher student confidence and lower competence independent of computer ownership. This pattern is reflected in many other situations in higher education (Beetham, McGill & Littlejohn, 2009).

Despite this apparently common, if under-reported, problem, the position of the digital in health care education remains largely limited to training around specific systems and software (Hobbs, 2002; Nguyen, Zierler, & Nguyen, 2011). Broader, transferable knowledge, skills or attitudes around digital literacy are almost entirely absent from accreditation requirements (the principal drivers for curricular design and reform) for health professional schools.

The assumption that health professional learners are intrinsically well prepared and able to work within digital environments is reinforced by a number of other phenomena:

- **Expert status risks:** The role of the academic or teacher is intrinsically based on their domain expertise. Trying to use unfamiliar technologies, particularly in front of learners, runs the risk of diminishing this expertise status. The risks associated with using IT in the classroom can therefore be disproportionately greater for teachers than for learners.
- **Division of labour:** IT support is generally carried out by professionals such as technologists and engineers, and it is more typically assigned to younger and less senior staff. Within the medical school culture the professions and the individuals associated with IT (and by association their work and interests) are typically considered to be of lower professional status than those of academics or clinicians.
- **Dominant academic paradigms:** Technology is more typically understood as a part of an operational or administrative paradigm rather than as a part of an academic one. It therefore tends to receive less critical consideration than other aspects of the medical education syllabus and the research that is carried out falls into well-established educational psychology or causal intervention measurement studies (Cook, 2009).
- **Overlooking technology integration in medical practice:** The advent of the stethoscope, the microscope, radiological investigations, laboratory tests and other technological inventions have changed the doctor-patient relationship as well as the practice of medicine as a whole (Reiser, 2009). Furthermore, the use of technology as a vehicle and as a tool in education is typically considered as something separate from the incorporation of technology into medical practice. Medical education programs create opportunities to learn clinical technologies as tools in patient care, with the potential of future specialization (e.g. certification in ultrasound, residency in lab medicine or radiology), while ironically disregarding the integration of technologies for learning in pedagogically sound ways. The hidden curriculum here is that digital prowess is not an intrinsic part of becoming a clinician.

Medical education is complex and curricula extremely busy and packed. This leads to a level of reticence to face NetGen issues in the context of so many other pressures. The NetGen meme can thereby prove a convenient, if unacknowledged, justification for a shift of responsibility for all things digital from teachers to learners. This shift also identifies the digital as something learners move away from rather than towards as they develop as health professionals. In other words, being a 'digital native' is not intrinsically advantageous to students pursuing the study of medicine. Indeed, digital prowess may be seen as a contraindication to the development of appropriate professional values and attitudes (Haas and Shaffir, 1991).

While many technologies are disruptive (Christensen, 2003) it is therefore arguable that it is the concept of NetGen itself rather than any specific technology that is the problem. Although there are many dimensions to this the problem can be illustrated in the form of three recurring errors:

Error #1: We Both Require and Disregard Technological Prosthesis

Digital media are often used as cognitive prosthetics; extending our mentalities beyond our organic boundaries (Clark, 2003). For instance, professional education used to be largely focused on the acquisition of a body of knowledge with recall as the primary assessment heuristic. This has changed over the last few decades to a focus on 'knowing in practice' where the information is accessed through various media rather than from memory (Ellaway, 2010a). Similarly the shift to point of care information systems is intended to mitigate the risks associated with variable healthcare provider memories (Brailer, 2005).

There is nothing intrinsically youth-oriented about this; older people can also make use of such prostheses. Indeed, the self-discipline developed in the absence of digital media may afford senior (and therefore more experienced) generations greater, rather than lesser, abilities with the digital. However, self-dependence also requires significant internalization of cognitive resources. Thus the degree of success in these cyborg relationships varies with an individual's capability or preparedness rather than age.

Accessing information at need, particularly when recall is uncertain is a legitimate and well-established use of cognitive prosthesis. This is a core tenet of the academic library; just as reference tools for proper dosages, treatment guidelines, and so on are critical to safe clinical practice. Despite this, there are concerns of students' over-dependence on cognitive prostheses and, simultaneously, a reluctance to permit or legitimize more than a basic use of cognitive prosthesis in the clinical learning environment.

There is a divergence between the cyborg learner and the construction of health professional education. It is important to consider the legitimate requirements of real-world medical practice alongside the advantages (and disadvantages) of digital technologies in medical education. Technologies for cognitive prostheses such as those for reference, patient education, or recording and reporting patient data are all legitimate applications. Cognitive prosthesis does not mean abdicating the need for internalized. Learners should be assessed independent of their cyborg prosthetics where memory, skill proficiency, and unaugmented performance of patient care are concerned. Similarly cyborg behaviours that authentically reflect evolving medical practices should be legitimized in both learning and assessment. Progressive and appropriate use of technologies in educational and clinical settings should be supported at all levels of health professional education.

Error #2: We Allow our Learners to Believe and Then Try to Fulfill the NetGen Model

The NetGen meme influences learners by shifting social expectations. Many learners try to be 'digital native' yet fall short of the ideal and there are social pressures on learners to have the latest technologies, and to know how to use them. An individual's competency with using digital media is often used by their peers as a reflection of their competence and standing in general. Current medical students are a significantly heterogeneous group when it comes to digital abilities. While some have grown up with computers others are still able to pass through the system without needing or desiring digital expertise. Furthermore, in order to get into medical school, learners need to commit much of their time to their studies and acts of public service so as to construct the most competitive medical school application. As such, they are by definition atypical of their generation.

Medical education involves more than the acquisition of knowledge; it involves learners displaying confidence and competence and adopting the social and cultural values associated with their intended profession (Haas & Shaffir, 1991). This can be a stressful, even debilitating process for those whose personal identities are at odds with aspects of the professional identities they are attempting to assume (Costello, 2005). The NetGen meme can be argued to add a third identity to those of the individual and of the profession and in doing so can further distract by requiring values and competences that do not fit with the other identities in play. This is particularly a problem where digital literacy is incongruent with the identity of a physician, or is at least perceived as such.

Error #3: We Allow Ourselves to Believe Learners Can and Should Follow the NetGen Model

Many teachers and administrators accept the NetGen meme without question. This can lead to a number of problems. Assuming the superiority of their learners' abilities with digital technologies can lead teachers to abdicate their oversight of all things digital to their learners. There is a need to reinstate leadership and positive role modeling by faculty and others in the environment around using new media effectively for teaching and learning (Beetham et al., 2009).

The binary division between the use and meaning of old and new media is not realized in practice. Not only are the two significantly blended in the classroom, the digital can be used to augment almost every aspect of the learning environment. While e-learning is still treated as something apart, there is also a tendency to disregard technology as inevitable and invisible.

The democratizing and 'flattening aspects' of digital media threaten the concept of "teacher" and other expert roles (Keen, 2007), particularly when better (or at least alternative) content and even instruction may be had online. Whether it is laptop use in lectures, or the use of Wikipedia as a primary source the legitimacy of creating and using knowledge, expertise has been wrested from the hands of the professor. Authority now rests with those who set the exams and then only as gatekeepers rather than as fellow travelers.

THE NetGen HIDDEN CURRICULUM

Given the errors and mixed messages expressed in and around the digital in health professional education many contemporary medical learners find themselves caught between the proverbial rock and its adjacent hard place, trying to resolve the contradictions between the pervasive although nebulous NetGen ideal and the divergent value systems of their chosen professions. These paradoxical situations in education are captured in the concept of a 'hidden curriculum' that may be expressed in benign ways (Hafferty, 1998) or disruptive, even destructive ways (Snyder, 1971). Hafferty's model (1998) is about identifying contradictions in medical education as expressed through institutional policy, evaluation, resource allocation and language. The hidden curriculum around NetGen-ism can be illustrated using these four dimensions:

- **Policies in education:** Include procedural rules, general codes of ethics and behaviour and more general regulatory structures such as curricula. Many institutions' responses to NetGen behaviours are to limit then through regulations and sanctions (Farnan, Gersh, Reddy & Moyer, 2009; Chretien et al., 2009). The primary hidden curriculum issue here is that digital literacy is framed by discipline and punishment rather than the more positive dimensions of developing competence and skill found in the rest of their studies.
- **Evaluation of learners:** Primarily undertaken through various kinds of exams set to test the individual's knowledge, attitude and skills. As digital competencies are almost entirely absent from accreditation structures they rarely find their way into exams in the first place. Even if technology is the medium for the evaluation, the default position is to minimize its effects rather than incorporating them as part the assessment (Amin et al, 2011). Similarly, faculty recruitment and promotion rarely value or acknowledge the value of digital activities in teaching (Ellaway, 2010b). As we have observed, the hidden curriculum message is the digital skills are of little value and have little legitimacy in clinical practice relative to the rest of their studies.
- **Resource allocation:** Although institutes of higher education spend a great deal on IT, only a small part is for directly educational purposes. The hidden curriculum here is that logistics are more important than learning and that the quality of the face-to-face experience is intrinsically better than working online (Davies, 2006).
- **Language:** The 'e-' prefix is (perhaps over-) used to denote the entity in question exhibits some aspects of the digital. The ubiquity of language along the lines of e-learning, e-assessment and e-portfolio explicitly sets them apart from 'normal' learning, assessment or portfolios even though the cognitive construct is essentially identical. The hidden curriculum message is that the digital is abnormal and 'other.'

As a result it is not surprising that the digital is a problem that the health professions have been trying to ignore. The NetGen meme, through its archetypes of intrinsic capabilities of youth, only exacerbates this. In the absence of any change to the system then the future health professional workforce may be less and less, rather than more and more, prepared to work in a digitized health environment. There are ways to address this. One that is gaining growing attention and attraction is that of affirmative modeling and teaching around the concept of digital professionalism.

DIGITAL PROFESSIONALISM

The current parlous state of the digital within medical education was not planned, and it passes largely unnoticed and unvalued by those involved. The contradictions between personal, professional and digital identities need to be resolved in affirmative, accessible, and meaningful ways. The key to this lies in the area of professionalism, a core pillar of medical practice: "a moral and ethical code is necessary because the asymmetry of information between physicians and patients makes the latter vulnerable to exploitation by the former" (Rothman and Blumenthal, 2010, p2). Ellaway (2010c) offers a digital professionalism framework (expanded upon here) to address this deficit of affirmative modeling and surfeit of punishment.

- **Keep Online Profiles Accurate and up to Date.** Asking learners to do Google searches on themselves and faculty can be very illuminating. Most (but not all, at least in 2011) learners have a Facebook profile and may also have a blog, a photo site or some other online presence. It is pointed out to them that as practicing doctors they are also likely to have an online professional profile made up of official and unofficial data, the latter consisting of patient ratings and comments as well as professional networking. Some will take online profiles as the literal truth; others will be intrinsically skeptical. Maintaining a principal of honesty, even if playful, is important in dealing with the reinterpretation and misinterpretation of a professional's profile. Principle: *Establish and sustain an on online professional presence that befits your responsibilities while representing your interests ... but be selective where you establish a profile.*

- **Work Responsibly and Positively Within Online Communities.** Although there may not be the same explicit duties of service and care within an online community, the professional's role within society should extend to the virtual as well as to the real. Learners are invited to explore the experience of working in online environments and how professional identities are translated and changed by doing so. They are also led through scenarios that involve ethical challenges in such circumstances. Principle: *Your professional identity extends into all online communities you join, and you are still a professional there.*
- **Manage Access to Different Parts of Online Profiles.** Social media can blur previously distinct professional and personal aspects of a physician's life. Learners are asked to discuss how their experiences have already mixed the two, perhaps inappropriately. They are then asked to ensure that they make personal dimensions more private otherwise they will tend to blur together with possibly serious consequences. *Principle: Use privacy controls to manage more personal parts of your online profile and do not make public anything that you would not be comfortable defending as professionally appropriate in a court of law or in front of a disciplinary panel.*
- **Reflect on How Individual Actions will be Perceived by Others.** Learners are invited to develop a more objective appreciation of how what they do is seen by others. In particular it can be very hard to judge how online postings and email will be received without taking a clear, conscientious approach to communicating online. Actions appropriate in one context may not be acceptable in another, particularly if an individual is linked to a profession or institution. Learners are asked to consider how different actions might reflect on their institutions and the profession of medicine and how the actions of the individual can be seen as reflecting or criticizing the position of the institution. Central to this is exploring the balance between freedom of speech and the need for professional discretion. Professional principles of honesty, integrity, and accuracy hold true across cases. *Principle: think carefully and critically about how what you say or do will be perceived by and reflect on others, including individuals and organizations. Act with appropriate restraint.*
- **Be Prepared to Deal with Ambient and Permanent Surveillance.** Almost everything done online can be monitored and recorded, including Google searches, Facebook postings and YouTube uploads. Learners are asked to reflect on how comments and postings may still be accessible years later and how they can impact on individuals' abilities to get or retain a job. *Principle: Think carefully and critically about how what you say or do will be per-*

ceived in years to come; consider every action online as permanent.

- **Promote Honesty and Accountability.** Impersonation and deception are easy in online environments. Health professionals should nonetheless be as open and transparent regarding their identity as possible. Learners are also invited to explore those circumstances where anonymity is required such as whistle blowing, error reporting, peer review and similar circumstances. *Principle: Pretence and deceit are inappropriate behaviors for health professionals. Do not impersonate or seek to hide your identity for malicious or unprofessional purposes.*
- **Be Prepared to Deal with Hostile Acts.** Individuals may seek to tarnish or even destroy another's reputation online (postings, ratings) or impersonate them (identity theft). Learners are invited to explore challenges of attack, defamation, slander, libel and identity theft through online media. *Principle: Be aware of the potential for digital attack or impersonation. Know how to protect your online reputation and what steps to take when it is under attack.*
- **Avoid Criminal Behaviour.** Just because materials or resources are online doesn't mean that they are free or available to do what you want with them. Learners are invited to explore how the rights and permissions to use and republish online materials works, as well as appropriate responses to piracy and theft. *Principle:* Theft, piracy, and bullying are not acceptable forms of behaviour for any professionals. Be aware of the digital rights and laws of the materials you use, and work within these.
- **Maintain Privacy and Confidentiality of Data.** Research and patient data need to be accessed, edited, stored and deleted in ways that maintain confidentiality and privacy. Persistent Internet access across personal and professional locations requires users pay careful attention to where and how they handle data. Ensure you are aware of the privacy standards in your professional context, both regarding data and the mechanisms for accessing it. *Principle: Curation of information is a serious responsibility. Do not expose information to unnecessary risk and consider wisely the potential impact of any use or exchange of information you make.*
- **Maintain Standards.** Respect and openness are not optional for health professionals. Learners are asked to explore issues of respect and consideration, especially when using email or texting. This includes appropriate responses to witnessing, or hearing of, unprofessional behaviour or attacks on others. *Principle: Behave professionally and respectfully in all venues and using all media. Take responsibility for modeling positive digital professionalism to others.*

This digital professionalism framework has been used to guide learner briefing and educational sessions, faculty development sessions and curriculum development in a number of institutions. However, progress is not without challenges.

Many medical schools have addressed the digital in terms of discipline and punishment. In a review of publicly accessible social media guidelines or policies of American medical schools, researchers found that policies and guidelines focus on what is forbidden, inappropriate or impermissible, or discussed online behaviours that should be discouraged (Kind, Genrich, Sodhi, & Chretien, 2010). Relying on static rules is an outmoded construct and neglects the reality that digital presence created by others persists even when an individual may not be active in a particular context (Palen & Dourish, 2003; Qualman, 2011). Uses of media, whether corporate, professional, personal, or social, interact in complex and interconnected ways that cannot be regulated by one organization.

Yet, those schools with publicly accessible policies on social media are the minority (Kind, Genrich, Sodhi, & Chretien, 2010). At the time of writing, digital professional principles are absent from regulatory frameworks for health professionals, and there are few rules or guidelines, often no more than exhortations to "do the right thing" (Bonilla-Warford, 2011; Chretien, Greysen, Chretien, & Kind, 2009; MacDonald, Sohn, & Ellis, 2010; Mondoux, 2010). It is hard in this context to know what the "right thing" is. Our realities are such that "a fine and shifting line between privacy and publicity exists, and is dependent on social context, intention, and the fine-grained coordination between action and the disclosure of that action" (Palen & Dourish, 2003, p.130). In the absence of concrete understanding of the underlying issues the responsibility for governing media use may be granted to specific committees (e.g. student disciplinary committees), individuals (e.g. IT, eLearning leads, information security leads; deanery) or dealt with at a policy level (e.g. student code of conduct, signed agreements, etc). Building a digitally professional environment may depend on first building basic media literacy, with guided examples (negative and positive) of use (Farnan et al., 2009; Farnan, Gersh, Reddy, & Moyer, 2010).

Where activities in the personal realm (e.g. a profile on a social network site) are counter to the rules and regulations of an individual's profession or institution (such as breaking patient confidentiality), the question of who is responsible for correcting the behavior, or even if correction is appropriate, remains unclear. Recently, a post-secondary institution sued two students for their critical posting about a faculty member on a social network site and cross-referenced to the faculty member's personal site. The judge upheld the freedom of speech of the students, even though the institution considered the posting an academic misconduct (Slade, 2010). Case law may therefore raise more issues than answers for administrators and their institutions.

Digital professionalism is about more than appropriate use of Facebook. Taking pictures or videos in many circumstances requires the permission of the subjects before they distributed by email, posted on office doors or as screensavers, or uploaded to social networking sites. While this may be relatively unambiguous in clinical contexts, it is less so regarding social gatherings, or in creating advertisements for student-run events. Even if the environment is not being sampled, inappropriate use of the digital, such as sending text messages during patient encounters, is contrary to standards of care. A key dimension of digital professionalism then is developing the self-discipline to use the digital in appropriate ways at the appropriate times.

FUTURE RESEARCH DIRECTIONS

Although contemporary medical students can still remember a pre-Internet world they will be the last ones to be able to do so. Claims that this differentiates them from those that preceded them clearly need to be challenged with a grounded research base that looks at the many interactions and emergent behaviours and social structures that thrive around the use of digital technologies and not just the technologies themselves. One sign of how things change has been the release of a report to the United Nations recommending that Internet access be recognized as a fundamental human right (La Rue, 2011).

Facebook is seven years old at the time of preparing this chapter and shows no sign of losing its dominant position, though its rival MySpace seems to be faring less well, while the latest competitor, Google+, is still too new to ascertain. Nonetheless all technologies intrinsically subvert themselves, both individually and collectively and value systems change in response to the possible (Graham, 1999). It is hard to tell at this point what will persist and what will prove less stable over time. The digital is also changing the organization and practice of healthcare and as a result the criticality of being digitally professional will grow but also change. Privacy and access will continue to be shaped by, and through, the use of technology. Large-scale initiatives such as analytics for the development of predictive algorithms in patient care will also influence, evolve and challenge existing paradigms of what it means to be a health care practitioner. There is both an opportunity and a need for programmatic research to track and map these changes.

It is arguable that the healthcare professions' slowness to react is partly based on coming to some comprehensive understanding of what it is dealing with before having the confidence to act decisively. Although we present a framework used to develop such understanding we appreciate that ongoing change is likely to continue to create caution and uncertainty in the health professions. Recasting the digital in a positive if somewhat risky light as demonstrated in this chapter is proving to be an appropriate strategy in creating an acceptable discourse for institutions and an accessible model for those entering the health professions. Future research will doubtless find some of this work to be flawed but even as the principles change with the ebb and flow of specific technologies it is hoped that the conceptual basis for the framework will prove to be more stable.

The grounds for future research are already being laid. For instance, emerging theories of value networks are proving successful in modeling how people cluster online and select the locus for their actions there. A parallel development to that of the Internet has been the inexorable rise of cognitive psychology. Although there is a great deal yet to be done, we increasingly understand the mind and its function both individually and socially in unprecedented ways. These and other techniques should also be brought to bear on the issues considered in this book. Possibly the most important challenge is not to consider technology-related social and cognitive issues as a separate discourse but to ground them in similar if not identical problems in the contexts in which they are to be applied.

CONCLUSION

The supposition that contemporary youth is intrinsically able to make good use digital media is flawed. We have demonstrated heterogeneity in media adoption and expertise across all generations. Educators must therefore be more active in helping their students to structure their approach to using and working with and around digital media. New technologies should be critically appraised, and digital literacy embraced as a core curriculum subject, alongside (and intertwined with) mathematics, physical sciences, and language arts (McDonough and Johnson, 2010).

The digital is implied in almost all contemporary professional frameworks through the move to accessing information sources rather than memorizing the required information to practice. The current default position of denial or punishment is perpetuating a hidden curriculum around the digital that misleads our learners and neglects their needs. By negatively impacting the training of healthcare providers not only are they likely to be less effective in practice but we may also be putting patients and the professions at risk.

However, preparing our existing faculty and students in the health professions, and by extension all disciplines, requires that digital professionalism be considered alongside digital literacy and critical appraisal skills. Individuals with lower levels of competence need support as much as more competent members need safe ways to express and utilize their abilities. Faculty must be more directly involved in how their learners use digital media and how they behave around it. They must also challenge the expectations and attitudes that flow from assuming the NetGen model is appropriate and applicable to their developing professional identities. Such a change would indicate a maturing relationship between the professions and the world in which they need to function. If such changes are not made then the professions risk becoming more and more distanced from the individuals and communities they are supposed to serve.

REFERENCES

American Medical Association. (2010). *Medical student debt*. Retrieved December 31, 2010, from http://www.ama-assn.org/ama/pub/about-ama/our-people/member-groups-sections/medical-student-section/advocacy-policy/medical-student-debt.shtml.

Amin, Z., Boulet, J., Cook, D., Ellaway, R., Fahal, A., Kneebone, R., & Ziv, A. (2011). (in press). Technology-enabled assessment of health professions education. *Medical Teacher*. doi:10.3109/0142159X.2011.565832

Barron, B. (2004). Learning ecologies for technological fluency: Gender and experience differences. *Journal of Educational Computing Research*, *31*(1), 1–36. doi:10.2190/1N20-VV12-4RB5-33VA

Beck, C., & Wade, M. (2004). *Got game: How the gamer generation is shaping business forever*. Harvard Business School Publishing.

Beetham, H., McGill, L., et al. (2009). *Thriving in the 21st century: Learning literacies for the digital age*. Glasgow, UK: Glasgow Caledonian University/JISC. Retrieved June 5, 2010, from http://www.jisc.ac.uk/media/documents/projects/llidareportjune2009.pdf.

Bonilla-Warford, N. (2011). Should you take the plunge into social media? *Optometry -. Journal of the American Optometric Association*, *82*(1), 51–52. doi:10.1016/j.optm.2010.11.004

Brailer, D. (2005). Interoperability: The key to the future health care system. *Health Affairs*, (w5.19-w5.20).

Caison, A. L., Bulman, D., Pai, S., & Neville, D. (2008). Exploring the technology readiness of nursing and medical students at a Canadian university. *Journal of Interprofessional Care*, *22*(3), 283–294. doi:10.1080/13561820802061809

Chretien, K., Greysen, S., Chretien, J.-P., & Kind, T. (2009). Online posting of unprofessional content by medical students. *Journal of the American Medical Association*, *302*(12). doi:10.1001/jama.2009.1387

Christensen, C. (2003). *The innovator's dilemma*. New York, NY: HarperBusiness.

Clark, A. (2003). *Natural-born cyborgs*. New York, NY: Oxford University Press.

Cook, D. (2009). The failure of e-learning research to inform educational practice, and what we can do about it. *Medical Teacher*, *31*(2), 158–162. doi:10.1080/01421590802691393

Costello, C. (2005). *Professional identity crisis: Race, class, gender, and success at professional schools*. Nashville, TN: Vanderbilt University Press.

Davies, W. (2006). Digital exuberance. *Prospect*, *119*, 30–33.

Dawkins, R. (1976). *The selfish gene*. Oxford University Press.

Dede, C. (2005). Planning for neomillennial learning styles. *Educause*, *28*(1). Retrieved from http://www.educause.edu/EDUCAUSE+Quarterly/EDUCAUSEQuarterlyMagazineVolum/PlanningforNeomillennialLearni/157325.

DiMaggio, P., Hargittai, E., Celeste, C., & Shafer, S. (2004). Digital inequality: From unequal access to differentiated use. In Neckerman, K. (Ed.), *Social inequality*. New York, NY: Russell Sage Foundation.

Dutton, W., & Loader, B. (Eds.). (2002). *Digital academe: The new media and institutions of higher education and learning*. London, UK: Routledge.

Ellaway, R. (2010a). eMedical Teacher # 33: Cyborg medical education. *Medical Teacher, 32*(3), 273–275. doi:10.3109/01421591003704360

Ellaway, R. (2010b). Developing learning resources. In Dornan, T., Mann, K., Scherpbier, A., & Spencer, J. (Eds.), *Medical education: Theory and practice* (pp. 265–282). Edinburgh, UK: Elsevier.

Ellaway, R. (2010c). eMedical Teacher # 38: Digital Professionalism. *Medical Teacher, 32*(8), 705–707. doi:10.3109/0142159X.2010.505849

Farnan, J., Paro, J., Higa, J., Reddy, S., Humphrey, H., & Arora, V. (2009). The relationship status of digital media and professionalism: It's complicated. *Academic Medicine, 84*, 1479–1481. doi:10.1097/ACM.0b013e3181bb17af

Farnan, J. M., Gersh, S., Reddy, S. T., & Moyer, D. (2010). A brave new world: Professionalism in the Digital Age. *Academic Internal Medicine Insight, 8*(2), 4-5,17.

Graham, G. (1999). *The Internet: A philosophical inquiry*. Routledge.

Grant, L. (2007). *Learning to be part of the knowledge economy: Digital divides and media literacy* (No. 816). England: FutureLab. Retrieved from http://www.futurelab.org.uk/resources/publications-reports-articles/discussion-papers/Discussion-Paper816.

Haas, J., & Shaffir, W. (1991). *Becoming doctors: The adoption of a cloak of competence*. Greenwich, CT: JAI Press Inc.

Hafferty, F. (1998). Beyond curriculum reform: Confronting medicine's hidden curriculum. *Academic Medicine, 73*(4), 403–407. doi:10.1097/00001888-199804000-00013

Hargittai, E., & Hinnant, A. (2008). Digital inequality: Differences in young adults' use of the internet. *Communication Research, 35*, 602–621. doi:10.1177/0093650208321782

Hobbs, S. D. (2002). Measuring nurses' computer competency: An analysis of published instruments. *Computers, Informatics, Nursing, 20*(2), 63–73. doi:10.1097/00024665-200203000-00012

Hoffman, J. (2010, December 5). As bullies go digital, parents play catch-up. *New York Times*, pp. A1, A26-27. Retrieved from http://www.nytimes.com/2010/12/05/us/05bully.html?ref=us.

Howe, N., & Strauss, W. (2000). *Millenials rising: The next great generation*. New York, NY: Random House.

Ito, M., Baumer, S., Bittanti, M., Boyd, D., Cody, R., & Herr, B. (Eds.). (2009). *Hanging out, messing around, geeking out: Living and learning with new media*. Cambridge, MA: MIT press.

Keen, A. (2007). *The cult of the amateur*. London, UK: Nicholas Brealey Publishing.

Kent, N., & Facer, K. (2004). Different worlds? A comparison of young people's home and school ICT use. *Journal of Computer Assisted Learning, 20*, 440–455. Retrieved from http://www.futurelab.org.uk/resources/publications-reports-articles/external-publications/External-Publication630. doi:10.1111/j.1365-2729.2004.00102.x

Kind, T., Genrich, G., Sodhi, A., & Chretien, K. C. (2010). Social media policies at US medical schools. *Medical Education Online, 15*.

Krause, N., Roulette, G., Papp, K., & Kaelber, D. (2006). Assessing medical informatics confidence among 1st and 2nd year medical students. *AMIA. Annu. Symp. Proc.* 2006, (p. 989).

La Rue, F. (2011). *Report of the Special Rapporteur on the promotion and protection of the right to freedom and expression. Human Rights Council*. United Nations.

MacDonald, J., Sohn, S., & Ellis, P. (2010). Privacy, professionalism and Facebook: A dilemma for young doctors. *Medical Education, 44*(8), 805–813. doi:10.1111/j.1365-2923.2010.03720.x

McDonough, B., & Johnson, J. (2010). *Inspiring education: A dialogue with Albertans*. Edmonton, Canada: Alberta Education.

Meng, J., Elliott, K., & Hall, M. (2010). Technology readiness index (TRI): Assessing cross-cultural validity. *Journal of International Consumer Marketing, 22*(1), 19–31. doi:10.1080/08961530902844915

Mondoux, S. (2010). *CFMS guide to medical professionalism*. Canadian Foundation of Medical Students.

Nguyen, D., Zierler, B., & Nguyen, H. (2011). A survey of nursing faculty needs for training in use of new technologies for education and practice. *The Journal of Nursing Education, 50*(4), 181–188. doi:10.3928/01484834-20101130-06

Oblinger, D., & Oblinger, J. (Eds.). (2005). *Educating the Net Generation*. Retrieved from net.educause.edu/ir/library/pdf/pub7101.pdf.

Palen, L., & Dourish, P. (2003). Unpacking "privacy" for a networked world. Paper presented at the CHI 2003, Ft. Lauderdale, Florida, USA.

Parasuraman, A. (2000). Technology readiness index (tri): A multiple-item scale to measure readiness to embrace new technologies. *J Service Rsch, 2*(4), 307–320. doi:10.1177/109467050024001

Prensky, M. (2001). Digital natives, digital immigrants. *Horizon, 9*(5). doi:10.1108/10748120110424816

Qualman, E. (2011). *Socialnomics: How social media transforms the way we live and do business*. John Wiley and Sons.

Reiser, S. (2009). *Technological medicine: The changing world of doctors and patients*. New York, NY: Cambridge University Press.

Rideout, V., Foehr, U., & Roberts, D. (2005). *Gen M: Media in the lives of 8–18 year-olds*. Henry J. Kaiser Family Foundation.

Rideout, V., Foehr, U., & Roberts, D. (2010). *Generation M2: Media in the lives of 8- to 18-year-olds*. Henry J. Kaiser Family Foundation.

Rideout, V., Foehr, U., Roberts, D., & Brodie, M. (1999). *Kids and media at the new millenium*. Henry J. Kaiser Family Foundation.

Rothman, D., & Blumenthal, D. (Eds.). (2010). *Medical professionalism in the new information age*. Rutgers University Press.

Slade, D. (2010). *Students win Facebook battle with U of C: Judge rules in favour of twins over defamation*. Calgary Herald. Retrieved from http://www.calgaryherald.com/technology/Students+Facebook+battle+with/3670183/story.html.

Slater, C., Crichton, S., & Pegler, K. (2010). *Understanding teaching technology use by generation, knowledge and career cycle* (p. 39). Calgary Board of Education.

Snyder, B. (1971). *The hidden curriculum*. Cambridge, MA: MIT Press.

Statistics Canada. (2010, May 10). Canadian internet use survey. *The Daily*. Retrieved from http://www.statcan.gc.ca/daily-quotidien/100510/dq100510a-eng.htm.

Tapscott, D. (1997). *Growing up digital: The rise of the net generation*. New York, NY: McGraw-Hill.

Thompson, L., Dawson, K., Ferdig, R., Black, E., Boyer, J., Coutts, J., & Black, N. (2008). The intersection of online social networking with medical professionalism. *Journal of General Internal Medicine, 23*(7), 954–957. doi:10.1007/s11606-008-0538-8

Tworek, J. (2007). *High school students' uses of media.* Calgary: M.Sc., University of Calgary.

United States Census Bureau. Population Division, Education & Social Stratification Branch. (2010). *Appendix table A: Households with a computer and internet use: 1984 to 2009.* Washington, DC: Government Printing Office.

United States Department of Commerce. (2010). *Exploring the digital nation: Home broadband internet adoption in the United States.* National Telecommunications and Information Association.

Warschauer, M. (2000). Technology and school reform: A view from both sides of the track. *Education Policy Analysis Archives, 8*(4), 1–21.

ADDITIONAL READING

Altman, I. (1977). Privacy Regulation: Culturally Universal or Culturally Specific? *The Journal of Social Issues, 33*(3), 66–84. doi:10.1111/j.1540-4560.1977.tb01883.x

Beetham, H., McGill, L., & Littlejohn, A. (2009). *Thriving in the 21st century: Learning Literacies for the Digital Age (LLiDA project).* Glasgow: Glasgow Caledonian University.

Cain, J., Scott, D., & Smith, K. (2010). Use of social media by residency program directors for resident selection. *American Journal of Health-System Pharmacy, 67*(19), 1635–1639. doi:10.2146/ajhp090658

Chretien, K., Greysen, S., Chretien, J., & Kind, T. (2009). Online Posting of Unprofessional Content by Medical Students. *Journal of the American Medical Association, 302*(12). doi:10.1001/jama.2009.1387

Ellaway, R. (2007). In Beetham, H., & Sharpe, R. (Eds.), *Discipline Based Designs for Learning: The Example of Professional and Vocational Education. Design for Learning: rethinking pedagogy for the digital age* (pp. 153–165). Routledge.

Ellaway, R., & Topps, D. (2010). In Wankel, C., & Malleck, S. (Eds.), *Preparing for Practice: Issues in Virtual Medical Education. Emerging Ethical Issues of Life in Virtual Worlds* (pp. 101–117). Information Age Publishing.

Farnan, J., Gersh, S., Reddy, S., and Moyer, D. (2010). A Brave New World: Professionalism in the Digital Age Academic Internal Medicine Insight 8(2), 4-5,17.

Guseh, J., Brendel, R., & Brendel, D. (2009). Medical professionalism in the age of online social networking. *Journal of Medical Ethics, 35*(9), 584–586. doi:10.1136/jme.2009.029231

Henning, E., & Van der Westhuizen, D. (2004). Crossing the digital divide safely and trustingly: how ecologies of learning scaffold the journey. *Computers & Education, 42*(4), 333–352. doi:10.1016/j.compedu.2003.08.006

Karasavvidis, I. (2009). Activity Theory as a conceptual framework for understanding teacher approaches to Information and Communication Technologies. *Computers & Education, 53*(2), 436–444. doi:10.1016/j.compedu.2009.03.003

Kennedy, G., Gray, K., & Tse, J. (2008). 'Net Generation' medical students: technological experiences of pre-clinical and clinical students. *Medical Teacher, 30*(1), 10–16. doi:10.1080/01421590701798737

Kind, T., Genrich, G., Sodhi, A. and Chretien, K.C. (2010). Social media policies at US medical schools. Medical Education Online, 15.

Kontos, E., Bennett, G., & Viswanath, K. (2007). Barriers and Facilitators to Home Computer and Internet Use Among Urban Novice Computer Users of Low Socioeconomic Position. *Journal of Medical Internet Research, 9*(4), e31. doi:10.2196/jmir.9.4.e31

Link, T., & Marz, R. (2006). Computer literacy and attitudes towards e-learning among first year medical students. *BMC Medical Education*, *6*(34).

Logan, R. (2007). Clinical, classroom, or personal education: attitudes about health literacy. Journal of the Medical Library Association, 95(2), 127-137; e148.

MacDonald, J., Sohn, S., & Ellis, P. (2010). Privacy, professionalism and Facebook: a dilemma for young doctors. *Medical Education*, *44*(8), 805–813. doi:10.1111/j.1365-2923.2010.03720.x

Mostaghimi, A., Crotty, B., & Landon, B. (2010). The Availability and Nature of Physician Information on the Internet. *Journal of General Internal Medicine*, *25*(11), 1152–1156. doi:10.1007/s11606-010-1425-7

Nardi, B. (1999). *Information ecologies: using technology with heart*. Boston, MA: MIT Press.

Norman, C., & Skinner, H. (2006). eHealth Literacy: Essential Skills for Consumer Health in a Networked World. *Journal of Medical Internet Research*, *8*(2), e9. doi:10.2196/jmir.8.2.e9

Palen, L., & Dourish, P. (2003). Unpacking "privacy" for a networked world. Paper presented at the Proceedings of the SIGCHI conference on Human factors in computing systems, Ft. Lauderdale, Florida, USA.

Qualman, E. (2011). *Socialnomics: How Social Media Transforms the Way We Live and Do Business*. John Wiley and Sons.

Wilkinson, A., While, A., & Roberts, J. (2009). Measurement of information and communication technology experience and attitudes to e-learning of students in the healthcare professions: integrative review. *Journal of Advanced Nursing*, *65*(4). doi:10.1111/j.1365-2648.2008.04924.x

KEY TERMS AND DEFINITIONS

Digital Literacy: A multi-dimensional construct that encompasses: a foundational knowledge or capability with using and appraising digital media; a practice without which a learner is impoverished in relation to culturally valued knowledge; the ability to communicate using a variety of digital media. This definition is grounded in the work of Beetham et al (2009).

Digital Professionalism: A set of principles and practices for appropriate and accountable use of digital media grounded in a particular professional domain.

Dynamic Boundary Regulation: Recognizing and redefining the boundary between the personal and the professional in acts of give and take between and among social entities and technical realities.

Medical Education: The process by which doctors (physicians and surgeons) are trained.

Meme: A model of how an idea, behaviour or style spreads from person to person within a culture. First termed by Richard Dawkins in "The Selfish Gene" (1976) it is the cultural analogue of the gene in as much as it models how ideas are transmitted, changed and adapted in response to the cultural environment in which they exist.

NetGen Meme: An aggregate of the ideas and symbols that depict contemporary youth as fluid, efficient and effective users of digital technologies and therefore intrinsically superior to their less able seniors.

Chapter 19
Utilizing Audio and Video Captures to Train and Engage the Net Generation in Effective Presentation Skills

Jessica Fargnoli
Bergen Community College, USA

ABSTRACT

This chapter examines the rationale and benefits for the use of audio and video capture as a pedagogical tool for engaging and instructing the Net Generation. It examines means of incorporating audio and video technology to guide students in developing effective presentation skills, and provides examples of how to utilize audio and video capture technology in other disciplines.

Specifically, this chapter provides (1) a pedagogical resource and strategy to engage the Net Generation; (2) provides an effective and applied approach for instruction through audio and video captures in the classroom; and (3) discusses increased level of student engagement through incorporating technology into the classroom. As a case example, self-report and survey results from college-level Speech Communication courses and remedial Basic Communication courses in which Echo 360 audio and video capture technology was utilized will be explored in respect to engaging the Net Generation.

INTRODUCTION

The Net Generation, born between 1980-2000, often referred to as "Digital Natives" by Marc Prensky, (2001a, p. 1) has been raised in a multimedia technology environment where using the Internet, blogging, instant messaging, social networking, text messaging, using smart phone applications, and posting videos is second nature as they connect with others and function in society. Due to this ubiquitous exposure to technology, the Net Generation has developed a particularly unique skill set that enables them to be independent, autonomous, innovative, emotionally and intel-

DOI: 10.4018/978-1-61350-347-8.ch019

lectually open, investigative, and collaborative learners (Tapscott, 1998). Because of this, the Net Generation desires options, choices, and a customized experience (Tapscott, 1998). To the Digital Native, technology is simply an "extension" of themselves and who they are (McLuhan, 1964, p. 54).

As can be seen from the above discussion, for the Net Generation student, technology is a means to connect as well as an activity in itself that fosters interaction and learning. One such technology is audio and video capture. Incorporating and applying audio and video capture software in college-level courses is a means to provide innovative, collaborative, and active learning. Audio and video capture technology engages a variety of learning styles, including aural, visual, and kinesthetic, in order to create a customized learning experience for the technologically savvy Net Generation student. This chapter therefore considers ways to approach and utilize an audio and video capture system as a presentation tool in the college classroom. It explores the effects of innovative teaching methods utilizing technology for digital learners.

BACKGROUND

The Net Generation communicates in ways that revolve around digital and media usage in the same ways that previous generations used the technology available to them. The Net Generation has been raised tech-savvy; it uses MP3 players, email, cell phones, smart phones, and voicemail. Net Generation members share their lives with the world via digital recordings and online sharing communities as YouTube®[1]. Because the Net Generation has been raised in an electronic environment, they also maintain a different skill set and ultimately, learn differently from prior generations (Oblinger & Oblinger, 2005; Prensky, 2006; Tapscott, 1998; Barnes, Marateo, & Ferris, 2007). The Net Generation is assertive, independent, autonomous, and savvy with technology, but oftentimes, they lack information literacy skills, critical thinking skills, and particularly reflection or analysis (Prensky, 2001b; Oblinger & Oblinger, 2005).

To better connect with a generation that has grown up with everything technological, how can educators utilize digital mediums to facilitate their learning? One means of doing so is through the use of digital technologies. Audio and video capture technology can help Net Generation students achieve self-reflection, critical thinking, and self-presentation skills (Wesch, 2009b). One technology in particular, video feedback, has been argued as the most effective method for improving oral communication skills (Brown, Bull & Pendlebury, 1997). Since Net Generation students gravitate toward the idea of posting and watching videos in online communities, adopting the basic concept of video recording and applying it to education can be useful. It can be easily integrated in the classroom through the use of audio and video capture technology.

SPEAKING THE LANGUAGE OF THE NET GENERATION

The Net Generation thrives on social networking, along with a combination of instant gratification, engagement, active learning, and collaboration (Tapscott, 1998). When instructing the Net Generation, educators should understand not only how to utilize technology in the classroom while upholding traditional teaching methodology, but also to communicate with students who live in a 24/7 communication environment.

Traditionally, as educators, we know how to motivate students to learn by "grounding learning activities in real world experience," "[inviting] learners to innovate," and "[celebrating] unique forms of participation," but do we "allow technology to foster adaptive activity"? (DeGennaro, 2008, p. 14-15). Educators must "craft learning designs that unite youth technology practices with effective learning practices" (DeGennaro, 2008, p. 1). Further, if useful technology is available, why *not* utilize it to engage the changing educational needs of the Net Generation?

Many Net Generation students are familiar with audio and video recording equipment as these products are widely available, easy to operate, and inexpensive to acquire. Their immersive use of video technologies can be seen in the following facts: Facebook®[2] has more than 500 million active users, and over 2 billion videos a day are watched on YouTube alone. Every minute there are 24 hours of video uploaded to YouTube (YouTube, 2011). There are more than 200 million active users currently accessing Facebook through mobile devices (Facebook, 2010). This demonstrates the unique digital climate where posting videos and photographs to social networking sites unites and connects an entire age.

As society moves toward the digitalization of business practices and the distribution of news via interactive company websites and online news videos, academics can also incorporate new technologies into education. The same audio and video tools that attract users to upload videos to the Internet or watch news segments online can be applied in a variety of disciplines in order to engage the Net Generation student and therefore, allow educators to speak the same language as their students by using the same technological media.

Further, with the shift from textual literacy to visual literacy, audio and video captures are the new screen language—the new currency for learning (Bleed 2005, p. 6). Educators can either join their Digital Native students or remain Digital Immigrants (Prensky, 2004, p. 8-11). This is supported by educators like Bleed, who argues that "the multimedia language of the screen has become the current vernacular" (Bleed, 2005, p. 6). When educators utilize a multimedia approach in the classroom, we will see that "the language of the screen is capable of constructing complex meanings independent of text" (Bleed, 2005, p. 6). With audio and video recordings, Net Generation students can shift from linear learning to hypermedia learning and experience a customized classroom experience that was not available 20 years ago.

Visual Literacy

The Net Generation has been raised in a fast-paced, highly visual society with high-definition television and broadband Internet, both with crystal clear, life-like videos and images. A rich visual environment has allowed Net Generation students to develop "hypertext minds" that allow them to entertain a variety of thoughts at once (Prensky, 2001b, p. 3).This allows the Net Generation to create and consume digital media and technology-enhanced texts of all kinds (Mabrito & Medley, 2008). Generally, these multimodal texts influenced by the digital world consist of words, graphics, sound, and video. Net Geners "prefer their graphics before their text rather than the opposite" (Prensky, 2001a, p. 2). For example, Adam Taylor, an e-marketing specialist for an insurance company and a borderline millennial, stated, "Video allows us to get sight and sound rather than someone just reading information off a static page" (in Chordas 2008, p. 89-90). Rather than reading large amounts of text, audio and video recordings allow the Net Generation to engage in an image rich environment.

Visual and kinesthetic learning allows the Net Generation to perform, participate, and experience by doing rather than just thinking or reading about things. Those Net Generation students who are kinesthetic learners, can simulate, role play, and become physically involved in the learning process through video recordings. By video recording their speeches, students can participate in the action of being the learner while simulating the thrill of filmmaking. For example, a topic as simple as a "how to," or speech of demonstration, puts the Net Generation learner in control of method and content as they show the audience what they think the best steps are to complete a process. In its basic form, countless self-made amateur videos are posted on YouTube, ranging from basic instructions in guitar playing to mimicking celebrity makeup applications, to performance art routines in singing, dancing, and acting. These types of videos, exemplify the desire of the Net Generation to disseminate many levels of knowledge and expertise of various subjects that are of personal interest to them.

The Net Generation also utilizes video as a way to document and record their thoughts and feelings. Video bloggers, also referred to as vloggers, create regular video diaries to express their thoughts in watchable videos in the same way that generations past wrote down their thoughts on paper (Young, 2007). Some educators utilize this propensity for self-documentation in their classrooms. For example, Michael Wesch, an assistant professor of cultural anthropology at Kansas State University, has his undergraduate students conduct ethnography of the online community of YouTube (Young, 2007). Wesch's students make their own regular vlogs and have the option to post their videos on YouTube. This has led Wesch to conceptualize the idea of speaking the language of video. In a speech at the "Personal Democracy Forum at Jazz at Lincoln Center, Wesch remarked, "They all speak video" (Wesch, 2009a).

Perhaps this phenomenon is not unique to the Net Generation. Over four decades ago the media ecologist Marshall McLuhan (1964) famously stated, "The medium is the message" (McLuhan 1964, p. 7).The message of a personal video recording is simple and yet complete: the aural and visual image of the individual is a truly powerful tool to communicate one's self. In the process, it also helps users develop a sense of self-awareness and self-presentation. There is nothing that promotes reflectiveness more than watching a video recording of oneself.

Action and Entertainment

According to the PEW Research Center, "69% of Internet users watch or download video online" and 84% of 18 to 29 year old young adult internet users watch or download videos (Purcell, 2010, p. 1, 4). The Net Generation uses digital media for entertainment, and consider excluding technology from the more "serious" aspects of life, such work and school, as peculiar. Urlocker (2006) highlights the ways in which the Net Generation does not separate work and school from entertainment. He states, "entertainment seems to be integrated into work as bite-sized snacks consumed through the day" (Urlocker, 2006, p. FP3).

This can have utility for education. When students are video recorded in the classroom, they can experience the feeling of a television and radio broadcast, while still experiencing the joyfulness of a semi-amateur video taken in the comforts of the classroom. The act of being video recorded is entertaining in itself, and the mere participation in such public activity is appealing to the Net Generation's desire for action and entertainment. When students watch their video recordings, they are integrating entertainment and education into their regular lives.

Since the Net Generation likes to incorporate devices that can be used for entertainment purposes into real-life work and school applications, audio and video capture assignments let students unite learning and entertainment. Students can learn by watching and re-watching themselves or their classmates on video, and can experience self-evaluation and peer critique outside of the classroom. Doug Edmunds, Assistant Dean for IT in UNC Law, stated it best, "I think students really do like to take their learning anywhere" (in Weyenberg, 2009, p. 39). Richard T. Sweeney, university librarian at the New Jersey Institute of Technology, remarks, "They [the Net Generation] like portability, and they are frustrated by technology that tethers them to a specific location" (in Carlson, 2005, p. A-34-A-37).

My personal experience from instructing the Net Generation shows the above to hold true. In my teaching, audio and video recordings allowed students to bring the elements of media entertainment into the classroom, thus engaging them with course material in ways that were previously impossible. By downloading the video files to a course learning management system or another private password protected website on the Internet, students experience web-browsing. Students may also view this process similar to the navigation of an online web portal as they browse and search through the downloaded student speech files. If students have Internet access on their mobile phone device, they can view their in-class video captured speeches on the device. Further, since audio files are downloadable as a podcast, students are able to download their file and upload to their MP3 player of their choice. This makes learning both active and entertaining.

Brown (2000) notes that the web fostered a shift in learning that has a "tendency toward action" and is based in discovery for digital learners, which encompasses navigation, discovery, and judgment (Brown, 2000, p. 15). With audio and video captures in the classroom, navigation, discovery, judgment, and action are all integrated parts of the process of creating and viewing video recordings. First, students experience many emotions as they *navigate* through the process of writing their presentation outlines, and as they *discover* the emotional aspect of presenting in front of a live audience. As students, deliver their speeches or presentations, they *take action* through the physical, mental, and emotional processes of speaking in front of an audience, while at the same time, mentally perceiving or *judging* how their delivery appears to the audience. After being in front of a live audience, students have the opportunity to *reflect* back on, and make judgments about, their performance. Students can critically analyze and draw conclusions from this interactive process.

Palfrey and Gasser (2008) reinforce the notion that Net Generation students are very creative and perceive information to be malleable. Essentially, information "is something that they can control and reshape in new and interesting ways" (Palfrey & Gasser, 2008, p. 6). Since information is perceived as something that can be reshaped, the Net Generation can shift attention from one idea, concept, and task to another quite rapidly (Oblinger, D.G., 2006, p. 9). This active process of experience building occurs with an audio and video recording.

APPLICATION IN THE CLASSROOM

Educators have a wide variety of e-learning and course capture systems to choose from and utilize in order to help create a customized learning experience for students. Such technologies include (but are not limited to) Accordent®[3], Echo 360®[4], Camtasia®[5], Mediasite®[6], Tegrity®[7], and Adobe® Connect™[8].[9] These capture systems allow instructors to create ad-hoc captures of classroom activities. Instructors can audio and video record their students delivering in-class presentations and then utilize an automatic upload feature where the audio and video files become available in the course learning management system.

If built-in classroom capture systems are not available in the instructor's respective colleges and universities, educators can utilize traditional camcorders or Flip Video®[10] cameras and require students to upload videos onto websites such as Vimeo®[11], YouTube, or Facebook.[12] Utilization of these methods is simple since students are accustomed to the idea of creating, broadcasting, or viewing online videos via these forums.

Video capture assignments can be utilized in various disciplines. Not only does it allow students to become better public speakers, but they can become more confident in their personal abilities, become empowered, and better engage themselves with course content. Students "learn by doing" and through self-expression, an important way in which the Net Generation student becomes engaged in the classroom (McNeely, 2005, p. 4.2).

Video capture has much potential for classroom application. Instructors can tailor assignments to their needs. Students can create video documentaries; script, record, and simulate a news broadcast; or create a talk show to highlight a particular concept discussed in class. Instructors can assign students to create, present, and record their interpretation of literary excerpts, a historical event, scientific experiment, or philosophical concept. In an art, music, or theatre class, students can showcase their artwork or musical talent via video capture systems that can be broadcast campus-wide or displayed at a later date for more audiences. In a science class, students can narrate, present, and record laboratory experiment results. Students can broadcast their work, become connected, and truly take part in learning and dissemination of information through the presentation experience. In addition, communication and business classes offer a natural opportunity for recording and critiquing presentations.

Audio and video recordings have been used in diverse educational environments. It is a useful technique in medical education (Ashbury, Iverson & Kralj, 2001; Kurtz, Laidlaw, Makoul & Schnabl, 1999; Whitehouse, 1991). For example, physicians and nurses in training have videotaped their patient simulations to analyze medical interactions (Byrne & Heath, 1980; Penner, Orom, Albrecht, Franks, Foster & Ruckdeschel, 2007; Winters, Hauck, Riggs, Clawson & Collins, 2003). Psychiatrists have also utilized video feedback to assist with training communication skills (Gask, 1998).

The above are some examples of disciplinary applications of the uses of audio and video capture in the classroom. Their optimal utilization depends on the instructor's need. For a Net Generation student, instructors are vital to their learning, but they appreciate extra guidance and mentoring (King, 1993). Instructors can equip students with the elements of effective communication theory, but Net Generation students thrive on the actual experience of doing and understanding without simply being told what to say, think or do. The Net Generation gravitates toward the challenge of learning through "inductive discovery" (Oblinger, D.G., 2006, p. 9). Oftentimes, Net Generation students appreciate this opportunity for self-reflection with audio and video recordings.

Instructor and Student Feedback

Feedback derived from viewing an audio-visual recording of oneself helps students imagine how others view, and inevitably judge them. Mead (1934, cited in Wesch 2009b) describes how "self-consciousness" arises out of the social process and through the understanding of himself or herself in relation to others (Morris, 1974, p. 91, 171, 172; Wesch, 2009b, p. 23). In the process of communication emerges a "conversation of gestures," which is either "conscious (significant)" or "unconscious (non-significant)" (Morris, 1974, p. 81). Mead argues that we cannot realize "significant symbols" or gestures until we engage in "reflective behavior" (Morris, 1974, p. 71, 91). For example, Mead is illustrating that we are not aware of our "sets of habits" as evidenced when we use particular vocal inflections when communicating joy (Morris, 1974, p. 163). We may sense joyousness and that we sent this meaning to another, but we do not realize the particular details that achieve this emotion. Our gestures may strike meaning with another individual, but it must make an impression on us in order to achieve awareness and significance.

For example, if an instructor simply tells a student that to be a better presenter she needs to "Stand up straight, look at the audience, and stop moving around," the student may perceive this as the instructor just being too strict or insensitive. With the video recordings, a student can see for herself exactly how she appears in a speaking situation. This personalized learning experience allows students to engage in the realistic self-appraisal. Through this self-reflection enabled by video recordings, students have the ability to form, change, mold, and transform their identities. This meets the Net Generational need to experiment and reinvent through different modes of expression, such as photographs, videos, and social networking (Palfrey & Gasser, 2008, p. 21).

As students progress in the development of their presentation skills, the instructor, the student, and oftentimes their peers witness a transformation from the initial audio and video recording to the final audio and video recording of the semester. This transformation of identity involves a greater level of self-awareness and emotional intelligence, which includes a positive difference in the development of confidence and a better understanding of verbal and nonverbal communication skills. In addition, students can also take the opportunity to mold their professional appearance, attire, or demeanor. For example, in an initial video recording, the student may under-dress for a formal presentation, with a t-shirt and jeans. However, after viewing their video recording, the student often looks at such video recordings and reflects back on the experience and realizes that he wants to look presentable to his peers. In future video recordings, the student may dress professionally or make an effort to impress his or her peers for the next recording. However, students are not only presenting to their classroom peers, "but also to one's own future self" (Wesch, 2009b, p. 24). For instance, instructors will notice that students will take pride in dressing up for the occasion of delivering their final speech of the semester. In essence, the video capture can promote an evolution of the student.

CASE EXAMPLE

To illustrate the potential of audio and video capture, a use of the Echo 360 audio and video capture software system is discussed in Basic Communication and Speech Communication courses at a community college in the north eastern United States of America. Echo 360 normally is marketed as lecture capture software to record instructor lectures; however, it can be easily utilized to record in-class activities, such as student speeches.

In this example, students delivered speeches to a live audience of peers and were videotaped with Echo 360 software, Echo 360 appliances, and the use of built-in classroom camera equipment. Speeches were only recorded in specifically designated Echo 360 classrooms on the college campus. Speeches were videotaped with the ad-hoc capture option, enhanced audio, an automatic upload feature, and screen-capture features. After the speeches were videotaped, students would access their presentations on their own computers via their course management system, where the recordings were uploaded. Students were then assigned to either write self-critique video reaction papers or peer-critique video reaction.

Utilizing Echo 360 audio and video capture allowed students to have instant access to their presentations, which were automatically uploaded to a web-based course application, available to only students registered for the course for student privacy (as opposed to a video camera device recording that is not automatically uploaded to the Internet). With 24/7 access to recorded speeches, Net Generation students are allowed the ability to navigate, view, and analyze recordings so they can independently draw their own emotional, intellectual, and academic conclusions.

In my personal experience, I have found that students who were asked to watch their recorded speeches and then write a self-critique assignment tended to note that they enjoy the experience of being video recorded in class and often cited that it helped them in identifying how they act and react as a speaker. They were more able to see their nonverbal communication and appearance as a speaker, hear their voice, and identify unique aspects in how they presented themselves in public.

Many students found the video recordings a rewarding challenge to identify public strengths and weaknesses for themselves. In the classroom, students often remarked that being able to see themselves from the audience's perspective allowed them to see what to improve upon, without solely relying on the professor's feedback.

Students who had thought that they were terrible speakers, or that they were too nervous, were able to view their performance in the video and are able to identify that they weren't as terrible or nervous as they thought. Other students who had an inflated sense of confidence watched their video and realized that their performance wasn't as amazing as they had originally thought. Basically, students came away with a realistic perspective of their public speaking skills. Some students took this experience as if they are actually performing in an entertainment or media role and imagine themselves or perform as if they were a reporter, newscaster, politician, or celebrity. When watching their speech videos online, they are able to learn from the audience's perspective, an experience not many speakers have the opportunity to do. Students become engaged and take a greater interest in improving their public speaking delivery, professional appearance, and nonverbal communication skills. Students also find watching their video recording a rewarding experience as many students are very proud of watching a presentation that they prepared and delivered. There is a sense of pride, accomplishment, and confidence building in the process.

AUDIO AND VIDEO CAPTURE SURVEY: RESULTS

This section discussed the results of a survey conducted over two semesters and administered through the online course learning management system in December 2010 and again in April 2011. The survey had 15 questions, with Yes/No options, and asked questions about of audio and video captures of recorded student speeches in the course. A total of 106 students voluntarily responded out of a total population of 181 students. Participants came from eleven classes: five remedial Basic Communication students and six 100-level Speech Communication classes voluntarily participated in the survey.

All survey results reported below were filtered and calculated based upon the integral self-report Yes/No Net Generation qualifier question, "Were you born between 1980 and 2000?"

Out of the 106 student respondents, 96 of the students identified themselves as Net Generation students, so the total number of respondents (n) can be considered n= 96 for this study.

Overwhelmingly, 94% of respondents reported that recorded speeches helped them understand and visualize public speaking concepts discussed in class, while 91% of respondents reported that the recorded speeches helped them improve their public speaking skills. Further, 83% reported that recording speeches helped build their confidence in public speaking.

In order to demonstrate how the use of audio and video capture has engaged students in class, respondents were asked to select all answers that applied to their level of engagement. The selections were "Engaged with the course content", "Engaged with the instructor", and "Engaged with other students." Here, 72% of respondents reported that the audio and video recordings engaged them in course content, 48% reported being engaged with the instructor, and 61% reported being engaged with other students in the course.

In further support of the use of audio and video captures in the classroom, 97% of respondents said that they would recommend audio and video capture classes to other students.

In addition to the above evidence, if survey results are drilled down further to include only those Net Generation students that reviewed and analyzed their recorded speeches online (n= 87), the percent of reported "Yes" increases for many questions, reinforcing that when a Net Generation student utilizes the full range of activities available from the audio and video capture technology, they will receive more educational benefits.

For instance, for the respondents who reviewed their recorded speech online, 99% reported that recorded speeches helped them understand and visualize public speaking concepts discussed in class; 93% reported that recorded speeches helped them improve their public speaking skills; 83% reported building their confidence in public speaking; and 75% reported that the video captured speeches engaged them in course content.

The mere act of having their speeches recorded, an experiential learning activity, engages students with each other and in the course content; however it is clear that when students actively view their recordings online, their level of engagement in course content also increases. A viewing and analysis process enables students to realize the connection between theory learned in class and application assignments.

Student Comments from Survey

Student comments on the survey further illustrate how they benefited from the usage of audio and video capture technology. In Question #12 in the survey, students were asked, "In your opinion, what are the benefits of Echo 360 technology in the classroom? What are the benefits of audio and video captures?" In response to this question, students cited several major benefits of audio and video captures including the ability to learn how one is perceived by other people, the ability to re-watch one's speech, the ability to see and hear one's self when giving a speech, the ability to build confidence and composure, the ability to learn without being lectured to, the ability to analyze body language while delivering a speech, and overall improvements in public speaking skills. One comment read, "[It is beneficial] Being able to possibly know how you might be perceived by other people. Knowing what needs to be improved in your public speaking."

Students felt that it was beneficial to see one's mistakes and flaws in order to learn and improve for the next presentation. Students cited that it was beneficial to see one's self from the audience's point of view as if one was in third person. Another comment response read "[it] allows you to see what the teacher critiques you on." Students also cited the added benefit of building self-confidence. One particular response read, "It helped me improve my public speaking skills and it also helped me to be more confident and composed when delivering a speech."

In Question #13 in the survey, students were asked, "How did the recorded speeches make you feel?" Students responded with a variety of thoughts on how it felt to be recorded while presenting a speech to how it felt to see one's self on camera. Responses varied in this question category. Overall, student responses showed an interesting sense of self and overall thought pattern of self-consciousness. Some students were very proud and happy with the recordings, while others felt that they knew that they could have done better. One comment read, "I learned from everyone else's eyes what I was doing." Some students felt that they weren't as bad a speaker as they had originally perceived. One comment read, "They made me feel better about myself. I got to see some negative and positive things that I do during a speech." Some felt that they were nervous seeing themselves on camera. Others cited that they had to become accustomed to being video recorded in class, but they became used to the video camera that they forgot it was there.

In Question #14 in the survey, students were asked, "Please explain how the recorded speeches affected your public speaking performance in the course." Students cited that recording speeches was a chance to identify public speaking mistakes and be able to assess and improve voice, body movement, gestures, pronunciation. One comment read, "I realized what I should do more in the next speech for example more eye contact." Another comment read, "It helped me realize how unprofessional I appeared when I felt I was in my niche." Students realized that audio and video recordings helped them identify points for improvement. One comment read, "By watching the video capture of one speech, it was easier to fix the mistakes for the next speech. Also, watching the video made me realize I didn't look or sound so bad, so it was easier to do the next speech after realizing that speaking didn't have to be such a big deal." Students also felt that this was an opportunity to increase self-awareness and experience a boost in self-confidence. Another comment read, "I now feel more confident about speaking in public than I did before I started this class."

In Question #15 in the survey, students were asked, "Please share any comments or suggestions on accessing captured speeches in your course this semester." In response to this question, students commented that they liked using the technology in the classroom and that it was a good invention. Responses highlighted that students never had been recorded in class before and were appreciative of this opportunity. In this particular question, several students used the word, "awesome" to describe the technology. They liked that they could apply the course material and critique themselves. One comment read, "It was a good, new way of learning and this time seeing yourself is a good way of improving yourself to do better next time rather then just hearing someone tell you what ways to improve." Another comment read, "I just think it was very effective in general. At my other school, all we had were the teachers remarks and sometimes you just think they are being hard on you [be]cause they don't like you. But to be able to see the speech and apply the critique was very helpful in improving my speeches."

Students also felt that the audio and video capture system should be used more frequently in class and in other classes. One comment read, "They should do this with every class." Students liked that they could receive feedback and get to know themselves and their classmates better. Another comment read, "I feel like it is a great idea to have captured speeches for all class[es] because it can really help a student get better at their speeches." Students agreed that the technology should be used again and they also offered ideas and suggestions to improve camera angles, wider panorama views, and to improve lighting in the classroom; thus, showing that they were engaged in the process, action, and entertainment of making and recording the student speech videos.

DISCUSSION: PRESENT AND FUTURE CONCERNS

Although the case discussed here illustrates the value of video capture in the classroom, it is important to consider, how faculty can effectively implement and communicate the pedagogy. With any technology, whether it be digital or traditional, it is necessary to underscore the need for self-correction and self-analysis through a variety of methods. Audio and video capture is simply one of these methods. Instructing students that their self-presentation skills can be developed and ultimately fine-tuned by utilizing video technologies that are normally used for entertainment, documentation, or "authenticity" of self is an additional benefit (Wesch, 2009a). Educators need to instruct the Net Generation in one main area: reflection (Prensky, 2001b, p. 5). With audio and video capture recordings, it allows the Net Generation to pause and reflect away from a fast-paced digital life to critically analyze and draw conclusions from their experiences.

Faculty may have questions, concerns, or complaints relating to the use of video capture technology that may stem from a few areas, including academic significance, personal technological deficiencies, close-mindedness to new methods, or inflexibility. While no technology in and of itself is a guarantee of improved teaching, adapting teaching methods to incorporate digital technology is vital to capturing the Net Generation's inquisitive, curious, and innovative minds. Faculty should remind themselves that making small steps to bridge the "tech gap" with their Net Generation students will go a long way.

Faculty must work to incorporate new technologies in teaching, and in doing so they will be able to challenge themselves to rethink the striking balance "between the physical (classroom) and the virtual world of learning" and perhaps even go as far as renovating the physical space to attract Net Generation learners (Skiba & Barton, 2006, p. 15; Mabrito & Medley, 2007). Net Generation students are "first person learners," and want to become a part of the learning process (Oblinger & Oblinger 2005, p. 2.12; in Skiba & Barton, 2006, p. 15). Academics should reconsider faculty and student perspectives on technology in order to make the connection between faculty participation in technology that draws student participation in the classroom.

The Need for Technology Funding

In the coming years with the addition of more Net Generation learners to classrooms, colleges and universities will need to invest in technology and professional faculty development training. In order to successfully implement audio and video capture technology and software, colleges and universities will need to allocate funding to purchase software licenses for e-capture or course capture systems or redevelop entire classrooms environments for built in cameras, computers, and software. If funding for technology is limited, colleges and universities may look toward implementing less expensive alternatives, such as purchasing hand-held camcorders and software for downloading videos to the Internet.

Faculty participation will be key in the success of audio and video recordings in the classroom, so faculty workshops will be important in order to ease any faculty concerns, apprehensions, or technological competency issues.

Legal Issues and Concerns for Privacy

The technology, media, and legal departments of colleges and universities will need to collaborate with faculty in order to quell any concerns for privacy by collaborating on the creation of privacy release forms. In order to release colleges and universities, faculty members, and other employed staff from potential claims, student privacy release forms are needed. The privacy release forms should be kept on file within the college's technology or media departments in the event such information is needed for future reference. With the influx of Net Generation students, college administrators and staff members should also be briefed about the proper use of technology systems and other rules of privacy.

Faculty syllabi should explicitly state the purpose of audio and video recordings and employ a brief description of the audio and video recording software chosen along with basic directions to access the technology. Net Generation students are curious, emotionally and intellectually open, and enjoy technology, but they will need to know the purpose of the assignment along with a strong commitment to privacy in order to achieve the appropriate level of "buy-in."

E-capture systems with features that allow automatic upload to course learning management systems generally have password-protected systems that allow only faculty and students access to the course and video recordings. Faculty members can also choose to require students to obtain their own video cameras or camcorders, videotape themselves outside of the classroom, and then require students to upload videos on a video sharing website, such as YouTube or Vimeo.[13] Students can share video links with the instructor or other classmates as required by course assignments.

ADA Accommodations: Visually and Hearing Impaired Students

Under the Americans with Disabilities Act, those Net Generation students with medical or physical accommodations will require certain accommodations to have access to audio and video recordings to complete self-evaluations or peer critiques about student presentation skills. Software applications can be obtained and downloaded to add captioning to video recordings to accommodate hearing impaired individuals. Visually impaired individuals can listen to the audio on the video captures to perceive the essence of their presentation.

It should be noted that video capture especially benefit remedial, academically challenged, and disabled students since the practicality of video capture can suit their individual learning styles. Many of these students may have a difficult time perceiving themselves as a good public speaker or presenter. However, being able to watch or listen to their video helps these students conquer their self-concept and learning issues, enabling them to move forward to accomplish additional assignments.

FUTURE RESEARCH DIRECTIONS

Since much research is currently focused on student engagement and participation in relation to lecture capture technology of instructors (Jones, 2008; Ullman, 2009; Weyenberg, 2009), that research needs to be extended. The significant difference between lecture capture and audio and video capture is that the Net Generation student appears at the center of the learning process. Further research in this area will need to be conducted.

Researchers will also need to further analyze the significance of audio and video capture technology on the Net Generation. By video recording the student, there is a shift in the dynamics of the classroom. Students become aware of themselves and are forced to give up the traditional passivity of sitting in the classroom avoiding speeches or presentations. Future research can investigate how audio and visual captures breakdown instructor and student barriers and engage students in active learning.

CONCLUSION

Audio and video capture software appeals to the Net Generation and brings modern technology together with active and collaborative learning, multi-tasking, learning by doing, and instant gratification. Educators can utilize these technologies to better relate to the Net Generation. Learning with audio and video capture allows the Net Generation to learn through active performance, reveal themselves in the classroom, and collaborate with each other in order to improve communication skills.

REFERENCES

Accordent Technologies, Inc. (2011, 15 April). *Hoover's company records, 116246*. (Document ID: 1605079501).

Adobe Systems Incorporated. (2011, 15 April). *Hoover's company records, 12518*. (Document ID: 168152191).

Ashbury, F. D., Iverson, D. C., & Kralj, B. (2001). Physician communication skills: Results of a survey of general/family practitioners in Newfoundland. *Medical Education Online 6*(1). Retrieved from www.med-ed-online.org.

Barnes, K., & Marateo, R. R., & Ferris, S. (2007, April/May). Teaching and learning with the net generation. *Innovate, 3*(4). Retrieved from http://www.innovateonline.info/index.php?view=article&id=382.

Bleed, R. (2005, August). *Visual literacy in higher education* (Educause Publication No. ELI4001). Retrieved from http://net.educause.edu/ir/library/pdf/ELI4001.pdf.

Boehret, K. (2007, September 12). An Easier way to make and share videos. *The Wall Street Journal*. Retrieved from http://online.wsj.com.

Brown, G., Bull, J., & Pendlebury, M. (1997). *Assessing student learning in higher education*. London, UK: Routledge.

Brown, J. (2000). Growing up digital: How the web changes work, education, and the ways people learn. *Change*, *32*(2), 10–20. doi:10.1080/00091380009601719

Byrne, P. S., & Heath, C. C. (1980). Practitioners' use of nonverbal behavior in real consultations. *The Journal of the Royal College of General Practitioners*, *30*(215), 327–331.

Carlson, S. (2005). The net generation in the classroom. *The Chronicle of Higher Education*, *52*(7), A34–A37.

Chordas, L. (2008). Y new technology? *Best's Review*, *109*(6), 88–90.

Cisco Systems, Inc. (2011, Oct. 7). Hoover's company records, 13494. United States, Austin: Dun and Bradstreet, Inc. (ProQuest Document ID: 230596963). Retrieved from http://search.proquest.com/docview/230596963?accountid=10818.

Connected Ventures, L. L. C. (2011, Oct. 6). *Hoover's company records*, 148343. United States, Austin: Dun and Bradstreet, Inc. (ProQuest Document ID: 230578498). Retrieved from http://search.proquest.com/docview/230578498?accountid=10818.

DeGennaro, D. (2008). Learning designs: An analysis of youth-initiated technology use. *Journal of Research on Technology in Education*, *41*(1), 1–20.

Echo360, Inc. (2011). *Echo 360 board of directors*. Retrieved from http://echo360.com/about/board-of-directors/.

Echo360, Inc. (2007, October). *Echo360 launches next generation lecture capture platform*. (Press Release). Retrieved from http://echo360.com/news-events/press-releases/pr102207/.

Facebook. (2010, December). *Facebook statistics*. Retrieved from http://www.facebook.com/press/info.php?statistics.

Facebook, Inc. (2011, 15 April). *Hoover's company records*, 148344. (Document ID: 1014566851).

Gask, L. (1998). Small group interactive techniques utilising video feedback. *International Journal of Psychiatry in Medicine*, *28*(1), 97–113. doi:10.2190/U8MM-JX7Y-LT0T-RKPX

Jones, M. (2008). Lecture capture technology lends a hand to community college students [Technology Update]. *Community College Week*, *20*, 20.

King, A. (1993). From sage on the stage to guide on the side. *College Teaching*, *41*(1), 30. doi:10.1080/87567555.1993.9926781

Kurtz, S., Laidlaw, T., Makoul, G., & Schnabl, G. (1999). Medical education initiatives in communication skills. *Cancer Prevention and Control*, *3*(1), 37–45.

Mabrito, M., & Medley, R. (2008, August/September). Why professor Johnny can't read: Understanding the Net Generation's texts. *Innovate*, *4*(6). Retrieved from http://www.innovateonline.info/index.php?view=article&id=510.

McLuhan, M. (1964). *Understanding media: The extensions of man*. New York, NY: McGraw-Hill Book Company.

McNeely, B. (2005). Using technology as a learning tool, not just the cool new thing. In D. G. Oblinger & J. L. Oblinger (Eds.), *Educating the Net generation* (pp. 4.1-4.10). Retrieved from http://net.educause.edu/ir/library/pdf/pub7101d.pdf.

Mead, G. H. (1934). *Mind, self, and society*. Chicago, IL: University of Chicago Press.

Morris, C. W. (Ed.). (1974). *Mind, self, and society: From the standpoint of a social behaviorist*. Chicago, IL: University of Chicago Press.

Murph, D. (2008, September). Vimeo now hosting one million videos, 10% in HD. *Engadget*. Retrieved from http://hd.engadget.com/2008/09/17/vimeo-now-hosting-one-million-videos-10-in-hd.

Oblinger, D. G. (2006, September). *Listening to what we're seeing*. Keynote address presented at Association for Learning Technology, Edinburgh, UK. Retrieved from http://www.alt.ac.uk/docs/diana_oblinger_20060905.pdf.

Oblinger, D. G., & Oblinger, J. L. (Eds.). (2005). *Educating the Net generation*. Washington, DC: Educause.

Oblinger, D. G., & Oblinger, J. L. (2006). Is it age or IT: First steps toward understanding the net generation. *CSLA Journal, 29*(2), 8–16.

Palfrey, J., & Gasser, U. (2008). *Born digital: Understanding the first generation of digital natives*. New York, NY: Basic Books.

Penner, L., Orom, H., Albrecht, T., Franks, M., Foster, T., & Ruckdeschel, J. (2007). Camera-related behaviors during video recorded medical interactions. *Journal of Nonverbal Behavior, 31*(2), 99–117. doi:10.1007/s10919-007-0024-8

Prensky, M. (2001a). Digital natives, digital immigrants, part 1. *Horizon, 9*(5), 1–6. Retrieved from http://www.marcprensky.com/writing/prensky%20-%20digital%20natives,%20digital%20immigrants%20-%20part1.pdf. doi:10.1108/10748120110424816

Prensky, M. (2001b). Digital natives, digital immigrants, part II: Do they really think differently? *Horizon, 9*(6), 1–6. Retrieved from http://www.marcprensky.com/writing/prensky%20-%20digital%20natives,%20digital%20immigrants%20-%20part2.pdf. doi:10.1108/10748120110424843

Prensky, M. (2004). Use their tools! Speak their language! *Connected, 10*, 8-11. Retrieved from http://www.ltscotland.org.uk/Images/connected_10_tcm4-122006.pdf.

Prensky, M. (2006). *"Don't bother me mom--I'm learning!" How computer and video games are preparing your kids for twenty-first century success and how you can help!*St. Paul, MN: Paragon House.

Purcell, K. (2010, June). *The state of online video*. Retrieved from http://www.pewinternet.org/~/media//Files/Reports/2010/PIP-The-State-of-Online-Video.pdf.

Pure Digital Technologies, Inc. (2011, Oct. 6). *Hoover's company records*, 140105. United States, Austin: Dun and Bradstreet, Inc. (ProQuest Document ID: 230629222). Retrieved from http://search.proquest.com/docview/230629222?accountid=10818.

Skiba, D. J., & Barton, A. J. (2006). Adapting your teaching to accommodate the net generation of learners. *Online Journal of Issues in Nursing, 11*(2), 15.

Sonic Foundry, Inc. (2011, 15 April). *Hoover's company records*, 56057. (Document ID: 168211121).

Tapscott, D. (1998). *Growing up digital: The rise of the net generation*. New York, NY: McGraw-Hill.

TechSmith Corporation. (2011, 15 April). Hoover's company records, 130509. (Document ID: 548579501).

Tegrity, Inc. (2010, October). *McGraw-Hill Education acquires Tegrity, provider of award-winning, automated service that captures class lectures for college students* (Press Release). Retrieved from http://www.tegrity.com/learn-more/press-releases/175-mcgraw-hill-education-acquires-tegrity.

Ullman, E. (2009). Lessons in video. *University Business, 12*(9), 28–34.

Urlocker, M. (2006, December 18). Rebels with a cursor. *National Post*, p. FP3. Retrieved from LexisNexis.

Wesch, M. (2009a, June). *The machine is (changing) us: YouTube and the politics of authenticity*. Keynote address presented at Personal Democracy Forum, Lincoln Center. Retrieved from http://www.youtube.com/watch?v=09gR6VPVrpw.

Wesch, M. (2009b). YouTube and you: Experiences of self-awareness in the context collapse of the recording webcam. *Explorations in Media Ecology*, *8*(2), 19–34.

Weyenberg, M. (2009). Technology in the classroom. *The National Jurist*, *19*(3), 38–39.

Whitehouse, C. R. (1991). The teaching of communication skills in United Kingdom medical schools. *Medical Education*, *25*(4), 311–318. doi:10.1111/j.1365-2923.1991.tb00072.x

Winters, J., Hauck, B., Riggs, C. J., Clawson, J., & Collins, J. (2003). Use of videotaping to assess competences and course outcome. *The Journal of Nursing Education*, *42*(10), 472–476.

Young, J. R. (2007). An anthropologist explores the culture of video blogging. *The Chronicle of Higher Education*, *53*(36), 39.

YouTube. (2011, July). *YouTube frequently asked questions*. Retrieved from http://www.youtube.com/t/faq.

YouTube, LLC. (2011, 15 April). *Hoover's company records*, 148460. (Document ID: 1014564471).

ADDITIONAL READING

Ayiter, E. (n.d). The history of visual communication. Retrieved from http://www.citrinitas.com/history_of_viscom/.

Benson, P. J. (1997). Problems in picturing text: A study of visual/verbal problem solving. [Retrieved from EBSCO*host*.]. *Technical Communication Quarterly*, *6*(2), 141–160. doi:10.1207/s15427625tcq0602_2

Beyers, R. N. (2009). A five dimensional model for educating the net generation. [Retrieved from EBSCO*host*.]. *Journal of Educational Technology & Society*, *12*(4), 218–227.

Bourne, J., & Burstein, D. (2009). *Web video: Making it great, getting it noticed*. Berkley, CA: Peachpit Press.

Burmark, L. (2002). *Visual Literacy: Learn to See, See to Learn*. Alexandria, VA: Association for Supervision & Curriculum Development.

Carlson, K. (2009). Delivering information to students 24/7 with Camtasia. *Information Technology and Libraries*, *28*(3), 154–156.

Carney, R. N., & Levin, J. R. (2002, March). Pictorial illustrations *still* improve students' learning from text. *Educational Psychology Review*, *14*(1), 5–26. Retrieved from http://users.cdli.ca/bmann/0_ARTICLES/Graphics_Carney02.pdf. doi:10.1023/A:1013176309260

Cunningham, B. (2007). *Digital native or digital immigrant, which language do you speak?* Retrieved from NACADA Clearinghouse of Academic Advising Resources website: http://www.nacada.ksu.edu/Clearinghouse/AdvisingIssues/Digital-Natives.htm.

Digital Media, J. I. S. C. (2011). Advice on moving images. Retrieved from http://www.jiscdigitalmedia.ac.uk/movingimages/.

Ekman, P. (2007). *Emotions Revealed: Recognizing faces and feelings to improve communication and emotional life* (2nd ed.). New York, NY: Owl Books- Henry Holt & Company.

Frand, J. (2000). The information age mindset: Changes in students and implications for higher education. *EDUCAUSE Review*, *35*(5), 15–24.

Germain, J. (2007, May 30). The net generation goes to college. *TechNewsWorld*. Retrieved from http://www.technewsworld.com/story/57590.html?wlc=1291393851&wlc=1293410197.

Jones, C. (2010). A new generation of learners? The net generation and digital natives. *Learning, Media and Technology*,*35*(4), 365–368..doi:10.1080/17439884.2010.531278

Jones, S. (2009). Second life, video games, and the social text. *PMLA*, *124*(1), 264. doi:10.1632/pmla.2009.124.1.264

Junco, R., & Mastrodicasa, J. (2007). *Connecting to the net. generation: What higher education professionals need to know about today's students*. Washington, D.C.: NASPA, Student Affairs Administrators in Higher Education.

Knapp, M. (1972). *Nonverbal communication in human interaction*. New York, NY: Reinhart and Winston Inc.

Marino, P. (2004). *3D game-based filmmaking: The art of machinima*. Scottsdale, AZ: Paraglyph Press.

Notay, B., & Grout, C. (2005, October). Looking for more than text? *Ariadne*, *45*. Retrieved from http://www.ariadne.ac.uk/issue45/notay.

O'Donoghue, M., & Cochrane, T. A. (2010). The role of live video capture production in the development of student communication skills. [Retrieved from EBSCO*host*.]. *Learning, Media and Technology*, *35*(3), 323–335. doi:10.1080/17439884.2010.509350

Pletka, B. (2007). *Educating the net generation: How to engage students in the 21st century*. Santa Monica, CA: Santa Monica Press.

Shohet, L. (2010). YouTube, use, and the idea of the archive. [Retrieved from EBSCO*host*.]. *Shakespeare Studies*, *38*, 68–76.

Skiba, D. J. (2007). Nursing education 2.0: YouTube. [Retrieved from EBSCO*host*.]. *Nursing Education Perspectives*, *28*(2), 100–102.

Stokes, S. (2002). Visual literacy in teaching and learning: A literature perspective. *Electronic Journal for the Integration of Technology in Education*, *1*(1), 10-19. Retrieved from http://ejite.isu.edu/Volume1No1/pdfs/stokes.pdf.

Strangelove, M. (2010). *Watching YouTube: Extraordinary videos by ordinary people*. Toronto, Canada: University of Toronto Press.

Tapscott, D. (2009). *Grown up digital: How the net generation is changing your world*. New York, NY: McGraw-Hill.

Taylor, P., & Keeter, S. (Eds.). (2010, February). *Millenials: A portrait of generation next*. Retrieved from Pew Research Center website: http://pewsocialtrends.org/files/2010/10/millennials-confident-connected-open-to-change.pdf.

KEY TERMS AND DEFINITIONS

Ad-Hoc Capture Option: The instructor can decide at any time when he or she wants to start video or audio recording classroom activities or lectures. Without an ad-hoc capture option, instructors must schedule with the college's technology department an appointed date and time when the video or audio recordings will commence.

Audio and Video Captures: A process and system by which classroom activities, such as student speeches and presentations, can be recorded in both audio and video file formats or one format or the other with the use of particular software that will automatically upload to the course learning management system. Students can listen and view their own in-class presentations. In this paper, the terminology of audio and video captures is used interchangeably with audio and video recordings.

Automatic Upload Feature: The raw audio and video files on the computer are automatically uploaded to the central data storage area to be processed for the web. The audio and video files are processed into podcast or vodcast files and can be published within the course management system.

E-Capture: An electronic or online system in which audio and video files of instructor lectures or classroom activities can be uploaded and placed in course learning management systems.

Enhanced Audio: The audio file is enhanced with screen captures.

Lecture Capture: A process and system by which instructor lectures can be recorded in both audio and video file formats or one format or the other with the use of particular software that will automatically upload to the course learning management system. Students can listen and view their instructor's in-class lectures.

Screen Captures: The audio and video capture of instructor lectures or student speeches can be videotaped while also recording the images, files, or presentations on the computer desktop. For example, instructor lectures and student speeches can also include the presentation slides within the file format. Any minor changes, such as a slide change, will be reflected in the video file.

ENDNOTES

1 YouTube, LLC was founded in 2005 by Steve Chen (former CEO) and Chad Hurley (former CEO). Salar Kamangar is the current CEO of YouTube, LLC. YouTube, LLC is a subsidiary of Google. Founders Sergey Brin and Larry E. Page are the current CEOs of Google Incorporated. (Youtube, Hoover's Company Records, 2011).

2 Facebook is owned by Facebook, Inc. Mark Zuckerberg is the current CEO of Facebook, Inc. (Facebook, Hoover's Company Records 2011).

3 Accordent is owned by Accordent Technologies, Inc., which is a subsidiary of Polycom, Inc. In 2011, Polycom acquired Accordent. Michael C. Newman is the current CEO of Accordent Technologies. Polycom's current Chairman is David DeWalt and the current President, CEO, and Director is Andrew M. Miller. (Accordent, Hoover's Company Records 2011).

4 Echo 360 is owned by and is a trademark of Echo360, Inc. Anystream Apreso acquired Lectopia resulting in the Echo 360 System. (Echo 360, 2007). Fred Singer is the current CEO of Echo 360, Inc. (Echo 360 Inc., 2011).

5 Camtasia is owned by TechSmith Corporation. William D. Hamilton is the current President of TechSmith Corporation. (TechSmith Corporation, Hoover's Company Records, 2011).

6 Mediasite is owned by Sonic Foundry, Inc. Rimas P. Buinevicius is the current Chairman of Sonic Foundry, Inc. Gerald R. Weis is the current CEO and Director of Sonic Foundry, Inc. (Sonic Foundry, Inc., Hoover's Company Records 2011).

7 On October 4, 2010, McGrawHill Education acquired Tegrity. Peter Davis is the current President of McGrawHill Education. (Tegrity, Inc., 2010).

8 Adobe Connect is owned by Adobe Systems Incorporated. Charles M. Geschke and John E. Warnock are current Co-Chairman of Adobe Systems Incorporated. (Adobe Systems Incorporated, Hoover's Company Records, 2011).

9 The listing of a variety of e-learning and course capture systems is not an endorsement of any system by the author or publisher.

10 Cisco Technology, Inc., also referred to as Cisco Systems, Inc., acquired Pure Digital Technologies, the maker of Flip Video, on May 21, 2009. John Chambers is the current Chairman and CEO of Cisco Systems. (Cisco Systems, Hoover's Company Records, 2011). Jonathan Kaplan is the Chairperson and CEO of Pure Digital Technologies.

(Boehret, 2007; Pure Digital Technologies, Hoover's Company Records, 2011).

11 Connected Ventures, LLC is the owner of Vimeo. InterActiveCorp (IAC) is the ultimate parent company of Connected Ventures, LLC and Vimeo. The President of Connected Ventures, LLC is Josh Abramson (Connected Ventures, LLC, Hoover's Company Records, 2011). The Current Chairman and Senior Executive of IAC is Barry Diller and the CEO is Gregory Blatt. Zach Klein and Jake Lodwick founded Vimeo in November 2004. (Murph, 2008).

12 The listing of a variety of video cameras and video sharing websites is not an endorsement of any product or system by the author or publisher.

13 The listing of a variety of video sharing websites is not an endorsement of any product or system by the author or publisher.

Chapter 20
Service-Learning as a Pedagogical Approach for Net Generation Learners:
A Case Study

Sally Blomstrom
Embry-Riddle Aeronautical University, USA

ABSTRACT

This chapter focuses on service-learning as a pedagogical approach for Net Generation learners, and presents a case study from a private technological institution in the United States as an example. The chapter covers details of the assignment as a case study, specific considerations in the assignment's design for Net Generation learners, ways in which the assignment followed principles of service-learning assignments, and how service-learning principles correspond with Net Generation learner characteristics. The case study focuses on an assignment for a speech class in which university students developed and delivered presentations on science topics to two audiences: children in an afterschool program and an online audience of teachers and adults. Issues and problems that arose are discussed followed by suggestions and recommendations for this service-learning project.

INTRODUCTION

This chapter explores service-learning as an effective pedagogical approach for teaching Net Generation learners, using a specific assignment as a case study. The assignment was for a speech course, which was a required general education class. The pedagogical method of service-learning has been incorporated in several sections of the speech class for four years. Data gathered during that period comparing service-learning with other pedagogies indicated students in the service-learning sections showed larger gains in

DOI: 10.4018/978-1-61350-347-8.ch020

the areas of content development, delivery, organization, team work, and personal skills (Blomstrom & Tam, 2010; Blomstrom & Tam, 2009). The assignment presented as a case study was a modification that added an online presentation as part of an ongoing service-learning project. The assignment was designed to address the problem of how to more effectively engage students while providing an effective learning experience. This paper suggests service-learning can be a solution to the problem of how to effectively engage Net Generation learners and examines characteristics of Net Generation learners, principles of effective service-learning practice, and how service-learning pedagogy corresponds with Net Generation learner characteristics.

BACKGROUND

The assignment was created for a speech course at Embry-Riddle Aeronautical University (ERAU) on the Prescott, AZ campus, located in the southwestern United States. The course was required of students majoring in engineering, aviation, space physics, and global security and intelligence studies. Speech was usually taken during the first year of study. The course had a defined structure, because the university has two residential campuses and a large worldwide campus and the course was offered through all three campuses. All instructors used a common syllabus, which stated the student learning objectives, and all students developed and delivered informative speeches, persuasive speeches, and team presentations. Instructors created specific assignments in their sections to meet the course objectives. The assignment for this chapter was designed to meet the objectives for the team presentation.

Many students taking the class were Net Generation learners, and the literature suggests those learners do not respond well in traditional classrooms (Howe & Strauss, 2000). In an effort to better address the students service-learning was selected as the pedagogical approach. Through service-learning students realize many benefits including helping them understand course material better, enjoying learning, liking service, receiving a professional development benefit, and gaining skills, experience, and confidence in their abilities and skills (Isaacson & Saperstein, 2005.) Communication is a practical discipline that can contribute to society through service (Applegate & Morreale, 1999), and the method has increased in popularity in the field of communication (Oster-Aaland, Sellnow, Nelson, & Pearson, 2004). Service-learning has also increased in popularity in engineering studies (Campus Compact, 2008). The engineering industry has a desire for well-rounded individuals equipped to work in a global context (Oakes, 2004). Engineering students who engage in service-learning develop an understanding of the social context and issues related to the problems they are solving, critical thinking skills, ethical standards, communication skills, an understanding of teamwork, and curiosity (Lima & Oakes, 2006).

Service-learning applications vary depending on the content area and the project; however, there are commonalities. Campus Compact (2011) defines service-learning this way: "Service-learning incorporates community work into the curriculum, giving students real-world learning experiences that enhance their academic learning while providing a tangible benefit for the community" (paragraph 1). Learn and Serve America (2011) adds that service-learning, "provides structured time for students to reflect on their service experiences and demonstrate knowledge or skills they have gained" (paragraph 1). Service-learning pedagogy is suited to how people learn (APA Learner-Centered Psychological Principles, 2008). The American Psychological Association (APA) described fourteen psychological principles pertaining to the learner and the learning process. Service-learning aligns particularly well with several of the principles in that it is goal-directed, involves strategic thinking and social influences, and can increase motivational and emotional influences on learning factors identified by APA. Researchers report service-learning can be beneficial in increasing teamwork skills. Eyler and Giles (1999) found 81% of the students surveyed reported that learning to "work with others" was either the most important or a very important thing they learned from service-learning. The report by the American Association of Community Colleges (Prentice & Robinson, 2010) indicated that in their study service-learning students scored significantly higher on 5 out of 6 institutional student learning outcomes, including communication and career/ teamwork skills.

The benefits of service-learning outlined above are as relevant to Net Generational learners as to traditional learners. However, to tailor the assignment for this particular group of Net Generation learners, it is helpful to look at characteristics of those learners. Before doing so it is important to mention that this discussion generalizes about the Net Generation, and generalizations do not hold true in all instances, but can provide some understanding of cohorts. The cohort born between 1980 and 2000 has been referred to as the Net Generation, Generation Y, Generation Next, the Digital Generation, and Millennials (Raines, 2010). Raines (2010) states,

"Net Generation, ...students must be actively involved in their classes, not just passive recipients of knowledge imparted by their teachers; they must be academically challenged and motivated enough by what they are learning and how we are teaching to put forth their best effort; they must have a lot of interaction with their teachers; and they must have the support they need to succeed (paragraph #11.)

Howe and Strauss (2000) described Millennials as individuals who, among other things, tend to like group activity, perceive that it is desirable to be smart, are intrigued by new technologies, and are interested in grades. The interest in grades extends to an interest in education. A study conducted by the Pew Research Center (2010) reported that 19% of Millenials have earned a degree; 39% are still in school with 8% in high school or trade school, 26% in college, and 5% in graduate school. Of those not in school, 30% reported they planned to earn a degree. In addition to an educational focus, the Millennials are digitally connected. The Pew study (2010) reported 96% of Millennials in college used the internet. Technology use among these learners apparently continues to increase. Bonamici, Hutto, Smith, and J. Ward (2005) stated the average Net Generation learner by age 21 typically has played 10,000 hours of video games, sent and received 200,000 emails, watched 20,000 hours of TV, spent 10,000 hours on the cell phone, and read less than 5,000 hours. More recently, Jones and Cross (2009) presented findings based on a survey of 596 first year college students' use of mobile phone messaging, instant messaging, participating in online social networks and other items. Their findings pointed to a complex and diverse group, calling into question some of the generalizations made about Net Generation's technological expertise and use. While it appears many people in the Net Generation have developed skills with video games, cell phone applications and their use, others in the Net Generation have not developed those same skills. Similarly some have developed skills with video conferencing, but many have not. Those who have developed skills with video conferencing may be adept at technical applications of the software and hardware, but not understand how to critically think about how to make the experience effective for presenters and for users, or how to implement the strategy. Knowing how to analyze the audience and how to involve the audience makes the experience more effective for all participants.

While many Net Generation learners come into college with well-developed technology skills, Barnes, Marateo, and Ferris (2007) caution that educators must find ways to put to use many of the skills Net Generation learners have developed, while not conforming to and encouraging the learners to seek instant gratification or to employ shallow thinking. The service-learning assignment discussed here sought to address this issue by providing an effective learning experience while avoiding potential pitfalls. In the next section the assignment will be described followed by a discussion of how the assignment was designed specifically for Net Generation learners and how it aligns with principles of best practice for service-learning projects.

THE ASSIGNMENT

This assignment built on a collaborative effort between Embry-Riddle Aeronautical University (ERAU) and the NASA Educator Resource Center (ERC) involving an ongoing service-learning project that has been offered each semester beginning in the fall of 2007. The students developed and delivered team presentations on science, technology, engineering, and math (STEM) topics to various audiences, primarily K-8 grade students. The project was created to address the problem of low interest and skill level in math and science among students in the state. Most ERAU students have a strong interest in STEM and they conveyed their enthusiasm to audience members.

The assignment described in this paper included sixty-three students enrolled in three sections of the speech course. The assignment involved two STEM presentations. The first presentation was delivered in a face-to-face setting to participants in the fall break program offered by the after-school provider for the local school district. The audience members were between the ages of 5-12. The young students displayed a natural curiosity about the sciences, and university students encouraged that curiosity through their presentations.

The innovation for this assignment was to add a second presentation on the same topic. Eight of the teams presented to an online audience and four teams presented face-to-face to an 8th-grade science class. The online audience members were invited by the NASA ERC and by students in the class. The online audience was composed primarily of teachers and other adults. The eight teams delivering their second presentation online used webinar software, which is a format the university students are likely to use in their career communication. The webinar platform provided a format in which students could use audio or a combination of audio and webcam video to accompany static slides. One team incorporated a video made during the first presentation, and several students included video clips to illustrate concepts. The topics were the same for both presentations, but students modified the content from their first presentations to better suit the online audience or the 8th grade science class.

Topics for the presentations were selected by our partner, the NASA ERC director. Students chose the topic they wanted to investigate from that list. Two teams from a given section worked on each topic. The titles for two of the teams under the NASA Missions topic illustrate how the students developed topics according to their interests (Table 1).

One indication that students were engaged was the observation that participants, audience members and students, appeared to enjoy the experience and to have fun, which was consistent with Shumer's (1997) observation that participants in successful service-learning programs had fun, and in addition to learning, their attitudes toward learning and group behavior were more positive. For college students the service-learning experiences provided a novel setting breaking the monotony of regular classes.

This assignment was designed for Net Generation learners and it also addressed the principles of effective service-learning suggested by the National Youth Leadership Council. In order to be effective, the basic foundation of the assignment needed to be strong. Table 2 illustrates how the assignment was structured with Net Generation

Table 1. Assigned topics and samples of team-developed topics for presentations

General Topic	Presentation Descriptions or Titles
Force and Motion on Land	Learn how Newton's Laws of Motion apply to cars, bikes, and other vehicles
Force and Motion in Water	Learn how velocity and Newton's 1st Law of Motion is demonstrated by a boat
Force and Motion in Air	Learn how mass, force, and acceleration apply to the Space Shuttle, helicopters, and jets
Force and Motion in Space	Learn how the Space Shuttle travels to and from the International Space Station.
NASA Aeronautics Missions	Unmanned Aerial Vehicles
	NASA Aeronautics Projects
NASA Aerospace Missions	Our Solar System … and Beyond!
	To Infinity and Beyond: Space Exploration's Past, Present and Future!

learners in mind. The table maps characteristics and attributes of the Net Generation, as noted by Oblinger and Oblinger (2005), with specific aspects of the assignment..

To look at the rigor and quality of the basic assignment, the eight principles of effective practice for K-12 service-learning projects from the National Youth Leadership Council were applied (Weah, 2007). The descriptions for the principles, which appear in quotes, are taken from the Learn and Serve America website (2011). While this assignment is a college-level assignment, the principles were deemed appropriate because the audience consisted primarily of K-12 students and teachers. In Table 3 each principle is listed followed by a description of how this assignment applied including references to the literature.

Service-learning assignments that meet these principles can be a good fit for Net Generation learners. Several of the principles of effective service-learning projects are listed with corresponding characteristics of Net Generation learners. Table 4 restates the characteristics of Net Generation learners and the principles of effective service-learning practice. Net Generation learners want to study things that matter and service-learning involves meaningful service. Net Generation learners like the social component and service-learning involves partnerships formed with community members and organizations providing interactions for students with people outside of their educational environment. Net Generation learners like immediate experiences and service-learning offers immediate and practical experience; furthermore students have a voice in determining what those experiences involve. Net Generation learners like experiential activities and service-learning is one form of experiential learning. An important element of service-learning is that the projects have sufficient duration and intensity to be meaningful and instructive. While Net Generation learners like to be connected, for learning to take place it is important that they not just be connected, but that connections are linked to the curriculum. Net Generation learners like to work in teams, and often service-learning projects incorporate teamwork. In addition service-learning projects often provide opportunities to gain appreciation for diversity, which is a benefit realized through teamwork. The structure preferred by Net Generation learners can be addressed by the progress monitoring in service-learning. While Net Generation learners like engagement and experience, service-learning theorists and practitioners have found that reflection is a critical part of relating the engagement and experience to learning.

Table 2. Description of how the assignment was designed to address characteristics and attributes of net generation learners identified byOblinger & Oblinger (2005)

Characteristic or Attribute of Net Generation Learner	Details of Assignment Design
Digitally Literate "Having grown up with widespread access to technology, the Net Gen is able to intuitively use a variety of IT devices and navigate the Internet. Although they are comfortable using technology without an instruction manual, their understanding of the technology or source quality may be shallow." (p. 16)	This service-learning assignment, even before the addition of the online component, was popular with students and evidence suggested it offered an effective way for students to learn the course content. Adding an online component fit well with the student population and it incorporated a skill the students were likely to use in the future. While students were digitally literate, the level of skills required for this assignment varied considerably between students with some demonstrating shallow knowledge and others incorporating features and functions beyond the basics.
Connected "While highly mobile, moving from work to classes to recreational activities, the Net Gen is always connected." (p. 16)	Having observed students frequently connected through laptops or cell phones, the thinking was that they would enjoy being connected to others for a class assignment. The commonly observed connections were likely with friends and family. The online audience they were connecting with consisted mostly of strangers, and the unknown aspect was anxiety producing for some students. Several other students responded quite favorably to the online audience. More investigation is needed to determine which students are more likely to experience anxiety, and then structure the assignment to reduce the anxiety.
Immediate "Whether it is the immediacy with which a response is expected or the speed at which they are used to receiving information, the Net Gen is fast." (p. 17)	Students like quick response times and they had to adapt during their online presentations. In some cases, their plan to show clips from YouTube failed because audience members in schools could not view the clips through the software links, nor could they access them independently through the internet when given the links. This was due to internet restrictions at the school. Consequently the students had to verbally describe what was being shown in the clips. The quick adaptations were handled better by some speakers than by others.
Experiential "Most Net Gen learners prefer to learn by doing rather by being told what to do." (p. 17)	Many students like to learn by doing. One challenge is to provide them sufficient information to carry out the tasks successfully. Moving ahead on an assignment without getting the details, resulted at times in false starts. Fortunately, at least one person from each team made sure to have all of the information before going ahead with an assignment. For example, all students were instructed to create PowerPoint presentations without animations because animations would be lost. One group member incorporated a number of animations in the slides. Only one group had that experience. Others either recalled the instruction or learned by observing that slides could not be animated.
Social "They seek to interact with others, whether in their personal lives, their online presence, or in class." (p. 17)	Students display a liking for social interaction. This assignment incorporated a social dimension online because of the availability of the text chat feature. Few people used the feature, but for those who did it was an effective means of communicating and connecting. For example, one teacher couldn't hear the audio and sent a text. Immediately the message was read and adjustments were made. The text chat feature was also used to send messages between audience members.
Teams "The Net Gen often prefers to learn and work in teams. A peer-to-peer approach is common, as well, where students help each other." (p. 18)	This assignment was the first major speech assignment of the term. Because the speech was a team presentation, the fear of public speaking appeared to be reduced. Moreover, in the reflective comments several students said they were more confident in giving a public speech after the assignment. A number of students wrote about how successfully their team performed. In the past many of them had dreaded team assignments, because one individual took on the work of the team, but in this assignment, the work was more equally distributed and the end result, according to students, was better than individual efforts would have been.

Continued on following page

Table 2. Continued

Characteristic or Attribute of Net Generation Learner	Details of Assignment Design
Structure "The Net Gen is very achievement oriented. "They want parameters, rules, priorities, and procedures...." (p. 18)	Students want to know what is required to achieve a goal. This assignment was involved and required many skills, so the instructions and parameters were given in chunks. The first day a 1 ½ page sheet was distributed. Several exemplars were displayed and discussed so students know what was expected of them and they could also identify high quality work. The evaluation sheet was included with the other documents for the assignment. A sample of the written work was also included. Later additional information such as software instructions were presented in class. That was followed with independent sessions using the software. Later still were instructions for the day of the presentation. This method seemed to work fairly well; however, a single written document or more likely, a more comprehensive collection of documents providing more details, may be generated for future assignments.
Engagement and Experience "The Net Gen is oriented toward inductive discovery or making observations, formulating hypotheses, and figuring out the rules." (p. 18)	The students appeared to be engaged and this was supported through their thoughtful reflective papers. The depth of thought presented in their writing was somewhat of a surprise, because the papers were graded pass/fail. The extra effort invested by students gave glimpses into their appreciation of the project and into what they learned.
Visual and Kinesthetic "The Net Gen is more comfortable in image-rich environments than with text." (p. 18)	Students have well-developed skills for presenting material visually. For this assignment with two audiences, those skills were put to use to create presentations for the different audiences so audience members could visually appreciate and enjoy the presentation. For example, the presentations on NASA Missions included many photos. When students were instructed on the software, one short component of the training was showing them how to use the laser pointer on slides. Within minutes students were using the pointer to draw attention to areas of their slides, focusing the attention of the audience.
Things that Matter "Given a choice, they seem to prefer working on things that matter, such as addressing an environmental concern or a community problem." (p. 18)	The Net Generation participates in community activities. For this assignment, students displayed respect for the community partners and the audiences through their dress and their respectful behavior. They answered questions clearly and respectfully and went beyond what was expected. Yet we sensed the students didn't see how the assignment fit within a larger context. We informed the students of the results of science scores for the state and talked explicitly about how their contributions could help. Students could reach more people (and possibly have a larger effect) through the online presentations. Students were asked to be more involved in reaching out to the education community to invite them to listen to their online presentations. The additional discussion of the larger community issue and how the students could make a difference may have resulted in a stronger connection during the online presentations. Overall, the students seemed very interested in the assignment and in their reflections they suggested the assignment be incorporated in future classes.

The revised assignment with an online component met the criteria for an effective service-learning project, and it seemed to appeal to most of the students. They worked in teams, had a lot of social interaction including several opportunities for feedback. They incorporated technology and they were addressing a real-world community problem. The addition of the online component is likely to become a regular part of the assignment, because the technology enables a broader outreach, which could provide a better, more robust solution to the problem motivating the service-learning project. In the face-to-face presentations, the younger students especially those who attended multiple sessions benefited in observable ways. They were more likely to answer questions during discussion. Their comments showed they grasped the material and that they had thought about the content presented. If similar experiences can be created for online audience members using webinar software, more people could be reached and perhaps more progress can be made toward addressing the problem of low interest in STEM.

Table 3. Description of how the assignment addresses principles of effective practice for service-learning projects (Learn and Serve America, 2011)

Principle	Details of Assignment Design
Duration and Intensity "Service-learning has sufficient duration and intensity to address community needs and meet specified outcomes." (p. 4)	Service-learning experiences that involved longer duration and more intensity resulted in higher perceived value of the project and higher likelihood of committing to further service (Eyler & Giles, 1997). Kraft and Krug (1994) reported the desired outcomes were found when students participated in 6 to 8 weeks of experience in service-learning with field work once a week. The service-learning project mentioned here took place over a 6-week period with students spending two hours presenting to the audiences and they had several meetings with the community partner.
Link to Curriculum "Service-learning is intentionally used as an instructional strategy to meet learning goals and/or content standards." (p. 4)	According to Eyler and Giles (1999), service and learning should have equal weight and enhance each other. This project involves university students applying the communication concepts and skills they were learning in their speech course in a service project. Through the project they learned audience analysis, content development, delivery skills, organizational skills, team skills, and personal skills. Data collected over the three-year period indicated that students in service-learning sections made significant gains in each of those five areas. The assignment also related to each of the five student learning outcomes specified for the course. The results from this project are consistent with the findings of evaluators who studied CalServe and reported that academic effects were related to clarity of goals and activities through focused reflection, which is an integral part of service learning (Ammon, Furco, Chi, & Middaugh, 2002).
Partnerships "Service-learning partnerships are collaborative, mutually beneficial, and address community needs." (p. 4)	Billig (2002) noted that a key factor for sustainability of service-learning projects was a reciprocal relationship with mutual high regard. These characteristics were achieved with all three partners in this project: the NASA ERC, Kids & Company, the after-school program for the local school district, and the 8th-grade science teacher. These partnerships enabled all parties to benefit from the project. Survey responses from the online audience members indicated they were interested in future presentations.
Meaningful Service "Service-learning actively engages participants in meaningful and personally relevant service activities." (p. 5)	The societal problem addressed in this project was the low interest and achievement in science for K-8 students in the state. The project was designed to try to increase STEM interest in the audiences. The extent of the problem was evidenced in the rankings on science scores for students in the state reported in The Nation's Report Card made available by the National Center for Education Statistics (2011). Based on test scores of eighth-graders in Arizona who took the 2009 test, 46% had test scores below the basic level, 32% had test scores at the basic level, 21% had test scores indicating a proficient level and 1% had test scores at the advanced Level. Only two states in the U. S. reported lower overall test scores. Because of the specialized nature of the majors and curriculum offered at ERAU, the students are in a unique position to speak about science-related topics. They engaged in meaningful service by communicating with younger students in public speaking settings, teaching them about science. They also shared their career goals, which seemed to interest the younger audience members.
Youth Voice "Service-learning provides youth with a strong voice in planning, implementing, and evaluating service-learning experiences with guidance from adults." (p. 5)	Fredericks, Kaplan, and Zeisler (2001, p. 1) defined youth voice as "the inclusion of young people as a meaningful part of the creation and implementation of service opportunities." The university students were given a project overview, a topic, expectations in terms of length of presentations and a list of equipment that would be available. Students developed the content of their presentations on their own. They received feedback along the way, yet the presentations and accompanying activities and demonstrations were created by the students. They were asked for their feedback and suggestions at the conclusion of the project.
Diversity "Service-learning promotes understanding of diversity and mutual respect among all participants." (p. 5)	Weah, Simmons, and McClellan (2000) commented that in service-learning students can move beyond their personal views to learn the perspectives of others. The university students worked in teams composed of students from different majors, ages, and experience so they learned from each other. The audience members were diverse in terms of race, educational expectations, and their interest in the topics. Young audience members enjoyed the international students and the diversity of the university students.

Continued on following page

Table 3. Continued

Principle	Details of Assignment Design
Reflection "Service-learning incorporates multiple challenging reflection activities that are ongoing and that prompt deep thinking and analysis about oneself and one's relationship to society." (p. 5)	The reflection component of service-learning is critical. Eyler & Giles (1999) report that reflection helps students gain a deeper understanding of what they learned. In the present project students wrote a minimum of two reflective papers. Throughout the process students were encouraged to ask questions and to comment on the process, the project, and their progress. Reflective comments written after the online presentation included, "What I liked about the online presentation is that I got to experience technology in online video, which is where a lot of business corporations are turning...," "Going into the speech I felt that I would be fairly comfortable presenting in a webinar however when I put the headset on, I really didn't like it. I did not like the fact that I couldn't see my audience. I couldn't tell if I was putting them to sleep like so many webinars do to me."
Progress Monitoring "Service-learning engages participants in an ongoing process to assess the quality of implementation and progress toward meeting specified goals, and uses results for improvement and sustainability." (p. 6)	The process of progress monitoring is to provide constructive feedback to participants. University students were given timelines and expectations, which included a dress rehearsal one week before the face-to-face presentations. Feedback was given to the students at the time of the dress rehearsals. Students provided feedback to the instructor on their efforts and those of their teammates. Students received immediate feedback from the audiences and additional feedback from the community partners. This project has undergone several modifications based on what was learned from data analysis and feedback. The data collection, analysis and feedback will continue. Data is gathered from the university students, students in the audience, the community partners, and online participants.

Table 4. Comparison of Net Generation learner characteristics and service-learning principles

Characteristics and Attributes of Net Generation Learners (Oblinger & Oblinger, 2005)	Principles of Effective Practice for K-12 Service-Learning Projects (Learn and Serve America 2011)
Things that Matter	Meaningful Service
Social	Partnerships
Immediate	Youth Voice
Experiential	Duration and Intensity
Connected	Link to Curriculum
Teams	Diversity
Structure	Progress Monitoring
Engagement and Experience	Reflection
Visual and Kinesthetic	
Digitally literate	

The service-learning project was well received by the community partners including the NASA ERC director, the director of the afterschool program and parents of the participants, the 8th grade science teacher, and the online participants. While considerable work remains to be done, the outcomes appear to be worth the effort and resources. Requests were made from the director of the afterschool program, the 8-th grade science teacher, and members of the online audience to continue the project in the future.

ISSUES, CONTROVERSIES, PROBLEMS

Several issues or challenges face anyone considering service-learning, and in particular, this assignment.

1. Faculty teaching Net Generation learners face decisions about how to best utilize their resources. Service-learning is a resource intensive teaching strategy leaving faculty who choose service-learning with less time to pursue other options. Net Generation learners have articulated their expectations for faculty, and these expectations require time for training and for skill development. Although the sample size in the study reported was small (25 students at the

University of Pittsburgh) the findings may be representative of a broader segment of the population. Students said they expect and value faculty who are knowledgeable in their fields. They rated the professor's experience and expertise as 8 on a 10 point scale of importance. The respondents rated "The professor's ability to professionally convey lecture points using contemporary software" as 7.68 out of 10 and they rated "The professor's ability to customize the class using the current technology available" as 7.64 out of 10 (Roberts, 2005 paragraph 11). To stay current in one's field takes time. If faculty teaching Net Generation learners must also be proficient in using technologies for their courses, that may leave little time for developing and implementing service-learning opportunities. Successful service-learning projects require partnerships and coordination of logistics. Establishing and building relationships with partners requires time, as does project coordination. As faculty choose among competing demands for their time, each person must ascertain how to invest their time as an instructor. Service-learning is highly rewarding, but the time commitment is considerable.

2. A problem worth mentioning is that not all students like working in teams. Regardless of the general description of Net Generation learners preferring social interaction and working in teams, some students are poor team members. The reasons gave for not wanting to work in teams were that some individuals had poor experiences on team projects in the past, some said their team experiences in the past seemed to just be repetitions of each other because they never learned about group dynamics or how to be effective, others required high grade point averages for scholarships and they did not want their grades negatively affected by poor performances of others in the group. The resistance expressed by students for working in teams was mitigated by grading each student individually, rather than assigning a group grade.
3. Some of the students said they experienced a higher level of anxiety presenting to an online audience than when presenting to a face-to-face audience, due to unknown factors of the audience and of the software. Several students commented that feedback from a face-to-face audience was important to them. This was somewhat surprising given the technological skills of the students and their frequent mediated communication, which was probably typical of Net Generation learners.
4. Delivery is an important part of public speaking. Several students used expressions such as "um" and "ah" (non-fluencies) which were distracting for the online audience more than they would be in a face-to-face situation because with fewer nonverbal cues available to the online audience the "ahs" and "ums" stood out. The non-fluency rate was probably higher due to increased anxiety of giving a speech and delivering it in a new venue. Net Generation learners are likely to use video conferencing or webinar formats to deliver presentations in their careers so practice can help them develop skills they will use in the future.
5. Some technically proficient students appeared anxious about using software to deliver a presentation. While Net Generation students have well-developed technical skills generally, those skills did not necessarily translate to the particular software application in this situation. This was consistent with Jones & Cross (2009) who found varying levels of confidence and skills among current college students in using tools and software, with 60% reporting no or minimal skills with video and audio software.

SOLUTIONS AND RECOMMENDATIONS

Solutions and recommendations for the problems identified are listed according to corresponding numbers of the problems.

1. A recommendation for determining how to best invest resources is to assess the outcomes and results through data collection and analysis. Assessment evidence gathered from students who participated in service-learning over several semesters at our institution indicated that service-learning was effective for student learning. Nearly all of the students were Net Generation learners. For students who participated in service-learning activities, gains were larger than for students in sections that did not incorporate service-learning. Final course evaluations for the service-learning sections were also reviewed. At our institution the evidence of larger gains on desired skills for students in service-learning sections coupled with the alignment of service-learning with our institution's mission statement, justify the investment of resources.
2. To address the problem of some students being poor team members a recommendation is to provide instruction in team dynamics and time management for teams. Tasks to complete the team project can be identified and discussed during class and placed on a timeline. Responsibility for each task can be assigned. Additionally teams can submit PowerPoint slides and team outlines in advance of the presentations as partial completion of the final project using the software to give them additional experience loading files. Students could be asked to give status reports to the instructor using the webinar software to gain experience using the software to deliver short status reports. For both the online and face-to-race presentations rehearsals should be mandatory, which helps with time management and which provide students with useful feedback.
3. To increase audience involvement which would likely decrease the anxiety experienced by students when presenting to an online audience, students need to have opportunities to practice using online features including the text function and the survey tool to ask questions of the audience. A recommendation is to have students observe more examples of how to involve the audience using these software features and have them practice to incorporate using the tools.
4. A recommendation to reduce non-fluencies is to have students prepare and use a manuscript for online presentations. Sounding natural when reading can be accomplished through practice. The combination of reading a manuscript and practicing deliver more would likely reduce non-fluencies. Using an extemporaneous delivery style in the face-to-face setting would provide students an opportunity to compare the two styles. A further recommendation is to have the manuscript delivery take place a week or two before the extemporaneous delivery. This would encourage students to be prepared in advance and would make the rehearsal time transitioning from manuscript to extemporaneous delivery more effective.
5. Spending more time using the software would allow students to respond more effectively and should reduce anxiety levels. A recommendation is to incorporate several practice sessions using the software. Awarding partial credit by asking that materials be submitted in advance through the software and by giving status reports at the time the materials are submitted would also increase familiarity with the program.

FUTURE RESEARCH DIRECTIONS

Several interesting questions arose when looking at this service-learning project with the online component. Would students gain the same benefits from the online presentation as from the face-to-face presentations? If not, in what area would differences become evident? How could the assignment be best structured for the students to maximize their learning and benefits? How do the presentations for the online audiences need to be structured? How much instruction do audience members need? How can the online presentations be structured to be most effective for the audience members? How much software instruction is the best amount of instruction for the university students and how should it be implemented? How can webinar exemplars best be included in instruction? Should the students develop portions of their online presentations in advance and test them?

Future research could focus on how to improve the process and outcomes for the students, for the community partners, and for the audience members. Research questions could address each of those groups. This project plans to collect quantitative and qualitative data to investigate those questions. Quantitative data will be gathered at ERAU through a skill survey completed by students at the beginning and the end of the semester. The skill survey has been used for four years, allowing comparisons to be made across semesters and across conditions. Quantitative data in the form of faculty evaluations of speeches can be used to identify areas of strength and areas needing improvement in future assignments. Quantitative data will be gathered from online audience members, who respond to questions at the end of the presentations. Qualitative data can also be gathered through reflective comments written by students and through interviews with the community partners. Additional reflective questions will be posed to students in the future. In-depth interviews will be conducted with the community partners to improve these relationships and thereby improve the quality of the experience for all involved. While this research will be case specific, the findings can have broader implications.

CONCLUSION

This chapter explored service-learning as a pedagogical method for instructing Net Generation learners, presenting an assignment as a case study. The service-learning assignment of students delivering similar presentations to a face-to-face audience and later to an online audience addressed several aspects of Net Generation learning preferences. Students worked in teams, had immediate experiences on a project that mattered, and incorporated digital elements. The assignment met with positive responses from students and from community partners, yet problems and issues were apparent. Solutions and recommendations were offered to address those problems. Additional research is recommended. More data, both quantitative and qualitative, needs to be gathered and analyzed to continue the process of improving instruction.

REFERENCES

Ammon, M. S., Furco, A., Chi, B., & Middaugh, E. (2002). *A profile of California's CalServe service-learning partnerships, 1997-2000*. Sacramento, CA: California Department of Education.

APA. (2008). *Learner-centered psychological principles: A framework for school reform and redesign*. Prepared by the Learner-Centered Principles Work Group of the American Psychological Associations Board of Educational Affairs (1997). Retrieved from http://www.apa.org/ed/lcp2/lcp14.html.

Applegate, J. L., & Morreale, S. P. (1999). Service-learning in communication: A natural partnership. In Droge, D., & Ortega Murphy, B. (Eds.), *Voices of strong Democracy: Concepts and models for service-learning in communication studies*. Sterling, VA: Stylus.

Barnes, K., Marateo, R., & Ferris, S. P. (2007). Teaching and learning with the Net Generation. *Innovate*. Retrieved from http://www.innovate.info/.

Billig, S. H. (2002). Adoption, implementation, and sustainability of K-12 service-learning. In A. Furco & S. H. Billig (Eds.), *Advances in service-learning research: Vol.1. Service-learning: The essence of the pedagogy* (pp. 245–267). Greenwich, CT: Information Age.

Blomstrom, S. A., & Tam, H. W. (2009, June). *How and to what extent does a service-learning pedagogy enhance communication and collaboration skill learning among first-year students?* Paper presented at the American Society for Engineering Education Conference Austin, TX.

Blomstrom, S. A., & Tam, H. W. (2010). Assessing service-learning to improve instruction. In Worley, D. W., Worley, D. A., Hugenberg, B., & Elkins, M. R. (Eds.), *Best practices in experiential and service learning in communication*. Dubuque, IA: Great River Technologies.

Bonamici, A., Hutto, D., Smith, D., & Ward, J. (2005). *The "Net Generation": Implications for libraries and higher education*. Retrieved from http://www.orbiscascade.org /council/c0510/Frye.ppt.

Campus Compact. (2008). *Service-learning in engineering resources*. Retrieved from: http://www.compact.org/resources/service-learning_resources/in_engineering/.

Campus Compact. (2011). *Service-learning*. http://www.compact.org/initiatives/service-learning/.

Eyler, J., & Giles, D. Jr. (1997). The importance of program quality in service-learning. In Waterman, A. (Ed.), *Service-learning: Applications from the research* (pp. 57–76). Mahwah, NJ: Erlbaum.

Eyler, J., & Giles, D. E. (1999). *Where's the learning in service-learning?* San Francisco, CA: Jossey-Bass.

Fredericks, L., Kaplan, E., & Zeisler, J. (2001). *Integrating youth voice in service-learning*. Denver, CO: Education Commission of the States.

Howe, N., & Strauss, W. (2000). *Millennials rising: The next great generation*. New York, NY: Vintage.

Isaacson, R., & Saperstein, J. (2005). *The art and strategy of service-learning presentations*. Belmont, CA: Wadsworth.

Jones, C., & Cross, S. (2009). *Is there a net generation coming to university?* Retrieved from http://oro.open.ac.uk/18468/1/ALTC_09_proceedings_090806_web_0299.pdf.

Kraft, R., & Krug, J. (1994). Review of research and evaluation on service-learning in public and higher education. In Kraft, R., & Swadener, M. (Eds.), *Building community: Service learning in the academic disciplines*. Denver, CO: Colorado Campus Compact.

Learn and Serve America. (2011). *Service-learning definition, elements, and examples*. Retrieved from http://www.learnandservearizona.com/#Service-Learning%20Standards.

Lima, M., & Oakes, W. C. (2006). *Service-learning engineering in your community*. Okemos, MI: Great Lakes Press.

National Center for Educational Statistics. (2011). *The nation's report card*. Retrieved from http://nces.ed.gov/nationsreportcard/pdf/main2009/2011451.pdf.

Oakes, W. (2004). *Service-learning in engineering: A resource guidebook*. Providence, RI: Campus Compact.

Oblinger, D. G., & Oblinger, J. L. (2005). Is it age or IT: First steps toward understanding the net generation. In D. G. Oblinger & J. L. Oblinger (Eds.), *Educating the net generation,* (pp. 2.1-2.20). Retrieved from http://www.educause.edu/educatingthenetgen/.

Oster-Aaland, L. K., Sellnow, T. L., Nelson, P. E., & Pearson, J. C. (2004). The status of service learning in departments of communication: A follow-up study. *Communication Education, 53*(4), 348–356. doi:10.1080/0363452032000305959

Pew Research Center. (2010). *Millennials*. Retrieved from http://pewresearch.org/millennials/.

Prensky, M. (2001). Digital natives, digital immigrants. *On the Horizon, 9*(5). MCB University Press.

Prentice, M., & Robinson, G. (2010). *Improving student learning outcomes with service learning*. American Association of Community Colleges. Retrieved from www.aacc.nche.edu/Resources/aaccprograms/horizons/Documents/slorb_jan2010.pdf.

Raines, C. (2010). *Millennials at work*. http://www.generationsatwork.com/ articles_millennials_at_work.php.

Roberts, G. R. (2005). In D. Oblinger & J. Oblinger, (Eds.), *Educating the Net generation*. Retrieved from http://www.educause.edu/Resources/EducatingtheNet Generation/TechnologyandLearning-Expectati/6056.

Shumer, R. D. (1997). Learning from qualitative research. In Waterman, A. S. (Ed.), *Service-learning: Applications from the research*. Mahwah, NJ: Lawrence Erlbaum Associates.

Weah, W. (2007). *Toward research-based standards for K-12 service-learning*. Retrieved from http://www.nylc.org/sites/nylc.org/files/files/2007G2G1.pdf.

Weah, W., Simmons, V., & McClellan, M. (2000). Service-learning and multicultural/ multiethnic perspectives: From diversity to equity. *Phi Delta Kappan, 81*(9), 673–675.

ADDITIONAL READING

Barnes, K., Marateo, R., & Ferris, S. P. (2007). Teaching and learning with the Net Generation. *Innovate*. Retrieved from http://www.innovate.info/.

Billig, S. H. (2002). Adoption, implementation, and sustainability of K-12 service-learning. In A. Furco & S. H. Billig (Eds.) *Advances in service-learning research: Vol.1. Service-learning: The essence of the pedagogy* (pp. 245–267). Greenwich, CT: Information Age.

Blomstrom, S., A. (2010). Identifying teacher effectiveness: Using student skill surveys, speech evaluations and quiz scores to inform instruction. *Communication and Theater Association of Minnesota Journal, 37*, 116–132.

Bringle, R. G. & Hatcher, J. A. (2009). Innovative practices in service-learning and curricular engagement in *New Directions for Higher Education (*247). 37-46.

Conville, R. L. (2001). Service-learning and the educated imagination. *Southern Communication Journal*. Spring, *Vol 66, Issue 3. (Note:* This is the first article in a special issue of the journal dedicated to service-learning in communication.).

Eyler, J. (2000). What do we most need to know about the impact of service-learning on student learning? *Michigan Journal of Community Service Learning*, (Special Issue) Fall, p11-17.

Eyler, J., & Giles, D. E. (1999). *Where's the Learning in Service-Learning?*San Francisco, CA: Jossey-Bass.

Furco, A. (2002). Advancing service-learning at research universities. *New Directions for Higher Education, 2001*(114), 67–78..doi:10.1002/he.15.abs

Furco, A., & Billig, S. H. (Eds.). (2002). *Service-learning: The essence of pedagogy*. Greenwich, CT: Information Age Publishing.

Gelmon, S. B., & Billig, S. H. (Eds.). (2007). *Service-learning: From Passion to Objectivity: International and cross-disciplinary perspectives on service-learning research.* Charlotte, NC: Information Age Publishing.

Holland, B. (1999). Factors and strategies that influence faculty involvement in public service. *The Journal of Public Service and Outreach, 4*, 37–43.

Holland, B. (2000). Institutional impacts and organizational issues related to service-learning. *Michigan Journal of Community Service-learning* (Special Issue), Fall, 54-60.

Isaacson, R., Dorries, B., & Brown, K. (2001). *Service learning in communication studies: A handbook*. Toronto: Wadsworth/Thompson Learning.

Prentice, M., & Robinson, G. (2010). Improving student learning outcomes with service learning. American Association of Community Colleges. Retrieved from http://www.aacc.nche.edu/Resources/aaccprograms/horizons/Documents/slorb_jan2010.pdf.

Soukup, P. A. (1999). Service-learning in communication: Why? In D. Droge & B. O. Murphy (Eds.), *Voices of strong democracy: Concepts and models for service-learning in communication studies* (pp. 7-12). Washington, DC: American Association of Higher Education in cooperation with the National Communication Association.

Worley, D. W., Worley, D. A., Hugenberg, B., & Elkins, M. R. (Eds.). (2010). *Best practices in experiential learning in communication*. Great River Technologies.

Zlotkowski, E. (1998). *Successful Service-Learning Programs. New Models of Excellence in Higher Education*. Bolton, MA: Anker Publishing.

Zlotkowski, E. (2000). Service-learning research in the disciplines. *Michigan Journal of Community Service-learning,* (Special Issue) Fall, 61-67.

KEY TERMS AND DEFINITIONS

Audience: The listeners who hear and respond to presentations.

Community Partners: Organizations and their representatives within the community who had an identified need the service-learning project addressed. In this case the problem was the need for increased interest in science with the hope of achieving higher science scores on state tests. The community partners provided important knowledge about the need and, importantly, the audience for the project.

Net Generation: Individuals born roughly between 1980 and 2000, who vary in important ways, but who generally want to be actively engaged in learning, who like to work in teams, who have technological skills, and who are interested in grades and learning.

Service-Learning: A method of teaching and learning that integrates academic content directly with meaningful community service and reflection to achieve curricular objectives.

Speech: The ability to effectively express thoughts, ideas, and emotions through oral communication, usually to an audience. The speech can be delivered face-to-face or it can be delivered using technology such as online webinars or television or radio.

STEM: Science, technology, engineering and math.

Technology: Refers to the use of video conferencing and use of PowerPoint and other file types within that structure.

Webinar: A workshop or lecture delivered over the web. In this case the audience members were invited to give feedback through the chat feature and through a survey at the end of the presentation.

Chapter 21
Teaching with PowerPoint in the Net Generation

Chris Gurrie
The University of Tampa, USA

Brandy Fair
Grayson County College, USA

ABSTRACT

This chapter focuses on students' perceptions of their professors' use, abuse, and success with PowerPoint presentation software. Both recent literature about the Net Generation and this study show that the novelty of PowerPoint is wearing off. The researchers found that student perceptions ranged from highly critical of professors' uses of PowerPoint, to delightfully engaged by the use of PowerPoint as a teaching tool. This research could benefit anyone looking to retool or calibrate current PowerPoint practices. The Net Generation of students has grown up with PowerPoint; its continued use is nothing new or novel when discussing student engagement and the transfer of knowledge. However, a return to best practices of teaching and engagement while implementing PowerPoint may help today's learners better retain course materials.

INTRODUCTION

Blank stares during boring lectures are nothing new to educators and students alike. It only takes a stroll through a college hallway to see instructors speaking with low lighting, PowerPoint screens ablaze, and students trying to stay awake, or worse yet, busily doing other tasks on iPhones, laptops, or notepads. Multitasking used to be a term that referred to the ability to do laundry while cooking dinner, or juggling projects while managing to maintain daily tasks. Yet, today, the Net Generation claims to have an excellent ability to multitask—but it may be during a professors' lecture or a trainer's lesson. Is this a bad thing? Has an overuse and lack of novelty with PowerPoint led students down the path of doing other things while "listening" to a speaker drone on during a PowerPoint lesson?

DOI: 10.4018/978-1-61350-347-8.ch021

Literature in this chapter supports the idea that the novelty of PowerPoint has worn off. This is really not surprising considering the program has been around for almost 30 years. The Net Generation, generally accepted to have been born in 1980 and later (also called GenY and Millennials), has had access to PowerPoint its whole academic life—no novelty there. So, as educators, it is important to rethink ways of engaging this group of learners to better express messages. This chapter highlights issues of PowerPoint in education and considers how those issues could help or hinder Net Generational learning and what could be done to improve teaching and learning.

BACKGROUND

In 1990 the first version of PowerPoint was released for Windows software. The software was originally created to enhance presentations and allowed for ease of presentation by the presenter. Adler and Elmhorst (2005) discussed how a good PowerPoint presentation is governed by good practice. For example, slides should consist of seven lines with no more than seven items per line, known as the "7×7" rule. Although some texts suggest a "6×6" rule or "8×8" rule the overarching idea is to keep the slides as simple as possible (Ball, 2009; Dobson, 2006; Gareis, 2007; Leyes, 2007).

In addition to simplicity, it is important to analyze the listeners,' learners,' and/or audience's perceptions of the material being presented, keeping in mind that people remember more when they are able to see, hear, and write material being introduced (Adler & Elmhorst, 2005). One of the best ways to use PowerPoint as a teaching tool would be to allow learners to see material and write notes on said material. However, this is not always the case in higher education classrooms despite being an important argument supporting the use of PowerPoint as a teaching tool. Many professors argue that using the program enables students to learn more information through a variety of channels, such as the instructor speaking and having the notes posted onto the screen simultaneously, thus appealing to the different learning styles that are present in the audience (Barnes, 2000; Doumont, 2005).

The authors of this chapter, being instructors in the communication field, have seen an array of issues dealing with PowerPoint and its use by faculty. Student advisees complain of lectures where professors pack data into 60 slides or more. Educators grumble about students using PowerPoint as a crutch to rely on when presenting final reports and papers. These issues are not unique; they affect today's learner group which arguably consists primarily of the Net Generation. The authors of this chapter suggest that there are better ways to reach this population for a more effective message and better teaching. Students are bored with current approaches to using PowerPoint and practitioners need to make the effort to address this issue.

Net Generation

According to Eubanks (2006), understanding people according to aggregated characteristics of those born in the same time period became popular with the emergence of the baby boom generation. Today's college students are no exception and are being labeled based on these characteristics that link them in age and in social characteristics. Eubanks defined the current group of traditional-aged college students as those born between 1980 and 2000 and calls them "Millennials." Eubanks was careful to note that others have researched this group and have given them different names including Generation Y, Generation Me, and Net Generation.

Raines (2002) found the learning preferences of the Net Generation include teamwork, technology, structure, entertainment and excitement, and experiential activities. Millennials expect instructors to use technology within the college classroom, but such use needs to be equivalent to or better than what they experienced in high school. Some researchers suggest that professors should use or offer online textbooks and the downloading of course materials to their iPods and laptops to address the issue of novelty. Raines findings would suggest that PowerPoint is simply tired compared to iPods and laptops, an issue which will be addressed later.

Pardue and Morgan (2008) found that the Net Generation has a propensity for multitasking that makes it difficult to focus on one activity, and the volumes of information available to them create additional, unique challenges for sorting through and evaluating critical data. Brown, Murphy, and Nanny (2003) suggested that Millennial students are often over confident because they equate their technology savvy with information literacy. Additionally, if students emulate the way some of their professors use PowerPoint (assuming the instructor is using it efficiently) they would be creating a vicious circle of ineffectiveness if those professors are not using PowerPoint correctly. This chapter aims at more specifically identifying what is liked and disliked about PowerPoint use from a learner's standpoint and considers how possible knowledge of this information could aid in teaching and learning the Net Generation.

PURPOSE OF THE CHAPTER

The purpose of the authors' ongoing research, and this chapter, is to investigate the Net Generation perceptions on the use of PowerPoint today, and consider potential ways to better use PowerPoint when teaching the Net Generation. Understanding this will help educators better use this tool when formulating a class or presentation. The first part of this chapter discusses the research on PowerPoint and the Net Generation; while the second part offers ideas and ways to connect with today's learners. While evidence points to the Net Generation's propensity toward technology, this does not mean it is wise to use technology for its own sake. After all, VCRs, record players, overhead projectors, and CD players are all forms of technology that may not catch the attention of the Net Generation learner. The same is true for PowerPoint. Replacing PowerPoint with other technology may not be the way to go either. So, what are the best practices and what connects with students when using PowerPoint? This question drives this chapter.

METHODOLOGY

In 2010 the authors conducted a larger study of PowerPoint use and Millennial behavior (Gurrie & Fair, 2010). The data set and themes from that study help to identify Net Generation learning motivations as they relate to PowerPoint. That study is the basis for this chapter. To understand the impact of using PowerPoint in the Net Generation classroom students at a mid-size private institution in the southeastern part of the United States as well as students enrolled at a public community college in the south were surveyed. All students were enrolled in an Introduction to Communication course and were instructed to answer questions about any/all professors who used PowerPoint as a teaching tool. Participation in the study was voluntary and all responses were submitted anonymously to encourage students to answer honestly on the survey. The survey was offered to 320 students, and after the removal of incomplete questionnaires, a total of 174 students voluntarily participated.

The survey tool included a series of questions focusing on PowerPoint use in class, students' perceptions of presentations, and peripheral uses of PowerPoint such as on-line posting of slides. The survey included 14 Likert 5-point scale questions to obtain quantitative data from the participants. In addition, two open-ended response questions were included to gain student perspectives on how PowerPoint was used within the higher education classroom. Answers were tabulated, reviewed, and categorized based on common themes concerning each of the above issues on PowerPoint in the classroom.

Ultimately, the questions were designed to gain information about students' perceptions of professors' usage of PowerPoint in the classroom. Previous researchers (Frey & Birnbaum, 2002) suggested that survey questions may elicit the necessary information to answer the question: how do students truly perceive their professors' use of PowerPoint in the classroom?

RESULTS AND DISCUSSION

As reported by us in an earlier study (Gurrie & Fair, 2010) a total of 89% of respondents reported having one or more professors who used PowerPoint as a lecture tool while teaching. Forty-two percent of students surveyed stated they preferred traditional lectures (using blackboard/whiteboard) versus PowerPoint lectures. Despite the high number of students who reported that their instructors used PowerPoint, the percentage of varied concerning which lecture format students preferred.

The results show the perception students have of their instructors' use PowerPoint varies. There were five major theme areas reported by students concerning their instructors' use of PowerPoint: (1) Mind-drift, (2) Reading, (3) Writing, Seeing, Listening, (4) Keep pace, and (5) Note-taking (see Table 1). In addition, the authors found that students reported both positive and negative associations with PowerPoint, even within each of these categories.

The same study (Gurrie and Fair, 2010) found that students reported liking PowerPoint for note taking and other functional classroom purposes, and almost half of the respondents reported they perceived PowerPoint was being used correctly by their instructors in the classroom. However, half of the respondents disagreed with the way PowerPoint was used by presenters.

Many of the participants in the study responded that the use of PowerPoint in the classroom helped to keep them focused on the course content. Responses that mentioned daydreaming, keeping focused, and being entertained, all classified under the category of mind drift. One student said, "Writing things down helps to keep my focus. Simply listening usually allows for my mind to wander and not fully comprehend what the teacher is discussion [*sic*]. PowerPoint helps because I am also a visual learner, so when it is heard, seen, and written, I tend to do much better."

Questions arising from our previous study, as well as themes from the literature, sparked this study on PowerPoint in the classroom. During the initial brainstorming phase for the research, the authors assumed that instructors were reading PowerPoint presentations word-for-word to students. Not surprisingly, eight percent of the respondents mentioned that the PowerPoint could be good unless they were being read to. In addition, the students' perceptions indicated that if a professor is reading the slides, then the PowerPoint is just as ineffective as the instructor (Gurrie & Fair, 2010).

Many participants (43%) illustrated how PowerPoint presentations and distribution of the PowerPoint slides impacted their writing, seeing, listening, and ultimately their ability to learn the material. One student noted, "I learn from listening to the professor, if I take notes, I feel I retain the information even more. PowerPoint information

Table 1. Responses concerning learning from instructor use of PowerPoint

Response Theme	Number of Responses	Percentage
Writing, Seeing, Listening	74	43%
Note Taking	51	29%
Mind Drift	27	16%
Reading	14	8%
Keep Pace	8	5%

is a recap of what needs to be learned. Most professors go over the most important points during a lecture and then send the PowerPoint presentation for studying too. I see no way possible for a PowerPoint presentation to hurt a student's way of learning."

According to Gurrie and Fair (2010) 17% of respondents liked PowerPoint notes to help them keep pace, or keep up with a lecture. One student said, "yes, so I can follow along without looking at the screen every two seconds." Another participant believed, "yes, in case I get lost I can look back." In addition another student added, "yes, it helps me follow along with the lecture better." One final participant thought, "yes I do, because it gives the students a chance to keep up with the pace of the instructor. Also, it is a lot easier to recall information for a test or quiz when you already have the information printed out. Also, it gives the student more of a chance of listening to what the instructor is saying, rather than just words up on the screen."

Keeping pace with lecture notes also fell in line with how students used PowerPoint for note taking in class. Forty-eight percent of respondents mentioned PowerPoint slides or notes in some way as they relate to note-taking. One student stated,

If I'm spending all my time trying to write down everything then I don't hear everything the teacher is talking about. And you have to write extremely fast just to get everything down before they move to the next slide and the extra notes. PowerPoint is an outline of the subject, your main points. The teachers always add extra comments during lecture. It's easier and helps me remember if I can follow along with the teacher and then just add their extra comments on my own.

The respondents mentioned above were traditional-aged college students and members of the Net Generation. Given our research, we hope that this chapter will give readers an insight into what Net Generation students think about the use of PowerPoint, since so many educators include it within their courses. In the literature review for this chapter and other research, very few questions were aimed at what students themselves think about PowerPoint. Numerous researchers have discussed the Net Generation, but often neglect surveying it to gain insight into their perspectives.. The following literature review helps us better understand Net Generation learners' technology profiles. Researchers know that Net Gen'ers are "hooked up," but hopefully understanding why they are connected will lead to solid teaching techniques that help connect pedagogically with the use of PowerPoint to reach this generation of learners.

NET GENERATION TECHNOLOGY CHARACTERISTICS

Research on the Millennial generation continuously and consistently mentions technology. According to Leidman and Piwinsky (2009), the accessibility of electronic mail and other portable communication devices has the potential of connecting the student and individual faculty members 24 hours a day, 7 days a week. This creates significant pressures on faculty time and raises issues of faculty workload that can be of particular concern in a unionized environment. According to the research of Leidman and Piwinsky (2009), e-mail has become a general accepted modality of faculty-student interaction, and faculty members do attempt to respond quickly to student e-mails.

Pardue and Morgan (2008) also found that educators often feel perplexed and frustrated in their ability to help Millennial students meet their learning needs. Cultivating awareness of one's own generational learning styles, biases, and prejudices can help faculty members address educational challenges. This concept will be addressed shortly in an attempt to better understand how to connect with students through PowerPoint as an effective teaching tool.

Park (2010) researched social networking sites and the characteristics of their users. Two characteristics emerged among the undergraduate group. First, the participants closely watched new trends related to information technologies but only in short usage cycles. The undergraduates—as the youngest group—appeared to be relatively responsive to new technology. They function as the trendsetters, closely watching for new gadgets and quickly incorporating them into their lives. The second finding in Park's (2010) research was that undergraduate students demonstrated a high desire for self-expression and exposure. Of nine participants in his study, six responded that they used profile service, (a function that helps identify characteristic patterns) the most. This reflected the fact that the undergraduates had a high desire for self-expression. Generally, compared to other services, the profile service is regarded as the best tool for decorating one's online space. Park's research was in line with other researchers in the way of self-expression and online lifestyle.

Despite the students' desire for self-expression and exposure, the instructor's concern becomes "what" information is shared online and how much information is appropriate to share with students. Mazer, Murphy, and Simonds (2007) examined students' reactions to three professors' Facebook accounts created with high, medium, and low levels of personal information disclosed. Results showed that the instructor pages that displayed either high or medium levels of disclosure received positive comments from the participants, noting the professors appeared more "real" because of the information revealed. The high-rated and medium-rated instructors gave some personal information about themselves, their families, likes/dislikes, etc. and came across as a person and not just a professor to the students.

However, despite the positive findings concerning instructor self-disclosure, Mazer, Murphy and Simonds. (2007) also noted that conflicting messages might occur. For example, a professor who appears friendly and caring on their webpage but acts extremely strict in the classroom setting can cause stronger negative reactions than if the professor had not revealed any personal information at all. When posting personal information, instructors need to consider the different ways a student may view the content. Is the information something the professor would be willing to share with anyone? Such concerns apply to text, pictures, quotes, icons, etc. that an instructor chooses to share with anyone who views their personal web page.

Kord and Wolf-Wendel (2009) conducted a series of research that explored how students' use of technology influenced their integration into higher education communities, including the examination of technology resources available for college students on college and university campuses, and the encouragement of its use for academic and social purposes. Their research shows how the integration of technology continues to shape college student experiences with each new generation that enters academia. The members of the Net Generation are a very mobile group who will willingly uproot to seek opportunity and find challenges and excitement in their lives (Walker et al., 2006).

McMahon and Pospisil (2005) stated that the newest Millennial learning style is characterized by social constructivist and experiential learning, including fluency in multiple media that utilizes each for the benefits it can offer, learning based on collectivity seeking, sieving, and synthesizing experiences, and active learning based on experience, including frequent opportunities for reflection, expression through nonlinear, mind mapping, and co design of learning experiences personalized to individual needs and preferences. They identified this generation as technologically savvy, responsible and focused on achievement, with a need to stay connected, zero tolerance for delays, and strengths in multitasking, goal orientation, and collaboration.

The Net Generation is nomadic and prolific communicators (Sweeney, 2006). They love and expect communication mobility. They have more friends and communicate with them more frequently and are much less likely to send a letter by U.S. mail than the generations before them. With these characteristics come possible changes for academe. According to Sweeney (2006), the impact on higher education is clear: colleges and universities must get students quick feedback, anytime, anywhere, on their desired communication channels.

With so much commentary on the characteristics of the Net Generation, it is necessary to better frame how the misuse of PowerPoint can hinder learning or connecting with the Net Generation. From this platform this chapter will offer suggestions to improve learning when using PowerPoint and working with the Net Generation. It is first necessary to identify potential problems with trying to categorize and understand the Net Generation and its acceptance of PowerPoint as a teaching tool.

POTENTIAL PROBLEMS

Examining the literature on characteristics of Net Gen'ers may be a bit overwhelming for the seasoned practitioner. Skepticism may arise about the validity of the claims and data describing this group. Some professors may simply think, "no technology is the way to go" and leave it at that. Others may spend so much time preparing PowerPoints and working to incorporate multiple technologies that they can miss rich learning objectives and outcomes. These are potential issues that may arise when instructors broach the subject of learning and teaching today's learners using technology.

Another potential concern surfaces when analyzing the literature on Net Gen technology habits from the perspective of PowerPoint in classrooms. As discussed, previous researchers suggest that students want interactive platforms that incorporate immediate response (e-mail), networking (Facebook, etc.), and instant feedback and gratification. PowerPoint, as referenced earlier, does not employ these tactics or principles, unless it is used in a more provocative way. To this point, faculty members must think of innovative ways to use PowerPoint in order to engage students in a way that aligns with the literature above on what is written about Net Gen'ers and their desires. Aside from time, this could pose issues for faculty that raise questions about their own teaching style, what they know, how to approach the program, where to start, or a myriad of other personal issues.

One thing to consider may be if PowerPoint is even relevant for desired classroom outcomes. Perhaps the discussion in the literature above has piqued an interest for other technology items such as clickers, or course management systems (CMS), podcasts, iBooks, etc. PowerPoint has been around since 1990. Rarely in other forms of learning do teachers use 21 year old forms of technology. Perhaps it is time to retool the technology arsenal for 2011 and realize it may not include the use of PowerPoint at all. Regardless of what route one chooses, understanding the Net Generation and its learning styles and technology use is the first step in using technology, and PowerPoint specifically, in a better manner.

SOLUTIONS AND RECOMMENDATIONS

So far this chapter has considered the historical roots of PowerPoint and some research related to it. Following this, literature addressed characteristics and learning styles relative to the Net Generation and its proclivity toward technology. Using these two sections as a spring board, several potential problems pertaining to Net Generation learning were discussed. These included boring PowerPoint presentations and subsequently bored students, the ineffective use of PowerPoint as a whole, or students preferring to be reached by new means and platforms. But the main purpose of this chapter is how to effectively aid the learning of students through the proper use of technology. The authors aim to do that here.

The first recommendation to better connect with students through the use of PowerPoint is by taking a PowerPoint inventory. This includes questions like: Do you use PowerPoint? What is your purpose in using PowerPoint? Do you use custom PowerPoint slides or slides from a publisher? Do you have time to use PowerPoint? Do you want to get better at the use of PowerPoint in order to help your students understand the material or encounter deep learning? Analyzing the answers to these questions will in turn help you when looking at other recommendations listed below.

Next, it is important to look at the research on PowerPoint and students which was mentioned earlier. Is the PowerPoint you are working on meeting best practices in the areas of (1) Mind-drift, (2) Reading, (3) Writing, Seeing, Listening, (4) Keep pace, and (5) Note-taking? Students reported in various response levels liking PowerPoint when it helped in these categories. Perhaps you can employ new techniques in each of the categories to better aid the connection to your students. To do this, it may help to keep in mind the literature characteristic of the Net Generation and technology.

Mind-Drift

Are your PowerPoint slides eye catching? Do they help alleviate mind-drift and keep the attention of the audience? The literature shows that Net Gen'ers like to multi-task while using and receiving technology. This is a good time to make sure slides are not all the same. Some slides could have videos. Other slides could ask for student feedback, pose a question for class discussion, or ask students to work in groups or individually on various tasks. Using slides with questions as transitions is also an excellent way to keep the audience's attention and reduce mind-drift when using PowerPoint. Students have already said they like PowerPoint to keep their attention. Working with the knowledge of what types of technology the Net Generation prefers may help to make PowerPoint presentations even more solid.

A user of PowerPoint must also ask, am I reading to the students? When working to alleviate mind-drift it is imperative to make sure you are not reading to the students (Figure 1). The best way to do this is to heed to the 7×7 rule where there is no more than seven lines of text and seven items per line on any given slide, and even less when possible (Figure 2). In addition, the presenter will want to make sure that he or she knows enough supplementary information about the material being presented that reading from the slide is not necessary. The slide should highlight points and not be laden with lengthy definitions and copious diagrams. The limited information on slides will require students to both listen and engage with the instructor to ensure that no important course information is missed beyond what is posted on the screen. For example, Figure 2 allows for students to observe and analyze the two graphs to determine the differences between the two examples. At first glance, the audience may believe that Graph A had higher cell phone use. However, after examining the models students would see that the left column listed as People has a smaller range on the left graph.

Reading

Reading problem is a major concern for students. It makes sense. How many times has an institution has hired a faculty member or teaching assistant to teach for the first time or teach a new course outside his or her scope of knowledge? Faculty members want students to get the most information possible and in a manner that is easy to understand during a given period. Unfortunately PowerPoint has provided a handrail for faculty to cling to when

Figure 1. Poor slide example

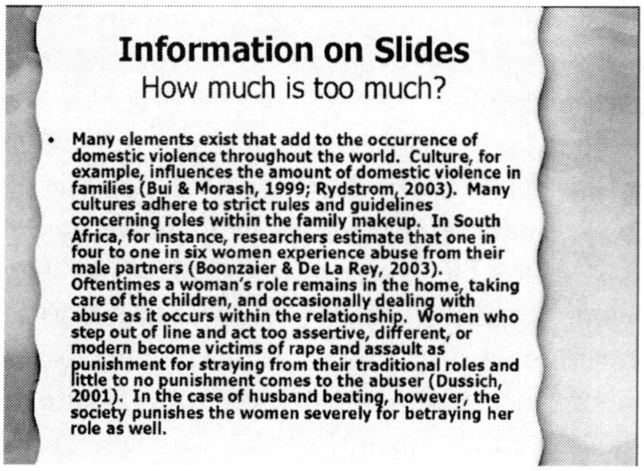

Figure 2. Limited information slide

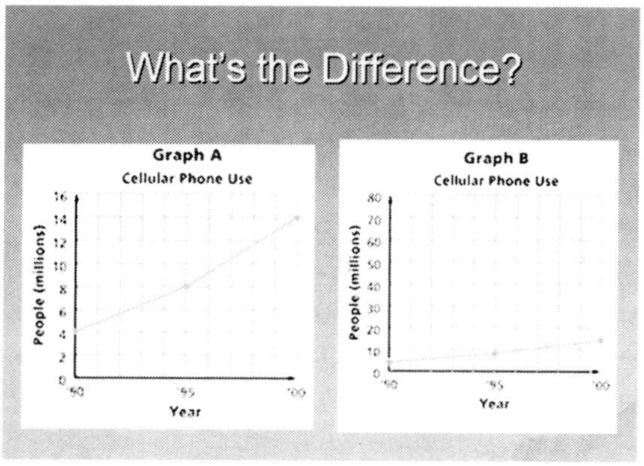

presenting new material. This has led presenters to read the material to the students (as shown in Figure 1). An additional consequence is that students may emulate their instructors' delivery styles for their own projects or presentations, believing "if this is how my professor presents information, then it must be the right way." There are ways to prevent this problem from occurring.

To begin, especially for new faculty and beginners in using PowerPoint, an instructor must be comfortable with the course information to efficiently deliver a presentation to students. This requires reviewing information, conducting some basic research, and reviewing course readings well before entering the classroom. In addition to content knowledge, awareness of certain public speaking delivery aspects would also benefit the instructor. Reviewing communication tips and tricks or joining public speaking organizations, such as Toastmasters, could help fine tune the distribution of course content. Figure 3 includes a link to a free online tutorial about putting effective PowerPoint presentations together. It is important for instructors to view various articles and techniques concerning the use of PowerPoint because there is not one "right way" to use the program. However, a clear understanding of the technology and what the Net Generation students expect will assist instructors in creating an engaging presentation.

Aside from basic public speaking skills and the ways of engagement mentioned in mind-drift, presenters can use other means within a presentation to avoid reading to students. One way is to make all of the PowerPoint slides pictures only (Figure 4). Using a symbol as a reference for students will help for even the simplest visual learners. A presenter's stories and information surrounding that picture can make the lecture all that more effective. Having movies embedded into a PowerPoint or links to the internet will break the monotony of over relying on the PowerPoint slides. Using outside technology like clickers, CMS, or online chat rooms can keep the in class of definitions and reading to a minimum and maximize the way PowerPoint is used. It is important to note that all of these suggestions may not work for every single lecture; however, the inclusion of movies, podcasts, etc. allows for variety and change beyond the traditional lecture format (Figure 5). Basically, an assortment of different approaches keeps students on their toes to see what will happen next.

Writing, Seeing, Listening

Reinforcement is extremely important when trying to engage students. Many students reported learning better when simultaneously hearing,

Figure 3. Free resources available for assistance

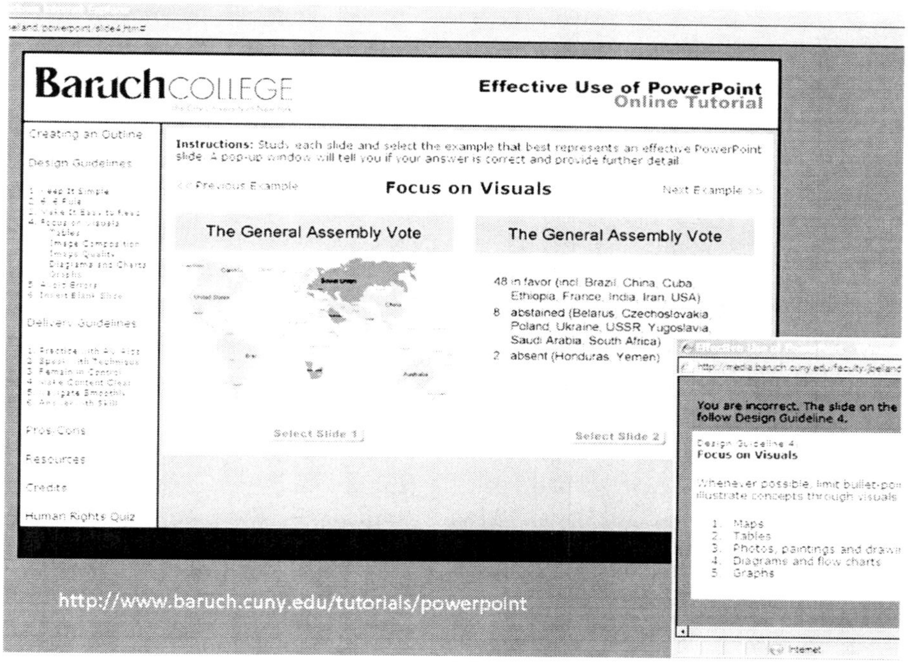

Figure 4. Grab the audience's attention

Figure 5. Including video in PowerPoint

seeing, and writing the information in the classroom setting. This form of reinforcement has been ingrained in lessons on teaching for years. If a presenter is simply clicking through slides it is quite possible that students are not getting the best possible connection to the material. So, to increase the way the Net Generation (and possibly all students) connects with the material it is important to identify and calibrate what one is doing with reinforcement in the way of writing, seeing, and listening. Figure 6 shows a PowerPoint slide used in an online communication course. The instructor has an opening slide instructing students that information will be presented both through text (seeing) and the instructor lecturing (listening) through the content as well. This format also allows students the opportunity to pause the lecture in order to take notes (writing) over the important course content and replay information if needed.

First, it may help to leave blanks in the material being presented on the slides. Students will have to be present and have to mentally participate to fill in the blanks with the pertinent information. Perhaps the material is posted early or sent to their iPhones, but only with blanks. This lets students be more involved with the presentation or lecture. Another technique is to take student writing samples and use them in the PowerPoint slides. Students have already written the material but will be on the lookout for their own as well as any peer reviewed material they have seen during the assignment. In addition, using student writing samples from previous semesters allows instructors to illustrate what an "A" assignment looks like versus a "C" assignment.

Next, it may help to discuss slides at length. Having fewer slides with more interaction and discussion will lead to deeper learning of the slide material. Asking students to discuss, analyze, and synthesize slides and slide material during a presentation session will help reinforce the writing, seeing, and listening goals. Students will use terminology and literature with each other and then hear the presenter use the material as well.

Figure 6. Incorporating audio

Finally, reinforcement with the Net Generation may come through the use of other forms of technology that help with writing, seeing, and listening. There are several ways to do this but most importantly when keeping the Net Generation in mind is—get creative! There are numerous simplistic and technological ways to reinforce presentation messages. CMS discussions or chat room posts may begin a discussion that is later carried on through PowerPoint during a lecture. If all students have text enabled mobile phones, the professor could Tweet or text certain talking points throughout the week with the plan to teach and reinforce the material during the PowerPoint lecture. Students could also be charged with creating their own multi-media messages that are required to use the necessary terms and concepts from the course material. This could be a precursor to the weekly lecture through PowerPoint and then serve as a study guide for themselves and classmates for upcoming assignments and exams. Above and beyond this a professor could ask students to upload their multimedia messages to a CMS where the professor could then embed the videos, music, or slides into his or her own PowerPoint lecture for the week. This is actively practicing reinforcement or seeing, hearing, and listening. In turn, this technique also employs the aspects of Net Generation learning and technology mentioned by scholars.

Keep Pace

Students reported one aspect of PowerPoint that helps them is its ability to aid in keeping pace with the lecturer and the material itself. Of course there are ways to do this that could optimize the presenter and students' time. The Net Generation says it likes to multi-task and that it can handle multiple things at one time. Yet, as a lecturer, it is difficult to control what *other* things a learner may be doing at any given time during a presentation. So, it is important to make sure that the student is focused on the PowerPoint because they may be giving more attention to other items. This is a valid concern.

After identifying other "tasks" it is important to structure a PowerPoint presentation that helps the student keep pace. The first and most important way to do this is to not place ALL of the information on the slide so that it shows when the slide is presented. Instead, it is important to hide lines of the slides so they appear only when they are clicked upon. Doing this helps the presenter control the pace of the lecture presentation and it also helps the students know how fast or slow they should be moving. It is quite possible that students are busily writing and taking notes on a slide that the presenter only has intentions of spending little time on. The opposite is also true. By controlling the clicks and information used on each slide a presenter can completely control the pace of the information during a presentation. This is especially true if an instructor wants to spend time discussing a particular item on the slide. If all of the slide content is in view, more than likely the students are busy copying down everything on the screen instead of engaging in the class dialogue. The "everything I need to know is on the slide" mentality will win out over discussions every time.

Another way to help students keep pace during a PowerPoint lecture is to remember essential elements of speech making. Although it may sound simple, treating each presentation as an individual "speech" or talk may help students understand where the material stands in the way of the course syllabus. In addition to doing this it may help to have an introduction slide that previews where the presentation will be going. This will help students anticipate what is coming and possibly take better notes or prepare note/computer space in a more calculated manner. It also helps with reinforcement by identifying the "need to know" information, excerpts from class readings than can be referred back to, or information the instructor has added to the discussion and is only obtained through listening to the presentation. The example below shows a slide discussing types of informative presentations (Figure 7). Although a few images are present, the instructor requires the students to give multiple examples of each type of presentation listed. This requires students to move away from only writing what is on the slide and engage in class discussion to provide examples of different types of speeches. Through writing and student engagement the audience gains a better understanding of the huge range of ideas for informative presentations.

After making an introductory slide (and having an introduction to the material) it also helps with keeping pace to have transition slides. Students can get lost in material during a PowerPoint presentation, especially if the presenter changes topics or moves quickly. Students taking courses outside their scope of expertise or major really benefit from transition slides. How these slides are set up is completely up to the creativity of the presenter. However, it may help here to think back to technology as it relates to the Net Generation. For example, each transition slide could be an embedded YouTube or other video. The videos will help diversify the type of technology being used and connect with the type of technology students may prefer. These transition slides or videos can serve as springboards for discussion

Figure 7. Providing some information but leaving room for discussion

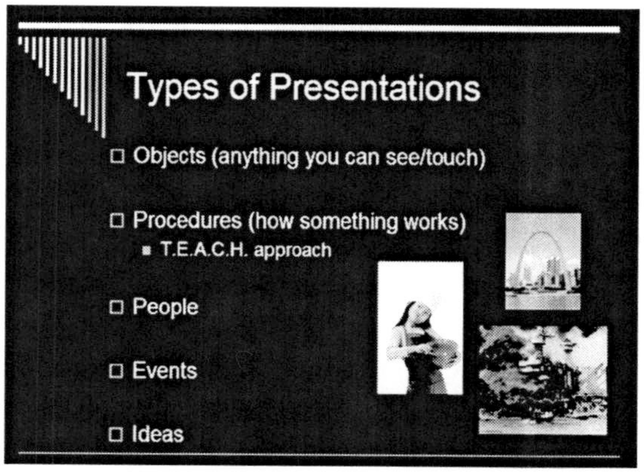

(writing, seeing, and listening) and also help the presenter move to the next topic of discussion. Transition slides can also serve as building blocks for the entire course period. It enables the student to understand how the information presented on the first slide relates to the last slide and all of the ones in between. They can help keep the flow of information clear for students to follow both the logistics of the content, the development of research in the specific area, and the thought process of the instructor delivering the information.

Simple slides as questions can also benefit students. Asking questions on transition slides may help students ponder to themselves what the shift in presentation may be, or where the lecture will go next. Another way to do this while infusing technology is asking questions of the students and then allowing them to use any means they choose to answer difficult transition slide questions. For example, the transition slide to a new chemistry concept may have a difficult formula or definition. The presenter may say, "what does this mean? Use any device you have with you to find out." Students could then use their phones, laptops, or friends to answer the question and be the first to do so.

Transition slides also help with breaking up monotonous lectures and may help with keeping the overall pace of the lecture. At some universities faculty members teach classes that meet once a week for three or four hours. It is never advisable to use a PowerPoint presentation for a three or four hour sitting. However, breaking module sections up with transition slides or activities helps the presenter keep pace and helps the students keep their sanity.

Finally, a conclusion slide will wrap up the day's presentation. Again this helps with reinforcement, but it also helps with pace. Signaling the end of PowerPoint presentation will help students look back at their notes and ponder if they have any unanswered questions. Too often presentations end because a presenter has far too many slides to get to in one session. Or, worse yet, the presenter says, "that's it" and sends the students on to their next class. Instead, it is important to have a conclusive slide that briefly reviews all information or points covered that day. Students will be glad to see this. It should look something like the introductory slide. Skip bibliography slides with references; the students do not care. Instead, place this important information on a CMS, and place citations within the body of the PowerPoint.

These suggestions will help some students keep better pace with the material and will help presenters control the pace of the overall presentation. In addition, introduction slides, transition slides, and conclusion slides help presenters who are less familiar with the presentation and its material move through the overall lecture. This tip is invaluable when redesigning a course or its contents. It also models best practices for students who themselves may be doing shortened versions of PowerPoint speeches in their own classes as reports, projects, or speeches. Demonstrating best practices in presenting is a great way to get best practices back from students, and also keeps faculty members from having to sit through a myriad of terribly boring emulative presentations.

Note Taking

The final PowerPoint theme of note taking incorporates aspects from the other areas of best practices and themes. The research found that students appreciate the use of PowerPoint to help when taking notes during a presentation. Of course from the sections above it was not recommended to load a bunch of slides up with hundreds of words and click through it while hoping that students take notes. If there is simply too much information or it is not presented correctly, the presenter is not going to connect with the Net Generation, or any student for that matter. There are ways to avoid doing this (some of which have already been mentioned) which will help connect with students for optimal learning outcomes.

Capitalizing on the students' impetus for multi-tasking may be one way to help them take notes during a PowerPoint presentation. One way to do this is through the use of student laptops or iPads. If an instructor is fortunate enough to have students with access to laptops or to host class in a computer lab, he or she can employ the following tactic. Load the PowerPoint presentation on a CMS so students have easy access to it during class. Make sure to have plenty of links and interactive technology through the PowerPoint presentation. During the presentation have students click on these links which will NOT be on the main presentation at the front of the lecture. They are instructed to make notes on the videos/links/websites they see. Upon the completion of the individual tasks, the greater class discussion can continue. At this point the presenter now has a student who has used multiple technologies, made notes, and practiced reinforcement. Students may also appreciate the different learning styles applied here.

A less technological method, yet simplistic and easy, is to provide handouts of the PowerPoint slides being presented with blanks where important information should be filled in. This was discussed earlier, but it is important to note that this could also aid in taking notes for students. Make sure to save trees and print PowerPoint slides in the "notes" format to print multiple slides on one page. Some people are unaware of this option when printing PowerPoint presentations (see Figure 8).

Sometimes it is important for reinforcement, as well as note taking, to use a capstone assignment to really drive home a point from the material or to help students master concepts. A good way to do this is through use of the CMS. Have students discuss the material from a PowerPoint lecture either before or after the presentation is made. Perhaps the instructor places a question on a chat board and students are required to respond to the question and to other students' responses. Without knowing it, the students now have notes using the lecture material in digital format. They could use these notes before the PowerPoint presentation to better understand the lecture.

The same activity could also be used *after* a PowerPoint presentation. Students could be charged with a discussion based on the material presented during a PowerPoint presentation. These answers to questions posed on the CMS could then be used for notes that could benefit the students for

Figure 8. How to print handouts

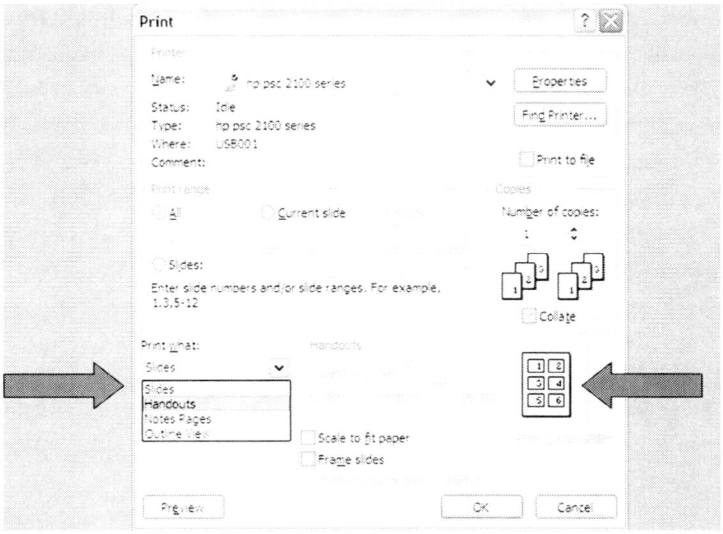

tests, discussion, or writing. Again, reinforcement of the material and the use of different technology platforms are important to connecting with the Net Generation and helping this population to learn better through the use of PowerPoint.

FINAL THOUGHTS

The ideas suggested above are not exhaustive; in fact it is the hope of the authors that this chapter serves as a springboard for greater ways to reach Net Generation students among all students when using PowerPoint as a tool for teaching. The important things to remember here are the research on the use and misuses of PowerPoint in classrooms, the literature on the Net Generation and its preferences and characteristics as rooted in technology, and the importance of combing the two areas for best practices in teaching when using PowerPoint as a medium for reaching student populations.

Keeping the areas of PowerPoint and Net Gen technology in mind, the creative practitioner can brainstorm many different ways to reach the Net Generation in order to aid in learning through new and old means alike. Remember it is important to not use technology for technology's sake, but rather to step back and analyze the pedagogy involved in a lesson where one is considering the use of PowerPoint. From there, begin to think of teaching activities like the ones in this chapter that will help students be better engaged with both the material AND the presenter. Surface learning is not learning that is rich, and therefore, PowerPoint slides for the passive listener may be forgotten the second the presentation has concluded. Instead, strive for deeper learning using active listening and engagement that connects with the students. Hopefully using the techniques and theories mentioned here will help practitioners continue their important work and add to their cadre of teaching tools.

Recommendations

One major recommendation that the authors can make is for presenters to attend as many teaching and career development workshops as possible. Technology is major factor that must be examined by today's higher education instructors. Hopefully the tips and techniques provided in this chapter can definitely help a current presenter or faculty member connect with his or her students through the use of PowerPoint in conjunction with data on the Net Generation.

However, one must not ever forget that technology is a *medium* by which a greater concept or theory is being presented. Today's PowerPoint is nothing more than yesterday's overhead projector, filmstrip reel, or VCR. To this end, it is important to know the material and how to teach it. It is important to know about the audience one is teaching and how to connect with them. Knowing and understanding people and their learning styles is the most important lesson anyone could have when it comes to connecting with students. It so happens that with today's Net Generation student the discussion of learning styles and technology are almost always married in some way or form. This is important to note, but it is also equally important to note there are other ways to reach this population without the use of technology. If one is not a technological person, there are other means to reach the Net Gen—your career is not over if you do not incorporate technology.

Therefore, thinking of ways to enhance the message being presented by PowerPoint is more important than ever before. Any person without any training could present a 60 slide PowerPoint presentation and hope that passive learners will sit idly by and "get" the material being discussed. However, it takes teachers skilled in connecting with students to present material that will come alive for students in a way that creates deeper meaning and learning. For this reason it is important to learn all one can about presentation, teaching, and students if one is to become a better user of PowerPoint for the sake of teaching and educating students. PowerPoint and technology are important, but they are not the end all to teaching with students. In the end knowing the audience, connecting with the students, and attempting to create relevance and meaning will be what helps students learn the best. It is up to the instructors to make the effort to connect with the students within their classrooms and find the style that best suits the learning environment. Through examining the audience, different technologies, and incorporating them into a delivery style, both instructors and students will benefit from a rich, fully-engaged learning experience.

FUTURE RESEARCH DIRECTIONS

As PowerPoint continues to be seen in classrooms there are different avenues that future researchers could take in order to better understand it as it relates to teaching and learning. One major study could be conducted using the same survey instrument used here in 2010, but only after the proposed teaching strategies have been implemented for a period of time. This style of post-test would analyze if the strategies have been, or continue to be effective.

A second area of future study could compare a group of Net Generation learners who use PowerPoint in one class to another group that does not use PowerPoint. The groups would need to have the same instructor for the same subject. It would be interesting to compare the outcomes and findings; and even survey both groups upon the completion of the term or study. This research could bolster the current research in this chapter. Both new directions mentioned here would be designed to improve teaching and learning with PowerPoint as it pertains to the Net Generation and students of all generations.

CONCLUSION

PowerPoint has permeated multiple facets of life from business presentations to higher education lectures. As previous research has shown, the Millennial generation has always been exposed to the Internet and computers, and thus is very familiar with PowerPoint. All presenters need to be aware of the message, the audience, and the overall specific purpose of the presentation when working with PowerPoint. This is especially true for instructors who not only make presentations but also serve as a model to their students. Acknowledging PowerPoint best practices and the intended goals of its use will hopefully lead to successful presentations to eager audiences for years to come.

REFERENCES

Adler, R. B., & Elmhorst, J. M. (2005). *Verbal and visual support in presentations. Communicating at Work* (pp. 370–399). New York, NY: McGraw Hill.

Ball, C. (2009). Avoiding death by PowerPoint. *Public Management*, *7*, 26–27.

Barnes, L. (2000). PowerPoint for terrified teachers. *Journal of Adolescent & Adult Literacy*, *44*(2), 184–187.

Brown, C., Murphy, T. J., & Nanny, M. (2003). Turning techno-savvy into info savvy: Authentically integrating information literacy into the college curriculum. *Journal of Academic Librarianship*, *29*, 386–398. doi:10.1016/j.jal.2003.08.005

Dobson, S. (2006). The assessment of student PowerPoint presentations – Attempting the impossible? *Assessment & Evaluation in Higher Education*, *31*(1), 109–119.. doi:10.1080/02602930500262403

Doumont, J. (2005). The cognitive style of PowerPoint: Slides are not all evil. *Technical Communication, 52*(1), 64–70.

Eubanks, S. (2006). *Millennials--Themes in current literature*. Retrieved from http://www.eubie.com/themes.pdf.

Frey, B. A., & Birnbaum, D. J. (2002). *Learners' perceptions on the value of PowerPoint in lectures*. (ERIC Document Reproduction Service No. ED467192).

Gareis, E. (2007). Active learning: A PowerPoint tutorial. *Business Communication Quarterly, 70*, 462–466. doi:10.1177/1080569907070004030 4

Gurrie, C., & Fair, B. (2010). PowerPoint: From fabulous to boring. *Journal of Communication, Speech, Theater, and Dance, 23*.

Kord, K., & Wolf-Wendel, L. (2009). The relationship between online social networking and academic and social integration. *College Student Affairs Journal, 28*(1), 103–124.

Leidman, M. B., & Piwinsky, M. J. (2009). *The perpetual professor in the 21st century university* [Scholarly project]. Indiana: Indiana University of Pennsylvania.

Leyes, M. (2007). Optimize your PowerPoint presentations. *Advisor Today, 11*, 76–77.

Mazer, J. P., Murphy, R. E., & Simonds, C. J. (2007). I'll see you on Facebook: The effects of computer-mediated teacher self-disclosure on student motivation, affective learning, and classroom climate. *Communication Education, 56*, 1–17. doi:10.1080/03634520601009710

McMahon, M., & Pospisil, R. (2005). Laptops for a digital lifestyle: Millennial students and wireless mobile technologies. In Goss, H. (Ed.), *ASCILITE 2005 Balance, Fidelity, Mobility: Maintaining the Momentum* (pp. 421–431). Brisbane, Australia: ASCILITE.

Pardue, K. T., & Morgan, P. (2008). Millennials considered: A new generation, new approaches, and implications for nursing education. *Nursing Education Perspectives, 29*(2), 74–79.

Park, J. (2010). Differences among university students and faculties in social networking site perception and use. *The Electronic Library, 28*, 417–431. doi:10.1108/02640471011051990

Raines, C. (2002). Managing millennials: Connecting generations. The sourcebook. *Generations at Work*. Retrieved from http://www.geneartion-satwork.com/ articles/millennials.htm.

Sweeney, R. (2006). *Millennial behaviors and demographics*. Newark, NJ: New Jersey Institute of Technology.

Walker, J. T., Martin, T., White, J., Elliott, R., Norwood, A., Mangum, C., & Haynie, L. (2006). Generational (age) differences in nursing students' preferences for teaching methods. *The Journal of Nursing Education, 45*, 371–374.

ADDITIONAL READING

Adams, C. (2006). PowerPoint, habits of mind, and classroom culture. *Journal of Curriculum Studies, 38*(4), 389–411.. doi:10.1080/00220270600579141

Anderson, R. (2004, June). Beyond PowerPoint: Building a new classroom presenter. *Syllabus.com*. Retrieved July, 2011, from www.syllabus.com.

Apperson, J. M., Laws, E. L., & Scepansky, J. A. (2008). An assessment of student preferences for PowerPoint presentation structure in undergraduate courses. *Computers & Education, 50*(1), 148–153. doi:10.1016/j.compedu.2006.04.003

Atkinson, C. (2011). *Beyond Bullet Points: Using Microsoft PowerPoint to Create Presentations that Inform, Motivate, and Inspire (Business Skills) (English and English Edition)*. Microsoft Press.

Burke, L. A., & James, K. E. (2008). PowerPoint-based lectures in business education: An Empirical Investigation of student-perceived novelty and effectiveness. *Business Communication Quarterly*, *71*(3), 277–296. doi:10.1177/1080569908317151

Clark, J. (2008). Powerpoint and pedagogy: maintaining student Interest in university lectures. *College Teaching*, *56*(1), 39–44. doi:10.3200/CTCH.56.1.39-46

Craig, R. J., & Amernic, J. H. (2006). PowerPoint Presentation technology and the dynamics of teaching. *Innovative Higher Education*, *31*, 147–160. doi:10.1007/s10755-006-9017-5

Duarte, N. (2008). *Slide:ology: the art and science of creating great presentations*. Beijing: O'Reilly Media.

DuFrene, D. D., & Lehman, C. M. (n.d.). Concept, content, construction, and contingencies: Getting the horse before the PowerPoint cartt. *Business Communication Quarterly*, *67*(1), 84-88.

Finkelstein, E., & Samsonov, P. (2008). *PowerPoint for teachers: dynamic presentations and interactive classroom projects (grades K-12)*. San Francisco: Jossey-Bass.

Holloway, R. (2008). Against the tyranny of PowerPoint: technology-in-use and technology abuse. *Organization Studies*, *29*(2), 255–276. doi:10.1177/0170840607079536

Kjeldsen, J. E. (2006). The rhetoric of PowerPoint. *Seminar.net - International Journal of Media, Technology and Lifelong Learning*, *2*(1).

Klemm, W. R. (2007). Computer Slide Shows: A Trap for Bad Teaching. *College Teaching*, *55*, 121–124. doi:10.3200/CTCH.55.3.121-124

Kosslyn, S. M. (2007). *Clear and to the point 8 psychological principles for compelling powerpoint presentations*. New York: Oxford University Press.

Kosslyn, S. M. (2010). *Better PowerPoint (R): Quick Fixes Based On How Your Audience Thinks*. Oxford University Press.

Mahin, L. (2004). PowerPoint pedagogy. *Business Communication Quarterly*, 67.

Ricer, R. E., Filak, A. T., & Short, J. (2005). Does a high tech (computerized, animated, PowerPoint) presentation increase retention of material compared to a low tech (black on clear overheads) presentation? *Teaching and Learning in Medicine*, *17*, 107–111. doi:10.1207/s15328015tlm1702_3

Savory, A., Proctor, R. W., & Salvendy, G. (2009). Information retention from PowerPoint™ and traditional lectures. *Computers & Education*, *52*(4), 858–867. doi:10.1016/j.compedu.2008.12.005

Szabo, A., & Hastings, N. (2000). Using IT in the undergraduate classroom: should we replace the blackboard with PowerPoint? *Computers & Education*, *35*(3), 175–187. doi:10.1016/S0360-1315(00)00030-0

Tufte, E. R. (2006). *The Cognitive Style of PowerPoint: Pitching Out Corrupts Within* (2nd ed.). Graphics Press.

Winn, J. (2003). Avoiding death by PowerPoint. *Journal of Professional Issues in Engineering Education and Practice*, *129*(3), 115–119. doi:10.1061/(ASCE)1052-3928(2003)129:3(115)

Witt, C. (2009). *Real leaders don't do PowerPoint: how to sell yourself and your ideas*. New York: Crown Business.

Worley, R. B., & Dyrud, M. A. (2004). Presentations and the PowerPoint problem. *Business Communication Quarterly*, *67*(1), 178–180. doi:10.1177/1080569903262027

KEY TERMS AND DEFINITIONS

Learning: The act of acquiring knowledge (as it pertains to the following topics).

Lecture: Stand and deliver presentation of information.

Millennials: The term given to the students/individuals born in the year 1980 or later.

Mind Drift: When a student's focus gravitates to something other than the immediate stimulus.

Net Generation: The generation of learners brought up on the Internet (synonomous with Millennial).

Pace: The rate at which a lecture or presentation is made.

PowerPoint: Microsoft Office program developed in 1990 for mediated presentations.

Reinforcement: The act of ensuring something is complete or understood.

Technology: Electronic development used to make things simpler, concise, or more advanced.

Chapter 22
Integrating Personal Experiences and Course Materials to Promote Net Generation Student Learning in an Online Health Communication Course

Rukhsana Ahmed
University of Ottawa, Canada

ABSTRACT

This study examines how technology-enhanced experiential learning methods, specifically the integration of personal experiences and course materials in an online course, can enhance Net Generation student learning. Drawing from undergraduate and graduate students' perspectives on their learning experiences gathered through an evaluation survey in an online health communication course, the study demonstrates how learning can be incorporated into everyday practice to meet the unique needs of digital learners. The study concludes with a discussion of implications of the findings for designing innovative methods of teaching and learning with the Net Generation in higher education institutions.

INTRODUCTION

In this day and age of computer technology, educators are in the midst of reflecting on current practices of teaching and learning. Today's students are inspired, enthused, and energized by technology making teaching an exciting, challenging, and rewarding experience for today's educators. Shaped by "a communications revolution," this young generation of learners – those born roughly between January 1977 to December 1997 – called the Net Generation (Tapscott, 1998, p. 2), is said to possess distinct learning styles from preceding generations (Barnes, Marateo, &

DOI: 10.4018/978-1-61350-347-8.ch022

Ferris, 2007; Oblinger & Oblinger, 2005; Tapscott, 2009). Among other learning styles, learning by doing – in its simplest form, known as experiential learning (Ahmed, 2005) – is deemed an important learning trait of the Net Generation (McNeely, 2005; Oblinger & Oblinger, 2005). This discourse on learning styles and generational differences seem to be in parallel with a shift in educational paradigms from instruction to learning (Barr & Tagg, 1995). Some scholars, however, challenge the notion that the Net Generation is "a distinctive new generation of students in possession of sophisticated technology skills and with learning preferences" underscoring the lack of sound empirical basis to (Bennett, Maton, & Kervin, 2008) support such claim. This study attempts to add to the empirical literature.

Against such a backdrop, this study begins with an examination of the intersection of the Net Generation and experiential learning. More specifically, with a view to explore how the application of technology-enhanced experiential learning contributes to advancing the learning of Net Generation student by connecting self with subject-matter, I examine undergraduate and graduate students' evaluations of an online health communication course. I close with a discussion of implications of the findings for designing innovative methods of teaching and learning with the Net Generation.

THE NET GENERATION AND EXPERIENTIAL LEARNING: CONNECTING SELF WITH SUBJECT-MATTER

The rapidly emerging digital media and web technologies, such as blogs (Ferdig & Trammell, 2004; Kerawalla, Minocha, Kirkup, & Conole, 2008), podcasts (King & Gura, 2008), wikis (Parker & Chao, 2007), instant messengers (IM) (Lu, Chiou, Day, Ong, & Hsu, 2006), social bookmarks (Abbitt, 2009), are creating mediated learning environments cultivating new approaches, novel applications, and increased flexibility to foster student learning (Beldarrain, 2006; Lansari, Tubaishat, & Al-Rawi, 2010). While these emerging web technologies are changing the way people communicate and access information, and the educational uses of these tools is on the rise, it is important to probe their potential in creating engaging learning environments and providing experiential learning opportunities to help students achieve personal growth and development. This humanistic orientation to learning (Maslow, 1970, Rogers & Freiberg, 1994) becomes crucial in the context of today's Net Generation who grew up with digital technology (Tapscott, 1998) and to whom "computers, the Internet, online resources, and instantaneous access are simply the way things are done" (Oblinger & Oblinger, 2005, pp. 2.1 -2.2.). How can learning be incorporated into every day practice to help Net Generation learners connect self with subject-matter in today's digital era? To explore how the application of technology-enhanced experiential learning contributes to advancing Net Generation student learning, this study examines undergraduate and graduate students' evaluations of an online health communication course.

Experiential leaning does not automatically equate with Net Generational learning, but it does offer key elements which can enhance the Net Generation learning. In the following section, I present an overview of the Net Generation learner traits and a discussion of experiential learning through the lens of the basic tenets of David Kolbs' (1984) theory of learning.

Net Generation Learners

The Net Generation, also called the Millenials (Howe & Strauss, 2000), Generation Y (Tapscott, 1998), Homo Zappiens (Veen, 2000), and Digital Natives (Prensky, 2001a, 2001b), has been characterized to "instinctively turn first to the Net to communicate, understand, learn, find, and do many things" (Tapscott, 2009, p. 9). Growing up with digital technology, the Net Generation is said to be distinct from previous generations—the Baby Boom (1946 – 1964) and the Baby Bust (1965 – 1976), also known as Generation X (Tapscott, 1998). The following arguments, from the many claims about the Net Generation found in the existing literature about the Net Generation learner traits, are spotlighted because of their relevance to the current study. Firstly, the Net Generation is different. Having grown up in an age of media saturation surrounded by multiple digital technologies, the Net Generation is described to be digitally literate, always connected through technology, fast, proficient in multitasking, active experiential learners, and socially oriented (Barnes, Marateo, & Ferris, 2007; Oblinger & Oblinger, 2005; Prensky, 2006; Tapscott, 1998, 2009). Secondly, the Net Generation has specific learning preferences. The Net Generation is said to learn by doing, through social interaction, and in teams; they prefer structure, engagement and experience, are visual and Kinaesthetic, and oriented towards things that matter (Howe & Strauss, 2000; McNeely, 2005; Oblinger & Oblinger, 2005; Prensky, 2006). And finally, the Net Generation has specific learning expectations. The Net Generation is argued to expect faculty members to be prepared and experts in and knowledgeable and passionate about their particular fields (Roberts, 2005).

Based on the above arguments regarding the distinctness of the Net Generation and their distinct learning preferences and expectations, some scholars argue for fundamental changes in education to accommodate these differences (Jones, 2002; Prensky, 2001; Tapscott, 1998, 2009). However, because research on the Net generation is still in its infancy, lacking empirical evidence and often supported by personal testimonials, other scholars call for a research agenda that is theoretically based and empirically informed (Bennett, Maton, & Kervin, 2008). Hence, the case for this study.

Experiential Learning

In its simplest form, experiential learning is learning through experience. According to David Kolb (1984), a renowned educational theorist, "learning is the process whereby knowledge is created through the transformation of experience. Knowledge results from the combination of grasping experience and transforming it" (p. 41). Kolb adopted a developmental perspective and recognized experience as the source of learning and development. He refined the model of experiential learning by drawing on and extending the earlier works in experiential learning by Dewey (1916, 1938), who argued for learning to be grounded in experience; Lewin (1951), who emphasized the importance of being active learners; and Piaget (1953), for whom intelligence is shaped by experience. Accordingly, Kolb developed a four-stage cyclical theory of learning that combines concrete experience (experience), observation and reflection (perception), abstract conceptualization (cognition), and testing in new situations (behaviour) (Kolb, 1984). Corresponding to these stages, Kolb & Fry (1975) identified four learning styles that underline conditions under which individuals learn better. These learning styles include orientation to/preference for the following: observation and collection of a wide range of information (diverger), sound logical theories (assimilator), practical application of concepts and theories (converger), and hands-on experiences (accommodator) (Kolb, 1976, 1981, 1984).

Although there are strengths and weaknesses associated with it, Kolb's model of experiential learning provides a useful framework for designing teaching and learning (Tennant, 1997).

Considering the Net Generation learner traits and key elements of Kolb's model of experiential learning as identified in the literature, the following research question was posed:

- **Research Question:** How does integrating personal experiences and course materials enhance student learning in an online health communication course?

METHODOLOGY

The purpose of this study was to find how technology-enhanced experiential learning methods, integration of personal experiences and course materials in an online course, can enhance Net Generation student learning. To this end, a survey was used to gather undergraduate and graduate students' responses to closed-ended and open-ended questions about their learning experiences in the online health communication course. This mixed methods approach was employed to get more complete and usable information for understanding Net Generation student learning. As Creswell, Fetters, and Ivankova (2004) noted, "When used in combination, both quantitative and qualitative data yield a more complete analysis, and they complement each other" (p. 7) because while the former can find statistical association between variables, the latter can discern potential explanation for particular behaviour.

Participants

All students (N = 16) enrolled in an online health communication course at a higher education institution based in eastern Canada were invited to participate in this study. Volunteer sampling method (Brain, 2000) was used which allowed students to self-select to participate in the study. A total of 11 students, four upper-level undergraduate students and seven master's level graduate students took part in the study. Among them, five were male and six were female. More detailed socio-demographic information about the students was not collected. Although the sample size was small, the data collected was rich in the quality of feedback and appropriate for the scope of this qualitative study. Such qualitative research is less concerned with generalizing and more interested in establishing trustworthiness in terms of providing rich and thick description of participants' responses (Lincoln & Guba, 1985; Schurink, 1998)

Overview of the Course

The seven week intensive course offered on the Blackboard Vista site was designed to examine theory and research in the field of health communication. The course aimed at providing a forum for a lively discussion among students on a variety of topics in health communication, including interaction between provider and patient, communication in health care organizations, health campaigns, and cultural meanings of health and illness.

Design of the course was informed by Kolb's cyclical theory of learning (Kolb, 1984) and Kolb & Fry's (1975) learning styles to facilitate different types of experiential education activities and support different learning styles. Being cognizant of the idea that learning becomes effective when learners' experiences are well designed and facilitated (Ahmed & Blankson, 2005; Dewey, 1916, 1938), the course assignments were created to encourage students to think/reflect, feel, observe, and do (Kolb, 1984), and to assist them move through concrete experience, reflective observation, abstract conceptualization, and active experimentation stages of learning (Kolb & Fry, 1975). Hence, viewing learning as a multidimensional process (Kolb, 1984), the highly interactive online course consisted of instructor notes and involved student engagement with the course materials, participation in online discussions, documents sharing, and applications over the Internet. Students were expected to read the equivalent of about 60-80 pages each week, from readings suggested in the course pack, some of which were also available online on the World Wide Web or through the university library databases.

Weekly online discussions and weekly shared activities formed significant parts of the course work. In order to participate in the course, students would need to be online about three to five hours a week to read and post discussion messages and complete activities according to the week's topic. Weekly reflection journal entries constituted another major and ongoing course assignment. The discussions, activities, and journal entries encouraged students to link concepts, theories, and central debates in health communication to their professional and/or to their personal lives. In order to help students make those links, the discussions, activities, and journal entries were centered around questions that asked students to describe how they were able to apply the theory they read about to their everyday lives; what and how specific article/discussion/activity influenced their thinking the most or changed their mind; what they learned that was new; what surprised them; how the course materials could be helpful to them on their job; and whether this would change how they would do things at work. In cases where students did not have any job experience at the time, they could respond to questions that asked them to picture themselves in their ideal job when they graduate and describe how they would see themselves using the course information. In this manner, the experiential learning assignments were designed to facilitate students to connect self with subject matter.

Data Collection Procedures

The study drew on students' learning experiences gathered through an online course evaluation survey with a focus on how technology-enhanced experiential learning contributes to advancing learning as self connected with subject-matter. For the purpose of this study, selected responses were drawn from the 30 questions (22 closed-ended and eight open-ended) in the original survey. The selected responses provided information on student learning experiences and student perception of improving the quality of the course and instruction for a better learning experience for future students. Students' participation in the survey were completely anonymous (using a tool built into Blackboard Vista) from the instructor and staff. Research Ethics Board (REB) approval was secured and informed consent forms were used to obtain permission from the participants to use their course evaluations as data for the study.

Data Analysis

To answer the research question, I read through students' course evaluations seeking broad themes "bringing together components or fragments of ideas or experiences, which often are meaningless when viewed alone" (Leininger, 1985, p. 60). Although primarily utilizing a qualitative data analysis tool, I blended thematic analysis (Taylor & Bogdan, 1984) of qualitative data with frequency analysis of quantitative data to identify and classify students' comments about their learning experiences.

RESULTS AND ANALYSIS

Here I present findings from survey results of students' responses to their learning experiences. Results are categorized into three broad themes—course structure, course instruction, and course knowledge.

Course Structure

A well-designed course is conducive to student learning in an online course.

In this study, course navigation, pace, contents, assignments, and means of communication were important considerations to students for effective learning. While 18% remained neutral, 82% of the students found that the course was well-organized and well-structured, and thus easy to navigate. One student commented: "I thoroughly enjoyed my experience! [the instructor] did an excellent job of organizing all of the material so that it was easily accessible." 73% of students thought that the pace of the course (the amount of time they had to spend doing their course work) was reasonable; 27% remained neutral. 82% of the students found the quality and relevance of the course assignments were above average and 18% found them as average. 73% of the students thought the quality and relevance of the other course content (readings, web links, lectures notes, and so on) were above average and 27% thought they were average. 64% of the students found the amount of interaction between them and other students was just enough, 27% thought it was adequate, and 9% thought it was not enough. 64% of the students thought the quality of interaction between them and other students was above average and 36% thought it was below average. Overall, student responses regarding course structure were positive.

Student response to the merit of having at least one face-to-face meeting with the instructor and fellow classmates was mixed. While 46% of the students did feel a face-to face meeting was necessary, 36% of them thought it would not had helped, and that they "enjoyed the independence of the online course," and 18% understood the constraints of arranging a face-to-face meeting. One student commented: "I didn't feel it hindered the progression of the class that we didn't [meet]. There were talks amongst the student to meet up but due to our schedules, that never happened. It would have been nice but not indispensable."

Those students who were in favour of a face-to-face meeting thought it would be nice just to get to know the professor and the people that they had been engaging in discussions with. One student elaborated:

A face to face interaction would allow me to be more comfortable with the course, and feel that I am a human and interacting with other humans. Everything being on the internet kind of makes me wonder who I am communicating with on the other end, and somewhat weird.

Another student suggested that face to face interaction be part of the curriculum, and that a meeting date and place be thought of in advance so that students have a chance to get to know the instructor and one another off screen.

Student responses on the merits of online versus face to face meetings in an online class were therefore mixed.

Overall, the students found the course assignments were appropriate, insightful, relevant to the course, and facilitated discussions. When asked about their favourite assignment, some students thought they had the most fun writing the reflection journals. The questions were stimulating and allowed them to apply their personal experiences to course work. The reflection journal assignment allowed them to be able to apply what they had read into real life situations. Others shared they enjoyed individual weekly activities that involved doing more research on a particular topic and thus they felt they learned a lot in those parts of the course. One student commented: "I really enjoyed the activity on a particular cultural group. It was interesting to do the activity on the health risk management project. This allowed us to do our own research and to ponder the effectiveness of such programs." Hence student responses reinforced the meaningfulness of experiential learning.

Course Instruction

The role of the teacher is not minimized in an online course. The students in this study felt that the following were important considerations for digital pedagogy: student-instructor interaction, student participation-instructor contribution ratio, instructor's demonstration of genuine concern towards students, being sensitive to student needs, providing them with adequate feedback, and evaluating their work constructively. Specific data on responses follow.

55% of the students thought the instructor was very effective and 36% thought the instructor was effective in teaching this course; 9% remained neutral. 55% of the students thought the quality of interaction between them and the instructor was excellent, 27% thought it was above average, and 18% thought it was average. 82% thought a very good balance of student participation and instructor contribution was achieved and 18% thought a good balance was achieved. All students felt that the instructor seemed genuinely concerned about their progress. 91% of the students found the instructor was always sensitive to student needs and concerns and 9% found the instructor was sometimes sensitive. Overall, student feedback indicated the positive role of the instructor in online learning.

While 73% of the students thought evaluations of their work were always made in a constructive manner, 27% thought they were sometimes made in a constructive manner. When asked about whether they felt they received adequate feedback from the instructor, the student response was mixed. 73% of the students thought that the instructor answered everything fast and effectively. Whenever they were in doubt, or needed confirmation that they were on the right track, the instructor was always quick to answer with insightful responses, especially on journal reflections weekly posts. Although 18% of the students felt that they received some good feedback from the instructor, they would have still liked that the instructor participate more actively in the course discussions. 9% of the students did not feel that adequate feedback had been provided; they would have liked to receive feedback each week on assignments and discussions. Yet, one student commented, "I would have maybe expected a weekly individual feedback, but I realized that it would have required far too much work considering the number of students!!" Overall, students felt positively about feedback from their instructor.

Course Knowledge

Carefully designed and pedagogically sound online course can provide rich and engaging learning experiences for students. For students in this study, the quality of readings, pedagogical strategies, and interactive methodologies were important considerations for increasing interest in the subject-matter. 73% of the students had taken online courses (1 - 6) before, while 27% of the students were taking an online course for the first time. Before the course, 18% of the students viewed health communication as a very important subject-matter, 73% thought it was important, and 9% thought it was not important. After completing this course, 82% of the students viewed health communication as a very important subject-matter and 18% viewed it as important. 91% of the students reported that this course increased their interest greatly in the subject-matter and 9% did not think so. One student shared:

If anything, I found it particularly informing. I did not know there was such thing as health communication before. Every reading brought with it a new discovery. I feel it will be very useful next time I find myself in a health care setting.

On the whole, the discussions, activities, and reflection journals in this course proved stimulating for all students (100%), reinforcing the importance of experiential learning for Net Generational learners. This perception is reinforced by other responses. When asked if the course enabled co-construction of knowledge, on the whole, the students responded favourably. Students felt co-construction was facilitated, especially through a combination of the useful readings, assignments, and the sharing of personal experiences. They thought it was interesting to read other students findings and opinions as well as share their knowledge with the class. One student commented: "Definitely, reading what others have to say broadened my horizons and way of thinking. It also allowed me to see things differently. In the end, my classmates' input helped me discover and learn more about health communication."

The ways in which learning in this class meaningfully impacted learning outside the class varied. When asked about the hours per week spent online doing related activities that were a direct result of taking the course, student responses ranged between one and 16 hours. In response to the course being intellectually stimulating, informing, and interactive, overall student response was positive. Students found that the course really had them thinking about the subject-matter. They found the course was stimulating, and that they learned a lot about health communication; the weekly discussions made the course more interactive. One student shared: "I gained a lot of information, as well as felt like I gave good information as well. I met and interacted with people of different cultures, ideas, and level of education, which made it more stimulating." Students felt the course stimulated them to read, research, and think deeply about health communication and its significance as an important field of study.

One student felt the course was interactive and somewhat stimulating. This student would have liked more recent journal articles on the subject rather than book chapters. Interestingly, for another student it was not the course material, rather the mode of interaction was more important: "I think it is informing to read all the articles. It is also interactive because people can respond to each other's answers, but I still prefer to express myself to others face-to-face."

When asked if they felt they had an opportunity to express themselves, 91% of the students responded optimistically. "Of course! That's what this course was about;" "I felt the whole course was an opportunity to express myself, the whole point was sharing my perception of things based on the readings or the research we did," shared a couple of students. Students felt they had the opportunity to express themselves in the course discussions, activities and journal entries. On the other hand, 9% of the students thought they could express themselves only at times; one student commented:

I feel, however, that the prompts provided often contained implicit conclusions that made the students often write very similar responses to each other, and thus may have made them feel ill at ease about expressing views at odds with those perceived to be those of the course convenor.

As students were asked to rate their overall experience in taking this course, 73% felt their overall experience was above average and 27% thought it was average. Thus most students' responses support the effectiveness of experiential learning.

DISCUSSION

This study examined how integration of personal experiences and course materials in an online course can enhance Net Generation student learning.

Analysis of undergraduate and graduate students' responses to closed-ended and open-ended course evaluation survey questions about their learning experiences in an online health communication course reveal that a well-designed and pedagogically sound online course can provide rich and engaging learning experiences for students. The findings also suggest that the quality and quantity of student-instructor interactions are important pedagogical considerations for effective learning in an online course. These results have important implications for designing innovative methods of teaching and learning with the Net Generation in higher education institutions. My discussion of these implications is broadly categorized into three areas- organizing the learning process, creating critical learning environment, and constructing diverse learning experiences.

Organizing the Learning Process

Communication modes, readings, and assignments are important considerations in an online course, and when integrated successfully with technology, a sound course structure offers students an idea of how the learning process is organized in an online environment. In this way, it paves the way for a rich and engaging learning experience for students and instructional opportunities for teachers. My findings show the importance to Net Generational learning of such course features as easy navigation and reasonable pace, quality and relevance of course contents and assignments, and the quantity and quality of peer interaction. These aspects were valued by students as important components of their learning experiences. Hence one implication of this study is that blending technology and content to facilitate learner interaction can promote Net Generation student learning by tapping into their preference for structure, social interaction, and orientation towards things that matter (McNeely, 2005; Oblinger & Oblinger, 2005; Prensky, 2006).

The mixed response of the students with regard to face-to-face meetings in the online course underscores the significance of technology-supported meaningful teacher-student and student-student connections. Since "relationships are a driving force in the learning process" (McNeely, 2005, p. 4.5) of the Net Generation, and since Net Generation learners "still crave interaction with their fellow students, even if they cannot see them" (Windham, 2005, p. 5.11), online interactive tools can be used to help learners make meaningful connections with each other. Such online learning tools include video presentations, chat rooms, and live teleconferences, among others.

The Net Generational learners in this study appreciated assignments that were insightful, relevant, and stimulating, which prompted them to draw on their life experiences to deepen disciplinary knowledge and increase their intellectual curiosity by engaging in further research. Since Net Generation learners have been described to learn better through discovery, prefer experiential learning (Oblinger & Oblinger, 2005) and learning experiences that are personally meaningful (Glenn, 2000), educators can make learning relevant to learners' daily lives and foster intellectual curiosity with integration of effective technology and appropriate variety of assignments.

Creating Critical Learning Environment

A critical learning environment encourages students to use independent thinking and connect course concepts to their everyday experiences. Here, the online health communication course cultivated a critical learning environment by maintaining the quality of student-teacher interaction and striking a balance between student participation and instructor contribution to promote learning. The findings in this study indicate that factors crucial to creating a critical learning environment, especially in an online setting, include maintaining instructor presence through showing concern for students, being sensitive to their needs, providing them with adequate feedback, and constructive evaluation of their work. Such instructor presence becomes effective when it creates a classroom environment that welcomes students' input, encourages them to take risks and accept constructive feedback, and offers a dynamic, collaborative dialogue through discussion and activities. It is interesting to note that the Net Generation learners have been described to expect teachers to be knowledgeable and passionate about their particular field (Roberts, 2005). This study suggests that to create a learning environment that nourishes Net Generation learners, educators should use their expertise to create experiential learning activities that can be facilitated through effective integration of appropriate online applications.

While Net Generation learners have been identified as having a need for immediacy (Oblinger & Oblinger, 2005), the findings in this study yielded mixed response from students with regard to the adequacy of instructor's feedback. With proper facilitation and course structure, educators can utilize various online applications, including Blackboard features, to cater to the differences in the ways that students learn. This study reinforces how important it is to be creative and flexible in interacting with students, to understand their learning needs, and to create significant learning experiences for them. Knowledgeable educators can thus provide more effective instruction through the design and facilitation of learning experiences.

Constructing Diverse Learning Experiences

Students learn best when they play an active role in their own education (Dewey, 1916, 1938; Rogers, & Freiberg, 1994). An educator can create diverse learning experiences for students by encouraging them to engage in open-ended, thought provoking discussions in which they need to tap into their analytical thinking skills and apply the knowledge to a given situation. Such diversity allows space for differences in the ways that students learn and use information. In this current study, the online health communication course integrated content, pedagogy, and technology to purposely design various elements of experiential learning—concrete experience, reflection, conceptualization, and application (Kolb, 1984). As indicated by the findings of the study, Net Generational students found the discussions, activities, and reflection journals helpful in facilitating co-construction of knowledge. Student learning was facilitated by connecting the subject-matter to their own everyday experiences.

Since the Net Generation students "learn well through discovery – by exploring for themselves or with their peers" (Oblinger & Oblinger, 2005, p. 2.6), educators can work to facilitate effective learning through experiential learning activities that help students learn by doing and through application. As evident from the findings of the current study, students learn better when subject-matter is connected to their own everyday experiences. With the help of various online tools, educators can develop strategies for engaging students in cooperative learning, design activities that enable sharing of experiences, and make the classroom more engaging and help students learn from each other.

Through constructing diverse learning experiences, educators can encourage students to be creative and act upon their ingenuity. When done well, these creative endeavors can contribute to connections between abstract conceptual learning and meaningful experiences.

FUTURE RESEARCH DIRECTIONS

This book provides an understanding of the Net Generation and features pedagogical resources for effectively teaching and learning with digital learners.

Growing up digital, today's students are motivated, enthused, and energized about learning by inventive, creative, and technology-enhanced teaching practices (Oblinger & Oblinger, 2005; Tapscott, 1998, 2009). However, while technological innovations can significantly enhance the learning process, the success of student learning is subject to educators' effective integration of these innovative tools into teaching and learning for supporting students' learning styles (Kolb, 1976, 1981, 1984; Kolb & Fry, 1975; Saeed, Yang, & Sinnappan, 2009) and reaching the instructional objectives in a classroom (Ahmed & Blankson, 2005; Dewey, 1916, 1938). Hence, future research should look into learners' characteristics, learning styles, and preferences, for effective incorporation of the rapidly emerging digital media and web technologies into everyday classroom experiences.

Technology-enhanced experiential learning methods can get students excited about school work. Whether in an online or traditional course, integration of personal experiences and course materials is key to creating a learning environment that optimizes student learning. In the online health communication course discussed in this study, course assignments were designed to help students critically think about their own practices and goals as learners, and to create a forum for co-construction of knowledge. The Internet and digital technologies offered promising tools for promoting student learning and potentially improving the learning process and outcomes. Future studies should continue to investigate the unique learning styles of digital learners and the changing interactions between students and instructors across disciplines because, while "web-based instruction becomes more common, differences among academic disciplines remain largely overlooked by researchers" (Smith, Heindel, & Torres-Ayala, p. 152.).

Evaluation, which elicits student reflection of the course structure, instruction, and learning, of an online course is an important component and should be built into course design. Carefully crafted online surveys can help improve the quality and effectiveness of a given online course and instruction. Such evaluation surveys can yield valuable information to aid in revising or enhancing a course in the future.

Lastly, web course management tools, such as Blackboard, allow higher education institutions to provide a standard platform for courses which can facilitate Net Generation learning. However, "for all learners, research points to the importance of learning environments which are active, social, and learner-centered" (Ramaley & Zia, 2005, p. 8.7), and which help promote self-development and personal growth. Educators should strive to provide a safe and optimal learning environment for students. Classroom activities and group discussions should be designed to enable students to discover and question and respect diverse values, beliefs, and opinions. This study discussed some simple ways to integrate technology into teaching to complement and enhance instruction that provided meaningful learning experiences for the Net Generation. Researchers should continue to share good practices in order to tap the potential of technology to reach today's digital learners.

CONCLUSION

The findings of this study indicate that students in the online health communication course under investigation preferred intellectually stimulating experiential learning, which is immediate and socially interactive. At the core of the course was the belief that education involves co-construction of knowledge. As a learner and teacher in the course, the instructor saw her own responsibility as stimulating critical thinking in students, engaging them in creative endeavors, and fostering a sense of community among them as they continued to wrestle with theory, research, and practice in health communication. Through the use of the Blackboard course management system, having daily access to a computer with reliable internet connection, a university e-mail account, and experience using the Blackboard course site, the students were offered a space to view the world through their own experiences (facilitated by the online discussions, weekly activities, and journal reflections) and place meaning upon them by engaging in a dialogue with self, others, and their environment.

As with any study, the findings here should be considered in light of some limitations. The generalizability of findings was limited by the small sample size. The study focused on a small class of 20 students maximum. Out of the 16 students enrolled in the course, only 11 students volunteered to participate in the study. Future research could investigate larger courses, use larger samples to promote generalizability of findings. It could also employ more sophisticated methodological tools. It is also important to note that this study focused on a health communication course. Future research should examine other disciplinary online courses to gather discipline specific findings. Nonetheless, on a scholarly level, this study provides insights into understanding how Net Generation student learning can be enhanced through the application of technology-enhanced experiential learning methods. On a practical level, the knowledge gained from this study offers educators, researchers, and administrators in higher education, insights into designing innovative methods of teaching and learning with the Net Generation in academic institutions.

REFERENCES

Abbitt, J. T. (2009). Evaluating the implementation of a social bookmarking activity for an undergraduate course. *Journal of Interactive Online Learning, 8*(1). Retrieved February 8, 2011, from http://www.ncolr.org/jiol/issues/pdf/8.1.5.pdf.

Ahmed, R. (November, 2005). *Experiential learning: The case study of rural action's environmental learning program.* Paper presented to the Experiential Learning in Communication Division, National Communication Association Annual Convention, Boston, MA, U.S.A.

Ahmed, R., & Blankson, H. (2005) Learning by (doing) Dewey: Enacting pragmatist philosophies in the basic communication course. In L.W. Hugenberg & B.S. Hugenberg (Eds.), *Teaching ideas for the basic communication course, volume 9*, (pp. 1-11). Dubuque, IO: Kendall Hunt Publishing.

Barnes, K., Marateo, R., & Ferris, S. (2007). Teaching and learning with the net generation. *Innovate, 3*(4). Retrieved December 7, 2010, from http://www.innovateonline.info/index.php?view=article&id=382.

Barr, R. B., & Tagg, J. (1995). From teaching to learning - A new paradigm for undergraduate education. *Change, 27*(6), 12–25.

Beldarrain, Y. (2006). Distance education trends: Integrating new technologies to foster student interaction and collaboration. *Distance Education, 27*(2), 139–153. doi:10.1080/01587910600789498

Benett, S., Maton, K., & Kervin, L. (2008). The digital natives debate: A critical review of the evidence. *British Journal of Educational Technology, 39*(5), 775–786. doi:10.1111/j.1467-8535.2007.00793.x

Brain, C. (2000). *Advanced subsidiary psychology: Approaches and methods.* Nelson Thornes Ltd.

Creswell, J. W., Fetters, M. D., & Ivankova, N. V. (2004). Designing a mixed methods study in primary care. *Annals of Family Medicine, 2*, 7–12. doi:10.1370/afm.104

Dewey, J. (1916). *Democracy and education: An introduction to the philosophy of education.* New York, NY: The Free Press.

Dewey, J. (1938). *Experience and education.* New York, NY: The Macmillan Company.

Ferdig, R. M., & Trammell, K. D. (2004). Content delivery in Blogsphere. *THE Journal.* Retrieved February 11, 2011, from http://thejournal.com/articles/16626.

Glenn, J. M. (2000). Teaching the Net generation. *Business Education Forum, 54*(3), 6–14.

Howe, N., & Strauss, W. (2000). *Millennials rising: The next great generation.* New York, NY: Vintage Books.

Kerawalla, L., Minocha, S., Kirkup, G., & Conole, G. (2008). Characterising the different blogging behaviours of students on an online distance learning course. *Learning, Media and Technology, 33*(1), 21–33. doi:10.1080/17439880701868838

King, K. P., & Gura, M. (2008). *Podcasting for teachers using a new technology to revolutionize teaching and learning* (Rev. 2nd ed.). USA: Information Age Publishing.

Kolb, D. A. (1976). *The learning style inventory: Technical manual*. Boston, MA: McBer.

Kolb, D. A. (1981). Learning styles and disciplinary differences. In Chickering, A. W. (Ed.), *The modern American college*. San Francisco, CA: Jossey-Bass.

Kolb, D. A. (1984). *Experiential learning: Experience as the source of learning and development*. Englewood Cliffs, NJ: Prentice-Hall Inc.

Kolb, D. A., & Fry, R. (1975). Toward an applied theory of experiential learning. In Cooper, C. (Ed.), *Theories of group process*. London, UK: John Wiley.

Lansari, A., Tubaishat, A., & Al-Rawi, A. (2010). Using a learning management system to foster independent learning in an outcome-based university: A Gulf perspective. *Issues in Informing Science and Information Technology*, *7*, 73–87.

Leininger, M. M. (1985). Ethnography and ethnonursing: Models and modes of qualitative data analysis. In Leininger, M. M. (Ed.), *Qualitative research methods in nursing* (pp. 33–72). Orlando, FL: Grune & Stratton.

Lewin, K. (1951). *Field theory in social science*. New York, NY: Harper Collins.

Lincoln, Y. S., & Guba, E. G. (1985). *Naturalistic inquiry*. Newbury Park, CA: Sage Publications.

Lu, C.-H., Chiou, G.-F., Day, M.-Y., Ong, C.-S., & Hsu, W.-L. (2006). Using Instant Messaging to provide an intelligent learning environment. *Lecture Notes in Computer Science*, *4053*, 575–583. doi:10.1007/11774303_57

Maslow, A. (1970). *Motivation and personality* (2nd ed.). New York, NY: Harper and Row.

McNeely, B. (2005). Using technology as a learning tool, not just the cool new thing. In D. G. Oblinger & J. L. Oblinger, (Eds.), *Educating the Net Generation* (pp. 4.1-4.10). Washington, DC: EDUCAUSE. Retrieved December 7, 2010, from http://www.kwantlen.ca/academicgrowth/resources/EduCausepub7101.pdf.

Oblinger, D. G., & Oblinger, J. L. (Eds.). (2005). *Educating the Net Generation*. Washington, DC: EDUCAUSE. Retrieved December 7, 2010, from http://www.kwantlen.ca/academicgrowth/resources/EduCausepub7101.pdf.

Oblinger, D. G., & Oblinger, J. L. (2005). Is it age for IT: First steps towards understanding the Net Generation. In D. G. Oblinger & J. L. Oblinger, (Eds.), *Educating the Net Generation* (pp. 2.1-2.120). Washington, DC: EDUCAUSE. Retrieved December 7, 2010, from http://www.kwantlen.ca/academicgrowth/resources/EduCausepub7101.pdf.

Parker, K. R., & Chao, J. T. (2007). Wiki as a teaching tool. *Interdisciplinary Journal of Knowledge and Learning Objects*, *3*, 57–72.

Piaget, J. (1953). *The origins of intelligence in children*. London, UK: Routledge and Kegan Paul.

Prenksy, M. (2001a). Digital natives, digital immigrants. *Horizon*, *9*(5), 1–6. doi:10.1108/10748120110424816

Prenksy, M. (2001b). Digital natives, digital immigrants, part II. Do they really think differently? *Horizon*, *9*(6), 1–6. doi:10.1108/10748120110424843

Prenksy, M. (2006). *Don't bother me Mom-I'm learning*. Minneapolis, MN: Paragon House Publishers.

Ramaley, J., & Zia, L. (2005). The real versus the possible: Closing the gaps in engagement and learning. In D. G. Oblinger & J. L. Oblinger, (Eds.), *Educating the Net Generation* (pp. 8.1-8.21). Washington, DC: EDUCAUSE. Retrieved December 7, 2010, from http://www.kwantlen.ca/academicgrowth/resources/EduCausepub7101.pdf.

Roberts, G. R. (2005). Technology and learning expectations of the Net Generation. In D. G. Oblinger & J. L. Oblinger, (Eds.), *Educating the Net Generation* (pp. 3.1-3.7). Washington, DC: EDUCAUSE. Retrieved December 7, 2010, from http://www.kwantlen.ca/academicgrowth/resources/EduCausepub7101.pdf.

Rogers, C., & Freiberg, H. J. (1994). *Freedom to learn* (3rd ed.). New York, NY: Merrill.

Saeed, N., Yang, Y., & Sinnappan, S. (2009). Emerging web technology in higher education: A case of incorporating blogs, podcasts and social bookmarks in a web programming course based on students' learning styles and technology preferences. *Journal of Educational Technology & Society*, *12*(4), 98–109.

Schurink, E. M. (1998). Designing qualitative research. In De Vos, A. S. (Ed). *Research at grass roots — A primer for the caring professions* (pp. 252-264). Pretoria, South Africa: van Schaik.

Smith, G. G., Heindel, A. J., & Torres-Ayala, A. T. (2008). E-learning commodity or community: Disciplinary differences between online courses. *Internet and Higher Education, 11*, 152–159. Retrieved January 15, 2011, from http://cgit.nutn.edu.tw:8080/cgit/PaperDL/TKW_090409063122.pdf.

Tapscott, D. (1998). *Growing up digital: The rise of the Net generation*. New York, NY: McGraw-Hill.

Tapscott, D. (2009). *Growing up digital: How the Net generation is changing your world*. New York, NY: McGraw-Hill.

Taylor, S. J., & Bogdan, R. (1984). *Introduction to qualitative research methods: The search for meanings*. New York, NY: John Wiley & Sons.

Tennant, M. (1997). *Psychology and adult learning* (2nd ed.). London, UK: Routledge.

Windham, C. (2005). The student's perspective. In D. G. Oblinger & J. L. Oblinger (Eds.), *Educating the Net Generation* (pp. 5.1-5.16). Washington, DC: EDUCAUSE. Retrieved December 7, 2010, from http://www.kwantlen.ca/academicgrowth/resources/EduCausepub7101.pdf.

ADDITIONAL READING

Bender, T. (2003). *Discussion-based online teaching to enhance student learning: theory, practice and assessment*. Sterling, Virginia: Stylus Publishing, LLC.

Boud, D., Keogh, R., & Walker, D. (Eds.). (1985). *Reflection turning experience into learning*. London: Kogan Page.

Boyer, N., Maher, P., & Kirkman, S. (2006). Transformative learning in online settings: The use of self-direction, metacognition, and collaborative learning. *The Journal of Transformative Education*, *4*(4), 335–361. doi:10.1177/1541344606295318

Breck, J. (2006). *109 ideas for virtual learning: How open content will help close the digital divide*. Lanham, Maryland: Rowman & Littlefield Publsihers, Inc.

Brown, J. S. (2000). Growing up digital. *Change*, *32*(2), 11–20. doi:10.1080/00091380009601719

Buckingham, D. (2007). *Beyond technology: children's learning in the age of digital culture*. Malden, MA: Polity.

Chickering, A. W. (2008). Strengthening democracy and personal development through community engagement. *New Directions for Adult and Continuing Education, 118*, 87–95. doi:10.1002/ace.298

Creswell, J. (1994). *Research design: Qualitative and quantitative approaches* (2nd ed.). Thousand Oaks, CA: Sage Publications.

Eastment, D. (2008). Social bookmarking. *ELT Journal, 62*(2), 217–218. doi:10.1093/elt/ccn007

Elgort, I., Smith, A. G., & Toland, J. (2008). Is wiki an effective platform for group course work? *Australasian Journal of Educational Technology, 24*(2), 195–210.

Ellison, N., & Wu, Y. (2008). Blogging in the classroom: A preliminary exploration of student attitudes and impact on comprehension. *Journal of Educational Multimedia and Hypermedia, 17*(1), 24.

Farmer, B., Yue, A., & Brooks, C. (2008). Using blogging for higher order learning in large cohort university teaching: A case study. *Australasian Journal of Educational Technology, 24*(2), 123–136.

Ferris, S. P., & Godar, S. (Eds.). (2006). *Teaching and learning with virtual teams*. Hershey, PA: Information Science Publishing, Idea Group Inc.

Howe, N., & Strauss, W. (2000). *Millenials rising: The next great generation*. New York: Vintage books.

Jarvis, P. (1987). *Adult learning in the social context*. London: Croom Helm.

Jones, S., Johnson-Yale, C., Millermaier, S., & Seoane Perez, F. (2008). Academic work, the Internet, and U.S. college students. *The Internet and Higher Education, 11*(3-4), 165–177. doi:10.1016/j.iheduc.2008.07.001

Kolb, D. A., & Fry, R. (1975). 'Toward an applied theory of experiential learning. In Cooper, C. (Ed.), *Theories of Group Process*. London: John Wiley.

Koszalka, T. A., & Ganesan, R. (2004). Designing online courses: A taxonomy to guide strategic use of features available in course management systems (CMS) in distance education. *Distance Education, 25*(2), 243–256. doi:10.1080/0158791042000262111

Malikowski, S. R., Thompson, M. E., & Theis, J. G. (2007). A model for research into course management systems: Bridging technology and learning theory. *Journal of Educational Computing Research, 36*(2), 149–173. doi:10.2190/1002-1T50-27G2-H3V7

Oravec, J. A. (2003). Blending by blogging: Weblogs in blended learning initiatives. *Journal of Educational Media, 28*(2–3), 225–233. doi:10.1080/1358165032000165671

Pratt, K. (2007). *Building online learning communities: Effective strategies for the virtual classroom*. San Francisco: Jossey-Bass.

Roberts, T. S. (2004). *Online collaborative learning: Theory and practice*. Hershey, PA: Information Science Publishing, Idea Group Inc.

Sandars, J., & Schroter, S. (2007). Web 2.0 technologies for undergraduate and postgraduate medical education: an online survey. *Postgraduate Medical Journal, 83*(986), 759–762. doi:10.1136/pgmj.2007.063123

Seels, B., & Glasgow, Z. (1998). *Making Instructional Design decisions* (2nd ed.). Upper Saddle River, NJ: Merrill.

Selwyn, N. (2006). Exploring the 'digital disconnect' between net-savvy students and their schools. *Learning, Media and Technology, 31*(1), 5–17. doi:10.1080/17439880500515416

Shea, P. (2006). A study of students" sense of learning community in online environments. *Journal of Asynchronous Learning Networks, 10*(1).

Strait, J., & Sauer, T. (2004). Constructing experiential learning for online courses: The birth of e-Service. *EDUCAUSE Quarterly, 27*(1).

Thompson, T. L., Dorsey, A. M., Miller, K. I., & Parrott, R. L. (Eds.). (2003). *Handbook of health communication*. Mahwah, NJ: Lawrence Erlbaum Associates.

Woods, R., Baker, J. D., & Hopper, D. (2004). Hybrid structures: Faculty use and perception of web-based courseware as a supplement to face-to-face instruction. *The Internet and Higher Education*, *7*(4), 281–297. doi:10.1016/j.iheduc.2004.09.002

Xie, Y., Ke, F., & Sharma, P. (2008). The effect of peer feedback for blogging on college students' reflective learning processes. *The Internet and Higher Education*, *11*(1), 18–25. doi:10.1016/j.iheduc.2007.11.001

Zheng, R. Z., & Ferris, S. P. (Eds.). (2008). *Understanding online instructional modeling: Theories and Practices*. Hershey, PA: Information Science Reference, IGI Global.

Zubizarreta, J. (2004). *The learning portfolio: Reflective practice for improving student learning*. Bolton, MA: Anker Publishing Company, Inc.

KEY TERMS AND DEFINITIONS

Course Evaluations: Use a paper-based or web-based questionnaire to elicit student reflection of the course structure, instruction, and learning.

Digital Learners: Those who grew up with digital technology and prefer to use digital media for learning.

Experiential Learning: In its simplest form, is learning through experience.

Health Communication: The study concerned with the interaction of people involved in the health care process and the dissemination and interpretation of health-related messages by individuals, groups, organizations, and/or the general public.

Mixed Methods Research: Refers to the collection and analysis of both quantitative and qualitative data within a particular study.

Net Generation: The cohort of young adults who has grown up in a technology-rich environment (e.g., computers, Internet, cellular phones, interactive video games).

Technology-Enhanced Experiential Learning: The integration of personal experiences and course materials in an online course.

Afterword

Teaching, Learning, and the Net Generation: Concepts and Tools for Reaching Digital Learners is one of those books that needed to be published, as the topics addressed are important, interesting, and timely. The anthology amplifies and builds on a body of literature that seeks to better understand the dynamic and complex processes involved in teaching and learning in our modern era. The chapters, although varied in perspective and purpose, share the theoretical and pedagogical positions that how we teach and learn is not only technologically-influenced, but simultaneously situated in cultural, spatial, and temporal contexts. Through interdisciplinary and applied research, the authors have questioned, studied, and analyzed common assumptions about Net Generation students, including learning expectations, preferences, course performance, and outcomes. While Net Generation students may have distinct new tools, skill sets, experiences, and attitudes toward learning, they are far from monolithic, and they share the historical bond of previous generations in negotiating and co-constructing with professional educators that which will constitute knowledge and link our present to the past.

Despite educational institutions generally lagging behind in adopting and implementing new technologies, there can be little doubt that our ways of teaching, learning, and knowing are changing more quickly than in the past. Perhaps, because of differential access and usage, these changes might still be better described as evolutionary rather than revolutionary. Use of information technology in courses can result in improved, with more engaged student-directed learning, convenience, and/or better preparation for the workplace. As this book goes to press, Net Generation students and their instructors are increasingly making use of Web-based textbooks, word processing and spreadsheet applications, simulations, wikis, blogs, bibliography and citation tools, video-sharing, and social networking. The research on technologies and their pedagogical applications presented herein offer not only relevant and practical possibilities for current educators but also provide a valuable historical document for the future. My own generation learned mostly face-to-face in a classroom, sometimes aided by noisy 16mm motion picture projectors, slippery overhead transparencies, and mimeographed printed handouts. Who can predict what the post-Net Generation, the children of the first digital learners studied here, will be like and what new tools they may have as they engage in knowledge acquisition and learning?

On a recent visit to the Gartner Group headquarters in Connecticut, a higher educational consultant joked that today's digital learners are incessantly hungry for new information technology in the classroom. Today's tech-savvy students say, "More please. Now please!" Yet Gartner estimates that only approximately 20 percent of faculty expends the considerable effort to use new information technologies in their teaching. The majority of faculty continues to be challenged, if not stressed, in trying to keep up with information technology, in an environment where there are few, if any, rewards for integrating information technology into existing courses. Therefore, while the Net Generation may be digital natives, for many, their day-to-day schooling harkens back to yesteryear.

One of the areas that I currently oversee at my University is a grant-funded community center that assists high school students in the Bronx to make up lost credits via online coursework during evenings and weekends so that they might graduate on time. For many of these teenagers, this is their first encounter with a digital, self-paced learning mode that is student-centered instead of teacher-centered. For their parents, who are invited to the center for basic computer training, the experience is a step toward narrowing the digital divide. For both Net Generation students and parents, it is about gaining access to tools and possibly life-changing educational opportunities. And, after all, that is the message behind *Teaching, Learning, and the Net Generation: Concepts and Tools for Reaching Digital Learners* -- to understand purposefully how the relationship of people and technology can help us re-conceptualize education for a more advanced society and a better world.

Ron Jacobson
Fordham University, USA

Ron Jacobson *holds a PhD from the University of Oregon in telecommunications and film; and is a Professor in the Department of Communication and Media Studies at Fordham University in New York City. He is the author of numerous articles and books, with research focusing on media education, literacy and technologies. He is co-editor of two editions of Communication and Cyberspace: Social Interaction in an Electronic Environment. He is serving in his 11th year as Associate Vice President in Fordham's Office of the Provost, where his current administrative portfolio includes new program development in professional and continuing studies, and facilitating University initiatives in online learning.*

Compilation of References

A few Twitter facts. (September 14, 2010). Retrieved November 2, 2010 from http://twitter.com/about#about.

Abbitt, J. T. (2009). Evaluating the implementation of a social bookmarking activity for an undergraduate course. *Journal of Interactive Online Learning, 8*(1). Retrieved February 8, 2011, from http://www.ncolr.org/jiol/issues/pdf/8.1.5.pdf.

About Quora. (n.d.). Retrieved February 12, 2011, from http://www.quora.com/about.

Accordent Technologies, Inc. (2011, 15 April). *Hoover's company records, 116246*. (Document ID: 1605079501).

Adler, R., & Brown, J. (2008). Minds on fire: Open education, the long tail, and learning 2.0. *EDUCAUSE Review*, *43*, 6–32.

Adler, R. B., & Elmhorst, J. M. (2005). *Verbal and visual support in presentations. Communicating at Work* (pp. 370–399). New York, NY: McGraw Hill.

Adler, R. B., & Rodman, G. (2009). *Understanding human communication*. New York, NY: Oxford.

Adobe Systems Incorporated. (2011, 15 April). *Hoover's company records, 12518*. (Document ID: 168152191).

Ahmed, R. (November, 2005). *Experiential learning: The case study of rural action's environmental learning program*. Paper presented to the Experiential Learning in Communication Division, National Communication Association Annual Convention, Boston, MA, U.S.A.

Ahmed, R., & Blankson, H. (2005) Learning by (doing) Dewey: Enacting pragmatist philosophies in the basic communication course. In L.W. Hugenberg & B.S. Hugenberg (Eds.), *Teaching ideas for the basic communication course, volume 9*, (pp. 1-11). Dubuque, IO: Kendall Hunt Publishing.

Alexander, P. A., & Murphy, P. K. (1993). *The research base for APA's learner-centered psychological principals. Taking research on learning seriously: Implications for teacher education.* Paper presented at the Annual Meeting of the American Psychological Association, New Orleans.

Allen, I. E., & Seaman, J. (2010). *Learning on demand: Online education in the United States, 2009*. Babson Park, MA: Babson Survey Research Group.

Allen, T. H. (2006). Is the rush to provide on-line instruction setting our students up for failure? *Communication Education*, *55*, 122–126..doi:10.1080/03634520500343418

Allen, I. E., & Seaman, J. (2008). *Staying the course: Online education in the United States, 2008*. Retrieved from http://sloanconsortium.org/sites/default/files/staying_the_course-2.pdf.

Althaus, S. L. (1997). Computer-mediated communication in the university classroom: An experiment with on-line discussions. *Communication Education*, *46*, 158–174. doi:10.1080/03634529709379088

Alvermann, D. (2001). *Effective literacy instruction for adolescents*. (Executive Summary and Paper). Chicago, IL: National Reading Conference.

American Foundation for Suicide Prevention. (2011). Facts and figures: National statistics. Retrieved from http://www.afsp.org/index.cfm?fuseaction=home.viewPage&page_id=050FEA9F-B064-4092-B1135C3A70DE1FDA.

American Medical Association. (2010). *Medical student debt*. Retrieved December 31, 2010, from http://www.ama-assn.org/ama/pub/about-ama/our-people/member-groups-sections/medical-student-section/advocacy-policy/medical-student-debt.shtml.

American Psychological Association Presidential Task Force on Psychology in Education. (1993). *Learner-centered psychological principles: Guidelines for school redesign and reform*. Washington, DC: American Psychological Association and the Mid-Continent Regional Educational Laboratory.

American Psychological Association. (2002). Ethical principles of psychologists and code of conduct. *APA Online*. Retrieved from http://www.apa.org/ethics/code/code-1992.aspx.

Amin, Z., Boulet, J., Cook, D., Ellaway, R., Fahal, A., Kneebone, R., & Ziv, A. (2011). (in press). Technology-enabled assessment of health professions education. *Medical Teacher*. doi:10.3109/0142159X.2011.565832

Ammon, M. S., Furco, A., Chi, B., & Middaugh, E. (2002). *A profile of California's CalServe service-learning partnerships, 1997-2000*. Sacramento, CA: California Department of Education.

An, Y. J., & Frick, T. (2006). Student perceptions of asynchronous computer-mediated communication in face-to-face courses. *Journal of Computer-Mediated Communication, 11*(2). Retrieved from http://jcmc.indiana.edu/vol11/issue2/an.html. doi:10.1111/j.1083-6101.2006.00023.x

Anderson, J. R. (1983). *The architecture of cognition*. Cambridge, MA: Harvard University Press.

Anderson, R., Davis, P., Linnell, N., Prince, C., Razmo, V., & Videon, F. (2007). Classroom presenter: Enhancing interactive education with digital ink. *Computer, 40*(9), 56–61..doi:10.1109/MC.2007.307

Anderson, J. R. (1983b). Retrieval of information from long-term memory. *Science, 220*, 25–30. doi:10.1126/science.6828877

Anderson, L., Krathwohl, D., Airasian, P., Cruikshank, K., Mayer, R., & Pintrich, P. ... Wittrock, M. (2001). *A taxonomy for learning, teaching, and assessing: A revision of Bloom's taxonomy of educational objectives*. New York, NY: Longman.

Anstey, M., & Bull, G. (2006). *Teaching and learning multiliteracies: Changing times, changing literacies*. Newark, DE: International Reading Association.

APA. (2008). *Learner-centered psychological principles: A framework for school reform and redesign*. Prepared by the Learner-Centered Principles Work Group of the American Psychological Associations Board of Educational Affairs (1997). Retrieved from http://www.apa.org/ed/lcp2/lcp14.html.

Applegate, J. L., & Morreale, S. P. (1999). Service-learning in communication: A natural partnership. In Droge, D., & Ortega Murphy, B. (Eds.), *Voices of strong Democracy: Concepts and models for service-learning in communication studies*. Sterling, VA: Stylus.

Arum, R., & Roksa, J. (2011). *Academically adrift: Limited learning on college campuses*. Chicago, IL: University of Chicago Press.

Ashbury, F. D., Iverson, D. C., & Kralj, B. (2001). Physician communication skills: Results of a survey of general/family practitioners in Newfoundland. *Medical Education Online 6*(1). Retrieved from www.med-ed-online.org.

Astin, A., Astin, H., & Lindholm, J. (2011). *Cultivating the spirit: How college can enhance students' inner lives*. San Francisco, CA: Jossey-Bass.

Astin, A. W., Astin, H. S., & Lindholm, J. A. (2011). *Cultivating the spirit: How college can enhance students' inner lives*. San Francisco, CA: Josey-Bass.

Atkinson, S. (2011). Embodied and embedded theory in practice: The student-owned learning-engagement (SOLE) model. *International Review of Research in Open and Distance Learning, 12*(2), 1–18.

Atkinson, S. (2009). *Revolution and pedagogy: Why e-learning can still transform university teaching* (proceedings). EQIBELT Workshop 2007-2008. Zagreb, Croatia: SRCE / University of Zagreb.

Attwell, G. (2007). E-portfolio: The DNA of the personal learning environment. *Journal of E-learning and Knowledge Society, 3*(2).

Augar, N., Raiman, R., & Zhou, W. (2004). *Teaching and learning online with wikis*. Paper presented at the Australian Society for Computers in Learning in Tertiary Education Conference, Perth, Australia.

Ayres, P. (2006). Impact of reducing intrinsic cognitive load on learning in a mathematical domain. *Applied Cognitive Psychology, 20*, 287–298. doi:10.1002/acp.1245

Baddeley, A. D. (1986). *Working memory*. Oxford, UK: Oxford University Press.

Baddeley, A. D. (1999). *Essentials of human memory*. Hove, UK: Psychology Press.

Baddeley, A. D., & Logie, R. H. (1992). Auditory imagery and working memory. In Reisberg, D. (Ed.), *Auditory imagery* (pp. 179–197). Hillsdale, NJ: Lawrence Erlbaum Associates.

Bailey, K. D. (1994). *Methods of social research* (4th ed.). New York, NY: Free Press.

Baker, E., Rozendal, M., & Whitenack, J. (2000). Audience awareness in a technology rich elementary classroom. *Journal of Literacy Research*, *32*(3), 395–419. doi:10.1080/10862960009548086

Baldwin, M. (2009, March 6). #FollowFriday: The anatomy of a Twitter trend. *Mashable*. Retrieved May 8, 2010, from http://mashable.com/2009/03/06/twitter-followfriday.

Ball, C. (2009). Avoiding death by PowerPoint. *Public Management*, *7*, 26–27.

Banas, J. A., & Raines, S. A. (2010). A meta-analysis of research on inoculation theory. *Communication Monographs*, *77*(3), 281–311. doi:10.1080/03637751003758193

Bandura, A. (1993). Perceived self-efficacy in cognitive development and functioning. *Educational Psychologist*, *28*, 117–148. doi:10.1207/s15326985ep2802_3

Bandura, A. (1986). *Social foundations of thought and action: A social cognitive theory*. Englewood Cliffs, NJ: Prentice-Hall.

Bandura, A. (1977). Self-efficacy: Toward a unifying theory of behavioral change. *Psychological Review*, *84*, 191–215. doi:10.1037/0033-295X.84.2.191

Bandura, A. (1994). Self-efficacy. In Ramachaudran, V. S. (Ed.), *Encyclopedia of human behavior* (*Vol. 4*, pp. 71–81). New York, NY: Academic Press.

Bargh, J. A. (1990). Auto-motives: Preconscious determinants of social interaction. In Higgins, E. T., & Sorrentino, R. M. (Eds.), *Handbook of motivation and cognition* (*Vol. 2*, pp. 93–130). New York, NY: Guilford.

Barkley, E. F., Cross, K. P., & Major, C. H. (2005). *Collaborative learning techniques: A handbook for college faculty*. San Francisco, CA: Jossey-Bass.

Barnes, L. (2000). PowerPoint for terrified teachers. *Journal of Adolescent & Adult Literacy*, *44*(2), 184–187.

Barnes, K., & Marateo, R. R., & Ferris, S. (2007, April/May). Teaching and learning with the net generation. *Innovate, 3*(4). Retrieved from http://www.innovateonline.info/index.php?view=article&id=382.

Barnlund, D. C. (1968). Therapeutic communication. In Barnlund, D. C. (Ed.), *Interpersonal communication: Survey and studies* (pp. 613–645). Boston, MA: Houghton Mifflin.

Baron, N. S. (2010). *Always on: Language in an online and mobile world*. Oxford, UK: Oxford University Press.

Baron, N. S. (2008). Adjusting the volume: Technology and multitasking in discourse control. In Katz, J. E. (Ed.), *Mobile communication and social change in a global context* (pp. 117–194). Cambridge, MA: The MIT Press.

Barr, R. B., & Tagg, J. (1995). From teaching to learning - A new paradigm for undergraduate education. *Change*, *27*(6), 12–25.

Barron, B. (2004). Learning ecologies for technological fluency: Gender and experience differences. *Journal of Educational Computing Research*, *31*(1), 1–36. doi:10.2190/1N20-VV12-4RB5-33VA

Bauerlein, M. (2008). *The dumbest generation: How the digital age stupefies young Americans and jeopardizes our future*. New York, NY: Penguin.

Baym, N. K. (2010). *Personal connections in the digital age*. Malden, MA: Polity Press.

Beck, C., & Wade, M. (2004). *Got game: How the gamer generation is shaping business forever*. Harvard Business School Publishing.

Becker, H. J., & Riel, M. (2000, December). *Teacher professional engagement and constructivist-compatible computer use*. Retrieved April 23, 2011, from http://www.crito.uci.edu/tlc/findings/report_7/.

Beetham, H., McGill, L., et al. (2009). *Thriving in the 21st century: Learning literacies for the digital age.* Glasgow, UK: Glasgow Caledonian University/JISC. Retrieved June 5, 2010, from http://www.jisc.ac.uk/media/documents/projects/llidareportjune2009.pdf.

Bejerano, A. R. (2008). Raising the question #11 – The genesis and evolution of online degree programs: Who are they for and what have we lost along the way? *Communication Education, 57*, 408–414. doi:10.1080/03634520801993697

Belal, A. R. (2011). Students perceptions of computer assisted learning: An empirical study. *International Journal of Management in Education, 5*(1), 63–78..doi:10.1504/IJMIE.2011.037755

Beldarrain, Y. (2006). Distance education trends: Integrating new technologies to foster student interaction and collaboration. *Distance Education, 27*(2), 139–153. doi:10.1080/01587910600789498

Benett, S., Maton, K., & Kervin, L. (2008). The digital natives debate: A critical review of the evidence. *British Journal of Educational Technology, 39*(5), 775–786. doi:10.1111/j.1467-8535.2007.00793.x

Bennett, S., & Maton, K. (2010). Beyond the digital natives debate: Towards a more nuanced understanding of students' technology experiences. *Journal of Computer Assisted Learning, 26*, 321–331. doi:10.1111/j.1365-2729.2010.00360.x

Benoit, P. J., Benoit, W. L., Milyo, J., & Hansen, G. J. (2006). *The effects of traditional vs. web-assisted instruction on student learning and satisfaction.* Columbia, MO: University of Missouri.

Berge, Z., & Myers, B. (2000). Evaluating computer mediated communication courses in higher education. *Journal of Educational Computing Research, 23*, 431–450.

Berger, K. A., & Topol, M. T. (2001). Technology to enhance learning: Use of a web site platform in traditional classes and distance learning. *Marketing Education Review, 11*, 15–26.

Bernard, R. M., Abrami, P. C., Borokhovski, E., Wade, C. A., Tamim, R. M., Surkes, M. A., et al. (2009). A meta-analysis of three types of interaction treatments in distance education. *Review of Educational Research, 79*(3), 1243-1289. doi: 1210.3102/0034654309333844.

Biggs, J., & Tang, C. (2007). *Teaching for quality learning at university: What the student does* (3rd ed.). Buckingham, UK: Open University Press.

Billig, S. H. (2002). Adoption, implementation, and sustainability of K-12 service-learning. In A. Furco & S. H. Billig (Eds.), *Advances in service-learning research: Vol. 1. Service-learning: The essence of the pedagogy* (pp. 245–267). Greenwich, CT: Information Age.

Bjork, R. A. (1988). Retrieval practice and the maintenance of knowledge. In Gruneberg, M. M., Morris, P. E., & Sykes, R. N. (Eds.), *Practical aspects of memory: Current research and issues* (*Vol. 1*, pp. 396–401). New York, NY: Wiley.

Black, P., & Wiliam, D. (1998). Inside the black box: Raising standards through classroom assessment. *Phi Delta Kappan, 80*, 139–148.

Bleed, R. (2005, August). *Visual literacy in higher education* (Educause Publication No. ELI4001). Retrieved from http://net.educause.edu/ir/library/pdf/ELI4001.pdf.

Bleicher, R. E., & Lindgren, J. (2005). Success in science learning and preservice science teaching self-efficacy. *Journal of Science Teacher Education, 16*, 205–225. doi:10.1007/s10972-005-4861-1

BlogPulse. (n.d.). *Stats.* Retrieved November 2, 2010, from http://www.blogpulse.com/.

Blomstrom, S. A., & Tam, H. W. (2010). Assessing service-learning to improve instruction. In Worley, D. W., Worley, D. A., Hugenberg, B., & Elkins, M. R. (Eds.), *Best practices in experiential and service learning in communication.* Dubuque, IA: Great River Technologies.

Blomstrom, S. A., & Tam, H. W. (2009, June). *How and to what extent does a service-learning pedagogy enhance communication and collaboration skill learning among first-year students?* Paper presented at the American Society for Engineering Education Conference Austin, TX.

Bloom, B. S. (1956). *Taxonomy of educational objectives, handbook I: The cognitive domain.* New York, NY: David McKay Co Inc.

Blumenfeld, P. C., Soloway, E., Marx, R. W., Krajcik, J. S., Guzdial, M., & Palincsar, A. (1991). Motivating project-based learning: Sustaining the doing, supporting the learning. *Educational Psychology, 26*(3 & 4), 369–398.

Blumer, H. (1969). *Symbolic interactionism*. Englewood Cliffs, NJ: Prentice-Hall.

Boehret, K. (2007, September 12). An Easier way to make and share videos. *The Wall Street Journal*. Retrieved from http://online.wsj.com.

Bok, D. C. (2006). *Our underachieving colleges: A candid look at how much students learn and why they should be learning more*. Princeton, NJ: Princeton University Press.

Bonamici, A., Hutto, D., Smith, D., & Ward, J. (2005). *The "Net Generation": Implications for libraries and higher education*. Retrieved from http://www.orbiscascade.org / council/c0510/Frye.ppt.

Bonilla-Warford, N. (2011). Should you take the plunge into social media? *Optometry -. Journal of the American Optometric Association*, *82*(1), 51–52. doi:10.1016/j.optm.2010.11.004

Bonk, C. J. (2008). *YouTube anchors and enders: The use of shared online video content as a macrocontext for learning*. Paper presented at the American Educational Research Association Annual Meeting.

Borgman, C. L., Abelson, H., Dirks, L., Johnson, R., Koedinger, K. R., Linn, M. C., et al. (2008). *Fostering learning in the networked world: The cyberlearning opportunity and challenge*. Report of the NSF Task Force on Cyberlearning. Retrieved October 15, 2009, from http://www.nsf.gov/pubs/2008/nsf08204/nsf08204.pdf.

Borgmann, A. (1984). *Technology and the character of contemporary life: A philosophical inquiry*. Chicago, IL: University of Chicago Press.

Bork, A. (1996). Highly interactive multimedia technology and future learning. *Journal of Computing in Higher Education*, *8*(1), 3–28. doi:10.1007/BF02942393

Boster, F. J., Meyer, G. S., Roberto, A. J., Inge, C., & Strom, R. (2006). Some effects of video streaming on educational achievement. *Communication Education*, *55*, 46–62. doi:10.1080/03634520500343392

Boud, D. (Ed.). (1993). *Using experience for learning*. Open University Press.

Boud, D., & Prosser, M. (2002). Appraising new technologies for learning: A framework for development. *Educational Media International*, *39*(3), 237. doi:10.1080/09523980210166026

Bouldin, A. S., Homes, E. R., & Fortenberry, M. L. (2006). Blogging about course concepts: Using technology for reflective journaling in a communications class. *American Journal of Pharmaceutical Education*, *70*(4), 1–8. doi:10.5688/aj700484

Bourdieu, P. (1977). *Outline of a theory of practice*. Cambridge University Press.

Brailer, D. (2005). Interoperability: The key to the future health care system. *Health Affairs*, (w5.19-w5.20).

Brain, C. (2000). *Advanced subsidiary psychology: Approaches and methods*. Nelson Thornes Ltd.

Briggs, M. (2010). *Journalism next*. Washington, DC: CQ Press.

Broadbent, D. E. (1958). *Perception and communication*. London, UK: Pergamon Press. doi:10.1037/10037-000

Brookfield, S. D. (1987). *Developing critical thinking*. San Francisco, CA: Jossey-Bass.

Brooks, D. (2011, March 21). Getting students to talk. *The Chronicle of Higher Education*. Retrieved from http://chronicle.com/article/Getting-Students-to-Talk/126826.

Brown, C., & Czerniewicz, L. (2010a). Debunking the "digital native": Beyond digital apartheid, towards digital democracy. *Journal of Computer Assisted Learning*, *26*, 357–369. doi:10.1111/j.1365-2729.2010.00369.x

Brown, C., & Czerniewicz, L. (2010b). Describing or debunking? The net generation and digital natives. *Journal of Computer Assisted Learning*, *26*, 317–320. doi:10.1111/j.1365-2729.2010.00379.x

Brown, J. S., & Adler, R. P. (2008). Minds on fire: Open education, the long tail, and learning 2.0. *EDUCAUSE Review*, *43*(1), 16–32. Retrieved from http://connect.educause.edu/Library/EDUCAUSE+Review/MindsonFireOpenEducationt/45823.

Brown, G., Bull, J., & Pendlebury, M. (1997). *Assessing student learning in higher education*. London, UK: Routledge.

Brown, J. (2000). Growing up digital: How the web changes work, education, and the ways people learn. *Change*, *32*(2), 10–20. doi:10.1080/00091380009601719

Brown, C., Murphy, T. J., & Nanny, M. (2003). Turning techno-savvy into info savvy: Authentically integrating information literacy into the college curriculum. *Journal of Academic Librarianship*, *29*, 386–398. doi:10.1016/j.jal.2003.08.005

Brown, M. (2005). In Oblinger, D., & Oblinger, J. (Eds.), *Educating the net generation* (pp. 12.1–12.22). Boulder, CO: EDUCAUSE.

Brown, M. (2005). Learning spaces. In D. G. Oblinger, & J. L. Oblinger (Eds.), *Educating the Net Generation* (pp. 12.1-12.22). Washington, DC: EDUCAUSE. Retrieved from http://www.educause.edu/educatingthenetgen.

Bruer, J. T. (1997). *Schools for thought: A science of learning in the classroom*. Cambridge, MA: The MIT Press.

Bruns, A., & Humphreys, S. (2007). *Building collaborative capacities in learners: The M/cyclopedia project revisited*. Paper presented at the International Symposium on Wikis, Montreal, Canada.

Bryson, M., & de Castell, S. (1998). New technologies and the cultural ecology of primary schooling: Imagining teachers as Luddites in/deed. *Educational Policy*, *12*(5), 542–567. doi:10.1177/0895904898012005005

Buckingham, D. (2007). *Beyond technology*. Cambridge, UK: Polity Press.

Bucy, E. (2004). Interactivity in society: Locating an elusive concept. *The Information Society*, *20*(5), 373–383.. doi:10.1080/01972240490508063

Bugeja, M. J. (2008). Harsh realities about virtual ones. *Inside Higher Ed.* Retrieved June 9, 2009, from http://m.insidehighered.com/views/2008/03/11/bugeja.

Bull, G. (November 2010). The always-connected generation. *Leading and Learning with Technology.* Retrieved January 30, 2011 from http://www.iste.org/learn/publications/learning-and-leading/digital-edition-november.aspx.

Bunderson, C. V., Wiley, D. A., & McBride, R. (2009). Domain theory for instruction: Mapping attainments to enable learner-centered education. In Reigeluth, C. M., & Carr-Chellman, A. A. (Eds.), *Instructional-design theories and models: Building a common knowledge base* (*Vol. III*, pp. 327–347). New York, NY: Routledge.

Bunz, U. (2003). Growing from computer literacy towards computer-mediated communication competence: Evolution of a field and evaluation of a new measurement instrument. *Information Technology. Education et Sociétés*, *4*(2), 53–84.

Bunz, U. (2001). *Usability and gratifications—Towards a website analysis model*. Paper presented at the 87th Annual Meeting of the National Communication Association.

Burhanna, K., Seeholzer, J., & Salem, J. Jr. (2009). No natives here: A focus group study of student perceptions of Web 2.0 and the academic library. *Journal of Academic Librarianship*, *35*, 523–532. doi:10.1016/j.acalib.2009.08.003

Burke, K. (1935). *Permanence and change*. New York, NY: New Republic.

Bush, M. (2008). What is contemplative pedagogy? In *Contemplative practices in higher education: A handbook of classroom practices* (pp. 5–7). Northhampton, MA: The Center for Contemplative Mind in Society.

Bush, M. D., & Mott, J. D. (2009). The transformation of learning with technology. *Educational Technology Magazine*, *49*(March-April), 3–20.

Bush, V. (1945). As we may think. *The Atlantic.* Retrieved February 12, 2011 from http://www.theatlantic.com/magazine/archive/1945/07/as-we-may-think/3881/.

Byrne, P. S., & Heath, C. C. (1980). Practitioners' use of nonverbal behavior in real consultations. *The Journal of the Royal College of General Practitioners*, *30*(215), 327–331.

Cacioppo, J. T., Petty, R. E., & Kao, C. F. (1984). The efficient assessment of need for cognition. *Journal of Personality Assessment*, *48*(3), 306–307. doi:10.1207/s15327752jpa4803_13

Caison, A. L., Bulman, D., Pai, S., & Neville, D. (2008). Exploring the technology readiness of nursing and medical students at a Canadian university. *Journal of Interprofessional Care*, *22*(3), 283–294. doi:10.1080/13561820802061809

Cambridge, B., Kahn, S., Tompkins, D., & Yancey, K. (Eds.). (2001). *Electronic portfolios: Emerging practices in student faculty, and institutional learning*. Washington, DC: American Association for Higher Education.

Cameron, A. F., & Webster, J. (2010). Relational outcomes of multicommunicating: Integrating incivility and social exchange perspectives. *Organization Science, Articles in Advance*, 1-18. doi: 10.1287/orsc.1100.0540.

Campus Compact. (2008). *Service-learning in engineering resources*. Retrieved from: http://www.compact.org/resources/service-learning_resources/in_engineering/.

Campus Compact. (2011). *Service-learning*. http://www.compact.org/initiatives/service-learning/.

Candy, P. C. (1991). *Self-direction for lifelong learning*. San Francisco, CA: Jossey-Bass.

Cao, L., & Nietfeld, J. L. (2007). College students' metacognitive awareness of difficulties in learning the class content does not automatically lead to adjustment of study strategies. *Australian Journal of Educational and Developmental Psychology*, *7*, 31–46.

Carlson, S. (2005). The net generation in the classroom. *The Chronicle of Higher Education*, *52*(7), A34–A37.

Carpenter, P., & Roberts, E. (2007). Going wiki in online technology education courses: Promoting online learning and service learning through wikis. *Technology Education Journal*, *9*, 58–64.

Carr, N. (2010). *The shallows: What the internet is doing to our brains*. New York, NY: Norton.

Carroll, M. (1995). Formative assessment workshops: Feedback sessions for large classes. *Biochemical Education*, *23*, 65–67. doi:10.1016/0307-4412(95)00001-J

Carswell, L., Thomas, P., Petre, M., Price, B., & Richards, M. (2000). Distance education via the Internet: The student experience. *British Journal of Educational Technology*, *31*, 29–46. doi:10.1111/1467-8535.00133

Castleberry, G., & Evers, R. (2010). Incorporate technology into the modern language classroom. *Intervention in School and Clinic*, *45*(3), 201–205. doi:10.1177/1053451209349535

Chadwick, S. A., & Russo, T. C. (2002). Virtual visiting professors: Communicative, pedagogical, and technological collaboration. In Comeaux, P. (Ed.), *Communication and collaboration in the online classroom* (pp. 75–91). Bolton, MA: Anker.

Chan, P., & Rabinowitz, T. (2006). A cross-sectional analysis of video games and attention deficit hyperactivity disorders symptoms in adolescents. *Annals of General Psychiatry*, *5*. Retrieved from http://www.ncbi.nlm.nih.gov/pmc/articles/PMC1635698/pdf/1744-859X-5-16.pdf. doi:10.1186/1744-859X-5-16

Cheney, G. (1982). *Identification as process and product: A field study*. Unpublished master's thesis, Purdue University, West Lafayette, IN.

Chordas, L. (2008). Y new technology? *Best's Review*, *109*(6), 88–90.

Chretien, K., Greysen, S., Chretien, J.-P., & Kind, T. (2009). Online posting of unprofessional content by medical students. *Journal of the American Medical Association*, *302*(12). doi:10.1001/jama.2009.1387

Christensen, C. (2003). *The innovator's dilemma*. New York, NY: HarperBusiness.

Chuang, H. (2010). Weblog-based electronic portfolios for student teachers in Taiwan. *Educational Technology Research and Development*, *58*(2), 211–227. doi:10.1007/s11423-008-9098-1

Cisco Systems, Inc. (2011, Oct. 7). Hoover's company records, 13494. United States, Austin: Dun and Bradstreet, Inc. (ProQuest Document ID: 230596963). Retrieved from http://search.proquest.com/docview/230596963?accountid=10818.

Clark, A. (2003). *Natural-born cyborgs*. New York, NY: Oxford University Press.

Clift, E. (2009, May 21). I'll never do it again. *The Chronicle of Higher Education*. Retrieved from http://chronicle.com/article/Ill-Never-Do-It-Again/44250/.

Clynes, M., & Raftery, S. (2008). Feedback: An essential element of student learning in clinical practice. *Nurse Education in Practice*, *8*(6), 405–411. doi:10.1016/j.nepr.2008.02.003

Coiro, J. (2003). Exploring literacy on the Internet: Reading comprehension on the Internet: Expanding our understanding of reading comprehension to encompass new literacies. *The Reading Teacher*, *56*(5), 458–464.

Collins, A., & Halverson, R. (2009). *Rethinking education in the age of technology: The digital revolution and the schools*. New York, NY: Teachers College Press.

Combes, B. (2008). *The Net generation: Tech-savvy or lost in virtual space?* Paper presented at the IASL Conference: World Class Learning and Literacy through School Libraries.

Compeau, D. R., & Higgins, C. A. (l995a). Application of social cognitive theory to training for computer skills. *Information Systems Research*, *6*(2), 118–143. doi:10.1287/isre.6.2.118

Compeau, D. R., & Higgins, C. A. (l995b). Computer self-efficacy: Development of a measure and initial test. *Management Information Systems Quarterly*, *19*(2), 189–211. doi:10.2307/249688

Compton, J., & Pfau, M. (2005). Inoculation theory of resistance to influence at maturity: Recent progress in theory development and application and suggestions for future research. In Kalbfleisch, P. (Ed.), *Communication yearbook 29* (pp. 97–145). Mahwah, NJ: Lawrence Erlbaum.

Cone Inc. in collaboration with AMP Agency (2006). *The 2006 Cone millennial cause study. The millennial generation: Pro-social and empowered to change the world.* Retrieved from http://www.greenbook.org/Content/AMP/Cause_AMPlified.pdf.

Connaway, L. S., Radford, M., Williams, J. D. A., & Confer, P. (2008). Sense-making and synchronicity: Information-seeking behaviors of millennials and baby boomers. *International Journal of Libraries and Information Services*, *58*, 123–135.

Connected Ventures, L. L. C. (2011, Oct. 6). *Hoover's company records*, 148343. United States, Austin: Dun and Bradstreet, Inc. (ProQuest Document ID: 230578498). Retrieved from http://search.proquest.com/docview/230578498?accountid=10818.

Connolly, P. J. (2001). A standard for success. *InfoWorld*, *23*(42), 57–58.

Connors, P. (2008). Assessing written evidence of critical thinking using an analytic rubric. *Journal of Nutrition Education and Behavior*, *40*(3), 193–194. doi:10.1016/j.jneb.2008.01.014

Conole, G., Dyke, M., Oliver, M., & Seale, J. (2004). Mapping pedagogy and tools for effective learning design. *Computers & Education*, *43*(1-2), 17–33. doi:10.1016/j.compedu.2003.12.018

Conole, G., & Fill, K. (2005). A learning design toolkit to create pedagogically effective learning activities. *Journal of Interactive Media in Education*, *1*. Retrieved from http://jime.open.ac.uk/jime/article/viewArticle/104.

Conole, G., Laat, M. D., Dillon, T., & Darby, J. (2006). *JISC LXP student experiences of technologies: Final report*. Joint Information Systems Committee. Retrieved from http://www.jisc.ac.uk/media/documents/programmes/elearningpedagogy/lxpprojectfinalreportdec06.pdf.

Cook, D. (2009). The failure of e-learning research to inform educational practice, and what we can do about it. *Medical Teacher*, *31*(2), 158–162. doi:10.1080/01421590802691393

New London Group. (2000). A pedagogy of multiliteracies: Designing social futures. In Cope, B., & Kalantzis, M. (Eds.), *Multiliteracies: Literacy learning and the design of social futures* (pp. 9–38). London, UK: Routledge.

Costello, C. (2005). *Professional identity crisis: Race, class, gender, and success at professional schools*. Nashville, TN: Vanderbilt University Press.

Craik, F. I. M., & Lockheart, R. S. (1972). Levels of processing: A framework for memory research. *Journal of Verbal Learning and Verbal Behavior*, *11*, 671–684. doi:10.1016/S0022-5371(72)80001-X

Creswell, J. W., Fetters, M. D., & Ivankova, N. V. (2004). Designing a mixed methods study in primary care. *Annals of Family Medicine*, *2*, 7–12. doi:10.1370/afm.104

Crews, T., & Wilkinson, K. (2010). Students' perceived preference for visual and auditory assessment with e-handwritten feedback. *Business Communication Quarterly*, *73*(4), 399. doi:10.1177/1080569910385566

Cronjé, J. (2006). Paradigms regained: Toward integrating objectivism and constructivism in instructional design and the learning sciences. *Educational Technology Research and Development*, *54*(4), 387–416. doi:10.1007/s11423-006-9605-1

Crook, C. (2008). *Web 2.0 technologies for learning: The current landscape – Opportunities, challenges and tensions*. Coventry, UK: BECTA.

Daniel, J. (1996). *Mega-universities and knowledge media: Technology strategies for higher education*. London, UK: Kogan Page.

Davidson, C. (2009). *The future of learning institutions in a digital age*. Cambridge, MA: MIT Press.

Davies, W. (2006). Digital exuberance. *Prospect, 119*, 30–33.

Dawkins, R. (1976). *The selfish gene*. Oxford University Press.

Daws, L. B., & Gleason, J. P. (2011). *Instructor perceptions of online office hours: Helping or hurting?* Paper presented at the 2011 Kentucky Conference on Converging Trends in Teaching & Learning, Erlanger, KY.

De Corte, E., & Verschaffel, L. Entwistle, & Van Merriëboer, J. (Eds.). (2003). *Unravelling basic components and dimensions of powerful learning environments*. Amsterdam, The Netherlands: Elsevier.

De Liddo, A. (2010). From open content to open thinking. *World Conference on Educational Multimedia, Hypermedia and Telecommunications 2010*, (pp. 3178-3183).

Dede, C. (2005). Planning for "Neomillenial" learning styles: Shifts in student's learning style will prompt a shift to active construction of knowledge through mediated immersion. *EDUCAUSE Quarterly, 28*, 7–12.

DeGennaro, D. (2008). Learning designs: An analysis of youth-initiated technology use. *Journal of Research on Technology in Education, 41*(1), 1–20.

Dennis, E. E., Meyer, P., Sundar, S. S., & Pryor, L., Rogers, Everett M., Pavlik, J. (2003). Learning reconsidered: Education in the digital age. *Journalism & Mass Communication Educator, 57*(4), 292–317.

DeStefano, D., & LeFevre, J. (2007, May). Cognitive load in hypertext reading: A review. *Computers in Human Behavior, 23*, 1616–1641. doi:10.1016/j.chb.2005.08.012

Dewey, J. (1916). *Democracy and education: An introduction to the philosophy of education*. New York, NY: The Free Press.

Dewey, J. (1938). *Experience and education*. New York, NY: The Macmillan Company.

Dick, W., Carey, L., & Carey, J. O. (2008). *The systematic design of instruction*. Boston, MA: Allyn & Bacon.

Digital Campus. (2010, May 8). *The Chronicle of Higher Education*. Retrieved from http://chronicle.com/section/The-Digital-Campus/529/.

DiMaggio, P., Hargittai, E., Celeste, C., & Shafer, S. (2004). Digital inequality: From unequal access to differentiated use. In Neckerman, K. (Ed.), *Social inequality*. New York, NY: Russell Sage Foundation.

Dobson, S. (2006). The assessment of student PowerPoint presentations – Attempting the impossible? *Assessment & Evaluation in Higher Education, 31*(1), 109–119.. doi:10.1080/02602930500262403

Doolittle, P., Terry, K., & Mariano, G. (2009). Multimedia learning and working memory capacity. In Zheng, R. (Ed.), *Cognitive effects of multimedia learning* (pp. 17–33). Hershey, PA: Information Science Reference/ IGI Global Publishing.

Doumont, J. (2005). The cognitive style of PowerPoint: Slides are not all evil. *Technical Communication, 52*(1), 64–70.

Downes, E., & McMillan, S. (2000). Defining interactivity: A qualitative identification of key dimensions. *New Media & Society, 6*(2), 157–179. doi:10.1177/14614440022225751

Downes, S. (2004). Educational blogging. *EDUCAUSE Review, 39*(5), 14–26. Retrieved from http://www.educause.edu/pub/er/erm04/erm0450.asp.

Downes, S. (2009, October 5). *Origins of the term "personal learning network."* Retrieved May 10, 2010, from http://halfanhour.blogspot.com/2009/10/origins-of-term-personal-learning.html.

Drews, F. A., Yazdani, H., Godfrey, C. N., Cooper, J. M., & Strayer, D. L. (2009). Text messaging during simulated driving. *Human Factors, 51*, 762–770. doi:10.1177/0018720809353319

Dreyfus, H. L. (2009). *On the Internet*. New York, NY: Routledge.

Driscoll, M. P. (2000). *Psychology of learning for instruction*. Needham, MA: Allyn & Bacon.

Duffy, P., & Bruns, A. (2006). *The use of blogs, wikis and RSS in education: A conversation of possibilities*. Paper presented at the Online Learning and Teaching Conference, Brisbane.

Dutton, W., & Loader, B. (Eds.). (2002). *Digital academe: The new media and institutions of higher education and learning*. London, UK: Routledge.

Duxbury, L., Dyke, L., & Lam, N. (2000, April 8). *Career development in the federal public service - Building a world-class workforce*. Treasury Board of Canada Secretariat. Retrieved from http://www.tbs-sct.gc.ca/pubs_pol/partners/workreport-PR-eng.asp?printable=True.

Eastin, M. S. (2005). Teen Internet use: Relating social perceptions and cognitive models to behavior. *Cyberpsychology & Behavior*, *8*(1), 62–75. doi:10.1089/cpb.2005.8.62

Ebner, M., Kickmeier-Rust, M., & Holzinger, A. (2008). Utilizing wiki-systems in higher education classes: A chance for universal access? *Universal Access in the Information Society*, *7*(4), 199–207..doi:10.1007/s10209-008-0115-2

Echo 360, Inc. (2007, October). *Echo360 launches next generation lecture capture platform*. (Press Release). Retrieved from http://echo360.com/news-events/press-releases/pr102207/.

Echo360, Inc. (2011). *Echo 360 board of directors*. Retrieved from http://echo360.com/about/board-of-directors/.

EduCause Learning Initiative. (2005, May). *7 things you should know about...social bookmarking*. Retrieved February 10, 2010 from http://net.educause.edu/ir/library/pdf/ELI7001.pdf.

Ekstrom, R. B., French, J. W., & Harman, H. H. with Derman, D. (1976). *Kit of factor-referenced cognitive tests*. Princeton, NJ: Educational Testing Service.

Ellaway, R. (2010a). eMedical Teacher # 33: Cyborg medical education. *Medical Teacher*, *32*(3), 273–275. doi:10.3109/01421591003704360

Ellaway, R. (2010c). eMedical Teacher # 38: Digital Professionalism. *Medical Teacher*, *32*(8), 705–707. doi:10.3109/0142159X.2010.505849

Ellaway, R. (2010b). Developing learning resources. In Dornan, T., Mann, K., Scherpbier, A., & Spencer, J. (Eds.), *Medical education: Theory and practice* (pp. 265–282). Edinburgh, UK: Elsevier.

Ellison, N., & Wu, Y. (2008). Blogging in the classroom: A preliminary exploration of student attitudes and impact on comprehension. *Journal of Educational Multimedia and Hypermedia*, *17*(1), 99–122.

Englert, C. (1992). Writing instruction from a sociocultural perspective: The holistic, dialogic, and social enterprise of writing. *Journal of Learning Disabilities*, *25*(3), 153–172. doi:10.1177/002221949202500303

Ennis, R. H. (1987). A taxonomy of critical thinking dispositions and abilities. In Baron, J. B., & Sternberg, R. J. (Eds.), *Teaching critical thinking skills* (pp. 9–26). New York, NY: Freeman.

Eubanks, S. (2006). *Millennials--Themes in current literature*. Retrieved from http://www.eubie.com/themes.pdf.

Evans, C., & Gibbons, N. J. (2007). The interactivity effect in multimedia learning. *Computers & Education*, *49*(4), 1147-1160. doi:1110.1016/j.compedu.2006.1101.1008.

Evans, P. (2006, January/February). The wiki factor. *BizEd*, (pp. 28-32).

Eyler, J., & Giles, D. E. (1999). *Where's the learning in service-learning?* San Francisco, CA: Jossey-Bass.

Eyler, J., & Giles, D. Jr. (1997). The importance of program quality in service-learning. In Waterman, A. (Ed.), *Service-learning: Applications from the research* (pp. 57–76). Mahwah, NJ: Erlbaum.

Eynon, R. (2009). *Harnessing technology: The learner and their context. How young people use technologies outside formal education. Survey Report*. Coventry, UK: Becta.

Facebook, Inc. (2011, 15 April). *Hoover's company records*, 148344. (Document ID: 1014566851).

Facebook. (2010, December). *Facebook statistics*. Retrieved from http://www.facebook.com/press/info.php?statistics.

Facione, P. A. (2011). Critical thinking: What it is and why it counts. *Insight Assessment*. Retrieved from http://www.insightassessment.com/pdf_files/what&why2010.pdf.

Farnan, J., Paro, J., Higa, J., Reddy, S., Humphrey, H., & Arora, V. (2009). The relationship status of digital media and professionalism: It's complicated. *Academic Medicine*, *84*, 1479–1481. doi:10.1097/ACM.0b013e3181bb17af

Farnan, J. M., Gersh, S., Reddy, S. T., & Moyer, D. (2010). A brave new world: Professionalism in the Digital Age. *Academic Internal Medicine Insight*, *8*(2), 4-5,17.

Farrell, E. F. (2008, February 29). Counseling centers lack resources to help troubled students. *The Chronicle of Higher Education*. Retrieved from http://chronicle.com/article/Counseling-Centers-Lack/33930/.

Faux, T. L., & Black-Hughes, C. (2000). A comparison of using the Internet versus lectures to teach social work history. *Research on Social Work Practice*, *10*, 454–466.

Feiertag, J., & Berge, Z. L. (2008). Training Generation N: How educators should approach the Net generation. *Education + Training*, *50*(6), 457–464. doi:10.1108/00400910810901782

Ferdig, R. M., & Trammell, K. D. (2004). Content delivery in Blogsphere. *THE Journal*. Retrieved February 11, 2011, from http://thejournal.com/articles/16626.

Fink, L. D. (2003). *Creating significant learning experiences: An integrated approach to designing college courses*. San Francisco, CA: Jossey-Bass.

Fisher, W. R. (1987). *Human communication as narration: Toward a philosophy of reason, value and action*. Columbia, SC: University of South Carolina Press.

Fishman, A. (2004). Understanding generational differences. *National Underwriter / Life & Health Financial Services*, *108*(2), 4-5.

Fletcher, D. (2003, September). *Unlocking the potential of gaming technology*. Higher Education Leaders Symposium. Symposium conducted at the Microsoft Corporation, Redmond, Washington.

Forte, A., & Bruckman, A. (2007). *Constructing text: Wiki as a toolkit for (collaborative?) learning*. Paper presented at the International Symposium on Wikis, Montreal, Canada.

Fountain, R. (2005). Wiki pedagogy. *Dossiers Technopedagiques*. Retrieved from http://www.profetic.org/dossiers/rubrique.php3?id_rubrique=110.

Frank, S., Dahler, L., Santurri, L. E., & Knight, K. (2010, November 9). *Hyper-texting and hyper-networking: A new health risk category for teens?* [Multimedia recording] Retrieved from http://apha.confex.com/apha/138am/webprogram/Paper224927.html.

Fredericks, L., Kaplan, E., & Zeisler, J. (2001). *Integrating youth voice in service-learning*. Denver, CO: Education Commission of the States.

Frederickson, J. R., & Collins, A. (1989). A systems approach to educational testing. *Educational Researcher*, *18*(9), 27–32.

Frey, B. A., & Birnbaum, D. J. (2002). *Learners' perceptions on the value of PowerPoint in lectures*. (ERIC Document Reproduction Service No. ED467192).

Friedman, T. L. (2006). *The world is flat - Updated and expanded: A brief history of the 21st century*. New York, NY: Farrar, Straus & Giroux.

Frietas, F. A., Myers, S. A., & Avtgis, T. A. (1998). Student perceptions of instructor immediacy in conventional and distributed learning classrooms. *Communication Education*, *47*, 366–372. doi:10.1080/03634529809379143

Frymier, A. B., & Houser, M. L. (2000). The teacher-student relationship as an interpersonal relationship. *Communication Education*, *49*, 207–219. doi:10.1080/03634520009379209

Frymier, A. B., Shulman, G. M., & Houser, M. (1996). The development of a learner empowerment measure. *Communication Education*, *45*(3), 181–199. doi:10.1080/03634529609379048

Gable, R. K., & Wolf, M. B. (1993). *Instrument development in the affective domain: Measuring attitudes and values in corporate and school settings* (2nd ed.). Boston, MA: Kluwer Academic Publishers.

Gabriel, T. (2010, November 4). Learning in dorm, because class is on the Web. *The New York Times*. Retrieved from http://www.nytimes.com/2010/11/05/us/05college.html.

Gagne, R. M., & Dick, W. (1983). Instructional psychology. *Annual Review of Psychology, 34*, 261–295. doi:10.1146/annurev.ps.34.020183.001401

Gareis, E. (2007). Active learning: A PowerPoint tutorial. *Business Communication Quarterly, 70*, 462–466. doi:10.1177/10805699070700040304

Garett, K. (2010). Professional learning communities allow a transformational culture to take root. *Education Digest, 76*(2), 4–9.

Garrett, R. K., & Danziger, J. N. (2007). IM=Interruption management? Instant messaging and disruption in the workplace. *Journal of Computer-Mediated Communication, 13*, 23–42..doi:10.1111/j.1083-6101.2007.00384.x

Garrison, D. R. (1992). Critical thinking and self-directed learning in adult education: an analysis of responsibility and control issues. *Adult Education Quarterly, 42*(3), 136–148.

Gask, L. (1998). Small group interactive techniques utilising video feedback. *International Journal of Psychiatry in Medicine, 28*(1), 97–113. doi:10.2190/U8MM-JX7Y-LT0T-RKPX

Gee, J. P. (2008). *Social linguistics and literacies: Ideology in discourses*. Routledge.

Gee, J. P. (2007). Affinity spaces. In Gee, J. P. (Ed.), *Good video games + good learning: Collected essays on video games, learning, and literacy* (pp. 87–103). New York, NY: Peter Lang.

George-Palilonis, J., & Filak, V. (2010). Visuals, path control, and knowledge gain: Variables that affect students' approval and enjoyment of a multimedia text as a learning tool. *International Journal on E-Learning, 9*(4), 463–480.

Gerlich, R. N., Greenlaw, S. A., & DeLoach, S. B. (2003). Teaching critical thinking with electronic discussion. *The Journal of Economic Education, 34*(1), 36–54. doi:10.1080/00220480309595199

Gibbons, A. S., Nelson, J. M., & Richards, R. (2002). The nature and origin of instructional objects. In Wiley, D. A. (Ed.), *The instructional use of learning objects: Online version*.

Gibson, S., & Nocente, N. (1998). Addressing instructional technology needs in faculties of education. *Alberta Journal of Educational Research Edmonton, 44*(3), 320–333.

Glass, A. L., & Holyoak, K. J. (1986). *Cognition* (2nd ed.). New York, NY: Random House.

Gleason, J. P. (2007). More than the medium: The unique role of content in user perception of interactivity. *International Journal of the Book, 5*(1), 77–84.

Gleason, J. P., & Lane, D. R. (2009). *Interactivity redefined: A first look at outcome interactivity theory.* Paper presented at the Annual Meeting of the National Communication Association.

Glenn, J. M. (2000). Teaching the Net generation. *Business Education Forum, 54*(3), 6–14.

Goffman, E. (1959). *The presentation of self in everyday life*. Garden City, NY: Doubleday.

Gokhale, A. (1995). Collaborative learning enhances critical thinking. *Journal of Technology Education, 7*(1), 1–7. Retrieved from http://scholar.lib.vt.edu/ejournals/JTE/jte-v7n1/gokhale.jte-v7n1.html.

Gonzalez, J. A., Jover, L., & Cobo, E. (2010). A web-based learning tool improves student performance in statistics: a randomized masked trial. *Computers & Education, 55*(2), 704–713. doi:10.1016/j.compedu.2010.03.003

Gonzalez, C. (2004). *The role of blended learning in the world of technology*. Retrieved from http://www.unt.edu/benchmarks/archives/2004/september04/eis.htm.

Gorman, P., Nelson, T., & Glassman, A. (2004). The Millennial generation: A strategic opportunity. *Organizational Analysis, 12*(3), 255–270.

Grabill, J., & Pigg, S. (2010). *Revisualizing composition: Mapping the writing lives of first-year college students.* Michigan State University, Writing in Digital Environments (WIDE) Research Center. Retrieved from http://wide.msu.edu/special/writinglives/WIDE_2010_writinglives_whitepaper.pdf.

Graham, G. (1999). *The Internet: A philosophical inquiry*. Routledge.

Grant, L. (2009). "I don't care do ur own page!" A case study of using wikis for collaborative work in a UK secondary school. *Learning, Media and Technology, 34*(2), 105–117. doi:10.1080/17439880902923564

Grant, L. (2007). *Learning to be part of the knowledge economy: Digital divides and media literacy* (No. 816). England: FutureLab. Retrieved from http://www.futurelab.org.uk/resources/publications-reports-articles/discussion-papers/Discussion-Paper816.

Gravois, J. (2005, October 21). Meditate on it. *The Chronicle of Higher Education*, A10–A12.

Greco, G. (2009, May 21). A reaffirmation of why I became an educator. *The Chronicle of Higher Education*. Retrieved from http://chronicle.com/article/A-Reaffirmation-of-Why-I/44254/.

Gregory, V. L. (2003). Student perceptions of the effectiveness of Web-based distance education. *New Library World*, *104*, 426–431. doi:10.1108/03074800310504366

Grossman, L. (2006). *Time's person of the year: You*. Retrieved May 5, 2008, from http://www.time.com/time/magazine/article/0,9171,1569514,00.html?aid=434.

Guiller, J., A., Durndell, A. Ross, A., & Thomson, K. (2008). Peer interaction and critical thinking: face-to-face or online discussion? *Learning and Instruction*, *18*(2), 187–200. doi:10.1016/j.learninstruc.2007.03.001

Guo, R. X., Dobson, T., & Petrina, S. (2008). Digital natives, digital immigrants: An analysis of age and ICT competency in teacher education. *Journal of Educational Computing Research*, *38*(3), 235–254. doi:10.2190/EC.38.3.a

Gurrie, C., & Fair, B. (2010). PowerPoint: From fabulous to boring. *Journal of Communication, Speech, Theater, and Dance, 23*.

Guth, S. (2007). *Wikis in education: Is public better?* Paper presented at the International Symposium on Wikis, Montreal, Canada.

Guzdial, M. (1999). *Teacher and students authoring on the Web for shifting agency*. Retrieved from http://home.cc.gatech.edu/csl/uploads/6/aera99.html.

Ha, L., & James, E. L. (1998). Interactivity reexamined: A baseline analysis of early business Web sites. *Journal of Broadcasting & Electronic Media*, *42*(4), 457–474.. doi:10.1080/08838159809364462

Haas, J., & Shaffir, W. (1991). *Becoming doctors: The adoption of a cloak of competence*. Greenwich, CT: JAI Press Inc.

Hafferty, F. (1998). Beyond curriculum reform: Confronting medicine's hidden curriculum. *Academic Medicine*, *73*(4), 403–407. doi:10.1097/00001888-199804000-00013

Haigh, M. M., & Pfau, M. (2006). Bolstering organizational identity, commitment, and citizenship behaviors through the process of inoculation. *The International Journal of Organizational Analysis*, *14*(4), 295–316. doi:10.1108/19348830610849718

Hailikari, T., Nevgi, A., & Lindblom-Ylänne, S. (2007). Exploring alternative ways of assessing prior knowledge, its components and their relation to student achievement: A mathematics based case study. *Studies in Educational Evaluation*, *33*(3-4), 320–337. doi:10.1016/j.stueduc.2007.07.007

Hamid, S., Chang, S., & Kurnia, S. (2009). Identifying the use of online social networking in higher education. In *Same Places, Different Spaces: Proceedings Ascilite*, Auckland. Retrieved from http://www.ascilite.org.au/conferences/auckland09/procs/hamid-poster.pdf.

Handley, K., & Williams, L. (2011). From copying to learning: Using exemplars to engage students with assessment criteria and feedback. *Assessment & Evaluation in Higher Education*, *36*(1), 95–108. doi:10.1080/02602930903201669

Harackiewicz, J. M., Barron, K. E., Tauer, J. M., Carter, S. M., & Elliot, A. J. (2000). Short-term and long-term consequences of achievement goals: Predicting interest and performance over time. *Journal of Educational Psychology*, *92*(2), 316–330. doi:10.1037/0022-0663.92.2.316

Harasim, L. (1990). *On-line education: Perspectives on a new environment*. New York, NY: Praeger.

Hargadon, S. (2010). *Educational networking: The important role web 2.0 will play in education*. Whitepaper. Scribd Online Journal.

Hargittai, E. (2010, February). Digital na(t)ives? Variation in internet skills and uses among members of the "net generation". *Sociological Inquiry*, *80*, 92–113. doi:10.1111/j.1475-682X.2009.00317.x

Hargittai, E., & Hinnant, A. (2008). Digital inequality: Differences in young adults' use of the internet. *Communication Research*, *35*, 602–621. doi:10.1177/0093650208321782

Harris, M., & Cullen, R. (2010). *Leading the learner-centered campus: An administrator's framework for improving student learning outcomes*. San Francisco, CA: Jossey-Bass.

Hart, T. (2004). Opening the contemplative mind in the classroom. *Journal of Transformative Education, 2*, 28–46. doi:10.1177/1541344603259311

Hartman, J., Moskal, P., & Dziuban, C. (2005). Preparing the academy of today for the learner of tomorrow. In D. G. Oblinger, & J. L. Oblinger (Eds.), *Educating the Net Generation* (pp. 6.1-6.15). Washington, DC: EDUCAUSE. Retrieved from http://www.educause.edu/educatingthenetgen.

Hattie, J., & Jaeger, R. (1998). Assessment and classroom learning: A deductive approach. *Assessment in Education, 5*(1), 111. doi:10.1080/0969595980050107

Havelka, D. (2003). Students beliefs and attitudes toward information technology. *Information Systems Education Journal, 1*(4), 3–9.

Haven, C. (2009). *The new literacy: Stanford study finds richness and complexity in students' writing*. Stanford Report, October 12, 2009. Retrieved from http://news.stanford.edu/news/2009/october12/lunsford-writing-research-101209.html.

Hawisher, G. E., & Pemberton, M. A. (1997). Writing across the curriculum encounters asynchronous learning networks or WAC meets up with ALN. [Online]. *Journal of Asynchronous Learning Networks, 1*(1).

Heeter, C. (1989). Implications of new interactive technologies for conceptualizing communication. In Salvaggio, J. L., & Bryant, J. (Eds.), *Media use in the information age* (pp. 217–235). Hillsdale, NJ: Lawrence Erlbaum.

Heidegger, M. (1995). *The fundamental concepts of metaphysics*. Bloomington, IN: Indiana University Press.

Henkel, M. (2005). Academic identity and autonomy revisited. In Bleiklie, I., & Henkel, M. (Eds.), *Governing knowledge* (*Vol. 9*, pp. 145–165). Berlin, Germany: Springer-Verlag. doi:10.1007/1-4020-3504-7_10

Hersh, R. H., & Merrow, J. (2006). *Declining by degrees: Higher education at risk*. New York, NY: Palgrave Macmillan.

Higdon, J., & Topaz, C. (2009). Blogs and wikis as instructional tools. *College Teaching, 57*(2), 105–109. doi:10.3200/CTCH.57.2.105-110

Hiltz, S. R., & Wellman, B. (1997). Asynchronous learning networks as a virtual classroom. *Communications of the ACM, 40*, 44–48. doi:10.1145/260750.260764

Hintzman, D. L. (1990). Human learning and memory: Connections and dissociations. *Annual Review of Psychology, 41*, 109–139. doi:10.1146/annurev.ps.41.020190.000545

Hmelo-Silver, C. E., Duncan, R. G., & Chinn, C. A. (2007). Scaffolding and achievement in problem-based and inquiry learning: A response to Kirschner, Sweller, and Clark (2006). *Educational Psychologist, 42*, 99–107. doi:10.1080/00461520701263368

Hobbs, S. D. (2002). Measuring nurses' computer competency: An analysis of published instruments. *Computers, Informatics, Nursing, 20*(2), 63–73. doi:10.1097/00024665-200203000-00012

Hodgins, H. W. (2002). The future of learning objects. In Wiley, D. A. (Ed.), *The instructional use of learning objects: Online version*.

Hoffler, T. N., Prechtl, H., & Nerdel, C. (2010). The influence of visual cognitive style when learning from instructional animations and static pictures. *Learning and Individual Differences, 20*(5), 479–483. doi:10.1016/j.lindif.2010.03.001

Hoffman, J. (2010, December 5). As bullies go digital, parents play catch-up. *New York Times*, pp. A1, A26-27. Retrieved from http://www.nytimes.com/2010/12/05/us/05bully.html?ref=us.

Holman, L. (2011). Millennial students' mental modes of search: Implications for academic librarians and database developers. *Journal of Academic Librarianship, 37*(1), 19–27. doi:10.1016/j.acalib.2010.10.003

Homik, M., & Melis, E. (2006). *Using blogs for learning logs*. Oxford, UK: Proceedings of e-Portfolio.

Hoover, E. (2006, May 19). Giving them the help they need. *The Chronicle of Higher Education*. Retrieved from http://chronicle.com/article/Giving-Them-the-Help-They/25347/.

Hoover, E. (2009, Oct. 11). The millennial muddle. How stereotyping students became a thriving industry and a bundle of contradictions. *The Chronicle of Higher Education*. Retrieved from http://chronicle.com/article/The-Millennial-Muddle-How/48772/.

Hosking, S. G., & Young, K. L. (2009). The effects of text messaging on young drivers. *Human Factors*, *51*, 582–592. doi:10.1177/0018720809341575

How to Use. (n.d.). *Twitter lists*. Retrieved February 10, 2010, from http://support.twitter.com/articles/76460-how-to-use-twitter-lists.

How to Use. (n.d.). *Twitter's suggestions for who to follow.* Retrieved February 10, 2010, from http://support.twitter.com/groups/31-twitter-basics/topics/108-finding-following-people/articles/227220-how-to-use-twitter-s-suggestions-for-who-to-follow.

Howe, N., & Strauss, W. (2000). *Millennials rising: The next great generation*. New York, NY: Vintage Books.

Howe, N. (2003). *Understanding the Millennial generation*. The Council of Independent Colleges' Presidents' Institute. Retrieved January 30, 2011, from http://www.cic.org/publications/independent/online/archive/winter-spring2003/PI2003_millennial.html.

Howe, N., & Strauss. W. (2003). *Millennials go to college*. American Association of College Registrars and Admissions Officers & LifeCourse Associates.

Hsu, H., & Wang, S. (2011). The impact of using blogs on college students' reading comprehension and learning motivation. *Literacy Research and Instruction*, *50*(1), 68–88. doi:10.1080/19388070903509177

Hsu, H., Wang, S., & Comac, L. (2008). Using audioblogs to assist English-language learning: An investigation into student perception. *Computer Assisted Language Learning*, *21*(2), 181–198. doi:10.1080/09588220801943775

Huang, H. (2002). Student perceptions in an online mediated environment. *International Journal of Instructional Media*, *29*, 405–422.

Huang, E. (2009). Teaching button-pushing versus teaching thinking the state of new media education in US universities. *Convergence: The International Journal of Research into New Media Technologies*, *15*(2), 233–247. doi:10.1177/1354856508101584

Hung, D. W. L., & Chen, D.-T. (2001). Situated cognition, Vygotskian thought and learning from the communities of practice perspective: Implications for the design of Web-based e-learning. *Educational Media International*, *38*(1), 3.

Isaacson, R., & Saperstein, J. (2005). *The art and strategy of service-learning presentations*. Belmont, CA: Wadsworth.

ISTE NETS. (2000). *Educational technology standards and performance indicators for all teachers*. Retrieved from http://www.iste.org/standards.aspx.

Ito, M., Baumer, S., Bittanti, M., Boyd, D., Cody, R., & Herr, B. (Eds.). (2009). *Hanging out, messing around, geeking out: Living and learning with new media*. Cambridge, MA: MIT press.

Jackson, M. (2009). *Distracted: The erosion of attention and the coming dark age*. Amherst, NY: Prometheus.

Jacoby, S. (2008). *The age of American unreason: Dumbing down and the future of democracy*. London, UK: Old Street.

Janicki, T., & Liegle, J. O. (2001). Development and evaluation of a framework for creating Web-based learning modules: A pedagogical and systems approach. *Journal of Asynchronous Learning Networks*, *5*(1). Retrieved from http://sloanconsortium.org/sites/default/files/v5n1_janicki_1.pdf.

Jenkins, H. (2009). *Confronting the challenges of participatory culture: Media education for the 21st century*. Cambridge, MA: The MIT Press.

Jiang, M., & Ting, E. (2000). A study of factors influencing student's perceived learning in a Web-based course environment. *International Journal of Educational Telecommunications*, *6*, 317–338.

Johnson, L. Smith, R., Willis, H., Levine, A., & Haywood, K., (2011). *The 2011 horizon report*. Austin, TX: The New Media Consortium.

Jonas-Dwyer, D., & Pospisil, R. (2004). The Millennial effect: Implications for academic development. *HERDSA 27th Annual Conference Proceedings*, (pp. 194-205).

Jonassen, D. H. (2000). *Computers as mindtools for schools*. Upper Saddle River, NJ: Merrill Prentice Hall.

Jonassen, D. H., Peck, K. L., & Wilson, B. G. (1999). *Learning with technology*. Columbus, OH: Prentice Hall.

Jone, C., & Czerniewicz, L. (2010). Describing or debunking? The Net generation and digital natives. *Journal of Computer Assisted Learning*, *26*(5), 317–320. doi:10.1111/j.1365-2729.2010.00379.x

Jones, C., & Healing, G. (2010). Net generation students: Agency and choice and the new technologies. *Journal of Computer Assisted Learning*, *26*(5), 344–356. doi:10.1111/j.1365-2729.2010.00370.x

Jones, C., Ramanau, R., Cross, S., & Healing, G. (2010). Net generation or digital natives: Is there a distinct new generation entering university? *Computers & Education*, *54*(3), 722–732. doi:10.1016/j.compedu.2009.09.022

Jones, M. G., Harmon, S. W., & O'Grady-Jones, M. (2005). Developing the digital mind: Challenges and solutions in teaching and learning. *Teacher Education Journal of South Carolina*, *2004-2005*, 17–24.

Jones, C., & Healing, G. (2010). Net generation students: Agency and choice and the new technologies. *Journal of Computer Assisted Learning*, *26*(5), 344–356. doi:10.1111/j.1365-2729.2010.00370.x

Jones, M. (2008). Lecture capture technology lends a hand to community college students [Technology Update]. *Community College Week*, *20*, 20.

Jones, C., & Cross, S. (2009). *Is there a net generation coming to university?* Retrieved from http://oro.open.ac.uk/18468/1/ALTC_09_proceedings_090806_web_0299.pdf.

Jones, M. G. (1997). *Learning to play, playing to learn: Lessons learned from computer games*. Retrieved April 29, 2010, from http://www2.gsu.edu/~wwwitr/docs/mjgames/index.html.

Joseph, R. C. (2010). Individual resistance to IT innovations. *Communications of the ACM*, *53*(4), 144–146. doi:10.1145/1721654.1721693

Jukes, I., McCain, T., & Crockett, L. (2010). *Understanding the digital generation: Teaching and learning in the new digital landscape*. Thousand Oaks, CA: Corwin.

Kabat-Zinn, J. (1994). *Wherever you go there you are: Mindfulness meditation in everyday life*. New York, NY: Hyperion.

Kalyuga, S. (2006). Assessment of learners' organized knowledge structures in adaptive learning environments. *Applied Cognitive Psychology*, *20*, 333–342. doi:10.1002/acp.1249

Kalyuga, S., Chandler, P., & Sweller, J. (2000). Incorporating learner experience into the design of multi-media instruction. *Journal of Educational Psychology*, *92*, 126–136. doi:10.1037/0022-0663.92.1.126

Kaplan, D., Rupley, W., Sparks, J., & Holcomb, A. (2007). Comparing traditional journal writing with journal writing shared over e-mail list serves as tools for facilitating reflective thinking: A study of preservice teachers. *Journal of Literacy Research*, *39*(3), 357–387.

Karau, S. J., & Williams, K. D. (1993). Social loafing: A meta-analytic review and theoretical integration. *Journal of Personality and Social Psychology*, *65*, 681–706. doi:10.1037/0022-3514.65.4.681

Karau, S. J., & Williams, K. D. (2001). Understanding individual motivation in groups: The collective effort model. In Turner, M. E. (Ed.), *Groups at work: Theory and research* (pp. 113–141). Mahwah, NJ: Lawrence Erlbaum Associates Publishers.

Katz, E., Blumler, J., & Gurevitch, M. (1974). Uses of mass communication by the individual. In Davidson, W. P., & Yu, F. (Eds.), *Mass communication research* (pp. 11–35). New York, NY: Praeger.

Kaya, T. (2010, November 16). Enrollment in online courses increases at the highest rate ever. *The Chronicle of Higher Education*. Retrieved May 16, 2011, from http://chronicle.com/blogs/wiredcampus/enrollment-in-online-courses-increases-at-the-highest-rate-ever/28204.

Keefe, J. W. (1982). Assessing student learning styles: An overview. In Keefe, J. W. (Ed.), *Student learning styles and brain behavior* (pp. 1–17). Reston, VA: National Association of Secondary School Principals.

Keen, A. (2007). *The cult of the amateur: How today's Internet is killing our culture*. London, UK: Broadway Business.

Kelan, E., & Lehnert, M. (2009, Feb.). The millennial generation: Generation Y and the opportunities for a globalised, networked educational system. *Beyond Current Horizons*. Retrieved from http://www.beyondcurrenthorizons.org.uk/the-millennial-generation-generation-y-and-the-opportunities-for-a-globalised-networked-educational-system/.

Keller, J. (2010, November 5). Mapping a virtual future at Penn State. *The Chronicle of Higher Education*, B16.

Kennedy, G., Judd, T., Dalgarnot, B., & Waycott, J. (2010). Beyond natives and immigrants: Exploring types of net generation students. *Journal of Computer Assisted Learning*, *26*, 332–343. doi:10.1111/j.1365-2729.2010.00371.x

Kennedy, G., Krause, K.-L., Judd, T., Churchward, A., & Gray, K. (2008). First year students' experiences with technology: Are they really digital natives? *Australasian Journal of Educational Technology*, *24*(1), 108–122.

Kent, N., & Facer, K. (2004). Different worlds? A comparison of young people's home and school ICT use. *Journal of Computer Assisted Learning*, *20*, 440–455. Retrieved from http://www.futurelab.org.uk/resources/publications-reports-articles/external-publications/External-Publication630. doi:10.1111/j.1365-2729.2004.00102.x

Kerawalla, L., Minocha, S., Kirkup, G., & Conole, G. (2008). Characterizing the different blogging behaviors of students on an online distance learning course. *Learning, Media and Technology*, *33*(1), 21–33.. doi:10.1080/17439880701868838

Khan, S. (2010, November 5). YouTube U. beats YouSnooze U. *The Chronicle of Higher Education*, B36–B38.

Kind, T., Genrich, G., Sodhi, A., & Chretien, K. C. (2010). Social media policies at US medical schools. *Medical Education Online, 15*.

King, R. C., & Xia, W. D. (1997). Media appropriateness: Effects of experience on communication media choice. *Decision Sciences*, *28*(4), 877–910. doi:10.1111/j.1540-5915.1997.tb01335.x

King, A. (1993). From sage on the stage to guide on the side. *College Teaching*, *41*(1), 30. doi:10.1080/87567555.1993.9926781

King, K. P., & Gura, M. (2008). *Podcasting for teachers using a new technology to revolutionize teaching and learning* (Rev. 2nd ed.). USA: Information Age Publishing.

Kinzie, S. (2009, June 26). Some professors losing their Twitter jitters. *Washington Post*. Retrieved from http://www.washingtonpost.com/wp-dyn/content/article/2009/06/25/AR2009062504027.html.

Kiousis, S. (2002). Interactivity: A concept explication. *New Media & Society*, *4*(3), 355–383.

Kirby, P. (1979). *Cognitive style, learning style and transfer skill acquisition*. Columbus, OH: The National Center for Research in Vocational Education, The Ohio State University.

Kirkpatrick, G. (2005). Online chat facilities as pedagogic tools: A case study. *Active Learning in Higher Education*, *6*, 145–159. doi:10.1177/1469787405054239

Kirschner, P. A., Sweller, J., & Clark, R. E. (2006). Why minimal guidance during instruction does not work: An analysis of the failure of constructivist, discovery, problem-based, experiential, and inquiry-based teaching. *Educational Psychologist*, *41*, 75–86. doi:10.1207/s15326985ep4102_1

Klein, A. (2011, Jan. 26). Incoming college students rate emotional health at record low, annual survey finds. *UCLA News*. Retrieved from http://www.heri.ucla.edu/PDFs/press/2010CIRPpressrelease.pdf.

Klingberg, T. (2005). Computerized training of working memory in children with ADHD—A randomized, controlled trial. *Journal of the American Academy of Child and Adolescent Psychiatry*, *44*, 177–186. doi:10.1097/00004583-200502000-00010

Klingberg, T. (2009). *The overflowing brain: Information overload and the limits of working memory*. New York, NY: Oxford University Press.

Kloss, R. J. (1994). A nudge is best: Helping students through the Perry Scheme of Intellectual Development. *College Teaching*, *42*, 151–158. doi:10.1080/87567555.1994.9926847

Knowles, M. (1984). *Using learning contracts*. San Francisco, CA: Jossey-Bass.

Knowles, M. (1975). *Self-directed learning: A guide for learners and teachers*. New York, NY: Cambridge.

Kochersberger, B. (2008, June 20). The healing power of a class. *The Chronicle of Higher Education*, B28.

Kofman, B., & Eckler, K. (2005). They are your future: Attracting and retaining Generation Y. *Canadian HR Reporter, 18*, 8. Retrieved from http://www.hrreporter.com/.

Kohut, A. (2008). *Audience segments in a changing news environment: Key news audiences now blend online and traditional sources*. Pew Research Center Biennial News Consumption Survey. The Pew Research Center for the People & Press.

Kolb, D. A. (1976). *The learning style inventory: Technical manual*. Boston, MA: McBer.

Kolb, D. A. (1984). *Experiential learning: Experience as the source of learning and development*. Englewood Cliffs, NJ: Prentice-Hall Inc.

Kolb, D. A. (1981). Learning styles and disciplinary differences. In Chickering, A. W. (Ed.), *The modern American college*. San Francisco, CA: Jossey-Bass.

Kolb, D. A., & Fry, R. (1975). Toward an applied theory of experiential learning. In Cooper, C. (Ed.), *Theories of group process*. London, UK: John Wiley.

Kolowich, S. (2011, May 16). Built for distance. *Inside Higher Ed.* Retrieved from http://www.insidehighered.com/layout/set/print/news/2011/05/16/online_faculty_burnout.

Kord, K., & Wolf-Wendel, L. (2009). The relationship between online social networking and academic and social integration. *College Student Affairs Journal, 28*(1), 103–124.

Kraft, R., & Krug, J. (1994). Review of research and evaluation on service-learning in public and higher education. In Kraft, R., & Swadener, M. (Eds.), *Building community: Service learning in the academic disciplines*. Denver, CO: Colorado Campus Compact.

Kramarski, B., & Michalsky, T. (2009). Investigating preservice teacher's professional growth in self-regulated learning environments. *Journal of Educational Psychology, 101*(1), 161–175. doi:10.1037/a0013101

Kramer, R., & Bernhardt, S. A. (1999). Moving instruction to the web: Writing as multi-tasking. *Technical Communication Quarterly, 8*(3), 319–336. doi:10.1080/10572259909364671

Krause, S. D. (2004). Blogs as a tool for teaching. *The Chronicle of Higher Education, 51*(42), 33. Retrieved from http://chronile.com/weekly/v51.i42/42b03301.htm.

Krause, N., Roulette, G., Papp, K., & Kaelber, D. (2006). Assessing medical informatics confidence among 1st and 2nd year medical students. *AMIA. Annu. Symp. Proc.* 2006, (p. 989).

Kreps, G. (1986). *Organizational communication*. White Plains, NY: Longman.

Kumar, S. (2008). Can we model wiki use in technology courses to help teachersuse wikis in their classrooms? In K. McFerrin, et al. (Eds.), *Proceedings of Society for Information Technology & Teacher Education International Conference 2008* (pp. 2068-2071). Chesapeake, VA: AACE. Retrieved from http://www.editlib.org/p/27507.

Kuo, Y. H. (2010). *Self-regulated learning: From theory to practice*. Kaohsiung, Taiwan: Wenzao Ursuline College of Languages (ERIC Document Reproduction Service No. ED 510 995).

Kurtz, S., Laidlaw, T., Makoul, G., & Schnabl, G. (1999). Medical education initiatives in communication skills. *Cancer Prevention and Control, 3*(1), 37–45.

Kvavik, R. B. (2005). Convenience, communications, and control: How students use technology. In Oblinger, D., & Oblinger, J. (Eds.), *Educating the net generation* (pp. 7.1–7.20). Boulder, CO: EDUCAUSE.

Kvavik, R. B., Caruso, J. B., & Morgan, G. (2004). *ECAR study of students and information technology, 2004: Convenience, connection, and control*, (p. 5). Retrieved from http://net.educause.edu/ir/library/pdf/ers0405/rs/ers0405w.pdf.

La Rue, F. (2011). *Report of the Special Rapporteur on the promotion and protection of the right to freedom and expression. Human Rights Council*. United Nations.

Lamb, B. (2004). Wide open spaces: Wikis, ready or not. *EDUCAUSE Review, 39*(5), 36–48.

Lancaster, L., & Stillman, D. (2003). *When generations collide: Who they are. Why they clash. How to solve the generational puzzle at work*. New York, NY: HarperCollins.

Landis, M., Swain, K. D., Friehe, M. J., & Coufal, K. L. (2007). Evaluating critical thinking in class and online: Comparison of the Newman Method and the Facione Rubric. *Communication Disorders Quarterly*, *28*(3), 135–143. doi:10.1177/15257401070280030301

Lang, J. M. (2010, November 2). The invisible curriculum. *The Chronicle of Higher Education*. Retrieved from http://chronicle.com/article/the-invisible-curriculum/125197/.

Lankshear, C., & Knobel, M. (2003). *New literacies: Changing knowledge and classroom learning*. Buckingham, UK: OU Press.

Lansari, A., Tubaishat, A., & Al-Rawi, A. (2010). Using a learning management system to foster independent learning in an outcome-based university: A Gulf perspective. *Issues in Informing Science and Information Technology*, *7*, 73–87.

LaRose, R., & Whitten, P. (2000). Re-thinking instructional immediacy for web courses: A social cognitive exploration. *Communication Education*, *48*, 320–338. doi:10.1080/03634520009379221

Laskey, M. L., & Hetzel, C. J. (2010). *Self-regulated learning, metacognition, and soft skills: The 21st century learner*. Milwaukee, WI: Cardinal Stritch University (ERIC Document Reproduction Service No. ED 511 589).

Latane, B., Williams, K., & Harkins, S. (1979). Many hands make light the work: The causes and consequences of social loafing. *Journal of Personality and Social Psychology*, *44*, 78–94.

Laurel, B. (1991). *Computers as theater*. Reading, MA: Addison-Wesley Publishing Company.

Laurel, B. (1986). *Toward the design of a computer-based interactive fantasy system*. Unpublished doctoral dissertation, The Ohio State University.

Laurillard, D. (1993). *Rethinking university teaching: A framework for the effective use of educational technology*. London, UK: Routledge.

Learn and Serve America. (2011). *Service-learning definition, elements, and examples*. Retrieved from http://www.learnandservearizona.com/#Service-Learning%20 Standards.

Lease, A. J., & Brown, T. A. (2009). Distance learning past, present and future. *International Journal of Instructional Media*, *36*, 415–426.

Lee, J.-S. (2000, August 9-12). *Interactivity: A new approach*. Paper presented at the AEJMC Annual Conference, Communication Technology & Policy Division, Phoenix.

Leidman, M. B., & Piwinsky, M. J. (2009). *The perpetual professor in the 21st century university* [Scholarly project]. Indiana: Indiana University of Pennsylvania.

Leininger, M. M. (1985). Ethnography and ethnonursing: Models and modes of qualitative data analysis. In Leininger, M. M. (Ed.), *Qualitative research methods in nursing* (pp. 33–72). Orlando, FL: Grune & Stratton.

Lenhart, A., Rainie, L., & Lewis, O. (2001). *Teenage life online*. Washington, DC: Pew Internet & American Life Project.

Lenhart, A., & Madden, M. (2005). *Testimony by Amanda Lenhart Senior Research Specialist, Pew Internet & American Life Project*. Testimony to the House Committee on Energy and Commerce.

Lenhart, A. (2009). *Adults and social network websites*. Pew Internet & American Life Project. Retrieved December 23, 2010, from http://www.pewinternet.org/Reports/2009/Adults-and-Social-Network-Websites.aspx.

Lenhart, A., & Fox, S. (2009). *Twitter and status updating*. Pew Internet & American Life Projects. Retrieved July 10, 2010, from http://www.pewinternet.org/~/media//Files/Reports/2009/PIP%20Twitter%20Memo%20FINAL.pdf.

Lenhart, L. R., Campbell, S. & Purcell, K. (2010). *Teens and mobile phones*. Pew Internet & American Life Project. Retrieved April 23, 2011, from http://pewinternet.org/Reports/2010/Teens-and-Mobile-Phones.aspx.

Lever-Duffy, J., McDonald, J. B., & Mizell, A. P. (2003). *Teaching and learning with technology*. Boston, MA: Allyn & Bacon/Pearson.

Levin, D., & Arafeh, S. (2002). *The digital disconnect: The widening gap between internet-savvy students and their schools*. Washington, DC: Pew Internet & American Life Project.

Levine, S. J. (2007). The online discussion board as a tool for online learning. *New Directions for Adult and Continuing Education, 113*, 65–74.

Levy, D. M., Nardick, D. L., Turner, J. W., & McWatters, L. (2011, May 8). No cellphone? No Internet? So much less stress. *The Chronicle of Higher Education*, B27–B28.

Lewin, K. (1951). *Field theory in social science*. New York, NY: Harper Collins.

Leyes, M. (2007). Optimize your PowerPoint presentations. *Advisor Today, 11*, 76–77.

Li, Q., Moorman, L., & Dyjur, P. (2010). Inquiry-based learning and e-mentoring via videoconferencing: A study of mathematics and science learning of Canadian rural students. *Educational Technology Research and Development, 58*(6), 729–753. doi:10.1007/s11423-010-9156-3

Liaw, S.-S., Huang, H.-M., & Chen, G.-D. (2007). Surveying instructor and learner attitudes toward e-learning. *Computers & Education, 49*, 1066–1080. doi:10.1016/j.compedu.2006.01.001

Lima, M., & Oakes, W. C. (2006). *Service-learning engineering in your community*. Okemos, MI: Great Lakes Press.

Lin, H. F. (2006). Understanding behavioral intention to participate in virtual communities. *Cyberpsychology & Behavior, 9*(5), 540–547. doi:10.1089/cpb.2006.9.540

Lin, S. Y., & Overbaugh, R. C. (2009). Computer-mediated discussion, self-efficacy and gender. *British Journal of Educational Technology, 40*(6), 999–1013. doi:10.1111/j.1467-8535.2008.00889.x

Lin, L. (2009). Breadth-biased versus focused cognitive control in media multitasking behaviors. *Proceedings of the National Academy of Sciences of the United States of America, 106*, 15521–15522..doi:10.1073/pnas.0908642106

Lincoln, Y. S., & Guba, E. G. (1985). *Naturalistic inquiry*. Newbury Park, CA: Sage Publications.

Lippincott, J. K. (2005). Net Generation students and libraries. In D. G. Oblinger, & J. L. Oblinger (Eds.), *Educating the Net Generation* (pp. 13.1-13.15), Washington, DC: EDUCAUSE. Retrieved from http://www.educause.edu/educatingthenetgen.

Liu, Z. (2005). Reading behavior in the digital environment. *The Journal of Documentation, 61*, 700–712. doi:10.1108/00220410510632040

Livingstone, S., & Bober, M. (2004). Taking up online opportunities? Children's use of the Internet for education, communication and participation. *E-learning, 1*(3), 395–419. doi:10.2304/elea.2004.1.3.5

Livingstone, S., Bober, M., & Helsper, E. J. (2005). Active participation or just more information? Young peoples' take up of opportunities to act and interact on the internet. *Information Communication and Society, 8*(3), 287–314. doi:10.1080/13691180500259103

Livingstone, S., Bober, M., & Helsper, E. (2005). *Internet literacy among children and young people*. London, UK: London School of Economics.

Locke, E. A., & Latham, G. P. (1990). *A theory of goal setting and task performance*. Englewood Cliffs, NJ: Prentice Hall.

Lodewyk, K. R., & Winne, P. H. (2005). Relations among the structure of learning tasks, achievement, and changes in self-efficacy in secondary students. *Journal of Educational Psychology, 97*, 1, 3–12. doi:10.1037/0022-0663.97.1.3

Lohnes, S., & Kinzer, C. (2007). Questioning assumptions about students' expectations for technology in college classrooms. *Innovate, 3*. Retrieved from http://innovateonline.info/index.php?view=article&id=431&action=article.

Long, L. W., & Javidi, A. (2001). *A comparison of course outcomes: Online distance learning versus traditional classroom settings.* Paper presented at the Annual Conference of the National Communication Association, Atlanta, Georgia.

Low, R., Jin, P. T., & Sweller, J. (2009). Cognitive architecture and instructional design in a multimedia context. In Zheng, R. (Ed.), *Cognitive effects of multimedia learning* (pp. 1–16). Hershey, PA: IGI Global.

Loyens, S. M. M., Magda, J., & Rikers, R. M. J. P. (2008). Self-directed learning in problem-based learning and its relationship with self-regulated learning. *Educational Psychology Review*, *20*, 411–427. doi:10.1007/s10648-008-9082-7

Lu, C.-H., Chiou, G.-F., Day, M.-Y., Ong, C.-S., & Hsu, W.-L. (2006). Using Instant Messaging to provide an intelligent learning environment. *Lecture Notes in Computer Science*, *4053*, 575–583. doi:10.1007/11774303_57

Luckin, R. (2010). *Re-designing learning contexts: Technology-rich, learner-centred ecologies*. London, UK: Routledge.

Luehmann, A. L., & Tinelli, L. (2008). Teacher professional identity development with social networking technologies: learning reform through blogging. *Educational Media International*, *45*(4), 323. doi:10.1080/09523980802573263

Lum, L. (2006). The power of podcasting. *Diverse Issues in Higher Education*, *23*(2), 32–35.

Lumsdaine, A. A., & Janis, I. L. (1953). Resistance to counterpropaganda produced by one-sided and two-sided propaganda presentations. *Public Opinion Quarterly*, *17*, 311–318. doi:10.1086/266464

Lund, A., & Smørdal, O. (2006). *Is there a space for the teacher in a wiki?* Paper presented at the International Symposium on Wikis, Odense, Denmark.

Lundsford, A. (2009). *The agenda - Andrea Lunsford* [Online video interview]. Retrieved from http://www.tvo.org/TVO/WebObjects/TVO.woa?video?TAWSP_Int_20091001_779626_0.

Lundstrom, K., & Baker, W. (2009). To give is better than to receive: The benefits of peer review to the reviewer's own writing. *Journal of Second Language Writing*, *18*(1), 30–43. doi:10.1016/j.jslw.2008.06.002

Mabrito, M., & Medley, R. (2008, August/September). Why professor Johnny can't read: Understanding the Net Generation's texts. *Innovate*, *4*(6). Retrieved from http://www.innovateonline.info/index.php?view=article&id=510.

MacDonald, J., Sohn, S., & Ellis, P. (2010). Privacy, professionalism and Facebook: A dilemma for young doctors. *Medical Education*, *44*(8), 805–813. doi:10.1111/j.1365-2923.2010.03720.x

MacKnight, C. (2000). Teaching critical thinking through online discussions. *EDUCAUSE Quarterly*, *4*, 38–41.

Mader, S. (2006). *Using wiki in education: Case studies from the classroom*. Retrieved from www.wikiineducation.com.

Magliaro, S. G., Lockee, B. B., & Burton, J. K. (2005). Direct instruction revisited: A key model for instructional technology. *Educational Technology Research and Development*, *53*(4), 41–55. doi:10.1007/BF02504684

Maki, R. H., Maki, W. S., Patterson, M., & Whitaker, P. D. (2000). Evaluation of a web-based introductory psychology course: I. Learning and satisfaction in on-line versus lecture courses. *Behavior Research Methods, Instruments, & Computers*, *32*, 230–239. doi:10.3758/BF03207788

Maki, W. S., & Maki, R. H. (2002). Multimedia comprehension skill predicts differential outcomes of web-based and lecture outcomes. *Journal of Experimental Psychology. Applied*, *8*, 85–98. doi:10.1037/1076-898X.8.2.85

Margaryan, A., Littlejohn, A., & Vojt, G. (2011). Are digital natives a myth or reality? University students' use of digital technologies. *Computers & Education*, *56*, 429–440. doi:10.1016/j.compedu.2010.09.004

Marshall, S. (2011, February 3). More face-to-face, less face-to-screen. *The Chronicle of Higher Education*. Retrieved February 19, 2011, from http://chronicle.com/article/More-Face-to-Face-Less/126163.

Martin, F. (2008). Effects of practice in a linear and non-linear web-based learning environment. *Journal of Educational Technology & Society*, *11*(4), 81–93.

Martin, C., & Dusenberry, L. (2008). Wiki lore and politics in the classroom. In Cummings, R. E., & Barton, M. (Eds.), *Wiki writing: Collaborative learning in the college classroom* (pp. 204–215). Ann Arbor: University of Michigan Press.

Marzano, R. J. (2006). *Classroom assessment and grading practices that work*. Alexandria, VA: Association for Supervision and Curriculum Development.

Maslow, A. H. (1970). *Motivation and personality* (2nd ed.). New York, NY: Harper & Row.

Mason, R. M., Barzilai-Nahon, K., & Lou, N. (2008). The organizational impact of digital natives: How organizations are responding to the next generation of knowledge workers. *Proceedings of the 17th Dubai International Conference on Management of Technology.* doi:10.1109/HICSS.2006.411.

Massey, B. L., & Levy, M. L. (1999). Interactivity, online journalism, and English-language Web newspapers in Asia. *Journalism & Mass Communication Quarterly, 76*(1), 138–151.

Matulich, E., Papp, R., & Haytko, D. L. (2008). Continuous improvement through teaching innovations: A requirement for today's learners. *Marketing Education Review, 18*, 1–7.

Mayer, R. E. (2001). *Multimedia learning*. Cambridge, UK: Cambridge University Press.

Mayer, R. E., & Anderson, R. (1991). Animations and narrations: An experimental test of a dual-coding hypothesis. *Journal of Educational Psychology, 83*, 484–490. doi:10.1037/0022-0663.83.4.484

Mayer, R. E., & Massa, L. J. (2003). Three facets of visual and verbal learners: Cognitive ability, cognitive style, and learning preference. *Journal of Educational Psychology, 95*, 833–846. doi:10.1037/0022-0663.95.4.833

Mayer, R. E., & Moreno, R. (1998). A split attention effect in multimedia learning: Evidence for dual processing systems in working memory. *Journal of Educational Psychology, 90*, 312–320. doi:10.1037/0022-0663.90.2.312

Mayer, R. E., & Moreno, R. (2000). A coherence effect in multimedia learning: The case for minimizing irrelevant sounds in the design of multimedia instructional messages. *Journal of Educational Psychology, 92*, 117–125. doi:10.1037/0022-0663.92.1.117

Mayer, R. E., & Moreno, R. (2003). Nine ways to reduce cognitive load in multimedia learning. *Educational Psychologist, 38*(1), 43–52. doi:10.1207/S15326985EP3801_6

Mayer, R. E., & Sims, V. K. (1994). For whom is a picture worth a thousand words? Extensions of a dual-coding theory of multimedia learning. *Journal of Educational Psychology, 86*(3), 389–401. doi:10.1037/0022-0663.86.3.389

Mayer, R. E. (1992). *Thinking, problem solving, cognition* (2nd ed.). New York, NY: W.H. Freeman.

Mayer, R. E. (1982). Learning. In Mitzel, H. E. (Ed.), *Encyclopedia of educational research* (pp. 1040–1058). New York, NY: Free Press.

Mazer, J. P., Murphy, R. E., & Simonds, C. J. (2007). I'll see you on Facebook: The effects of computer-mediated teacher self-disclosure on student motivation, affective learning, and classroom climate. *Communication Education, 56*, 1–17. doi:10.1080/03634520601009710

McCaffrey, R., & Gulbrandsen, K. (2007, October). *Wiki-Who? Using wikis to teach audience in the classroom.* Paper presented at the Association for Business Communication Annual Conference. Yosemite, CA.

McCain, T. (2005). *Teaching for tomorrow: Teaching content and problem-solving skills*. Thousand Oaks, CA: Corwin Press.

McCombs, B., & Whisler, J. (1997). *The learner-centered classroom and school*. San Francisco, CA: Jossey-Bass.

McCombs, B. L., & Vakili, D. (2005). A learner-centered framework for e-learning. *Teachers College Record, 107*(8), 1582–1600. doi:10.1111/j.1467-9620.2005.00534.x

McDaniel, M. A., & Fisher, R. P. (1991). Tests and test feedback as learning sources. *Contemporary Educational Psychology, 16*, 192–201. doi:10.1016/0361-476X(91)90037-L

McDonough, B., & Johnson, J. (2010). *Inspiring education: A dialogue with Albertans*. Edmonton, Canada: Alberta Education.

McEuen, S. F. (2001). How fluent with information technology are our students? *EDUCAUSE Quarterly, 4*, 8–17.

McFarland, D., & Hamilton, D. (2005). Factors affecting student performance and satisfaction: Online versus traditional course delivery. *Journal of Computer Information Systems, 46*(2), 25–32.

McGuire, W. J. (1964). Inducing resistance to persuasion: Some contemporary approaches. In Berkowitz, L. (Ed.), *Advances in experimental social psychology* (*Vol. 1*, pp. 191–229). New York, NY: Academic Press. doi:10.1016/S0065-2601(08)60052-0

McKeachie, W. J., & Svinicki, M. (2006). *McKeachie's teaching tips: Strategies, research and theory for college and university teachers*. New York, NY: Houghton Mifflin.

McLuhan, M. (1964). *Understanding media: The extensions of man*. New York, NY: McGraw-Hill Book Company.

McMahon, M., & Pospisil, R. (2005). Laptops for a digital lifestyle: Millennial students and wireless mobile technologies. In Goss, H. (Ed.), *ASCILITE 2005 Balance, Fidelity, Mobility: Maintaining the Momentum* (pp. 421–431). Brisbane, Australia: ASCILITE.

McMillan, S. J. (2002). A four-part model of cyber-interactivity: Some cyber-places are more interactive than others. *New Media & Society*, *6*(2), 271–291. doi:. doi:10.1177/146144480200400208

McNeely, B. (2005). Using technology as a learning tool, not just the cool thing. In D. G. Oblinger, & J. L. Oblinger (Eds.), *Educating the Net Generation* (pp. 4.1-4.10). Washington, DC: EDUCAUSE. Retrieved http://www.educause.edu/educatingthenetgen.

McWilliam, E. L. (2002). Against professional development. *Educational Philosophy and Theory*, *34*(3), 289–300. doi:10.1080/00131850220150246

Mead, G. H. (1934). *Mind, self, and society*. Chicago, IL: University of Chicago Press.

Menand, L. (2010). *The marketplace of ideas: Reform and resistance in the American university*. New York, NY: W.W. Norton.

Meng, J., Elliott, K., & Hall, M. (2010). Technology readiness index (TRI): Assessing cross-cultural validity. *Journal of International Consumer Marketing*, *22*(1), 19–31. doi:10.1080/08961530902844915

Merrill, M. D., & ID2 Research Group. (1998). ID Expert: A second generation instructional development system. *Instructional Science*, *26*(3-4), 242–262.

Merrill, D. M. (2002). First principles of instruction. *Educational Technology Research and Development*, *50*(3), 43–59. doi:10.1007/BF02505024

Merrill, M. D. (2009). First principles of instruction. In Reigeluth, C. M., & Carr-Chellman, A. A. (Eds.), *Instructional-design theories and models: Building a common knowledge base* (*Vol. III*). New York, NY: Routledge.

Mezirow, J. (1978). *Perspective transformation. Adult Education Quarterly, 28(2), Pachler, N., Bachmair, B., Cook, J., & Kress, G. (2010). Mobile learning: Structures, agency, practices*. New York, NY: Springer.

Milliron, M. D. (2010, November 5). 2010). Online education vs. traditional learning: Time to end the family feud. *The Chronicle of Higher Education*, B31–B32.

Minocha, S., & Roberts, D. (2008). Social, usability, and pedagogical factors influencing students' learning experiences with wikis and blogs. *Pragmatics & Cognition*, *16*(2), 272–306.

Minocha, S., Schencks, M., Sclater, N., Thomas, P., & Hause, M. (2007). Collaborative learning in a wiki environment: Case study of a requirements engineering course. *Proceedings of the European Distance and E-learning Network (EDEN) Annual Conference on New Learning 2.0 Emerging Digital Territories, Developing Continuities, New Divides*, Naples. Retrieved from http://www.eden-online.org/eden.php?menuId=353&contentId=587.

Mishra, P., Koehler, M. J., & Kereluik, K. (2009). The song remains the same: Looking back to the future of educational technology. *TechTrends*, *53*(5), 48–53. doi:10.1007/s11528-009-0325-3

Mitchell, R. (1992). *Testing for learning*. New York, NY: The Free Press.

Mitchell, S. (2003). *American generations. Who they are. How they live. What they think*. Ithaca, NY: New Strategist Publications Inc.

Mondoux, S. (2010). *CFMS guide to medical professionalism*. Canadian Foundation of Medical Students.

Montgomery, K. (2007). *Generation digital: Politics, commerce, and childhood in the age of the internet*. Cambridge, MA: MIT Press.

Montgomery, J. L., & Baker, W. (2007). Teacher-written feedback: Student perceptions, teacher self-assessment, and actual teacher performance. *Journal of Second Language Writing*, *16*(2), 82–99. doi:10.1016/j.jslw.2007.04.002

Moody, M. (2010). Teaching Twitter and beyond: Tips for incorporating social media in traditional courses. *Journal of Magazine & New Media Research*, *3*(11), 1–9.

Moore, M. (1993). Three types of interaction. In Boyd, R. D., & Apps, J. W. (Eds.), *Redefining the discipline of adult education*. San Francisco, CA: Jossey-Bass.

Moreno, R., & Mayer, R. E. (1999). Cognitive principles of multimedia learning: The role of modality and contiguity. *Journal of Educational Psychology*, *91*, 358–368. doi:10.1037/0022-0663.91.2.358

Morris, C. W. (Ed.). (1974). *Mind, self, and society: From the standpoint of a social behaviorist*. Chicago, IL: University of Chicago Press.

Mottet, T. P., Frymier, A. B., & Beebe, S. A. (2006). Theorizing about instructional communication. In Mottet, T. P., Richmond, V. P., & McCroskey, J. C. (Eds.), *Handbook of instructional communication: Rhetorical and relational perspectives* (pp. 255–282). Boston, MA: Allyn and Bacon.

Mousavi, S. Y., Low, R., & Sweller, J. (1995). Reducing cognitive load by missing auditory and visual presentation modes. *Journal of Educational Psychology*, *87*, 319–334. doi:10.1037/0022-0663.87.2.319

Mousavi, S. Y., Low, R., & Sweller, J. (1995). Reducing cognitive leads by mixing auditory and visual presentation modes. *Journal of Educational Psychology*, *92*, 724–733.

Moxley, J. (2007). *For teachers new to wikis*. Retrieved from http://writingwiki.org/default.aspx/WritingWiki/For%20Teachers%20New%20to%20Wikis.html.

Murph, D. (2008, September). Vimeo now hosting one million videos, 10% in HD. *Engadget*. Retrieved from http://hd.engadget.com/2008/09/17/vimeo-now-hosting-one-million-videos-10-in-hd.

Myers, G. (2010). *Discourse of blogs and wikis*. New York, NY: Continuum.

Nackerud, S. & Scaletta, K. (2008). Blogging in academy. *New Directions for Students Services, 124*. DOI: 10 1002/ss_296.

Nadler, M. K., & Nadler, L. B. (2000). Out of class communication between faculty and students: A faculty perspective. *Communication Studies*, *51*(2), 176–188.. doi:10.1080/10510970009388517

Nardi, B., Whittaker, S., & Bradner, E. (2000). Interaction and outeraction: Instant messaging in action. In *CSCW '00: Proceedings of the 2000 ACM Conference on Computer Supported Cooperative Work* (pp. 79-88). Philadelphia, PA: ACM Press.

Nasah, A., DaCosta, B., Kinsell, C., & Seok, S. (2010). The digital literacy debate: An investigation of digital propensity and information and communication technology. *Educational Technology Research and Development*, *58*(5), 531–555. doi:10.1007/s11423-010-9151-8

National Center for Education Statistics. (2007). *National assessment of educational progress, the nation's report card: Writing 2007* (NCES Publication No. 2008468). Retrieved from http://nces.ed.gov/pubsearch/pubsinfo.asp?pubid=2008468.

National Center for Educational Statistics. (2011). *The nation's report card*. Retrieved from http://nces.ed.gov/nationsreportcard/pdf/main2009/2011451.pdf.

Nesson, R., & Nesson, C. (2008). The case for education in virtual worlds. *Space and Culture*, *11*, 273–284. doi:10.1177/1206331208319149

Neuman, W. R. (1991). *The future of the mass audience*. Cambridge University Press.

Nguyen, D., Zierler, B., & Nguyen, H. (2011). A survey of nursing faculty needs for training in use of new technologies for education and practice. *The Journal of Nursing Education*, *50*(4), 181–188. doi:10.3928/01484834-20101130-06

Nielsen, J. (2006, April 17). F-shaped pattern for reading web content. *Alertbox*. Retrieved from http://www.useit.com/alertbox/reading_pattern.html.

Nnazor, R. (1998). *Understanding the advent of information technology in teaching at the university: A case study of the University of British Columbia*. Unpublished Doctoral dissertation, University of British Columbia, BC.

Norman, D. K. (2008). *Predicting the performance of interpreting instruction based on digital propensity index score in text and graphic formats*. Unpublished dissertation, University of Central Florida.

NSSE. National Survey of Student Engagement. (2009). *NSSE: National Survey of Student Engagement* (Online). Retrieved June 13, 2010, from http://nsse.iub.edu/nsse_2009/in.

Numberof.net. (2010). *Number of blogs*. Retrieved from http://www.numberof.net/number-of-blogs/.

O'Brien, P. M. (2009). *Accreditation: Assuring and enhancing quality, new directions for higher education*. San Francisco, CA: Jossey-Bass.

Oakes, W. (2004). *Service-learning in engineering: A resource guidebook*. Providence, RI: Campus Compact.

Oblinger, D. G., & Oblinger, J. L. (Eds.). (2005). *Educating the Net generation*. Boulder, CO: EDUCAUSE.

Oblinger, D. G., & Oblinger, J. L. (2006). Is it age or IT: First steps toward understanding the net generation. *CSLA Journal*, *29*(2), 8–16.

Oblinger, D. G. (2006, September). *Listening to what we're seeing*. Keynote address presented at Association for Learning Technology, Edinburgh, UK. Retrieved from http://www.alt.ac.uk/docs/diana_oblinger_20060905.pdf.

Ophir, E., Nass, C., & Wagner, A. D. (2009). Cognitive control in media multitaskers. *Proceedings of the National Academy of Sciences of the United States of America*, *106*, 15583–15587..doi:10.1073/pnas.0903620106

Oppenheimer, T. (2003). *The flickering mind: Saving education from the false promise of technology*. New York, NY: Random House.

Oster-Aaland, L. K., Sellnow, T. L., Nelson, P. E., & Pearson, J. C. (2004). The status of service learning in departments of communication: A follow-up study. *Communication Education*, *53*(4), 348–356. doi:10.1080/0363452032000305959

Paas, F. (1992). Training strategies for attaining transfer of problem-solving skill in statistics: A cognitive load approach. *Journal of Educational Psychology*, *84*, 429–434. doi:10.1037/0022-0663.84.4.429

Paas, F., Renkl, A., & Sweller, J. (2003). Cognitive load theory and instructional design: Recent developments. *Educational Psychologist*, *38*, 1–4. doi:10.1207/S15326985EP3801_1

Paivio, A. (1986). *Mental representations: A dual coding approach*. Oxford, UK: Oxford University Press.

Palen, L., & Dourish, P. (2003). Unpacking "privacy" for a networked world. Paper presented at the CHI 2003, Ft. Lauderdale, Florida, USA.

Palfrey, J., & Gasser, U. (2008). *Born digital: Understanding the first generation of digital natives*. New York, NY: Basic Books.

Palloff, R. M., & Pratt, K. (1999). *Building learning communities in cyberspace: Effective strategies for the online classroom*. San Francisco, CA: Jossey-Bass.

Palmer, P. J. (1998). *The courage to teach: Exploring the inner landscape of a teacher's life*. San Francisco, CA: Jossey-Bass.

Palmgreen, P., Wenner, L. A., & Rayburn, J. D. (1980). Relations between gratifications sought and obtained: A study of television news. *Communication Research*, *7*, 161–192..doi:10.1177/009365028000700202

Palmgreen, P., & Rayburn, J. D. (1985). An expectancy-value approach to media gratifications. In Rosengren, K. E., Wenner, L. A., & Palmgreen, P. (Eds.), *Media gratifications research* (pp. 61–72). Beverly Hills, CA: Sage.

Parasuraman, A. (2000). Technology readiness index (tri): A multiple-item scale to measure readiness to embrace new technologies. *J Service Rsch*, *2*(4), 307–320. doi:10.1177/109467050024001

Parbooteeah, S., & Anwar, M. (2009). Thematic analysis of written assignment feedback: Implications for nurse education. *Nurse Education Today*, *29*(7), 753–757. doi:10.1016/j.nedt.2009.02.017

Pardue, K. T., & Morgan, P. (2008). Millennials considered: A new generation, new approaches, and implications for nursing education. *Nursing Education Perspectives*, *29*(2), 74–79.

Paretti, M. C., McNair, L. D., & Holloway-Attaway, L. (2007). Teaching technical communication in an era of distributed work: A case study of collaboration between U.S. and Swedish students. *Technical Communication Quarterly*, *16*, 327–352. doi:10.1080/10572250701291087

Park, J. (2010). Differences among university students and faculties in social networking site perception and use. *The Electronic Library*, *28*, 417–431. doi:10.1108/02640471011051990

Parker, K. R., & Chao, J. T. (2007). Wiki as a teaching tool. *Interdisciplinary Journal of Knowledge and Learning Objects*, *3*, 57–72.

Parr, J., & Timperley, H. (2010). Feedback to writing, assessment for teaching and learning and student progress. *Assessing Writing, 15*(2), 68–85. doi:10.1016/j.asw.2010.05.004

Parr, J. M., & Limbrick, L. (2010). Contextualising practice: Hallmarks of effective teachers of writing. *Teaching and Teacher Education, 26*(3), 583–590. doi:10.1016/j.tate.2009.09.004

Parry, M. (2009, August 31). Professors embrace online courses despite qualms about quality. *The Chronicle of Higher Education.* Retrieved from http://chronicle.com/article/Professors-Embrace-Online/48235.

Parry, M. (2010, July 4). Linked in with: A writer who questions the wisdom of teaching with technology. *The Chronicle of Higher Education.* Retrieved from http://chronicle.com/article/Is-Technology-Making-Your/66128/.

Parry, M. (2010, May 4). Most professors use social media. *The Chronicle of Higher Education.* Retrieved May 8, 2010, from http://chronicle.com/blogPost/Most-Professors-Use-Social/23716.

Partlow, K. M., & Gibbs, W. J. (2003). Indicators of constructivist principles in Internet-based courses. *Journal of Computing in Higher Education, 14*(2), 66–95. doi:10.1007/BF02940939

Patterson, B. R., & Gojdycz, T. K. (2000). The relationship between computer-mediated communication and communication related anxieties. *Communication Research Reports, 17*(3), 278–287. doi:10.1080/08824090009388775

Paul, R., & Elder, L. (2007). *The miniature guide to critical thinking: Concepts & tools.* Dillon Beach, CA: Foundation for Critical Thinking.

Pavela, G. (2006). *Questions and answers on college student suicide: A law and policy perspective.* Asheville, NC: College Administration Publications.

Pellegrino, J., & Quellmalz, E. (2010). Perspectives on the integration of technology and assessment. *Journal of Research on Technology in Education, 43*(2), 119–134.

Penner, L., Orom, H., Albrecht, T., Franks, M., Foster, T., & Ruckdeschel, J. (2007). Camera-related behaviors during video recorded medical interactions. *Journal of Nonverbal Behavior, 31*(2), 99–117. doi:10.1007/s10919-007-0024-8

Perlmutter, D. D. (2010). *Promotion and tenure confidential.* Cambridge, MA: Harvard University Press.

Perry, N. E., Phillips, L., & Hutchinson, L. (2006). Mentoring student teachers to support self-regulated learning. *The Elementary School Journal, 106*(3), 237–254. doi:10.1086/501485

Pew Research Center. (2010). *Americans spending more time following the news.* Pew Research Center. Retrieved May 18, 2011, from http://people-press.org/http://people-press.org/files/legacy-pdf/652.pdf.

Pew Research Center. (2010). *Millennials.* Retrieved from http://pewresearch.org/millennials/.

Pfau, M., & Burgoon, M. (1988). Inoculation in political campaign communication. *Human Communication Research, 15*(1), 91–111. doi:10.1111/j.1468-2958.1988.tb00172.x

Pfau, M., Compton, J., Parker, K. A., Wittenberg, E. M., An, C., & Ferguson, M. (2004). The traditional explanation for resistance based on the core elements of threat and counterarguing and an alternative rationale based on attitude accessibility: Do these mechanisms trigger distinct or overlapping process of resistance? *Human Communication Research, 30*, 329–360. doi:10.1093/hcr/30.3.329

Pfau, M., & Kenski, H. C. (1990). *Attack politics: Strategy and defense.* New York, NY: Praeger.

Pfau, M., Semmler, S. M., Deatrick, L., Mason, A., Nisbett, G., & Lane, L. (2009). Nuances about the role and impact of affect in inoculation. *Communication Monographs, 76*(1), 73–98. doi:10.1080/03637750802378807

Pfau, M., & Van Bockern, S. (1994). The persistence of inoculation in conferring resistance to smoking initiation among adolescents: The second year. *Human Communication Research, 20*, 413–430. doi:10.1111/j.1468-2958.1994.tb00329.x

Pfau, M. (1995). Designing messages for behavioral inoculation. In Maibach, E., & Parrott, R. L. (Eds.), *Designing health messages: Approaches from communication theory and public health practice* (pp. 99–113). Newbury Park, CA: Sage Publications.

Phillipson, M. (2008). Wikis in the classroom: A taxonomy. In Cummings, R. H., & Barton, M. (Eds.), *Wiki writing: Collaborative learning in the college classroom* (pp. 19–43). Ann Arbor, MI: University of Michigan Press.

Piaget, J. (1953). *The origins of intelligence in children.* London, UK: Routledge and Kegan Paul.

Pintrich, P. R., Smith, D. A., Garcia, T., & McKeachie, W. J. (1993). Reliability and predictive validity of the motivated strategies for learning questionnaire (MSLQ). *Educational and Psychological Measurement, 53*(3), 801–813. doi:10.1177/0013164493053003024

Pintrich, P. R. (1995). Understanding self-regulated learning. [San Francisco, CA: Jossey-Bass.]. *New Directions for Teaching and Learning, 63*, 3–12. doi:10.1002/tl.37219956304

Pintrich, P. R. (1988). A process-oriented view of student motivation and cognition. In Stark, J. S., & Mets, L. A. (Eds.), *New directions for institutional research, no. 57: Improving teaching and learning through research* (pp. 65–79). San Francisco, CA: Jossey-Bass.

Piolat, A., Olive, T., & Kellogg, R. T. (2005). Cognitive effort during note taking. *Applied Cognitive Psychology, 19*(3), 291–312. doi:10.1002/acp.1086

Pivec, M., & Pivec, P. (2008). *Games in schools: Executive summary.* Retrieved fromhttp://www.paulpivec.com/Games_in_Schools.pdf.

Plass, J., Homer, B., & Haywood, E. (2009). Design factors for educationally effective animations and simulations. *Journal of Computing in Higher Education, 21*, 31–61. doi:10.1007/s12528-009-9011-x

Pogue, L., & Ahyun, K. (2006). The effect of teacher nonverbal immediacy and credibility on student motivation and affective learning. *Communication Education, 55*, 331–344. doi:10.1080/03634520600748623

Pohl, M. (2000). *Learning to think, thinking to learn: Models and strategies to develop a classroom culture of thinking.* Cheltenham, UK: Hawker Brownlow.

Põldoja, H., & Väljataga, T. (2010). *Externalization of a PLE: Conceptual design of LeContract.* The PLE Conference. ISSN 2077-9119. Retrieved July 24, 2011, from http://pleconference.citilab.eu/cas/wp-content/uploads/2010/06/ple2010_submission_68.pdf.

Powers, W. (2010). *Hamlet's BlackBerry: A practical philosophy for building a good life in the digital age.* New York, NY: HarperCollins.

Prenksy, M. (2001). Digital natives, digital immigrants. *Horizon, 9*(5), 1–6..doi:10.1108/10748120110424816

Prenksy, M. (2006). *Don't bother me Mom-I'm learning.* Minneapolis, MN: Paragon House Publishers.

Prensky, M. (2001). Digital natives, digital immigrants. *Horizon, 9*, 1–6. doi:10.1108/10748120110424816

Prensky, M. (2010). *Teaching digital natives: Partnering for real learning.* Thousand Oaks, CA: Corwin.

Prensky, M. (1998). *Twitch speed: Keeping up with young workers.* Retrieved from http://www.twitchspeed.com/site/article.html#twitch.

Prensky, M. (2004). Use their tools! Speak their language! *Connected, 10*, 8-11. Retrieved from http://www.ltscotland.org.uk/Images/connected_10_tcm4-122006.pdf.

Prensky, M. (2009). H. sapiens digital: From digital immigrants and digital natives to digital wisdom. *Innovate 5*(3). Retrieved February 9, 2009, from http://innovateonline.info/index.php?view=article&id=705.

Prentice, M., & Robinson, G. (2010). *Improving student learning outcomes with service learning.* American Association of Community Colleges. Retrieved from www.aacc.nche.edu/Resources/aaccprograms/horizons/Documents/slorb_jan2010.pdf.

Purcell, K. (2010, June). *The state of online video.* Retrieved from http://www.pewinternet.org/~/media//Files/Reports/2010/PIP-The-State-of-Online-Video.pdf.

Pure Digital Technologies, Inc. (2011, Oct. 6). *Hoover's company records*, 140105. United States, Austin: Dun and Bradstreet, Inc. (ProQuest Document ID: 230629222). Retrieved from http://search.proquest.com/docview/230629222?accountid=10818.

Qualman, E. (2011). *Socialnomics: How social media transforms the way we live and do business.* John Wiley and Sons.

Rafaeli, S. (1988). Interactivity: From new media to communication. In *Sage Annual Review of Communication Research: Advancing Communication Science* (*Vol. 16*, pp. 110–134). Beverly Hills, CA: Sage.

Rafaeli, S., & Sudweeks, F. (1997). Networked interactivity. *Journal of Computer-Mediated Communication, 2*(4).

Raines, C. (2002). Managing millennials: Connecting generations. The sourcebook. *Generations at Work*. Retrieved from http://www.geneartionsatwork.com/ articles/ millennials.htm.

Raines, C. (2010). *Millennials at work*. http://www.generationsatwork.com/ articles_millennials_at_work.php.

Rainie, L. (2006). *Americans and their cell phones*. Washington, DC: Pew Research Center. Retrieved from http:// www.pewinternet.org/~/media//Files/Reports/2006/ PIP_Cell_phone_study.pdf.pdf.

Ramaley, J., & Zia, L. (2005). The real versus the possible: Closing the gaps in engagement and learning. In D. G. Oblinger & J. L. Oblinger, (Eds.), *Educating the Net Generation* (pp. 8.1-8.21). Washington, DC: EDUCAUSE. Retrieved December 7, 2010, from http://www.kwantlen.ca/academicgrowth/resources/EduCausepub7101.pdf.

Ranson, S., Martin, J., Nixon, J., & McKeown, P. (1996). Towards a theory of learning. *British Journal of Educational Studies, 44*(1), 9–26. doi:10.1080/00071005.1996.9974055

Ravitz, J. L., Becker, H. J., & Wong, Y.-T. (2000). *Constructivist compatible beliefs and practices among US teachers*. (Teaching, Learning & Computing Report 4.) Irvine, CA: Center for Research on Information Technology and Organizations, University of California. Retrieved May 18, 2011, from http://www.crito.uci.edu/ TLC/findings/report4/.

Rebora, A. (2010, October 11). Change agent. *Education Week Teacher Professional Development Sourcebook*. Retrieved July 26, 2011, from http://www.edweek.org/ tsb/articles/2010/10/12/01richardson.h04.html.

Reda, M. M. (2010, September 5). What's the problem with quiet students? Anyone? Anyone? *The Chronicle of Higher Education*. Retrieved from http://chronicle.com.

Reed, S. (2006). Cognitive architectures for multimedia learning. *Educational Psychologist, 41*, 87–98. doi:10.1207/s15326985ep4102_2

Reid, J. (1972). *Alienation*. Speech delivered at the University of Glasgow, U.K. Retrieved February 8, 2011, from http://www.gla.ac.uk/media/media_167194_en.pdf.

Reigeluth, C. M., & Carr-Chellman, A. A. (Eds.). (2009). *Instructional-design theories and models: Building a common knowledge base* (*Vol. III*). New York, NY: Routledge.

Reigeluth, C. M., & Garfinkle, R. J. (1994). Envisioning a new system of education. In Reigeluth, C. M., & Garfinkle, R. J. (Eds.), *Systemic change in education* (pp. 59–70). Englewood Cliffs, NJ: Educational Technology Publications.

Reinsch, N. L., Turner, J. W., & Tinsley, C. H. (2008). Multicommunicating: A practice whose time has come? *Academy of Management Review, 33*, 391–403. doi:10.5465/AMR.2008.31193450

Reiser, S. (2009). *Technological medicine: The changing world of doctors and patients*. New York, NY: Cambridge University Press.

Rennecker, J., Dennis, A. R., & Hansen, S. (2006). Reconstructing the stage: The use of instant messaging to restructure meeting boundaries. *Proceedings of the 39th Hawaii International Conference on System Sciences*. doi: 10.1109/HICSS.2006.411.

Rheingold, H. (2008). Using social media to teach social media. *New England Journal of Higher Education*, (Summer): 25–26.

Rheingold, H. (2009, June 30). Crap detection 101. *San Francisco Gate*. Retrieved February 8, 2011 from http://www.sfgate.com/cgi-bin/blogs/rheingold/detail? entry_id=42805.

Richard, J., & Ting, E. (1999). *Making the most of interaction: What instructors do that most affects students' perceptions of learning*. Paper presented at the 5th International Conference on Asynchronous Learning, College Park, MD.

Richardson, W. (2006). *Blogs, wikis, podcasts, and other powerful web tools for classrooms*. Thousand Oaks, CA: Corwin Press.

Rideout, V., Foehr, U., & Roberts, D. (2010). *Generation M2: Media in the lives of 8- to 18-year-olds*. Henry J. Kaiser Family Foundation.

Rideout, V., Foehr, U., Roberts, D., & Brodie, M. (1999). *Kids and media at the new millenium*. Henry J. Kaiser Family Foundation.

Rideout, V., Foehr, U., & Roberts, D. (2005). *Gen M: Media in the lives of 8–18 year-olds*. Henry J. Kaiser Family Foundation.

Roberts, G. (2005). Technology and learning expectations of the Net Generation. In D. G. Oblinger, & J. L. Oblinger (Eds.), *Educating the Net Generation* (pp. 3.1-3.7). Washington, DC: EDUCAUSE. Retrieved from http://www.educause.edu/educatingthenetgen.

Roberts, G. R. (2005). In D. Oblinger & J. Oblinger, (Eds.), *Educating the Net generation*. Retrieved from http://www.educause.edu/Resources/EducatingtheNet Generation/TechnologyandLearningExpectati/6056.

Rogers, R. D., & Monsell, S. (1995). Costs of a predictable switch between simple cognitive tasks. *Journal of Experimental Psychology*, *124*, 207–231.

Rogers, C., & Freiberg, H. J. (1994). *Freedom to learn* (3rd ed.). New York, NY: Merrill.

Rose, D., & Meyer, A. (2002). *Teaching every student in the digital age: Universal design for learning*. Alexandria, VA: Association for Supervision & Curriculum Development.

Rosen, L., Carrier, M., & Cheever, N. (2010). *Rewired: Understanding the iGeneration and the way they learn*. New York, NY: Macmillan.

Rothman, D., & Blumenthal, D. (Eds.). (2010). *Medical professionalism in the new information age*. Rutgers University Press.

Rueda, M., Rothbart, M., & Posner, M. (2005). Training, maturation and genetic influences on the development of executive attention. *Proceedings of the National Academy of Sciences of the United States of America*, *102*, 14931–14936. doi:10.1073/pnas.0506897102

Rushkoff, D. (2006). *ScreenAgers: Lessons in chaos from digital kids*. New York, NY: Hampton Press.

Russell, T. (1999). *The no significant difference phenomenon*. Chapel Hill, NC: Office of Instructional Telecommunication, North Carolina State University.

Russo, T., & Benson, S. (2005). Learning with invisible others: Perceptions of online presence and their relationship to cognitive and affective learning. *Journal of Educational Technology & Society*, *8*(1), 54–62.

Russo, T. C., & Chadwick, S. A. (2001). Making connections: Enhancing classroom learning with a virtual visiting professor. *Communication Teacher*, *15*, 7–9.

Ružić-Dimitrijević, L., & Maja Dimitrijević, M. (2010). Challenges IT instructors face in the self-education process. *Journal of Information Technology Education*, *9*, 35–48.

Ryan, M., & Switzer, L. (2001). Balancing arts and sciences, skills, and conceptual content. *Journalism & Mass Communication Educator*, *56*(2), 55–68.

Saeed, N., Yang, Y., & Sinnappan, S. (2009). Emerging web technology in higher education: A case of incorporating blogs, podcasts and social bookmarks in a web programming course based on students' learning styles and technology preferences. *Journal of Educational Technology & Society*, *12*(4), 98–109.

Safer, M. (2007, May 25). The "millennials" are coming. *CBS News.com: 60 Minutes*. Retrieved from http://www.cbsnews.com/stories/2007/11/08/60minutes/main3475200.shtml.

Salaway, G., & Caruso, J. B. (2007). *The ECAR study of undergraduate students and information technology*. EDUCAUSE Center for Applied Research. Retrieved from http://connect.educause.edu/library/abstract/TheECARStudyofUnderg/45075.

Salisbury, D. F. (1990). Cognitive psychology and Its implications for designing drill and practice programs for computers. *Journal of Computer-Based Instruction*, *17*(1), 23–30.

Sanders, S. (2011, January). *Investigating learning in sciences and professions*. Powerpoint presentation at Better Learning through Technology Institute, Youngstown, OH.

Sandmann, A. (2006). Nurturing thoughtful revision using the focused question card strategy. *Journal of Adolescent & Adult Literacy*, *50*(1), 20–28. doi:10.1598/JAAL.50.1.3

Sang, G., Valcke, M., van Braak, J., & Tondeur, J. (2010). Student teachers' thinking processes and ICT integration: Predictors of prospective teaching behaviors with educational technology. *Computers & Education*, *54*, 103–112. doi:10.1016/j.compedu.2009.07.010

Scaletta, K. R. (2006). *To whom are these texts valuable? An inquiry into student blogging*. Master's project, University of Minnesota. Retrieved from http://inms.umn.edu/events/past/newresearch_2006/scaletta.html.

Scheffler, F. L., & Logan, J. P. (1999). Computer technology in schools: What teachers should know and be able to do. *Journal of Research on Computing in Education, 31*, 305–326.

Schiller, S. Z. (2009). Practicing learner-centered teaching: Pedagogical design and assessment of a Second Life project. *Journal of Information Systems Education, 20*(3), 369–381.

Schlechty, P. (2002). *Working on the work*. New York, NY: John Wiley & Sons.

Schrire, S. (2004). Interaction and cognition in asynchronous computer conferencing. *Instructional Science, 32*, 475–502..doi:10.1007/s11251-004-2518-7

Schrodt, P., Witt, P. L., Myers, S. A., Turman, P. D., Barton, M. H., & Jernberg, K. A. (2008). Learner empowerment and teacher evaluations as functions of teacher power use in the college classroom. *Communication Education, 57*(2), 180–200..doi:10.1080/03634520701840303

Schunk, D. H. (1990). Goal setting and self-efficacy during self-regulated learning. *Educational Psychologist, 25*(1), 71–86. doi:10.1207/s15326985ep2501_6

Schunk, D. H. (1991). Self-efficacy and academic motivation. *Educational Psychologist, 26*(3), 207–231. doi:10.1207/s15326985ep2603&4_2

Schurink, E. M. (1998). Designing qualitative research. In De Vos, A. S. (Ed). *Research at grass roots — A primer for the caring professions* (pp. 252-264). Pretoria, South Africa: van Schaik.

Schwartz, D. L., Lin, X., Brophy, S., & Bransford, J. D. (1999). Toward the development of flexibly adaptive instructional designs. In Reigeluth, C. M. (Ed.), *Instructional-design theories and models: A new paradigm of instructional theory* (*Vol. II*, pp. 183–213). Mahwah, NJ: Lawrence Erlbaum.

Scriven, M., & Richard, P. (2009). Defining critical thinking. Retrieved January 29, 2009, from http://www.criticalthinking.org/page.cfm?PageID=410HYPERLINK.

Seaman, J. (2009). Online learning as a strategic asset, volume II: The paradox of faculty voices. Retrieved from http://www.aplu.org/NetCommunity/Document.Doc?id=1879.

Selwyn, N. (2009). *The digital native - Myth and reality*. Paper presented at the CILIP (Chartered Institute of Library and Information Professionals) London seminar series. Retrieved from http://www.scribd.com/doc/9775892/Digital-Native.

Shapiro, W., & Gonick, L. (2008). Learning 2.0: Who's in control now? In *Sparking Innovative Learning and Creativity, Summer Conference at Princeton University Proceedings*, (pp. 64-71).

Shenk, D. (1997). *Data smog: Surviving the information glut*. New York, NY: HarperOne.

Sherblom, J. C. (2010). The computer-mediated communication (CMC) classroom: A challenge of medium, presence, interaction, identity, and relationship. *Communication Education, 59*, 497–523. doi:10.1080/03634523.2010.486440

Shieh, D. (2009, February 10). Professors regard online instruction as less effective than classroom learning. *The Chronicle of Higher Education*. Retrieved from http://chronicle.com/article/Professors-Regard-Online/1519/.

Shneiderman, B., & Kearsley, G. (1999). Engagement theory: A framework for technology-based teaching and learning. *Journal of Educational Technology, 38*(5), 20–23.

Shumer, R. D. (1997). Learning from qualitative research. In Waterman, A. S. (Ed.), *Service-learning: Applications from the research*. Mahwah, NJ: Lawrence Erlbaum Associates.

Shute, V. J., & Towle, B. (2003). Adaptive e-learning. *Educational Psychologist, 38*(2), 105–114. doi:10.1207/S15326985EP3802_5

Shute, V. J., & Torreano, L. A. (2003). Formative evaluation of an automated knowledge elicitation and organization tool. In Murray, T., Ainsworth, S., & Blessing, S. (Eds.), *Authoring tools for advanced technology learning environments: Toward cost-effective adaptive, interactive, and intelligent educational software* (pp. 149–180). The Netherlands: Kluwer Academic Publishers.

Shute, V. J., & Zapata-Rivera, D. (2008). Adaptive technologies. In Spector, J. M., Merrill, D., van Merrienboer, J., & Driscoll, M. (Eds.), *Handbook of research on educational communications and technology* (3rd ed., pp. 277–294). New York, NY: Lawrence Erlbaum Associates, Taylor & Francis Group.

Siemens, G. (2005). Connectivism: A learning theory for the digital age. *International Journal of Instructional Technology and Distance Learning, 2*(1). Retrieved from http://www.itdl.org/Journal/Jan_05/article01.htm.

Siemens, G. (2008). *Learning and knowing in networks: Changing roles for educators and designers.* Paper presented at the University of Georgia IT Forum. Retrieved from http://it.coe.uga.edu/itforum/Paper105/Siemens.pdf.

Simmons, C. D., Willkomm, T., & Behling, K. (2010). Professional power through education: Universal course design initiatives in occupational therapy curriculum. *Occupational Therapy in Health Care, 24*(1), 86–96. doi:10.3109/07380570903428664

Skiba, D. J., & Barton, A. J. (2006). Adapting your teaching to accommodate the net generation of learners. *Online Journal of Issues in Nursing, 11*(2), 15.

Skylar, A. (2009). A comparison of asynchronous online text-based lectures and synchronous interactive web conferencing lectures. *Issues in Teacher Education, 18*(2), 69–84.

Slade, D. (2010). *Students win Facebook battle with U of C: Judge rules in favour of twins over defamation.* Calgary Herald. Retrieved from http://www.calgaryherald.com/technology/Students+Facebook+battle+with/3670183/story.html.

Slater, C., Crichton, S., & Pegler, K. (2010). *Understanding teaching technology use by generation, knowledge and career cycle* (p. 39). Calgary Board of Education.

Sledzik, B. (2011, February 2). Trying to figure out Quora? Me, too! *ToughSledding* [Blog]. Retrieved February 10, 2011, from http://et.kent.edu/toughsledding/?p=6696.

Small, G., & Vorgan, G. (2008). *iBrain: Surviving the technological alteration of the modern mind.* New York, NY: CollinsLiving.

Smart, B., & Desouza, K. (2007). Overcoming technology resistance. *Business Strategy Review*, 25-28.

Smith, S., & Caruso, J. (2010). *The ECAR Study of undergraduate students and Information Technology, 2010.* Boulder, CO: Educause.

Smith, P. L., & Ragan, T. J. (2005). *Instructional design* (3rd ed.). Hoboken, NJ: John Wiley & Sons.

Smith, G. G., & Ferguson, D. (2003). The Web versus the classroom: Instructor experiences in discussion-based and mathematics-based disciplines. *Journal of Educational Computing Research, 29*, 29–59. doi:10.2190/PEA0-T6N4-PU8D-CFUF

Smith, S. D., & Caruso, J. B. (2010). *The ECAR study of undergraduate students and information technology, 2010.* Boulder, CO: Educause Center for Applied Research.

Smith, P. L., & Ragan, T. J. (2005). *Instructional design.* Danver, MA: John Wiley & Sons, Inc.

Smith, G. G., Heindel, A. J., & Torres-Ayala, A. T. (2008). E-learning commodity or community: Disciplinary differences between online courses. *Internet and Higher Education, 11*, 152–159. Retrieved January 15, 2011, from http://cgit.nutn.edu.tw:8080/cgit/PaperDL/TKW_090409063122.pdf.

Smith, S., Caruso, J., & Kim, J. (2010). *ECAR study of undergraduate students and information technology.* Retrieved at http://www.educase.edu.edu/Resources/ECARStudyofUndergraduateStuden/217333.

Snyder, B. (1971). *The hidden curriculum.* Cambridge, MA: MIT Press.

Solomon, G., Allen, N., & Resta, P. (2002). *Toward digital equity: Bridging the divide in education.* Boston, MA: Allyn & Bacon.

Soloway, E., Guzdial, M., & Hay, K. E. (1994). Learner-centered design: The challenge for HCI in the 21st century. *Interaction, 1*(2), 36–48. doi:10.1145/174809.174813

Sonic Foundry, Inc. (2011, 15 April). *Hoover's company records*, 56057. (Document ID: 168211121).

Spector, J. M. (2001). An overview of progress and problems in educational technology. *Interactive Educational Multimedia, 3*, 27–37.

Spigelman, C., & Grobman, L. (Eds.). (2005). *On location: Theory and practice in classroom-based writing tutoring*. Logan, UT: Utah State University Press.

Stapleton, A. J. (2004). *Beyond entertainment: Games as learning technologies.* Paper presented at the AIMIA Game Based-Learning Seminar, Melbourne, VIC.

Statistics Canada. (2010, May 10). Canadian internet use survey. *The Daily.* Retrieved from http://www.statcan.gc.ca/daily-quotidien/100510/dq100510a-eng.htm.

Stephens, K. K. (2008). Optimizing costs in workplace instant messaging use. *IEEE Transactions on Professional Communication*, *51*, 369–380..doi:10.1109/TPC.2008.2007864

Stephens, K. K., & Davis, J. D. (2009). The social influences on electronic multitasking in organizational meetings. *Management Communication Quarterly*, *23*, 63–83..doi:10.1177/0893318909335417

Stephens, K. K., & Mottet, T. M. (2008). Interactivity in a Web conferencing training context: Effects on trainers & trainees. *Communication Education*, *57*, 88–104..doi:10.1080/03634520701573284

Steuer, J. (1992). Defining virtual reality: Dimensions determining telepresence. *The Journal of Communication*, *42*(4), 73–93..doi:10.1111/j.1460-2466.1992.tb00812.x

Stith, B. (2000). Web-enhanced lecture course scores big with students and faculty. *Technology Horizons in Education Journal*, *27*, 20–28.

Stromer-Galley, J. (2004). Interactivity-as-product and interactivity-as-process. *The Information Society*, *20*(5), 391–394. doi:10.1080/01972240490508081

Stroop, J. R. (1935). Studies of interference in serial verbal reactions. *Journal of Experimental Psychology*, *18*, 643–662. doi:10.1037/h0054651

Student Poll. (2010). Research dispels Millennial theories: Millennials appear more like than different from their parents' generation. *The CollegeBoard.* Retrieved from http://professionals.collegeboard.com/data-reports-research/trends/studentpoll/millennial.

Stupnisky, R. H., Renaud, R. D., Daniels, L. M., Haynes, T. L., & Perry, R. P. (2008). The interrelation of first-year college students' critical thinking disposition, perceived academic control, and academic achievement. *Research in Higher Education*, *49*, 513–530. doi:10.1007/s11162-008-9093-8

Subcommitteeon Telecommunications and the Internet hearing on H.R. 5319, The Deleting On-line Predators Act of 2006. Retrieved from http://www.pewinternet.org/~/media//Files/Presentations/2006/2006%20-%207.11.06%20-%20Testimony%20by%20Amanda%20Lenhart.pdf.

Sun, P. C., Tsai, R. J., Finger, G., Chen, Y. Y., & Yeh, D. (2008). What drives a successful e-Learning? An empirical investigation of the critical factors influencing learner satisfaction. *Computers & Education*, *50*(4), 1183-1202. doi:1110.1016/j.compedu.2006.1111.1007.

Sundar, S. S. (2004). Theorizing interactivity's effects. *The Information Society*, *20*(5), 385–389..doi:10.1080/01972240490508072

Swan, K. (2001). Virtual interaction: Design factors affecting student satisfaction and perceived learning in asynchronous online courses. *Distance Education*, *22*, 306–331. doi:10.1080/0158791010220208

Sweeney, R. (2006). *Millennial behaviors and demographics*. Newark, NJ: New Jersey Institute of Technology.

Sweeney, R. (2007, Sep). *Millennial behaviors and higher education focus group results*. Presentation at William Paterson University. Retrieved from http://library1.njit.edu/staff-folders/sweeney/.

Sweeny, S. M. (2010). Writing for the instant messaging and text messaging generation: Using new literacies to support writing instruction. *Journal of Adolescent & Adult Literacy*, *54*(2), 121–130. doi:10.1598/JAAL.54.2.4

Sweller, J., & Chandler, P. (1991). Evidence for cognitive load theory. *Cognition and Instruction*, *8*(4), 351–362. doi:10.1207/s1532690xci0804_5

Sweller, J., & Chandler, P. (1994). Why some material is difficult to learn. *Cognition and Instruction*, *12*(3), 185–233. doi:10.1207/s1532690xci1203_1

Sweller, J. (2006). The worked example effect and human cognition. *Learning and Instruction, 16*, 165–169. doi:10.1016/j.learninstruc.2006.02.005

Swenson, L. C. (1980). *Theories of learning: Traditional perspectives/contemporary developments*. Belmont, CA: Wadsworth.

Szabo, M., & Flesher, K. (2002). *CMI theory and practice: Historical roots of learning managment systems.* Paper presented at the E-Learn 2002 World Conference on E-Learning in Corporate, Government, Healthcare, & Higher Education, Montreal, Canada.

Tabachnick, B. G., & Fidell, L. S. (2001). *Using multivariate statistics* (4th ed.). Needham Heights, MA: Allyn & Bacon.

Tackett, L., & Cator, K. (2011). *The promise of communities of practice*. ED.gov. Retrieved from: http://www.ed.gov/oii-news/promise-communities-practice.

Taguchi, N., & Ogawa, T. (2010). OSCEs in Japanese postgraduate clinical training Hiroshima experience 2000-2009. *European Journal of Dental Education, 14*(4), 203–209. doi:10.1111/j.1600-0579.2009.00610.x

Tapscott, D. (2009). *Grown up digital: How the Net generation is changing your world.* New York, NY: McGraw Hill.

Tapscott, D. (1998). *Growing up digital: The rise of the Net generation.* New York, NY: McGraw-Hill Companies.

Taylor, S. J., & Bogdan, R. (1984). *Introduction to qualitative research methods: The search for meanings*. New York, NY: John Wiley & Sons.

TechSmith Corporation. (2011, 15 April). Hoover's company records, 130509. (Document ID: 548579501).

Tegrity, Inc. (2010, October). *McGraw-Hill Education acquires Tegrity, provider of award-winning, automated service that captures class lectures for college students* (Press Release). Retrieved from http://www.tegrity.com/learn-more/press-releases/175-mcgraw-hill-education-acquires-tegrity.

Tennant, M. (1997). *Psychology and adult learning* (2nd ed.). London, UK: Routledge.

The net generation, unplugged. (2010, March 4). *The Economist,* Retrieved from http://www.economist.com/node/15582279.

Thiroux, J. P., & Krasemann, K. W. (2009). *Ethics: Theory and practice*. Upper Saddle River, NJ: Pearson.

Thirunarayanan, M. O., & Perez-Prado, A. (2001-2002). Comparing Web-based and classroom-based learning: A quantitative study. *Journal of Research on Technology in Education, 34*, 131–137.

Thompson, B. (2008). Characteristics of parent-teacher e-mail communication. *Communication Education, 57*, 201–223. doi:10.1080/03634520701852050

Thompson, L., Dawson, K., Ferdig, R., Black, E., Boyer, J., Coutts, J., & Black, N. (2008). The intersection of online social networking with medical professionalism. *Journal of General Internal Medicine, 23*(7), 954–957. doi:10.1007/s11606-008-0538-8

Thompson, C. (2006). The early years. *New York Magazine*. February. Retrieved from http://nymag.com/news/media/15971/.

Timmerman, C. E., & Kruepke, K. A. (2006). Computer-assisted instruction, media richness, and college student performance. *Communication Education, 55*, 73–104.

Too many interruptions at work? (2006, June). *Gallup Management Journal.* Retrieved from http://gmj.gallup.com/content/23146/too-many-interruptions-at-work.aspx

Tulving, E. (1983). *Elements of episodic memory*. Oxford, UK: Clarendon Press.

Tulving, E. (1972). Episodic and semantic memory. In Tulving, E., & Donaldson, W. (Eds.), *Organization of memory* (pp. 381–403). New York, NY: Academic Press.

Turkle, S. (2011). *Alone together: Why we expect more from technology and less from each other*. New York, NY: Basic Books.

Turner, K., & Katic, E. (2009). The influence of technological literacy on students' writing. *Journal of Educational Computing Research, 41*(3), 253–270. doi:10.2190/EC.41.3.a

Turner, J. W., & Reinsch, N. L. (2010). Successful and unsuccessful multicommunication episodes: Engaging in dialogue or juggling messages? *Information Systems Frontiers*, *12*, 277–285..doi:10.1007/s10796-009-9175-y

Turner, L. (2005). 20 technology skills every educator should have. *THE Journal.* Retrieved January 4, 2011, from http://thejournal.com/articles/17325_1.

Twenge, J. M. (2009). Generational changes and their impact in the classroom: Teaching generation me. *Medical Education*, *43*(5), 398–405..doi:10.1111/j.1365-2923.2009.03310.x

Twitter (2010). *Twitter help center: Frequently asked questions*. Retrieved from http://support.twitter.com/groups/31-twitter-basics/topics/104-welcome-to-twitter-support/articles/13920-frequently-asked-questions.

Tworek, J. (2007). *High school students' uses of media.* Calgary: M.Sc., University of Calgary.

Ullman, E. (2009). Lessons in video. *University Business*, *12*(9), 28–34.

Umphrey, L. R., Wickersham, J. A., & Sherblom, J. C. (2008). Student perceptions of the instructor's relational characteristics, the classroom communication experience, and the interaction involvement in face-to-face versus video conference instruction. *Communication Research Reports*, *25*, 102–114. doi:10.1080/08824090802021954

United States Census Bureau. Population Division, Education & Social Stratification Branch. (2010). *Appendix table A: Households with a computer and internet use: 1984 to 2009*. Washington, DC: Government Printing Office.

United States Department of Commerce. (2010). *Exploring the digital nation: Home broadband internet adoption in the United States*. National Telecommunications and Information Association.

United States Distance Learning Association. (n.d.) *Definition: Distance learning*. Retrieved January 17, 2007, from http://www.usdla.org.

Urlocker, M. (2006, December 18). Rebels with a cursor. *National Post*, p. FP3. Retrieved from LexisNexis.

Väljataga, T., & Fiedler, S. (2009). Supporting students to self-direct intentional learning projects with social media. *Journal of Educational Technology & Society*, *12*(3), 58–69.

van Merrienboer, J. J. G., & Sweller, J. (2005). Cognitive load theory and complex learning: Recent developments and future directions. *Educational Psychology Review*, *17*, 147–177. doi:10.1007/s10648-005-3951-0

Vess, D. (2005). Asynchronous discussion and communication patterns in online and hybrid history courses. *Communication Education*, *54*, 355–364.. doi:10.1080/03634520500442210

Vie, S., & DeWinter, J. (2008). Disrupting intellectual property: Collaboration and resistance in wikis. In Cummings, R. E., & Barton, M. (Eds.), *Wiki writing: Collaborative learning in the college classroom* (pp. 109–122). Ann Arbor, MI: University of Michigan Press.

Vogel, J. J., Vogel, D. S., Cannon-Bowers, J., Bowers, C. A., Muse, K., & Wright, M. (2006). Computer gaming and interactive simulations for learning: A meta-analysis. *Journal of Educational Computing Research*, *34*(3), 229–243. doi:10.2190/FLHV-K4WA-WPVQ-H0YM

Vonderwell, S. (2003). An examination of asynchronous communication experience and perspectives of students in an online course: A case study. *The Internet and Higher Education*, *6*, 77–90. doi:10.1016/S1096-7516(02)00164-1

Wade, C. (1995). Using writing to develop and assess critical thinking. *Teaching of Psychology*, *22*(1), 24–28. doi:10.1207/s15328023top2201_8

Walker, J. T., Martin, T., White, J., Elliott, R., Norwood, A., Mangum, C., & Haynie, L. (2006). Generational (age) differences in nursing students' preferences for teaching methods. *The Journal of Nursing Education*, *45*, 371–374.

Walsh, L. (2010). Constructive interference: Wikis and service learning in thetechnical communication classroom. *Technical Communication Quarterly*, *19*(2), 184–211. doi:10.1080/10572250903559381

Walther, J. B., & Parks, M. R. (2002). Cues filtered out, cues filtered in: Computer-mediated communication and relationships. In Knapp, M. L., & Daly, J. A. (Eds.), *Handbook of interpersonal communication* (pp. 529–563). Thousand Oaks, CA: Sage.

Wang, L. (2010). Integrating communities of practice in e-portfolio assessment: Effects and experiences of mutual assessment in an online course. *The Internet and Higher Education*, *13*(4), 267–271. doi:10.1016/j.iheduc.2010.07.002

Wang, S., & Hsu, H. (2008). Reflection from using blogs to expand in-class discussion. *TechTrend*, *52*(3), 81–85. doi:10.1007/s11528-008-0160-y

Warlick, D. (2009). Grow your personal learning network: New technologies can keep you connected and help you manage information overload. *Learning and Leading with Technology*, *36*(6), 12–16.

Warlick, D. (2010). *The art & technique of personal learning networks or: A gardener's approach to learning.* Retrieved from http://davidwarlick.com/wiki/pmwiki.php/ Main/TheArtAmpTechniqueOfCultivatingYourPersonalLearningNetwork.

Warschauer, M. (2004). *Technology and social inclusion: Rethinking the digital divide*. Cambridge, MA: MIT Press.

Warschauer, M. (2000). Technology and school reform: A view from both sides of the track. *Education Policy Analysis Archives*, *8*(4), 1–21.

Watson, W. R., & Watson, S. L. (2007). An argument for clarity: What are learning management systems, what are they not, and what should they become? *TechTrends*, *51*(2), 28–34. doi:10.1007/s11528-007-0023-y

Watson, J. M., & Strayer, D. L. (2010). Supertaskers: Profiles in extraordinary multi-tasking ability. *Psychonomic Bulletin & Review*, *17*, 479–485. doi:10.3758/PBR.17.4.479

Watson, W. R., Lee, S., & Reigeluth, C. M. (2007). Learning management systems: An overview and roadmap of the systemic application of computers to education. In Neto, F. M. M., & Brasileiro, F. V. (Eds.), *Advances in computer-supported learning* (pp. 66–96). London, UK: Information Science Publishing.

Waycott, J., Bennett, S., Kennedy, G., Dalgarno, B., & Gray, K. (2010). Digital divides? Student and staff perceptions of information and communication technologies. *Computers & Education*, *54*(4), 1202-1211. doi:1210.1016/j.compedu.2009.1211.1006.

Weah, W., Simmons, V., & McClellan, M. (2000). Service-learning and multicultural/ multiethnic perspectives: From diversity to equity. *Phi Delta Kappan*, *81*(9), 673–675.

Weah, W. (2007). *Toward research-based standards for K-12 service-learning*. Retrieved from http://www.nylc.org/sites/nylc.org/files/files/2007G2G1.pdf.

Weimer, M. (2002). *Learner-centered teaching*. San Francisco, CA: Jossey-Bass.

Weisgerber, C., & Butler, S. (2011). Social media as a professional development tool: Using blogs, microblogs and social bookmarks to create personal learning networks. In Wankel, C. (Ed.), *Teaching arts & science with social media*. Bingley, UK: Emerald. doi:10.1108/S2044-9968(2011)0000003020

Weller, M. (2009). Using learning environments as a metaphor for educational change. *Horizon*, *17*(3), 181–189. doi:10.1108/10748120910993204

Wernet, S. P., Olliges, R. H., & Delicath, T. A. (2000). Postcourse evaluations of WebCT (Web Course Tools) classes by social work students. *Research on Social Work Practice*, *10*, 487–504.

Wesch, M. (2009b). YouTube and you: Experiences of self-awareness in the context collapse of the recording webcam. *Explorations in Media Ecology*, *8*(2), 19–34.

Wesch, M. (2009a, June). *The machine is (changing) us: YouTube and the politics of authenticity*. Keynote address presented at Personal Democracy Forum, Lincoln Center. Retrieved from http://www.youtube.com/watch?v=09gR6VPVrpw.

Wessels, P. L., & Steenkamp, L. P. (2009). Generation Y students: Appropriate learning styles and teaching approaches in the economic and management sciences faculty. *South African Journal of Higher Education*, *23*(5), 1039–1058.

Weyenberg, M. (2009). Technology in the classroom. *The National Jurist*, *19*(3), 38–39.

What is following? (n.d.). Retrieved February 10, 2011 from http://support.twitter.com/ articles/14019-what-is-following.

White, S. E. (1999). *The effectiveness of Web-based instruction: A case study.* Paper presented at the joint meeting of the Central States Communication Association and the Southern States Communication Association, St Louis, MO.

Whitehouse, C. R. (1991). The teaching of communication skills in United Kingdom medical schools. *Medical Education*, *25*(4), 311–318. doi:10.1111/j.1365-2923.1991.tb00072.x

Wiggins, G. (1998). *Educative assessment: Designing assessments to inform and improve student performance*. San Francisco, CA: Jossey-Bass Publishers.

Wiley, D. (2002). Connecting learning objects to instructional design theory: A definition, a metaphor, and a taxonomy. In Wiley, D. A. (Ed.), *The instructional use of learning objects: Online version*.

Williams, J. P. (1984). Categorization, macrostructure, and finding the main idea. *Journal of Educational Psychology*, *76*(5), 874–879. doi:10.1037/0022-0663.76.5.874

Williams, J. B., & Jacobs, J. (2004). Exploring the use of blogs as learning spaces in the higher education sector. *Australasian Journal of Educational Technology*, *20*(2), 232-247. Retrieved from http://www.ascilite.org.au/ajet/ajet20/williams.html.

Wilson, S., Liber, O., Johnson, M., Beauvior, P., Sharples, P., & Milligan, C. (2006). *Personal learning environments: Challenging the dominant design of educational systems*. Paper presented at the ECTEL Workshop on Learner-Oriented Knowledge Management and Knowledge Management-Oriented Learning, Heraklion, Crete.

Windell, D., & Wieber, E. N. (2007). *Measuring cognitive load in multimedia instruction: A comparison of two instruments*. Paper presented at American Educational Research Association Annual Conference, Chicago, IL.

Windham, C. (2005). The student's perspective. In D. G. Oblinger, & J. L. Oblinger (Eds.), *Educating the Net Generation* (pp. 5.1-5.16). Washington, DC: EDUCAUSE. Retrieved from http://www.educause.edu/educatingthenetgen.

Winter, J., Cotton, D., & Gavin, J. (2010). Effective e-learning? multi-tasking, distractions and boundary management by graduate students in an online environment. *ALT-J: Research in Learning Technology*, *18*(1), 71–83. doi:10.1080/09687761003657598

Winters, J., Hauck, B., Riggs, C. J., Clawson, J., & Collins, J. (2003). Use of videotaping to assess competences and course outcome. *The Journal of Nursing Education*, *42*(10), 472–476.

Witt, P. L., Wheeless, L. R., & Allen, M. (2004). A meta-analytical review of the relationship between teacher immediacy and student learning. *Communication Monographs*, *71*, 184–207..doi:10.1080/03645204200022805 4

Woelk, K. (2008). Optimizing the use of personal response devices (clickers) in large-enrollment introductory courses. *Journal of Chemical Education*, *85*(10), 1400–1405. doi:10.1021/ed085p1400

Wood, M. L. M. (2007). Rethinking the inoculation analogy: Effects on subjects with differing preexisting attitudes. *Human Communication Research*, *33*, 357–378. doi:10.1111/j.1468-2958.2007.00303.x

Wood, A. F., & Fassett, D. L. (2003). Remote control: Identity, power, and technology in the communication classroom. *Communication Education*, *52*, 286–296.. doi:10.1080/0363452032000156253

Worley, W. L., & Tesdell, L. S. (2009). Instructor time and effort in online and face-to-face teaching: Lessons learned. *IEEE Transactions on Professional Communication*, *52*, 138–151. doi:10.1109/TPC.2009.2017990

Wu, G. (2005). The mediating role of perceived interactivity in the effect of actual interactivity on attitude toward the Website. *Journal of Interactive Advertising*, *5*(2).

Xie, Y., Ke, F., & Sharma, P. (2008). The effect of peer feedback for blogging on college students' reflective learning processes. *The Internet and Higher Education*, *11*(1), 18–25. doi:10.1016/j.iheduc.2007.11.001

Yin, R. K. (2009). *Case study research: Design and methods* (4th ed.). Thousand Oaks, CA: Sage Publications.

Yoo, C. Y. (2007). Implicit memory measures for Web advertising effectiveness. *Journalism & Mass Communication Quarterly*, *84*(1), 7–23.

Yorke, M. (2003). Formative assessment in higher education: Moves towards theory and the enhancement of pedagogic practice. *Higher Education*, *45*(4), 477–501. doi:10.1023/A:1023967026413

Young, J. R. (2007). An anthropologist explores the culture of video blogging. *The Chronicle of Higher Education*, *53*(36), 39.

Young, J. (2010, December 9). 18 percent of college students who go online use Twitter. *The Chronicle of Higher Education*. Retrieved February 8, 2011, from http://chronicle.com/blogs/wiredcampus/18-percent-of-college-students-use-twitter/28642.

YouTube, LLC. (2011, 15 April). *Hoover's company records*, 148460. (Document ID: 1014564471).

YouTube. (2011, July). *YouTube frequently asked questions*. Retrieved from http://www.youtube.com/t/faq.

Yucht, A. (2009). Building your personal learning network. *Information Searcher*, *19*(1), 11–14.

Zaichkowsky, J. L. (1985). Measuring the involvement construct. *The Journal of Consumer Research*, *12*, 341–352. doi:10.1086/208520

Zajonc, A. (2008). What is contemplative pedagogy? In *Contemplative practices in higher education: A handbook of classroom practices* (p. 9). Northhampton, MA: The Center for Contemplative Mind in Society.

Zawillinski, L. (2009). Hot blogging: A framework for blogging to promote higher order thinking. *The Reading Teacher*, *62*(8), 650–651. doi:10.1598/RT.62.8.3

Zeidan, F., Johnson, S. K., Diamond, B. J., David, Z., & Goolkasian, P. (2010, June). Mindfulness meditation improves cognition: Evidence of brief mental training. *Consciousness and Cognition*, *19*(2), 597–605. doi:10.1016/j.concog.2010.03.014

Zemke, R., Raines, C., & Filipczak, B. (2000). *Generations at work: Managing the clash of veterans, Boomers, Xers, and Nexters in your workplace*. New York, NY: AMACOM American Management Association.

Zemsky, R. (2009). *Making reform work: The case for transforming American higher education*. Piscataway, NJ: Rutgers University Press.

Zhao, Y., Lei, J., Lai, B. Y. C., & Tan, H. S. (2005). What makes a difference? A practical analysis of research on the effectiveness of distance education. *Teachers College Record*, *107*, 1836–1884. doi:10.1111/j.1467-9620.2005.00544.x

Zheng, R. (Ed.). (2009). *Cognitive effects of multimedia learning*. Hershey, PA: Information Science Reference/IGI Global Publishing.

Zheng, R. (2010). Effects of situated learning on students' knowledge acquisition: An individual differences perspective. *Journal of Educational Computing Research*, *43*(4), 463–483. doi:10.2190/EC.43.4.c

Zheng, R., Flygare, J., & Dahl, L. (2009a). Style matching or ability building? An empirical study on FDI learners' learning in well-structured and ill-structured asynchronous online learning environments. *Journal of Educational Computing Research*, *41*(2), 195–226. doi:10.2190/EC.41.2.d

Zheng, R., McAlack, M., Wilmes, B., Kohler-Evans, P., & Williamson, J. (2009b). Effects of multimedia on cognitive load, self-efficacy, and multiple rule-based problem solving. *British Journal of Educational Technology*, *40*(5), 790–803. doi:10.1111/j.1467-8535.2008.00859.x

Zheng, R., Miller, S., Snelbecker, G., & Cohen, I. (2006). Use of multimedia for problem-solving tasks. *Journal of Technology, Instruction. Cognition and Learning*, *3*(1-2), 135–143.

Zheng, R., Yang, W., Garcia, D., & McCadden, B. P. (2008). Effects of multimedia on schema induced analogical reasoning in science learning. *Journal of Computer Assisted Learning*, *24*, 474–482. doi:10.1111/j.1365-2729.2008.00282.x

Zheng, R. (2007). Cognitive functionality of multimedia in problem solving. In Kidd, T., & Song, H. (Eds.), *Handbook of research on instructional systems and technology* (pp. 230–246). Hershey, PA: Information Science Reference/IGI Global Publishing. doi:10.4018/978-1-59904-865-9.ch017

Zhu, L., & Grabowski, B. L. (2006). Web-based animation or static graphics: Is the extra cost of animation worth it? *Journal of Educational Multimedia and Hypermedia*, *15*(3), 329–347.

Zickuhr, K. (2010). [Report from the Pew Internet and American Life Project.]. *Generations (San Francisco, Calif.)*, 2010.

Zimmerman, B. J. (1990). Self-regulated learning and academic achievement: An overview. *Educational Psychologist*, *25*(1), 3–17. doi:10.1207/s15326985ep2501_2

Zimmerman, B. J. (1998). Academic studying and the development of personal skills: A self-regulatory perspective. *Educational Psychologist*, *33*(2/3), 73–86.

Zimmerman, B. J. (2002). Becoming a self-regulated learner: An overview. *Theory into Practice*, *41*(2), 64–70. doi:10.1207/s15430421tip4102_2

About the Contributors

Sharmila Pixy Ferris (PhD Penn State) is Professor in the department of Communication at the William Paterson University in New Jersey, where she recently completed a six year term as Director of the Center for Teaching Excellence. She teaches undergraduate and graduate courses in the areas of interpersonal, organizational and communication theory. Her research brings an interdisciplinary focus to computer-mediated communication, in which she has published in a variety of print and electronic journals. Previous books with IGI Global include *Virtual and Collaborative Teams: Theories, Process and Practice* (2004, with Sue Godar), *Teaching and Learning with Virtual and Collaborative Teams* (2006, with Sue Godar), and *Online Instructional Modeling* (2007, with Robert Zheng).

***

Rukhsana Ahmed (PhD, University of Ohio) is an Assistant Professor in the Department of Communication at the University of Ottawa. Her research interests lie at the intersections of health, interpersonal, intercultural, media, and other realms of communication, including pedagogy, gender, and development. Her research has been published in *Communication Studies, Intercultural Communication Studies, Women's Health & Urban Life: An International and Interdisciplinary Journal, Journal of Cancer Education, Medical Informatics & the Internet in Medicine, Identity, Culture and Politics: An Afro-Asian Dialogue,* and in several book chapters. She has presented numerous papers at regional, national, and international conferences and conventions.

Rachel Angel has been known to text classmates ten minutes before class to ask whether an assignment is due and spends her seconds of leisure time dreaming up the perfect dessert. Despite this, she has somehow managed to complete her M.Ed. in school counselling and plans to pursue her license in professional counselling so she can afford to continue feeding people. She feels passionately about helping others reach their full potential, blogging, and making the perfect béchamel sauce. She is currently writing a children's book series featuring pirates and ninjas, which is designed to help children adjust to the expectations of the school environment. She is a full-time worker bee and mother and a dedicated lifelong learner.

Simon Paul Atkinson has served in continuing education roles with Exeter University (UK) and Victoria University (New Zealand), in faculty development for distance education roles with the Open University (UK) and Massey University (New Zealand). He has held a number of academic and professional development roles teaching on faculty development programs including the London School of Economics. Simon has held senior faculty roles in Learning Development with the University of Hull, where he was Head of e-Learning and Director of Learning & Teaching Support and he is currently the Associate Dean for Teaching Enhancement at BPP University College in the UK. He served as external expert consultant for the Croatian national e-Learning development project EQIBELT, and has contributed to distance education capacity building initiatives in Kenya. Simon writes, teaches, and presents on learning design for emerging digitally enabled university contexts.

Charles Aust is in his 23rd year as a full-time college professor and has taught in the Department of Communication at Kennesaw State University since 1995. Prior appointments were at Stillman College in Tuscaloosa, Alabama and University of West Georgia in Carrollton. His areas of interest include media effects, media literacy, using media to grieve, communication and positive psychology, and effective teaching methods in the classroom. Dr. Aust's mass media experience includes public relations for a non-profit social service agency, news writing, and photography. He also served as a caseworker for 3 years and a drug and alcohol education specialist for 2 years. Dr. Aust has a PhD in Mass Communication from the University of Alabama. His Master's degree is in Telecommunication from Indiana University. His Bachelor's degree in Psychology is from the University of Pittsburgh. He was born and raised in Johnstown, Pennsylvania.

Sally Blomstrom, PhD is an Associate Professor at Embry-Riddle Aeronautical University in Prescott, AZ, where she teaches communication courses and conducts research in service-learning, assessment, and student attitudes toward research. She also works with students on digital history projects.

Shannan H. Butler, PhD, is an Assistant Professor of Communication at St. Edward's University in Austin, Texas. Shannan conducts research in the area of visual communication, new media, pedagogy, and rhetorical criticism of visual media. He was invited to present his work on visualization at the 2010 *Horizon Report* general meeting. Together with his colleague, Dr. Corinne Weisgerber, he has just finished editing a special issue (Communication Pedagogy in the Age of Social Media) for the *Electronic Journal of Communication*.

Steve Buzinski is a graduate of Lebanon Valley College and is currently a doctoral candidate in the Social, Decision, & Organizational Sciences (SDOS) program at the University of Maryland. He is completing a dissertation investigating the influence of goal demands on self-regulatory success. In addition to goal systems and self-regulation, Steve's research interests include the scholarship of teaching and learning (SoTL) and psychological distance. He has taught courses in social psychology, psychological research methods, and the psychology of communication and persuasion. While at Maryland Steve found a passion for teaching, as he has served as a Lilly Teaching Fellow and has won several teaching awards. This fall, Steve will take his dedication to evidence-based pedagogy back to Lebanon Valley College, where he will serve as a teaching Fellow in the department of Psychology for the 2011-2012 academic year.

Erin E. Carr has a BA in Communication Studies from Virginia Tech and will receive an MEd in Counselor Education from Virginia Commonwealth University in December 2011. After six years of sports marketing, hospitality, and corporate event planning experience, Erin decided she wanted a more fulfilling career and that education was her true passion. She has since worked in the Honors College and with student athletes at VCU. Erin enjoys the numerous different aspects of student affairs and how there are so many ways to positively affect students' experiences in higher education. Having been born and raised in Virginia, Erin loves to spend her free time with her two dogs either exploring Richmond, or traveling to the nearby beach or mountains.

Josh Compton (PhD, University of Oklahoma, 2004) is Senior Lecturer in Speech in the Institute for Writing and Rhetoric at Dartmouth College. His scholarship of inoculation theory, political humor, and speech pedagogy has appeared in *Human Communication Research, Journal of Applied Communication Research, Health Communication, Communication Theory, Arts and Humanities in Higher Education*, and other journals. His political humor analyses have been included in several books, including Routledge's *Laughing Matters* (2008) and Lexington's The Daily Show *and Rhetoric* (2011). He was a recipient of the National Speakers Association's Outstanding Professor Award, and his teaching has been recognized by the International Communication Association and Pi Kappa Delta National Honorary. He also maintains an active public speaking schedule, presenting interactive workshops on such topics as public speaking and inoculation theory.

Susanne Croasdaile is a program specialist in curriculum and instruction at the Virginia Department of Education's Training and Technical Assistance Center at Virginia Commonwealth University. Her research interests include reflective practice, Universal Design for Learning, instructional strategies to support all learners, and creative uses of digital media.

Boaventura DaCosta is a researcher with Solers Research Group in Orlando, FL. He holds a PhD in instructional systems design. In addition to his research interests in cognitive psychology and information and communication technology innovations, Dr. DaCosta is also interested in how games can be used in learning. Complementing his work as a researcher, Dr. DaCosta has worked in the commercial and government training sectors for the past 16 years as a software engineer.

Laura Beth Daws (PhD- Mass Communication, University of Kentucky) is an Assistant Professor of Communication at Georgia Highlands College in Marietta, GA, teaching courses in Human Communication, Public Speaking, and Mass Media. Her current program of research explores the implications of technology in classroom settings, as well as new media's influence on in-person and online out-of-classroom interactions. Other research interests include the relationship between mass communication and gender identity, as well as gender and identity performance online. She has presented her work at various regional and national conferences and published in *Communication Teacher*.

Scott C. D'Urso (PhD, 2004, University of Texas at Austin) is an Assistant Professor of Communication Studies at Marquette University, where he teaches courses focused on organizational and corporate communication and new communication technology. Scott's primary research interests include organizational use of communication technologies such as e-mail, instant messaging, and social media. He has published manuscripts on privacy and surveillance in the workplace, communication channel selection, crisis communication, and stakeholder issues. He is currently working on several projects including digital divides in organizations, virtual team decision-making, and the role of online identity creation and privacy concerns with social networking websites. Prior to a career in academia, Scott worked for several years as a multimedia Specialist/Manager of a multimedia production department for a government defense contractor in the Southwest.

Maureen Ebben (PhD, University of Illinois) is a Lecturer in the Communication and Media Studies Department at the University of Southern Maine. Her research focuses on the nexus of culture, technology, gender, and communication. Her critical work with the net generation explores the material and discursive deployment of technology for teaching and learning across the shifting landscape of higher education. She is interested in identifying and addressing gaps between popular discursive promises of technology and every day, real practices of many college students. She is co-editor of the volume *Women, Information Technology, and Scholarship,* and her work has been published in journals such as *Women's Studies in Communication, UCLA Law Review,* and *Women and Language.*

Rachel Helen Ellaway, PhD, is the Assistant Dean for Informatics and an Associate Professor at the Northern Ontario School of Medicine. Her work concentrates on online learning, simulation and the use of new technologies for teaching and assessment. Dr. Ellaway's work in developing and implementing profession-focused educational systems was recognized in the award of a Queen's Anniversary Prize for Higher and Further Education to the University of Edinburgh in 2005, the first such award given to work involving learning technologies.

Jessica Fargnoli, MA, is a faculty member at Bergen Community College, where she instructs Speech Communication. She has incorporated audio and video capture technology in her teaching methodology and pedagogy for the past 3 years.

Brandy Fair is a Communication Professor and the Department Chair for the Arts and Communication programs at Grayson County College. She currently teaches Introduction to Communication and Business and Professional Communication courses, both in face-to-face and hybrid course designs. Her research interests include technology and education, student readiness for online courses, and issues concerning plagiarism and cheating in the classroom. She has served on the Faculty Association, the Distance Learning Advisory Council, and several other committees at her institution. In addition, Fair has presented at local, national, and international conferences and published articles in scholarly communication and education research journals.

William J. Gibbs is an Associate Professor in the Journalism and Multimedia Arts Department at Duquesne University where he teaches courses in Digital media production, multimedia technology, instructional design, and human-computer interaction and interface design. He received a PhD in Instructional Systems from The Pennsylvania State University. His research interests include technology-based learning environments, usability engineering, and human-computer interactions. Most recently his research has examined learning and behavioral changes that occur during human-computer interactions.

James Gleason is an Assistant Professor of Communication at Eastern Kentucky University. His research interests include mass communication, new media, advertising, public relations, and instructional design. He received his PhD from the University of Kentucky. An experienced business communicator and Public Relations professional, he previously was Director of Worldwide Employee Communications for Lexmark International, and President and Chief Information Architect of Buzzword, a regional interactive development firm. He is accredited by the Public Relations Society of America (PRSA), and is a member of the National Communication Association. He is also an accomplished guitarist, composer, and recording artist, and is a member of the *American Society of Composers, Authors and Publishers (ASCAP).*

Chris Gurrie is an Assistant Professor and the Director of the Speech Communication Program at the University of Tampa in Florida. Aside from teaching, his research interests center on communication immediacy and nonverbal cues, communication education, first year students and programming, and technology education and communication. Aside from teaching and researching, Gurrie presents programs on faculty development in first year programming, communication and relationships for Campuspeak, and on-campus honors seminars. A key component of his work at the University of Tampa is the education abroad program where he has led six faculty-led study abroad opportunities for students of all majors. When not at school Gurrie is an avid traveler, wake boarder and boater, and reader.

Carrie Eunyoung Hong, PhD, is an Assistant Professor in the Department of Educational Leadership and Professional Studies at William Paterson University. She has a variety of teaching experience in elementary and middle schools, providing individualized literacy instruction for struggling readers and writers. She is currently teaching undergraduate and graduate courses on reading and literacy. Her research interests include reading and literacy, literacy instruction for English learners, and teacher preparation. She has conducted numerous workshops at the state and national levels.

Lucy Hudson is the Founder and Director of Hannah's Women, Inc, a faith based organization whose primary goal is to provide developmental programs and address literacy issues, in an effort to combat problems involving youth and families in rural areas. She has been employed with Virginia Commonwealth University in Richmond, Virginia since 2006 and is skilled in organizational development, program coordinating, and instructional technology development. She is a graduate of Virginia Commonwealth University with a Bachelor of Science in Urban Studies and Planning and Bachelor of Arts in Religious Studies. She is a native of Emporia, Virginia, a graduate of Greensville County High School, and is currently obtaining a Master of Education in Adult Learning and Family Literacy from Virginia Commonwealth University.

Marsha M. Huber is an Associate Professor of Accounting at Youngstown State University. She earned her PhD from The Ohio State University. Her research areas are positive psychology, course re-design, classroom assessment, and resilience. Her articles have appeared in *Case Research Journal*, *New Directions in Teaching and Learning*, and in the recent American Accounting Association monograph, *Accounting Student Learning*. She is also a featured presenter at the Lilly conferences on teaching and learning and a speaker at conferences. She has served as a member on several panels including those on "accounting innovations" and "best practices." She is also a multiple award winner for her innovations in accounting education.

Kerk F. Kee (PhD, University of Texas, 2010) is an Assistant Professor of Communication Studies at Chapman University. His research interests include emerging technologies, social media, organizational communication, and health dissemination. His published work appears in journals such as *Journal of Computer-Mediated Communication, Computer Supported Cooperative Work, CyberPsychology, Behavior & Social Networking*, and *IEEE Computer*. A co-authored chapter on positive organizational communication will appear in the *Oxford Handbook of Positive Organizational Scholarship*. He teaches courses in organizational communication, communication & workplace technologies, and research methods.

Jean P. Kelly has been on the faculty of Otterbein University since 1997. Her teaching specialties include publication design, online technologies, and magazine writing and editing. Many of her classes also include service learning, an approach that integrates community service with academic study in order to enrich learning, teach civic responsibility, and strengthen communities. Her current research includes investigations of how directed classroom use of new online social media might improve critical thinking skills of college students. Dr. Kelly has extensive professional experience as a magazine editor and writer, web site designer, and public relations consultant for non-profits and arts organizations. As editor of *OHIO* magazine, her writing and editing work has won both local and national awards.

Russell Kivatisky (PhD, Bowling Green State University) is an Assistant Professor in the Communication and Media Studies Department at the University of Southern Maine. His research centers on group communication, especially how students perceive the effects of technology on relationships and group outcomes. He aims to develop critical insights and best practices for teachers who work with the net generation in higher education. He teaches Small Group Communication and Business & Professional Communication among other courses, and directs the Communication Internship Program. Largely, he explores the intersections of the net generation, technology, education, and the professional world. His work has appeared in *The Guide to Simulations & Games for Education & Training, Simulation & Gaming News,* and *Communication Quarterly.*

Carolyn Kinsell is President of Solers Research Group. She holds a PhD in instructional technology and a certificate in human performance. Dr. Kinsell's career spans almost two decades, during which she has focused on the application of training, ranging from analysis, to the development of virtual environments, to defining requirements and solutions for human performance standards; more recently, she led continuous investigation to determine links between blending training, gaming, and simulation techniques to establish exemplar training conditions and methods. Dr. Kinsell has worked closely with the military to include the Navy, Army, and Marine Corps programs.

Shirine Mafi is a Professor of Management at Otterbein College. She earned her BS and MBA at Marshall University. She earned her PhD in Human Resource Development from The Ohio State University in 2000. Her articles have appeared in *Case Research Journal* and *Advances in Developing Human Resources*. Her research interests include studying the impact of philanthropy on learning and innovation in teaching. She has also worked as a management consultant and written in the area of quality service. She is also an award winner for her work in philanthropy in education.

Geraldine Mongillo, PhD, is an Associate Professor in the Department of Educational Leadership and Professional Studies at William Paterson University and department Chair. Over the past 4 years she has coordinated the university Basic Skills Reading Program where she revised the program for struggling freshmen yielding improved student achievement and test scores. Research interests include new literacies, intervention strategies for struggling readers, and the professional development of reading teachers. Recent publications appeared in *Contemporary Issues in Technology & English Language Arts Teacher Education, The Association of Teacher Educators Yearbook, XVI,* and *i-Manager's Journal of Educational Technology.*

Star A. Muir is an Associate Professor of Communication at George Mason University and received his PhD in Rhetoric and Communication from the University of Pittsburgh. His research focuses on digital natives and on presentational and instructional technology, including the use of PowerPoint and social networking. He has won several teaching excellence awards, and his work on distance delivery of video modules won both Communicator and Telly awards for educational programming. He is the Program Planner for the Human Communication and Technology Division of the National Communication Association, and has previously published in *Critical Studies in Mass Communication*, *Philosophy and Rhetoric*, *The Technology Source*, and *Inventio: Creative Thinking about Teaching and Learning*. He was a debate coach for top-ranked college debate programs for seventeen years.

Melissa Murphy (BS University of Cincinnati, 2008) is an MA student and Teaching Assistant in the department of Communication Studies at University of Texas at Austin. Her research interests include technology use in romantic relationships and organizational friendships. She has examined the effects of strategic ambiguity in non-profit organizations and communication practices in local organizational culture. She is the 2011-2012 Master's Representative for the Communication Studies Graduate Community and is a 2011 summer fellow at the Bodo Graduate School of Business at the University of Nordland. Prior to graduate school, Melissa worked in digital sales and marketing in the music industry in Los Angeles, California.

Angelique Nasah is Researcher with Solers Research Group in Orlando, FL, and she holds a PhD in Instructional Technology. Her research interests include the reduction of cognitive load through instructional design principles. Dr. Nasah is also interested in how information and communication technology innovation and usage impacts learning outcomes for various learning audiences. In addition to her work as a researcher, Dr. Nasah has worked in the education and training sector for more than 17 years; she has experience in secondary and higher education settings, as well as in the area of defense training.

Daniel A. Panici (PhD, University of Missouri) is an Associate Professor in the Communication and Media Studies Department at the University of Southern Maine. His research interests include the areas of pedagogy and technology, popular media and framing of technology, and children and media. Daniel recently developed a course titled "Understanding Technology" which examines the relationship between media, technology, and society from a variety of perspectives and disciplines. The recipient of several teaching awards, Daniel also serves as a manuscript reviewer for *Journalism and Mass Communication Quarterly* and *Journal of Broadcasting and Electronic Media.* His articles have been published in journals such as *Journalism and Mass Communication Educator* and *Communication Studies.*

Charles Reiguleth received a BA in Economics from Harvard University. He was a high school teacher for three years before earning his doctorate in instructional psychology at Brigham Young University. He was a Professor at Syracuse University for 10 years, culminating as Program Chair. He has been a Professor in the Instructional Systems Technology Department at Indiana University's School of Education in Bloomington since 1988, and served as Chair of the department from 1990-1992. His major professional focus is the district-wide paradigm change process for public education. He is internationally known for his work on instructional methods and theories. Currently, his major research goal is to advance knowledge to help school districts successfully navigate paradigm change, including advancing knowledge about personalized, integrated, technology systems that support the learner-centered paradigm of education.

Scott Roberts earned his Bachelor's degree from Denison University where he focused on comparative cognition and conducted independent research with the Ohio State Chimpanzee Center. He then spent three years working as a Research Associate and Senior dolphin Trainer at the University of Hawaii's Kewlo Basin Marine Mammal Lab, contributing to studies of the dolphins' cognitive, linguistic, and sensory capacities. His doctorate from the University of Maryland involved the development and testing of a novel approach to detecting deception via cognitive activity. Widely recognized for his dedication to teaching, Scott taught various undergraduate and graduate courses at the University of Maryland and has been active in research on the scholarship of teaching and learning (SoTL). After two years serving as a Research Psychologist for the Federal Government, Scott returned to the University of Maryland as the Director of Undergraduate Studies for the Department of Psychology where he continues to teach.

Craig R. Scott (PhD, Arizona State University, 1994) is an Associate Professor and PhD Program Director in the School of Communication, Information and Library Studies at Rutgers University. His research related to anonymity and new communication technologies has been published in journals such as *Communication Theory, Management Communication Quarterly, Journal of Computer-Mediated Communication, Western Journal of Communication*, and *Communication Quarterly* as well as the *Free Speech Yearbook*. His scholarly work related to teams and group communication technologies has been published in outlets such as *Communication Monographs, Communication Research, Small Group Research, Communication Education, Communication Reports*, and several book chapters. Scott also teaches graduate and undergraduate courses in this area and conducts training workshops related to appropriate use of communication technologies in the workplace.

Keri K. Stephens (PhD, University of Texas, 2005) is an Assistant Professor of Communication Studies at University of Texas at Austin. Her research examines how people use information and communication technologies (ICTs) in organizations and how that affects workplace overload and emergency/crisis communication. Her published work appears in places like *Communication Theory, Management Communication Quarterly, Journal of Computer-Mediated Communication, Communication Education, Journal of Health Communication, Communication Research, Journal of Public Relations Research, and The Handbook of Crisis Communication.* She is a co-author of the book, *Information and Communication Technology in Action: Linking Theory and Narratives of Practice*. She has won several teaching awards and has taught research methods courses in Norway. She teaches courses in organizational communication, sales communication, and workplace technology use. Prior to academia, Dr. Stephens spent eight years in industry working in technical sales, corporate training, and project management roles.

Janet Tworek is Manager of eLearning for Undergraduate Medical Education, and a doctoral candidate in Educational Technology at the University of Calgary. She is the recipient of the ASCD award for Innovative Teaching with Technology in Science and in 2009 was recognized as a Future Leader in Medicine by the Association of Faculties of Medicine of Canada. She leads her team in building and supporting digital tools for medical students through all phases of their MD degree. Her PhD work focuses on the complex layers of activity involved in technology-enabled education interventions, such as virtual patients.

Carin Usrey graduated from the University of Virginia in 2007 with a B.A. in Sociology and a minor in French. After working abroad at the American School in London as a first grade teaching intern for a year, she returned to her hometown of Arlington, Virginia to tutor high school students with a local tutoring and test preparation group, Georgetown Learning Centers. Her interest in career development and her passion for working one on one with students in an academic setting has led Carin back to graduate school to pursue a future in counseling. She now lives in Richmond, Virginia and attends VCU where she is working towards her Master's in Counselor Education with a concentration in College Student Development Services.

Sunnie Lee Watson is an Assistant Professor of Educational Technology in the Department of Educational Studies at Ball State University. Dr. Watson holds her dual major doctorate in Instructional Systems Technology and Educational Leadership & Policy Studies with a focus on International and Comparative Education from Indiana University. She earned her Master of Science degree in Instructional Systems Technology from Indiana University. Her Bachelor of Arts in Educational Technology is from Ewha Womans University in Seoul, South Korea. Dr. Watson has taught at the elementary, high school, and college levels for over 10 years. She has also worked in human resources development for Fortune 100 companies and developed educational software for P-16 students. She teaches and conducts scholarly work in the field of international technology policies and leadership for digital equity, multicultural education, and peace education in South Korea, and critical systems theory/thinking for educational change and research.

William R. Watson is an Assistant Professor of Learning Design and Technology in the Department of Curriculum and Instruction at Purdue University. He established and is the director of the Purdue Center for Serious Games and Learning in Virtual Environments, which conducts research on and provides support for implementing, designing and developing serious games and virtual environments for learning. Watson earned a PhD in Education and a MS in Information Science from Indiana University. His research interest focuses on the critical, systemic change of education to realize a learner-centered paradigm, including the application of technology such as video games, virtual environments, and learning management software in order to create customized and personalized learning environments.

Corinne Weisgerber, PhD, is an Assistant Professor of Communication at St. Edward's University in Austin, Texas where she teaches social media, interpersonal communication, and public relations classes. Corinne has been studying computer-mediated communication and how people develop and maintain online relationships since the beginning of her doctoral studies at the Pennsylvania State University. Her research interests include new media, pedagogy, and interpersonal communication. She developed one of the first social media for public relations classes – a course which explores emerging social media technologies and studies their application in contemporary PR practice and which she has been teaching since 2007.

Hilary Wilder, EdD, is an Associate Professor in the Educational Leadership and Professional Studies department in the College of Education at William Paterson University of New Jersey in the United States. She teaches undergraduate and graduate courses in Educational Technology and also directs a M.Ed. program in Learning Technologies. Her research includes the use of online and as well as low-cost cellphone-based social networking technologies to promote writing literacies and afford effective written communication skills. She is especially interested in the use of these technologies to promote writing in disadvantaged and/or previously marginalized student populations.

Robert Zheng is a Faculty Member and Director of Instructional Design and Educational Technology (IDET) program in the Department of Educational Psychology at the University of Utah. His research interest includes online instructional design, cognition and multimedia learning, and human-computer interaction. He has edited and co-edited two books, published nine book chapters, and a dozen of research papers on the above topics.

Index

A

B

C

D

E

F

O

P

R

S

T

U

V

W

CPSIA information can be obtained at www.ICGtesting.com
Printed in the USA
BVOW011549101111

275514BV00006B/1/P

9 781613 503478